Palgrave Studies in European Union Politics

Following on the sustained success of the acclaimed *European Union Series,* which essentially
publishes research-based textbooks, *Palgrave Studies in European Union Politics* publishes
cutting-edge, research-driven, monographs.

The remit of the series is broadly defined, both in terms of subject and academic discipline.
All topics of significance concerning the nature and operation of the European Union
potentially fall within the scope of the series. The series is multidisciplinary to reflect the
growing importance of the EU as a political, economic and social phenomenon.

Eva Gross
THE EUROPEANIZATION OF NATIONAL FOREIGN POLICY
Continuity and Change in European Crisis Management

Hussein Kassim and Handley Stevens
AIR TRANSPORT AND THE EUROPEAN UNION
Europeanization and its Limits

Katie Verlin Laatikainen and Karen E. Smith (*editors*)
THE EUROPEAN UNION AND THE UNITED NATIONS
Intersecting Multilateralisms

Esra LaGro and Knud Erik Jørgensen (*editors*)
TURKEY AND THE EUROPEAN UNION
Prospects for a Difficult Encounter

Ingo Linsenmann, Christoph O. Meyer and Wolfgang T. Wessels (*editors*)
ECONOMIC GOVERNMENT OF THE EU
A Balance Sheet of New Modes of Policy Coordination

Hartmut Mayer and Henri Vogt (*editors*)
A RESPONSIBLE EUROPE?
Ethical Foundations of EU External Affairs

Philomena Murray (*editor*)
EUROPE AND ASIA
Regions in Flux

Daniel Naurin and Helen Wallace (*editors*)
UNVEILING THE COUNCIL OF THE EUROPEAN UNION
Games Governments Play in Brussels

David Phinnemore and Alex Warleigh-Lack
REFLECTIONS ON EUROPEAN INTEGRATION
50 Years of the Treaty of Rome

Sebastiaan Princen
AGENDA-SETTING IN THE EUROPEAN UNION

Palgrave Studies in European Union Politics
Series Standing Order ISBN 978–1–4039–9511–7 (hardback)
ISBN 978–1–4039–9512–4 (paperback)

You can receive future titles in this series as they are published by placing a standing order. Please contact your bookseller or, in case of difficulty, write to us at the address below with your name and address, the title of the series and one of the ISBNs quoted above.

Customer Services Department, Macmillan Distribution Ltd, Houndmills, Basingstoke, Hampshire RG21 6XS, UK

Research Agendas in EU Studies

Stalking the Elephant

Edited by

Michelle Egan
Associate Professor and Jean Monnet Chair of
European Integration
American University, USA

Neill Nugent
Professor of Politics and Jean Monnet Professor of
European Integration
Manchester Metropolitan University, UK

and

William E. Paterson
Honorary Professor of European and German Politics
Aston University, UK

palgrave
macmillan

First published 2010 by
PALGRAVE MACMILLAN

Palgrave Macmillan in the UK is an imprint of Macmillan Publishers Limited,
registered in England, company number 785998, of Houndmills, Basingstoke,
Hampshire RG21 6XS.

Palgrave Macmillan in the US is a division of St Martin's Press LLC,
175 Fifth Avenue, New York, NY 10010.

Palgrave Macmillan is the global academic imprint of the above companies
and has companies and representatives throughout the world.

Palgrave® and Macmillan® are registered trademarks in the United States,
the United Kingdom, Europe and other countries.

ISBN 978–0–230–55524–2   hardback
ISBN 978–0–230–55525–9   paperback
10068449 0
This book is printed on paper suitable for recycling and made from fully
managed and sustained forest sources. Logging, pulping and manufacturing
processes are expected to conform to the environmental regulations of the
country of origin.

A catalogue record for this book is available from the British Library.

A catalog record for this book is available from the Library of Congress.

10   9   8   7   6   5   4   3   2   1
19 18 17 16 15 14 13 12 11 10

Printed and bound in Great Britain by
CPI Antony Rowe, Chippenham and Eastbourne

Contents

List of Tables and Figures

Tables

Figures

List of Abbreviations

AFSJ	area of freedom, security and justice
ASEAN	Association of South-East Asian Nations
CAP	Common Agricultural Policy
CEE	Central and Eastern Europe
CEEC	Central and Eastern European country
CFI	Court of First Instance
CFSP	Common Foreign and Security Policy
Coreper	Committee of Permanent Representatives
CSW	(UN) Convention on the Status of Women
DG	Directorate General
EC	European Community
ECB	European Central Bank
ECJ	European Court of Justice
ECOFIN	Council of Economic and Finance Ministers
ECSC	European Coal and Steel Community
EEA	European Economic Area
EEC	European Economic Community
EES	European Employment Strategy
EFTA	European Free Trade Association
EIB	European Investment Bank
EMU	Economic and Monetary Union
ENP	European Neighbourhood Policy
EP	European Parliament
EPC	European Political Cooperation
ERM	Exchange Rate Mechanism
ESDP	European Security and Defence Policy
EU	European Union
EWL	European Women's Lobby
FPA	foreign policy analysis
GATT	General Agreement on Tariffs and Trade
GCC	German Constitutional Court
HI	historical institutionalism
IGC	intergovernmental conference
IMF	International Monetary Fund
IO	Intergovernmental Organization
IR	International Relations
JHA	Justice and Home Affairs
LI	liberal intergovernmentalism

MEP	Member of the European Parliament
MLG	multilevel governance
NATO	North Atlantic Treaty Organisation
NBS	Nash Bargaining Solution
NGO	non-governmental organization
OCA	optimal currency area
OECD	Organisation for Economic Co-operation and Development
OMC	open method of coordination
SEA	Single European Act
SEM	Single European Market
TCE	Treaty Establishing a Constitution for Europe
TEC	Treaty Establishing the European Community
TEU	Treaty on European Union
UK	United Kingdom
UN	United Nations
US	United States
WTO	World Trade Organization

Notes on the Contributors

Anthony Arnull is Barber Professor of Jurisprudence and Head of the Birmingham Law School at the University of Birmingham in the United Kingdom.

Derek Beach is Associate Professor of Political Science at the University of Aarhus, Denmark.

Susana Borrás is Professor at the International Center for Business and Politics at the Copenhagen Business School, Denmark.

Christina Boswell is Senior Lecturer in the School of Politics and International Relations at the University of Edinburgh, UK.

Michelle Egan is Associate Professor and Jean Monnet Chair in the School of International Service, American University, Washington, DC, USA.

Theofanis Exadaktylos is a PhD candidate in the Department of Politics at the University of Exeter, UK, and a research assistant at the Jean Monnet Chair in EU Policy Analysis.

Heather Grabbe is Director of the Open Society Institute in Brussels, Belgium, and was formerly special advisor to Olli Rehn, the European Commissioner for Enlargement.

Wade Jacoby is Professor of Political Science at Brigham Young University, USA, where he also directs the Center for the Study of Europe.

Johanna Kantola is Senior Lecturer in Politics at the University of Helsinki, Finland.

N. Piers Ludlow is Senior Lecturer in the Department of International History at the London School of Economics and Political Science, UK.

Sophie Meunier is a research scholar in Public and International Affairs at the Woodrow Wilson School, Princeton University, USA, where she is also the co-director of the EU Programme.

Neill Nugent is Professor of Politics and Jean Monnet Professor of European Integration at Manchester Metropolitan University, UK.

William E. Paterson is Honorary Professor at the Aston Centre for Europe, Aston University, UK.

B. Guy Peters is Maurice Falk Professor of American Government at the University of Pittsburgh, USA, and also Professor of Comparative Government at Zeppelin University, Friedrichshafen, Germany.

Claudio Radaelli is Professor of Political Science and Jean Monnet Chair in EU Policy Analysis at the University of Exeter, UK, where he directs the Centre for European Governance.

Berthold Rittberger is Professor of Political Science and Contemporary History at the University of Mannheim and is the project leader at the Mannheim Centre for European Social Research (MZES), Germany.

Waltraud Schelkle is Senior Lecturer in Political Economy at the European Institute of the London School of Economics and Political Science, UK.

Frank Schimmelfennig is Professor of European Studies at the Center for Comparative and International Studies (CIS) at the Swiss Federal Institute of Technology (ETH), Zurich, Switzerland.

Ulrich Sedelmeier is Senior Lecturer in International Relations at the London School of Economics and Political Science, UK.

Karen E. Smith is Reader in International Relations at the London School of Economics and Political Science, UK.

Preface

This volume has its origins in a symposium held in March 2007 to mark the successful establishment of the book series entitled 'Palgrave Studies in European Union Politics'. At the symposium, a number of leading EU scholars presented papers mapping out 'the state of the art' of existing research on the EU and identifying future research challenges.

The symposium was highly successful in bringing a number of perspectives to bear on the issues at hand and in stimulating debate on current and future research on the EU. As editors of the series it seemed to us that a book emerging from the symposium, but ranging more widely and including also contributions from leading scholars who were not present at the symposium, would be useful to those who are interested in EU studies. Such a book, which did not restrict itself to taking stock of the current state of EU studies but also mapped out future directions, would complement the innovative and research-driven, but inevitably more narrowly focused, books being published in the series. In essence, therefore, the purpose of this book is to establish the state of health of research across key substantive areas within the field of EU studies and to identify where the need for more and different research is most pressing. We seek to advance understanding of the integration process, both in theoretical and methodological terms, and in so doing offer helpful and critical insights into EU studies. A multidisciplinary approach is taken, with contributors drawing from prevailing frameworks and disciplinary and methodological debates in history, economics, law, political science and international relations.

Whether or not they stem from contributions made at the symposium, all of the chapters are new and written specifically for this book. Whilst we took a deliberate decision as editors not to impose a rigid template on the contributors, all were asked to do two main things in their subject areas: review the current state of research and suggest where further work is necessary.

We should explain the bibliographic system we have used. There was quite a debate between us on the respective merits of each chapter having its own bibliography versus there being one collated bibliography at the end of the book. There are arguments for both systems, but ultimately we opted for the former on the grounds that most readers are likely to find specialized bibliographies – on, for example, 'Europeanization' or 'Economic and Monetary Union' – to be the more useful.

We received valuable assistance from several quarters during the preparation of the book. The Germany Embassy in London kindly hosted the symposium as part of its Council Presidency programme. Susannah Atkins undertook, with great efficiency, much of the organizational work on the symposium. Our Palgrave Macmillan editors, Alison Howson (who had the original idea for the series) and Amy Lankester-Owen, were, as always, supportive and extremely helpful throughout. And the book's contributors were all responsive to editorial suggestions and, at times, chivvying.

MICHELLE EGAN
NEILL NUGENT
WILLIAM E. PATERSON

Chapter 1

Introduction: Researching the European Union

Michelle Egan, Neill Nugent and William E. Paterson

The 'explosion' in European Union studies

The European Union (EU) has become the subject of intense academic interest in recent years. This has been because it has grown greatly in importance since the mid-1980s. There have been three main dimensions to this growing importance. First, and most obviously, the EU has extended its membership: from ten member states in 1985 to 27 in 2009. Having hitherto been strictly a West European organization, the fall of the Berlin Wall in 1989 paved the way for the EU coming to cover most of the European continent west of Russia. It is, moreover, a covering that is not yet complete, with a long list of potential further members, many of which will involve very difficult decisions for the EU. Second, the EU has greatly extended its policy reach. Across most spheres of public policy it now has some sort of direct involvement, and in a significant number of crucially important policy areas – including market regulation, agriculture, fishing, and monetary policy for eurozone members – the nature of that involvement is extensive. Perhaps the most novel and challenging extension of competences has been in the area of Justice and Home Affairs (JHA), which traditionally has been seen as being at the heart of state sovereignty but now is an arena of very extensive EU activity. Third, in a series of treaty reform rounds starting with 1986 Single European Act (SEA), the EU has strengthened its policy-making capacity, with many of its key decisions now being taken on a largely supranational basis.

This increasing importance of the EU has resulted in an ever widening academic 'clientele'. Prior to the 'relaunch' of the European integration project in the mid-1980s, relatively few academics specialized in the study of the EU. Now, however, it is a major academic industry, with most European universities containing EU specialists of various kinds, with many universities in other parts of the world also containing such specialists, and with there having been over the last 20 years or so a veritable proliferation of EU-focused academic publications, conferences and organizations.

Not only has EU-related academic activity greatly increased in volume but it has also become much more variegated in nature. Scholars working within different discipline areas – but particularly history, international relations and politics, law, economics and sociology – have been attracted in large numbers to EU studies and have offered a variety of important insights into the multifaceted and hybrid nature of European integration. Historians, for example, have worked to capture the early post-war relationships by unravelling the successes and failures of integration through archival research that illuminates the diverse panorama of choices and constraints that faced European governments, their different intentions and the subsequent realities for them of accepting legal, political and economic reforms. Amongst the subjects that have been analysed by political scientists have been the exercise of political power and authority in the EU, the role of institutional developments on the evolution of public policy at EU and member state levels, and the extent to which, and the ways in which, EU decision-making processes are democratic in character. Economists have shifted from an earlier focus on the impact of European integration on economic growth, general welfare gains and economies of scale and scope to focus increasingly on the role of innovation and technology in fostering competitiveness, the tradability of goods and services, and globalization. Sociologists have focused on culture, norms and ideas, rather than material interests, in seeking to explain how the EU and its member states act and operate. And lawyers have emphasized doctrinal analysis and uniform applications of law, as well as contextual features that influence EU legal outcomes.

Not only have different disciplines cast light on different aspects of the integration process and of the EU but so has there been a mushrooming of varying approaches to EU studies within disciplines. This is nowhere more clearly demonstrated than within political science where the traditional international relations-based approaches of realism, transactionalism and neofunctionalism – that for so many years dominated the framing of debates, the choice of language and empirical analyses – have been supplemented by newer approaches, most notably rational choice and constructivism. As issues of group theory, public choice and formal modelling have come to vie with ideational, discursive and governance approaches to understanding the integration process and the nature of the European polity, political science-based EU studies has become increasingly eclectic. This increasing eclecticism is no more clearly seen than in the expansion of comparative politics and policy analysis approaches into EU studies, which has inevitably fostered increasing heterogeneity in ideas, models and methods, and which has called into question traditional distinctions between subdiscipline areas within academic political science (Hix, 1994; Jupille and Caporaso, 1999; Jupille *et al.* 2003; Franchino, 2006; Hooghe and Marks, 2009).

The focus of the book

In the early 1970s, Donald Puchala, in what was to become a famous and much-cited article, wrote the following:

> The story of the blind men and the elephant is universally known. Several blind men approached an elephant and each touched the animal in an effort to discover what the beast looked like. Each blind man, however, touched a different part of the large animal, and each concluded that the elephant had the appearance of the part he had touched. Hence, the blind man who felt the elephant's trunk concluded that an elephant must be tall and slender, while his fellow who touched the beast's ear, concluded that an elephant must be oblong and flat. Others of course reached different conclusions. The total result was that no man arrived at a very accurate description of the elephant. Yet, each man had gained enough evidence from his own experience to disbelieve his fellows and to maintain a lively debate of the nature of the beast.
>
> The experience of scholars who have been grappling with contemporary international integration is not unlike the episode of the blind men and the elephant ... Part of the problem stems from the fact that different researchers have been looking at different parts, dimensions or manifestations of the phenomenon. Furthermore, different schools of researchers have exalted different parts of the integration 'elephant' ... Added conceptual confusion has followed from the fact that the phenomenon under investigation ... has turned out to be more complex than anyone initially suspected. (Puchala, 1972: 267–8)

Puchala's metaphor of the elephant has been much applied over the years to the study of European integration and of the EU. It is applied here too for it does much to capture the diffuse nature of both the subject matter on which EU scholars focus and the methods and approaches they use in their descriptions and analyses. It is with this diffuseness that this book is concerned: how has the elephant – that is, the EU and the associated European integration process – been stalked, and what further stalking is required?

In essence, the purpose of the book is to establish the state of health of research across key substantive areas within the field of EU studies and to identify where the need for more and different research is most pressing. The contributors were asked to provide analytical surveys of existing academic debates, to consider how earlier debates and critiques have informed, shaped and reacted to new theoretical and empirical developments, and to diagnose where research is weak and to suggest future areas of research. Regarding the latter, one of the goals of the book is to foster research in new and interesting directions.

In the book we attempt to advance understanding of the phenomenon of integration, both in theoretical and methodological terms. In so doing we draw on a multidisciplinary approach, with contributions and inputs from history, economics, law, political science and international relations, and sociology. Key questions are addressed from both long-established and new perspectives and are explored via the material, ideational and political processes that shape integration and the operation of the EU.

By tracing the historiography of analytical developments, mapping out the main debates and providing fresh perspectives for future areas of research, we seek to both bring out core features of current understanding about the European integration process and the nature of the EU and also to identify where understanding is lacking. Amongst the many broad topics explored by the book's contributors are: the impact of the EU upon existing institutional and socio-economic arrangements; the complexity of Europeanization's simultaneously integrating and fragmenting forces; the operation of the market; the reordering of political relations and the restructuring of territoriality; and the configuration of new practices of governance upon different sectors within the European polity.

Themes of the book

Given that this book is much taken up with mapping research across what are now the very broad plains of EU studies, there is naturally no one overarching central theme or argument running through it. Or, at least, there is no one overarching theme or argument beyond the core belief and assertion on which the book may be said to be based: that there are a great variety of disciplines and approaches that have something useful to say about European integration and the functioning of the EU.

This variety in the application of different disciplines and approaches is seen in the way researchers utilize and apply both well-established and newer methodological tools. So within political science, the long-since created 'sub' fields of public administration, comparative politics and organizational analysis all still provide very important frameworks to understand the European institutions, political actors and policy processes, whilst international relations is still the dominant way through which statecraft, interstate bargaining and EU external power relations are conceptualized and analysed. But such traditional approaches, which have their counterparts in other disciplines, have increasingly been joined by newer approaches, which may be said to stem in large part from the vitality of EU studies, which has witnessed the development of strong critiques by scholars from many perspectives about the methods, tools and frameworks that should be used to analyse European integration.

So, whether it is via formal modelling and quantitative analysis or cultural analysis and social theory, the study of European integration has evolved in new directions.

But, although there is no one overarching central theme to the book beyond the assertion that EU studies has greatly benefited from the application of a variety of different disciplines and approaches, a number of subthemes do recur, though they do not necessarily feature in all chapters. Amongst these themes is the increasing interest displayed by academics in EU governance and its various configurations. This interest has resulted in an emphasis on the different constitutive forms of governance in different sectors, with much attention focused on explaining the emergence of new patterns of rules, processes and outcomes and new relations between state and non-state actors. So, as well as focusing on established and mainstream governance patterns in which the EU's main institutions serve as the primary reference for understanding political developments, academics have also examined more specialized areas such as security governance and economic governance. This has resulted in a focus on the way that a range of institutions, agencies and actors have sought to pursue economic and welfare goals, assert economic interests and cultural values, and expand security and foreign policy objectives. Several chapters of this book consider such governance issues and focus on, for example, key features of EU governance, the relationships between political and economic institutions, and the institutionalization of differing forms of political representation.

Attuned to the growing complexity of European integration, the interaction between national, European and global forces in shaping the integration process is another theme of the book. As a number of chapters show, integration which simultaneously internationalizes domestic politics and domesticates international politics has generated significant interest in the 'top-down' and 'bottom-up' impacts of integration, and has encouraged greater attention to the impact of domestic politics on the European polity and the role of the European polity in shaping both domestic and international political developments.

A consequence of Europeanization and globalization has been to thrust the role and functions of the state into the centre of political controversy, which has promoted academic interest in how state-centred paradigms have been adjusted and modified to incorporate the shift in functional and territorial boundaries. As territoriality – reflected in central concepts such as state-centred nationalism, state borders and state sovereignty – has been altered, and more particularly fragmented, so has there been an increasing focus on the external roles and influence of the EU. The global impact of European political economy and foreign policy, and whether they are capable of wielding significant interventionist, persuasive and regulatory power on the world stage, have been the subject of extensive academic comment and analysis. Particular attention has been given to how, and to what extent, external policy actions have facilitated territorial expansion through enlargements, economic leverage and an ability to use the European market as a platform to foster broader foreign policy objectives and ideas. The end of the Cold War created a space for a greater European role in the provision of security, and these efforts have also been the subject of much academic enquiry. These, and related issues, are addressed in several chapters of the book.

As domestic autonomy has changed, and arguably been 'weakened' – by the pressures of Europeanization and globalization, the advancement of market mechanisms and economic reforms, and the spread of democratic and liberal norms – the contributors to the book offer a fresh look at such matters as the changing nature and roles of EU political institutions and the process of instituting a European market economy. They consider fundamental questions of political citizenship, identity and participation in the European polity. And they demonstrate how the state that commanded considerable strength in different policy domains has been transformed by transnational networks, norms and rules which strongly influence choices at the national level and foster denser cooperation and rule making at the international level (Slaughter, 2004). Such processes have generated new social and political dynamics that have restructured territoriality and national boundaries through new governance mechanisms in which production, exchange and property rights have been transformed, collective security cooperation has been enhanced and societal mobilization has significantly altered rules, norms and structures deriving from earlier paths of state formation and nation-state consolidation.

The existence and consequences of resistance to Europeanization also feature in the book, with several chapters pointing to the contentious politics that have arisen around efforts to deepen European integration. As Europeanization has led to an unbundling and reorganization of aspects of national economies and political systems, so has it also led to efforts to protect the familiar and to resist, or at least be cautious about, continued integration.

The varying degrees of resistance to and caution about integration is, of course, a key reason why the EU's institutional and decision-making systems are so complex and multifaceted. This complexity and multifacetedness – which are manifested in such features of the EU as its changing treaties and treaty structures, its sheer number of policy-making processes, its multilevel governance character in some policy areas and its increasing differentiation (policy activity without all member states fully participating) – are explored in several chapters of the book. The explorations emphasize that the complexity and multifacetedness result in problems of directional coordination and coherence which, in turn, impact on efforts to exercise coherent political control. The complexity and multifacetedness impact also on the transparency, accountability and efficiency of the political system, thereby raising concerns about democratic control (Scharpf, 1999). Yet, as recent debates illustrate, some aspects of the complexity, such as multilevel governance, may – ironically it may be thought – actually help the EU's democratic quality by enhancing deliberation and allowing states to achieve policy coordination, reciprocal benefits and credible commitments through delegating and pooling sovereignty (Keohane *et al.*, 2009).

How integration has proceeded in differing ways and to differing degrees between policy sectors is another theme of the book. A number of reasons account for this, not least, as was suggested in the previous paragraph, that decision-making in a multilevel polity, where the lower levels exercise considerable power, inevitably faces problems of fragmented decision-making and coordination. Another important reason is that the organizational configuration of the European polity – with its powerful executive, legislative and judicial institutions, and its mixed bag of highly influential political actors – means that the institutional system provides no shortage of opportunities for the polity to take on a sharply contested form. Variation across different economic policy domains, for example, highlights that integration has not been driven only by the logic of uniform market principles but reflects also the salience of social solidarity and the preservation of sectoral and national diversity in the economic sphere within Europe (Schmidt, 2002; Menz, 2005; Hancké *et al.*, 2007). Similarly, while collective security has been enhanced, there remain distinct national strategic cultures and different approaches to the management of internal security.

A final theme of the book that should be stressed is the way in which book chapters demonstrate that the chronicling and understanding of European integration must consider the nature of, and the intersections and interactions between, both the old and the new. As regards chronicling, the character of, for example, new modes of governance, new forms of production and new issues in the public affairs' arena are all important in their own right, but so too is their impact on established practices and patterns. As regards understanding, academics have sought to analyse issues and problems through new frameworks and perspectives, but they have also continued to use and borrow from older models and approaches.

The contents of the book

A very wide range of topics are covered in the chapters of this book. Whilst space limitations have necessarily not permitted every institution, political actor or policy to be fully analysed, and not every theoretical, empirical or methodological approach to be explored in depth, the principal issues and debates that have attracted academic attention in recent years are, we believe, all given due consideration.

In Chapter 2, Piers Ludlow focuses on the historiography of European integration, indicating how scholars have generated new avenues of historical research that are increasingly cross-national in character. Bolstered by an emphasis on state calculations and strategic interests, the early work on individual states has been supplemented by greater attention to internal developments in a variety of European policies. Yet despite the breadth and variety of historical research, and the focus on ideas, institutions and identity, Ludlow argues that we need to blend methodological insights from law, economics and politics with studies of the historical past and link the historiography of the integration process with broader questions about how much European integration has shaped or altered patterns of economic cooperation, electoral politics and social mobilization, and security cooperation.

Frank Schimmelfennig, in Chapter 3, examines the evolution of integration theory, which derives largely from international relations and political science. He focuses on the emergence of rational approaches that have served to generate new questions on the EU's institutional evolution and policy developments, and he compares this to constructivism, with its focus on social learning, deliberation and norms. He concludes with a survey of new avenues for theoretical research on the varying institutional arrangements that have emerged as part of the transformation of European governance and suggests that this requires a greater exchange between integration theories and comparative politics.

Chapter 4 is on the EU institutions, with Neill Nugent and William Paterson focusing particularly on the conceptual and theoretical work on the main institutions. They survey the main debates in international relations on institutional power and influence, and highlight the growth of research using rational, sociological and historical institutionalist approaches. They make the point that newer conceptual approaches have not been slow to 'borrow' from neighbouring approaches, including organizational culture, transaction cost economics and bureaucratic politics, to explain institutional dynamics.

Derek Beach, in Chapter 5, examines the role of leadership, drawing on literature in public administration and organization studies, to understand the dynamics of supply and demand of leadership in European negotiations. He focuses on the constraints upon leadership, through empirical cases of intergovernmental negotiations, to highlight the role of informational advantages, trust and entrepreneurship in fostering collective institutionally agreed outcomes.

In Chapter 6, Guy Peters and Susana Borrás examine the complexity of governance, emphasizing the multiplicity of processes and institutions involved in European decision-making. They highlight how the multilevel segmented nature of policy-making poses constraints on coherence and coordination across the public sector. While high-lighting performance problems, they also point to the need for thinking about the importance of democratic accountability. The advent of new forms of collaborative governance has altered traditional policy styles and organizational structures so that the styles of governing in Europe have to be stretched to meet a multitude of actual needs.

Berthold Rittberger, in Chapter 7, undertakes an ambitious and sys-tematic analysis of the debate about the EU's democratic quality. In his account, he looks at the standard version before turning to the scep-tical view associated with communitarian and republican theorists. This is followed by a consideration of the more positive view of the deliberative theorists and an analysis of the regulatory state school. In the final sections of his chapter he takes issue with deliberative democ-racy and concludes with a powerful argument on the lack of systematic empirical knowledge and the failure to test theoretical claims.

Chapter 8, by Anthony Arnull, lays out the character of legal scholar-ship and its effect on the field of European law, as well as the impact of different legal traditions on the context and study of European law. While acknowledging the role of political science in theorizing the evo-lution of the legal structure, and stressing the critical role that the courts have played in market-making, Arnull highlights the methodological divisions, the continuing requirement for doctrinal analysis and the increasing specialization that play a role in European legal analysis.

Claudio Radaelli and Theofanis Exadaktylos, in Chapter 9, focus on Europeanization. They point to the diffusion of Europeanization research across both international relations and comparative politics, noting that scholarship on European integration has always dealt with the transformation of state processes. As such, Europeanization as a concept, method and explanation has evolved into a more nuanced understanding of the reshaping of identities, interests and institutions of political representation at both the national and European level. The causal measurement of the usage and pressures stemming from Europeanization is, they argue, critical for determining whether the importance of the concept as a key mechanism in promoting adapta-tion and change is to be fully understood.

In Chapter 10 Michelle Egan focuses on the political process of insti-tuting a market economy, the operations of the market and the efforts to balance efficiency goals with broader social equity goals that are increasingly constrained by European rules regarding regulation, liber-alization and market competition. She analyses the increasing political salience of market integration within domestic politics, and how distinctive institutional configurations of capitalism make the deep-ening of market integration more difficult.

Egan's chapter on the political economy of market integration ties in with Chapter 11 by Waltraud Schelkle, who focuses on macroeconomic policy, especially monetary policy, to highlight the structural problems faced by maintaining fiscal policy within member states. In her chapter, Schelkle outlines the need for both fiscal policy coordination and welfare reform, and the political and economic challenges created by these competing agendas in the context of the current fiscal crisis and economic climate.

Christina Boswell in Chapter 12 outlines how an amorphous set of policies constitute JHA. While scholars have examined developments within immigration and asylum, judicial cooperation and law enforcement, and border controls and management, she argues that they have not engaged in enough cross-sectoral analysis or linked JHA policy development sufficiently to broader debates on neo-institutionalism, constructivism or critical theory. The framing of discourse in this area is crucial in understanding the legitimation problems, the modes of governing and the organizational constraints that cooperation faces in the area of internal security.

In Chapter 13 Johanna Kantola focuses on how feminist scholars perceive European integration as well as how European integration has impacted and affected women in terms of access, equality, labour markets and social exclusion. She traces the framing of gender issues within the EU and feminist critiques of European actions in the contexts of market citizenship, social values and civil society.

Karen Smith in Chapter 14 highlights the expansion of research in European external relations. She notes that whilst attempts to meet the challenge of explaining the motives of foreign policy cooperation mainly derive from international relations, the challenges of implementing and evaluating the effects of such policies draw upon research in trade, development, and peace and conflict resolution. She also emphasizes that studies of foreign policy can engage with broader integration debates on Europeanization to assess the impact on the foreign policy cultures and orientations of member states, as well as being useful in engaging in debates on the implementation and the effectiveness of coordinated action or the consequences of lack of action.

In Chapter 15 Wade Jacoby and Sophie Meunier consider the relationship between globalization and integration. They highlight how globalization constitutes a set of ideas that centre on heightened market integration, which has led to a primary focus on the territorial effects of globalization on states or regions. They examine the relationship between Europeanization and globalization in terms of deregulation, liberalization and privatization to tease out the causal relationship between the two processes and to analyse both the impact of globalization on different European sectors and the impact of European market integration in shaping global rules and norms. They also analyse the diffusion of ideas and the rhetoric of globalization to determine the causal effects of globalization on European politics and how European states are attempting to 'manage globalization'.

The future shape of the EU is the subject of Chapter 16, by Heather Grabbe and Ulrich Sedelmeier. They take stock of the transformation of functional and territorial boundaries in understanding the external governance role of the Union. Focusing on Europeanization beyond the nation-state, the chapter illustrates the cross-temporal and cross-regional effects of enlargement on state capacity and domestic governance. The complexity of building market institutions and the interplay of sociological, political and economic factors in sustaining enlargement negotiations serve to illustrate the challenges still facing the European polity.

In the final chapter, we, as the book's editors, draw out a number of general points that emerge from the chapters. Perhaps the most important of these points is that although there has been an enormous amount of research undertaken on the EU in recent years – and, indeed, one can talk of a partial reinvention of EU studies through such developments as the governance turn, the policy turn, the constructivist turn and the quantitative turn – some areas and approaches have been relatively neglected and/or underdeveloped. An example of such an area is the theoretical work on EU policies that are not part of the EU's first pillar. The chapter also explores the relationship of EU studies to cognate areas and the implications of this relationship for the debate about whether the EU is best studied in an interdisciplinary mode or by applying disciplinary tools. Looking to the future of EU research, a number of potentially important and fruitful areas are identified.

The European Union and European Union studies: both advancing, largely successfully, but with some failures

As we examine the EU after five decades of its existence, it is indisputable that the academic study of its development and nature has achieved a great deal. The chapters of this book demonstrate the achievements, with explanations given of the very considerable insights we now have in aspects of the integration process, ranging from EU governance to the impact of globalization. But the chapters also show that much further research is necessary, and that in some respects – of which the relative paucity of interdisciplinary work is perhaps the most obvious and important instance – EU studies may be said to have partially failed.

In seeking to evaluate what research on European integration has accomplished, where it has lagged and where it should go, the book covers a lot of ground. It does so by looking at both empirical realities and theoretical debates from many perspectives and by focusing on many key aspects of the integration process. For example, attention is given to why and how the assumption that the single market would foster economic growth and development – through eliminating restrictions to the movement of goods, capital, labour and services – did not anticipate the recurrent economic crises that have occurred or the impact of globalization on European competitiveness. Enlargement is also considered, with attention given to how it can be seen as the EU's attempt to come to terms with the realities of a post-Cold War world, to how the EU has played an unprecedented role in shaping states and markets in Central and Eastern Europe, and to how the transformation of relations with Central and Eastern European states through the ambitious enlargement agenda has served as a catalyst for deeper integration in areas of immigration, border enforcement and internal security. The challenges of institutional and political actor adaptation are examined too, with a focus on, amongst other things, how European governments have changed the way they deal with one another as they have shifted from nation-states to member states. Another important area that is analysed is the extension of the EU's foreign profile, from its limited intergovernmental origins to the current position whereby the EU is often able to advance a common economic and political agenda when dealing with third countries in bilateral and multilateral forums.

Rather like the mixed record of EU studies, the EU's own record also shows successes and failures, and in the book instances of both are examined. So, for example, whilst major institutional reforms have been made over the years, for many practitioners and commentators the difficulty in pushing through in the 2000s a treaty reform that had as its main purpose making the Union more coherent, effective and visible to both its citizens and to other states must be viewed as a major failure. Economically, the EU has been successful in its efforts to reduce transaction costs and foster economic coordination. Further, trade and investment have increased, mergers and acquisitions have surged, and there has been an unprecedented degree of social and economic integration – most notably in the form of monetary union. But as the European economic strategy has shifted from that of market liberalization and market access to the language of competitiveness, impact assessment, growth and market-based alternatives, so has success been less clear, and so has, in the opinions of many, insufficient attention been paid to social solidarity and welfare goals. Security policy has also been less developed than many would have liked to see, with efforts to create an intergovernmental defence and security policy having been marked by difficulties in translating sentiment into credible policy commitments.

On these and other matters, academic commentators, including some contributors to this book, reach significantly different conclusions. They do so in large part as a result of approaching their subjects in different ways, covering different time scales and focusing on different issue areas. Such differences encapsulate some of the problems European studies has as a subject area. But, it is nonetheless a subject area that has made great advances over the years, as this book's chapters demonstrate.

References

Franchino F. (2006) *The Powers of the Union: Delegation in the EU* (Cambridge: Cambridge University Press).

Hancké, B., Rhodes, M. and Thatcher, M. (eds) (2007) *Beyond Varieties of Capitalism: Conflict, Contradictions and Complementarities in the European Economy* (Oxford: Oxford University Press).

Hix, S. (1994) 'The Study of the European Community: The Challenge to Comparative Politics', *West European Politics* 17(1): 1–30.

Hooghe, L. and Marks, G. (2009) 'A Postfunctionalist Theory of European Integration: From Permissive Consensus to Constraining Dissensus', *British Journal of Political Science* 39(1): 1–23.

Jupille, J. and Caporaso, J.A. (1999) 'Institutionalism and the European Union:

Beyond Comparative Politics and International Relations', *Annual Review of Political Science* 2: 429–44.

Jupille, J., Caporaso, J.A. and Checkel, J.T. (eds) (2003) 'Integrating Institutions: Rationalism, Constructivism, and the Study of the European Union', special issue of *Comparative Political Studies*, 36(1–2).

Keohane, R., Macedo, S. and Moravscik, A. (2009) 'Democracy Enhancing Multilateralism', *International Organization* 63(1): 1–31.

Menz, G. (2005) *Varieties of Capitalism and Europeanization – National Response Strategies to the Single European Market* (Oxford: Oxford University Press).

Puchala, D. (1972) 'Of Blind Men, Elephants and International Integration', *Journal of Common Market Studies* 10(3): 267–84.

Scharpf, F. (1999) *Governing in Europe: Effective and Democratic?* (Oxford: Oxford University Press).

Schmidt, V. (2002) *The Futures of European Capitalism* (Oxford: Oxford University Press).

Slaughter, A.M. (2004) *A New World Order* (Princeton: Princeton University Press).

Chapter 2

History Aplenty: But Still Too Isolated

N. Piers Ludlow

Like most political anniversaries, the fiftieth anniversary of the signature of the Treaty of Rome, marked by multiple events in the spring of 2007, has rapidly faded from memory. In its brief moment of prominence, however, the occasion did serve to underline quite how long the European integration process has lasted. The EC/EU itself is more than 50 years old; some form of institutionalized level of cooperation at a European level has been in existence now for over six decades; and the idea of European unity and cooperation has a much longer history even than that. There is hence plenty for historians of European integration to get their teeth into, even making allowances for the normal reluctance of historians to study subjects which are too close to the present and for which access to archival documents is limited. A varied and wide ranging historiography has been the result. The first part of this chapter will briefly review what has been written by historians about the integration process; the second part will then assess the strengths and weaknesses of this work; and a third part will suggest a number of fields to which historians appear to be (or, in some cases, ought to be) turning their attention.

From ideas to states and institutions and back again?

The first focus of European integration history was the Second World War, or, more precisely, the Europeanist ideas which emerged amongst resistance groups and governments-in-exile during the 1940–45 period. The work of Walter Lipgens, in particular, identified those engaged in a battle against Nazism as the pioneers in that change of European attitudes towards nations and nationalism that would make possible post-war cooperation and integration. Nazism and Fascism had discredited nationalism; still more importantly, the experience of military defeat and/or occupation undergone by all European states except Britain and a handful of neutrals demonstrated the inability of individual nation-states, acting alone, to fulfil their most basic obligation of protecting their citizens. As a result, wartime opponents of Nazism came to a shared realization that the international architecture of the post-war world could not be built upon fully sovereign nation-states alone. This readiness to transcend the nation-state was a vital precondition for the success of post-war integration (Lipgens and Loth, 1977, 1988, 1991). The voluminous primary documents collected by Lipgens and his team did also provide striking evidence of how Europeanist ideas had circulated amongst both German and collaborationist thinkers in wartime Europe as well as amongst their adversaries – but significantly perhaps Lipgens in his overview of his findings chose to de-emphasize this fact.

The association between resistance and Europeanism fitted well with the multiple memoirs of protagonists in the early integration process which had been published in the 1960s and early 1970s (Adenauer, 1965, 1966, 1967, 1968; Spaak, 1969; Hallstein, 1972; Monnet, 1978; Pineau and Rimbaud, 1991). These too tended to present the European integration experiment as an attempt to break away from the nationalistic rivalries which had twice led Europe into war in the twentieth century. It also fitted well with the rhetoric of the European institutions which again liked to present themselves as being fundamentally about peace rather than merely economics. And it seemed to have the additional merit of explaining Britain's ambivalence towards European integration. The UK, it was argued, had not suffered defeat or occupation during the Second World War and had hence come out of the conflict with faith in its own institutions and in its own ability to steer an independent course in the world reinforced rather than weakened. Britain had thus looked askance at the ambitious supranational schemes espoused by its continental neighbours and rejected invitations to participate. This failure to join either the European Coal and Steel Community (ECSC) or the European Economic Community (EEC) from the outset – a choice later British governments appeared to regret – was, in Monnet's telling phrase, 'the price of victory' (Charlton, 1983).

Unfortunately, though, the identification of the Second World War resistance leaders as the originators of a major break with Europe's nationalist path did little actually to explain how the integration process began. The first effective move towards supranational integration had after all only been accomplished with the Schuman Plan in 1950, by which time the majority of those politicians who had emerged into prominence through their role in the wartime resistance movements had either lapsed back into obscurity or had been compelled to reinvent themselves in a decidedly more nationalistic mode so as to survive in the rough and tumble of peacetime politics. Neither chronology nor continuity of personnel thus suggested a strong link between wartime ideas and the actual decisions which led to the ECSC or the EEC. Explaining the breakthroughs of 1950 or 1955 would need another type of explanation.

In the event, two rival schools emerged, one emphasizing the political motivations which underlay the establishment of the ECSC and the EEC, the other highlighting an economic chain of causality. The former was most closely associated with the two so-called *Power in Europe* volumes, which gathered contributions from an impressive array of the most prominent international historians at work in France, Germany, Italy and the UK (Becker and Knipping, 1986; Di Nolfo, 1992). These presented the key integration choices (or non-choices in the British case) of the four main Western European states as being a result of their altered power status within post-war international relations. The Treaty of Rome was thus, as Pierre Guillen put it, 'a cure for French impotence'. In similar fashion integration represented an opportunity for Germany and Italy to regain some of the status and international respectability forfeited by wartime defeat and, for the Federal Republic of Germany, a means to bind itself securely to the West in such a fashion that neither its allies nor subsequent German governments could cast doubt on its Western alignment (Küsters, 1982). For exponents of the second school, by contrast, led by the economic historian Alan Milward, these same choices could be explained primarily in economic terms. The Schuman Plan thus constituted a French scheme designed to prevent its post-war economic recovery plan (masterminded by none other than Jean Monnet) from being thrown off course by the re-emergence of West Germany as a major steel producer (Milward, 1984). The EEC meanwhile began life as a Dutch device, intended to make irreversible the degree of trade liberalization within Western Europe which had already occurred by the early 1950s and upon which small, advanced economies like that of the Netherlands had come to rely (Milward *et al.*, 1992). The success of this Dutch idea was greatly facilitated, however, when it was seized upon by a small coterie of French leaders as a mechanism which could wean France off its traditional protectionism by offering the opportunity of controlled liberalization within a small and potentially tightly regulated common market (Lynch, 1997).

Despite their very obvious differences, however, both schools shared two important assumptions. The first was that the key actors in the integration story were states and not the loose collection of Europeanist thinkers who had populated the pages of Lipgens's account. It was through the actions of the governments of France, Germany, Italy, the Netherlands and Britain that the emergence of the ECSC and the EEC could best be explained. Second, both the contributors to the *Power in Europe* volumes and Milward and his entourage, de-emphasized the role of Europeanist idealism and instead stressed the vital importance of hard-headed calculation. Those national bureaucrats and politicians who made the key choices which initiated the integration process were not motivated by a desire to transcend the nation-state and nationalism, but instead to further national needs and ambitions (either economic or political) through a strategy based on far-reaching cooperation and the pooling of sovereignty. Milward's striking title, *The European Rescue of the Nation-State*, could in essence apply to either school.

This was an important breakthrough. Both the writings of Lipgens and the early memoir accounts had suggested a level of altruism and idealism in the early decisions about European integration which sat uncomfortably with the normal behaviour of national politicians. The new explanations, by contrast, whether emphasizing economic or political factors, were much more akin to the type of arguments that historians have employed to explain other international phenomena like the outbreak of the two world wars, the decolonization process or the breakdown of East–West relations. The emphasis on state actions, furthermore, indicated that historians of the integration process could make use of the well-trodden research paths leading to the national archives of each of the states involved. A huge outpouring of literature ensued, much of it probing the actions and motivations of individual national governments or even of individual ministries or ministers within these governments.

A significant amount of this research took the form of contributions to edited volumes. The conference volume seemed a particularly appropriate vehicle in the field of European integration history, able to bring together studies of how each country took the decision for or against involvement in the nascent European institutions. Collaborative works of this sort also meant that a new field could make the most of the pre-existing reservoir of expertise on national political histories. The usual pattern of work was hence for the contributions on French policy to be written by well-established French historians, those on Germany to be penned by German specialists and those on the UK to be the work of leading British historians. The key series of volumes taking this approach re-examined wartime cooperation, the Schuman Plan, the failed European Defence Community project and the chain of events leading from the Messina conference of 1955 to the signature of the Rome Treaties themselves in 1957 (Poidevin, 1986a; Schwabe, 1988; Serra, 1989; Trausch, 1993). Another more thematically organized collection investigated the theme of European identity – although again with a lot of emphasis on national calculation and governmental action (Girault and Bossuat, 1993; Bossuat and Girault, 1994; Girault, 1994; Deighton, 1995; Fleury and Frank, 1997; Bitsch *et al.*, 1998).

The tendency of European integration history writing to be organized around national studies was also visible in the first wave of monographs on the subject. One striking example was Gérard Bossuat's heavyweight study of France, the Marshall Plan and European integration (Bossuat, 1997). Others to follow a similar approach included Laschi's work on Italian agriculture and Europe, Rhenisch's investigation of German business and early European integration, and Hitchcock's account of early post-war French policy (Hitchcock, 1998; Rhenisch, 1999; Laschi, 2000). Thiemeyer, Noël and Weilemann did constitute valuable exceptions to this rule, with their multinational focus on individual policy areas, but they did not seriously undermine the trend (Weilemann, 1983; Noël, 1988; Thiemeyer, 1999). Nor was this concentration on the policy of individual states confined to books about the six states which did participate in the first European institutions. On the contrary, a sizeable literature emerged both on the policies of the most prominent sceptic towards European integration – the United Kingdom – and on the actions of European unity's greatest external cheerleader, the United States. The former ranged from John Young's investigation of British policy towards European integration under the first post-war Labour government, via two detailed assessments of why Britain chose not to accept the Schuman Plan, to James Ellison's analysis of the free trade area scheme with which London had hoped to temper the harmful effects of its self-willed exclusion from the EEC (Young, 1984; Dell, 1995; Lord, 1996; Ellison, 2000). Mention also should be made of the three detailed monographs written on British policy towards the European Defence Community project and the question of German rearmament (Dockrill, 1991; Mawby, 1999; Ruane, 2000). The most thorough investigation of Washington's supportive role was probably that by Pascaline Winand (Winand, 1993). But there were also useful studies by Lundestad, Killick, Giauque and Skogmar, as well as highly relevant sections in the biographical studies of McCloy, Dulles and Conant (Immerman, 1990; Schwartz, 1991; Hershberg, 1993; Killick, 1997; Lundestad, 1998; Giauque, 2002; Skogmar, 2004). All of these confirmed the degree of activism shown by US policy makers in encouraging Europe to unite.

The biographical approach was also effectively used on some of the European figures who had played leading roles in the early history of integration. Possibly the first major contribution in this respect was Raymond Poidevin's reconstruction of Robert Schuman's political life (Poidevin, 1986b). But this was followed by the equally accomplished studies of Adenuaer, De Gasperi, Bidault, Van Zeeland, Spaak, Eden, Macmillan, de Gaulle, Pompidou and Monnet himself (Schwarz, 1986, 1991; Horne, 1989; Lacouture, 1991; Duchêne and Monnet, 1994; Roussel, 1994, 1996, 2002; Dujardin and Dumoulin, 1997; Dutton, 1997; Dumoulin, 1999; Bézias, 2006; Craveri, 2006). Most of these sought to contextualize each politician's European decisions within the wider framework of their approach to foreign policy, thereby reinforcing the trend away from an emphasis on Europeanist ideology and towards integration as a means of advancing national interest. Schuman's decision-making in the run-up to the European plan that would bear his name was not thus intrinsically different from that which led to his decisions in the fields of East–West relations or of France's bilateral relations with the United States (Poidevin, 1986b). Likewise, the most recent and thorough study of De Gasperi rejects the portrayal of the Italian statesman by earlier biographers as a convinced federalist, and suggests instead that his enthusiasm for Italian involvement in the integration process was a much more complex and multicausal affair (Craveri, 2006).

The fact that all of this literature was based primarily on archival materials from national collections also influenced the chronological focus of the research. Western governments tend to operate what is known as a 'thirty year rule' – a system under which previously secret government materials are made available to historians three decades after they were written. This means that the frontier of historical scholarship usually lies a little over 30 years before the present (allowing for the time needed to process and write up the archival findings). Thus the 1990s saw the beginning of substantial work on the operation and initial development of the European Community in the 1960s. One focus for attention was the way in which the EEC's early success obliged those European countries which had originally chosen not to take part to reconsider their position. A succession of volumes thus investigated the Community's first encounters with the issue of enlargement in 1961–63 and again in 1967 (Griffiths and Ward, 1996; Kaiser, 1996; Tratt, 1996; Ludlow, 1997; Wilkes, 1997; Schaad, 2000; Daddow, 2002; Milward, 2002; Parr, 2006; Pine, 2007).

The British case naturally loomed large in most of these books – decisions taken in London were, after all, the trigger for all three rounds of enlargement discussions in the 1961–73 period – but many of the edited volumes also contained work looking at the manner in which the Danes, Irish and Norwegians applied for membership alongside the British, as well as the positions adopted by countries like Sweden or Spain. Some of these titles also analysed the enlargement episode from the Community's point of view, demonstrating that while the terms 'widening' and 'deepening' only entered general usage after the Hague Summit of December 1969, the perceived tension between these two ambitions dated back to 1961 at least.

Work on the actual first enlargement, by contrast, has been somewhat slow to emerge. The general overview by Kaiser and Elvert of how the Community's membership has grown did offer some discussion of the 1970–72 negotiations, as did the special issue of the *Journal of European Integration History* (vol. 11, issue 2, 2005) dedicated to enlargement (Kaiser and Elvert, 2004). A further special issue of the same journal (vol 9, issue 1, 2003) also provided valuable analysis of the Hague Summit which arguably cleared the way for EC expansion. Previously unknown details of the Heath–Pompidou discussions at the May 1971 summit were revealed in Roussel's biography of the French

President (Roussel, 1994). And the official British history of the negotiations, written up by Sir Con O'Neill, was made public by Frank Cass (O'Neill, 2000). But none of the detailed doctorates devoted to the membership negotiations of the early 1970s, which are underway or have recently been completed, have yet been published.

Books on the Community's internal development also gradually proliferated. The best starting point for someone wanting to master this literature are the three edited volumes which resulted from the conferences organized by the EU Liaison Committee of Historians (Milward and Deighton, 1999; Loth, 2001; Varsori, 2006). These demonstrated the way in which a focus on the post-1958 period obliged authors to flank the traditional studies centring on individual member states (which naturally continued) with new research on both the Community institutions and the gradual emergence of common policies. Such institutional investigations followed a trail which had been successfully blazed by the well-produced official history of the High Authority of the ECSC (Spierenburg and Poidevin, 1993). This was followed by a series of other volumes exploring the early growth of the EC's institutional system (Heyen, 1992; Bitsch *et al.*, 1998; Loth, 2005; Varsori, 2006; Kaiser *et al.*, 2009). The year 2007 also saw the emergence of a second official history, this time focusing on the European Commission between 1958 and 1972 (Dumoulin and Bitsch, 2007). This contained some genuinely useful new material, but did highlight the dangers of the Commission's decision not to accompany the writing of an official history with the type of systematic attempt to catalogue and organize its archives in the manner which had so strengthened the Poidevin and Spierenburg volume. Few of the historians involved in the new project appear to have found the oral testimonies of ageing former *fonctionnaires* a fully adequate replacement for the multiple gaps in the Commission's archival record.

Book-length studies of the Community's policies have been slow to appear: the first monograph devoted to a common policy looks likely to be an in-depth investigation of the Common Agricultural Policy (CAP) (Knudsen, 2009), but the succession of recent doctorates devoted to other Community policies, from the common commercial policy and the Kennedy Round of GATT negotiations to competition policy, suggest the beginnings of an overdue and highly welcome trend. There have been several chapters and articles devoted to common policies (Ludlow, 2005; Varsori, 2006; Kaiser *et al.*, 2009). Ludlow meanwhile made a first attempt to combine national, institutional and policy-oriented approaches so as to produce a comprehensive overview of the Community's evolution in the second half of the 1960s (Ludlow, 2006).

National studies have continued of course. Good examples include Henning Turk's investigation of the European policies of the Grand Coalition government in Germany between 1966 and 1969 and Antonio

Varsori's multiple collections, both of individual chapters on different aspects of policy-making in Rome and of core documents relating to Italy's European policy (Ballini and Varsori, 2004; Türk, 2006; Varsori and Romero, 2006). Gehler's work on Austria or Crespo MacLennan's on Spain also demonstrates that the path towards involvement with the EC of those states who had initially not been members remains a subject of ongoing investigation (Gehler, 2005; MacLennan, 2000). National chapters have gone on being a feature, moreover, of the first few edited volumes devoted to European integration in the 1970s (Knipping and Schönwald, 2004; Van der Harst, 2007). A healthy subgenre of bilateral studies has also emerged, exploring the development of European cooperation through a focus on the relations between key European states. Predictably, perhaps, the relationship between France and Germany has been the most extensively investigated (Soutou, 1996; Bitsch and Mestre, 2001; Lappenküper, 2001), but there have also been detailed investigations of relations between Italy and France, Italy and Germany, Britain and Germany, Britain and France, Britain and the Netherlands, and Germany and the Netherlands (Bagnato, 1995; Masala, 1997; Wielenga, 1997; Decup, 1998; Schaad, 2000; Ashton and Hellema, 2001).

The last few years has also seen a significant re-emergence of interest in the ideas that underpinned European integration and the political movements within which they flourished. Christian Democracy, the political tradition out of which emerged the majority of those dubbed the 'founding fathers', is understandably the political tradition focused upon most (Gehler and Kaiser, 2004; Kaiser, 2007; Risso, 2007). But there has also been work both on the Socialists and Europe (Anaya, 2002) and upon those who rejected Europe. Robert Dewey's forthcoming study on British Euroscepticism in the 1960s will be of great significance in this respect (Dewey, 2009), but interesting work is also being done on the opposition of the Italian Communists to their country's participation in the building of Europe. Over two decades on from the decisive rejection by historians of Walter Lipgens's earlier emphasis on ideas and idealism as the main motivating forces behind European integration, a new generation of specialists seems to be rediscovering that neither national nor institutional motivations alone are sufficient to explain the transformation of Europe since 1950. Instead the ideas, beliefs, fears and political milieux of those politicians and officials who took the crucial decisions is once again coming under deserved historical scrutiny.

Broad but too uncritical and isolated?

The key strength of this historiography has been its breadth and variety. The topics covered range from the precise economic incentives of prominent European industrialists (Dumoulin, 1993) to the world view of military thinkers, passing en route the motivations of civil servants, politicians and intellectuals, and the anxieties and aspirations of those who chose to promote the process and those who chose to contest it. Geographically there has also been an encouraging diversity, both in terms of the countries written about and the national provenance of those doing the historical research. Only the countries which used to lie behind the Iron Curtain have been largely untouched by the spread of interest in European integration history – an understandable situation given that points of intersection between the national development of these countries and the integration process were few and far between prior to 1989. In the last five to ten years, there has also been a welcome loosening of the assumption that only scholars from a given country can study in depth the European policies of that country. A healthy number of the younger specialists are thus working on nations other than their own, not to mention those other researchers who have focused on institutions, policies or political parties instead of national governments. The days of the conference paper on France being reserved for the senior French historian, or the young English researcher being automatically expected to do the 'Britain and x' chapter in a volume, would appear to be numbered.

Also welcome has been the relatively high degree of institutionalization which the field has undergone. This matters greatly in a subject area where so many depend upon receiving information about and assistance in using archival resources elsewhere in Europe. Similarly, the existence of established networks helps the flow of information about key new publications in the field and dissemination of information about conferences, workshops or collaborative projects. The oldest of these networks is what is now called the EU Liaison Committee of Historians, which began life over 25 years ago as a Commission funded initiative. Direct EC funding has long since dried up, but the group continues to meet regularly, to organize periodic conferences designed to showcase the latest research and to publish the *Journal of European Integration History*. Another larger and slightly looser network, with a membership which overlaps substantially with that of the Liaison Committee, is the product of the large transnational project, originally set up by René Girault, to explore European identity, and now directed by Robert Frank in its investigation of 'Les Espaces Européennes'. Professor Frank has also just put in place a further collaborative network linking specialists in the field across Europe for a project which will study the 'dimensions and dynamics of European integration'.

Alongside these networks of well-established specialists, there are also two highly active networks of younger researchers, both of which have emerged in the course of the last five years. One, originally based in Paris, but now with members across Europe and beyond, is called RICHIE (Reseau International de Chercheurs de l'Histoire d'Intégration Européenne); the other, which emerged in Britain but has also spread substantially, is called HEIRS (History of European Integration Research Society). Both organize regular conferences and share an email circulation list which has become vital for spreading information about publications and events. This matters all the more in a field where researchers are widely spread geographically and often lack fellow specialists in their own universities. And like the existence of a specialist journal and the more senior networks, both RICHIE and HEIRS serve an important role in insulating emerging scholars against the current unfashionability of international history and especially international political history within the wider historical profession. The numbers involved in each network, and the geographic and methodological variety of their output, also suggests a degree of intellectual vitality which is highly encouraging.

Writing the history of the integration process is not without its difficulties or controversies, however. As Mark Gilbert has pointed out in a thoughtful recent piece in the *Journal of Common Market Studies*, writing about the EC can all too easily drift into patterns associated with Whig History – that is narrating the establishment of the Communities and then the Union as if they were part of some progressive and possibly teleological tale, the positive outcome and import of which is beyond doubt (Gilbert, 2008). This can involve the careless use of emotive language about 'advance', 'relaunch' and 'stagnation', all of which imply unquestioningly that the progress of integration is a good thing and its slowing or even reversal an unwelcome development. It can also overemphasize the personal role of the founding fathers, and of Monnet in particular, in a fashion which most branches of history rejected decades ago as outdated and hagiographic. And it can lead to a portrayal of those, like de Gaulle or Thatcher, who have harboured serious misgivings about the integration process, as blinkered reactionaries, standing in the way of enlightened advance.

Another set of potential difficulties is related to the way in which historical attention has for the most part focused on the making of institutions and policies and not upon their wider impact. This means that the main documentary sources have been the records of those governments and institutions that devised and pushed for further integration – that is precisely those who are likely to have regarded this 'advance' in the most positive light – whereas the views of those who may have been affected by the integration process, but who had no role in its genesis, have seldom been taken into account. Inevitably some of the language, and to a lesser extent some of the judgements reflecting this lopsided source–base, find their way into historians' accounts. Similarly, judgements about the 'success' or 'failure' of an institution or policy have tended to be grounded upon the institution's or policy's repercussions within the integration process – on whether, for instance, it strengthened or weakened French governmental support for further integration, or helped create the momentum for some subsequent institutional 'advance' – rather than being based upon the repercussions of the institution or policy on the citizens of Europe or of the world beyond. This point was well illustrated at a recent historical conference on the origins and development of the CAP, where the papers emphasizing the 'success' of the policy in the 1960s and 1970s as measured by its effect in galvanizing the integration process, stood in stark contrast to other contributions which assessed the farm policy's overall commercial impact or, still more strikingly, the deleterious effects which European agricultural protectionism had on the groundnut producers of Senegal. Needless to say, the judgements and choice of language in the latter papers were much more negative about this aspect of European integration than papers in the first category had been.

Equally serious, to my mind, is the highly fragmented nature of most detailed work on European integration history. As is the case with a lot of contemporary history writing, those analysing the Community/Union's past have often preferred to write densely footnoted and impeccably researched microstudies of small and isolated episodes in integration history rather than seeking to explain the broader pattern of development. Such studies are in part a function of the sheer volume of archival material that any one twentieth century national government, let alone multiple governments plus assorted Community institutions, produce in any given month or year. With so mountainous a pile of paper to analyse it is perhaps not surprising that most sensible historians choose to master a small portion, rather than generalize on the basis of much less in-depth research. This choice may also reflect the current unfashionability amongst historians of anything which might be denounced by postmodernist critics as a 'metanarrative'. And at an even more prosaic level, the tendency to produce small miniatures rather than vast frescos may partly reflect a university culture which, all over Europe, becomes ever more obsessed with the regular production of detailed research articles and books, rather than tolerating the type of long gestation which a truly commanding overview of the integration process between 1947 and 1990, for example, would require. An academic Michelangelo of the late twentieth or early twenty-first century might well find him or herself obliged to churn out small scale portraits, rather than painting the Sistine Chapel ceiling!

The overall effect, however, is to produce a very patchy tableau of integration history, with some areas filled in with huge levels of detail, but other equally large portions lacking any real paint at all. The missing interconnections between the various points where details have been painted in, and the vast areas where only the barest outline of events has been sketched out, rob the overall picture of any easily discernible shape or structure. As a result, the existing historical literature often fails to offer fully convincing answers to the questions that historians specializing in other fields or European specialists from other intellectual disciplines might be most expected to ask, such as 'did this all matter?', 'has integration changed Europe, for better or worse, in the way that its proponents (and opponents) have claimed?', or even 'why has a process begun over five decades ago been able to sustain itself, let alone expand in both geographical scope and the range of policy areas involved?'. Instead integration historians have been somewhat prone to expend most of their energies in detailed discussions of why exactly the Community evolved as it did over a brief five-year period, without being able to communicate effectively why such minutiae matter.

The end result has been an unacceptable degree of isolation from both the discussions of other historians and the debates of European specialists looking at the EC/EU from within political science, international relations, economics or law. As far as other historians are concerned, the problem is evident both from the missing integration dimension of many discussions of twentieth-century European history and from the tendency of integration historians to produce works which fail, and often barely even try, to link the integration story with the wider evolution of Europe in the post-1945 period. The first of these difficulties becomes apparent from even a brief look at recent survey texts. Some confine their discussion of the integration process entirely to its economic effects – and even at this level regard it as a secondary factor (James, 2003). Others, like Tony Judt's *Postwar*, pay greater lip service to the idea that integration has somehow transformed Europe, but they seem unable to provide much indication of how this transformation might actually have been wrought (Judt, 2007). In-depth discussion of how the progressive institutionalization of interaction between European countries might have altered the manner in which they related to one another – not merely making intra-European conflict less likely, if not impossible, but fundamentally blurring the dividing line between domestic and foreign policy – is largely absent, as is any real debate about how the growth of a European level of governance may or may not have affected national politics. Nor are integration historians much better at making linkages between their own specialist concerns and the wider sweep of European history. Americanization, the Cold War, the decolonization process or the development across Western Europe of a highly distinctive pattern of welfare states all play a much less prominent role in many accounts of the EC's development than might be expected.

A similar lack of dialogue characterizes the relationship between integration historians and their peers in other academic fields. A few brave political scientists have sought to engage with the Community's historical development and begin a conversation with those who work primarily on its past – Andrew Moravcsik and Craig Parsons would be the most obvious examples – although their results have sometimes been as eloquent about the mutual frustrations involved in such exchanges as about their potential (Moravcsik, 1998; Parsons, 2003). And a minority of integration historians have responded in kind, seeking to deploy a limited number of concepts and ideas borrowed from those who work on the contemporary EU to an analysis of its development over time (Kaiser *et al.*, 2009). But such exceptions barely dent a generalized rule of non-communication. The 'background' chapters of many a political science textbook on the EU thus remain a frightening redoubt of myths about the institutions' past which most historians discredited years ago; and the writings of those who dub themselves 'historical institutionalists' contain next to nothing that a historian would recognize as relating to his or her own work. Meanwhile, much of the output of historians remains wide open to the charge of being conceptually underdeveloped and based on scant working knowledge of how the EU is viewed as functioning today.

The situation is even worse, furthermore, when it comes to engagement with the fields of law and economics. The former is particularly striking given the centrality of law to the whole integration process and the way in which academic specialists on European law were among the first university experts to begin serious study of what was happening in Luxembourg, Strasbourg and Brussels. Yet in the main, historians neither read lawyers – past or present – nor lawyers read historians. The development of the European Court of Justice (ECJ) thus remains largely uncharted; the allusions to the landmarks of European jurisprudence are brief and sparing in most history texts; and the legal literature itself seems deeply uninterested in the way that the emergence of European law interacted with the parallel development of the Community/Union, still less the evolving Western European political and social context. Nor has the prominence of a number of economic historians in the historiography of European integration led to a much better situation with regard to interchange with economics. Milward's writings for instance show a distinct preference for engaging with economic theorizing dating back to the 1950s and 1960s, rather than tangling with any economic debate of more recent vintage. His *Politics and Economics in the History of the European Union* refers to Viner, Meade, Lipsey and Sciatovsky – all of whom were writing when the integration process had barely begun – but contains only two footnotes which mention an economic text published since 1980 (Milward, 2005). Needless to say, such disdain is returned in more than equal measure by most economists who continue to write about the economics of European integration in a fashion which suggests hardly any interest in, or knowledge of, anything which occurred before 1985.

So where now?

The easiest future trend of European-integration historiography to predict is the gradual advance of that chronological barrier represented by the thirty-year rule. The focus of much research has already shifted from the 1960s to the 1970s, and it is almost certain that over the next decade increasing forays will be made by historians forward into the largely unexplored territory of the 1980s. For integration specialists this means that a variety of new topics are likely to become the subject of enquiry. These range from the consequences of enlargement (both the first and the second) to the broadening of the EC's policy agenda in the 1970s and 1980s. Also predictable – indeed already underway to some extent – is a more general reconsideration of the 1970s, which are all too often still labelled as a stagnant decade, despite the series of vital institutional, policy and legal changes that occurred. And also likely in the medium term is a growing interest not merely in the historical roots of the 1980s *relance*, but also in the extent to which the Community/Union affected and was affected by the geopolitical transformation of the European continent in 1989–90. Hopefully this last will oblige integration historians to engage with the historiography of the Cold War – and force Cold War historians to acknowledge the importance of European integration – to a degree which has not occurred so far.

There is also some chance that the rigid adherence to the thirty-year rule will begin to fade. This reflects the way in which several European countries and the Community institutions themselves have begun to alter their legislation on the release of confidential government documents. Both Britain and the EU institutions have thus adopted freedom of information legislation which ought to make possible targeted requests for the early release of documents; France has shifted from a thirty-year rule to a twenty-five year rule, and also allows outgoing presidents or their heirs to set independent rules for access to Elysée papers. Frustratingly this means that most of the papers of General de Gaulle are still locked up, but those of Valéry Giscard d'Estaing and François Mitterrand have already been profitably raided by some historians. The Netherlands has long operated a twenty-year rule. The United States, moreover, which has often been the EC/EU's key interlocutor, also releases many documents well before three decades have elapsed. A resourceful researcher thus might well be able to range well into the 1980s and possibly beyond substantially earlier than would traditionally have been the case under the thirty-year rule.

This ability to overcome the usual chronological restrictions on European integration history might become even more pronounced were historians to jettison some of their customary hesitations about the use of oral history. At present oral history within a Community context has tended to be restricted to interviewing eyewitnesses about events well over three decades old. Inevitably this has placed clear limits upon the reliability of such evidence – memories are seldom entirely accurate after such a long interval – as well as severely restricting the number of potential interviewees. But Pierre Gerbet demonstrated over 50 years ago, and Peter Ludlow has confirmed, both with his work on the making of the European Monetary System written in the late 1970s and early 1980s and with his much more recent writings on European Council meetings over the last five years, that valuable results can be obtained by marrying the approach of a historian with off-the-record interviewing of protagonists more usually employed by journalists or political scientists (Gerbet, 1956; Ludlow, 1982, 2004). Such work could also benefit from the multiple EU related documents that are already within the public domain, and the many more which are likely to be shown unofficially to a determined but tactful investigator. A historian willing to break with convention and focus his or her attention on a much more recent period of EU history might therefore reap substantial rewards. This is all the more true given the widespread doubts that exist about the extent to which good archiving practices persist in national and Community civil services which now work primarily by email, telephone and informal face-to-face meetings. The treasure trove of official papers relating to the 1980s and beyond may, in other words, prove less valuable, when it finally does emerge, than has been the case for the first three quarters of the twentieth century.

Another welcome change would be an increased level of investigation into the impact of integration. To a certain extent this is almost bound to happen as the chronological centre of gravity of historical research rolls forward. In the 1950s and 1960s, the period upon which the bulk of historical research has been done hitherto, the main protagonists of the integration story were elite decision-makers, able to act in a manner which was relatively unencumbered by public opinion. Prior to 1968 there is little evidence of strong popular engagement either for or against European unity. From the 1970s onwards, however, the appearance of public referendums on European topics, the entry into the Community of a number of countries with a strong current of Euroscepticism and the beginning of direct elections to the European Parliament all mean that historians will be obliged to address public sentiment about European integration to a much greater degree than before. Research into such topics from the 1970s onwards is likely to be further facilitated by the greater availability of opinion poll data. The rediscovery of pro- and anti-European ideas as legitimate subjects for historical research and the renewed attention given to the role of political parties in mobilizing for and against European integration, both noted above, are also likely to encourage movement in the same direction. But even in such favourable circumstances, a conscious effort will need to be made to flank the current top-down emphasis of most historical research, with a greater degree of investigation into popular attitudes towards Europe and the views and opinions of those groups directly affected by the integration process but largely uninvolved in shaping its course. Farmers, fishermen, steel workers, scientists receiving EUREKA and other funding from the early 1980s onwards, the first generation of ERASMUS students, as well as those European business leaders pressing for a truly uniform European market prior to 1985, would all be worthy subjects of detailed studies into how European policy was received rather than conceived.

Another valuable area of future enquiry would be the way in which the European institutions functioned. It has already become clear from research into the 1960s that patterns of behaviour in Brussels fairly quickly diverged from the expectations of those who had initiated the integration process. Equally clearly this was not simply – or even mainly – due to de Gaulle. But we still know much too little about how the early institutions interacted with one another, about who populated Community Brussels, about the interchange between the European level of governance and the national, and about the way in which the second generation of Community policies – early monetary initiatives, the initial stirrings of regional policy, etc. – were affected by the successes and shortcomings of the first. Did the Community back away from the type of automatic spending commitments involved in the CAP, as farm expenditure mushroomed out of control in the 1970s and 1980s? What was the impact upon the workings of the whole institutional system of the European Council's creation in 1974? How did the arrival of cohorts of British, Danish and Irish Eurocrats alter the way Brussels operated? Or was the pioneer spirit already ebbing away sometime before the newcomers took up their new posts in the enlarged Community? These and many other questions need to be investigated by the next generation of historians who pore over the records of the Brussels institutions and the multiple national ministries involved in playing the European game.

Even more fundamentally, however, some of those interested in European integration history need to start debating the overall importance and impact of the integration process in a way which might capture the interest both of other historians and of political scientists, lawyers and economists. At one level this is likely to involve beginning to answer the currently unaddressed questions about how much European integration has contributed to Europe's overall development since the Second World War. Has it really been the key factor in maintaining peace in what had been a highly volatile continent? Or did this have much more to do with NATO, the American military presence and the overarching Cold War framework? How much, if at all, has economic integration shaped the continent's economic fortunes in the course of the 50 plus years since 1958? How has institutionalized cooperation in Brussels affected the course of party politics within each member state, the range of policy options available to national leaders, and the trends of public opinion across Europe? Has European integration contributed to those elements of social convergence across Europe identified by social historians like Hartmut Kaeble (2007)? Or was such convergence instead a precondition without which integration could not have worked? And if the impact of European integration on the course of national politics has only been gradual and has become of major significance only in its latter stages, when and why did a process which began so long ago begin to have an important effect upon national politics? Beginning to answer such queries would turn integration history into a field which other historians of Europe since 1945 could not afford to ignore, even if they were intent upon suggesting a rather different assessment of its overall importance.

Likewise, integration history ought to become a little more self-assertive in its interaction with other aspects of European studies, broadly defined. To a limited extent, this may involve borrowing or importing concepts and vocabulary developed by political scientists, sociologists, economists or legal experts who also work on the EU. More crucial, however, is a readiness to point out when historical research suggests that ideas developed to interpret the current integration process do not fit with its past and may hence be debatable analyses of its present. Integration historians do need to read a bit more of what other European specialists write – not primarily so that they can parrot the rival terminology, but instead so that they can deploy their expertise in order to challenge some of the rival fields' assumptions. Such challenges may well of course be contested. But at the very least contestation should lead to a rather more intensive and extensive dialogue across disciplinary boundaries than tends to occur at present. And dialogue between different approaches is likely to become even more feasible were some historians at least to swallow their qualms about writing about periods of history rather more recent than three decades ago.

Conclusion

Overall then, integration history, while not without achievements, has a great deal still to discover. It has already put forward quite an extensive set of competing, but ultimately complementary, explanations as to why the process got underway. It has also gone a long way in adding both complexity and depth to the rather simplistic account of the Community's early decades of operation promulgated by the memoirs and public pronouncements of those who took part. In addition it has devised both the structures and the patterns of behaviour to ensure a lively ongoing debate about the details of the integration process in the 1960s, increasingly the 1970s, and before too long the 1980s. But its most urgent challenge is to break out of its largely self-imposed isolation and establish channels of communication both with the wider community of historians working on the making of the contemporary world and with the multiple other specialists from other academic disciplines who take part in the never-ending attempt to demystify and explain the EU. No individual aged 50 plus could be sensibly analysed or assessed without extensive reference to his or her past; likewise, no political system which has been in constant evolution for over five decades can seriously be dissected and understood without a much greater contribution from those who specialize in understanding its past.

References

Adenauer, K. (1965) *Erinnerungen 1945–53* (Stuttgart: Deutsche Verlags-Anstalt).

Adenauer, K. (1966) *Erinnerungen 1953–55* (Stuttgart: Deutsche Verlags-Anstalt).

Adenauer, K. (1967) *Erinnerungen 1955–59* (Stuttgart: Deutsche Verlags-Anstalt).

Adenauer, K. (1968) *Erinnerungen 1959–63* (Stuttgart: Deutsche Verlags-Anstalt).

Anaya, P.O. (2002) *European Socialists and Spain: The Transition to Democracy, 1959–77* (Basingstoke: Palgrave Macmillan).

Ashton, N.J. and Hellema, D. (eds) (2001) *Unspoken Allies: Anglo-Dutch Relations since 1780* (Amsterdam: Amsterdam University Press).

Bagnato, B. (1995) *Storia di una illusione europea. Il progetto di unione doganale italo-francese* (London: Lothian Foundation Press).

Ballini, P.L. and Varsori, A. (eds) (2004) *L'Italia e l'Europa: 1947–1979* (Catanzaro: Soveria Mannelli).

Becker, J. and Knipping, F. (eds) (1986) *Power in Europe?: Great Britain, France, Italy, and Germany in a Postwar World, 1945–1950* (Berlin: W. de Gruyter).

Bézias, J.-R. (2006) *Georges Bidault et la politique étrangère de la France: Europe, Etats-Unis, proche-orient, 1944–1948* (Paris: Harmattan).

Bitsch, M.-T., Loth, W. and Poidevin, R. (eds) (1998) *Institutions européennes et identitées européennes* (Brussels: Bruylant).

Bitsch, M.-T. and Mestre, C. (eds) (2001) *Le couple France-Allemagne et les institutions européennes: une postérité pour le plan Schuman ?* (Brussels: Bruylant).

Bossuat, G. (1997) *La France, l'aide américaine et la construction européenne, 1944–1954* (Paris: Comité pour l'histoire économique et financière de la France).

Bossuat, G. and Girault, R. (eds) (1994) *Europe brisée, Europe retrouvée: nouvelles réflexions sur l'unité européenne au XXe siècle* (Paris: Publications de la Sorbonne).

Charlton, M. (1983) *The Price of Victory* (London: Parkwest Publications Incorporated).

Craveri, P. (2006) *De Gasperi* (Bologna: Il Mulino).

Daddow, O.J. (ed.) (2002) *Harold Wilson and European Integration: Britain's Second Application to Join the EEC* (London: Cass).

Decup, S.M. (1998) *France-Angleterre: les relations militaires de 1945 à 1962* (Paris: Economica).

Deighton, A. (ed.) (1995) *Building Postwar Europe: National Decision-makers and European Institutions, 1948–63* (London: Macmillan).

Dell, E. (1995) *The Schuman Plan and the British Abdication of Leadership in Europe* (Oxford: New York: Oxford University Press).

Dewey, R. (2009) *British National Identity and Opposition to Membership of Europe, 1961–63: The Anti-marketeers* (Manchester: Manchester University Press).

Di Nolfo, E. (1992) *Power in Europe? II: Great Britain, France, Germany and Italy and the Origins of the EEC, 1952–1957* (Berlin: W. de Gruyter).

Dockrill, S. (1991) *Britain's Policy for West German Rearmament, 1950–1955* (Cambridge: Cambridge University Press).

Duchêne, F. and Monnet, J. (1994) *Jean Monnet: The First Statesman of Interdependence* (New York: Norton).

Dujardin, V. and Dumoulin, M. (1997) *Paul van Zeeland, 1893–1973* (Brussels: Racine).

Dumoulin, M. (ed.) (1993) *L'Europe du patronat: de la guerre froide aux années soixante* (Berne: Peter Lang).

Dumoulin, M. (1999) *Spaak* (Brussels: Editions Racine).

Dumoulin, M. and Bitsch, M.-T. (2007) *The European Commission, 1958–72: History and Memories* (Luxembourg: Office for Official Publications of the European Communities).

Dutton, D. (1997) *Anthony Eden: A Life and Reputation* (London: Arnold).

Ellison, J. (2000) *Threatening Europe: Britain and the Creation of the European Community, 1955–58* (Basingstoke: Palgrave Macmillan).

Fleury, A. and Frank, R. (eds) (1997) *Le rôle des guerres dans la mémoire des Européens* (Berne: Peter Lang).

Gehler, M. (2005) *Österreichs Aussenpolitik der Zweiten Republik: von der alliierten Besatzung bis zum Europa des 21. Jahrhunderts* (Innsbruck: StudienVerlag).

Gehler, M. and Kaiser, W. (2004) *Christian Democracy in Europe since 1945 Volume 2* (London, New York: Routledge).

Gerbet, P. (1956) La genèse du Plan Schuman, des origines à la déclaration du 9 mai 1950. *Revue Française de Science Politique* (juillet-septembre): 525–53.

Giauque, J.G. (2002) *Grand Designs and Visions of Unity: The Atlantic Powers and the Reorganization of Western Europe, 1955–1963* (Chapel Hill: University of North Carolina Press).

Gilbert, M. (2008) 'Narrating the Process: Questioning the Progressive Story of European Integration', *Journal of Common Market Studies* 46(3): 641–62.

Girault, R. (ed.) (1994) *Identité et conscience européenne au XXe siècle* (Paris: Hachette).

Girault, R. and Bossuat, G. (eds) (1993) *L'Europe des européens* (Paris: Publications de la Sorbonne).

Griffiths, R.T. and Ward, S. (eds) (1996) *Courting the Common Market: The First Attempt to Enlarge the European Community, 1961–1963* (London: Lothian Foundation).

Hallstein, W. (1972) *Europe in the Making* (London: George Allen & Unwin).

Hershberg, J. (1993) *James B. Conant: Harvard to Hiroshima and the Making of the Nuclear Age* (New York: Knopf).

Heyen, E.V. (ed.) (1992) *Die Anfänge der Verwaltung der Europäischen Gemeinschaft* (Baden-Baden: Nomos).

Hitchcock, W.I. (1998) *France Restored: Cold War Diplomacy and the Quest for Leadership in Europe, 1944–1954* (Chapel Hill: University of North Carolina Press).

Horne, A. (1989) *Macmillan, Vol. 2, 1957–1986* (London: Macmillan).

Immerman, R.H. (1990) *John Foster Dulles and the Diplomacy of the Cold War* (Princeton: Princeton University Press).

James, H. (2003) *Europe Reborn: A History, 1914–2000* (Harlow: Longman).

Judt, T. (2007) *Postwar: A History of Europe since 1945* (London: Pimlico).

Kaeble, H. (2007) *Sozialgeschichte Europas* (Munich: Beck).

Kaiser, W. (1996) *Using Europe, Abusing the Europeans: Britain and European Integration, 1945–63* (London: Macmillan).

Kaiser, W. (2007) *Christian Democracy and the Origins of European Union* (Cambridge: Cambridge University Press).

Kaiser, W. and Elvert, J. (eds) (2004) *European Union Enlargement: A Comparative History* (London: Routledge).

Kaiser, W., Leucht, B. and Rasmussen, M. (2009) *The History of the European Union: Origins of a Trans- and Supranational Polity 1950–72* (Abingdon: Routledge).

Killick, J. (1997) *The United States and the European Reconstruction, 1945–1960* (Edinburgh: Keele University Press).

Knipping, F. and Schönwald, M. (eds) (2004) *Aufbruch zum Europa der zweiten Generation : die europäische Einigung 1969–1984* (Trier: WVT, Wissenschaftlicher Verlag).

Knudsen, A.-C. L. (2009) *Farmers on Welfare: The Making of Europe's Common Agricultural Policy* (Ithaca: Cornell University Press).

Küsters, H.J. (1982) *Die Gründung der Europäischen Wirtschaftsgemeinschaft* (Baden-Baden: Nomos Verlagsgesellschaft).

Lacouture, J. (1991) *De Gaulle : the ruler, 1945–1970* (London: Harvill).

Lappenküper, U. (2001) *Die deutsch-französischen Beziehungen 1949–63* (Munich: Oldenbourg).

Laschi, G. (2000) *L'agricultura italiana e l'integrazione europea* (Berne: Peter Lang).

Lipgens, W. and Loth, W. (1977) *Die Anfänge der europäischen Einigungspolitik 1945–1950* (Stuttgart: Klett).

Lipgens, W. and Loth, W. (1988) *Documents on the History of European Integration Vol.3, The Struggle for European Union by Political Parties and*

Pressure Groups in Western European Countries 1945–1950 (Berlin: W. de Gruyter.).

Lipgens, W. and Loth, W. (1991) *Documents on the History of European Integration: Volume 4, Transnational Organisations of Political Parties and Pressure Groups in the Struggle for European Union, 1945–1950* (Berlin: W. de Gruyter).

Lord, C.J. (1996) *Absent at the Creation: Britain and the Formation of the European Community, 1950–1952* (Aldershot: Dartmouth Publishing).

Loth, W. (ed.) (2001) *Crises and Compromises: The European Project 1963–1969* (Baden-Baden: Nomos Verlag).

Loth, W. (ed.) (2005) *La gouvernance supranationale dans la construction européenne* (Brussels: Bruylant).

Ludlow, N.P. (1997) *Dealing with Britain: The Six and the First UK Application to the EEC* (Cambridge: Cambridge University Press).

Ludlow, N.P. (2005) 'The Making of the CAP: Towards a Historical Analysis of the EU's First Major Policy', *Contemporary European History* 14(3): 347–71.

Ludlow, N.P. (2006) *The European Community and the Crises of the 1960s: Negotiating the Gaullist Challenge* (London: Routledge).

Ludlow, P. (1982) *The Making of the European Monetary System: A Case Study of the Politics of the European Community* (London: Butterworths).

Ludlow, P. (2004) *The Making of the New Europe: The European Councils in Brussels and Copenhagen 2002* (Brussels: Eurocomment).

Lundestad, G. (1998) *Empire by Integration: The United States and European Integration, 1945–1997* (Oxford: Oxford University Press).

Lynch, F.M.B. (1997) *France and the International Economy: From Vichy to the Treaty of Rome* (London: Routledge).

MacLennan, C. (2000) *Spain and the Process of European Integration, 1957–85: Political Change and Europeanism* (Basingstoke: Palgrave Macmillan).

Masala, C. (1997) *Italia und Germania: die deutsch-italienischen Beziehungen 1963–1969* (Vierow bei Greifswald: SH).

Mawby, S. (1999) *Containing Germany: Britain and the Arming of the Federal Republic* (New York: St Martin's Press).

Milward, A.S. (1984) *The Reconstruction of Western Europe 1945–51* (London: Methuen).

Milward, A.S. (2002) *The Rise and Fall of a National Strategy, 1945–1963* (London: Whitehall History Publishing in association with Frank Cass).

Milward, A.S. (2005) *Politics and Economics in the History of the European Union* (Oxford: Routledge).

Milward, A.S., Brennan, G. and Romero, F. (1992) *The European Rescue of the Nation-state* (London: Routledge).

Milward, A.S. and Deighton, A. (eds) (1999) *Widening, Deepening and Acceleration: The European Economic Community, 1957–1963* (Baden-Baden: Nomos).

Monnet, J. (1978) *Memoirs* (London: Collins).

Moravcsik, A. (1998) *The Choice for Europe: Social Purpose and State Power from Messina to Maastricht* (Ithaca: Cornell University Press).

Noël, G. (1988) *Du pool vert à la politique agricole commune: les tentatives de Communauté agricole européenne entre 1945 et 1955* (Paris: Economica).

O'Neill, C. (2000) *Britain's Entry into the European Community: Report by Sir Con O'Neill on the Negotiations of 1970–1972* (Portland: Frank Cass).

Parr, H. (2006) *Britain's Policy toward the European Community: Harold Wilson and Britain's World Role, 1964–1967* (London: Routledge).

Parsons, C. (2003) *A Certain Idea of Europe* (Ithaca: Cornell University Press).

Pine, M. (2007) *Harold Wilson and Europe: Pursuing Britain's Membership of the European Community* (London: Tauris Academic Studies).

Pineau, C. and Rimbaud, C. (1991) *Le grand pari: l'aventure du traité de Rome* (Paris: Fayard).

Poidevin, R. (ed.) (1986a) *Histoire des débuts de la construction européenne (Mars 1948–Mai 1950): actes du colloque de Strasbourg 28–30 novembre 1984* (Brussels: Bruylant).

Poidevin, R. (1986b) *Robert Schuman: homme d'état* (Paris: Imprimerie nationale).

Rhenisch, T. (1999) *Europäische Integration und industrielles Interesse: die Deutsche Industrie und die Gründung der Europäischen Wirtschaftsgemeinschaft* (Stuttgart: Steiner).

Risso, L. (2007) *Divided We Stand: The French and Italian Political Parties and the Rearmament of West Germany, 1949–1955* (Newcastle: Cambridge Scholars Publishing).

Roussel, E. (1994) *Georges Pompidou, 1911–1974* (Paris: J.C. Lattès).

Roussel, E. (1996) *Jean Monnet, 1888–1979* (Paris: Fayard).

Roussel, E. (2002) *Charles de Gaulle* (Paris: Gallimard).

Ruane, K. (2000) *The Rise and Fall of the European Defence Community: Anglo-American Relations and the Crisis of European Defence, 1950–55* (Basingstoke: Palgrave Macmillan).

Schaad, M.P.C. (2000) *Bullying Bonn: Anglo-German Diplomacy on European Integration, 1955–61* (Basingstoke: Palgrave Macmillan).

Schwabe, K. (ed.) (1988) *Anfänge des Schuman-Plans 1950–51* (Baden-Baden: Nomos Verlagsgesellschaft).

Schwartz, T.A. (1991) *America's Germany: John J. McCloy and the Federal Republic of Germany* (Cambridge, MA: Harvard University Press).

Schwarz, H.-P. (1986) *Adenauer: der Aufstieg, 1876–1952* (Stuttgart: Deutsche Verlags-Anstalt).

Schwarz, H.-P. (1991) *Adenauer: der Staatsmann, 1952–1967* (Stuttgart: Deutsche Verlags-Anstalt).

Serra, E. (ed.) (1989) *Il Rilancio dell'Europa e i trattati di Roma* (Brussels: Bruylant).

Skogmar, G. (2004) *The United States and the Nuclear Dimension of European Integration* (Basingstoke: Palgrave Macmillan).

Soutou, G.-H. (1996) *L'alliance incertaine: les rapports politico-stratégiques franco-allemands, 1954–1996* (Paris: Fayard).

Spaak, P.-H. (1969) *Combats inachevés* (Paris: Fayard).

Spierenburg, D.P. and Poidevin, R. (1993) *Histoire de la Haute Autorité de la Communauté Européenne du Charbon et de l'Acier: une expérience supra-nationale* (Brussels: Bruylant).

Thiemeyer, G. (1999) *Vom 'Pool Vert' zur Europäischen Wirtschaftsgemeinschaft: europäische Integration, kalter Krieg und die Anfänge der gemeinsamen europäischen Agrarpolitik 1950–1957* (Munich: Oldenbourg).

Tratt, J. (1996) *The Macmillan Government and Europe: A Study in the Process of Policy Development* (London: Macmillan).

Trausch, G. (ed.) (1993) *Die Europäische Integration vom Schuman-Plan bis zu den Verträgen von Rom: Pläne und Initiativen, Enttäuschungen und Misserfolge: Beiträge des Kolloquiums in Luxemburg, 17–19 Mai 1989* (Baden-Baden: Nomos Verlag).

Türk, H. (2006) *Die Europapolitik der Grossen Koalition 1966–1969. 1. Aufl. ed.* (Munich: Oldenbourg).

Van Der Harst, J. (2007) *Beyond The Customs Union: The European Community's Quest for Deepening, Widening and Completion, 1969–1975* (Brussels: Bruylant).

Varsori, A. (ed.) (2006) *Inside the European Community: Actors and Policies in the European Integration 1957–1972* (Baden-Baden: Nomos).

Varsori, A. and Romero, F. (eds) (2006) *Nazione, interdipendenza, integrazione. Le relazioni internazionali dell'Italia (1917–1989)* (Rome: Carocci).

Weilemann, P. (1983) *Die Anfänge der Europäischen Atomgemeinschaft : zur Gründungsgeschichte von EURATOM 1955–1957* (Baden-Baden: Nomos).

Wielenga, F. (ed.) (1997) *Nachbarn: Niederländer und Deutsche und die Europäische Einigung* (Bonn: Niederländische Botschaft, Presse- und Kulturabteilung).

Wilkes, G. (ed.) (1997) *Britain's Failure to Enter the European Community, 1961–63: The Enlargement Negotiations and Crises in European, Atlantic, and Commonwealth Relations* (London: Frank Cass).

Winand, P. (1993) *Eisenhower, Kennedy, and the United States of Europe* (London: Macmillan).

Young, J.W. (1984) *Britain, France and the Unity of Europe: 1945–1951* (Leicester: Leicester University Press).

Chapter 3

Integration Theory

Frank Schimmelfennig[1]

Introduction

In the early days of European integration 'integration theory' was equivalent to political science theorizing on the European Community and neofunctionalism was *the* theory of European integration. Since then, theorizing has strongly diversified. On the one hand, neofunctionalism has been rivalled by intergovernmentalist theories of European integration since the 1960s. On the other hand, and more importantly, theories of European integration have been complemented by theories of European politics and policies. The theoretical division of labour is now between theories of European integration as theories of institutional change and theories of European governance as theories of politics, decision-making and policy-making within a given institutional framework.

Theories of European integration stipulate the conditions and mechanisms under which competencies and boundaries shift between levels and agents of governance in the European multilevel system. These shifts occur in three dimensions (Schimmelfennig and Rittberger, 2006). *Sectoral integration* (or 'broadening') refers to a process through which policy areas or sectors, which were previously governed exclusively at the national level, become (partially or exclusively) regulated by the EU. *Vertical integration* (or 'deepening') refers to the distribution of competencies between EU institutions in integrated policy sectors. An increase in vertical integration occurs when previously national competencies are shared across EU member states (including changes from unanimity to qualified majority decision-making) or delegated to autonomous supranational institutions. *Horizontal integration* (or 'widening') refers to the territorial extension of a given state of sectoral and vertical integration. Enlargement is the most important process of horizontal integration, but widening also takes place when non-member states adopt partial regulatory regimes of the EU (such as 'Schengen') or member states broaden their integration (e.g. when they introduce the euro at a later date).

Integration theories thus seek to explain how and under what conditions new policies come under European regulation, competencies are devolved from the nation-state to the European level, and European rules expand in space. They also explain why some sectors and states were integrated sooner, and are integrated more deeply, than others.

In this chapter, I will, first, give a brief account of how integration theory has developed in the past. The main part of the chapter will review the two major current agendas in integration theory: constructivism and enlargement. Finally, I will make some suggestions for the future agenda in integration theory.

Theory development

The basic divide in integration theory has been that between supranationalist and intergovernmentalist theories. Both families of theories differ most fundamentally on the question as to whether or not integration is a self-reinforcing and transformative process. Intergovernmentalists deny this. For them, integration remains under the control of member state governments, which collectively determine the speed and substance of any further steps of integration. Supranationalists, however, assert that the institutions created by member state governments trigger a self-reinforcing process which begets further integration and escapes member state control. It transforms not only the organization of the EU but also the member states and societies.

There are two general sources of development and change in theories of European integration (see also Rosamond, 2007). On the one hand, change can be inspired by theoretical developments in the larger discipline of Political Science and, above all, International Relations (IR). General theoretical innovations and refinements tend to be tried out in, and adapted to, the study of European integration sooner or later as well. On the other hand, theoretical change may reflect political developments in European integration itself. Dynamic growth in specific areas of European integration is likely to trigger increased scholarly interest in these areas and a focus on the driving forces of integration, whereas periods of stagnation and crisis favour reflection on the obstacles to integration.

Histories of the field tend to draw on both sources of theoretical change to account for the development of integration theory (see e.g. Battistelli and Isernia, 1993; Caporaso and Keeler, 1995). In this perspective, the debate between supranationalism and intergovernmentalism mirrors the IR debate between idealism (or liberalism) and realism. Neofunctionalism, the most important starting point of supranationalist theorizing, drew on and elaborated functionalist theories of international cooperation and organization. Its initial dominance in integration theory (Haas, 1968) resulted from the upswing of supranational economic integration in the 1950s, which conformed to the functional model. By contrast, intergovernmentalism reflected realist, state-centred assumptions. Its rise in the mid-1960s (Hoffmann, 1966) correlated with the De Gaulle era and the ('empty-chair') crisis in integration. The ensuing 'doldrums era' (Caporaso and Keeler, 1995: 13), which was characterized by the absence of any big leaps in integration, reoriented research on the European Community (EC) away from integration theory altogether and toward analyses of policy-making within the existing institutional framework. It was at that time that Ernst Haas, the most influential neofunctionalist, declared regional integration theory 'obsolescent' (Haas, 1975).

The *'relance Européenne'* of the 1980s was duly followed by a new wave of theorizing on European integration in the 1990s, which reproduced the supranationalist–intergovernmentalist divide in a modified form. Both sides started from different strands of institutionalism in social science. The supranationalist theorizing of the 1990s drew heavily on 'historical institutionalism' to explain the momentum in European integration and the loss of control of the member states. In this view, the complexity of levels and actors in the Community and the short time horizons of policy-makers account for why European integration produces unintended consequences. In turn, the Community's decision rules explain why it is so difficult to correct these consequences (Pierson, 1996; Stone Sweet and Sandholtz, 1997).

By contrast, Andrew Moravcsik's 'liberal intergovernmentalism' (1993, 1998) applied central assumptions of 'neoliberal institutionalism' in IR. In line with neoliberal institutionalism's focus on international institutions facilitating and stabilizing cooperation among rational state actors, Moravcsik viewed the EC as an 'international regime for policy coordination' (1993: 480), in which member state governments, first, bargain hard to realize the interests of powerful domestic social groups and, second, delegate competencies to supranational organizations in order to ensure their mutual commitment to the cooperative solutions they find. Yet, in line with general intergovernmentalist tenets, integration outcomes are still attributed to constellations of state preferences and power.

In hindsight, however, the theoretical divide narrowed considerably and appears to have resulted mainly from differences in emphasis and a division of labour. Both theories adhered to a broadly rationalist framework of analysis. In contrast to older, realist versions of intergovernmentalism, liberal intergovernmentalism incorporates a liberal theory of state preferences as well as factors traditionally attributed to supranationalist accounts of European integration: international interdependence as a catalyst of societal demand for integration (Stone Sweet and Sandholtz, 1998: 7; Caporaso, 1999: 163) and delegation of competencies to supranational organizations capable of acting against the short-term preferences of governments (Stone Sweet, 2003). In turn, supranationalist explanations do not deny the relevance of

intergovernmental bargaining in treaty-making or treaty-revising negotiations (e.g. Pierson, 1996).

Consider, for instance, the explanations of the internal market programme that triggered the theory debate of the 1990s. In their 'supranationalist' explanation, Sandholtz and Zysman (1989) stipulate a
combination of change in the international economic power structure,
policy leadership by the Commission (in conjunction with a transnational business coalition) and a favourable (pro-market) domestic
context. In his 'intergovernmentalist' explanation, Moravcsik (1991)
also emphasizes structural economic trends and the convergence of
national economic preferences. Later, he concedes that in this case
supranational entrepreneurs in the Commission (and the Parliament)
played a relevant role in overcoming domestic coordination problems
in the member states by initiating the SEA, mobilizing a latent transnational constituency and generating a more efficient outcome (Moravcsik,
1999: 292–8). Differences in emphasis aside, the ingredients of both
explanations are very similar.

In other respects, there is an apparent division of labour between the
two theories. Moravcsik focuses on the 'major steps toward European
integration' (1998: 4), that is, the formal introduction of new (mainly
economic) policies and competencies through treaty negotiations. By contrast, supranationalism concentrates on what happens after the treaties
are put in place, that is on the informal constitutional changes resulting
from the interpretation and use of the treaties by the organizations of the
EU in day-to-day policy-making. In particular, liberal intergovernmentalism is silent on the ECJ and the legal integration it has promoted.

Like earlier developments in integration theory, the current agenda
has been fuelled by theoretical developments in IR as well as real-world
developments in European integration. First, the debate between intergovernmentalism and supranationalism has largely subsided in recent
years – not unlike the 'neo-neo' debate in IR between neorealism and
neoliberalism. In its stead, the debate between rationalism and constructivism in IR has spilled over into the study of European integration.
Second, enlargement – arguably the most important development in
European integration in the past decade – has become a major subject
of integration theory for the first time. In the two following sections, I
will deal with both theoretical developments in greater detail.

Constructivism

Theory

Constructivism (understood as a family of IR theories that share fundamental assumptions in the same way as rationalist IR theories do)

has two main foundations – one relating to structure, the other relating to actors. First, it assumes the primacy of ideational, intersubjective structures such as collective identities, knowledge, culture, values and norms in international politics. Ideas, rather than material structures and interests, shape social preferences and outcomes. Second, rather than behaving instrumentally or strategically, actors follow the 'logic of appropriateness' (March and Olsen, 1989: 160). They do not judge alternative courses of action by the consequences for their own utility but for their conformity to norms, rules and identities.

Although a constructivist (grand) theory of European integration has not been formulated, the main building blocks of such a theory can be derived from constructivism's general propositions about international politics. In addition, there exist a number of analyses of EU politics inspired by constructivist theorizing (for recent overviews, see e.g. Risse, 2004; Wiener, 2006; Checkel, 2007). In the constructivist perspective, European integration is at its core a process of community-building. Communities are groups or associations based on common ideas. They share a collective identity and possess common causal or normative beliefs. Ideas and integration are causally linked in two ways. First, institutional integration depends on community-building: the stronger the collective 'European' identity and the larger the pool of common beliefs, the more institutional integration we will see. By contrast, weak European collective identities generate resistance to institutional integration and without shared normative and causal beliefs common institutions and integrated policies are hard to agree on. Second, existing institutional integration promotes community-building. Integrated policy-making generates intense and frequent contacts and cooperation which, in turn, transform identities and promote learning processes, leading to common beliefs. In the longer run, this community-building process generates considerable momentum in favour of further integration.

In this respect, constructivist integration theory takes up ideas proposed by early integration theories. Karl Deutsch, in his study of security communities, defined the transformation of identities as the core of integration and stipulated compatible values (together with mutual responsiveness) as essential conditions of functioning 'pluralistic' communities (1957). He thus emphasized the intersubjective *prerequisites* of integration. By contrast, neofunctionalists focused on the intersubjective *consequences* of integration. They expected European integration to lead to the socialization of actors involved in the integrated policy-making process and to the transfer of identity and loyalty away from the nation-state and towards the EC.

Identity and socialization are core concepts in the constructivist analysis of European integration, too. The central mechanisms capturing identity-transforming processes of socialization are social learning mechanisms, processes of imitation, persuasion and social influence. Checkel (2001: 562–3) and Johnston (2001: 498–9) established a catalogue of conditions under which these mechanisms are likely to be effective (see also Risse, 2000: 19; Schimmelfennig, 2005: 63–9). Social learning is most likely when actors face *novel* situations characterized by high *uncertainty* and the presence of a socializing agent which possesses the *authority* to act on behalf of a community with which a particular actor *identifies* (or to which an actor desires to belong). The social learning process affects norms and rules, which enjoy a high degree of *legitimacy* in the community and takes place in an environment corresponding to an 'ideal speech situation' which encourages *deliberation* that is characterized by the absence of external and political constraints, and in which the domestic or societal *resonance* of international norms and rules is high (or, at least, when domestic/societal rules and norms do not contradict international rules and norms).

Evidence

What do empirical studies tell us about the relevance of identity and socialization in European integration? The results are ambivalent. On the one hand, there is evidence that ideas and identities shape European integration significantly. Constructivist integration theory complements rationalist integration theory, where it is indeterminate, and provides alternative explanations where it fails. On the other hand, however, there is only weak evidence for the social learning and identity-transforming effects of European integration.

First, rationalist intergovernmentalists admit that they are best at explaining state preferences on integration when an issue has clear material, distributional consequences for powerful domestic interest groups. Otherwise, ideas-based preferences will be dominant (Moravcsik and Nicolaidis, 1999: 82). This is, above all, the case for constitutional issues where constructivist analyses show evidence of resonance effects: constitutional preferences for European integration mirror national constitutional traditions and ideas. For instance, many authors argue that federally organized member states are more likely to advocate supranational institutional solutions than unitary member states (see e.g. Wagner, 2002; Koenig-Archibugi, 2004; Risse, 2005). Yet constructivists show that ideas also matter in macroeconomic policy. Kathleen McNamara (1999) argues that Economic and Monetary Union (EMU) resulted from the dominance of neoliberal economic ideas which redefined the member states' monetary policy preferences during the 1980s and created policy consensus in a situation of uncertain distributional consequences. In addition, the fact that Denmark,

Sweden and the UK have not introduced the euro has less to do with a lack of economic convergence, let alone opposition to neoliberal monetary policy, but with identity- and resonance-based scepticism toward sovereignty transfers in the populations of these countries (Risse *et al.*, 1999). Finally, Craig Parsons shows that early French integration policy cannot be explained by structural economic conditions or domestic interest group preferences alone, but needs to take account of community-minded leadership as well (2002).

Second, community ideas and identity constructions affect not only state preferences but also integration outcomes. Again, this is most relevant for constitutional issues. In my own work on the Eastern enlargement of the EU, I have argued that the community's liberal-democratic identity explains that the EU offered membership to democratic Central and Eastern European countries, although many member states were reticent to do so, precisely because they feared adverse distributional consequences (Schimmelfennig, 2001). This identity also explains why the EU established the norm of restricting membership to democratic countries, even though the big member states had been in favour of giving Franco's Spain a membership perspective in the early 1960s (Thomas, 2006).

Finally, the progressive parliamentarization and institutionalization of human rights in the EU can be attributed to the shared liberal democratic norms of the community (Rittberger, 2005; Rittberger and Schimmelfennig, 2006). Functional, efficiency-oriented integration undermines national parliamentary competencies and national mechanisms of human rights' protection. The ensuing legitimacy deficit generates pressure for compensation at the EU level which constrains the decision-making power of the member state governments.

Whereas identities strongly affect integration outcomes, this does not seem to hold the other way round. First of all, there is no evidence for a shift of mass loyalties and change of identities. True, identities are only inadequately categorized as either national or European, and are better conceived of as multiple, layered or nested (Risse, 2004, 2005: 295–6). Survey data, however, shows that national identities and allegiances clearly predominate in the European Union – either as purely national identities or as national identities with a modicum of European identity. Moreover, purely and moderately national identities have remained extraordinarily stable since the early 1990s (Gillespie and Laffan, 2006: 145–7; Kelemen, 2007: 60). What is more, whereas mass attitudes toward European integration have indeed become more politicized as a result of integration, as expected by neofunctionalists (Schmitter, 1969), this politicization has resulted in undermining the 'permissive consensus' in favour of European integration, reasserting territorial and national identities and divisions, and proliferating and strengthening Eurosceptical parties (Hooghe and Marks, 2009). As shown by the referenda on treaty revisions since the 1990s, and most clearly on the Constitutional Treaty in 2005, electoral participation in European integration has weakened rather than strengthened the growth of integration.

Second, there is only weak evidence of far-reaching socialization at the elite level – despite the fact that political elites are much more involved in EU policy-making than the masses. This general finding holds for various groups of elite actors. Markus Jachtenfuchs *et al.* have found that the EU-related constitutional ideas of the major parties in the major member states have remained remarkably stable over the decades (1998). Morten Egeberg (1999) and Jarle Trondal (2004) argue that *national bureaucrats* involved in Commission and Council committees do develop conceptions of new roles but that their primary allegiance remains with their state of origin. Roger Scully shows that the views on integration of members of the *European Parliament* are little different from those of the members of national parliaments. Moreover, the length of service in the European Parliament (EP) has no significant effect (Scully, 2005). Jan Beyers finds that the extensive exposure of *Council officials* to the EU does not systematically lead to supranational role-playing. Rather, domestic factors affect the adoption of supranational role conceptions (Beyers, 2005). Finally, Liesbet Hooghe demonstrates that EU socialization is not even strong in the Commission (2005). Although there is high support for the EU among Commission officials, this is not a result of preference shifts or internalization generated by involvement in EU policy-making but a result of previous socialization in national contexts.

In sum, institutional integration does not seem to require identity transformation at either the mass or the elite level. From the late 1980s to the late 1990s, institutional integration has progressed strongly without an upsurge in European identity preceding or following this development. In addition, institutional integration does not seem to have strong socialization effects at either the mass or the elite level. The primary and predominant political socialization takes place at the national level. To what extent citizens as well as officials involved in EU policy-making have European, integration-friendly attitudes and preferences is also mainly determined at the national level. Thus, identities are best seen as a set of stable intersubjective structures. This applies to the liberal democratic identity of the community, the predominantly national feelings of belonging as well as the different constitutional ideas and attitudes towards European integration. These intersubjective structures have been established as indispensable elements of a full account of European integration. They are mobilized and have become effective in the constitutional politics of the EU in particular.

Enlargement

Theory

If constructivism has been the major recent theoretical innovation, the study of enlargement has been the major real-world challenge for integration theory. Until recently, enlargement was a largely neglected issue in the theory of regional integration (Schimmelfennig and Sedelmeier, 2002: 501). The classical approaches to the study of integration only mentioned 'widening' in passing. This is understandable because analysing the establishment and stabilization of regional organizations logically precedes studying their territorial expansion and the heyday of regional integration theory had come to an end before the European Community's first enlargement in 1973. It is more surprising that the revival of the theoretical debate at the beginning of the 1990s and the theoretical debate between 'intergovernmentalism' and 'supranationalism' still focused exclusively upon issues of 'deepening', such as the SEA, the EMU or legal integration.

In the meantime, the study of horizontal integration has caught up theoretically with the study of sectoral and vertical integration. The theoretical debate on enlargement, however, has not followed the older lines of 'supranationalism' vs 'intergovernmentalism' but the contemporary rationalist–constructivist debate. Integration–theoretical studies of enlargement typically seek to answer two sets of questions: Why do states want to join the EU? Why and under what conditions does the EU decide to admit new member states? According to rationalist theory, applicant as well as member states calculate the costs and benefits of enlargement. The EU admits a new member state if membership increases the marginal utility of all old member states and the new member state in comparison with non-membership and alternative institutional relationships such as association. States that do not benefit from enlargement need to be compensated, for example through side-payments. By contrast, constructivist theory stipulates that enlargement depends on collective identities and a community of values and norms. States seek to join the EU – and the EU will be ready to admit them – if they identify themselves with the EU, share its fundamental values and accept its norms.

These questions and hypotheses have informed the theoretical debate on Eastern enlargement during the past decade. However, the European Free Trade Association (EFTA) enlargement of 1995 and Eastern enlargement have presented researchers with different puzzles. Whereas in the EFTA case the main questions were why these countries only applied to join in the early 1990s and why some joined and others (Norway and Switzerland) did not, the analysis of Eastern enlargement focused on explaining why the EU decided to admit 12 additional members in 2004 and 2007 (Schimmelfennig and Sedelmeier, 2002, 2006).

State preferences

Both in a rationalist and a constructivist perspective, member state preferences on EFTA enlargement were unproblematic. Not only had the EFTA countries been a part of the liberal democratic West for a long time, they were also small and rich countries which were not expected to produce any major redistribution of political power and financial allocations in the Union. Rather, the key question was why the EFTA countries, after a long period of deliberate non-membership in the EC, developed an interest in joining at the beginning of the 1990s. There is broad agreement in the literature that three major systemic developments, which fit well with a rationalist framework, can account for the timing of the EFTA countries' interest in EU membership: the end of the Cold War, globalization, and the deepening of EC integration (Fioretos, 1997; Ingebritsen, 1997; Mattli, 1999). The end of the Cold War removed an obstacle to EU membership, since the majority of the EFTA countries (except for Iceland and Norway) were neutral and non-aligned. In addition, globalization and the negative externalities resulting from the deepening of EC integration created positive incentives for a stronger institutional relationship. Ingebritsen (1997: 174) argues that, as a result of the oil shock, the Scandinavian countries moved closer to the economic model of the EC countries. When the EC launched its internal market programme, the EFTA economies performed worse than the EC and experienced a dramatic increase in outward investment. The internal market therefore provided a strong pull, as it offered the prospect of increasing competitiveness, while the threat of a relocation of investment had a push effect. This explanation is in line with both a liberal intergovernmentalism (LI) focus on international interdependence and the 'geographic spillover' mechanism already put forward by Ernst Haas in *The Uniting of Europe* (1968: 313–5).

But how do we then explain the variation in outcomes? Drawing on aggregate data on economic performance, Mattli attributes the negative outcome of the Norwegian referendum to the fact that, for the second time after 1972, the economic performance gap with the EU had disappeared between application and ratification (1999: 85–6). By contrast, Ingebritsen (1998) attributes the variation to different leading sectors. Whereas Sweden and, to a lesser degree, Finland are capital-intensive, manufacturing exporters (which makes them sensitive to changes in their export markets and to the threat of disinvestment), Norway's income is dominated by the petroleum sector which not only makes this country less dependent on the European market, but also allows it to protect its agriculture and fisheries at higher levels than the EU. This analysis is mirrored by Moses and Jenssen (1998) whose analysis of the referenda at the county level shows that (subnational) regions that depend on sheltered sectors were less likely to support membership than those dependent on manufacture and trade. Rationalist explanations, however, are less convincing in the Swiss case. Observers attribute the Swiss 'no' to membership to adverse identity constructions and voters' concerns about neutrality, sovereignty and direct democracy (e.g. Mattli, 1999: 93–4; Gstöhl, 2002).

In the Eastern enlargement, the Central and Eastern European countries' (CEECs') applications for membership seem obvious and overdetermined. In the constructivist perspective, they result from the end of Communism and the end of the Cold War, which permitted the CEECs to 'return to Europe' and transform into liberal democracies. Applications for membership are an expression of a sense of belonging to, as well as a desire to be recognized by, the community of liberal democratic European countries. In the rationalist perspective, the CEECs were generally dependent on trade with and investments from the EU and were poorer than the member states. They therefore stood to gain from full access to the internal market, subsidies from the EU budget and decision-making power in the EU's institutions. In a more policy-oriented perspective, Mattli and Plümper (2002, 2004) argue that democratic governments are more willing to implement the liberal, market-oriented economic reforms the EU demands of its future members than authoritarian governments who are engaged in rent-seeking and can afford to cater to special interests. The rationalist and constructivist explanations thus converge on the expectation that states are more likely to seek membership the more democratic they are. Since there are, however, many cases of non-democratic governments aspiring to EU membership, the rationalist explanation is the more encompassing one.

By contrast, rationalist and constructivist expectations and explanations diverge for the Eastern enlargement preferences of the member states. According to constructivism, socialization to the EU's enlargement norms should have produced largely homogeneous enlargement preferences. In the case of Eastern enlargement, member states should thus have favoured admitting European liberal democratic countries regardless of the costs of membership. This was not the case, however: member states diverged both with regard to the desirability of enlargement as such and with regard to their preferred new member states. Most of the divergence can be explained by different degrees of interdependence with the CEECs and different distributional implications of enlargement. Countries at the eastern border of the EU have tended to favour enlargement to the East, and the poorer and less highly industrialized member states have tended to oppose enlargement because they feared financial and economic competition with the relatively poor and low-tech CEECs (Schimmelfennig, 2001). In sum, the rationalist explanation of enlargement preferences is stronger overall. With the possible exception of Switzerland, it accounts more convincingly for state preferences in those cases in which rationalism and constructivism generate different expectations and predictions.

Enlargement decisions

Why and how did the member states come to the decision to admit the EFTA countries and the CEECs? The EFTA enlargement is an easy case for both rationalism and constructivism because the candidate countries did not pose any major distributional or identity problems for the EU. The theoretical debate therefore focused on eastern enlargement. In this case, member state preferences diverged, distributional issues came to the fore and questions of identity and norm compliance were unavoidable.

Rationalist explanations of eastern enlargement come in three main varieties: EU bargaining power, discriminatory membership, and geopolitical interest. Andrew Moravcsik and Milada Vachudova (2003) argue that the costs of eastern enlargement are modest enough to prevent severe distributional problems for the old member states. If that was the case, however, why did the enlargement preferences of the member states differ? By contrast, Thomas Plümper and Christina Schneider (Plümper and Schneider, 2007; Schneider, 2009) start from the assumption that enlargement gains and losses were unevenly distributed among the member states. As a consequence, some member states faced net losses and therefore opposed eastern enlargement. These member states, however, could be compensated by 'discriminatory membership': the EU could use the extremely asymmetrical interdependence between old and new member states to impose accession conditions – such as initially reduced agricultural subsidies and temporary restrictions on the freedom of movement for labour – that would reduce the costs of enlargement for the losers among the member states to the point that they agreed to enlargement.

This explanation provides a plausible causal mechanism for transforming initial opposition into eventual agreement. Two strong assumptions need to be made here, however. First, the opponents of enlargement agreed to it before the distributional bargaining had even started. They therefore must have been certain that they would be sufficiently compensated eventually. Second, the explanation assumes that the temporary discrimination agreed in the accession negotiations would fully compensate the potential losers. Finally, this account does not explain why the EU started accession negotiations in waves. In line with this account, the EU should have invited the least costly new member states first – but Poland is an obvious counter-example.

Lars Skålnes (2005) argues that the member states were predominantly interested in a secure and stable neighbourhood. So when the wars broke out in former Yugoslavia, first in Croatia and Bosnia-Herzegovina, then in Kosovo, the EU went forward with Eastern enlargement in spite of possible economic losses. The geographical distribution of member state preferences is compatible with this view because the easternmost countries of the EU were the first to be affected by instability. By contrast, this perspective has no explanation for the distributional conflicts and bargaining that are an important part of enlargement negotiations. It also does not explain why the EU first offered membership to those countries that were the most stable in the region and turned to the most unstable regions only when violent conflict was largely contained.

Constructivist explanations focus on identity constructions and normative obligations. Such explanations refer to the general liberal democratic identity of the EU, which creates the obligation to admit democratic European countries (Schimmelfennig, 1998, 2001), or they refer to more specific identity constructions with regard to Central and Eastern Europe. This is true for the Western promise of inclusion and support for reform during the Cold War (Fierke and Wiener, 1999), for the 'special responsibility' (Sedelmeier, 2000, 2005) and the 'sense of "kinship-based duty"' (Sjursen, 2002: 508) of the EU to Central and Eastern Europe, or for the 'collective guilt' of the West for having betrayed the CEECs before and after the Second World War (Lasas, 2008). These identities created moral obligations that would have threatened the identity of the EU in the case of non-enlargement (Fierke and Wiener, 1999) and that could be used by the self-interested proponents of enlargement in the East and the West to put normative pressure on the reluctant member states (Schimmelfennig, 2001; cf. also Lasas, 2008).

Are these constructivist explanations able to account for the sequence and the scope of Eastern enlargement, that is the common weakness of rationalist accounts? Explanations based on identity constructions for the entire Central and Eastern European region may be able to predict where Eastern enlargement will end. According to Sjursen, the kinship-based duty does not extend to countries like Turkey (2002: 504), and, according to Lasas, countries like Ukraine and Georgia will not benefit from collective guilt. But these explanations do not account for the differentiation among the CEECs. By contrast, if enlargement is driven by the liberal democratic identity of the EU, applicant countries will be differentiated according to their state of democratization and given the opportunity to join when they consolidate their democracy. This explains the actual selection of candidates for membership plausibly (Schimmelfennig, 2001, 2002, 2008).

In sum, the results match the preliminary conclusions of constructivist integration theory. First, there is no strong evidence for socialization effects on enlargement preferences. All in all, the enlargement preferences of member and non-member states can be explained by material, economic self-interest. Second, however, intersubjective structures at the EU level have been established as a necessary component of a full account of enlargement. At least in the case of Eastern enlargement, identity constructions and enlargement norms (in particular the liberal democratic identity and the associated selection criteria for new member states) are needed to explain, first, how the EU differentiated among the applicant countries and, second, why the EU committed itself to enlargement in spite of the superior bargaining power of the reluctant member states and at a time when it was highly uncertain whether and to what extent their perceived losses would be compensated. Finally, however, enlargement has proven to be a complex process which cannot be explained by one theory alone.

Future agendas

Constructivism and the study of enlargement have closed two important gaps in integration theory. Integration theory has caught up with theory development in IR and, under the impression of EFTA and eastern enlargement, it has been extended to the hitherto neglected dimension of horizontal integration. Based on our 50-year experience with European integration theory, we may expect that future developments will also be driven by IR theory as well as the course of European integration.

From dynamism to consolidation?

In this perspective, we would hardly expect a dynamic and innovative development of integration theory in the near future. For one, paradigmatic theoretical debate in IR has died down. The great debate between rationalism and constructivism has given way to 'peaceful coexistence' and a quest for 'synthesis'. In the general discipline of IR (e.g. Fearon and Wendt, 2002) and in EU studies, more recent contributions to the debate emphasize that the metatheoretical and methodological dividing lines between rationalism and constructivism are far from clear cut (Checkel and Moravcsik, 2001) and that synthetic explanations drawing on rationalist as well as constructivist mechanisms and conditions are not only possible but also fruitful (Jupille *et al.*, 2003). Another 'great debate' in IR that could provide a fresh impetus to integration theory is currently not on the horizon.

The dynamic growth in integration that characterized the decade from the mid-1980s to the mid-1990s has died down as well. The grand integration projects that were launched during this time and have inspired much of the academic production and debate in integration theory have been completed: those on the internal market, the currency union and enlargement. Treaty revisions from Amsterdam to Lisbon were concerned with institutional consolidation and the incremental continuation of the Maastricht agenda, rather than with supranational integration projects in new policy sectors. Just as Ernst Haas declared integration theory 'obsolescent' in the mid-1970s (Haas, 1975), Andrew Moravcsik (2007) now speaks of a stable 'constitutional settlement' in European integration.

Does that mean that integration theory is doomed to stagnate as well? In general, there is nothing inherently problematic with a 'normal science' of European integration, in which theories mature and are refined, past events and developments are analysed and reanalysed, and remaining puzzles are solved. A dynamic, developmental theory such as integration theory does not per se require the constant change of its subject. Even if the current state of integration remained stable, the history of European integration would provide many opportunities for uncovering new facts and testing theoretical arguments longitudinally and with historical material.

In addition, Moravcsik's assessment applies mainly to intergovernmentalism. Assuming that integration as such – and thus also any form of 'constitutional settlement' – will transform actor preferences and relationships and carry the seeds of future institutional change, supranationalists would draw much less pessimistic conclusions on the future relevance of integration theory.

Blind spots, new challenges

However, integration theory has been limited by several biases and blind spots that need to be addressed under the current circumstances. First, integration theory has focused mainly on the *first pillar*, that is supranational integration, the Community method and economic policies such as market integration, monetary integration and the CAP. This is obviously true of liberal intergovernmentalism but also of supranationalism with its focus on legal integration. Constructivist studies of identity and socialization have been mainly interested in the development of supranational identity and of socialization in supranational organizations as well. Finally, enlargement is a process of supranational integration, too, and can be understood as the Community method of horizontal integration.

Second, integration theory has focused on *formal* institutional change, above all the making and remaking of the Treaties. To be sure, this applies more to intergovernmentalism than to supranationalism and constructivism. Supranationalists have always put a special emphasis on the informal institutional processes that take place beyond intergovernmental treaty-making and which constrain and influence future treaty revisions. However, the theoretical debate between inter-governmentalism and supranationalism has focused on the explanation of formal, treaty-based changes in the SEA or at Maastricht and the new integration projects that were launched by these treaties. The explanation of enlargement has further contributed to this focus on formal, treaty-based institutional change.

Third, integration theory has focused on the *elite* level. Although the focus is on different constellations of actors, both intergovernmen-talism and supranationalism explain integration outcomes purely as the result of elite interactions. Both operate under the assumption of either a 'permissive consensus' or decision-making processes that sys-tematically circumvent participation by and accountability to citizens. None of the major explanations of enlargement regards citizens' atti-tudes and political behaviour as a relevant factor. Constructivism has put more emphasis on mass-level identities in relation to the EU and their role as an obstacle to integration but has not developed a model of integration that systematically integrates electorates or social groups into the explanation.

Why bother? For the more remote past, it is entirely plausible to argue that the most important developments in European integra-tion belong to the supranational first pillar and have been initiated and decided by elites in treaty-making or treaty-amending intergov-ernmental negotiations. More recent developments in European inte-gration, however, raise doubts on whether this is still true. These developments indicate a *shift in the focus of integration from the first to the second and third pillars, from formal and rigid to less formal and flexible forms of integration, and an increasing relevance of citizens.*

The second and third pillars of the EU – the Common Foreign and Security Policy (CFSP), the European Security and Defence Policy (ESDP) and the JHA – have proven the most dynamic policy areas in recent years. On the whole, and despite the migration of much of JHA issues to the first pillar, these new policies continue to be governed less formally and supranationally than the traditional first pillar issues. Even for the economic policies that make up the core of the first pillar, the advent of the open method of coordination (OMC) and other new, coordinative modes of governance signal a reorientation from the supranational, formal and hard law focus of the past. Moreover, the failure of formal treaty revision after 2000 slowed formal institutional change, stopped further 'deepening' moves to qualified majority-voting and more parliamentary competencies, and highlighted the relevance of citizens in integration. Flexible or differentiated integration was agreed in the Treaty of Amsterdam and continues to be practised in such core policies as Monetary Union and Schengen.

Finally, enlargement is markedly slowing down and loses its importance as the dominant way of integrating the neighbours of the EU. The cases of Norway and Switzerland and, more recently, Turkey demonstrate the growing importance of citizens' attitudes as a constraint on enlargement. The European Economic Area (plus the bilateral treaties with Switzerland) as well as the complex setup of neighbourhood policies with the Mediterranean and Eurasian countries are more likely to develop into stable alternatives to membership rather than transitional arrangements on the way to enlargement.

Under these circumstances, integration theory needs to focus more on varying institutional arrangements of European governance, including more informal and intergovernmental ones, on the one hand, and on public opinion and domestic electoral and party politics, on the other. This requires, in turn, a stronger connection between integration theory, on the one hand, and theories of (comparative) politics as well as theories of governance, on the other. In other words, the division of labour between integration theory – as the theory of shifting boundaries and competences – and theories of politics and governance as theories of decision- and policy-making is inadequate. To be sure, the reconnection requirement cuts both ways. That is, political–sociological analyses (i.e. the study of public opinion, political mobilization, electoral politics and party politics) as well as analyses of governance modes and arrangements need to make (sectoral, vertical and horizontal) integration their dependent variable and to develop hypotheses on the level, scope and growth of integration.

Two recent publications provide exemplary connections between political sociology and integration theory. In their 'postfunctionalist theory of European integration', Liesbet Hooghe and Gary Marks (2009) link public opinion, party competition and European integration and thereby overcome the elite focus of integration theory. They develop a model which stipulates under which domestic, party-political conditions the politics of integration follow the distributional logic assumed by intergovernmentalism and neofunctionalism and when it follows the identity logic postulated by constructivism. The model explains why European integration has increasingly been following identity logic since the 1990s.

By contrast, Stefano Bartolini (2005) takes a macrosociological and historical perspective that breaks completely with the intergovernmentalist–supranationalist debate. Starting from the Hirschman-Rokkan model of boundary formation and political structuring in the modern nation-state, Bartolini theorizes European integration as the formation of a new centre, which partially redraws the boundaries of the nation-state and thereby creates new (partial) exit options for societal and political actors. On this basis, he analyses the effects that the imbalance and partiality of the political restructuring of Europe has on actor strategies and behaviours, political cleavages and collective action problems as well as the sustainability of the democratic welfare state and European integration.

One of the major challenges for reconnecting the analysis of governance with integration theory is a *theory of informal institutional change* arising out of the EU's governance practices and everyday politics. In general, such a theory can build on supranationalist theorizing, which has stipulated historical–institutionalist causal mechanisms and focused on how supranational organizations in the EU have used their competencies as well as ambiguities and loopholes in the formal treaty rules to expand their own competences and strengthen European integration. Two recent special issues – one edited by Berthold Rittberger and Jeffrey Stacey for the *Journal of European Public Policy* in 2003, another edited by Henry Farrell and Adrienne Héritier for *West European Politics* in 2007 – have gone in this direction.

Finally, integration theory needs to move from analysing and theorizing the growth of supranational integration to analysing and *theorizing differentiated integration*. Differentiated integration is not strictly a new phenomenon. The presence of the concept has strongly increased since the 1990s, and has not gone unnoticed in the literature. Authors have categorized differentiated integration (e.g. Stubb, 1996) and begun capturing it in metaphorical ways – such as de Neve's (2007) 'onion' – or by historical analogy (see e.g. Zielonka, 2005, on neomedievalism). There are explanations of integration in foreign and security policy (e.g. Smith, 2004; Jones, 2007) as well as JHA (e.g. Niemann, 2008) that take up factors and hypotheses from integration theory, but systematic theorizing and comparative empirical analysis across pillars and sectors have been rare. Alkuin Kölliker's (2001, 2006) functionalist approach, which explains differentiated integration and its centripetal effects by public goods theory, and Christina Schneider's (2009; see also Plümper and Schneider, 2007) analysis of discriminatory membership in the context of enlargement, provide useful starting points. In principle, however, the entire set of variables featured by existing integration theories could be used to explain the patterns of differentiated integration and their change over time.

In sum, the future agenda for integration theory is to become both more inclusive and differentiated: inclusive in the meaning of expanding to mass politics and informal change, and differentiated in terms of capturing and explaining the increasing cross-issue and cross-country variation in European integration.

Note

1. For comments on an earlier version, I thank Dirk Leuffen, Guido Schwellnus and William Paterson.

References

Bartolini, S. (2005) *Restructuring Europe. Centre Formation, System Building, and Political Structuring Between the Nation State and the European Union* (Oxford: Oxford University Press).

Battistelli, F. and Isernia, P. (1993) 'Europa und die Integrationstheorien. Obsoleszenz oder Wachstumskrise?', in A. von Bogdandy (ed.), *Die Europäische Option. Eine interdisziplinäre Analyse über Herkunft, Stand und Perspektiven der europäischen Integration* (Baden-Baden: Nomos Verlag) 171–98.

Beyers, J. (2005) 'Multiple Embeddedness and Socialization in Europe: The Case of Council Officials', *International Organization* 59(4): 899–936.

Caporaso, J. A. (1999) 'Toward a Normal Science of Regional Integration', *Journal of European Public Policy* 6(1): 160–4.

Caporaso, J. A. and Keeler, J. T.S. (1995) 'The European Union and Regional Integration Theory', in C. Rhodes and S. Mazey (eds), *The State of the European Union. Vol. 3: Building a European Polity?* (Boulder: Lynne Rienner): 29–62.

Checkel, J. T. (2001) 'Why Comply? Social Learning and European Identity Change', *International Organization* 55(3): 553–88.

Checkel, J. T. (2007) 'Constructivism and EU Politics', in K. E. Jorgensen, M. A. Pollack, and B. Rosamond (eds), *Handbook of European Union Politics* (London: Sage) 57–76.

Checkel, J. T. and Moravcsik, A. (2001) 'A Constructivist Research Program in EU Studies?', *European Union Politics* 2 (2): 219–49.

Deutsch, K. W. (1957) *Political Community and the North Atlantic Area: International Organization in the Light of Historical Experience* (Princeton: Princeton University Press).

Egeberg, M. (1999) 'Transcending Intergovernmentalism? Identity and Role Perceptions of National Officials', *Journal of European Public Policy* 6(3): 456–74.

Fearon, J. and Wendt, A. (2002) 'Rationalism v. Constructivism: A Skeptical View', in W. Carlsnaes, T. Risse and B. A. Simmons (eds), *Handbook of International Relations* (London: Sage) 52–72.

Fierke, K. and Wiener, A. (1999) 'Constructing Institutional Interests: EU and NATO Enlargement', *Journal of European Public Policy* 6(5): 721–42.

Fioretos, K.-O. (1997) 'The Anatomy of Autonomy: Interdependence, Domestic Balances of Power, and European Integration', *Review of International Studies* 23(3): 293–320.

Gillespie, P. and Laffan, B. (2006) 'European Identity: Theory and Empirics', in M. Cini and A. K. Bourne (eds), *European Union Studies* (Basingstoke: Palgrave Macmillan) 131–50.

Gstöhl, S. (2002). *Reluctant Europeans. Norway, Sweden, and Switzerland in the Process of European Integration* (Boulder: Lynne Rienner).

Haas, E. B. (1968) *The Uniting of Europe. Political, Social, and Economic Forces 1950–1957* (Stanford: Stanford University Press).

Haas, E. B. (1975) *The Obsolescence of Regional Integration Theory* (Berkeley: Institute of International Studies).

Hoffmann, S. (1966) 'Obstinate or Obsolete? The Fate of the Nation-State and the Case of Western Europe', *Daedalus* 95(3): 862–915.

Hooghe, L. (2005) 'Several Roads Lead to International Norms, but Few Via International Socialization: A Case Study of the European Commission', *International Organization* 59(4): 861–98.

Hooghe, L. and Marks, G. (2009) 'A Postfunctionalist Theory of European Integration: From Permissive Consensus to Constraining Dissensus', *British Journal of Political Science* 39(1): 1–23.

Ingebritsen, C. (1997) 'Pulling in Different Directions: The Europeanization of Scandinavian Political Economies', in P. J. Katzenstein (ed.), *Tamed Power. Germany in Europe* (Ithaca: Cornell University Press) 167–94.

Ingebritsen, C. (1998) *The Nordic States and European Unity* (Ithaca: Cornell University Press).

Jachtenfuchs, M., Diez, T., and Jung, S. (1998) 'Which Europe? Conflicting Models of a Legitimate European Political Order', *European Journal of International Relations* 4(4): 409–45.

Johnston, A. I. (2001) 'Treating International Institutions as Social Environments', *International Studies Quarterly* 45(4): 487–515.

Jones, S. G. (2007) *The Rise of European Security Cooperation* (Cambridge: Cambridge University Press).

Jupille, J., Caporaso, J. A., and Checkel, J. T. (2003) 'Integrating Institutions. Rationalism, Constructivism, and the Study of the European Union', *Comparative Political Studies* 36(1/2): 7–40.

Kelemen, R. D. (2007) 'Built to Last? The Durability of EU Federalism', in S. Meunier and K. R. McNamara (eds), *Making History. European Integration and Institutional Change at Fifty* (Oxford: Oxford University Press) 51–66.

Koenig-Archibugi, M. (2004) 'Explaining Government Preferences for Institutional Change in EU Foreign and Security Policy', *International Organization* 58(1): 137–74.

Kölliker, A. (2001) 'Bringing Together or Driving Apart the Union? Towards a Theory of Differentiated Integration', *West European Politics* 24(4): 125–51.

Kölliker, A. (2006) *Flexibility and European Unification: The Logic of Differentiated Integration* (Lanham: Rowman & Littlefield).

Lasas, A. (2008) 'Restituting Victims: EU and NATO Enlargements Through the Lenses of Collective Guilt', *Journal of European Public Policy* 15(1): 98–116.

March, J. G. and Olsen, J. P. (1989) *Rediscovering Institutions: The Organizational Basis of Politics* (New York: Free Press).

Mattli, W. (1999) *The Logic of Regional Integration. Europe and Beyond* (Cambridge: Cambridge University Press).

Mattli, W. and Plümper, T. (2002) 'The Demand-Side Politics of EU Enlargement: Democracy and the Application for EU Membership', *Journal of European Public Policy* 9(4): 550–74.

Mattli, W. and Plümper, T. (2004) 'The Internal Value of External Options: How the EU Shapes the Scope of Regulatory Reforms in Transition Countries', *European Union Politics* 5(3): 307–30.

McNamara, K. (1999) 'Consensus and Constraint: Ideas and Capital Mobility in European Monetary Integration', *Journal of Common Market Studies* 37(3): 455–76.

Moravcsik, A. (1991) 'Negotiating the Single European Act. National Interests and Conventional Statecraft in the European Community', *International Organization* 45(1): 651–88.

Moravcsik, A. (1993) 'Preferences and Power in the European Community: A Liberal Intergovernmentalist Approach', *Journal of Common Market Studies* 31(4): 473–524.

Moravcsik, A. (1998) *The Choice for Europe: Social Purpose and State Power from Messina to Maastricht* (Ithaca: Cornell University Press).

Moravcsik, A. (1999) 'A New Statecraft? Supranational Entrepreneurs and International Cooperation', *International Organization* 53(2): 267–306.

Moravcsik, A. (2007) 'The European Constitutional Settlement', in S. Meunier and K. R. McNamara (eds), *Making History. European Integration and Institutional Change at Fifty* (Oxford: Oxford University Press) 23–50.

Moravcsik, A. and Nicolaidis, K. (1999) 'Explaining the Treaty of Amsterdam: Interests, Influence, Institutions', *Journal of Common Market Studies* 37(1): 59–85.

Moravcsik, A. and Milada, A. V. (2003) 'National Interests, State Power, EU Enlargement', *East European Politics and Societies* 17(1): 42–57.

Moses, J. W. and Todal Jenssen, A. (1998) 'Nordic Accession: An Analysis of the EU Referendums', in B. Eichengreen and J. Frieden (eds), *Forging an Integrated Europe* (Ann Arbor: University of Michigan Press) 211–46.

de Neve, J.-E. (2007) 'The European Onion? How Differentiated Integration is Reshaping the EU', *Journal of European Integration* 29(4): 503–21.

Niemann, A. (2008) 'Dynamics and Countervailing Pressures of Visa, Asylum, and Immigration Policy Treaty Revision: Explaining Change and Stagnation from Amsterdam to the IGC of 2003–04', *Journal of Common Market Studies* 46(3): 559–91.

Parsons, C. (2002) 'Showing Ideas as Causes. The Origins of the European Union', *International Organization* 56(1): 47–84.

Pierson, P. (1996) 'The Path to European Integration. A Historical Institutionalist Analysis', *Comparative Political Studies* 29(2): 123–63.

Plümper, T. and Schneider, C. (2007) 'Discriminatory European Membership and the Redistribution of Enlargement Gains', *Journal of Conflict Resolution* 51(4): 568–87.

Risse, T. (2000) '"Let's Argue!" Communicative Action in World Politics', *International Organization* 54(1):1–39.

Risse, T. (2004) 'Social Constructivism and European Integration', in A. Wiener and T. Diez (eds), *European Integration Theory* (Oxford: Oxford University Press) 159–76.

Risse, T. (2005) 'Neofunctionalism, European Identity, and the Puzzles of European Integration', *Journal of European Public Policy* 12(2): 291–309.

Risse, T., Engelmann-Martin, D., Knopf, H.-J. and Roscher, K. (1999) 'To Euro or Not to Euro? The EMU and Identity Politics in the European Union', *European Journal of International Relations* 5(2): 147–87.

Rittberger, B. (2005) *Building Europe's Parliament. Democratic Representation Beyond the Nation-State* (Oxford: Oxford University Press).

Rittberger, B. and Schimmelfennig, F. (2006) 'Explaining the Constitutionalization of the European Union', *Journal of European Public Policy* 13(8): 1148–67.

Rosamond, B. (2007) 'The Political Sciences of European Integration: Disciplinary History and EU Studies', in K. E. Jorgensen, M. A. Pollack and B. Rosamond (eds), *Handbook of European Union Politics* (London: Sage) 7–30.

Sandholtz, W. and Zysman, J. (1989) 'Recasting the European Bargain', *World Politics* 42(1): 95–128.

Schimmelfennig, F. (1998) 'Liberal Norms and the Eastern Enlargement of the European Union: A Case for Sociological Institutionalism', *Österreichische Zeitschrift für Politikwissenschaft* 27(4): 459–72.

Schimmelfennig, F. (2001) 'The Community Trap: Liberal Norms, Rhetorical Action, and the Eastern Enlargement of the European Union', *International Organization* 55(1): 47–80.

Schimmelfennig, F. (2002) 'Liberal Community and Enlargement. An Event-History Analysis', *Journal of European Public Policy* 9(4): 598–626.

Schimmelfennig, F. (2005) 'Transnational Socialization: Community-Building in an Integrated Europe', in W. Kaiser and P. Starie (eds), *Transnational European Union. Towards a Common Political Space* (London: Routledge) 61–82.

Schimmelfennig, F. (2008) 'EU Political Conditionality After the 2004 Enlargement: Consistency and Effectiveness', *Journal of European Public Policy* 15(6): 918–37.

Schimmelfennig, F. and Rittberger, B. (2006) 'Theories of European Integration: Assumptions and Hypotheses', in J. Richardson (ed.), *European Union: Power and Policy-Making*, 3rd edn (Abingdon: Routledge) 73–95.

Schimmelfennig, F. and Sedelmeier, U. (2002) 'Theorizing EU Enlargement: Research Focus, Hypotheses, and the State of Research', *Journal of European Public Policy* 9(4): 500–28.

Schimmelfennig, F. and Sedelmeier, U. (2006) 'The Study of Enlargement: Theoretical Approaches and Empirical Findings', in M. Cini and A. K. Bourne (eds), *European Union Studies* (Basingstoke: Palgrave Macmillan) 96–116.

Schmitter, P. C. (1969) 'Three Neo-Functional Hypotheses about International Integration', *International Organization* 23(1): 161–6.

Schneider, C. J. (2009) *Conflict, Negotiation and European Union Enlargement* (Cambridge: Cambridge University Press).

Scully, R. (2005) *Becoming Europeans? Attitudes, Behaviour, and Socialization in the European Parliament* (Oxford: Oxford University Press).

Sedelmeier, U. (2000) 'Eastern Enlargement: Risk, Rationality, and Role-Compliance', in M. Green Cowles and M. Smith (eds), *Risks, Reforms, Resistance and Revival* (Oxford: Oxford University Press).

Sedelmeier, U. (2005) *Constructing the Path to Eastern Enlargement. The Uneven Policy Impact of EU Identity* (Manchester: Manchester University Press).

Sjursen, H. (2002) 'Why Expand? The Question of Legitimacy and Justification in the EU's Enlargement Policy', *Journal of Common Market Studies* 40(3): 491–513.

Skålnes, L. S. (2005) 'Geopolitics and the Eastern Enlargement of the European Union', in F. Schimmelfennig and U. Sedelmeier (eds), *The Politics of European Union Enlargement. Theoretical Approaches* (London: Routledge) 213–33.

Smith, M. E. (2004) *Europe's Foreign and Security Policy. The Institutionalization of Cooperation* (Cambridge: Cambridge University Press).

Stone Sweet, A. (2003) 'European Integration and the Legal System', in T. Börzel and R. Cichowsky (eds), *Law, Politics, and Society* (Oxford: Oxford University Press) 18–47.

Stone Sweet, A. and Sandholtz, W. (1997) 'European Integration and Supranational Governance', *Journal of European Public Policy* 4(3): 297–317.

Stone Sweet, A. and Sandholtz, W. (1998) 'Integration, Supranational Governance, and the Institutionalization of the European Polity', in W. Sandholtz. and A. Stone Sweet (eds), *European Integration and Supranational Governance* (Oxford: Oxford University Press) 1–26.

Stubb, A. C.G. (1996) 'A Categorization of Differentiated Integration', *Journal of Common Market Studies* 34(2): 283–95.

Thomas, D. C. (2006) 'Constitutionalization Through Enlargement: The Contested Origins of the EU's Democratic Identity', *Journal of European Public Policy* 13(8): 1190–210.

Trondal, J. (2004) 'Re-Socializing Civil Servants: The Transformative Powers of EU Institutions', *Acta Politica* 39(1): 4–30.

Wagner, W. (2002) 'The Subnational Foundations of the European Parliament', *Journal of International Relations and Development* 5(1): 24–36.

Wiener, A. (2006) 'Constructivism and Sociological Institutionalism', in M. Cini and A. K. Bourne (eds), *European Union Studies* (Basingstoke: Palgrave Macmillan) 35–55.

Zielonka, J. (2005) *Europe as Empire: The Nature of the Enlarged European Union* (Oxford: Oxford University Press).

Chapter 4

The European Union's Institutions

Neill Nugent and William E. Paterson

Until the early 1990s the literature on the EU's institutions, like the literature on the European integration process more generally, was somewhat sparse. Not only was it sparse but much of it was also narrowly focused, not least in that it was mainly of an essentially descriptive and non-theoretical nature. Since the early 1990s, however, published work on the institutions has mushroomed, both in its empirical range and in that it has become increasingly conceptually and theoretically based.

In this chapter we review these developments in the study of EU institutions. In so doing, we seek to highlight the main features of the different approaches that have been used, show what sort of knowledge has been attained, and identify key areas where understanding is still lacking and where further research and analysis is necessary. Given space constraints, we do not attempt to provide a complete literature review, but rather a broad overview of trends in research and the associated writing.

The chapter focuses primarily on the EU's four main 'political' institutions: the European Commission, the European Parliament, the Council of the European Union (commonly referred to as the Council of Ministers) and the European Council. The EU's courts are covered in Chapter 8, the European Central Bank in Chapter 11, and there are passing references to some of the minor institutions in other chapters.

An overview of the unfolding of the research and associated literature

Scholarly research on the EU's (then EC's) institutions took a long time to get going following the launch of the European integration process in the 1950s. Indeed, it was not until the early 1990s that there began to be much coverage at all, and even then it was initially somewhat limited – in both volume and scope.

Until the take-off in the early 1990s, published work on the institutions tended to fall into three broad categories. First, there was a scattering of studies of individual institutions. Books included those by David

Coombes (1970) on the Commission, by Michael Palmer (1981) on the EP and by Simon Bulmer and Wolfgang Wessels (1987) on the European Council. Tellingly, in terms of the dearth of the literature, there was no full-scale book on the Council of Ministers. Of the books that were available on individual institutions, most were essentially descriptive and atheoretical in nature. The most notable exception was Coombes's book on the Commission, which explored whether it was possible for the Commission to combine advocacy roles on the one hand with mediating and managerial roles on the other. Second, the early theoretical debate on the nature and driving forces of the integration process focused on the roles and powers of EU institutions, especially the Commission and the Council of Ministers. This debate is outlined below, so suffice it to say here that intergovernmentalists saw power as ultimately lying with the Council, with the Commission exercising little more than a facilitating role, while neofunctionalists saw the Commission as exercising significant powers in an independent, or at least quasi-independent, manner. Third, such studies of EU policies and policy processes as existed – of which the first major one was that by Wallace *et al.* (1977) – naturally commented on the institutions, usually from a perspective that was placed somewhere towards the middle of the supranationalist/intergovernmentalist spectrum.

The surge in published work on the EU's institutions from the early 1990s had its starting point in the perceived increasing importance of European integration from the mid-1980s. It was a perception that was perhaps a little exaggerated, for significant integrationist advances had in fact occurred during the so-called Eurosclerotic years of the 1970s and early 1980s – not least on the institutional front with the creation of the European Council in 1975 and the holding of the first direct elections to the EP in 1979. Nonetheless, European integration was seen as being relaunched in 1985–86 with the Single European Market (SEM) programme and the SEA. This relaunch served to promote a generally increased academic interest in the integration process and in the institutions that, nominally at least, guided and managed it. As part of this increasing interest, a growing number of scholars who had been working on, or who had been trained in, disciplines that were close to and/or touched on European integration studies began to take an interest in what was happening in the EU. Foremost amongst these disciplines were international relations, comparative politics and public policy studies. The importing of approaches and ideas drawn from these discipline areas resulted in studies of the EU's institutions increasing in volume and also becoming more varied in nature and range. The variations particularly took the form of studies taking a more theoretically based direction, with conceptual frameworks increasingly being used to explore the compositions, structures, roles, operations and powers and influences of the institutions.

Conceptually based approaches facilitating an understanding of EU institutions

Since EU studies took a more theoretical turn from the early 1990s, so a variety of conceptually based approaches have increasingly been used to help throw light on aspects of the EU's institutions. Most of the approaches have not had institutions as their sole concern. Rather, questions relating to institutions have been part of a broader focus, such as the nature of the European integration process, the characteristic features of EU policy processes and the relative powers of EU policy actors. Nonetheless, though the concerns of these approaches have normally been broader than institutions as such, they all have been interested in institutions and have imparted insights of various kinds as to how EU institutions can be analysed and understood.

It is not possible here to provide a complete logging of the very large number of approaches that have been used in recent years to assist research and writing on the EU's institutions. It is possible, however, to provide an overview of the main approaches. These approaches overlap and intertwine in various ways, but it is of some analytical value to group them under three – very broad – headings.

Modernized grand theory

Much of the early academic writing on European integration was framed within a debate about the nature of the integration process. Two schools dominated: intergovernmentalism and neofunctionalism. Intergovernmentalism, led by Stanley Hoffmann (1966, 1982), saw integration as being essentially limited in scope (in that it was confined largely to 'low' politics areas) and as being a consequence of agreements between national governments whose close working relationships could sometimes be mutually beneficial. Neofunctionalism, led by Ernst Haas (1958), Leon Lindberg (1963) and Lindberg and Stuart Scheingold (1970), had at its heart the notion of spillover, by which was meant that once integration began – and it was likely to do so initially in economic and social policy areas – it would almost inevitably expand because of functional spillover (policy areas are not self-contained but impact on one another in many ways), political spillover (new political elites would be constituted with a self-interest in advancing integration) and cultural spillover (attitudes would change, with an increasing acceptance of power being exercised at the regional level). These two theoretical approaches had quite different interpretations of the role of the EU's institutions within the integration process. For intergovernmentalists, all key decisions were taken by representatives of the national governments in the Council of Ministers with the other main institutions – the Commission, the EP and the ECJ – being little more than supporting agencies. For neofunctionalists, these other institutions – especially the Commission – were independent and influential actors in their own right.

These 'grand' or 'macro-' theories about the nature of the integration process fell somewhat into disuse from the mid-1970s, largely because their explanatory power seemed to be wanting in key respects. However, with the intensification of the integration process that began in the mid-1980s there was something of a revival of the debate between intergovernmentalists and neofunctionalists. It is a debate that continues to the present day, albeit in updated, and in many respects more sophisticated and nuanced, terms.

The relaunch of the theoretical debate on the driving forces behind European integration owes much to Andrew Moravcsik (1991, 1993, 1995, 1998), who has advanced a sophisticated version of intergovernmentalism, which he calls liberal intergovernmentalism. It is beyond the scope of this chapter to examine this theoretical approach in detail (see Schimmelfennig, 2004, for a good summary) but in essence it has three main elements. First, the external actions of states are assumed to be based on maximizing utility – that is, states are assumed to act rationally. Second, there is a liberal theory of national preference formation, which suggests that state goals are at least partly shaped by domestic pressures. Third, interstate relations are seen as being largely constructed via governments, with the outcome of intergovernmental relations being the consequence of relative bargaining powers and perceptions of whether deals serve national interests.

Crucially, from the viewpoint of this chapter's focus on EU institutions, liberal intergovernmentalism postulates that real power and influence in the EU is in the hands of the national governments operating within the framework of the European Council and the Council of Ministers. The supranational institutions – the Commission, the EP and the ECJ – are seen as being little more than adjuncts and facilitators. To the numerous empirical studies that purport to show the supranational institutions, especially the Commission, bringing forward and helping to drive through EU policies in an independent way, Moravcsik's response is that '*intergovernmental demand* for policy ideas, not the *supranational supply* of these ideas, is the fundamental exogenous factor driving integration' (Moravcsik, 1995: 618).

Liberal intergovernmentalism quickly became, and has continued to be, an important reference point for research and writings both on the nature of the European integration process as a whole and on the role and influence of the EU's institutions. Regarding the latter, some of this research and writing has been essentially neofunctionalist in nature, or at least heavily neofunctionalist in tone. This is no more clearly seen than in the work of Alec Stone Sweet and Wayne Sandholtz (Stone Sweet and Sandholtz, 1997; Sandholtz and Stone Sweet, 1998) who, though preferring to use the word 'supranationalist' to describe their approach, build from a clear neofunctionalist base. From this base they draw also on other conceptual approaches – notably globalization and transactionalism – to explain the development of supranational governance in the EU and to show why the development varies considerably between policy areas. They develop a theory in which 'transnational exchange provokes supranational organizations to make rules designed to facilitate and to regulate the development of a transnational society' (Sandholtz and Stone Sweet, 1998: 25). These supranational organizations – notably the Commission and the ECJ – are shown as exercising significant power and influence in core policy areas.

Institutional approaches based on how political actors behave

Since the early 1990s the so-called new institutionalism has impacted considerably on the study of EU institutions, with two articles that were published in the mid-1990s having a particular impact in showing the potential use of new institutionalism in EU studies (Bulmer, 1994; Pollack, 1996). As Bulmer (2009) notes, the new institutionalism has offered two clear insights: 'that institutions mattered and *how* they mattered'. As such, new institutionalism has, in part at least, been a reaction against what many view as the overbehavioural and overquantitative nature of much of American political science.

A key feature of new institutionalism is that institutions are understood in a broad way. In the EU context this means that they are seen as consisting not just of the structures and personnel of the EU institutions but also of the rules, norms and values that are associated with and that surround them. (For a review of new institutionalism and EU studies, see Pollack, 2008.)

New institutionalism has, as Hall and Taylor (1996) noted in a much quoted article, three broad strands: rational choice institutionalism; historical institutionalism; and sociological institutionalism. These three institutionalisms are examined in depth in the EU context in Aspinwall and Schneider (2000), and are now outlined.

Rational choice institutionalism

Put simply, rationalist approaches assume that the behaviour of political actors is largely conditioned by desires to maximize utility. It is assumed that actors have goals they wish to achieve and that their behaviour can largely be explained by drives to maximize benefits and minimize costs in relation to the goals. (For overviews of rational choice approaches to the study of the EU, see Scully, 2006; Pollack, 2006.)

Liberal intergovernmentalism is a rationalist-based approach in that it assumes: the governments of the member states have preferences they pursue in the forums of the European Council and the Council of Ministers; decisions are taken in these forums to pursue a particular direction – be it treaty reform, EU enlargement or the deepening of the internal market – when there is a convergence of the national preferences; and some limited powers may be assigned to the supranational institutions if that suits national governmental purposes – by, for example, reducing transaction costs.

Rational institutionalism goes beyond rationalism as applied by liberal intergovernmentalists in that, whilst it shares the assumption that political actors seek to act rationally, it also asserts that their ability to do so is shaped and constrained by institutional considerations. Much of the work undertaken within this approach makes extensive use of formal modelling and advanced quantitative methods. Reviews of the application of some of these methods in the study of EU institutions are given by Hörl *et al.* (2005), Selk (2006) and Rittberger (2007).

The EU institution that has been most subject to analysis by rational institutionalists is the EP, where a veritable plethora of studies have been published on the voting behaviour of MEPs (see pp. 74–5). One reason for the abundance of this literature is that in the 1990s a number of American scholars were attracted to EU studies and brought with them, and have since helped to spread to EU studies, rational choice-based models and analytical devices that cut their teeth on analyses of US Congressional voting behaviour. Another reason is that, until recently, there was not much quantitative information available on EU institutional operational matters other than voting in the EP (and even this was, and indeed still is, only partial, since not all EP votes involve roll calls).

Since the late 1990s, the use of modelling techniques and of quantitative analysis has also increasingly been used in studies of the Council of Ministers. One reason for this has doubtless been academic discipline development, but another has been the appearance of much fuller information on votes in the Council. Prior to the late 1990s, information about voting in the Council was not published, so although some information about the extent and nature of voting could be gleaned – mainly from briefings, leaks and interviews – it was neither systematic nor comprehensive. The opening up of information about Council voting since the late 1990s has resulted in a considerable number of published works, many of them as part of a major study of EU decision-making led by Robert Thomson.

Associated with their interest in how institutional factors shape the behaviour of political actors, rational choice institutionalists have also had much to say about the impact of institutional environments on institutional power and influence. Again, most of the early work on this was focused primarily on the EP, with George Tsebelis and Geoffrey Garrett being particularly prominent in examining the impact of the cooperation, and more especially of the co-decision, legislative decision-making procedures on the EP's impact on EU legislation (Tsebelis, 1994; Tsebelis and Garrett 1997, 2000). The general consensus was that the new procedures – institutional rules – would increase the EP's influence, but suggestions from Tsebelis, and Tsebelis and Garrett, that co-decision, at least in its Maastricht version (the co-decision procedure was established by the Maastricht Treaty and then amended to the EP's advantage by the Amsterdam Treaty), would result in a decrease in the EP's legislative powers, did little for the standing of 'dry' modelling amongst most EU scholars. Indeed, the Tsebelis and Garrett position was reviewed in 2000 with a mixture of puzzlement, bordering on incredulity, by Richard Corbett, an academically cognizant MEP, who is a leading expert on EU, and especially EP, institutional affairs (Corbett, 2000). Corbett's scepticism was based primarily on a belief that the modelling was too divorced from the 'real world': the researchers relied far too heavily on formal treaty rules and did not take sufficient account of practical realities or of how MEPs seek to interpret and use the rules to their advantage.

Corbett's core criticism – that modelling is just too theoretical and insufficiently based on realities – still very much resonates in academic debates on how EU institutions and decision-making processes are best studied. Indeed, the debate has intensified as rationalist-based modelling and quantitative approaches have increasingly been used by EU scholars – with one prominent journal, *European Union Politics*, which was launched in 2000, largely taken up with such approaches.

As part of the debate on the uses of modelling, many of those who are sympathetic to the general approach have recognized that formal procedural models – that is, models based on the formal rules applying – do contain a number of weaknesses, including that they rest on oversimplistic assumptions, that they overestimate the impact of formal decision-making rules and that they have not done well in terms of empirical verification. On the latter, for example, formal procedural models would anticipate extensive voting in the Council when voting is permitted by the rules, but all the studies of Council voting in fact indicate that the great majority of decisions are adopted by consensus and without any formal vote being taken. Recognition of such weaknesses with procedural models has produced a developing academic literature, which is still in its early stages, in which efforts are being made to theoretically extend procedural models to embrace not just the formal rules by which decisions are taken but also the informal processes and understandings that accompany them. Much of this fledgling literature is based on bargaining models, which distinguish between different decision-making stages and seek to identify the informal processes at work before decisions are formally taken. (For useful reviews of the limitations of formal modelling and how it needs to be extended, see Achen, 2006; Sullivan and Selck, 2007.)

Of course, by no means all academics are persuaded of the merits of modelling and quantitative approaches. A particularly graphic instance of the key elements being aired in the debate about the merits of these approaches is seen in a spirited exchange between Dorothee Heisenberg (2008) and Gerald Schneider (2008) on how the Council of Ministers is best researched. Heisenberg argues that whilst formal and quantitative approaches may have their place in the study of some aspects of the EU, they are not appropriate for examining an institution such as the Council, where there is a relatively limited number of decision-makers, where operating norms do much to shape decision-making processes, where many key issues – such as member state preferences and informal operation practices (of which the most important is the seeking of consensus whenever possible) – are not readily subject to measurement, and 'where most of the important work is done behind closed doors and over dinner tables' (263). Rather, she argues, the Council lends itself better to qualitative, empirical study. What new insights into the Council has, she asks, formal- and statistical-based work provided? In response, Schneider – the founding editor of *European Union Politics* – accepts that traditionalist approaches to studying the Council have something to offer, but they are, he suggests, too often overdescriptive, insufficiently rigorous and just too unscientific. He vigorously argues that the use of game-theoretic modelling to study the Council is fully warranted as its underlying assumption of strategic rational behaviour on the part of Council actors is justified. Moreover, he argues, there is nothing inherent in rational choice models that privileges quantitative over qualitative testing.

Historical institutionalism

Historical institutionalism is focused on the temporal aspects of institutional behaviour and influence. In particular it is used to analyse how decisions taken at one point (decisions, perhaps, on institutional rules or on policy matters) can limit and constrain decision-making at later points in time. Fritz Scharpf's famous 1988 article on the 'joint-decision trap' is, in effect, an early instance of historical institutionalist thinking. In the article, Scharpf argues that the differing positions of national governments as EU decision-makers coupled with their heavy reliance on unanimity when making decisions combine to produce 'an institutional arrangement whose policy outcomes have an inherent (non-accidental) tendency to be sub-optimal' (Scharpf, 1988: 165). (For a later version of Scharpf's thinking on the joint-decision trap, see Scharpf, 2006.) Historical institutionalism has subsequently been developed more fully from a theoretical perspective by, amongst others, Bulmer (1994), Armstrong and Bulmer (1998) and, most notably, Pierson (1996, 2000, 2004). They, like all historical institutionalists, see EU operations as being part of a process than can only be understood if placed in an evolutionary context. As such, historical institutionalism has much in common with neofunctionalism, especially insofar as it emphasizes the sometimes unintended consequences of decisions and the tendency of initial decisions to later produce functional spillovers.

Key historical institutional concepts are 'path-dependency' and 'lock-in', which draw attention to how decisions taken at one point in time – such as decisions on decision-making rules or on the adoption of new policy priorities – can make it difficult for institutions to be flexible and open to change at later points in time, even though the decisional outcomes at these later points may be undesirable and/or inefficient. This helps to explain why some policies become 'set' and difficult to reform even when there appears to be considerable support for reform amongst decision-making actors. The CAP, which the Commission has long wanted to reform in a more radical way than has proved possible, is the most obvious policy area where this is so. The related problems in reforming the EU's budget also lend themselves to explanation in historical institutionalist terms, as Ackrill and Kay (2006) have shown with their demonstration of how member states, faced with reform pressures, may build new 'layers' into existing frameworks so as to preserve existing trajectories.

But though historical institutionalism is useful in helping to explain difficulties in effecting policy change – by highlighting, for example, the importance of decision-making rules that make policy-changing decisions difficult and the emergence of vested interests attached to the outcomes of previous decisions – it is perhaps less useful in helping to explain when, why and how EU institutions can drive through change. It has been seen as being of only limited value in providing insights into, for example, the ways in which the Commission has had considerable success in driving forward EU enlargement and the internal market programme, even though both of these policy initiatives have met with considerable resistance.

Sociological institutionalism

Sociological institutionalists are interested in the social contexts within which political actors operate and the effect these contexts have on attitudes and behaviour. Whereas rational institutionalists see the goals and actions of political actors as being determined by self-interested calculation, sociological institutionalists see them as being conditioned by interests, identities, norms and expectations that are generated by operational contexts, including those that emanate from the institutions themselves. Political actors are seen not only as being unable to divorce themselves from their operational contexts but also as being profoundly influenced by them. This results in them acting according to a 'logic of appropriateness' rather than, as rationalists would argue, a 'logic of consequences'.

Sociological institutionalism is closely associated with constructivism. So much so, indeed, that the two are, in practice, very difficult to separate. Bulmer (2009) suggests that in constructivism structures and agencies are more explicitly seen as mutually constitutive, but in practice much of what is thought of as sociological institutionalist work indicates something similar. (For reviews of constructivist and sociological institutionalist approaches to the study of the EU, see Christiansen *et al.*, 1999; Risse, 2004; Wiener, 2006; Checkel, 2006.)

Sociological institutionalist and constructivist work on the EU's institutions takes many different forms. The extensive publications of Liesbet Hooghe on the backgrounds and attitudes of Commission officials illustrates well what such approaches can bring to the table, with a picture drawn of officials who are, amongst other things, much more European in their identities than are 'ordinary' EU citizens (Hooghe, 1999, 2001, 2005). A quite different instance of sociological institutionalist and constructivist work with important things to say about the EU's institutions is that of Frank Schimmelfennig and Uli Sedelmeier on EU enlargement. Why, Schimmelfennig and Sedelmeier ask, when it was seemingly not in the interests of some existing EU member states to permit the 2004 enlargement, and when the support of all existing national governments meeting in the forums of the European Council and Council of Ministers was necessary for EU enlargement to be able to proceed, did enlargement nonetheless take place? The answer, they argue, is to be found partly in norms and values, with all governments in the European Council and the Council of Ministers subscribing to the view that fellow democratic governments should be supported. With some EU-15 governments still wavering, a process of 'rhetorical entrapment' took place, with 'promises' to the applicant states gradually being upgraded through a series of European Council Presidency Conclusions: to the point that it became all but impossible for doubters to backtrack and say no (Schimmelfennig, 2001, 2002; Schimmelfennig and Sedelmeier, 2005).

Approaches based on different conceptualizations of the EU

There is a considerable volume of academic literature focused on broadly conceptualizing the EU. The main purpose of this literature is to try and capture the main features of the EU and so further understanding of it.

Conceptualizing is, of course, common in the social sciences. But what is distinctive about conceptualizations of the EU is the sheer number of different conceptualizations that have been advanced. To take just some of the more prominent ones offered by political scientists, these include conceptualizations of the EU as a quasi-state; as a federal, near federal or confederal system; as a consociation; as a multilevel system; as a regulatory state; and as a special sort of international organization. All such conceptualizations present different pictures of the EU's institutions. They do so in large part because, as Donald Puchala noted in his still much-cited article, though it dates from the early 1970s, they are usually focusing on different 'body parts' of the 'elephant' (Puchala, 1972). That is to say, the analysts who present different conceptualizations are focusing on different institutions – or processes or policies – of the EU.

In terms of the ways in which the EU institutions are presented in conceptualizations, a particular focus is on the extent and nature of their powers and influence. Two sets of linked questions have dominated academic enquiry on the matter: which institutions exercise what power(s) in what context?; and to what extent is power exercised independently and to what extent is it framed and conditioned by other institutional actors? In very broad terms, the answers to these questions can be thought of as being spread along spectrums, with the conceptual literature having shown a particular interest in the extent of independent impact made by non-governmental institutions, and especially by the Commission, on EU decision-making. Two contrasting conceptualizations of the EU may be taken to illustrate the different sorts of 'power and influence' portrayals of the EU's institutions that different conceptualizations contain.

The EU as an international organization

Scholars approaching the EU from an intergovernmental perspective tend to see it as being a special sort of Intergovernmental Organization (IO). It is accepted that it is a particularly sophisticated and developed IO, but the core features of IOs are nonetheless seen to pertain: decision-making is in the hands of national representatives, with major decisions controlled by national governments (in the European Council and the Council of Ministers), acting usually on the basis of unanimity; decisions on major and controversial issues cannot be imposed by central institutions on unwilling member states; there is a central secretariat (the Commission), but it has few independent decision-making powers; the ethos of institutional functioning is 'cooperation', not 'integration'. This view accords a less heroic role to the Commission than the neofunctionalists but does stress the need for a very high level of competence among Commission employees. This competence is however of a traditional kind which privileges, as an early commentator on the Commission noted, technical, managerial and diplomatic skills rather than the political entrepreneurial skills favoured by the neofunctionalist approach (Siotis, 1964).

In this IO view, EU institutions are best viewed not as external agencies imposing their views on unwilling national authorities, but rather as frameworks or networks in which national actors attempt to coordinate their interests and preferences. As Paul Magnette, a leading advocate of the IO interpretation, notes: 'The EU is not about depriving the states of their sovereignty. Rather it is about encouraging them to exercise their prerogatives in new and more cooperative ways' (Magnette, 2005: 3).

The EU as a regulatory state

Giandomenico Majone has led the way in characterizing the EU as 'a regulatory state' (Majone, 1992, 1994, 1996; see also McGowan and Wallace, 1996; Jordana and Levi-Faur, 2004). This model emphasizes two key, interrelated, features of the EU: its functions and its institutional nature. Regarding the functions, they primarily involve regulating policy areas that are either economic in nature or are in large part driven by economic considerations. At the front of these policy areas are a range of internal market and internal market-related matters – including product specifications, consumer protection, competition rules and aspects of environmental and social policy. However, there is little in the way of distributive and redistributive policies, which results in most EU policies being relatively inexpensive for the EU to implement. Where there are heavy implementation costs, as with much of environmental policy, they fall mainly on public authorities and private companies in the member states. Regarding the institutions, a number of regulatory and non-majoritarian institutions are seen as exercising key roles in respect of the development and operation of the EU's policies. The most important of these institutions are the Commission and the EU's courts, but the growing number of EU agencies that have been created in recent years are also seen as exercising some influence (on European agencies, see Gerardin *et al.*, 2005; Majone, 2006). A number of reasons are identified as explaining why these institutions and agencies are able to exercise such influence, most of which have to do with the nature of the policies themselves. In particular: many of the policy issues on the EU's agenda are highly specific and technical in character, which advantages the Commission and the agencies because of their subject expertise and their knowledge of existing practices across the EU; the policies are mostly in areas where high-profile sovereignty issues tend not to arise, so national governments are not so concerned about sovereignty implications; the outcomes of proposed regulatory policies on member states are not usually so clear as are the outcomes of proposed distributive and redistributive policies, which can result in less resistance to them by national governments; and because EU policies do not – with the exception of the CAP and the Structural Funds – result in high levels of EU expenditure, they do not generally result in member states trying to stop Commission-led initiatives because they will increase the size of the EU's budget (although, of course, they may try to stop or amend them for other reasons). The regulatory nature of so many EU policies is thus seen as offering opportunities to non-governmental-based institutions, most notably the Commission, to push the policy portfolio forward, which in turn can strengthen their own institutional positions.

Taking stock of existing knowledge on the institutions

The previous sections of this chapter have provided an overview of the range of issues addressed, the types of approaches taken and the sorts of information and knowledge provided by those who have researched and written about the EU's institutions. In this section we look at the four main political institutions separately, noting major themes in the work undertaken on them and suggesting where further research is required.

The European Commission

The Commission has been subject to extensive academic scrutiny. More has been published on it than any other EU institution. There are three main reasons for this. The first is that the Commission is in many respects a unique institution. There is no other international institution that displays the Commission's mixture of being partly a political and partly an administrative body, and of being a powerful executive while also undertaking important legislative roles. The second reason is that many academic analysts take the view that the Commission exercises very considerable power and influence in the EU system. They see many policy areas – from the internal market regulation, through external trade negotiations, to EU enlargements – where the Commission has been, and still is, a policy mover and prompter as much as a servant of the national governments. Intergovernmentalists may argue that the power and influence of the Commission is of a second order and that it is essentially controlled by the governments of the member states, but this is not the majority view. And a third reason is that, until relatively recently at least, the Commission has been more accessible to academic study than either the European Council or the Council of Ministers. While the latter two have been cautious about opening up, and in any event are logistically difficult to study because the key actors are scattered around the member states, the Commission is located in one spot and its members and officials have usually been receptive to academic investigation.

So, the literature on the Commission is extensive and diverse. Much of it is, of course, like the writings on other EU institutions, contained in broadly based studies of the European integration process, and especially that on EU policy processes. This stock of published work is far too wide and voluminous to summarize here, so two examples will have to suffice to illustrate its range. The first example is the application of conceptually based approaches to policy processes in ways that highlight the strengths and weaknesses of Commission power – such as Peterson and Bomberg's (1999) use of policy networks, which helps to highlight how the Commission is a key policy actor in respect of middle and lower levels of policy-making but is less key in respect of 'history-making' decisions. The second example is the application of leadership models to EU decision-making – which as used by Beach (2005) and by Beach and Mazzucelli (2007) shows that the Commission has resources that can, in certain circumstances, be used to exercise significant influence even in seemingly 'pure' intergovernmental contexts.

As for work that focuses wholly on the Commission, broadly based texts include those by Cini (1996), Edwards and Spence (1997), Nugent (2000, 2001), Dimitrakopoulos (2004) and Spence (2006). Amongst the many studies that have focused on the Commission's power resources and the power it exercises are Schmidt (1998, 2000), Burns (2004) and Woll (2006). Work on the Commission's individual services includes Stevens and Stevens (2001) and Hooghe and Nugent (2006).

On the Commission's powers, a number of works have used a principal–agent framework to explore two sets of key questions: for what reasons and in what circumstances do the governments of the member states (the principals in this instance) delegate powers to the Commission (the agent)?; and to what extent and by what means is the Commission able to 'escape' control by the governments? Most authors who have taken such a principal–agent approach (and they include, most notably, Pollack, 1997, 2003; Franchino, 2002, 2004, 2007) emphasize that the key reason for the delegation of powers to the Commission is a reduction in the transaction costs of policy-making, via the likes of the speedier adoption of legislation and more efficient policy implementation. As for the ability of the Commission to escape the control of the national governments – perhaps to the point of pursuing divergent policy preferences – this is seen as varying very much according to context, but as being most possible when, for example, the policy preferences of governments are unclear or are conflicting, and/or when the operating rules and controls under which the Commission operates are weak.

A number of studies of 'the culture' of the Commission have also been published in recent years, in which the attitudes and orientations of Commissioners and Commission officials have been examined. These studies have taken a number of different forms. Cini (2000), for instance, in her comparison of the different cultures existing in the Competition and Environment Directorate Generals (DGs) relied largely on interviews. Egeberg (2006), in his study of the role behaviour of Commissioners, also relied on interviews, in his case with a small number of people who were in a position to observe Commissioners 'in action'. Abélès and Bellier (1996) and McDonald (2000), in their studies of Commission officials, took almost a social anthropological approach. And Hooghe, whose work on Commission officials was cited above, undertook extensive interviews and also made use of surveys, as did Trondal (2007) in his study of seconded national officials in the Commission.

The European Parliament

If the Commission is the EU institution that has been most explored by academics, the EP 'comes in second'. For years it received relatively little attention at all, other than in a handful of general texts (Palmer, 1981; Robinson and Webb, 1985; Jacobs and Corbett, 1990), and from 1979 in a few studies of EP elections (for example, Reif, 1985; Lodge, 1985, 1990, 1996). However, since the mid-1990s, research and publications on the Parliament have taken off, due in part to the generally increased academic interest in the EU but also in response to two specific factors. First, the EP has simply become a much more important institution than it used to be, and therefore more worthy of attention. Starting with the SEA, successive rounds of treaty reform have advanced the EP's powers and influence from being a special sort of advisory body to being a first rank institutional actor. Indeed, in important respects, especially regarding the making of legislation, the EP now exercises more influence in its domains than do most of the parliaments of the member states. Second, academics who were interested in applying modelling techniques and in using data analysis became interested in EU studies and for them the EP was the most obvious institution to focus on because of the availability of voting records.

Much of the literature that is focused exclusively on the EP (that is, excluding the broader policy process literature in which, like the other institutions, the EP naturally features), falls under five broad categories. First, there are general texts, of which two are especially prominent: Corbett *et al.* (2007) – the successor to the above cited Jacobs and Corbett – and Judge and Earnshaw (2009). Second, there are attempts to gauge and measure the EP's influence, much of this being conducted by modelling the likely outcomes of decision-making procedures (Tsebelis, 1994; Tsebelis and Garrett, 1997, 2001) and/or by statistical analyses of what happens to EP policy actions – especially tabled amendments to legislative proposals (Kreppel, 1999; Kasak, 2004). Third, there are analyses of the factors that shape voting behaviour in the EP, with the single most important factor being shown to be ideology as measured by political group membership (Kreppel, 2000; Hix, 2001, 2004; Hix *et al.*, 2007). Fourth, there are studies of the role and nature of political parties, and of the associated political groups, in the EP (Hix and Lord, 1997; Kreppel, 2002; several articles in a special edition of the *Journal of European Public Policy*, 2008). Fifth, the relationships between the EP and EU legitimacy and democracy are, quite naturally given that the EP is the EU's only directly elected institution, much examined. Different perspectives on this much-debated issue include those provided by Beetham and Lord (1998), Hix (2002), Koepke and Ringe (2006) and Kohler-Koch and Rittberger (2007).

The Council of Ministers

Given its importance in the EU system – it is the day-to-day intergovernmental institution and is (now usually in co-decision with the EP) the EU's legislative authority – the Council of Ministers was, until recently, relatively unexplored. Three main factors accounted for this. First, it was difficult to obtain objective and wholly reliable information about proceedings at the Council's most senior and important decision-making level – the ministerial level. Meetings were held behind closed doors and official information about what happened in meetings was sparse and dry. Second, the absence of any published information on what many academic researchers regard as the most interesting aspect of the operation of the Council – voting – meant that hard statistical work on the Council could not be undertaken. Third, unlike the Commission, the EP and the EU's courts, the Council was not interested in proselytizing the role of the institution since its main members – ministers – had 'day jobs' as members of national governments. By contrast, the other institutions were able to devote a lot of resources to speaking about their institutions at academic conferences and inviting academics to come and study them.

Until recently, published work specifically on the Council was thus relatively sparse. There were a few texts, of which the best were those by Hayes-Renshaw and Wallace (2006 [1997]), Sherrington (2000) and Westlake (1995, third edition – with Galloway – 2004). There were also a few studies of specific aspects of the Council – such as by Hayes-Renshaw and Wallace (1995) on the powers of the Council; by Hayes-Renshaw *et al.* (1989) on the Permanent Representations and the Committee of Permanent Representatives; and by Wallace and Edwards (1976) and Nuallain (1985) on the Council Presidency. Overall, however, the published literature on the Council was much thinner than that on the Commission or the EP.

This situation is, however, changing, with a decided upturn in research and publications on the Council now well underway. Unquestionably an important reason for this has been a move on the Council's part to greater transparency. Ministerial meetings are still mostly held in private, but voting records are now in the public domain and so are subject to academic analysis. Unsurprisingly, this development has attracted new scholars, most of them well-armed with sophisticated theoretical approaches and a solid grounding in the use of (sometimes advanced) statistical techniques. Amongst aspects of Council operations to have become the subject of increased scrutiny in the 2000s are: the powers of the Council Presidency (Tallberg, 2003, 2004; Schalk *et al.*, 2007; Thomson, 2008a; Warntjen, 2008); the relative powers of member states in Council forums (Thomson, 2008b); the level of the Council hierarchy at which decisions are taken (Häge, 2008); the use that is made of voting provisions in ministerial meetings and the existence of voting coalitions in the meetings (Mattlila and Lane, 2001; Mattila, 2004; Hayes-Renshaw *et al.*, 2006; several chapters in Thomson *et al.*, 2006, and in Naurin and Wallace, 2008); the 'culture' of the Council (Beyers, 2005); and the party political dimension of Council activity (Hagemann and Hoyland, 2008).

Perhaps the most important area where further work needs to be undertaken is in respect of the 'informal' and 'off the record' dimensions of the Council's operations. It is, for example, well known that prior to Council meetings – at working group, Committee of Permanent Representatives (Coreper) and ministerial levels – there are numerous pre-meetings and exchanges between the officials and politicians who represent the member states, but the scale and outcomes of such meetings and exchanges tend to be wrapped in generalities. And there is very little comparative work on the different procedures and cultural requirements that shape the behaviour and effectiveness of national representatives in the Council (though Bulmer and Lequesne, 2005, provide some insights). Of course, undertaking research on such aspects of the functioning of the Council is difficult, both methodologically and logistically. But, more of it needs to be done – as indeed it does on the other EU institutions too.

The European Council

The European Council is the most under-researched and least written about of all the EU's main institutions. That this should be so into the 1980s is not surprising, for the European Council was not constituted as such until 1975 and then for some years it was not at all clear just what its role and importance would be. France's then president, Valéry Giscard d'Estaing, who, along with Germany's then chancellor, Helmut Schmidt, was instrumental in creating the European Council, spoke of it as being an informal gathering designed to promote under-standing between national leaders and to give general policy direction to the Community – but this was obviously extremely vague and open to challenge.

However, over the years, and especially following the rows over the EC's budget in the early-to-mid 1980s, which were resolved at European Council rather than ministerial level, it increasingly became clear that most major issues facing the EC, then EU, were being referred to summits. Today, virtually all such issues – be they concerned with treaty reform, enlargements, financial perspectives or significant new policy initiatives – are referred to summits. Additionally, a host of other important issues – from monitoring the Lisbon Process to issuing CFSP and ESDP guidelines – regularly appear on summit agendas.

But academic research on the European Council cannot be said to have kept pace with the increasing importance of the institution. Published work on the European Council is somewhat thin on the ground with, as compared with the literature on the Commission, the EP and the Council of Ministers, relatively few works focusing specifi-cally on the European Council. A handful of general books on the European Council have been published over the years, including Bulmer and Wessels (1987) and Werts (2008). There are a few papers and book chapters that take an overview of the nature and functioning of the European Council (including de Schoutheete and Wallace, 2002; Nugent, 2006; de Schoutheete, 2006). There are a handful of analyses of the distribution of power in the European Council (see especially, Tallberg, 2008; Tallberg and Johansson, 2008). And there are accounts of some individual summits – notably in a series written by Peter Ludlow in the early-to-mid 2000s (see, for example, Ludlow, 2002, 2004). Beyond these types of publication, however, there is not much else, other, of course, than that which is found in more general works on EU politics and in studies of such issue areas as treaty-making and enlargement policy, where the European Council is at the fore (as, for example, in Beach, 2005; Beach and Mazzucelli, 2007). The relative paucity of the literature on the European Council is no more clearly demonstrated than in the way in which most of the mainstream texts on EU government and politics – including those by Bache and George (2006), Richardson (2006) and Cini (2007) – subsume consideration of the European Council within chapters on the Council of Ministers and assign but a few pages at best to the former.

Why has the European Council been relatively neglected by academic analysts? One reason may be that prior to the Lisbon Treaty it did not have its own institutional status and was presented as a sort of adjunct of the Council of Ministers. Many academics who did give attention to it treated it in precisely this manner: as a special part of the Council of Ministers. Under the Lisbon Treaty, the European Council became an

EU institution in its own right. Another reason is that it just is very difficult to research – with meetings held in secret and with most of the key participants difficult to access. And a third reason is that virtually all European Council decisions are taken by consensus – so there is little for the statistically inclined to get their teeth into.

In consequence, there is no shortage of research that needs to be undertaken on the European Council. More needs to be known, for example, about the impact of the pre-summit meetings and gatherings of various kinds that have become increasingly common between European Council participants. And more knowledge is needed on the factors that determine the influence wielded by national leaders in summit meetings, such as, for example, 'personality' traits and the impact of the size of the member states that the national leaders represent.

The impact of enlargement on EU institutions

The 2004–07 enlargement of the EU was accompanied, as have been all enlargement rounds, by a debate about the relationship between widening and deepening. The scale of this enlargement precipitated an especially wide-ranging debate on the institutional front, with attention focused on whether the addition of so many new member states would make it difficult for some institutions, especially the European Council and the Council of Ministers, to operate effectively. Would, indeed, enlargement lead to decision-making gridlock and a decline in the supranational character of EU institutions? These fears lay behind a determined German attempt, from Foreign Minister Joschka Fischer's 2001 Humboldt speech onwards, to strengthen the EU institutions.

Initially, much of the writing on enlargement was of an inside-out character, being focused especially on the impact of conditionality on the political, economic and legal systems of the acceding states (see, for example, Sedelmeier and Schimmelfennig, 2005; Grabbe, 2005, 2007). More recently, however, increasing attention has been focused on how the EU institutions have fared in an EU of 27 members (see Hagemann and De Clerck-Sachsse, 2007; Wallace, 2007; Kurpas *et al.*, 2008; Best *et al.*, 2009). The central concern of these studies has been on whether enlargement has resulted in the decision-making stalemates that some anticipated – which would make further institutional reform an urgent imperative – or whether the EU has been able to operate with reasonable efficiency. The conclusion of the various studies is quite clear: stalemates have not occurred, or at least they have not done so if the total amount of legislation passed each year is taken as the basis of judgement. Hagemann and De Clerck-Sachsse (2007: 10), for example, have shown the total amount of legislation being passed has quickly returned to former levels after an immediate post-enlargement dip.

Wallace (2007: 5) reports that there has only been a very modest drop in Commission proposals. Wallace also shows a decrease in time taken from proposal to decision (Wallace, 2007: 6). Contrary to much writing in advance of enlargement, the number of opposing votes has not risen in the Council of Ministers and there have been no persisting differences in voting patterns between 'old' and 'new' members (Hagemann and De Clerck-Sachsse, 2007: 18–19).

Unpacking the causal nexus of this near 'business as usual' is, of course, complicated and merits further research. Early research on the topic suggests a number of causal variables. In terms of the operation of the Commission, for example, Kurpas *et al.* (2008: 48) suggest that 'less controversy and better management have been the two "leitmotifs" of the Commission's successful adaptation to enlargement up till now'. Regarding the 'less controversy', the Commission is seen in particular as being more willing to use soft law measures and as being more reluctant to pursue controversial proposals. Regarding the 'better management', changes have included an enhanced role for the President, a stronger Secretariat General and increased use of planning instruments. In terms of the operation of the Council, a significant finding reported by Hagemann and De Clerke-Sachsse (2008: 24), that certainly goes some way to explaining the absence of decision-making gridlock, is an increased role of intermediary actors, especially the Council Presidency. Council meetings are now more formalized, with 'real' negotiations normally occurring outside the formal meetings and with the Presidency playing a leading role. 'Negotiations now take place elsewhere, presidencies have bilateral contacts with people ... it all happens but it happens in a much more informal manner outside the meeting room, in bilateral or multilateral contacts ... so the presidency has to go round and hear all the major member states and actually push them to see how far they will go ... the bilaterals have, in a way, become more important than plenary sessions' (ibid.). Another intermediary, the Council Secretariat, is also reported in the literature as increasing in importance, as illustrated by the creation in the Secretariat prior to enlargement of a special section (the dorsal) with responsibility for co-decision legislation.

Early studies of the EU-27 thus indicate 'business as usual'. This is so both in terms of the real world and of academic analysis. On the one hand, the institutions have avoided gridlock and are able, with some adjustments, to carry on as usual. Indeed, in the institutions where one would have expected the addition of new members to have had most impact – the European Council and the Council of Ministers – enlargement does not seem to have had a great impact on decision-making. There have, to be sure, been some changes in operating procedures with, for example, more formal statements being made and less 'real negotiating' taking place in formal European Council and

Council of Ministers meetings, but there have been only marginal changes to decision-making capacities. On the other hand, enlargement has not led to any major innovations in the methods of studying institutions. The early studies have yielded informative results using conventional analytical tools. Pressures for new analytical tool kits appear to be largely absent, save perhaps from those who are searching for more sophisticated ways of applying quantitative techniques.

Enlargement is, of course, a constantly ongoing and unfolding process, as must be the research on it. This is no more clearly demonstrated than with the Commission, where much further work remains to be done on how, for instance, the College has adapted to the 2004/07 enlargement. Has, for example, enlargement reduced the collegial character of the Commission? How are the 'working groups', which post-enlargement are now managing College business in broad areas, operating? And has, as Wallace (2007: 9) suggests, the reduction of the number of Commissioners to one per member state (which was occasioned by enlargement) increased the pressure on Commissioners to become advocates of their home countries and, if so, how is this impacting on their behaviour?

Institutions in the Lisbon Treaty

The Lisbon Treaty, like the Constitutional Treaty on which it was built, was intended to represent a definitive answer to a number of long-running issues surrounding the nature and operation of the EU's institutions (see the Preamble to the Lisbon Treaty). Assuming the Treaty is eventually ratified (and at the time of writing – September 2009 – that is dependent on the Irish people approving the Treaty in a second referendum on it) then most of the major institutional issues are indeed likely to remain settled for at least the medium term. For after the long and exhaustive institutional quarrels that characterized the making of the Constitutional Treaty and then the Lisbon Treaty, the member states have no appetite for another major round of negotiations on such matters as voting provisions in the European Council and Council of Ministers or the EP's powers. And, in any event, the onset of the global recession will necessitate a concentration on policy matters.

Assuming the Lisbon Treaty is eventually ratified, there will be no shortage of matters to be researched, for the institutional changes contained in the Treaty are quite far-reaching. The most important of these changes relate to the various presidencies. The Treaty makes provision for a full time President of the European Council elected by a qualified majority of the members of the European Council for a term of two and a half years. Apart from in the sphere of foreign affairs, the various formations of the Council of Ministers will be presided over by pre-established groups of three member states for a period of 18 months, with member states chairing Council meetings in six monthly rotations. The Foreign Affairs Council will be chaired on a permanent basis by the High Representative of the Union for Foreign Affairs and Security Policy, who will be appointed by a qualified majority of the European Council with the agreement of the Commission President. The reason for the Commission President being involved in the appointment of the High Representative is that as well as presiding over the Council of Ministers for Foreign Affairs, the High Representative will also become a Vice President of the Commission, responsible for handling external affairs, though unlike other Commissioners his or her term can be ended by the European Council at any point. The status of the President of the Commission is slightly strengthened in that as compared with the Nice Treaty position, under which he or she is 'approved' by the EP on the basis of a European Council nomination, under the Lisbon Treaty the European Council must, when making its nomination for the post, take into account the elections to the EP, with the President-designate then being 'elected' by the EP.

Taken as a whole, the Lisbon Treaty changes would appear to strengthen the national as opposed to the supranational dimension of the institutions but at the price of potential instability. The differing electoral bases of the Presidents of the Council and the Commission seem likely to generate tensions, while the potential for tension developing between both offices and the High Representative is high. This is an obvious area for future research on the institutions.

Another important area for research is the impact of the changed voting arrangements in the Council of Ministers that are made by the Lisbon Treaty. These are not, however, to be introduced until 2014, and even then on a three-year phasing-in basis. The key feature of the changes is that the weighting of Council of Ministers votes that were made in the Nice Treaty giving larger member states an increased voting weight were abolished in the Lisbon Treaty and replaced by a double majority system based partly on demographic weight which is even more advantageous to the large member states (see Baldwin and Widgren, 2004).

Amongst other important institutional changes, the Lisbon Treaty strengthens the European Parliament in a range of areas. This strengthening includes the elevation of the co-decision procedure to the status of 'ordinary legislative procedure' and the requirement of EP approval for some decisions – such as decisions to initiate enhanced cooperation – that hitherto have been the sole prerogative of the Council. These proposals are partially balanced by other measures that seek to enhance the monitoring and supervisory role of national parliaments.

The institutional changes contained in the Lisbon Treaty have naturally attracted the attention of scholars. Youri Devuyst (2008), for example, takes a detailed legal approach in which he emphasizes that a key feature of the Treaty is enhanced intergovernmentalism and a (further) decline in the Community method. He regrets this develop-ment, arguing that it bodes badly for the future operation of the EU: 'the main result of these changes is not necessarily an increased effi-ciency of the EU's decision-making, representation, and internal equity, but rather a strengthened control by the larger member States and their agents over the European integration process' (317). In a more concep-tually based article, Hofmann and Wessels (2008) look at the Treaty under three perspectives: the degree to which it rebalances the member state (they use the term 'sovereignty reflex') and the supranational ele-ments; the degree to which the Treaty's changes increase the ability of the EU to act; and the degree to which the changes increase legitimacy. Amongst their conclusions are that the Treaty: faces both ways on the member state–supranational dimension (by, for example, removing the explicit reference to the primacy of European law while giving the EU 'a legal personality'); potentially contributes to a greater capacity for the EU to act legitimately; and, a point we have already made, lays foundations for increased institutional tensions.

On a final point about the Lisbon Treaty, while the governments of the member states have all been keen to give assurances that no further significant institutional changes are foreseeable, the assurances may have been given more to ease ratifications in reluctant member states than in a spirit of conviction. For the fact is that at some point, possibly in the none too distant future, institutional questions will be revisited, partly perhaps in response to enlargement to include the Balkans and Turkey and/or, as Hofmann and Wessels suggest (2008: 20), in response to changing elite and mass preferences and the emergence and redefini-tion of issues. Questions concerning institutional reform are thus likely to remain firmly on the academic research agenda.

Future perspectives for research

Future research on EU institutions will continue to be driven both by new theoretical approaches and by new empirical developments. The main question that underlies much work on the institutions is whether the system has reached some sort of equilibrium in recent years and is acquiring the characteristics of a 'normal' political system (Hix, 2004, 2005). If this view is taken, then future research on institutions will be dominated by tools drawn from mainstream political science, in partic-ular comparative politics. This does, of course, cover a very wide field of possible approaches, from qualitative to quantitative and from rationalist to constructivist. As we have seen in this chapter, the increasing use of such approaches has resulted in a considerable 'mainstreaming' of EU studies: a theme to which we will return in the conclusion to this volume.

The comparative politics approach is, however, contested by scholars whose key point of reference is international relations. Scholars working in this framework bring quite different perceptions to the study of the EU. Crucially, for them the EU is essentially a state-centred forum of intergovernmental negotiations. As such, their work is unlikely to assume that any stable equilibrium will be reached since any state-centred explanation assumes that the power of particular states waxes and wanes and that all states attempt to make their institutional preferences prevail. The changing balance between state preferences is then reflected in the institutions, as institutional developments in the financial/credit crisis that began unfolding in the autumn of 2008 arguably showed. State preferences, especially those of the major states, were much more central to EU discussions than were those of the Commission, and the UK under the premiership of Gordon Brown exercised a major impact on decisions despite the UK not being a member of the eurozone. This whole area of state preferences and their impact on the EU institutions requires a great deal of research. Hitherto the role of state preferences has been analysed mainly through the lens of 'history-making decisions' rather than at the 'day to day' policy level.

Whether the EU will eventually arrive at a stable equilibrium in institutional terms remains to be seen. Certainly there are at least three, inter-related and overlapping, reasons to doubt that such a scenario is imminent. First, there is the EU's rolling enlargement programme, which envisages the eventual membership of most of the states of the former Yugoslavia and Turkey. It is true that the grand enlargement of 2004–07 did not lead to the gridlock, implosion and destruction of the institutional equilibrium that some predicted, but enlargements always raise important institutional concerns. One such concern is how decision-making efficiency and effectiveness can be preserved, and if possible increased, in a larger EU. Another concern is the effects of accessions on the EU's institutional balances – between, for example, the relative powers of large and small member states, and between the two potentially conflicting principles of the equality of member states and the 'democratic right' of larger member states to have greater institutional presence and power. Second, the Lisbon Treaty most certainly did not put all institutional questions 'to bed'. Indeed, the impact of the Treaty, assuming it is eventually ratified, is uncertain, containing as it does a light privileging of the sovereignty reflex over the supranational impulse and a recipe for heightened inter-institutional tensions. Third, the global financial crisis and economic recession that began in 2008 present a huge challenge for the EU's institutions given that the institutions were created in, and only have experience of, economic fair weather. Indeed, the nature of this institutional challenge was no more clearly seen than in the closing months of 2008 when there was great uncertainty, and no little disagreement, in EU elite circles concerning what policy responsibilities lay at the EU level and what lay at the national level, and concerning also who should be taking the policy lead at the EU level. At varying times, institutional leads of some kind were offered by the (French) Council Presidency, the Heads of Government of the larger member states meeting in various combinations, the Commission, the Eurogroup (with the Eurogroup meeting for the first time at Heads of Government level, though with the UK Prime Minister invited also to attend), and the European Council.

These issues facing the EU, alongside the lack of clarity about the EU's *finalité*, lie at the heart of many of the future challenges for research on the institutions. They are challenges for research on individual institutions, but perhaps even more so for research on the ensemble of institutions. For, perhaps somewhat surprisingly, there is something of a dearth of explicit comparative work on the EU's institutions. Of course, much work is implicitly comparative, but it would be helpful if there was much more that is explicitly comparative. Certainly there is no shortage of comparative questions to be addressed, ranging from issues concerning the cultures of the institutions to the precise circumstances in which institutional actors are most able to exercise power.

References

Abélès, M. and Bellier, I. (1996) 'La Commission Européenne: Du Compromis Culturel à la Culture Politique du Compromis', *Revue Française de Science Politique* 46(3): 431–56.

Achen, C.H. (2006) 'Evaluating Political Decision-Making Models', in R. Thomson, F.N. Stokman, C.H. Achen and T. König (eds) *The European Union Decides* (Cambridge: Cambridge University Press) 264–98.

Ackrill, R. and Kay, A. (2006) 'Historical Institutionalist Perspectives on the Development of the EU Budget System', *Journal of European Public Policy* 13(1): 113–333.

Armstrong, K. and Bulmer, S. (1998) *The Governance of the Single European Market* (Manchester: Manchester University Press).

Aspinwall, M and Schneider, G. (2000) 'Same Menu, Separate Tables: The Institutionalist Turn in Political Science and the Study of European Integration', *European Journal of Political Science* 38(1): 1–36.

Bache, I. and George, S. (2006) *Politics in the European Union* (2nd edn) (Oxford: Oxford University Press).

Baldwin, R. and Widgren, M. (2004) 'Council Voting in the Constitutional Treaty. Devil in the Details', Brussels, Centre for European Policy Studies Brief, 6–7 July.

Beach, D. (2005) *The Dynamics Of European Integration: Why and When EU Institutions Matter* (Basingstoke: Palgrave Macmillan).

Beach, D. and Mazzucelli, C. (2007) *Leadership in the Big Bangs of European Integration* (Basingstoke: Palgrave Macmillan).

Beetham, D. and Lord, C. (1998) *Legitimacy and the European Union* (London: Longman).

Best, E., Christiansen, T. and Settembri, P. (eds) (2009) *The Institutions of the Enlarged European Union, Governance of the Wider Europe: EU Enlargement and Institutional Change* (Cheltenham: Edward Elgar).

Beyers, J. (2005) 'Multiple Embeddedness and Socialization in Europe: The Case of Council Officials', *International Organization*, 59(4)): 899–936.

Bulmer, S. (1994) 'The Governance of the European Union: A New Institutionalist Approach', *Journal of Public Policy* 13(4): 351–80.

Bulmer, S. (2009) 'Institutional and Policy Analysis in the European Union: From the Treaty of Rome to the Present', in D. Phinnmemore and A. Warleigh-Lack (eds), *Reflections on European Integration: 50 Years of the Treaty of Rome* (Basingstoke: Palgrave Macmillan) 109–24.

Bulmer, S. and Lequesne, C. (2005) (eds) *The Member States of the European Union* (Oxford: Oxford University Press).

Bulmer, S. and Wessels, W. (1987) *The European Council: Decision-Making in European Politics* (London: Macmillan).

Burns, C. (2004) 'Codecision and the European Commission: A Study of Declining Influence?', *Journal of European Public Policy* 11(1): 1–18.

Checkel, J.T. (2006) 'Constructivism and EU Politics', in K.A., Pollack, M.A. and B. Rosamond (eds), *Handbook of European Union Politics* (London: Sage) 57–76.

Christiansen, T., Jørgensen, K-E., and Wiener, A. (1999) 'The Social Construction of Europe', special edition of *Journal of European Public Policy* 6(4).

Cini, M. (1996) *The European Commission: Leadership, Organisation and Culture in the EU Administration* (Manchester: Manchester University Press).

Cini, M. (2000) 'Administrative Culture in the Commission: The Cases of Competition and Environment', in N. Nugent (ed.) *At the Heart of the Union: Studies of the European Commission* (2nd edn) (Basingstoke: Palgrave Macmillan) 73–90.

Cini, M. (2007) *European Union Politics*, (Oxford: Oxford University Press).

Coombes, D. (1970) *Politics and Bureaucracy in the European Community: A Portrait of the Commission of the EEC* (London: George Allen & Unwin).

Corbett, R. (2000) 'Academic Modelling of the Codecision Procedure: A Practitioners Puzzled Reaction', *European Union Politics* 1(3): 373–81.

Corbett, R., Jacobs, M., and Shackleton, M. (2007) *The European Parliament* (7th edn) (London: John Harper).

Devuyst, Y. (2008) 'The European Union's Institutional Balance After the Treaty of Lisbon: Community Method and Democratic Deficit Reassessed', *Georgetown Journal of International Law* 39(2): 247–326.

Dimitrakopoulos, D.G. (2004) *The Changing European Commission* (Manchester: Manchester University Press).

Edwards, G. and Spence, D. (1997) (eds) *The European Commission* (2nd edn) (London: Cartermill).

Egeberg, M. (2006) 'Executive Politics as Usual: Role Behaviour and Conflict Dimensions in the College of European Commissioners', *Journal of European Public Policy* 13(1): 1–15.

Franchino, F. (2002) 'Efficiency or Credibility: Testing the Two Logics of Delegation to the European Commission, *Journal of European Public Policy* 9(5): 677–94.

Franchino, F. (2004) 'Delegating Powers in the European Community', *British Journal of Political Science* 34(2): 449–76.

Franchino, F. (2007) *The Powers of the Union: Delegation in the EU* (Cambridge: Cambridge University Press).

Gerardin, D., Munoz, R. and Petit, N. (2005) *Regulation Though Agencies: A New Paradigm of European Governance* (Cheltenham: Edward Elgar).

Grabbe, H. (2007) *The EU's Transformative Power: Europeanization through Conditionality in Central and Eastern Europe* (Basingstoke: Palgrave Macmillan).

Haas, E.B. (1958) *The Uniting of Europe: Political, Social and Economic Forces 1950–57* (Stanford: Stanford University Press).

Häge, F.M. (2008) 'Who Decides in the Council of the European Union?', *Journal of Common Market Studies* 46(3): 533–58.

Hagemann, S. and de Clerck-Sachsse, J. (2007) *Old Rules, New Game: Decision-Making in the Council of Ministers After the 2004 Enlargement*, CEPS Special Report, (Brussels: Centre for European Policy Studies), March; available at <http://www.ceps.eu>

Hagemann, S. and Hoyland, B. (2008) 'Parties in the Council?', *Journal of European Public Policy* 15(8): 1205–21.

Hall, P.A. and Taylor, R.C.R. (1996) 'Political Science and the Three New Institutionalisms' *Political Studies* 44(5): 936–57.

Hayes-Renshaw, F. and Wallace, H. (1995) 'Executive Power in the European Union: The Functions and Limits of the Council of Ministers', *Journal of European Public Policy* 2(4): 559–82.

Hayes-Renshaw, F. and Wallace, H. (2006 [1997]) *The Council of Ministers* (2nd edn) (Basingstoke: Palgrave Macmillan).

Hayes-Renshaw, F., Lequesne, C, and Lopez, P.M. (1989) 'The Permanent Representations of the Member States to the European Communities', *Journal of Common Market Studies* 28(2): 119–37.

Hayes-Renshaw, F., Van Aken, W. and Wallace, H. (2006) 'When and Why the EU Council of Ministers Votes Explicitly', *Journal of Common Market Studies* 44(1): 161–94.

Heisenberg, D. (2008) 'How Should We Best Study the Council of Ministers?', in D. Naurin, and H. Wallace (eds), *Unveiling the Council of the European Union: Games Governments Play in Brussels* (Basingstoke: Palgrave Macmillan) 261–76.

Hix, S. (2001) 'Legislative Behaviour and Party Competition in the Post-1999 European Parliament: An Application of NOMINATE to the EU', *Journal of Common Market Studies* 39(4): 663–88.

Hix, S. (2002) 'What Role for the European Parliament in a More Democratic European Union?', *One Europe or Several? – Newsletter*, 7, Brighton: University of Sussex.

Hix, S. (2004) 'Electoral Systems and Legislative Behaviour: Explaining Voter-Defection in the European Parliament', *World Politics* 56(1): 194–223.

Hix, S. (2005) *The Political System of the European Union* (2nd edn) (Basingstoke: Palgrave Macmillan).

Hix, S. and Lord, C. (1997) *Political Parties in the European Union* (London: Macmillan).

Hix, S., Noury, A.G. and Roland, G. (2007) *Democratic Politics in the European Parliament* (Cambridge: Cambridge University Press).

Hofmann, A. and Wessels, W. (2008) 'Der Vertrag von Lissabon –eine tragfaehige und abschliessende Antwort auf konstitutionelle Grundfragen?', *Integration* 21(1): 3–20.

Hoffmann, S. (1966) 'Obstinate or Obsolete: The Fate of the Nation State and the Case of Western Europe', *Daedelus* 95: 862–915.

Hoffmann, S. (1982) 'Reflection on the Nation State in Western Europe Today', *Journal of Common Market Studies* 21(1–2): 21–37.

Hooghe, L. (1999) 'Images of Europe: Orientations to European Integration Among Senior Officials of the European Commission', *British Journal of Political Science* 29(2): 345–67.

Hooghe, L. (2001) *The European Commission and the Integration of Europe: Images of Governance* (Cambridge: Cambridge University Press).

Hooghe, L (2005) 'Many Roads Lead to International Norms, But Few Via International Socialization', *International Organization* 59(4): 861–98.

Hooghe, L. and Nugent, N. (2006) 'The Commission's Services', in J. Peterson and M. Shackleton (eds), *The Institutions of the European Union* (2nd edn) (Oxford: Oxford University Press) 147–68.

Hörl, B., Warntjen, A., and Wonka, A. (2005) 'Built on Quicksand? A Decade of Procedural Spatial Models on EU Legislative Decision-Making', *Journal of European Public Policy* 12(3): 592–606.

Jacobs, F. and Corbett, R. (1990) *The European Parliament* (London: Longman).

Jordana, J. and Levy-Faur, D. (eds) (2004) *The Politics of Regulation* (Cheltenham: Edward Elgar).

Judge, D. and Earnshaw, D. (2009) *The European Parliament* (2nd edn) (Basingstoke: Palgrave Macmillan).

Kasak, C. (2004) 'The Legislative Impact of the European Parliament Under the Revised Co-Decision Procedure', *European Union Politics*, 5(2): 241–60.

Koepke, J.R. and Ringe, N. (2006) 'The Second Order Election Model in an Enlarged Europe', *European Union Politics* 7(3): 321–46.

Kohler-Koch, B. and Rittberger, B. (2007) *Debating the Democratic Legitimacy of the European Union* (Lanham: Rowman & Littlefield).

Kreppel, A. (1999) 'The European Parliament's Influence Over EU Policy Outcomes', *Journal of Common Market Studies* 37(3): 521–38.

Kreppel, A. (2000) 'Rules and Ideology and Coalition Formation in the European Parliament: Past, Present and Future', *European Union Politics* 1(3): 340–62.

Kreppel, A. (2002) *The European Parliament and the Supranational Party System: A Study in Institutional Development* (Cambridge: Cambridge University Press).

Kurpas, S., Grøn, C., and Kaczyński, P.M. (2008) *The European Commission After Enlargement: Does More Add Up to Less?*, CEPS Special Report, (Brussels: Centre for European Policy Studies), March; available at <http://www.ceps.eu>

Lindberg, L. (1963) *The Political Dynamics of European Economic Integration* (Stanford: Stanford University Press).

Lindberg, L. N., and Scheingold, S.A. (1970) *Europe's Would-Be Polity: Patterns of Change in the European Community* (New York: Prentice Hall).

Lodge, J. (1985) (ed.) *Direct Elections to the European Parliament, 1984* (London: Macmillan).

Lodge, J. (1990) (ed.) *Direct Elections to the European Parliament, 1989* (London: Macmillan).

Lodge, J. (1996) (ed.) *The 1994 Elections to the European Parliament* (London: Macmillan).

Ludlow, P. (2002) *The Seville Council* (Brussels: Eurocomment).

Ludlow, P. (2004) *The Making of the New Europe: The European Councils in Brussels and Copenhagen 2002* (Brussels: Eurocomment).

Magnette P. (2005) *What is the European Union?* (Basingstoke: Palgrave Macmillan).

Majone, G. (1992) 'Regulatory Federalism in the European Community', *Environment and Planning C: Government and Policy* 10(3): 299–316.

Majone, G. (1994) 'The Rise of the Regulatory State in Europe', *West European Politics* 17(3): 77–101.

Majone, G. (1996) *Regulating Europe* (London: Routledge).

Majone, G. (2006) *Managing Europeanization: The European Agencies*, in J. Peterson and M. Shackleton (eds) *The Institutions of the European Union*, 2nd edn, (Oxford: Oxford University Press) 190–209.

Mattila, M. (2004) 'Contested Decisions – Empirical Analysis of Voting in the EU Council of Ministers', *European Journal of Political Research* 31(1): 34–51.

Mattila, M. and Lane, J-E. (2001) 'Why Unanimity in the Council? A Roll Call Analysis of Council Voting', *European Union Politics* 2(1): 31–52.

McDonald, M. (2000) 'Identities in the European Commission', in Nugent, N. (ed.), *At the Heart of the Union: Studies of the European Commission* (2nd edn) (Basingstoke: Palgrave Macmillan) 51–72.

McGowan, F. and Wallace, H. (1996) 'Towards a European Regulatory State', *Journal of European Public Policy* 3(4): 560–76.

Moravcsik, A. (1991) 'Negotiating the Single European Act: National Interests and Conventional Statecraft in the European Community', *International Organization* 45(1): 19–56.

Moravcsik, A. (1993) 'Preferences and Power in the European Community: A Liberal Intergovernmentalist Approach', *Journal of Common Market Studies* 31(4): 473–524.

Moravcsik, A. (1995) 'Liberal Intergovernmentalism and Integration: A Rejoinder', *Journal of Common Market Studies* 33(4): 611–28.

Moravcsik, A. (1998) *The Choice for Europe: Social Purpose and State Power from Messina to Maastricht* (Ithaca: Cornell University Press).

Naurin, D. and Wallace, H. (eds) (2008) *Unveiling the Council of the European Union: Games Governments Play in Brussels* (Basingstoke: Palgrave Macmillan).

Nuallin, C.O. (1985) (ed.) *The Presidency of the European Council of Ministers* (London: Croom Helm).

Nugent, N. (2000) *At the Heart of the Union: Studies of the European Commission* (2nd edn) (Basingstoke: Palgrave Macmillan).

Nugent, N. (2001) *The European Commission* (Basingstoke: Palgrave Macmillan).

Nugent, N. (2006) *The Government and Politics of the European Union* (6th edn) (Basingstoke: Palgrave Macmillan) 219–39.

Palmer, M. (1981) *The European Parliament* (London: Pergamon).

Peterson, J. and Bomberg, E. (1999) *Decision-Making in the European Union* (London: Macmillan).

Pierson, P. (1996) 'The Path to European Integration: A Historical Institutionalist Analysis', *Comparative Political Studies* 29(2): 123–63.

Pierson, P. (2000) 'Increasing Returns, Path Dependence, and the Study of Politics', *American Political Science Review* 94(2): 251–67.

Pierson, P. (2004) *Politics in Time: History, Institutions, and Social Analysis* (Princeton: Princeton University Press).

Pollack, M.A. (1996) 'The New Institutionalisms and EU Governance: The Promise and Limits of Institutionalist Analysis', *Governance* 9(4): 429–58.

Pollack, M.A. (1997) 'Delegation, Agency and Agenda Setting in the European Community', *International Organization* 51(1): 99–135.

Pollack, M.A. (2003) *The Engines of European Integration: Delegation, Agency and Agenda-Setting in the European Union* (Oxford: Oxford University Press).

Pollack, M.A. (2006) 'Rational Choice and EU Politics', in K.E. Jørgenson, M.A. Pollack and B. Rosamond (eds) *Handbook of European Union Politics* (London: Sage) 31–55.

Pollack, M.A. (2008) 'The New Institutionalisms and European Integration', *conWEB-webpapers on Constitutionalism and Governance Beyond the State*, 2008:1, available at <www.bath.ac.uk/esm1/conWEB>

Puchala, D.J. (1972) 'Of Blind Men, Elephants and International Integration', *Journal of Common Market Studies* 10(3): 267–84.

Reif, K. (1985) (ed.) *Ten European Elections: Campaigns and Results of the 1979/81 First Direct Elections to the European Parliament* (Aldershot: Gower).

Richardson, J. (ed.) (2006) *European Union: Power and Policy-Making* (3rd edn) (London: Routledge).

Risse, T. (2004) 'Social Constructivism and European Integration', in A. Wiener and T. Diez (eds), *European Integration Theory* (Oxford: Oxford University Press) 159–76.

Rittberger, B. (2007) 'Political Preferences, Revealed Positions and Strategic Votes: Explaining Decision-Making in the EU Council', *Journal of European Public Policy* 14(7): 1150–61.

Robinson, A. and Webb, A. (1985) *The European Parliament in the EC Policy Process* (London: Policy Studies Institute).

Sandholtz, W. and Stone Sweet, A. (eds) (1998) *European Integration and Supranational Governance* (Oxford: Oxford University Press).

Schalk, J., Torenvlied, R., Weesie, J., and Stokman, F. (2007) 'The Power of the Presidency in EU Council Decision-Making', *European Union Politics* 8(2): 229–50.

Scharpf, F.W. (1988) 'The Joint Decision Trap: Lessons From German Federalism and European Integration', *Public Administration* 66(3): 239–78.

Scharpf, F.W. (2006) 'The Joint Decision-Trap Revisited', *Journal of Common Market Studies* 44(4): 845–64.

Schimmelfennig, F. (2001) 'The Community Trap: Liberal Norms, Rhetorical Action, and the Eastern Enlargement of the European Union', *International Organization* 55(1): 47–80.

Schimmelfennig, F. (2002) 'Liberal Community and Enlargement: An Event History Analysis', *Journal of European Public Policy* 9(4): 598–626.

Schimmelfennig, F. (2004) 'Liberal Intergovernmentalism', in A. Wiener and T. Diez (eds) *European Integration Theory* (Oxford: Oxford University Press): 75–94.

Schimmelfennig, F. and Sedelmeier, U. (2005) *The Politics of European Union Enlargement: Theoretical Approaches* (London: Routledge).

Schmidt, S.K. (1998) 'Commission Activism: Subsuming Telecommunications and Electricity Under European Competition Law', *Journal of European Public Policy* 5(2): 169–84.

Schmidt, S.K. (2000) 'Only an Agenda Setter? The European Commission's Power Over the Council of Ministers', *European Union Politics* 1(1): 37–61.

Schneider, G. (2008) 'Neither Goethe Nor Bismarck: On the Link between Theory and Empirics in Council Decision-Making Studies', in D. Naurin, and H. Wallace (eds), *Unveiling the Council of the European Union: Games Governments Play in Brussels* (Basingstoke: Palgrave Macmillan) 277–89.

de Schoutheete, P. (2006) 'The European Council', in J. Peterson and M. Shackleton (eds), *The Institutions of the European Union* (2nd edn) (Oxford: Oxford University Press).

de Schoutheete, P. and Wallace, W. (2002) *The European Council* (Paris: Notre Europe), accessible at <http://www.notre-europe.eu/en/>

Scully, R. (2006) 'Rational Institutionalism and Liberal Intergovernmentalism', in M. Cini and A.K. Bourne (eds), *Palgrave Advances in European Union Studies* (Basingstoke: Palgrave Macmillan) 19–34.

Sedelmeier, U. and Schimmelfennig, F. (eds) (2005) *The Europeanisation of Central and Eastern Europe* (Cornell: Cornell University Press).

Selk, T.J. (2006) *Preferences and Procedures: European Union Legislative Decision-Making* (Dordrecht: Springer).

Siotis, J. (1964) 'Some Problems of European Secretariats', *Journal of Common Market Studies* 2(3): 222–5.

Spence, D. (ed.) (2006) *The European Commission* (3rd edn) (London: John Harper).

Stevens, A. and Stevens, H. (2001) *Brussels Bureaucrats? The Administration of the European Union* (Basingstoke: Palgrave Macmillan).

Stone Sweet, A. and Sandholtz, W. (1997) 'European Integration and Supranational Governance', *Journal of European Public Policy* 4(3): 297–317.

Sullivan, J. and Selck, J. (2007) 'Political Preferences, Revealed Positions and Strategic Votes: Explaining Decision-Making in the EU Council', *Journal of European Public Policy* 14(7): 1150–61.

Tallberg, J. (2003) 'The Agenda-Shaping Powers of the EU Council Presidency', *Journal of European Public Policy* 10(1): 1–19.

Tallberg, J. (2004) 'The Power of the Presidency: Brokerage, Efficiency and Distribution in EU Negotiations, *Journal of Common Market Studies* 42(5): 999–1022.

Tallberg, J. (2008) 'Bargaining Power in the European Council', *Journal of Common Market Studies* 46(3): 685–708.

Tallberg, J. and Johansson, K.M. (2008) 'Party Politics in the European Council', *Journal of European Public Policy* 15(8): 1222–42.

Thomson, R. (2008a) 'The Council Presidency in the European Union: Responsibility With Power', *Journal of Common Market Studies* 46(3): 593–617.

Thomson, R. (2008b) 'The Relative Power of Member States in the Council: Large and Small, Old and New', in D. Naurin, and H. Wallace (eds) *Unveiling the Council of the European Union: Games Governments Play in Brussels* (Basingstoke: Palgrave Macmillan).

Thomson, R., Stokman, F.N., Achen, C.H. and König, T. (2006) (eds) *The European Union Decides* (Cambridge: Cambridge University Press).

Trondal, J. (2007) 'Is the Commission a "Hothouse" for Supanationalism?', *Journal of Common Market Studies* 45 (5): 1111–33.

Tsebelis, G. (1994) 'The Power of the European Parliament as a Conditional Agenda Setter', *American Political Science Review* 88(1): 128–42.

Tsebelis, G. and Garrett, G. (1997) 'Agenda Setting, Vetoes and the European Union's Co-Decision Procedure', *Journal of Legislative Studies* 3: 74–92.

Tsebelis, G. and Garrett, G. (2000) 'Legislative Politics in the European Union', *European Union Politics* 1: 5–32.

Tsebelis, G. and Garrett, G. (2001) 'The Institutional Foundations of Intergovernmentalism and Supranationalism in the European Union', *International Organization* 55(2): 357–90.

Wallace, H. (2007) *Adapting to Enlargement of the European Union: Institutional Practice Since May 2004* (Brussels: TEPSA).

Wallace, H. and Edwards. G. (1976) 'European Community: The Evolving Role of the Presidency of the Council', *International Affairs* 57(4): 535–50.

Wallace, H., Wallace, W. and Webb, C. (1977) (eds) *Policy-Making in the European Communities* (Chichester: John Wiley).

Warntjen, A. (2008) 'The Council Presidency: Power Broker or Burden? An Empirical Analysis', *European Union Politics* 9(3): 315–38.

Werts, J. (2008) *The European Council* (London: John Harper Publishing).

Westlake, M. (1995) *The Council of the European Union* (London: Cartermill).

Westlake, M. and Galloway, D. (2004) *The Council of the European Union* (3rd edn) (London: John Harper Publishing).

Wiener, A. (2006) 'Constructivism and Sociological Institutionalism', in M. Cini, and A.K. Bourne (eds), *Palgrave Advances in European Union Studies* (Basingstoke: Palgrave Macmillan) 35–55.

Woll, C. (2006) 'The Road to External Representation: The European Commission's Activism in International Air Transport', *Journal of European Public Policy* 13(1): 52–69.

Chapter 5

Leadership and Intergovernmental Negotiations in the European Union

Derek Beach

Introduction

Within EU studies, there has been an increasing recognition that the celebrated 'big bangs' agreements do not materialize by themselves. History-making negotiations that conclude constitutional negotiations in intergovernmental conferences (IGCs) or major reform packages like Agenda 2000 are not what can be termed 'spot markets', where governments and EU institutions relatively effortlessly sit down and find and agree upon a deal that both maximizes utility gains while reflecting patterns of relative actor power. Recent advances point out that these types of complex negotiations are not self-organizing, which means that the 'demand' for cooperation amongst governments does not necessarily create its own supply of efficient agreements (Tallberg, 2004, 2006; Beach and Mazzucelli, 2007). Factors such as agenda overload and issue complexity can act as a barrier for agreement, creating the risk that either inefficient outcomes are reached or even that the negotiations collapse. Negotiation theory points out that the provision of leadership is a necessity to overcome these transaction cost related factors and is a crucial intervening variable between actor preferences and outcomes.

Yet who provides leadership matters. Would the SEA have been as ambitious and far-reaching a document if the Commission had not been informally granted control of the agenda by the Luxembourg Presidency? Would the Eastern enlargement with ten states have been successfully concluded in the manner that is was in 2002 if an opponent of enlargement held the Presidency instead of pro-enlargement Denmark?

While many scholars acknowledge its importance, leadership has been a quite vacuous theoretical concept in political science/international relations. What we have often seen have been studies that focused upon the 'great men' (and women) and their impact, with the inevitable over/underestimation of his or her influence depending upon the author's interpretation of the person. In recent years the concept of

92

leadership has been utilized in a more systematic fashion, both within political science/international relations more generally, and within EU studies more specifically. We have seen the use of principal–agent theorizing on leadership, with scholars looking at legislative politics (Fiorina and Shepsle, 1989), executive politics and delegation (Pollack, 2003; Tallberg, 2006), along with the broader IR literature on regime creation and change and interstate negotiations (Young, 1991; Zartman, 2003).

Common to these approaches is the contention that leadership is a necessary condition for the conclusion of efficient intergovernmental negotiations due to high transaction costs. Transaction costs can range from the costs of gathering and analysing all of the information necessary to understand a given negotiating context, to the difficulties of finding mutually beneficial deals in situations where communication is difficult and actors have incentives to exaggerate their bottom lines. Complex, multiparty negotiations are therefore not necessarily efficient, given that transaction costs can present formidable barriers between the 'best deal possible' and what can actually be attained (for an accessible introduction to the debate on transaction costs and their impact upon negotiations, see Scharpf, 1997).

Leadership is usually defined as the exercise of functions that help the parties overcome transaction costs that hinder efficient collective action, enabling the attainment of more efficient outcome than would have occurred without coordination. These functions can either be functions formally delegated by the parties, such as the chair, or be a more informal delegation of agenda-setting or brokerage powers, where the parties ask an actor to manage the agenda, table proposals that potentially form focal points for further discussions, and help find and broker compromises without granting them formal powers. This definition of leadership echoes what Young termed 'instrumental' leadership (Young, 1991).

While outcomes can, at least in theory, be pushed through the Council using majority votes and where the Commission enjoys significant institutional powers, in the history-making decisions, such as treaty reform, enlargements or major reform packages, negotiations are intergovernmental and all governments have to agree unanimously. Given this need for consensus, the concept of leadership used to study these history-making decisions should be differentiated from the leadership theories used in hegemonic stability theory, where the focus is upon the need for a hegemonic actor to provide public goods (Kindleberger, 1981, 1986), and from the supranational bargaining theory developed by Haas (1961), where strong supranational powers enable the leader to 'upgrade the common interest'.

Leadership alone is naturally not *sufficient* for a negotiation to reach a mutually acceptable, Pareto-efficient outcome: there must be some form of political demand for agreement amongst the parties. Yet, as I develop in the following, the provision of leadership is a *necessary* condition for efficient outcomes when institutional bargaining is affected by high transaction costs. In this chapter, leadership is treated as a key intervening variable between governmental preferences and outcomes.

This chapter proceeds in three steps. First, I review the theoretical debate within EU studies, showing that the study of leadership has developed in the past decade, but also that there is a bifurcation in the literature between proponents of principal–agent models inspired by rational choice and scholars who utilize similar models but replace the comprehensive rationality assumption with a more realistic bounded-rationality assumption. This distinction between using the assumptions of full and bounded rationality results in two slightly different sets of expectations regarding when and why leadership matters. Second, the chapter then turns to an empirical analysis that investigates the broad trends in the variations in the explanatory factors that determine the demand and supply of leadership in EU history-making decisions. As the EU has become more complex and heterogeneous, this has increased the reliance of governments upon the Presidency and experts such as the Council Secretariat; something that can explain the gradual shift towards a more Council-based EU over the past two decades. The chapter concludes by pointing towards future research directions, including necessary work on improving the theoretical and methodological basis of the study of leadership in the EU's history-making decisions.

The theoretical debate on the importance of leadership

It is important to first note that leadership models are *not* complete integration theories, but are only *mid-range* theories that describe what happens in one phase of the intergovernmental negotiations in the EU.

As depicted in Figure 5.1, leadership theories do *not* attempt to explain the preference formation process, that is the sources of demands for integration. In this first stage the key debates in the past two decades have been between LI and its neofunctionalist and social constructivist critics.

The following review will only discuss the supply-side of integration theories. Since social constructivism only focuses upon explaining the construction and reconstruction of national preferences and not variations in the supply of integration, it will not be reviewed.

Leadership theories form a part of the debate in integration theory about what determines outcomes in EU intergovernmental negotiations, that is theories explaining the supply of integration. Are outcomes merely the product of patterns of asymmetric interdependence, reflecting the preferences of those governments least dependent upon agreement, as LI theorizes, or is leadership a key intervening variable between national preferences and intergovernmental outcomes?

Figure 5.1 *Analytical stages of EU intergovernmental politics*

Theories accounting for demands for integration	+	Theories explaining the supply of integration	→	Dependent variable
Liberal intergovernmentalism • Economic interests		*Liberal intergovernmentalism* • Governments are key actors • Outcomes reflect patterns of asymmetric interdependence		
Neofunctionalism • Economic and political interests • Spillover dynamics		*Neofunctionalism* • Supranational leadership *between* IGCs		Outcomes of EU intergovernmental negotiations
Social constructivism • Economic and political interests • Interaction effects		*Leadership theories* • Leadership is key explanatory variable linking demand and supply of integration		

Liberal intergovernmentalism: no need for leaders

Within scholarship on the history-making decisions of European integration, the base hypothesis has been LI. Moravcsik's LI is in many respects an 'anti-paradigm' in EU studies, with almost every theory-informed study of major EU decisions defining itself in *opposition* to LI. While the centrality of his theory is a testament to the rigour of his scholarship and his theoretical eloquence, the anti-paradigm status has been arguably gained due to the unrealistic nature of the assumptions that underlie his model of EU intergovernmental bargaining.

Drawing upon functionalist theories of international cooperation, such as Keohane's neoliberal institutionalism, Moravcsik's model of intergovernmental bargaining utilizes the Nash Bargaining Solution (NBS) as a predictor of bargaining outcomes. In an eloquent 1950 article, Nash developed a model that predicted that two actors in a negotiation will evenly split utility. This is illustrated in Figure 5.2, where two parties (X and Y) each have a most preferred outcome (respectively A and B), but compromise and equitably split the difference by agreeing to point C, measured in utility space.

For the NBS to be an accurate predictor of intergovernmental outcomes the negotiations must fulfil a set of *very strict* assumptions. These include low (if not zero) transaction costs and the postulate that institutional positions do not matter. Moravcsik argues that while transaction costs in history-making negotiations are high, they are low

Figure 5.2   *The Nash Bargaining Solution and the impact of institutional positions*

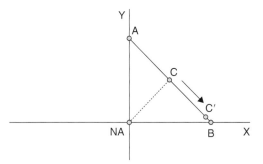

relative to the gains that states get from cooperation (1999). However, while the point of relatively low transaction costs holds when we analyse the broad contours of these negotiations, when we investigate actual negotiations it becomes clear that they are not self-organizing. For example, if one actor does not have the responsibility for managing the agenda in complex multiparty negotiations there would be a significant risk of bargaining failure, as each party has incentives to table its preferred outcome. This results in what is termed 'cycling', where the agenda cycles between the preferred positions of each actor in turn, and never settles upon a single proposal that can form the basis for further negotiations. The rational solution to the agenda-cycling problem is to delegate the management of the agenda to one actor. In EU intergovernmental negotiations this is the role delegated to the EU Presidency (Tallberg, 2004, 2006).

Unfortunately, Moravcsik's theory and empirical analysis assumes away the importance of institutional positions. This is partially due to the fact that Keohane's neoliberal institutionalism upon which Moravcsik's theory is based was developed *prior* to the institutionalist turn in political science in the early 1990s. What new institutionalist theories (in particular principal–agent theorizing) have conclusively proven is that a delegated institutional position is a significant power resource that can be exploited for private gains. In terms of Figure 5.2, if actor X has been delegated a strong institutional position, such as management of the agenda, actor X can choose to exploit this to propose a deal that is at C' instead of C. Actor Y would still accept C' over the no agreement outcome, but the final outcome is far from the NBS due to actor X exploiting its institutional position.

While Moravcsik (1998, 1999) investigated the role of EU institutions, his neglect of the impact of institutional positions has resulted in omitted variable bias, as shown by numerous competing studies of EU intergovernmental negotiations which have provided strong evidence that institutional positions matter (see especially Beach and Mazzucelli, 2007).

Neofunctionalism: supranational leadership

The main focus of neofunctionalist research has been upon the formation and transformation of national preferences. As the major integrative steps until the mid-1980s took place within the day-to-day operations of the EU, the study of leadership within EU intergovernmental negotiations was not focused upon in the heyday of neofunctionalism. Early neofunctionalists did investigate supranational leadership, but the focus was upon EU institutions acting within the supranational community (e.g. Haas, 1961). One exception to the lack of explicit theorization on leadership in neofunctionalism was the Easton-inspired model of integration created by Lindberg and Scheingold in 1970, where leadership was seen as a 'crucial activator' of the demands for system growth and had the function of identifying problems, processing and storing information, articulating goals and building support for the system, and helping to 'engineer consensus' (Lindberg and Scheingold, 1970: 128–33). It could be provided by either national governments or supranational actors. However, variance in the demand and supply of leadership were under-theorized in the model, and in the resultant case studies leadership is only used as an ad hoc variable to explain why outcomes did not always reflect the underlying demand for integration.

Leadership theories and integration theory

The study of leadership has recently emerged from this relative neglect, in particular as the result of the introduction of principal–agent theories into EU studies. As a result, we have seen a proliferation of recent studies that have focused upon the role and impact of the Presidency (Tallberg, 2006; Crum, 2007), other actors such as the Commission (Beach, 2005; Kassim and Dimitrakopoulos, 2007) and the European Parliament (Corbett, 1998; Maurer, 2002). These theories can be differentiated according to whether they are based upon the assumption of full/comprehensive or bounded rationality, which then have theoretical implications regarding what types of functions are most demanded.

A world of rational actors: principal–agent models of leadership

The assumption of full or comprehensive rationality implies a world where each actor is able to engage in a close to synoptic decision-making process, rationally determining which action maximizes utility for the lowest cost. Transaction costs that can prevent the realization of Pareto-efficient outcomes are related to the structure of a given negotiating situation. In a situation where parties have perfectly overlapping interests, cooperation will be self-organizing (Coase, 1960; see

Scharpf, 1997 for a good introduction to these different ideal situations). Yet while governments frequently have interests in common action, they rarely want the exact same form of cooperation (Calvert, 1992). In other words, negotiations are about both increasing the efficiency of cooperation and distributing the gains from cooperation.

In this rational world, governments that desire different outcomes on the Pareto frontier primarily face two collective action problems. First is the problem of *agenda failure*, described above as a situation that occurs when all parties have equal agenda-setting opportunities. Instead of agreeing upon a common focal point for the negotiations, rational parties will keep tabling their own preferred outcome. A rational solution to this is for the parties, if they have interests in reaping the benefits of collective action, to delegate agenda control to an actor (Tallberg, 2006).

Second, in negotiations that have a distributive dimension, the parties have incentives to conceal information about their true preferences. This is what Lax and Sebenius (1986) termed the 'Negotiator's dilemma', where sincere cooperative moves such as the disclosure of one's bottom-line can be exploited by other actors that are not as forthcoming, impacting upon one's ability to maximize gains. Tallberg (2006) argues that the functional solution to this dilemma is to delegate brokerage responsibilities to an actor, enabling the broker to gain information about the private preferences of the parties and formulate an acceptable compromise based upon this information that would otherwise elude the parties.

A less perfect world: bounded rationality and complexity in EU negotiations

A competing set of theories is based upon the bounded rationality assumption, which describes a world of informational asymmetries and experts. This theory was proposed by Young (1991) in the international negotiation literature, and has been introduced into EU studies by Beach and Mazzucelli (2007). These models suggest that governments are more dependent upon the provision of leadership in order to overcome transaction costs related to high information costs that are a function of complexity, and further that the margin of discretion for the leader is greater due to significant informational asymmetries due to these high information costs. In the following I will briefly introduce the bounded rationality assumption and illustrate its implications.

First, though, it is important to note that these approaches are not what Moravcsik and Nicolaïdis (1999) term 'garbage can' approaches, where problems and solutions are randomly matched in a form of primeval policy soup. Instead, these models build upon principal–agent theorization, but use a different conception of the size of information costs and the ability of actors to match solutions to problems, creating a greater demand for leadership by actors with strong relevant informational resources than envisioned by transaction cost-free models of negotiations (see for example Coase, 1960).

The assumption of bounded rationality describes actors as intelligent, goal-seeking individuals, but it also argues that there are natural cognitive limitations that prevent them from undertaking a fully synoptic, utility-maximizing search for the perfect coupling of a problem with an optimum solution (Simon, 1997; Jones, 2001; Rosati, 2001). This thicker, more realistic conception of actor rationality posits that ambiguity and uncertainty are two factors that define complex-choice situations faced by actors. In any given complex-choice situation, actors face a mesmerizing multitude of information that needs to be translated into operational knowledge. Further, under these conditions actor behaviour tends to be 'satisfying' and *not* utility-maximizing, and therefore will also be more prone to accept delegation costs than utility-maximizing actors.

But why should governments ever face these types of problems, for are bureaucratic organizations such as foreign ministries not specifically created to compensate for the cognitive limitations of the individual? I argue, based upon data gathered in participant interviews and archives, that bounded rationality is applicable at the organizational level within EU governments for three reasons. First, in any given international negotiation there will only be a handful of national negotiators that have *direct* access to the actual negotiations, with the rest of the national bureaucracy several steps removed. While a given negotiator can in theory fully mobilize his or her ministry in order to compensate, in practice this is often very difficult given the difficulties of painting a fully synoptic picture of a fast-moving negotiation dealing with hundreds of immensely complex issues to civil servants sitting in offices back in the national capital. Second, even if it was possible to paint a synoptic picture, only the largest governments have the informational resources necessary to understand fully both the substantive issues and to have an accurate map of the distribution of preferences in very complex international negotiations. Often, smaller governments will merely focus upon a handful of issues that are important to them. (This assertion is further backed by archival evidence gained in national foreign ministerial archives that clearly shows that smaller governments are only able to digest fully all of the substantive and legal implications of a handful of salient issues.)

Third, when the chips are down in major EU intergovernmental negotiations, politicians take over in order to settle the final contentious points. The high level politicians that take the stage in the endgame are the epitome of bounded rationality. They are purposive and goal-seeking, wanting a deal that furthers national interests; but they simply do not possess the substantive expertise or the drafting and negotiating skills necessary to translate their preferences into a specific, mutually acceptable, contractual agreement. They are therefore very dependent upon the informational skills of their own civil servants and those of the Presidency and the Council Secretariat – and in final deal-clinching summits, national civil servants are purposively held outside the negotiating room in order for politicians to cut deals, making the dependence of politicians upon the Presidency and CS even greater, as they are the only 'experts' in the room.

The implication of the bounded rationality assumption is that the demand for leadership is greater than what we would expect in the full rationality model due to higher information costs. History-making negotiations in the EU involve laborious efforts in first identifying often ill-understood problems created by interdependence between EU states, and in then finding and reaching mutually acceptable solutions in the form of contractual agreements. This can lead either to less efficient agreements or even to bargaining failure (Hopmann, 1996: 258; Stubb, 2002; Tallberg, 2003). Even in an extremely information rich setting such as the EU, one well-informed participant described this 'fog of negotiation' in the following terms: 'Governments and their negotiators do not always know what they want and the situation changes unpredictably with the dynamics of the negotiations where written and oral proposals are floated around the table by all the participants at frequent intervals' (Stubb, 2002: 27). In such circumstances, leadership that diagnoses the problems facing states and helps craft solutions is necessary to help governmental negotiators *find* the Pareto frontier of mutually acceptable agreements (Young, 1991: 283).

In what types of situations should we then expect leadership to be necessary, and when should we expect a given actor to be able to supply leadership? The following section will develop clear, testable hypotheses based upon the leadership model coupled with the bounded rationality assumption in order to explain the variation in the demand for and supply of leadership. The model is depicted in Figure 5.4 below.

The demand for leadership

A necessary condition for leadership to be demanded is that governments must want some form of collective agreement. The demand for leadership is a function of the strength of the political will for agreement: the greater the will, the greater the interests governments have in delegating functions to a leader in order to overcome high transaction costs that prevent collective action. In this respect leadership theories make no explicit arguments about the sources and nature of national preferences, and the theory can in principle be coupled with both LI and neofunctionalist theories of preference formation.

When governments want a contractual agreement but are unable to easily reach it due to high transactions costs, they have strong incentives to delegate the provision of leadership functions, such as drafting texts, shaping the agenda in ways that promote integrative bargaining, building coalitions, and brokering key compromises in order to reach a mutually acceptable, efficient outcome. Transaction costs can range from the costs of gathering and analysing all of the information necessary to understand a given negotiating context, to the difficulties of finding mutually beneficial deals in situations where communication is difficult and actors have incentives to exaggerate their bottom-lines. Complex, multiparty negotiations are therefore not necessarily efficient, given that transaction costs can present formidable barriers between the 'best deal possible' and what can actually be attained (for an accessible introduction to the debate on transaction costs and their impact upon negotiations, see Scharpf, 1997).

What forms of transactions costs prevent governments from achieving cooperative deals? Here I will focus upon three negotiating 'bottlenecks' that create a demand for leadership. First is the problem of *agenda failure* which can occur when all parties have equal agenda-setting opportunities (Tallberg, 2006). A rational solution to this is for the parties, if they have interests in reaping the benefits of collective action, to delegate agenda control to an actor. The leader can then act as a centripetal force, utilizing agenda-management techniques such as deciding what issues are to be debated and proposing a focal point around which negotiations coalesce (ibid.). The size of demand for agenda-management is therefore a function of the heterogeneity of preferences and the number of parties in the negotiations: the greater the number of parties with disparate interests, the greater the demand for agenda control in order to reach Pareto-efficient outcomes (see Figure 5.3).

Figure 5.3 *The leader as a centripetal force in multiparty negotiations*

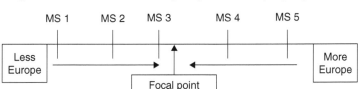

Second, in negotiations that have a distributive dimension, the parties have incentives to conceal information about their true preferences. Tallberg (2006) argues that the functional solution to this dilemma is to delegate brokerage responsibilities to an actor, enabling the broker to gain information about the private preferences of the parties and formulate an acceptable compromise based upon this information that would otherwise elude the parties. The size of demand for brokerage therefore relates to the strength of the cleavages splitting actors.

Third, issue complexity is often a significant transaction cost that can hinder governments from achieving maximum gains from cooperation. Many issues negotiated within the EU involve laborious efforts in first identifying often ill-understood problems created by interdependence between states, and then in finding and reaching mutually acceptable solutions in the form of contractual agreements. For instance, in the Fifth enlargement negotiations in 2000–02, the substance of the negotiations dealt with ensuring that the candidate countries faithfully implemented the 80,000 pages of EU legislation (the *acquis communautaire*) while also granting transition periods in certain areas. However, the negotiation of the transition periods demanded a very high level of expertise on the internal workings of the EU's *acquis* along with the state of the sector in the given accession country, without which the negotiations could not have progressed. The demand for the leadership functions of providing information and drafting texts increases as the level of issue complexity increases.

The ability to supply leadership

What factors determine variations in the ability to supply leadership? Leadership theorists focus upon three factors that increase the probability that an actor can supply leadership. The first two factors relate to the informational and procedural resources of a potential leader, whilst the third – which is usually seen is being the most critical – is trust/acceptance.

A potential leader must possess strong informational and/or procedural resources. For example, in order to act as a successful broker the potential leader needs to possess both the bargaining skills (informational resources) and the procedural tools, such as having responsibility for managing the agenda, that can enable the actor to break through an impasse and propose an acceptable compromise. In order to help governments understand issues the potential leader must possess sufficient technical and legal expertise in order to be able to provide assistance with defining problems and formulating solutions to them.

The third condition for the ability to supply leadership is that the potential leader enjoys the trust/acceptance of governments. This is a necessary condition due to the consensual nature of Council decision-making. Even the largest EU governments are unable to *impose* solutions upon other EU governments. Further, governments holding the Presidency do possess relatively strong procedural powers, but even the EU Presidency cannot unilaterally impose solutions, as was clearly illustrated by the failure of the Dutch Presidency in 1991 to replace an intergovernmental treaty draft with a more supranational draft. Trust, or level of acceptance, is however not necessarily synonymous with neutrality, but instead is based on recognition of the utility of the actor's contributions (Haas, 1990: 87–8; Bercovitch and Houston, 1996: 25–7; Hopmann, 1996: 225; Tallberg, 2003). Often, governments will know that the leader has his or her own agenda, but will still choose to delegate leadership functions when they perceive that the delegation costs are lower than the gains.

Matching demand with supply

Figure 5.4 depicts three potential situations regarding the delegation of leadership functions. The first scenario is one where there is a lack of supply of leadership. The results of a lack of leadership are suboptimal outcomes – either poor deals where gains are left on the table, or even bargaining failure.

Figure 5.4   *Leadership in EU intergovernmental negotiations*

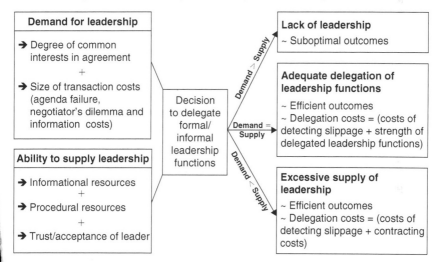

The second scenario is where the demand for leadership matches the supply. Here governments want a deal but the deal is not 'self-organizing' due to high transaction costs. Governments therefore either rely upon an effective EU Presidency or upon leadership provided by both the Presidency and other actors, such as the Council Secretariat, in order to reach a Pareto-efficient outcome.

In the third scenario there is an excess supply of leadership. Governments can freely pick and choose between different leaders, but there are still delegation costs, as once governments have accepted the provision of a leadership function by one particular leader, the leader can still exploit these functions for private gain. Whereas the leader in scenario two can exploit the lack of an acceptable substitute, enabling him or her to exploit fully his or her delegated powers, the presence of other potential leaders means that the size of delegation costs are only a function of the size of the costs of detecting slippage and the costs of delegating the same functions to another leader.

However, principal–agent leadership models also imply that the gains of delegating leadership functions come at a price, as a leader can exploit his or her delegated powers for private gain. The degree of divergence between what the collective principals want and the actual outcome influenced by the leader are termed 'delegation costs'. The size of these costs vary according to the strength of the delegated powers themselves and the ability of governments to detect slippage. Delegation costs are relatively low in comprehensive rationality models, since: (1) transaction costs are relatively low, as they primarily relate to bargaining impediments; and (2) governments can relatively easily monitor whether the gains of delegation exceed the costs due to lower information costs. Therefore the size of delegation costs in works such as Tallberg's primarily relate to the strength of the procedural powers delegated to the leader. The size of the costs of delegation are viewed as being somewhat larger in bounded rationality models, since: (1) transaction costs are larger due to higher information costs; (2) it is more difficult for governments to detect slippage due to high information costs; and (3) governments tend to accept more slippage due to the 'satisfying' assumption of bounded rationality models.

Concluding, both leadership models described above imply that leadership is a critical determinant of the success or failure in the 'big bangs' of European integration. Where the two models differ is in the level of demand for leadership created by informational costs and the degree of discretion available to a leader in a given situation.

The empirical record: leadership during the past 25 years of European integration

The intention of the following is not to provide an in-depth assessment of the analytical predictions of leadership theory, but instead to shed light on the broad trends in the variation of demands and supply of leadership in the history-making intergovernmental decisions on treaty reforms of the past 25 years. The section first describes major variations in the demands for specific forms of leadership and then discusses, based upon variations in demands, whether there have been changes in what types of actors have been able to supply leadership.

The demand for leadership

As argued above, when there is no political will for agreement, no amount of instrumental leadership can help. Here only stronger forms of leadership supplied by actors with 'muscles', termed structural leadership in the literature, or alternatively longer-term entrepreneurial leadership as theorized by neofunctionalism, can potentially create a degree of common interest in a deal. Therefore, arguably the major difference between the two major integrative jumps forward (the SEA and the Treaty of Maastricht) and later rounds of constitutional reform (like Amsterdam and Nice) was the differing levels of political will. Governments had strong common interests in achieving a functioning common market in the mid-1980s, and following the economic and political upheavals of the late 1980s they were interested in solving the problems created by an increase in German economic and political might (Moravcsik, 1998; Beach, 2005). In comparison, the Treaty of Amsterdam is a good example of a lack of political will, where governments lacked the will to engage in serious discussions about the far-reaching institutional changes that were the reason for convening the negotiations (McDonagh, 1998).

Demands for agenda-management have increased significantly since the mid-1980s. While the agenda for the 1985 IGC dealt with a large handful of salient issues, by the late 1990s the number of issues dealt with in treaty reform negotiations was over 200. Further, the expansion of the EU from a relatively homogeneous club of nine member states in the late 1970s to a more heterogeneous club of 15 states by the mid-1990s greatly increased the need for agenda-management functions in Council/European Council decision-making. One tool to do this was the use of a single negotiating text, the control of which became an ever more important prerogative of the Presidency (Tallberg, 2006). The demand for agenda-management has become even greater since the 2004 enlargement due to the increase in Union membership, resulting in debates amongst EU governments about the necessity to delegate even stronger agenda-management functions to the Presidency and/or a form of permanent President/chair (see below).

The demand for brokerage has also increased substantially since the mid-1980s due to the nature of the cleavages splitting governments on key issues. While governments in the 1985 IGC (SEA) were split on the central questions, such as whether more majority voting was necessary and what the scope of the definition of the internal market should be; and in the 1990–91 IGC (Treaty of Maastricht) were split on key questions, such as whether a political union should be a strong intergovernmental or supranational union and what issues should be included and the form that a single currency should take – the cleavages that split governments could be bridged through the provision of brokerage and in particular leadership that linked issues and offered side-payments to recalcitrant governments. In contrast, the key issues that have split governments in the past decade have dealt with the future institutional balance-of-power in the Union: issues that have a more zero-sum character. (Public choice theory predicts that if negotiations are only about distribution, there is little point in negotiating, as negotiations will only reproduce existing power inequities (Scharpf, 1997: ch. 6). However, while the zero-sum issue of the institutional balance-of-power has predominated treaty reform negotiations since the 1996–97 IGC, there have been a sufficient number of other issues involved to ensure that the negotiations were not only about the distribution of gains, but also the 'production' of gains.) To prevent negotiating deadlock, clever brokerage tactics are required to enhance the salience of the Pareto-improving proposals on the agenda, and also to formulate creative proposals that can reduce the conflictual nature of the institutional questions. (One method that has proved effective has been to postpone the implementation of institutional reforms until a date that is so far in the future that the current governments will not be affected.)

Finally, as predicted by historical institutionalist theory (Pierson, 1996), the complexity of the Union has increased over time, creating a strong demand for expert assistance in order for governments to comprehend key issues and draft legally sound proposals. For instance, the 1996–97 IGC that drafted the Treaty of Amsterdam had over 200 salient issues on the agenda, with many of these very technical issues such as how areas of JHA cooperation could be 'communitarized'. In this type of issue there was a strong demand for the provision of expertise to help parties understand the implications of communitarization of JHA, along with demands for assistance in order to formulate treaty provisions that would both protect the supranational character of the Community while ensuring that the political sensitivities of the policy-area were respected.

The supply of leadership

Which actors have been able to supply the agenda-management, brokerage and informational assistance demanded in EU intergovernmental negotiations? In particular, which actors have possessed relevant informational and procedural resources and the requisite acceptance amongst governments in order to supply the leadership demanded in specific circumstances? The following will review which actors have been able to supply leadership, which actors were unsuccessful, and why. The potential leaders investigated include the Commission, the Council Secretariat, select Presidencies (Netherlands in 1991 and France in 2000) and the Franco-German tandem.

The high-water mark of Commission leadership was the 1985 IGC due to the combination of the possession of strong relevant informational resources and the acceptance of Commission leadership in the issues under negotiation. The issues dealt with were core areas of European cooperation: areas where the Commission had decades of policy experience that no other actor could rival (Budden, 2002: 81, 90). Basically, the revision of the workings of the Community requires intimate knowledge of how it works: knowledge that only the Commission possessed (Beach, 2005). Key Commission officials like Emile Noël had a breadth of experience that no other actor possessed (ibid.: 44). As most of the issues in the IGC were core areas of Community cooperation they were also seen as legitimate areas for Commission leadership in comparison to foreign policy areas that were seen as the province of governments.

In the actual negotiations the Commission succeeded in matching the strong demand for leadership with a supply. As the Luxembourg Presidency did not have the informational resources to chair effectively the negotiations, governments accepted that Luxembourg would informally delegate agenda-setting and brokerage functions to the Commission. This allowed the Commission to table legitimately a series of proposals on the most important issues that created a range of focal points for further debate. Additionally, the Commission was central in the actual drafting of texts, giving it the power of the pen (ibid.: 54–5). The result of Commission leadership was an arguably more efficient treaty than would otherwise have been agreed upon, but the final SEA was broader and more ambitious in scope than it would have been in the absence of Commission leadership.

The fate of Commission leadership in the next two IGCs is illustrative of when actors are *unsuccessful* in providing leadership due to a lack of informational resources and/or acceptance. In the issues negotiated in the two parallel IGCs in 1990–91 (on EMU and on political union), the Commission had few comparative informational advantages in monetary or foreign policy issues, but it did have strong advantages in internal market related issues such as social and environmental policy. The situation was similar in the 1996–97 IGC; whereas the Commission expertise was unsurpassed in core Community issues, many of the issues under debate were either simple (like the institutional issues related to voting weights etc.) or were areas like foreign policy where the Commission had a relative disadvantage.

This was not helped by the reputation that the Commission had gained in the late 1980s. Delors did work behind-the-scenes in helping to push the negotiations forward in monetary issues in the late 1980s, playing a key role in chairing the so-called Delors Committee that ensured the co-optation of central bankers behind the idea of monetary union (Dyson and Featherstone, 1999). Yet by the start of the actual IGC, the Delors Commission had decided to eschew the behind-the-scenes leadership that had been so successful in the 1985 IGC, instead deciding to try to play a more proactive 'Champion of Europe' role. This seriously impacted upon the acceptance of its role by governments. The result was that attempts by the Commission to provide leadership, such as the attempt to create a focal point for the negotiations by tabling a full draft treaty on EMU, were increasingly ignored by governments (Beach, 2005; see also Kassim and Dimitrakopoulos, 2007).

Turning to the role of the Council Presidency, Tallberg (2006) argues that it is the key leader in intergovernmental EU negotiations, with the institution being a rational functional solution to match the demand for leadership with a supply. He contends that by having a strong delegated position the government holding the Presidency gains private information on the distribution of actor preferences that can be exploited for private gains. Further, acceptance is not seen by Tallberg to be a key factor, as the rotation of the role gives governments incentives to 'swallow bitter pills' until it is their turn to exploit the Presidency.

However, even before enlargement, governments only had the Presidency once every seven years, raising the question of why rational governments would accept being exploited so strongly over such a long period for the relatively short period of gains during their own six-month Presidency. Furthermore, with the possible exception of the French Presidency in 2000, evidence clearly shows that attempts to exploit *excessively* the Presidency will be ignored. The Dutch Presidency in the autumn of 1991 is the best example of this. On 30 September, in what has gone into EU lore as 'Black Monday', the Dutch exploited its role as President by presenting a new, more federal draft treaty that it preferred over the one that it had inherited from the preceding Luxembourg Presidency. The Dutch draft was however resoundingly rejected by ten of the twelve delegations as the basis for further negotiations (Corbett, 1998: 310). The main criticism was that the draft clearly broke with what had been agreed upon in the Luxembourg Summit's conclusions in June – even antagonizing those who preferred the more federal treaty structure that was advocated in the Dutch draft (Ross, 1995: 172). In the face of massive opposition, the Dutch were embarrassingly forced to return to the second Luxembourg draft as the basis for the negotiations (Christoffersen, 1992: 97; Christiansen, 2002: 48), showing the limits of Presidency leadership when it clearly and very visibly oversteps the boundaries of excessive partiality. (Admittedly, it can be difficult for the analyst to detect this line a priori. Given that governments are boundedly rational, this line is also relatively fuzzy, and therefore often only the most blatant and visible transgressions are detected by governments.)

France, in the autumn of 2000, is arguably the one exception to the rule that successful leaders in the EU need to possess both informational resources and trust/acceptance. During the negotiations, the general impression from other delegations was that the French were excessively partial towards their own interests and did not listen to the concerns of other delegations (interviews with Finnish civil servant,

Brussels, April 2002; Danish civil servant, Copenhagen, May 2001; British civil servant, telephone interview, July 2004). French partiality was particularly obvious in the debates on the reweighting of Council votes, especially in the actual Nice Summit that concluded the negotiations (Beach, 2005; Schout and Vanhoonacker, 2006). On 10 December the French Presidency tabled a proposal on voting weights that was very favourable to larger member states. The proposal: compensated Spain in terms of voting weights for giving up its second Commissioner; kept Franco-German parity in voting weights; introduced a demographic 'safety net' that mandated that if one government asked for it, then a proposal under QMV must be adopted by governments representing 62 per cent of the EU's population. After it was rejected the negotiations spun dangerously out of control, with the French Presidency more interested in maintaining Franco-German parity than in brokering a fair compromise. A majority of governments demanded a new proposal based upon the Commission's proposed simple double-majority solution – but the French Presidency after long debates and bilateral discussions reintroduced its own proposal, with the crucial difference that many of the medium-sized countries gained an additional vote. This was then grudgingly accepted by all of the governments except the Belgians, who demanded and got compensation for accepting that the Dutch gained more votes than themselves (*Economist*, 2000; interviews with two British civil servants, London, February 2002, and telephone interview, July 2004). However, the one-time nature of French exploitation of its position became obvious in the aftermath of the Summit, where a chorus of voices started the chant 'never another Nice' that led to the change in how constitutional reform is conducted by removing the strong Presidency role during the preparatory stage of negotiations – instead creating a preparatory 'Convention' to prepare the agenda for the IGC. Concluding, in order to effectively supply leadership, a Presidency must possess a combination of informational resources and the trust/acceptance of its role amongst other governments.

Given these factors, it also becomes obvious that the Presidency is not the only leader in the history-making decisions of European integration. First, many smaller governments simply lack the informational resources in the form of the necessary legal expertise, substantive knowledge and bargaining skills to lift the full burden of the Presidency (this assertion is backed by extensive research in foreign ministerial archives and participant interviews by the author). The best example of this was the Luxembourg Presidency in 1985 that decided to ask the Commission (with the acceptance of other governments) informally to provide many of the functions normally provided by the Presidency. However, other governments like Ireland also routinely ask for assistance, although their preferred assistant is the Council Secretariat, as will be discussed below. Often what we see therefore is that a smaller state Presidency will strategically choose to focus its efforts on a few priority issues, while on other issues they usually delegate functions, such as managing the agenda and drafting texts, to the Council Secretariat.

Second, while larger EU governments holding the Presidency (usually) have the necessary informational resources to go it alone, smaller states will often not trust a larger state Presidency with the *exclusive* task of formulating and securing agreement. For example, a text drafted by the Council Secretariat on a sensitive issue is seen as more acceptable to other delegations than one that originates in London or Paris, other things being equal. Therefore, a larger state Presidency often has incentives to delegate sensitive leadership functions such as drafting and brokerage to the Council Secretariat in order to ensure that all the potential gains from agreement are reached in an issue.

An unsung hero in the 'big bangs' of integration has therefore been the Council Secretariat. What are the comparative informational advantages of the Secretariat? Crucially, a given EU government has the Presidency for six months, whereas the Secretariat is permanent – which means that the Secretariat in many respects acts as the institutional memory for how to conduct effectively negotiations in the Council. If we look at the staff of the Secretariat that has dealt with IGCs, there has been a core team that took part in every IGC since 1985, giving them an institutional memory and experience unparalleled by any other actor (Galloway, 2001: 38–9; Christiansen, 2002: 47). While the staff of the Secretariat cannot compete with the Commission in their substantive knowledge of the workings of the treaties, the Secretariat has a breadth of knowledge on conducting both daily EU negotiations and treaty reform and strong legal expertise. Given their role of being the vital cog in Council decision-making, this provides the Council Secretariat with detailed knowledge of the workings of the EU treaties, the preferences of Member States and extensive and unsurpassed experience with brokering compromises in the EU (Westlake and Galloway, 2004).

I now turn to look at the trust/acceptance of the Secretariat. Despite changing its role from that of an unimportant '*notaire*' to the 'right-hand man' of the Presidency during the 1980s (Westlake and Galloway, 2004), most national delegates saw (and still see) the Secretariat as a relatively neutral institution that can be trusted to produce issue briefs of the highest quality, formulate fair compromises and in general help the Member States achieve their wishes (interview with former Council Secretariat official, Copenhagen, January 2002; interviews with national civil servants, Brussels, May 2001 and April 2002, and London, February 2002). This does vary though, and when the Secretariat attempted openly to pursue its own interests, its acceptability as a useful and trusted assistant to the Presidency declined. This was seen in the Spanish Presidency in the autumn of 1995, and in the Dutch Presidency in the spring of 1997 (Beach, 2005).

The combination of strong informational resources and trust/ acceptance has given governments and Presidencies strong incentives to delegate informally leadership functions to the Secretariat. The Secretariat often works behind the Presidency, using its extensive network of contacts at multiple levels to increase the efficiency of decision-making. This is especially the case with sensitive functions such as drafting texts and brokering compromises (for more evidence, see Beach, 2007). By playing the role of trusted assistant, the Secretariat gains many opportunities to provide leadership to the parties. For instance, during the drafting process governments often put forward relatively vague ideas that then have to be translated into draft legal text. In the 1996–97 IGC almost all of the draft texts were written and developed by the Secretariat.

However, by providing leadership, this enables the Secretariat to skew outcomes towards its own institutional preferences of ensuring the effectiveness of the Union while also strengthening the Council in the process. As insiders point out, and as can be seen when papers prepared by the Secretariat are carefully scrutinized, drafts written by the Secretariat often contain points that either were not on the agenda or that were even opposed by a majority of Member States (interview with former Council Secretariat official, January 2002; national civil servants, Brussels, May 2001 and April 2002, and London, February 2002; for more evidence, see Beach, 2005). These inclusions are though often masked by the opaque, legal language that they are written in – giving the Secretariat considerable leeway to exploit its informational advantages.

Perhaps the best example of Secretariat leadership was in the 1990–91 IGC. Here the French representative put forward the idea that the Treaty should be split into three separate 'pillars' in order to keep intergovernmental cooperation on foreign affairs and police cooperation separate from the supranational parts of the Treaty. But while the French government had the informational resources to produce such a draft legal text, a French authored draft would have been met with suspicion by other governments. The French, with the support of several other governments, therefore asked the Council's General Secretariat to produce a draft, which it duly did. The Secretariat's draft echoed its own institutional interests, and was a more integrated draft than what France would have produced, as it included strong common provisions that bound the three pillars of the Treaty together (Beach, 2005: 109).

EU governments are not stupid. They are aware that delegating leadership functions to the Secretariat has 'delegation costs'. However, delegation to the Secretariat is usually a more attractive option in a given negotiation than any alternative source of leadership. First, as we are dealing with informal delegation, governments are under no obligation to listen to their agent, meaning that they can easily revoke delegated functions from the Secretariat. This means that governments and in particular the Presidency can delegate leadership functions to the Secretariat and still feel that they are firmly in control of the process, although high information costs place limits on the ability of the principals (governments/Presidency) to detect 'slippage' by the agent (the Secretariat).

The final potential leader that will be examined is the ad hoc leadership of the Franco-German tandem. Indeed, some authors argue that integration has been an elite, Franco-German compromise (Pedersen, 1998). However, despite their 'great power' status in the EU, they are not individually or collectively strong enough to provide what can be termed 'hegemonic' leadership, where they are able to deploy an array of positive and negative incentives to other governments to force a deal through in consensual history-making negotiations. As described in a recent analysis by Mazzucelli, Guérot and Metz (2007), France and Germany are only able to supply leadership when their role is 'accepted' by other governments. What determines whether Franco-German leadership is acceptable? The authors argue that the key to Franco-German leadership has been their ability to craft a compromise between them that neatly bridges the key cleavages in a given negotiation. While these compromises have to be fleshed out in legal texts, the basic outlines of compromises such as the Franco-German compromise on the second and third pillars in the Treaty of Maastricht created a focal point for further negotiations. (There are also many notable instances such as the Franco-German compromise on flexibility in 1996 that were so vague that they were unable to serve as a focal point.)

When a Franco-German compromise has not bridged key cleavages, they have either been ignored or contested. While France and Germany stood on opposite sides of the intergovernmentalist–supranationalist cleavage in the 1980s and 1990s, on the institutional balance-of-power issues they both stand clearly on the side of bigger Member States. The result has been that instead of providing acceptable compromises, Franco-German leadership has increasingly been an 'improbable core' acceptable only to the other bigger states (ibid.).

Directions for future research

Further work is needed in order to improve both the theoretical and methodological underpinnings of leadership theory as applied to EU history-making decisions. The first challenge is to improve leadership models by specifying even more clearly what type of evidence would falsify the theory, although this is a weakness shared with transaction-cost-inspired negotiation theories more generally. For instance, while leadership theory moves us to expect that when the issues being dealt with are very complex and technical (high information costs) and that they will demand expert 'assistance', the exact relationship between specific forms of complexity (e.g. legal and substantive) and the demand for specific leadership functions can be improved. Further work should also focus upon improving the empirical measurement of the explanatory variables. How can we improve the validity of measures of political cleavages or a strong shared will for agreement amongst governments?

Additional work is also needed in order to assess the explanatory power of leadership models versus other competing models explaining outcomes. Do leadership models merely explain residuals, or does the provision of leadership by specific actors make such an impact upon outcomes that we cannot understand the history-making decisions of European integration without investigating who provided leadership?

Finally, how should we relate leadership models to the longer-term 'leadership' theorized by neofunctionalism, where the Commission subtly cultivated demands for integration amongst political elites with the actual history-making negotiations? Should we also incorporate actions aimed at moulding governmental preferences into our leadership models?

Conclusions

This chapter first developed the two variants of leadership theory: the comprehensive and bounded rationality models. Both variants posit that when governments want agreement but are hindered by high transaction costs there exists a strong demand for leadership to help them find and agree upon a mutually acceptable outcome. Both models see delegation of leadership functions as a 'rational' trade-off between efficiency gains and delegation costs, with delegation taking place when efficiency gains exceed delegation costs. Where the two models differ is regarding: (1) the size of informational costs that form part of the transaction costs and can act as a barrier to efficient negotiations; and (2) the ability of governments to detect 'delegation costs'. The bounded rationality model opens for a broader range of demands for leadership, especially as regards the technical, behind-the-scenes drafting process, and also for a lessened ability of governments to 'rationally' (read synoptically) calculate delegation costs.

As was seen in the empirical review, while leadership can in theory be exclusively supplied by the Presidency, the Presidency is often prevented from providing the leadership demanded by either: (1) a lack of the informational resources necessary (smaller-state Presidency); or (2) a lack of trust/acceptance amongst governments of its leadership (larger-state Presidency). A further factor that limits the ability of an individual Presidency to provide leadership is its short duration. As most history-making decisions are several years underway, an individual Presidency is unable to follow a proposal from genesis to agreement. In contrast, while the past two decades has seen the decline in the role of the Commission due to its lack of relevant informational resources and acceptance, the Council Secretariat has become an increasingly important supplier of expert leadership in the EU due to its combination of expertise and acceptance. The unseen provision of leadership by the Secretariat can partially explain the increasing shift in power towards the Council.

To conclude, the study of leadership has emerged as a vital area of EU scholarship in recent years, shedding important light on what happens in the actual negotiation of the 'big bangs' of integration. Yet we have only taken the first steps, and much more empirical and theoretical work is necessary.

References

Beach, D. (2005) *The Dynamics of European Integration: Why and When EU Institutions Matter* (Basingstoke: Palgrave Macmillan).

Beach, D. (2007) 'Oiling the Wheels of Compromise: The Council Secretariat in the 1996–97 and 2003–4 IGCs', in D. Beach and C. Mazzucelli (eds) *Leadership in the 'Big Bangs' of European Integration* (Basingstoke: Palgrave Macmillan).

Beach, D. and Mazzucelli, C. (2007) (eds) *Leadership in the Big Bangs of European Integration* (Basingstoke: Palgrave Macmillan).

Bercovitch, J. and Houston, A. (1996) 'The Study of International Mediation: Theoretical Issues and Empirical Evidence', in J. Bercovitch (ed.), *Resolving International Conflicts: The Theory and Practice of Mediation* (London: Lynne Rienner) 11–35.

Budden, P. (2002) 'Observations on the Single European Act and the "Relaunch of Europe": A Less "Intergovernmental" Reading of the 1985 Intergovernmental Conference', *Journal of European Public Policy* 9(1): 76–97.

Calvert, R. (1992) 'Leadership and its Basis in Problems of Social Coordination', *International Political Science Review* 13(1): 7–24.

Christiansen, T. (2002) 'The Role of Supranational Actors in EU Treaty Reform', *Journal of European Public Policy* 9(1): 33–53.

Christoffersen, P. S. (1992) *Traktaten om Den Europæiske Union* (Copenhagen: Jurist og Økonomforbundets Forlag).

Coase, R.H. (1960) 'The Problem of Social Cost', *Journal of Law and Economics* 3: 1–44.

Corbett, R. (1998) *The European Parliament's Role in Closer EU Integration* (London: Macmillan).

Dyson, K. and Featherstone, K. (1999) *The Road to Maastricht: Negotiating Economic and Monetary Union* (Oxford: Oxford University Press).

Economist (2000) 'At Two in the Morning', 357(8201): 26.

Galloway, D. (2001) *The Treaty of Nice and Beyond: Realities and Illusions of Power in the EU* (Sheffield: Sheffield University Press).

Haas, E. B. (1961) 'International Integration: The European and the Universal Process', *International Organization* 15(3): 366–92.

Haas, E. B. (1990) *When Knowledge is Power: Three Models of Change in International Organizations* (Berkeley: University of California Press).

Hopmann, P. T. (1996) *The Negotiation Process and the Resolution of International Conflicts* (Columbia: University of South Carolina Press).

Jones, B. D. (2001) *Politics and the Architecture of Choice: Bounded Rationality and Governance* (Chicago: University of Chicago Press).

Kassim, H. and Dimitrakopoulos, D. (2007) 'Leader or Bystander? The European Commission and EU Treaty Reform', in D. Beach and C. Mazzucelli (eds), *Leadership in the Big Bangs of European Integration* (Basingstoke: Palgrave Macmillan) 94–114.

Kindleberger, C.P. (1981) 'Dominance and Leadership in the International Economy: Exploitation, Public Goods, and Free Rides', *International Studies Quarterly* 25(2): 242–54.

Kindleberger, C.P. (1986) 'International Public Goods without International Government' *American Economic Review* 76(1): 1–13.

Lax, D. A. and Sebenius, J. K. (1986) *The Manager as Negotiator* (London: The Free Press).

Lindberg, L. N. and Scheingold, S. A. (1970) *Europe's Would-Be Polity* (Englewood Cliffs: Prentice-Hall).

Mazzucelli, C., Guérot, U., and Metz, A. (2007) 'Big versus Small' in D. Beach and C. Mazzucelli (eds) *Leadership in the Big Bangs of European Integration* (Basingstoke: Palgrave Macmillan) 158–77.

McDonagh, B. (1998) *Original Sin in a Brave New World: An Account of the Negotiation of the Treaty of Amsterdam* (Dublin: Institute of European Affairs).

Moravcsik, A. (1998) *The Choice for Europe: Social Purpose and State Power from Messina to Maastricht* (Ithaca: Cornell University Press).

Moravcsik, A. (1999) 'A New Statecraft? Supranational Entrepreneurs and International Cooperation', *International Organization* 53(2): 267–306.

Moravcsik, A. and Nicolaïdis, K. (1999) 'Explaining the Treaty of Amsterdam: Interests, Influence, Institutions.', *Journal of Common Market Studies* 37(1): 59–85.

Nash, J. F. Jr (1950) 'The Bargaining Problem', *Econometrica* 18(2): 155–62.

Pierson, P. (1996) 'The Path to European Integration: A Historical Institutionalist Analysis', *Comparative Political Studies* 29(2): 123–63.

Rosati, J. A. (2001) 'The Power of Human Cognition in the Study of World Politics', *International Studies Review* 2(3): 45–75.

Ross, G. (1995) *Jacques Delors and European Integration* (Cambridge: Polity).

Scharpf, F. (1997) *Games Real Actors Play: Actor-Centered Institutionalism in Policy Research* (Oxford: Westview Press).

Schout, A. and Vanhoonacker, S. (2006) 'Evaluating Presidencies of the Council of the EU: Revisiting Nice', *Journal of Common Market Studies* 44(5): 1051–77.

Simon, H. A. (1997) *Administrative Behavior: A Study of Decision-Making Processes in Administrative Organizations* (4th edn) (New York: The Free Press).

Stubb, A. (2002) *Negotiating Flexibility in the European Union* (Basingstoke: Palgrave Macmillan).

Tallberg, J. (2003) 'The Agenda-Shaping Powers of the EU Council Presidency', *Journal of European Public Policy* 10(1): 1–19.

Tallberg, J. (2004) 'The Power of the Presidency: Brokerage, Efficiency and Distribution in EU Negotiations', *Journal of Common Market Studies* 42(5): 999–1022.

Tallberg, J. (2006) *Leadership and Negotiation in the European Union* (Cambridge: Cambridge University Press).

Westlake, M. and Galloway, D. (2004) *The Council of Ministers* (3rd edn) (London: John Harper).

Young, O. R. (1991) 'Political Leadership and Regime Formation: On the Development of Institutions in International Society', *International Organization* 45(3): 281–308.

Chapter 6

Governance and European Integration

B. Guy Peters and Susana Borrás

Introduction

Governance remains a scarce commodity for much of the world. The European Union has been able to provide governance for its population, but the style of governance and particularly its democratic content remains the subject of substantial controversy (Olsen, 2007). Further, as the EU has both deepened and widened, the style of governing has changed, and will necessarily continue to change as a wider range of challenges are confronted. While there is certainly change in almost all systems of governing, changes within the EU are perhaps more visible. This visibility is to a large extent a function of the unique nature of governance in the EU, the contested nature of the governance process and the related possibilities for developing new forms of governing.

Despite the squabbling, academic and otherwise, that has taken place around the idea of governance, the fundamental argument of this chapter is that utilizing the governance perspective provides important insights into European integration and the capacity of the European Union to fulfil the goals and dreams of its leaders and of its citizens. We might even take the argument further, noting that to some extent the creation of governance capacity for the institutions within the EU is actually the goal of much of the process of integration. European integration has been historically almost an end in itself, intended to reduce conflict among countries, but that integration may also be the means for attaining the capacity to govern a large territory with complex economic and social structures. Further, as the processes of working in a more united Europe become more routinized, governance questions will outweigh integration questions.

The political process through which European policies are selected and implemented are complex, involve a number of actors and may be less determinate even than those in many national policy processes. That complexity does not eliminate the capacity for effective governance, but it does reduce its probability, with the resulting possibility of unintended consequences for the capacity and legitimacy of the governing system. The internal complexity may, therefore, produce a need

117

for additional mechanisms for steering and control that can augment the activities of the formal EU institutions.

Despite the complexity and its being enshrined in multiple treaties and summit agreements, governance within the EU is not immutable and some important changes have been occurring, and continue to occur. Some of these transformations of governing have been dictated by formal changes in the institutions and processes of the EU. Other governance changes, however, represent more creative solutions to governance problems. Further, the changes are far from unidirectional but rather represent alternative, and almost contradictory, approaches to solving governance problems.

What is governance?

At its most fundamental level governance implies the capacity of a society to develop some means of making and implementing collective choices (Pierre, 2000; Tiihonen, 2005). Dror (2001) has considered governance as simply designing ways of improving the future, using collective mechanisms or as imposing some architecture on the processes of making decisions (Parsons, 2004). Another way of considering governance is the capacity to overcome collective action problems in ways that are agreed upon by the participants in the society.[1] The basic logic of the governance concept, therefore, is that an effective society requires some set of mechanisms for identifying common problems, deciding upon goals and then designing and implementing the means to achieve those purposes. This perspective is quite obviously functionalist and rests upon the need to have some mechanisms for managing collective needs and maintaining the social order.

The broad steering perspective on governance also implies that the concept means more than simply making public policy. For some scholars governance becomes very much the 'empirical constitutionalism' discussed by Hjern and Hull (1982) in reference to implementation. That is, studying governance implies studying comprehensive patterns of making and implementing policy, as well as the processes and institutions involved in that decision-making. Further, governance approaches attempt not to consider policies one by one but rather to examine patterns of policy. Finally, governance involves not only the formal institutions of the public sector but also the manner in which those institutions are linked with civil society and involve civil society actors in policy. Thus, a governance approach to some extent blurs the usual boundaries we impose for understanding the complexity of governing, but, by doing so, it also includes elements that might otherwise be excluded.

Taken from this broadened perspective, a governance approach is agnostic about how this fundamental steering function is performed in any society, and about who does it. Some definitions of governance have contrasted governance with government, arguing that governance implies performing that steering function without the involvement of official governmental actors: self-organizing networks are assumed to be able better to provide direction to society (Rhodes, 1996; Bogason and Musso, 2006) than are the clumsy, bureaucratic institutions to be found in government. In this chapter we will, however, be considering governments as one of many potential sources of the broader process of governance. Further, rather than assuming a stark dichotomy between government and social actors, we will emphasize that these actors often cooperate, often to the point that it is difficult to separate the one from the other. Governance therefore provides an approach to comparative politics in which researchers examine empirical mixtures of state and society involvement, and also look at the relative success of the alternative formats.

One way out of some of the definitional issues involved in utilizing the governance concept is to use modifiers to delimit the types of governance, as well as the issues involved in governing societies. For example, any number of scholars have attempted to clarify what might be meant by 'democratic governance' (March and Olsen, 1995). We also can use the term 'network governance' to describe the domination of governance processes by non-governmental actors and more specifically the dominance of social actors organized in network structures (Koopenjaan and Klijn, 2006). Likewise, some scholars and practitioners have focused on the idea of 'good governance', implying largely the capacity to minimize corruption and increase transparency in the public sector (Kaufman, Kraay and Mastruzzi, 2007). The 'new governance' implies moving away from conventional command and control mechanisms for public intervention in economy and society in favour of 'softer' forms of intervention (Salamon, 2001; Mörth, 2005).[2]

It is important to remember that all of the governance strategies, whether dependent upon civil society or not, are being conducted in the 'shadow of hierarchy' (Scharpf, 1997). That is, even if social actors are empowered to become involved in making policy or to be involved in other forms of societal steering, those activities ultimately are being conducted in the name of the state (Pierre and Peters, 2001). Because those activities involve delegation of public power (Huber, 2004), if that power is abused or it is not used at all, then the state has the residual powers to reclaim decision-making and to exert its own control over the policy area. Advocates of informal mechanisms of governance do not like the concept of delegation, but the hierarchy of the state always remains ready if it is required.

As well as a shadow of hierarchy, the groups and individuals designing public programmes also function in the 'shadow of new governance'. That is, when conventional mechanisms for hierarchy are ineffective or unacceptable, there is the option of developing alternative approaches that appear, and actually may be, somewhat softer and less reliant upon authority to achieve their ends. This shadow is perhaps especially relevant for the EU where the familiar 'community method' has proven itself to be perhaps less acceptable and less capable of achieving the range of goals now deemed necessary for the Union.

The above discussion is written primarily in terms of governance within rather conventional nation states, but much of the same logic applies to the EU. As the governance system of the EU has become more institutionalized over time, it has assumed ever more of the attributes of one of those conventional states. That is not to deny the uniqueness of the EU, but it is meant to point to the basic similarities in the conduct of governing between the Union and other types of government. The governance perspective may be especially important for understanding the transformations occurring outside the formal institutions and processes usually associated with the EU (Kohler-Koch and Jachtenfuchs, 2004). That said, the legalism of many aspects of EU governance may make the use of less formal mechanisms for governance more difficult to place within the overall pattern of governing.

Propositions about European governance

With some better idea of what governance means, we now need to consider how this set of ideas apply to the EU and in particular how they apply to the changes occurring within EU governance. We will do this through five propositions that we believe to be important about this linkage, though these are highly contested among scholars of the EU. This degree of contestation may be in part a function of different intellectual understandings about the process of integration (the classic distinction between neofunctionalism and LI) as well as some of the normative debates concerning what the EU should be. We will tend to avoid the normative debates and instead will focus attention on the manner in which governance is being conducted and the implications of those styles of organizing public action, and of making and implementing public policy. Further, the propositions should help to point to a research agenda concerning European governance and its distinctive (or not?) nature. The propositions are:

1. European governance is conducted at many levels;
2. EU governance is crucial for output legitimation;
3. Governance affects the presumed 'democratic deficit' of the EU;
4. EU governance is highly segmented;
5. EU governance is being transformed.

Multilevel governance

The first obvious feature of European governance is that most of its activities of making and implementing policy involve multilevel activity. The idea of multilevel governance (MLG) was developed largely in reference to the EU (Marks *et al.*, 1996; Bache and Flinders, 2004), although most of the features associated with this concept would be familiar to the citizens of federal states, or indeed most unitary states. The MLG model recognizes not only the existence of national governments in the EU, but also emphasizes the importance of regional governments, whether natural regions (the German Länder, for example) or regions that have been constructed for purposes of regional policy.

Although multilevel governance is discussed as a general attribute of European governance, it is perhaps most important for understanding the implementation of European directives. The formal logic of EU governance is that the Commission has the right of initiating legislation, although in reality the agenda-setting process (Peters, 2001) may be more open to influence from both national and social actors. The EU has, however, little implementation capacity of its own, and therefore depends upon the member states and their components in order to be able to put policy choices into effect. The assumption is that the directives coming from Brussels will be implemented as intended by appropriate national agencies.

Although it might be considered a technical aspect of implementation, MLG also has a number of important political consequences. Most importantly, it empowers, or in some instances virtually creates, regional entities with European member states. This empowerment may help to legitimate the EU, given that it involves and recognizes lower level governments which tend to have greater legitimacy (especially in multiethnic countries) than do national governments. In addition, the development of these relationships gives potential influence to social and political groups which otherwise might have relatively little sway over policy in other circumstances.

The positive, democratic nature of multilevel governance should not, however, be exaggerated, and there may be some ways in which the development of complex MLG systems tend to strengthen EU and even national bureaucratic actors at the expense of subnational actors Peters and Pierre, 2004). The largely unstructured nature of many of the interactions involved in multilevel governance may appear to provide opportunities for the regions or other actors outside official positions to impose priorities on policies and over the preferences of 'Brussels' actors, or even formal national actors, on policy. In practice, however, such unstructured situations permit actors with clearly defined priorities to prevail and to be able to push through their priorities.

The multilevel nature of European governance is one aspect of the complexity within this policy-making system. The existence of multiple veto points makes effective governance more difficult and produces more need for bargaining. As Scharpf (1988) has pointed out, bargaining among the regions, or nations, in turn may produce suboptimal policy choices. The actors involved in multilevel governance may be forced to adopt solutions that correspond to the lowest common denominator among them. If European policy-making is to move forward, the actors involved at the multiple levels must thus find some means of bargaining across issues and across time to create more positive outcomes. Thus, there are crucial research questions about the actual impact of MLG on the distribution of power and resources within Europe in general, as well as within the individual member states. This question is perhaps especially interesting in relation to unitary states in which the subnational units may have avenues of access that have never been available to them.

Governance is crucial for output legitimation

As any relatively new political entity must, and indeed as well-established political entities must, the EU must legitimate itself. The legitimation of any political system may be problematic, but the EU faces more challenges than most in ensuring a position for itself in the governance of its constituent parts. One of the crucial legitimation challenges is the (in)famous democratic deficit (Follesdal and Hix, 2006). That is, while operating in societies that are accustomed to institutionalized forms of democratic governing, the EU is often described as lacking effective democracy. This may be in large part because of the lack of democratic accountability of the executive – the European Commission. The European Parliament has been able to gain significant powers over policy and mechanisms, and so require some accountability from the Commission, but the characterization of the democratic deficit is still applied commonly, and perhaps appropriately, to the EU (see below).

As well as being characterized as being undemocratic, the governing style of the EU may also be characterized as excessively bureaucratic. As contrasted to the member states in which governance has been transformed by both market principles and principles of network governance, much of the output of Brussels is formal rules made by bureaucratic organizations. Not only is the source of the regulations bureaucratic but these often appear to be concerned with incredibly minute details of economic life. A citizen need not be a student of von Hayek to think that the degree of curvature of a cucumber might be something that consumers could decide for themselves.

One of the fundamental weaknesses of the EU from the perspective of output legitimation is that it addresses only slightly and indirectly some of the policy areas that have been most important for legitimating European national governments. In particular, given its economic roots, the EU has a limited role in the welfare state programmes that have been so important in post-war Europe.

The democratic credentials of European governance

Although the democratic deficit has been a very common characterization of European governance, the extent to which the governance system within the EU is democratic remains an open and vibrant question. A democratically elected EU Parliament has become more important in the policy process, particularly with the extension of the co-decision procedure on most important policy issues (Selck and Steunenberg, 2004). The de facto veto power of the European Parliament, in an increasing number of central policy issues, permits a greater democratic control. Likewise, the growing number of mechanisms that allow for influence from social actors and stakeholders in the everyday governance of many policy areas of the EU permit some more direct involvement of European citizens.

Two crucial issues remain at the core of the democratic deficit debate in the EU context. The first one has to do with the nature of the EU itself, and whether a supranational organization can be the object and subject of normative aspirations of democratic systems. This is not a trivial matter. The conventional mechanism for legitimizing democratically any sort of international organization is the indirect mechanism of national representation, assuming that the member states of that particular organization are democratic. This holds true as much for any type of international organization as for the supranational EU. However, the early 1990s' legitimacy crises, that impacted on most significant international organizations (including the IMF, the World Bank, the UN, as well as the EU), have shown in very vivid terms the real limits of indirect democratic legitimization to these increasingly complex governance systems. For that reason, there is a growing understanding that the democratic credentials of these governance systems need to be assessed on the basis of their own ability to function according to democratic rules of the game (Held and Koenig-Archibugi, 2004). This holds particularly true for the EU, as the recurring crises of Treaty ratifications since the early 1990s have shown poor ratios of popular endorsement.

The second and perhaps the most important issue has to do with the different theoretical approaches and social normative understandings about how a democracy should work. Admittedly, there is a wide range of normative theories of democracy emphasizing cultural or procedural aspects. From liberal representative democratic theories to communitarian, participatory or deliberative theories, each of these theoretical approaches contributes not only to the scholarly discussions about the EU but, above all, to the practical debates about how to democratize it. From the point of view of participatory democracy, the softening of European law and rule-making can be seen to some extent as democratizing European governance (Eriksen and Fossum, 2000). In particular, the continuing increases in the powers of different advisory and decision-making committees (Christiansen and Larsson, 2007) and the active involvement of stakeholders in most of the soft law and new modes of governance arrangements have tended to open the system to influences beyond the preferences of the bureaucrats themselves (Borrás and Conzelmann, 2007). These developments are, however, not without their critics, partly because the developments might undermine traditional representative democracy (Tsakatika, 2007) and partly too because they generally do not allow the range of representation that policy networks may have at the national level in many European countries. But, that said, the developments do provide an opening into the policy-making system and do permit greater influence from outside than has been possible in the past. We still need to see, through research, just what the effects of the continued opening of participation will be and whether they can approximate the style of 'corporate pluralism' in Northern Europe.

European governance is highly segmented

Almost all governing systems are segmented. The functional specialization of government organizations and programmes into the various 'stovepipes' is logical from the perspective of the capacity of those organizations to focus attention on a narrow range of problems and to bring expertise to bear on those problems, but it generates significant problems for governance when considered more broadly. Very few public programmes can perform well in isolation from other policies: agriculture, for example, needs to be related to industry (especially the food industry), to the environment, and to health programmes. Effective governance, therefore, requires creating greater coherence and coordination across the public sector and the capacity to govern horizontally as well as vertically (Peters, 1998).

EU governance is perhaps more segmented than most national systems. First, the EU system does not have such effective political instruments for coordination as do most national political systems. In national systems, political parties and governing coalitions are usually able to produce some levels of coordination. Further, despite the general power of the Commission, most of the operative powers over policy reside in the individual DGs rather than in the collectivity. The EU also lacks strong central agencies that can impose controls (financial, personnel, etc.) across the governing system as a whole. The creation of a more established Presidency in the EU and other aspects of treaty change may help to integrate the political system, but a high level of segmentation remains. Finally, the linkages of programmes and organizations to powerful interests in society, notably agriculture and some industries, reinforces the structural segmentation found in the system.

While the creation of policy coordination is important for effective governance it may also have consequences for the development of the European polity. As noted above, effective governance may be important for legitimation in a governing system that does not have such effective instruments for input legitimation as do most national systems. Further, achieving several of the dominant European policy goals, such as those associated with the Lisbon Strategy on growth and employment, will require effective coordination. Some innovative mechanisms, notably the 'Open Method of Coordination' (Borrás and Jacobssen, 2004), have been devised to cope with these demands, but these softer instruments may yet be inadequate for achieving the level of coordination necessary for effective governance. The result of this segmentation is that integration may be very effective in some policy areas and less effective in others. This is a matter that requires further research.

European governance is being transformed

The governance arrangements of all contemporary political systems are transforming, and often transforming very rapidly (Pierre and Peters, 2006), but the EU is transforming perhaps more extensively than others. This is in part because it is changing not only how it performs its governance functions, but also what it does. These two changes are linked, but yet should be discussed separately for analytic purposes.[3]

Changing governance styles

Giadomenico Majone (1996), amongst others, has characterized EU governance as having a dominant regulatory style. That is, the vast majority of the interventions made by the EU to steer the economies and societies of its member states have employed law as the instrument to achieve the desired results.[4] The Union typically operates primarily through issuing regulations that then must be implemented by the member states, with the assumption that there will be uniform implementation in all those states, even recently acceded states, despite their having less capacity to do so (Falkner *et al.*, 2005).

This style of governance has been effective in many ways. It has enabled the EU to steer society without developing an extensive bureaucracy of its own. The critics of the Union have delighted in referring to it as a highly bureaucratic governance system, but in reality it has had a quite small administrative system compared to its national governments (Page, 1997). The style of governing may have been legalistic and bureaucratic, but it has been carried out through a small structure. Indeed, the domination of policy-making by the specialized bureaucracies in the Commission's DGs reinforces the regulatory style and empowers bureaucracies against more political forces in the process of governing.

The legalistic, regulatory style of governing is well entrenched, but at the same time it is being transformed in a number of ways. The changes are having an effect on the nature of the EU system and its relationship with society and the member states. The first dimension of transformation is that the EU is becoming more directly involved with the delivery of public services. The EU bureaucracy has been expanding significantly through the creation of a number of agencies, analogous to the administrative agencies now found in most of the member states (Majone, 2001; Pollitt and Talbot, 2004). Most of the actions undertaken by these agencies are performed through legalistic, regulatory means, but the agencies do have more capacity to intervene directly.

Even for the more conventional components of the European Commission, the style of governing has to some extent become more interventionist. For example, the competition authorities within the Commission have begun to use their own powers to raid premises and to confiscate possible evidence. In the relatively recently acquired policy area of criminal justice, the use of instruments such as European arrest warrants are a further example of interventionist approaches. The limited number of employees of the EU per se will prevent there being much direct action of this sort, but still there is the sense of a greater action orientation for EU officials and a tendency to make European policy more directly effective within the member states. Of course, this style of intervention may be seen by some European citizens as excessively interventionist and as violating the presumed limits of the powers of the EU. Further, the creation of European agencies to govern policy areas that once had been governed informally (Pierre and Peters, 2009) indicates some hardening of the stances towards governing.

At the same time that the European governance style is becoming more extensive and more interventionist, it is also becoming less interventionist in some ways. As noted above, the emergence of 'soft law' is reducing the requirements for the DGs in the Commission to make and implement so many of their own regulations, instead involving social actors as well as a range of other actors from the public sector in negotiating their own solutions to some policy problems facing Europe (Mörth, 2004).[5] The community method of making decisions depended upon uniformity and authority, but the newer forms depend more upon negotiation and interaction of the actors.

Further, in this style of governance, compliance is not expected to be as precise as in conventional forms of European governance, and there are ranges of acceptable outcomes rather than a single form. This style of governing then allows the participants to make more of their own choices about the actual policies as implemented and represents some deinstitutionalization of the legalistic community method. The research question, however, appears to be what difference it actually makes, and whether the policy outcomes are really different from what they might have been had there been a greater emphasis on uniformity.

The shift towards softer forms of implementation, when combined with the shift towards multilevel governance, might make the potential federal nature of the EU more of an actuality. The linkages among these transformations are not yet obvious but they may become more so as the increasingly vertical nature of governing combines with greater latitude in implementation. The conventional means of transposing EU regulations into national law becomes less constraining when there is more room for decisions and for choices about how to reach goals.

In sum, there are numerous 'new forms of governance' that are being implemented within the European Union[6] and these new instruments all enable governance without the intrusive, bureaucratic style usually associated with the EU. There is, however, still a long 'shadow of hierarchy', with the European Commission retaining much of its capacity to initiate legalistic approaches and to make decisions in a bureaucratic manner.

Changing policy issues

As well as changing the forms of intervention, the EU is also changing what it does. European governance is becoming involved directly in policy areas that once were the exclusive domain of the individual member states. The policy domain of the Union has expanded gradually since the original Treaty of Rome, but the movement into areas such as defence and foreign policy has made governance in the EU more like that of a nation state. The constitutional changes that will be implemented with the adoption of the Treaty of Lisbon mean that the emerging role of a European foreign secretary becomes further institutionalized, and the role of its main official – the High Representative – becomes more clearly defined in representing Europe as a whole in international fora.

The familiar functionalist arguments about the processes of political integration also appear to be manifested in the changing policy domains of the Union. The increasing movement of the EU into social policy is the most obvious case of this spillover into areas that were not originally part of its policy domain. The drive to make Europe more competitive and to enhance employment opportunities that generated the Open Method of Coordination discussed above also has generated some need for the EU to become more involved in social policy, and especially issues of the social costs of employment. If the social costs of employment deter firms from locating in Europe, or if there are any significant competitive advantages of one member state over another as a result of social policy and/or its costs, then the EU is to some extent obliged to become involved.

The expansion of the EU into a number of consumer and safety issues has been closely associated with the formation of the European agencies mentioned above. This movement to greater involvement in consumer protection also reflects the functionalist logic of spillovers in integration theory (Wiener and Diez, 2004). The regulation and standardization of products for competition reasons very easily leads on to the standardization of products to protect consumers and to ensure safety – for example, food safety and airline safety. A major question therefore is: what degree of standardization is required before the level of policy integration is sufficient for adequate economic and social governance? The habit of the EU has been to press for very close standardization, while the administrative methods now appear to be allowing greater latitude for local action. This creates a potential conflict of styles and in so doing raises more questions about governance capacity.

Changing policy and European integration

The changes that have just been noted in the EU governance style and the EU policy portfolio may have some interesting, if contradictory, effects on the continuing integration of Europe. On the one hand, the changes may create the image (correctly or not) of a kinder, gentler EU. The bargaining style evolving through the Open Method of Coordination and other soft law instruments of the EU soften the possibly draconian and legalistic image of Brussels and also permit greater adaptation of European policy to local circumstances. Further, despite the numerous critiques of the growing numbers of and increasingly myriad nature of EU committees, the bargaining and representation implied in this format for policy-making make the system appear more open and adaptable than the usual stereotype. At the same time, it changes the previous institutional balance of powers in Brussels (Borrás, 2009) allowing social actors greater influence.

On the other hand, however, the increased range of policy concerns of the EU, as well as its more direct intervention in some policy areas, may create the opposite image. For some member states the creation of the Common Foreign and Security Policy has been seen as a threat to their sovereignty in a way that many of the economic policies of the Union have not (Smith, 2000). In addition, the EU has begun to exercise something like police powers in enforcing some of its other policy areas (Mastenbroek, 2005), creating the appearance of a more interventionist and even more bureaucratic form of governance. While some inconsistency in governance styles is not uncommon, the contradictory tendencies in the EU – as a somewhat less institutionalized system of governance when compared to others – may present greater problems for citizens and for their officials.

The question then is whether either of these types of changes or the imagery associated with them really affects the capacity of European governance to produce effective integration. Looked at in one way, the more interventionist style might be seen as creating an effective governance system not dissimilar to that of many of the member states. Further, the changed style can be seen as reinforcing norms of equality across the member states and perhaps across individuals within those member states. Thus, output legitimation of the policy-making system can be enhanced by a more active European 'government'. But, looked at in another way, the interventionist and perceived bureaucratic nature of these attempts to steer only reinforces the perception of a remote and unwelcomed system which continues to lack fundamental input legitimization. This is the paradox of European legitimacy, namely, that output legitimation (popular support based on active and effective solution of problems), although necessary, does not bring more input legitimation to the EU system (popular support based on the feeling of a political community), because the latter is still solidly anchored in national imageries that seem to be socially or culturally exclusive rather than inclusive. This trend has in fact been exacerbated during the past few years. Several decades of efforts put into an increasing democratization of the EU machinery do not show that levels of input legitimation have improved substantially.

Summary and conclusions

The most fundamental question that must be asked about governance in the EU is whether or not there is adequate governing capacity within the political system not only to cope with day-to-day policy issues but also to move European governance forward in ways that could steer society and the economy strategically and effectively (Pierre and Peters, 2006). Related to this, governance must be brought about in a sufficiently democratic form to satisfy citizens who are accustomed to highly democratic governance. If the structures of the EU are not able to be this effective and this open in the manner in which they govern then continuing integration may not be possible.

The evidence discussed above indicates that the Union has substantial governance capacity when it is seen from some perspectives, but has limited capacity when considered from others. The EU has proven itself very effective in using the regulatory approach contained within the community method to generate legalistic compliance from member states and entities within them, largely through bureaucratic mechanisms. This governance style was appropriate so long as the goals and policy areas involved in European governance were focused largely on economic competition policy and reducing internal trade barriers. Further, this focus for governance activity corresponded to the bureaucratic style of the EU and the dominance of the Commission in making policy. But, as the tasks of the Union have expanded, then so has the style of governing had to adapt. It will have to continue to do so.

The changing tasks and the changing instruments used in governance reflect the need to use more democratic means to make and implement policy. Thus, the democratization of the EU may not come through the usual means of mass politics and ministerial responsibility but rather through more indirect means. These means may not correspond to the usual understandings of political democracy, but they do increase public involvement in EU governance and so may in fact open the governance system to a greater extent than a model of democratization based more on conventional parliamentary democracy.

The increased availability of democratic mechanisms for governance within the EU does not eliminate the need for effective governance. EU governance may become more democratic, which certainly would be a positive development, but in the end output legitimation appears to remain the more crucial aspect of the activities of the EU. Several of the changes in the style of European governance may be designed to improve the implementation of programmes, but these reforms also run the risk of further disaggregating a governance system already beset by excessive fragmentation.

The above discussion should indicate that EU governance is thus intimately related to the possibilities of further European integration, or to the maintenance of such integration that has been achieved. This relationship can be seen in the real world of governing, but it also exists in the academic literature. As we have conceptualized the shifts occurring in how the EU is governed, as well as the tasks that are being undertaken, the suggestion has been that the governance system may become incapable of providing the type of bureaucratic governance in which it has been so skilled. Atthe same time, it has yet to become capable of providing the more open, flexible and adaptive form of governance that many of the public may favour. There is therefore presented a formidable and continuing challenge to European governance.

Notes

1. Sørensen and Torfing (2007) define governance as a notion capturing the sense of an increasingly differentiated polity in which networks account for the multidimensional patterns of political interaction between actors in the process of governing a society.

2. Much of the literature does assume (implicitly perhaps) that the public sector will remain the principal actor in governance and that the important change involved in governance will be in the instruments through which that public sector chooses to intervene (Lascoumes and Le Gales, 2007).
3. Indeed, sometimes the discussion of governance in the EU becomes muddled because these two dimensions of change are not seen as analytically separate.
4. The extensive instruments literature on policy analysis identifies regulation as one of a wide range of styles for intervention. Hood (1976), for example, discusses law (as an instrument) as the use of authority, while other commentators on instruments see law generally as the use of a legal stick to force action.
5. Again, these are being done in the 'shadow of authority', with the agenda to some extent determined by the EU and not by the autonomous interactions of the social actors and national actors involved.
6. See the website of the New Modes of Governance Research Group at http://www.eu-newgov.org

References

Bache, I. and Flinders, M.V. (2004) *Multi-Level Governance* (Oxford: Oxford University Press).

Bogason, P. and Musso, J.A. (2006) 'The Democratic Prospects of Network Governance', *The American Review of Public Administration* 36: 3–18.

Borrás, S. (2009) 'The Politics of the Lisbon Strategy: Explaining the Changing Role of the Commission', *West European Politics* 32(1): 97–118.

Borrás, S. and Conzelmann, T. (2007) 'Democracy, Legitimacy and Soft Modes of Governance in the EU: The Empirical Turn', *Journal of European Integration* 29(5): 531–48.

Borrás, S. and Jacobsson, K. (2004) 'The Open Method of Coordination and the New Governance Patterns in Europe', *Journal of European Public Policy* 11(2): 185–208.

Christiansen, T. and Larsson, T. (2007) *The Role of Committees in the Policy Process of the EU* (Cheltenham: Edward Elgar).

Dror, Y. (2001) *The Capacity to Govern* (London: Routledge).

Eriksen, E.O. and Fossum, J.E. (2000) *Democracy in the European Union: Integration Through Deliberation* (London: Routledge).

Falkner, G., Treib, O., Hartlapp, M. and Leiber, S. (2005) *Complying With Europe: EU Harmonization and Soft Law in Member States* (Cambridge: Cambridge University Press).

Follesdal, A. and Hix, S. (2006) 'Why There is a Democratic Deficit in the EU: A Response to Majone and Moravcsik', *Journal of Common Market Studies* 44(3): 533–62.

Held, D. and Koenig-Archibugi, M. (2004) 'Introduction to Special Issue on Global Governance and Public Accountability', *Government and Opposition* 39(2): 125–31.

Hjern, B. and Hull, C. (1982) 'Implementation Research as Empirical Constitutionalism', *European Journal of Political Research* 10: 105–15.

Hood, C. (1976) *The Tools of Government* (Chatham: Chatham House).

Huber, J.D. (2004) Deliberate *Delegation* (Cambridge: Cambridge University Press).

Kaufman, D., Kraay, A. and Mastruzzi, M. (2007) Governance Matters V: Aggregate and Individual Governance Indicators, World Bank Research Papers (Washington, DC: The World Bank).

Kohler-Koch, B. and Jachtenfuchs, M. (2004) 'Governance and Institutional Development', in A. Wiener and T. Diez, (eds) *European Integration Theory* (Oxford: Oxford University Press).

Koopenjaan, J. and Klijn, E.-H. (2006) *Managing Uncertainty in Policy Networks* (London: Routledge).

Lascoumes, P. and Le Gales, P. (2007) 'Introduction: Understanding Public Policy through Its Instruments: From the Nature of Instruments to the Sociology of Public Policy Instrumentation', *Governance* 20(1): 1–21.

Majone, G. (1996) *Regulating Europe* (London: Routledge).

Majone, G. (2001) 'Two Logics of Delegation: Agency and Fiduciary Relations in the European Union', *European Union Politics* 2(1): 103–22.

March, J.G. and Olsen, J.P. (1995) *Democratic Governance* (New York: The Free Press).

Marks, G., Hooghe, L. and Blank, K. (1996) 'European Integration from the 1980s: State-Centric vs. Multi-Level Governance', *Journal of Common Market Studies* 34(3): 341–78.

Mastenbroek, E. (2005) 'EU Compliance: Still a 'Black Hole'?, *Journal of European Public Policy* 12(6):1103–20.

Mörth, U. (2005) *Soft Law in Governance and Regulation* (Cheltenham: Edward Elgar).

Olsen, J.P. (2007) *Europe in Search of Political Order* (Oxford: Oxford University Press).

Page, E.C. (1997) *People Who Run Europe* (Oxford: Oxford University Press).

Parsons, W. (2004) 'Not Just Steering but Weaving: Relevant Knowledge and Craft of Building Policy Capacity', *Australian Journal of Public Administration* 63 (1): 43–57.

Peters, B.G. (1998) 'Managing Horizontal Government: The Politics of Policy Coordination', *Public Administration* 76: 295–311.

Peters, B.G. (2001) 'Agenda-Setting in the European Union', in J.J. Richardson (ed.) *European Union: Power and Policy-Making* (2nd edn) (London: Routledge).

Peters, B.G. and Pierre, J. (2004) 'Multi-Level Governance: A Faustian Bargain?', in I. Bache and M. Flinders (eds) *Multi-Level Governance* (Oxford: Oxford University Press).

Pierre, J. (2000) *Debating Governance. Authority, Steering and Democracy* (Oxford: Oxford University Press).

Pierre, J. and Peters, B.G. (2001) *Politics, Governance and the State* (Basingstoke: Palgrave Macmillan).

Pierre, J. and Peters, B.G. (2006) *Governing Complex Societies* (London: Routledge).

Pierre, J. and Peters, B.G. (2009) From a Club to a Bureaucracy: JAA, EASA and European Aviation Regulation, Journal of European Public Policy 16, 337–55.

Pollitt, C. and Talbot, C. (2004) *Unbundled Government: A Critical Analysis of the Global Trend to Agencies, Quangos and Contractualisation* (London: Routledge).

Rhodes, R.A.W. (1996) 'The New Governance: Governance Without Government', *Political Studies* 44: 652–67.

Salamon, L.M. (2001) 'Introduction', in L.M. Salamon (ed.) *The Handbook of Policy Instruments* (New York: Oxford University Press).

Scharpf, F.W. (1988) 'The Joint-Decision Trap: Lessons from German Federalism and European Integration', *Public Administration* 66(3): 239–78.

Scharpf, F.W. (1997) *Games Real Actors Play: Actor-Centered Institutionalism in Policy Research* (Boulder: Westview).

Selck, T.J. and Steunenberg, B. (2004) 'Between Power and Luck: The European Parliament in the EU Legislative Process', *European Union Politics* 5(1): 25–46.

Smith, M.E. (2000) 'Conforming to Europe: The Domestic Impact of EU Foreign Policy Coordination', *Journal of European Public Policy* 7: 613–31.

Sørensen, E. and Torfing, J. (2007) 'Introduction: Governance Network Research: Towards a Second Generation', in E. Sørensen and J. Torfing (eds) *Theories of Democratic Network Governance* (Basingstoke: Palgrave Macmillan) 1–24.

Tiihonen, S. (2005) *From Governing to Governance: The Process of Change* (Tampere: Tampere University Press).

Tsakatika, M. (2007) 'A Parliamentary Dimension for EU Soft Governance', *Journal of European Integration* 29(5): 549–64.

Wiener, A. and Diez, T. (eds) (2004) *European Integration Theory* (Oxford: Oxford University Press).

Chapter 7

Democracy and European Union Governance

Berthold Rittberger

The state of the debate: democratic legitimacy and EU governance

If one were to set the date of birth for the EU's often acclaimed 'democratic deficit', 9 May 1950 should be considered a hot candidate. Once Robert Schuman's plan to create the ECSC was in the open, the prospective member states and their officials puzzled over the implications of this plan not only for their economic and security-related concerns but also for the democratic legitimacy of policy-making in the context of the new supranational political order. The proposal to institute a supranational High Authority was considered highly problematic in this regard: while the Dutch and Benelux officials saw the looming threat of a 'dictatorship of experts' that needed to be put firmly under (inter-) governmental control (Küsters, 1988: 79), the German officials at the Schuman Plan conference saw in the High Authority a quasi-executive that had to be democratically controlled by a supranational parliament. Concerns about democratic accountability and interest representation have been regular characteristics of EU politics since the inception of the ECSC; over time, the institutional features of representative democracy have thus been gradually transplanted onto the EU level (Rittberger and Schimmelfennig, 2007).

Against this background, the academic literature addressing the democratic quality of the EU is of much more recent origin. The Maastricht Treaty and the concomitant substantial transfers of sovereignty – such as in the case of EMU or the extension of sectoral integration, with CFSP and cooperation in JHA being cases in point – have sparked a debate about how much sovereignty nation states can relinquish without endangering popular sovereignty 'at home' and how 'democracy' at the EU level should be organized. Similarly, the rejection of the Maastricht Treaty in the Danish referendum and the French referendum, which was won merely by a whisker, sent shockwaves down the European capitals and put a painful end to the cherished assumption that there was a 'permissive consensus' supporting the moves of political elites towards more integration.

The debate on the EU's democratic quality has followed a particular path, which will be systematically elaborated in the course of this chapter. Initial treatises of the democratic quality of the EU were wedded to the standards of liberal representative democracy and its focus on the 'input' side, emphasizing the democratic process and associated institutional mechanisms granting influence and control, for example, via the directly elected and increasingly influential EP. Against the focus on 'input legitimacy', another group of scholars has emphasized that the EU possesses sufficient 'output legitimacy' given the predominantly regulatory nature of EU policies, which produces outcomes beneficial to all.[1] At the same time, a different cluster of work inspired by republican ideas came to argue that democratically legitimate rule and one of its central corollaries – the adoption of majority rule – requires the existence of a demos – a community identity. How could political decisions with potentially redistributive implications be otherwise legitimized? Against the conception that democratically legitimate policy-making rests on the existence of a 'thick' community identity, proponents of deliberative democracy have come to argue against liberal and republican conceptions of democracy, pointing instead at the context and process of political debate and stressing the conditions under which outcomes that are perceived to be fair and just by all can be obtained. While deliberative theory continues to be the most thriving underpinning of democratic theory applied to the EU, other scholars have come to take for granted that the EU *is* a democratic polity and focus instead on explaining why the EU and its institutions mirror key tenets of representative democratic institutions.

Against the background of this brief 'teaser', in this chapter I thus adopt a decidedly theory-driven approach for exploring the literature addressing the EU's democratic quality and legitimacy. I follow Dahl in charting the literature by introducing a set of dimensions along which different positions in the debate can be distinguished (Dahl, 1989: 6–9). The first distinction is based on the assumption that arguments on the EU's democratic legitimacy and quality can be differentiated according to the nature of the argument. While some defend a position and argument on rather 'philosophical' or normative grounds, others employ more empirically founded arguments. Questions pertaining to the former include, among others: should the EU be a democratic polity? Is the EU the type of 'association' for which the democratic process is desirable? If this question is answered in the affirmative, what is the model of democracy informing how the democratic process should be designed? As to the more empirically driven questions, we could envisage asking: does the EU meet the criteria or conditions laid down by one or several of the models of democracy? Under what conditions is the EU likely to live up to (some of) the normative expectations? Furthermore, I will also discuss a strand of research adopting a historical perspective in its assessment of the democratic potential of the EU. Here, the guiding question is whether the EU actually can be democratic if we employ the kind of yardsticks that, for example, comparative work on democratization has on offer.[2]

This chapter is organized as follows. The following section will present a panorama of theoretic positions on democracy, addressing normative and empirical concerns. Can the EU be democratic? What are the normative foundations of its democratic legitimacy? Can the conditions that derive from the normative yardsticks be met by the EU? First, I will present the 'standard version', which reflects standards of liberal democracy. Second, the 'sceptical' view propagated by communitarian and republican theorists will be developed. Third, I turn to the 'positive' assessment of deliberative democrats, notwithstanding that they constitute a heterogeneous group of thought. Fourth, I will introduce a position which is 'critical' if not opposed to applying standards of democratic legitimacy to the EU polity – the 'Regulatory State' thesis. Fifth, I will move away from normative underpinnings to examing a macrohistorical perspective investigating the socio-economic and political conditions that are conducive for or inhibit democratization in the EU. In the third section of the chapter, on new research agendas, I will take issue with deliberative democracy and sketch some of the challenges facing this school of thought with regard to assessing the EU's democratic quality. I will conclude with a plea to encourage 'deliberation' between more theoretically and more empirically oriented work on deliberative democracy.

Can and should the EU be democratic? Answers and trajectories from different models of democracy

The notion of democracy is intimately bound to the question as to whether there is a 'will of the people' and how it can be discovered (Shapiro, 2003). Normative democratic theory offers two very different perspectives towards answering this question. According to the 'aggregative' perspective, the central challenge is to devise rules and decision-making processes such that citizens' preferences add up to the 'general will' or the 'common good'. The contrasting view, deliberative democracy, posits that the 'will of the people' cannot simply be discovered by designing and employing 'correct' decision rules, but has to be 'manufactured': 'deliberation can alter preferences so as to facilitate the search for the common good' (ibid.: 3). The ensuing paragraphs introduce liberal democracy and its 'applications' to the EU.

The extended 'standard version': liberal democracy

Liberal democracy shares with the aggregative perspective the assumption that the interests of citizens are fixed and that democracy is about devising the 'right' kinds of majority rules to govern such that citizens' interests can be 'rationally' translated into policy. Yet, social-choice theory questions the possibility that aggregation mechanisms, that is decision-making rules to reach the 'common good' (Arrow, 1951; Riker, 1982), can be devised, and hence it concludes that 'majority rule can lead to arbitrary outcomes and even to minority tyranny' (Shapiro, 2003: 11). The prevention of arbitrary rule, whether by a tyrannical majority or by minority 'factions', is the central challenge for liberal democracy: the protection of citizens and their individual liberties requires that every citizen is granted the right to protect his or her interests from arbitrary rules (Held, 1996: 88). This presupposes that citizens possess a set of negative rights (which they hold *vis-à-vis* the state and fellow citizens) enabling them to assert their interests and protect them from government intervention (Habermas, 1994: 2). If the justification for liberal democracy is the principle that citizens require protection from the state as well as from each other so that government pursues policies 'commensurate with citizens' interests as a whole' (Held, 1996: 99), which institutional features are conducive to uphold this principle? To make abuse of power difficult, liberal democrats place a premium on systems with multiple vetoes, separation of powers and elaborate 'feedback' structures between citizens *qua* voters and those who govern: 'the governors must be held accountable to the governed through political mechanisms (the secret ballot, regular voting and competition between political representatives, among other things) which give citizens satisfactory means for choosing, authorizing and controlling political decisions' (ibid.: 88–9).

Many of the early treatises of the EU's democratic quality rest on liberal underpinnings, even though often only implicitly. This can be illustrated by briefly extracting some elements of the so-called 'standard version' of the EU's democratic deficit (see Weiler et al., 1995; Follesdal and Hix, 2006 for prominent overviews). According to the standard version, accountability in modern liberal democracies is ensured such that governments are accountable to voters via parliaments. This 'chain of accountability' is corrosive in the EU since EU integration has empowered national executives acting in the European Council or in the Council of Ministers at the expense of national parliaments (Moravcsik, 1994; O'Brennan and Raunio, 2007; Goetz and Meyer-Sahling, 2008), while the 'compensation' offered by the EP, as a directly elected assembly, is considered to be too weak. Furthermore, elections to the EP are considered to be deficient, since – empirically – they are not 'European' but merely 'second order elections': EP elections 'are not about the personalities and parties at the European level or the direction of the EU policy agenda. ... The absence of a "European" element in national and European elections means that EU citizens' preferences on issues on the EU policy agenda at best have only an indirect influence on EU policy outcomes' (Follesdal and Hix, 2006: 536). As these two examples suggest, the institutions of representative democracy, which have been 'transplanted' to the EU level, do not serve citizens' interests well. Yet, there also exist more optimistic views about the democratic quality of the EU, which share with the standard version its liberal democratic assumptions.

According to Andrew Moravcsik, the claim about the EU's 'democratic deficit' is largely misplaced. Taking recourse to liberal justifications for democracy, Moravcsik argues that the EU can be neither characterized as a 'superstate' nor as a technocracy ruled by unaccountable bureaucrats. Turning the standard version on its head, Moravcsik argues that 'constitutional checks and balances, indirect democratic control via national governments, and the increasing powers of the European Parliament are sufficient to ensure that EU policy-making is ... transparent, effective and politically responsive to the demands of the European citizens' (Moravcsik, 2002: 605). Moravcsik concludes that when the EU is compared with the practice of democratic governance in most liberal democratic systems, the EU behaves quite favourably. Zweifel (2002) echoes this assessment, evaluating the EU's democratic quality by introducing a set of established democracy scales. Along the dimensions essential to the liberal model of democracy – the protection of civil liberties, guarantee of political rights, constraints on the exercise of power, competitive elections, to name the most important ones – the EU scores on par or only slightly below the 'democracy scores' of the United States and Switzerland: 'based on widely accepted scales for measuring democracy, the EU does *not* suffer from a democratic deficit significantly greater than that of most liberal democracies' (ibid.: 834).

A sceptical view: communitarians and republicans

The centrality of community: the communitarian position

The second strand of research discussed in this chapter – which I label the communitarian position – is informed by the idea that the legitimate exercise of authority rests on a shared conception of a common good or a shared way of life within a community of free and equal citizens. For communitarians, communities are 'social facts' bound together through 'common social practices, cultural traditions and shared social understandings' (Kymlicka, 1993: 367). Communitarians view the community as an 'independent principle', which can be rooted in 'shared nationality, language, culture, religion, history or way of life' (ibid.: 366), rather than 'derivative of freedom and equality' (ibid.: 376), as proponents of liberal democracy would argue. Communitarians thus claim that these quasi-primordial communities have to be respected and protected since only in a community of shared language and experience can citizens engage in political debate to discover and probe their goals and values (ibid.).

Communitarianism-inspired positions in the debate about the EU's democratic legitimacy deficit are in a minority position, which does not imply, however, that they are marginal. The most 'prominent' position is commonly referred to as the 'no-demos' thesis (Weiler, 1995). In a paper with the provocative title 'The State "über alles"', Weiler takes issue with the (in)famous 'Maastricht Decision' of the German Constitutional Court (GCC).[3] In its decision, the GCC evokes its concern with the potential for democratizing the EU system of governance, while – at the same time – it also addresses the repercussions of further European integration on the integrity of Germany's democratic structures. According to Weiler, the GCC has exposed itself as a defender of the 'no-demos' thesis which – in a nutshell – posits 'that absent a demos, there cannot, by definition, be a democracy or democratization at the European level' (ibid.: 6). Majority rule, according to this perspective, is only legitimate within a 'demos', 'when Danes rule Danes' and not when Danes were – by way of a thought experiment – given full representation in the German Bundestag, thereby enshrining a permanent minorityship (ibid.: 5–6).

What are the arguments advanced by the GCC to defend the no-demos thesis? What are the characteristics of a 'demos' when it is claimed that the 'authority and legitimacy of a majority to compel a minority exists only within political boundaries defined by a demos' (ibid.: 2)? Weiler's interpretation of the GCC's decision posits that membership within a demos rests on 'organic cultural-national criteria' (ibid.: 6); furthermore, the GCC takes recourse to an implicit assumption, namely that there exists 'an ethno-culturally homogenous Volk' (ibid.: 3) which forms the basis of democratically legitimate rule-making. It is fairly obvious that the EU falls short of this requirement: there simply is no European demos. Absent the organic national-cultural conditions upon which a sense of identity and solidarity could emerge, it is unrealistic to think that the EU could be democratized.

Former GCC judge Dieter Grimm presents a somewhat 'softer' version of the no-demos thesis. He claims that a common political identity does not necessarily rest on an 'organic' or 'essentialist' conception of a *Volk*-ish identity, as exposed by Weiler. Grimm argues, however, that there exist structural deficiencies which render the formation of European identity unlikely. At the heart of the problem is the absence of a Europe-wide discursive space which Grimm considers crucial for the forging of a common identity and, in turn, for the functioning of a democratic polity (Grimm, 2001: 243–50). Institutional reforms, such as the empowerment of the EP, are unlikely to provide a remedy for this state of affairs. Yet, it is unclear what the remedy could be. This is where the model of republicanism enters the stage.

Softening the communitarian position: enter republicanism

Grimm's position already points at the potential of public debate for community- and identity-building processes. Here I present two positions which address the potential for community building from a republican perspective. Republicanism places a strong emphasis on the role of political debate for discussing value orientations in the context of democratic will-formation. The first position sees the potential for the creation of a value-based community in the EU in rather positive terms, while the second position is rather sceptical.

Amitai Etzioni argues that for the EU to be democratic, an EU-wide 'normative-affective community' has to be in place, that is the 'members of the social entity involved have formed a core of shared values (i.e. a moral culture) and a web of bonds of affection' (Etzioni, 2007: 24). Democratic rule does, however, not require an 'organic' demos, but socio-cultural ties and particularistic values which can be forged and can come to define a supranational political *and* social community. Etzioni claims that the EU has not just a democratic deficit but also a community deficit; yet for the democratic deficit to be reduced, the community deficit has to be overcome first. Why is the EU in need of developing a normative-affective community? With further economic and political integration, the EU has come to impact profoundly on the lives of individuals to the degree that integrated policies, such as monetary policy, have repercussions on domestic fiscal and economic policies. Etzioni argues that the sacrifices entailed in such decision-making are only acceptable to EU citizens if they come 'to value the EU common good and the purpose it serves' (ibid.: 32; see Scharpf, 1997, for a similar argument). A democratic community then has to be a social community 'whose members share a core of values, whose common good and purpose they find compelling and whose institutions are considered legitimate to the extent that their design and actions are compatible with the shared values' (Etzioni, 2007: 34). For the EU to form such a value-based community, Etzioni suggests that this can come about through engaging in moral dialogue among citizens, 'public discussions that engage values rather than merely interests or wants ... [that] are mainly ethical, rather than empirical' (ibid.: 36). Etzioni expresses the hope that these kinds of dialogues and discussions on EU issues (preceding, say, an EU-wide referendum) allow for a debate about 'who *we* are' and 'what *we* want' as a community – such as the question of a Turkish entry into the EU – which, in turn, may serve as a community-building device.

A more sceptical argument is advanced by Peter Graf Kielmansegg. He equally dismisses an essentialist reading of the no-demos thesis and equally posits that 'only when all those who are affected by a decision perceive themselves to be part of a common, all-encompassing political identity is it possible to differentiate between majority rule which can be consented to and the rule of strangers which will then be considered illegitimate' (Kielmansegg, 2003: 57). In the EU, however, there is not such a 'common, all-encompassing identity' which would render majority rule acceptable (or, at least, less threatening), especially when authoritative decisions impose duties and create 'winners and losers'. Why is Kielmansegg more sceptical with regard to the community-building potential inside the EU? Historically, collective political identities have formed around communities of memory, experience and communication. The EU is not a community of communication: multilingualism hampers the emergence of common structures of communication and understanding; the EU is also hardly a community of memory, even though attempts to construct a common European heritage have been mushrooming in the recent past (take the discourse surrounding the Constitutional Convention or the question of Turkey's entry into the EU as examples and focal points). Yet, European states have distinct national histories, each with its own interpretation of the past. Lastly, the EU is only a rudimentary community of experience. Kielmansegg argues that it is this 'community' which has the largest identity-forming potential. For instance, the commonly shared threat in the years of block confrontation marks a common experience for (Western) European states. All in all, Europe has been very poor in identifying and defining common experiences which could carry the potential to generate a 'we-feeling' among EU citizens (Lepsius, 1999; Cederman, 2001; Seidendorf, 2007; Maier and Rittberger, 2008).

Both Etzioni and Kielmansegg combine republican with communitarian positions. According to the republican model, democratic will-formation places a premium on those structures that enable and foster the type of communication and discourse constitutive of a political community; against the aggregative view of democratic will-formation which underpins the liberal model, republicanism stresses that political discourses 'are meant to allow one to discuss value orientations and interpretations of needs and wants, and then to change these in an insightful way' (Habermas, 1994: 4). For 'communitarian republicans', political discourses are, according to Habermas, 'ethically constricted', which implies that they serve the purpose of clarifying the value basis of a political community (Fossum and Eriksen, 2003) by pointing to 'the type of ethical questions ... we, as members of a community, ask ourselves [such as] who we are and who we would like to be' (Habermas,

1994: 4). Following this perspective, democratic will-formation is legit-imized by the 'previous convergence of settled ethical convictions' (ibid.).

What are the implications for the democratic legitimacy of the EU if we were to adopt a republican communitarian perspective and hence accept the argument that democratic legitimacy rests on a 'thick', value-based common identity? As we have seen above, the empirical evidence shows little signs that the EU meets this requirement. According to Fossum and Eriksen, the EU is a 'post-communitarian entity, with different value systems. For it to function, some modicum of a common will has to be articulated. Such a common will cannot simply be based on the commonalities of the existing collectives, i.e. the nation states' (Fossum and Eriksen, 2003: 42). The viability of the communitarian republican view is not only challenged on empirical but also on normative grounds. Fossum and Eriksen voice their criticism of the communitarian perspective by pointing to the normative status of human rights. From the republican communitarian perspective, these rights derive their validity and legitimacy from the collective delibera-tion of a particular community. Fossum and Eriksen find this perspec-tive highly problematic: 'the problem of this kind of communitarian republicanism is that it pictures democracy as a process of collective self-discovery, which only gives human rights a binding status as long as they correspond with the collective self-understanding of that society' (ibid.: 43). For them, the particularism espoused in the com-munitarian republican model is much less desirable than the universal-istic premises upon which the model of deliberative democracy is founded. It is to this perspective that I will now turn.

A positive view: deliberative democracy

Against the notion of a 'substantively integrated ethical community' (Habermas, 1994: 4), the discourse-theoretic interpretation of democ-ratic will-formation – introduced by Habermas and 'popularized' under the banner of deliberative democracy – differentiates itself from both republican communitarian and liberal-aggregative models of the democratic process: 'in the discourse theoretical reading of procedural democracy, both the atomistic individual and the supra-individual subject – the nation – disappear. It is the flow of communication in and between associational networks of civil society and the parlia-mentary complex that constitutes and ensures popular sovereignty, not the formal aggregative procedures that liberals place their trust in or the coming together in fora and "halls" that republicans salute' (Eriksen and Fossum, 2000: 20–1). What renders the deliberative model of democracy particularly attractive for contemplating democ-ratic legitimacy beyond the nation state is the claim that democratic will-formation does not presuppose a pre-existing community where membership is based on the sharing of common values or a common sense of destiny. Deliberative democracy separates politics from culture and hence from a 'thick' identity based on the particularism of nationally and culturally separated 'life forms' (see, for example, Cederman, 2001). Instead, Habermas stresses that the type of ethical questions which underpin the republican model of democracy are actually 'subordinate to moral questions and connected with pragmatic questions' (Habermas, 1994: 5). For him, questions of justice are the type of moral questions that are deemed to be given priority in the democratic process: the 'politically enacted law of a ... legal community must, if it is to be legitimate, at least be compatible with moral tenets that claim universal validity going beyond the legal community' (ibid.). In short, democracy is a process whereby citizens deliberate on 'what is fair or just' (Eriksen and Fossum, 2000: 19). Any type of political decision in societies characterized by cultural and societal pluralism, whereby a multitude of interests and values normally conflict, in order to be legitimate, 'depends on a prior regulation of fair terms for achieving results, which are acceptable for all parties on the basis of their differing preferences' (Habermas, 1994: 5).

Normatively, deliberative democracy thus places a premium on political debate, which precedes political decisions in the political-administrative realm. Deliberation in the discourse-theoretic interpretation of deliberative democracy is fundamentally different from the liberal model of democracy and conventional conceptions of interest representation since the former is 'talk-centric' while the latter are 'voting-centric'. According to the voting-centric, liberal model, 'public decisions result from the aggregation of fixed interests and preferences that compete through the mechanisms of power and money in voting-centric, representative politics' (Fung, 2003: 525). By contrast, decision-making qua deliberation 'reflects the result of an equal and open communication process in which participants appeal to reasons that others can accept, rather than to force, money, sheer numbers, or status' (ibid.).

The discourse-theoretic underpinnings of deliberative democracy and its focus on communicative processes implies that the democratic quality of governance is not assessed by solely focusing on the parliamentary arena or on political-administrative actors, 'but also on the possibility for wielding influence via institutions of civil society – press media, non-governmental organizations – and the possibility of participation in opinion formation and the shaping and channelling of communicative power into the institutional complex' of political decision systems (Eriksen and Fossum, 2000: 21).[4] It comes as little surprise then that researchers have come to focus increasingly on concepts such as the public sphere and civil society and their contribution to the democratic legitimacy of the EU in both normative and empirical terms (see Neyer, 2006 for an overview).

In the following, I will address the normative and empirical arguments and statements highlighting the desirability and relevance of civil society and the public sphere for the EU's democratic quality from the purview of deliberative democracy.

The public sphere and the EU's democratic legitimacy

The concept of the 'public sphere' is usually referred to as a 'space or arena for (broad, public) deliberation, discussion and engagement in societal issues' (de Vreese, 2007: 4). It is a 'space that exists outside the institutions of the state but in which all who are concerned with questions of public interest and the conduct of civil society may engage in debate' (Schlesinger and Kevin, 2000: 207). From the perspective of deliberative democracy, the existence of a public sphere is vital for the democratic process: 'democratic legitimation requires mutual contact between, on the one hand, institutionalized deliberation and decision-making within parliaments, courts and administrative bodies and, on the other, an inclusive process of informal mass communication' (Habermas, 2001: 17). In this context the means of mass communication play an important role as they help to 'turn relevant societal problems into topics of concern, and allow the general public to relate, at the same time, to the same topics' (ibid.: 18). Not only is the existence of a public sphere central to democracy, as it presupposes freedom of expression, it also serves 'a rational, well-informed conversation between equals capable of resolving their differences by non-coercive means' (Schlesinger and Kevin, 2000: 207). Since the existence of a public sphere is normatively desirable from the purview of deliberative democracy, two (empirically driven) questions are shaping the debate in the literature: is there an EU-wide public sphere? If the answer is in the affirmative, how do we know it when we see it? And if the answer is negative, what are the prospects of there being one?

As to the first question, the answer is (almost) unanimous. The 'notion of a singular, supra-national, pan-European public sphere ... conceptualized as communicative space requiring a common language, shared identity and a transnational media system' (de Vreese, 2007: 8; but see Risse and Van de Steeg, 2003) is by-and-large rejected, both on conceptual and empirical grounds. Habermas, for instance, acknowledges that an EU-wide public sphere should not simply be considered as the extension or projection of national public spheres onto the EU level, 'it [an EU-wide public sphere] will rather emerge from the mutual opening of existing national universes to one another, yielding to an interpenetration of mutually translated national communications'

(Habermas, 2001: 18). Habermas thus alludes to a strand of investigation which highlights the 'Europeanization' of national public spheres. According to this more 'realistic' approach (de Vreese, 2007: 9), researchers have engaged in cross-national comparisons of the news media to assess the degree of horizontal and vertical Europeanization of national public spheres. Whereas vertical Europeanization refers to national actors addressing EU actors, and EU issues as well as EU actors addressing domestic audiences on EU issues, horizontal Europeanization captures the degree to which domestic actors address issues and actors in another EU country (ibid.). The research strategy employed to assess these two dimensions of the Europeanization of national public spheres often involves large scale comparative analyses of national news media (newspapers and television). The evidence provided by several larger research projects is mixed with regard to the scope of Europeanization along the two aforementioned dimensions. According to de Vreese (2007), this is mostly due to different sets of criteria for operationalization and measurement, which thus render comparisons of different studies difficult. Moreover, there are differences in the degree of Europeanization according to media type. While cross-national comparisons of quality newspapers find evidence for Europeanization, analyses of national television news has found 'virtually no trace of a European public sphere and only occasional, and brief, indications of Europeanization' (ibid.: 11).

The democratizing potential of civil society

The concept of 'civil society' has made its inroads into research on the EU's democratic quality in the context of a resurfacing of the notion of participatory democracy (Finke, 2007; see Greven, 2007 for a critical appraisal of the concept) and an open dissatisfaction with proposals to legitimize democratically the EU via the 'traditional' institutions of representative democracy.[5] Scholarly discourse is also reacting to shifts in focus among political actors who increasingly focus on means of direct democracy and participatory democracy as 'supplements' to representative democracy.[6] According to one observer, 'while the traditional concerns of democratic theory with state-centered institutions remain importantly crucial and ethically central, they are increasingly subject to the limitations we should expect when nineteenth-century concepts meet twenty-first century realities' (Warren, 2001: 226). Numerous EU-level developments are indicative of the 'participatory' turn that is propagated by policy-makers and academics alike. For example, the famous White Paper on European Governance by the European Commission echoes the importance attributed to non-electoral and non-legislative channels for citizen participation, stressing consultation practices and dialogue with civil society groups and citizens (European

Commission, 2001). The Treaty Establishing a Constitution for Europe (TCE), as well as its 'successor', the Lisbon 'Reform Treaty', contain explicit marks of participatory governance mirroring the increasing prominence of upgrading civil society and unmediated channels for citizen participation. In the TCE, for example, the principle of participatory democracy finds explicit mention (Article I-47). The principle extends to an open, transparent and regular dialogue between EU institutions and representative associations and civil society. In particular, the Commission is called on to carry out broad consultations with parties concerned and be responsive to a new instrument, the citizens' initiatives, whereby one million citizens, from any number of member countries, will be able to ask the Commission to present a proposal in any of the EU's areas of responsibility. These provisions intended to provide citizens with 'voice' and to open a 'civil dialogue' reflect some of the core ideas of the White Paper on Governance and the follow-up initiatives by the Commission. Just like the White Paper, the incorporation of participatory democracy in the TCE has met a mixed response in the academic EU community (Joerges et al., 2001). From the purview of deliberative democracy, the crucial contribution of encouraging civil society participation in the democratic process is to facilitate public deliberation by way of constituting a public sphere in which 'social problems and priorities ... are ... initially articulated and transmitted to political and economic spheres' (Fung, 2003: 525).

There is a nascent but fast-growing research agenda which addresses how civil society contributes to the EU's democratic legitimacy from the purview of deliberative democracy (see Finke, 2007 for an overview). Assuming the normative value of civil society for the democratic process, one question in this context asks how the potential contribution of civil society to a functioning public sphere can be assessed in empirical terms. Kohler-Koch and Finke (2007: 216) argue that, according to a 'principled conception of participation', participation can only be deemed democratic if it lives up to meeting the two criteria of 'equal chance of access' and 'equal representation in turnout'. Analysing the Commission's consultation 'regime', the authors suggest – with regard to the first criterion – to enquire into the 'accessibility of the political process in general, measure the openness and transparency of consultation processes, check the real thresholds of access for different kinds of interest associations, and evaluate the turnout of the collective actors involved' (ibid.). As to the second criterion – equal representation – assessing the representation of civil society follows a different logic than that of 'traditional' electoral representation. The authors thus propose to evaluate the representativeness of the Commission's consultations with reference to policy-relevant cleavage structures whereby they seek to tap those societal groups which 'broadly reflect the social composition of society' (ibid.).

There is a variety of case studies addressing the contribution of civil society participation in EU decision-making from the perspective of deliberative democratic theory (see, for example, De Schutter, 2002; Curtin, 2003; Persson, 2007; see Finke, 2007 for an overview).[7] Yet, we find little convergence in terms of the concepts and measures employed to assess empirically the contribution of civil society in different realms to the EU's democratic legitimacy: while Kohler-Koch and Finke (2007) seem to have in mind variable issue-specific social interest constellations, De Schutter (2002) points to 'fixed' and 'variable' attributes of representativeness. Irrespective of the criteria employed, conceptual vagueness is one problem of what this nascent field research has to grapple with. Furthermore, the important link between 'society' and 'state' is both undertheorized and conceptually underspecified. One key argument in the debate about deliberative democracy holds that civil society actors and the public sphere 'can set a public agenda and steer formal political systems in directions set by fair deliberations' (Fung, 2003: 525). This is an empirically testable claim which goes further than analysing accessibility and representativeness of civil society actors.

Institutional engineering and deliberation

While the discussion about the public sphere and civil society has stressed the democratizing potential of societal actors and transnational processes of communication, deliberative democracy does not have an exclusively society-centred understanding of the democratic process. Habermas stresses that 'the success of deliberative politics depends not on a collectively acting citizenry but on the institutionalization of the corresponding procedures and conditions of communication' (Habermas, 1994: 7). It is thus equally important to shift the analytical focus to those structures and conditions promoting or inhibiting discursive processes (see Niesen, 2007: 21–3 for an overview). Habermas argues, for instance, that the resistance and growing scepticism that the EU project is confronted with by the 'overwhelming majority of the population' can only be 'won for Europe if the project is extricated from the pallid abstraction of administrative measures and technical discourse: in other words, is politicized' (Habermas, 2001: 25–6).

This argument ties in with some of the more recent treatises on how to overcome the EU's democratic deficit. Follesdal and Hix (2006) argue that the lamented apathy and lack of engagement with EU affairs 'is partly endogenous, a consequence of lack of political contestation' (551). Their argument runs counter to a purely 'voting-centric', aggregative conception of the democratic process in that they stress that political competition on EU issues ('politicization') 'fosters political debate, which in turn promotes the formation of public opinion on different policy options' (ibid.: 550). This argument is also directed against the communitarian perspective and the no-demos thesis: 'rather than assuming that a European *demos* is a prerequisite for genuine EU democracy, a European democratic identity might well form through the practice of democratic competition and institutionalized cooperation' (ibid.). Follesdal and Hix go on to argue that constitutional and institutional features of the EU inhibit political contestation, insulating the EU from political competition.[8] In order to connect political decision-making on the EU level with national publics, they suggest that the introduction of some rather simple and small-scale institutional reforms will help spur political contestation and controversies engendering EU-wide debates on EU issues. In order to intensify political debate and contestation about EU politics, Follesdal and Hix (2006: 554) propose inter alia to allow for an electoral contest for the office of Commission President by national parliaments or citizens with the express optimism that this would induce open and transparent competition 'with candidates declaring themselves before the European elections, issuing manifestos for their term in office, and the transnational parties and the governments then declaring their support for one or the other candidates' (ibid.). From this perspective, deliberation carries a 'politicizing' impetus which can be engendered via institutional engineering. I will return to this position later.

A 'category mistake': the EU as a regulatory state

While the positions discussed so far in the chapter all have in common that they consider the EU to suffer from some kind of democratic deficit, they disagree strongly as to whether or not this democratic deficit is remediable and what the apposite remedy is.[9] The position which is presented in this section takes a different starting point. Those who attest that the EU suffers from a democratic deficit commit a '"category mistake", which consists in discussing certain facts as if they belonged to one logical type or category, when they actually belong to another' (Majone, 2006: 618). While this implies that the EU may well suffer from a lack of legitimacy, it also implies that any real or potential legitimacy deficit does not pertain to a lack of *democratic* legitimacy.

How can we make sense of this? The EU has to be seen, first and foremost, as an economic and a regulatory community which is committed to producing Pareto-improving policies for its citizens. Regulatory policies, such as competition policy, the removal of trade barriers or monetary policy, are destined to address and redress market failures to the benefits of all and hence do not carry redistributive implications. For these Pareto-improving policies to be effective, they have to be taken in a 'non-majoritarian' fashion. This implies that they must be excluded from the adversarial power-play of electoral and parliamentary politics. Otherwise decisions would be unduly politicized and their credibility and Pareto-efficient effects would be undermined and the EU's (output) legitimacy would suffer (Majone 2000, 2002). Since most EU policies are regulatory in nature, they can only be dealt with effectively by delegating these types of policy decisions to non-majoritarian institutions, such as courts, central banks and regulatory agencies, that is institutions that are not directly accountable to voters or their elected representatives. Their legitimacy is not vested in the democratic process; instead their legitimacy is generated by 'the belief of being, of all feasible institutional arrangements, the most appropriate one for a given range of problems' (Majone, 2006: 619).

While Majone thus vehemently defends his argument that the yardstick of *democratic* legitimacy should not be employed to evaluate the legitimacy of the EU polity (and thus commit a 'category mistake') mostly on theoretical and conceptual grounds, other scholars base their arguments about the unwarranted democratic deficit on empirically observed, more 'realistic', standards to evaluate the democratic quality of the EU polity. Akin to Majone, Moravcsik argues that it is a category mistake to assess the EU according to standards derived from democratic theories. Yet, whereas Majone's complaint is directed against the use of democratic theory given its alleged regulatory nature and the concomitant requirement of non-majoritarian decision-making structures, Moravcsik claims that the standards commonly employed by democratic theory are overly 'idealistic' and are not even met by any modern democratic government (Moravcsik, 2002: 605). By sticking to these 'idealistic' standards, analysts overlook 'the social context of contemporary European policy-making – the real-world practices of existing governments and multi-level political system in which they act' (ibid.). Echoing Majone's characterization of the EU as a regulatory state, Moravcsik argues that the treaties impose strict limits on EU activities since the EU's core activity remains regulatory in nature: trade in goods and services, movement of the factors of production, trade-related environmental and consumer policy, monetary policy, etc. Policies such as taxation, social welfare provision, defence and education policy – despite the 'modest inroads' made by the EU – are still firmly in the hands of the nation state. Furthermore, he points out that 'there is little distinctively "European" about the pattern of delegation we observe in the EU' (ibid.: 613). EU officials such as central bankers, judges in the ECJ and Commissioners enjoy the highest degree of decision-making autonomy precisely in those areas in which policymakers in modern democracies have also insulated themselves from 'majoritarian' decision-making and hence electoral and parliamentary contestation. His point is that critics should not employ double-standards: one may well quibble over the question whether insulation from majoritarian contestation is normatively desirable or justifiable by the standards of democratic theory, yet it cannot be ignored that insulation is an empirical fact both in the EU and in advanced democracies all over the world. Moravcsik concludes that 'as long as political proce-dures are consistent with existing national democratic practice and have a *prima facie* normative justification ... we cannot draw negative conclusions about the legitimacy of the EU from casual observation of the non-participatory nature of its institutions' (ibid.: 622).

These positions have been heavily criticized on theoretical and empir-ical grounds. Follesdal and Hix posit, for instance, that Majone and Moravcsik 'extol the virtues of "enlightened" bureaucracy against the dangers of untrammelled "popular" democracy, or "majoritarian" rule in the current parlance' (Follesdal and Hix, 2006: 546). More specifi-cally, criticism has been voiced that policies that are purely Pareto effi-cient in their effects are actually hard to identify. Follesdal and Hix challenge the dichotomous distinction Majone and Moravcsik draw between regulatory and non-regulatory policies on the ground that 'the empirical reality of decisions is a continuum between policies that are predominantly efficient and policies that are predominantly redistribu-tive, with many mixes' (ibid.: 542). They provide empirically based arguments that 'many EU regulatory policies have identifiable winners and losers' (ibid.: 543) and are thus by no means Pareto efficient and, as a consequence, should be subjected to the democratic process.

Table 7.1 summarizes the positions and arguments advanced hitherto and presents an overview of the different assessments of the EU's democratic quality from different theoretical perspectives.

The historical perspective: conditions for democratization

So far I have presented a range of models of democracy from which several arguments, both normative and empirical, have been derived with a view to assessing the EU's democratic potential and quality. Furthermore, I have presented a set of arguments which are rather crit-ical of applying democratic theory to the EU polity. Looking at our map of democratic theory, we have thus travelled a considerable dis-tance. In the sections that follow, I intend to draw attention to a set of contributions which adopt a macrohistorical perspective, exploring the historical origins of democratic institutions at the EU level as well as in the context of the formation of the modern state. From these perspec-tives we can also draw conclusions with regard to the 'democratizing potential' of the EU.

Institutional democratization: crafting the institutions of representative democracy on to the EU level

For democratic theorists, the extension of the powers of the directly elected EP constitutes an interesting research question. Since parliaments

Table 7.1. *The EU's democratic quality from different theoretical perspectives*

	Liberalism	*Republicanism*	*Deliberative democracy*	*Regulatory state*
Democratic process	Reflection of (exogenous) interests of pre-politically constituted society	Constitutes political society and citizens	Improves epistemic quality and legitimacy of policy	Enhances regulatory efficiency
Mechanisms	Elections (aggregation of interests)	Deliberation (collective 'self-determination')	Deliberation (truth-tracking and legitimizing potential)	Credible commitments and expertise
EU as …	Systems of 'checks and balances'	Normative–affective community	Post-national community	Regulatory state
Legitimacy deficit as …	Institutional deficit	Community deficit	Procedural deficit	Efficiency deficit
Instruments and preconditions	Separation of powers; rights protection	Public sphere: citizen autonomy and equality	Public sphere: inclusion, transparency, reasoned consensus	Non-majoritarian institutions

are constitutive features of representative government, the question of why the EU – as the only such organization within the universe of international organizations – contains a representative parliamentary institution with considerable decision-making powers, making it one of the strongest parliamentary assemblies in the world (Hix et al., 2003), is ever more pressing. Looking at the EP's legislative powers, we find that they have been gradually extended at every IGC since the adoption of the SEA. Until the entry into force of the SEA, the EP merely had to be consulted on matters of secondary legislation. Since then, the so-called 'cooperation procedure' endowed the EP for the first time with the formal right to propose amendments to legislation which – if supported by the Commission – were easier for the Council to accept than to reject (Tsebelis, 1994). In subsequent Treaty revisions, the legislative powers of the EP have been gradually enhanced. The 'co-decision procedure' first introduced by the Maastricht Treaty and amended by the Amsterdam Treaty further enhances the power of the EP *vis-à-vis* the Council (Thomson et al., 2006). The co-decision procedure's 'reach' has since been extended by all of the treaties since Maastricht and – in a symbolic acknowledgement of its mainstreaming – was renamed the 'ordinary legislative procedure' by the Libson Treaty.

How can this form of institutional democratization be accounted for? Research on the empowerment of the EP addresses two paths to empowerment. The first path is through 'interstitial institutional change' (Farrell and Héritier, 2007), which takes place in-between the 'grand bargains', viz. IGCs. Explanations for the empowerment of the EP highlight the 'incompleteness' and ambiguities of existing treaty rules. Employing principal–agent theory, it is argued that the incompleteness of treaty rules and information asymmetries between the principals (in the Council) and the agent (the EP) tend to lead to contestation over the existing treaty rules. The EP is expected to take these ambiguities as a lever in day-to-day politics in order to obtain an interpretation of treaty rules that enhance its competencies *vis-à-vis* other EU actors, such as the Council or the Commission (Hix, 2002; Héritier, 2007). Institutional change is thus triggered by means of rule interpretation and bargaining over these rules among EU actors. At subsequent IGCs, member state governments are expected to formalize the hitherto informal rules that resulted from interinstitutional bargaining.

The second path to empowerment points to changes of the formal treaty rules, reflecting qualitative differences either in scope (a 'net-empowerment' compared to existing formal or informal rules) or function (a new category of powers has been added, e.g. budgetary powers). In order to explain why member state governments enhance the Parliament's competences, the often-lamented 'deparliamentarization' of national parliaments, i.e. the reduction of their prerogatives as a result of European integration, provides a crucial impetus. Recent research has demonstrated that it is precisely the expected or perceived undermining of domestic parliamentary prerogatives resulting from further integration that has fuelled demands for expanding the powers of the EP (Rittberger, 2003, 2005; Rittberger and Schimmelfennig, 2007). The argument runs as follows. If proposed or implemented steps of EU integration are perceived to curb the competencies of national parliaments, the perceived 'democratic deficit' of European integration becomes particularly salient in the eyes of (some) EU actors. EU actors then try to exercise normative pressure – such as shaming or shunning – on those member states unwilling to redress this situation. In order for normative pressure to be effective, it is assumed that member states in the EU are embedded in a liberal democratic community environment (Schimmelfennig, 2003). Members of this kind of environment share a common ethos which, if violated by any of its members, will trigger efforts of 'abiding' actors to bring the recalcitrant state in line with the community ethos. In a community sharing a common ethos the pursuit of political goals is not only dependent on the bargaining power and preference constellation of the relevant actors, but on conformity with the community ethos. Actors may, however, use the community ethos strategically to bolster the legitimacy of their own goals against arguments brought forward by their opponents (Schimmelfennig, 2001; see also Rittberger and Schimmelfennig, 2007). What does this argument imply for the expansion of the EP's powers? Even though augmenting legislative powers may not reflect the collective institutional interest or normative consensus of the member states at the respective IGCs, their collective identity as democratic states and as members of a liberal democratic community environment obliges them in principle to conform to basic norms of liberal democracy. The explanatory power of this approach has been demonstrated empirically with regard to the increase of the EP's legislative and budgetary powers, as well as with a view to hold the Commission to account (Lindner and Rittberger, 2003; Rittberger, 2005; Schimmelfennig *et al.*, 2006).[10]

Providing a socio-political 'infrastructure' for democracy: lessons from modern state-building

Even though the EP can be seen as an important feature of institutional democratization, most EU scholars addressing the question of the EU's democratic quality (rightly) argue that institutional democratization in and of itself – the empowerment of the EP being a case in point – does not necessarily improve the democratic legitimacy of the EU. Stefano Bartolini argues that the EU's institutional infrastructure inhibits the kinds of political structuring processes – interest differentiation and associated conflict lines and their manifestation in political movements, alliances and parties – which have historically accompanied democrati- zation processes. He posits that 'institutional democratization without political structuring may turn into facade electioneering, at best, or dangerous experiments, at worst' (Bartolini, 2005: xv).

Historically, processes of state- and nation-building – which refer to the cultural standardization and nationalization of the mass population – have triggered widespread opposition and conflict among culturally dis- tinct groups. Furthermore, socio-economic changes, most notably the rise of capitalism, have generated opposition among actors in the mar- ketplace and led to a politicization of conflicts which the state had to accommodate (ibid.: 364). These 'cultural, economic and politico- administrative lines of conflict and opposition ... overlapped and some- times reinforced each other, contributing to the political "vertebration" of civil society and to the accommodation of different interests within the state through representation and incorporation' (ibid.). Bartolini locates the process of European integration as the (hitherto) last of a set of developmental trends which formed European states, nations, democracies and welfare systems.

The onset of the European integration process can thus be interpreted in Bartolini's reading by taking recourse to a set of structural factors 'as a response by national elites to the weakening of the European state system and to the new pressure brought to bear by capitalist world development' (ibid.: 365). From this perspective, European integration was instrumental for the consolidation and economic viability of the post Second World War system of *nation* states in Western Europe (see also Milward, 1992). Furthermore, European integration set into motion processes whereby the overlapping economic, cultural and politico- administrative boundaries of the nation state become gradually disjoined: the territorially expanding scope of economic and legal integration 'places the legitimation triangle of the nation state under severe pressure, based as it is on cultural homogeneity, political participation and social sharing institutions' (Bartolini, 2005: 375).

For the purpose of our discussion, the impact of European integration on the political structures of representation and hence the links between citizens and their political elites is of particular relevance. Bartolini posits that European integration leads to a 'destructuring' of 'previous locally rooted political structures and systems of representation' (ibid.: 386). This is mirrored in a weakening of partisan alignments and in domestic parties' self-imposed 'gag rule' to keep EU issues off the elec- toral plate (see also Mair, 2007). As a result, this 'lack of any party thematization of EU issues leaves the mass public attitudes towards the EU largely unstructured' (Bartolini, 2005: 385). He concludes that the prospects for political 'restructuring' at the EU-level are bleak. This sit- uation cannot be compensated for by institutional democratization at the EU level: for 'top-down' democratization to work, political structures representing different interests and identities need to be in place. The present form of 'democratic engineering' in the EU, not least the above-mentioned empowerment of the EP or 'experimentation' with a Philadelphia-style Constitutional Convention, cannot work in the EU as long as possibilities for 'exit' and boundary transcendence are pervasive: under these conditions, the EU will neither be able to 'enforce "positive" costly integration' nor generate 'incentives to structure "voice" at the European level' (ibid.: 408).

New research agendas

I will now pick up the thread provided by Dahl at the outset of this chapter. Dahl's 'map' of democratic theory distinguishes inter alia among arguments which are more 'philosophical', for instance by providing justifications for the democratic process and how it should be designed, and arguments which are more empirically oriented, for instance by empirically assessing normative claims about the democratic process. The previous sections have hinted at vibrant debates between more normatively oriented and more empirically oriented scholars studying the EU's democratic quality. My last task is to highlight some of the current problems and potential solutions that have been engendered in these debates.

Linking normative and empirical democratic theory

One of the most thriving and voluminous literatures in democratic theory at present can undoubtedly be found in the area of deliberative democracy. This does not only apply to democratic theory in general (see the overviews by Thompson 2008 and Rosenberg 2007a) but also to the study of the democratic quality of the EU (see Neyer, 2006 for an overview). One of the key challenges facing scholars on deliberative democracy, at present, lies in linking normative theory with empirical political science research (see, among others, Dryzek, 2007; Mutz, 2008; Thompson, 2008). Diana Mutz asks provocatively: 'for many political scientists, regarding theorists' accounts of deliberative democracy can be aggravating. On the one hand, many of the assertions seem to cry out for empirical verification. On the other hand, much of the empirical work in this vein has been deemed irrelevant to the theory of deliberative democracy by political theorists' (Mutz, 2008: 522).

These two challenges are equally germane to the study of democracy in the EU. Even though there is broad agreement among 'theorists' and 'empirical analysts' about the desirability of outcomes of the democratic process – which reflect, inter alia, more and better informed citizens, a higher degree of public-spiritedness, more social trust, fairness of outcomes and (a concomitant) increase in the perceived legitimacy of political decisions – the question is still open as to which factors (help) generate these outcomes. Some would even go further and argue that deliberative processes also carry the potential to engender identity-building processes. Scholarship on deliberative democracy has developed a broad set of conditions which are deemed relevant for deliberation to succeed in generating the above-mentioned outcomes (see, for example, Rosenberg, 2007b: 9–10; Mutz, 2008). For deliberation to 'succeed', e.g. to lend legitimacy to political decisions, Eriksen (2006, 2007) argues that two distinct strands of arguments – a 'participatory' and 'rationalistic' strand – can be distinguished in the literature, both emphasizing different requirements for successful deliberation. The former stresses process-related factors geared towards ensuring equal opportunities for participation (and a concomitant focus on political rights, elections and representative institutions), while the latter points at the conditions promoting 'rational argumentation' – based on a free and open discourse – so that qualitatively 'superior' decisions which are acceptable to all can be obtained (ibid.).

Both theoretical perspectives have received ample attention in the EU-related literature. Yet, a lot of work still has to be done to engage normatively and empirically oriented scholars in a more productive discourse. Scope for improvement is primarily to be found with those research efforts which are geared towards empirically scrutinizing the claims advanced by deliberative theory. At present, most of the literature applying deliberative theory to the EU concentrates on the conditions and requirements that are considered necessary for deliberative politics to ensue and be 'successful' in producing the purported beneficial outcomes. Most contributions to the burgeoning literatures on the 'public sphere' and 'civil society' and their potential to contribute to the EU's democratic legitimacy are written against the backdrop of a deliberative democratic perspective. Most of the studies address a set of conditions which are deemed relevant for 'successful' deliberation to ensue. For the sake of illustration, I take two prominent examples from recent scholarship on 'civil society' and its potential to contribute to the EU's democratic legitimacy.[11] Steffek and Nanz (2008: 10) present four criteria which are deemed 'to bring about free, informed and inclusive deliberation': access to deliberation, transparency and access to information, responsiveness to the concerns of stakeholders, and inclusion of all voices. In their assessment of the European Commission's consultation regime, Kohler-Koch and Finke (2007: 216–17) argue that participatory practices need to live up to three standards: the Commission has to listen to 'a maximum range of (authentic) voices existing in the "lifeworld" and stimulating a reasoned debate', a 'spread of the (controversial) discussion on EU political issues' should be engendered, as well as the emergence of a media-sustained European public space.

As I alluded to above, there are some problems that arise from this focus on conditions and requirements for successful deliberation. Most scholars, 'testing' or 'applying' deliberative theory to the EU, work on the assumption that meeting the evaluative standards deemed necessary for 'good' or 'successful' deliberation actually produces 'good' and 'successful' deliberation. How do we know whether the evaluative standards actually produce the desired outcomes ('more' democratic legitimacy) via deliberative processes? In most studies so far, the link between conditions and outcomes is 'black boxed' and the beneficial results of deliberative democracy are assumed rather than explored and explained. This type of research strategy may be less problematic in a research context where both theoretical and empirical knowledge about the mechanisms operating within the 'black box' are well known and established. However, such a strategy is highly problematic when such knowledge is lacking or, even worse, when previously developed theories and gathered evidence fly in the face of deliberative theory (Mutz, 2008: 533–5). Diana Mutz proposes to be more sceptical with regard to the claims advanced by deliberative theory, and thus treat what has hitherto been assumed by most theorists as something that needs to be explained: 'before we set a goal of equality within a deliberative context, or attempt to change decision-making processes to meet any other deliberative standard, we should first have evidence that the theory works as advertised and that these particular standards are crucial to its beneficial outcomes' (ibid.: 528). Many claims about the design and consequences of institutional EU treaty reforms are reviewed against the backdrop of their potential to enhance the EU's democratic legitimacy. To assess these claims scientifically, scholars should take Mutz's advice seriously and empirically explore whether the claims that deliberative theorists have voiced in conjunction with the debate about constitutional reform in the EU can be supported empirically. An illustration of how this research agenda could be advanced follows in the next section and is related to the recent debate about the potential promises and pitfalls of the 'politicization' of EU politics.

The challenge of politicization

'Finally some politics in the EU!' is heralded by Simon Hix whereby he refers to the taking up of rhetorical arms by different partisan camps in Brussels and national capitals following the rejection of the Constitutional Treaty in France and the Netherlands: 'Neo-liberals' defending a large-scale market are pitted against 'social Europe' protagonists in a political battle about the future of the European project. This, Hix believes, 'is exactly what Europe needs' (Hix, 2006: 3). Given the advanced state of European integration, most EU policies inevitably produce winners and losers and are by no means Pareto efficient as the proponents of the 'Regulatory State' thesis suggest. Hence, 'there is no inherent reason why these policies should be isolated from democratic contestation' (ibid.: 7).

From the perspective of deliberative theory, politicizing EU politics is deemed to produce beneficial outcomes, for not only does it induce deliberation, but it also creates a more and better informed citizenry and contributes to 'enlightened understanding' (Dahl, 1989), which some democratic theorists consider to be integral to the democratic process. In the current EU-related literature, champions of the 'politicization thesis' make explicit or implicit arguments linking institutional variables, with participatory opportunities and deliberative practices, which in turn are assumed to produce beneficial outcomes flowing from deliberation, such as greater democratic legitimacy, social trust, identification, etc. (Moravcsik, 2006; cf. the discussion of Mutz, 2008 above). To advance the conversation between theorists and more empirically oriented scholars, this chain of arguments should be dissected into analytically distinct empirical claims. According to the first claim, institutional reform creates opportunities for more (and 'better') participation as well as more (and 'better') deliberation; second, deliberation is considered to produce a set of beneficial outcomes, such as higher legitimacy, compliance, trust, etc. There is not yet an advanced empirical–analytical literature testing these different claims. However, a debate is emerging which provides both theoretical and empirically 'informed' arguments as to the explanatory leverage of the different causal claims in the 'politicization chain'. These arguments will be reviewed in brief in what follows.

For Follesdal and Hix (2006) the crucial challenge facing the EU and its democratic aspirations is to bridge the gap between an increasingly politicized political structure in the Brussels orbit and the attitudes of EU citizens who have 'very little information about the emerging politics inside the EU institutions, and so cannot identify the protagonists and the positions they represent' (Hix, 2006: 23). As we have seen, Follesdal and Hix (2006) suggest that this gap can be narrowed by (even rather small-scale) institutional reforms that induce political competition (see also Hix, 2006). Yet, there exists disagreement over the consequences of more participation of a more and better informed citizenry: the referenda on the TCE and the Irish referendum on the Lisbon 'Reform Treaty' are cases in point. While these referenda demonstrate that there is definitely a potential for politicization *in* the EU (and actually *of* the EU), the political battles that took place domestically were directed at 'fundamental constitutional issues and not on the specific policy content within a particular constitutional status quo' (Follesdal and Hix, 2006: 551). From this perspective, referenda can be considered 'ineffective mechanisms for promoting day-to-day competition, or contestation between policy platforms, or indeed articulation and opposition in the EU policy process' (ibid.: 552). Not only can referenda be seen as 'undue' instruments to incite political contestation on the left/right dimension, the Irish Referendum of 12 June 2008 has demonstrated that politicization may play into the hands of smaller opposition groups inside and, as in the Irish case, particularly outside the parliamentary arena (only three Irish MPs opposed the ratification legislation!).[12]

Others in the discipline are much more sceptical than Follesdal and Hix about the effects of politicization on the structure of political contestation. While Follesdal and Hix express confidence that contestation of EU policies can and eventually will be integrated into left/right politics, there are sceptical voices arguing that political contestation of EU issues in domestic arenas may have rather damaging effects. For one, there is the 'sleeping giant' thesis by van der Eijk and Franklin (2004). They show empirically that 'the pro/anti-EU orientation, despite its apparent irrelevance for political behaviour in the domestic sphere, constitutes something of a "sleeping giant" that has the potential, if awakened, to impel voters to political behaviour that ... undercuts the bases for contemporary party mobilization in many, if not most, European polities' (van der Eijk and Franklin, 2004: 32–3). They bolster this claim by demonstrating that voter attitudes display greater dispersion of attitudes on Europe than on the left/right dimension: 'it is surely only a matter of time before policy entrepreneurs in some countries seize the opportunity, presented to their parties by these quite polarized opinions, to differentiate themselves from other parties in EU terms' (ibid.: 47). The consequences that ensue from the politicization of EU issues may well be negative on grounds of decision-making effectiveness as well as with a view to inciting political structuring processes. Van der Eijk and Franklin speculate that politicization could be a stumbling block for the development of a European party system given the incoherence of party positions on the left/right and pro/anti-EU dimensions; regarding decision-making effectiveness, party group cohesion inside the EP may well be put under increasing stress (but see Hix *et al.*, 2007). In a similar vein Bartolini (2006) wonders whether the politicization of the EU would not throw the baby out with the bathwater. If politicization does not merely affect 'isomorphic issues', which are similar to the political issues discussed and debated at the national level, but 'constitutive issues' pertaining to constitutional questions, such as EU membership and institutional design, this could prove 'disastrous' (Bartolini, 2006: 35). He echoes van der Eijk and Franklin's concern that politicization could lead to party splits and a widening gap between political elites and their electorates, an issue which is regularly coming to the fore in referenda (which are held on constitutive issues such as treaty revision or EU membership). In sum, Bartolini is highly sceptical that politicization 'will apply to the benign left–right issues rather than threatening constitutive issues' (ibid.).

There is a third position, which seeks to qualify both Hix's and the sceptics' positions, adding yet another layer of empirical argument to the politicization debate. According to Magnette and Papadopoulos (2008) both Hix and Bartolini are overly 'optimistic' that institutional design choices can either induce welcome politicization (Hix) or help avoiding it (Bartolini). Magnette and Papadopoulos argue instead that the consociational character of the EU – reflected in the style of consensual politics and power diffusion along horizontal and vertical dimensions – 'narrows the scope for polarization, and thus reduces the effect in terms of clarification' which Hix hopes to obtain via politicization (ibid.: 77). While left–right polarization has also grown in consociational democracies such as Belgium and Switzerland, the authors claim that this 'does not prevent majorities to be formed around centrist compromises' in order to overcome multiple veto points (ibid.: 84; see also Moravcsik, 2002). Furthermore, they claim that there is no evidence demonstrating that politicization in consociational systems has a (negative) direct bearing on civic interest, the point being that 'civic interest is not only a function of party competition' (Magnette and Papadopoulos, 2008: 84). Even though consociational politics is often equated with elite collusion, Magnette and Papadopolous suggest that consociational systems with their emphasis on compromise-building can nevertheless improve their democratic capacity – stimulating and popularizing debate on EU issues – by allowing for a 'dose' of participatory democracy via an increased use of referenda via the envisaged citizens' initiative.

One evident observation that can be drawn from the previous discussion is the unequivocal agreement that democratic will-formation among informed citizens is a crucial ingredient for democratically legitimate governance. Some scholars have identified politicization as a promising mechanism to induce deliberative politics; however, assessments of the conditions for and consequences of politicization differ profoundly. There is thus not only a myriad of claims and arguments as well as growing confusion in this debate; future research should address questions providing some structure to this debate. Going back to first principles, concept specification is a key issue: 'politicization' can mean many things to different researchers. Questions of concept measurement and of employing the appropriate indicators to assess degrees of 'contestation', 'ideological competition' and 'polarization' suggest themselves. The literature on political parties and party systems has, thankfully, many suggestions to make in this respect. The same holds for deliberation and the boundaries of the two concepts, 'politicization' and 'deliberation'.[13] The most obvious lacuna, however, is the lack of systematic empirical knowledge and the concomitant lack of testing theoretical claims. As the 'politicization' example demonstrated, three different works have produced three different arguments about the likely consequences of politicization. Future research must pay attention to the empirical implications, both at the macro- as well as at the microlevel, of these alternative conjectures. Deliberation between deliberative theorists and more empirically oriented scholars requires that both listen to each other and reflect on the others' claims and positions. Recent developments in democratic theory provide an optimistic outlook that this debate reaches further into the field of EU studies.

Notes

1. See Scharpf (1999) for the distinction between 'input' and 'output legitimacy'.
2. Others have provided excellent overviews on the literature addressing the EU's democratic quality (see, for example, Schäfer, 2006). While existing overviews often map arguments as to whether they are rather 'optimistic' or 'pessimistic' about the prospects of enhancing the democratic legitimacy of the EU, this overview is decidedly theory-driven.
3. BVerfGE 89, 155.
4. The literature elaborating and applying standards from deliberative democratic theory to assess and evaluate the democratic credentials of the EU polity display a rapid growth. The EU-funded Integrated Project RECON (Reconstituting Democracy in Europe) headed by ARENA (Oslo) is at the forefront of scholarship in this context (see Eriksen, 2005; Eriksen and Fossum, 2007; see also their online working paper series at: http://www.reconproject.eu).
5. Following Habermas, civil society is 'composed of those more or less spontaneously emergent associations, organizations, and movements that, attuned to how societal problems resonate in the private life sphere, distil and transmit such reactions ... to the public sphere' (Habermas, 1996: 367).
6. The following section draws from Kohler-Koch and Rittberger (2007: 10–11).
7. There are similar questions about the democratic legitimating potential of civil society actors in the context of international governance (Steffek *et al.*, 2008).
8. Arguments about the causes of a lack of political contestation on EU issues are manifold. Some emphasize the lack of institutional provisions that could facilitate political contestation (Follesdal and Hix, 2006); others argue that the lack of political contestation is a deliberate strategy among national political parties (see, for example, Mair, 2007).
9. This section draws from Kohler-Koch and Rittberger (2007: 4–6).

10. It is not just the EP that can consider itself a beneficiary of previous IGCs: arguments about 'deparliamentarization' at the domestic level have also triggered discussions about enhancing the role of national parliaments in EU policy-making via EU Treaty reform (Raunio, 2005, 2007; O'Brennan and Raunio, 2007; Rittberger, 2007).
11. For the literature addressing the existence or 'quality' of an EU-wide public sphere, see, for example, the contributions in *European Political Science* to the symposium edited by Bee *et al.* (2008) entitled 'The Development of a European Public Sphere: A Stalled Project?'.
12. See Hobolt (2006) for an overview of the literature on referenda.
13. See Steiner (2008) on deliberation and concept specification.

References

Arrow, K. J. (1951) *Social Choice and Individual Values* (New Haven: Yale University Press).

Bartolini, S. (2005) *Reconstructing Europe. Centre Formation, System Building, and Political Structuring between the Nation State and the European Union* (Oxford: Oxford University Press).

Bartolini, S. (2006) 'Should the Union be "Politicized"? Prospects and Risks', Policy Paper 19, Paris: Notre Europe: 29–50.

Bee, C., Scartezzini, R. and Scott, A. (2008) 'The Development of a European Public Sphere: A Stalled Project?', *European Political Science* 7(3): 257–63.

Cederman, L.-E. (2001) 'Political Boundaries and Identity Trade-Offs', in L.-E. Cederman (ed.) *Constructing Europe's Identity. The External Dimension* (London: Lynne Rienner Publishers) 1–32.

Curtin, D. (2003) 'Private Interest Representation or Civil Interest Deliberation? A Contemporary Dilemma for European Union Governance', *Social Legal Studies* 12(1): 55–75.

Dahl, R. (1989) *Democracy and Its Critics* (New Haven: Yale University Press).

De Schutter, O. (2002) 'Europe in Search of its Civil Society', *European Law Journal* 8(2): 198–217.

Dryzek, J. S. (2007) 'Theory, Evidence, and the Tasks of Deliberation', in S. W. Rosenberg (ed.) *Deliberation, Participation and Democracy. Can the People Govern?* (Basingstoke: Palgrave Macmillan) 237–50.

Eijk, C. van der and Franklin, M. N. (2004) 'Potential for contestation on European matters at national elections in Europe', in G. Marks and M. R. Steenbergen (eds) *European Integration and Political Conflict* (Cambridge: Cambridge University Press).

Eriksen, E. O. (ed.) (2005) *Making the European Polity. Reflexive Integration in the EU* (London: Routledge).

Eriksen, E. O. (ed.) (2006) 'Deliberation and the problem of democratic legitimacy in the EU. Are working agreements the most that can be expected?' ARENA Working Paper No. 8.

Eriksen, E. O. (ed.) (2007) 'A Comment on Schmalz-Bruns', in B. Kohler-Koch and B. Rittberger (eds) *Debating the democratic Legitimacy of the European Union* (Lanham: Rowman & Littlefield): 304–10.

Eriksen, E. O. and Fossum, J. E. (2000) 'Post-national integration', in Ebd. (eds), *Democracy in the European Union. Integration through Deliberation?* (London: Routledge) 1–28.

Eriksen, E. O. and Fossum, J. E. (2007) *Europe in Transformation. How to Reconstitute Democracy?* Recon Online Working Paper 01.

Etzioni, A. (2007) 'The Community Deficit', *Journal of Common Market Studies* 45(1): 23–42.

European Commission (2001) 'European Governance, A White Paper.' 428 final.

Farrell, H. and Héritier A. (2007) 'Contested competences in Europe: Incomplete contracts and interstitial institutional change', *West European Politics* 30(2): 227–43.

Finke, B. (2007) 'Civil society participation in EU governance', *Living Reviews in European Governance* 2(2): 1–31.

Follesdal, A. and Hix S. (2006) 'Why There is a Democratic Deficit in the EU: A Response to Majone and Moravcsik', *Journal of Common Market Studies* 44(3): 533–62.

Fossum, J. E. and Eriksen, E. O. (2003) 'Europe in search of its legitimacy. Assessing strategies of legitimation', in E. O. Eriksen, C. Joerges and J. Neyer (eds) *European Governance, Deliberation and the Quest for Democratisation* (Oslo: Arena Report) 23–56.

Fung, A. (2003) 'Associations and Democracy: Between Theories, Hopes, and Realities', *Annuals Review of Sociology* 29: 515–39.

Goetz, K. H. and Meyer-Sahling, J.-H. (2008) 'The Europeanisation of National Political Systems: Parliaments and Executives', *Living Reviews in European Governance* 3(2): 1–30.

Greven, M. T. (2007) 'Some Consideration on Participation in Participatory Governance', in B. Kohler-Koch and B. Rittberger (eds) *Debating the democratic legitimacy of the European Union* (Lanham: Rowman & Littlefield Publishers) 233–48.

Grimm, D. (2001) *Die Verfassung und die Politik. Einsprüche in Störfällen* (München: C.H. Beck).

Habermas, J. (1994) 'Three Normative Models of Democracy', *Constellations* 1(1): 1–10.

Habermas, J. (1996) *Between Facts and Norms: Contributions to a Discourse Theory of Law and Democracy* (Cambridge MA: MIT Press).

Habermas, J. (2001) 'Why Europe needs a Constitution', *New Left Review* 11: 5–26.

Held, D. (1996) *Models of Democracy* (Cambridge: Polity Press).

Héritier, A. (2007) *Explaining Institutional Change in Europe* (Oxford: Oxford University Press).

Hix, S. (2002) 'Constitutional Agenda-Setting through Discretion in Rule Interpretation: Why the European Parliament Won at Amsterdam', *British Journal of Political Science* 32(2): 259–80.

Hix, S. (2006) 'Why the EU needs (Left–Right) politics? Policy reform and accountability are impossible without it', Policy Paper No. 19, Paris: Notre Europe: 1–28.

Hix, S., Raunio, T. and Scully, R. (2003) 'Fifty Years on: Research on the European Parliament', *Journal of Common Market Studies* 41(2): 191–202.

Hix, S., Noury, A. G. and Roland, G. (2007) *Democratic Politics in the European Parliament* (Cambridge: Cambridge University Press).

Hobolt, S. B. (2006) 'Direct Democracy and European Integration', *Journal of European Public Policy* 13(1): 153–66.

Joerges, C., Mény, Y. and Weiler, J. H. H. (2001) *Mountain or Molehill? A Critical Appraisal of the Commission White Paper on Governance*, New York School of Law, Jean Monnet Working Paper Series 6 (1).

Kielmansegg, P. G. (2003) 'Integration und Demokratie', in M. Jachtenfuchs and B. Kohler-Koch (eds), *Europäische Integration* (Opladen: Leske and Budrich).

Kohler-Koch, B. and Finke, B. (2007) 'The Institutional Shaping of EU-Society Relations: A Contribution to Democracy via Participation?' *Journal of Civil Society* 3(3): 205–21.

Kohler-Koch, B. and Rittberger, B. (2007) 'Charting Crowded Territory: Debating the Democratic Legitimacy of the European Union', in B. Kohler-Koch and B. Rittberger (eds) *Debating the democratic Legitimacy of the European Union* (Lanham: Rowman & Littlefield) 1–29.

Küsters, H. J. (1988) 'Die Verhandlungen über das institutionelle System zur Gründung der Europäischen Gemeinschaft für Kohl and Stahl', in K. Schwabe (ed.) *Die Anfänge des Schuman Plans 1950/51 – The Beginnings of the Schuman Plan* (Baden-Baden: Nomos).

Kymlicka, W. (1993) 'Community', in R. E. Gooding and P. Petit (eds), *A Companion to Contemporary Political Philosophy* (Malden: Blackwell Publishing Ltd) 366–78.

Lepsius, R. M. (1999) 'Bildet sich eine Kulturelle Identität innerhalb der Europäischen Gemeinschaft?', in W. Reese-Schäfer, *Identität und Interesse: Der Diskurs der Identitätsforschung* (Opladen: Leske and Budrich).

Lindner, J. and Rittberger, B. (2003) 'The Creation, Interpretation and Contestation of Institutions—Revisiting Historical Institutionalism', *Journal of Common Market Studies* 41(3): 445–73.

Magnette, P. and Papadopoulos, Y. (2008) 'On the Politicisation of the European Consociation: A Middle Way Between Hix and Bartolini', *European Governance Papers (Eurogov)*, C-08-01.

Maier, J. and Rittberger, B. (2008) 'Shifting Europe's Boundaries: Mass Media, Public Opinion and the Enlargement of the EU', *European Union Politics* 9(2): 243–67.

Mair, P. (2007) 'Political Opposition and the European Union', *Government and Opposition* 42(1): 1–17.

Majone, G. (2000) 'The Credibility Crisis of Community Regulation', *Journal of Common Market Studies* 38(2): 273–302.

Majone, G. (2002) 'Delegation of Regulatory Power in a Mixed Polity', *European Law Journal* 38(3): 319–39.

Majone, G. (2006) 'The common sense of European Integration', *Journal of European Public Policy* 13(5): 607–26.

Milward, A. S. (1992) *The European Rescue of the Nation-State* (London: Routledge).

Moravcsik, A. (1994) 'Why the European Community Strengthens the State: Domestic Politics and International Institutions', Center for European Studies Working Paper Series 52 (Cambridge: Center for European Studies).

Moravcsik, A. (2002) 'In Defense of the "Democratic Deficit": Reassessing Legitimacy in the European Union', *Journal of Common Market Studies* 40(4): 603–23.

Moravcsik, A. (2006) 'What Can We Learn from the Collapse of the European Constitutional Project?', *Politische Vierteljahresschrift* 47(2): 219–41.

Mutz, D. C. (2008) 'Is Deliberative Democracy a Falsifiable Theory?', *Annual Review of Political Science* 11: 521–38.

Neyer, J. (2006) 'The Deliberative Turn in Integration Theory', *Journal of European Public Policy* 13(5): 779–91.

Niesen, P. (2007) 'Anarchie der kommunikativen Freiheit – ein Problemaufriss', in P. Niesen and B. Herborth (eds), *Anarchie der kommunikativen Freiheit. Jürgen Habermas und die Theorie der internationalen Politik* (Frankfurt am Main: Suhrkamp Verlag).

O'Brennan, J. and Raunio, T. (2007) 'Introduction. Deparliamentarization and European integration', in J. O'Brennan and T. Raunio (eds) *National parliaments within the enlarged European Union. From 'victims' of integration to competitive actors?* (London: Routledge) 1–26.

Persson, T. (2007) 'Democratizing European Chemicals Policy: Do Consultations Favour Civil Society Participation?', *Journal of Civil Society* 3(3): 223–38.

Raunio, T. (2005) 'Holding governments accountable in European affairs: Explaining cross-national variation', *Journal of Legislative Studies* 11(3/4): 319–42.

Raunio, T. (2007) 'National legislatures in the EU Constitutional Treaty', in J. O'Brennan and T. Raunio (eds) *National parliaments within the enlarged European Union. From 'victims' of integration to competitive actors?* (London: Routledge) 79–92.

Riker, W. H. (1982) *Liberalism Against Populism: A Confrontation Between the Theory of Democracy and the Theory of Social Choice* (Prospect Heights: Waveland Press).

Risse, T. and Van de Steeg, M. (2003) 'An Emerging European Public Sphere? Empirical Evidence and Theoretical Clarifications', Paper presented to the conference on the 'Europeanization of Public Spheres, Political Mobilization, Public Communication and the European Union,' Science Center Berlin, June 20–22.

Rittberger, B. (2003) 'The Creation and Empowerment of the European Parliament', *Journal of Common Market Studies* 42(2): 203–25.

Rittberger, B. (2005) *Building Europe's Parliament. Democratic Representation Beyond the Nation State* (Oxford: Oxford University Press).

Rittberger, B. (2007) 'Constructing Parliamentary Democracy in the European Union: How Did It Happen?', in B. Kohler-Koch and B. Rittberger (eds) *Debating the democratic Legitimacy of the European Union* (Lanham: Rowman & Littlefield) 111–37.

Rittberger, B. and Schimmelfennig, F. (eds) (2007) *The Constitutionalization of the European Union* (London: Routledge).

Rosenberg, S. W. (ed.) (2007a) *Deliberation, Participation and Democracy. Can the People Govern?* (Basingstoke: Palgrave Macmillan).

Rosenberg, S. W. (2007b) 'An Introduction: Theoretical Perspectives and Empirical Research on Deliberative Democracy', in S. W. Rosenberg (ed.),

Deliberation, Participation and Democracy. Can the People Govern? (Basingstoke: Palgrave Macmillan) 1–22.

Schäfer, A. (2006) 'Nach dem permissiven Konsens. Das Demokratiedefizit der Europäischen Union', *Leviathan* 34(3): 350–76.

Scharpf, F. W. (1997) 'Introduction: the problem-solving capacity of multi-level governance', *Journal of European Public Policy* 4(4): 520–38.

Scharpf, F. W. (1999) *Governing in Europe. Effective and Democratic?* (Oxford: Oxford University Press).

Schimmelfennig, F. (2001) 'The Community Trap: Liberal Norms, Rhetorical Action, and the Eastern Enlargement of the European Union', *International Organization* 55(1): 47–80.

Schimmelfennig, F. (2003) *The EU, NATO and the Integration of Europe. Rules and Rhetoric* (Cambridge: Cambridge University Press).

Schimmelfennig, F., Rittberger, B., Bürgin, A. and Schwellnus, G. (2006) 'Conditions for EU constitutionalization: a qualitative comparative analysis', *Journal of European Public Policy* 13(8): 1168–89.

Schlesinger, P. and Kevin, D. (2000) 'Can the European Union become a sphere of publics?', in E. O. Eriksen and J. E. Fossum (eds), *Democracy in the European Union. Integration through Deliberation?* (London: Routledge) 206–29.

Seidendorf, S. (2007) *Europäisierung nationaler Identitätsdiskurse? Ein Vergleich französische und deutscher Printmedien* (Regieren in Europa Bd. 13) (Baden-Baden: Nomos).

Shapiro, I. (2003) *The State of Democratic Theory* (Princeton: Princeton University Press).

Steffek, J. and Nanz, P. (2008) 'Emergent patterns of Civil Society Participation in Global and European Governance', in J. Steffek, C. Kissling and P. Nanz (eds), *Civil Society Participation in European and Global Governance. A Cure for the Democratic Deficit?* (Basingstoke: Palgrave Macmillan).

Steffek, J., Kissling, C. and Nanz, P. (2008) *Civil Society Participation in European and Global Governance. A Cure for the Democratic Deficit?* (Basingstoke: Palgrave Macmillan).

Steiner, J. (2008) 'Concept stretching: the case of deliberation', *European Political Science* 7(2): 186–90.

Thompson, D. F. (2008) 'Deliberative Democratic Theory and Empirical Political Science', *Annual Review of Political Science* 11: 497–520.

Thomson, R., Stokman, F. N., Achen, C. H. and T. König (2006) *The European Union Decides* (Cambridge: Cambridge University Press).

Tsebelis, G. (1994) 'The Power of the European Parliament as a Conditional Agenda-Setter', *American Political Science Review* 88: 128–42.

De Vreese, C. H. (2007) 'The EU as a public sphere', *Living Reviews in European Governance* 2(3): 1–20.

Warren, M. E. (2001) *Democracy and Association* (Princeton: Princeton University Press).

Weiler, J.H.H. (1995) 'The State "über alles": Demos, Telos and the German Maastricht Decision', Jean Monnet Working Paper Series 6/95 (Cambridge, MA: Harvard Law School).

Weiler, J. H. H., Haltern, U. and Mayer, F. C. (1995) 'European Democracy and its Critique', *West European Politics* 18(1): 4–39.

Zweifel, T. D. (2002) 'Who is without sin cast the first stone: the EU's democratic deficit in comparison', *Journal of European Public Policy* 9(5): 812–40.

Chapter 8

European Union Law: A Tale of Microscopes and Telescopes

Anthony Arnull

Among the many fields of legal study is a subject known as comparative law, which involves comparing different national legal systems. To help make this daunting exercise more manageable, comparative lawyers divide the world's legal systems into families based on their distinctive features or style (Zweigert and Kötz, 1998: 67). Legal scholarship generally reflects the family to which its author belongs.

While there is no universally accepted set of legal families, the original six Member States of what is now the EU may be described as belonging to a single such family, that of the civil law. At considerable risk of oversimplification, it may be said that a characteristic feature of civil law countries is the importance they attach to codified abstract rules. The civil law tradition inevitably had a major influence on the design and development of the legal order of the then EC.

The first enlargement in 1973 brought into the Community two Member States – the United Kingdom and Ireland – from one of the world's other great legal families, that of the common law (though Scotland, albeit part of the UK, is a mixed legal system with common law and civil law features: ibid.: 201–2). The common law family also embraces many nations outside Europe including the United States of America. The special characteristic of the common law is the importance it attaches to decisions of the courts and the capacity it accords such decisions to bind other courts in the future in accordance with the doctrine of precedent.

Distinctions between the civil law and the common law systems should not be exaggerated: there is much judge-made law on the continent of Europe and a mass of legislation in the United Kingdom and Ireland (ibid.: 70). However, the visible distinctions between the two systems reflect underlying differences in modes of thought. In the context of the EU, those differences have given rise to much misunderstanding but also to a rich and enlightening dialogue.

This chapter is written from the perspective of someone trained in the common law system of England and Wales but who has worked, both in an academic and a practical context, alongside lawyers trained in the civil law system. This inevitably affects the view presented here of the development of EU law scholarship and the challenges it faces. However, the growing dominance of English as the main medium of communication about EU law (Shaw, 2003: 333–5), as well as the very nature of the subject, means that exchange between scholars from a variety of national backgrounds is perhaps more common in EU law than it is in some other areas of legal study.

Changing perspectives

The doctrinal tradition

In the United Kingdom, law was a late arrival in the academy. In the latter part of the nineteenth century, early British legal academics sought to establish their scholarly and professional credentials by organizing and analysing court judgments and focusing on what the law was rather than what it ought to be. Central to this endeavour was the legal text-book, which attempted to set out clearly and systematically the rules applicable in particular areas of the law and to deduce general principles on which those rules were based. Such textbooks were aimed principally at students intending to enter into legal practice (Sugarman, 1986).

This so-called 'doctrinal' or 'black-letter' tradition of legal writing became well established. In the years immediately following UK accession, it was reflected in the leading textbooks on EC law published in English (although by then academic writers did not hesitate to express views on what the law ought to be). Examples are Dominik Lasok and John Bridge's *An Introduction to the Law and Institutions of the European Communities* (1973); Derrick Wyatt and Alan Dashwood's *The Substantive Law of the EEC* (1980); and Trevor Hartley's *The Foundations of European Community Law* (1981). These were all doctrinal works of great authority in the classical English textbook tradition. Thus, the preface to Wyatt and Dashwood stated: 'our book is aimed first and foremost at students ... At the same time, it is hoped that the book will be useful to members of the legal profession' (1980: v). According to the foreword to Hartley, the purpose of the book was 'to describe the more general aspects of Community law, what one might call the constitutional and administrative law of the Community' (1981: v). Dashwood and Hartley came from South Africa, a country with a mixed legal system drawing on both the common law and the civil law (Zweigert and Kötz, 1998: 231–5). Like Edinburgh's John Mitchell and Birmingham's L. Neville Brown, a specialist in French law, they were particularly well placed to explain to a common law audience the essentially civilian legal system of the EC (Brown and Jacobs, 1977; Bates *et al.*, 1983).

British scholars writing about EC law were not out of line with their colleagues across the Channel. The authors referred to above were influenced by authoritative doctrinal works by continental European authors (e.g. Mégret, 1970; Schermers, 1976; Vandersanden and Barav, 1977). Indeed, until the 1980s, much of the literature on Community law had two essential characteristics: first, it was 'based on the exposition of legal doctrine and the analysis of judicial decisions' (Snyder, 1990: 1); second, it was essentially sympathetic to the integration project. Both characteristics reflected the backgrounds of the leading authors. Many were officials of one of the Community institutions (Schepel and Wesseling, 1997: 173). Of the academics who had been drawn to the study of Community law, many were specialists in public international law. That was a field in which scholars, preoccupied for much of the post-war period with establishing the relevance of international law to the way in which international life was ordered (Slaughter Burley, 1993), had tended to resort to 'a kind of positivist doctrinalism, that is a dry, seemingly value-free analysis of international rules, and, conversely, a general distrust of theory' (Twining *et al.*, 2003: 942). To academic writers who belonged to this school, Community law showed what treaties could achieve. As Joseph Weiler, then of the Harvard Law School and the European University Institute, Florence, explained:

> In some ways, Community law and the European Court were everything an international lawyer could dream about: the Court was creating a new order of international law in which norms were norms, sanctions were sanctions, courts were central and frequently used, and lawyers were important. Community law as transformed by the European Court was an antidote to the international legal malaise. (Weiler, 1999a: 205–6)

Nearly all writers, whatever their specialist background, 'embraced their subject with something approaching a missionary zeal' (Walker, 2005: 586). Community law was special 'because the European supranational project was an indisputably good cause, a triumph of rationality over the passions, of common interest over national insularity, and ... of law over politics' (ibid.). The absence of a 'powerful critical tradition' (Weiler, 1999a: 206) in Europe led such writers to see their main task as describing and analysing the intricacies of this 'new legal order'. Its gathering complexity made it hard for outsiders to challenge the prevailing orthodoxy. However, the winds of change were blowing from the other side of the Atlantic (Arnull, 2008: 421–4).

The American influence

In the early decades of the twentieth century, the American legal realists had attacked the idea that legal reasoning involved nothing more than logical deduction from first principles or general legal concepts

(Bix, 2003: 979). The realists saw the law as a tool designed to serve policy objectives. The extent to which it achieved those objectives therefore required analysis. The realist approach undermined what is sometimes called the autonomy of law, the notion that legal reasoning is self-sufficient and does not need to be supported by recourse to non-legal sources. If the crucial question was whether or not the law was achieving its policy objectives, then extra-legal considerations would sometimes have to be taken into account.

Until the 1960s, however, it was not widely thought that 'the keys to understanding law were held by disciplines other than law' (Posner, 1987: 763). All that was required, apart from a knowledge of legal texts and the ability to analyse and interpret them, was the general knowledge possessed by a reasonably well-educated person with a modicum of common sense. In the 1960s, the shattering of the political consensus caused the law to become 'deeply entangled with political questions' (ibid.: 767). At the same time, there was 'a boom in disciplines that are complementary to law', such as economics and philosophy. This led to the emergence in that decade of a new type of legal scholarship which involved the application to legal problems of perspectives drawn from other disciplines (ibid.: 772). If doctrinal analysts of the law identified more with the legal than the academic community, the emerging body of contextualists and interdisciplinarians saw themselves as part of the community of scholars rather than that of lawyers (Posner, 1981: 1122).

The trend towards interdisciplinarity seems to have been fuelled by the culture of the American legal academy. Richard Posner, an academic turned judge, suggested that the most imaginative scholars wanted to be 'innovators rather than imitators' and to 'strike out in a new direction' (Posner, 1987: 772). They found a ready audience among their students, already graduates in disciplines other than law, often political science. Traditional legal scholarship began to seem 'work for followers rather than leaders' (ibid.). That theme was taken up by Neil Duxbury, who underlined both the advantages and the disadvantages of this trend:

> What is especially noticeable is the extent to which American juristic culture has emphasized originality and counter-intuitiveness, and how, in the quest to exhibit these qualities, American legal academics – much as they often purport to behave otherwise – have tended increasingly to value legal scholarship by how visible and in vogue it happens to be. (Duxbury, 2003: 951)

Duxbury acknowledged 'the imaginativeness, particularly the capacity for lateral thinking, demonstrated by some American jurists with interdisciplinary leanings'. However, he went on to remark on 'an astonishing amount of cross-disciplinary chutzpah in the American law reviews.

American law professors ... are remarkably willing and confident to wander into disciplinary domains within which they have no professional training' (ibid.: 957).

The quantity and quality of American interdisciplinary literature on the law may have been affected by the prevalence in the United States of law reviews edited by students, perhaps too easily taken in by fashionable scholarship 'complete with the cute title, the epigraphs, the fusion of high theory and popular culture, and so on' (ibid.: 964). Posner went so far as to suggest that, while student editors were good at dealing with doctrinal scholarship, their failure to make regular use of referees to help in deciding which submissions should be published, or in offering contributors' suggestions for improvement, resulted in 'the publication of social scientific papers on law that should not be published at all, in the occasional failure to publish good papers, and in the publication of papers that would have been improved greatly by the publication process characteristic of academic fields other than law' (Posner, 1981: 1124).

Economics may also have influenced the changing character of American legal scholarship. It has been argued that the increasing demand for legal education in the US made American law schools richer and increased the number of law professors able to concentrate on academic work, to the exclusion of any involvement in practice (Twining *et al.*, 2003: 931). It has also been suggested that many doctrinal analysts in US law schools were enticed into practice by a growing disparity in salaries and the expectation of greater job satisfaction (Posner, 1981: 1117).

The American trend towards interdisciplinarity was not without its critics. In an article published in 1992, Harry Edwards, a judge and former academic, lambasted 'abstract scholarship that has little relevance to concrete issues, or addresses concrete issues in a wholly theoretical manner' (Edwards, 1992: 34). He believed 'that judges, administrators, legislators, and practitioners have little use for much of the scholarship that is now produced by members of the academy' (ibid.: 35). Edwards argued that there was no longer a 'healthy balance' between what he called 'impractical' and 'practical' scholars and lamented the 'waning *prestige*' of the latter within the academy (ibid.: 36). Support for this view was provided by Brian Bix, who commented: 'doctrinal work is still done [by American legal scholars], but it has been overshadowed (particularly in "high status" law journals) by interdisciplinary and theoretical work of various kinds' (Bix, 2003: 981). Duxbury concurred:

> By the 1980s, if not before then, this tendency of many [American] law professors to wander unself-consciously into other disciplinary domains was beginning to demoralise many of their doctrinally oriented colleagues, who felt that regular black-letter scholarship was

being undervalued: it seemed that law professors had an incentive to neglect that body of knowledge over which they had some expertise and begin professing on matters about which they had little or no expertise. (Duxbury, 2003: 957–8)

The effect on EU law scholarship

The change in the character of American legal scholarship eventually came to influence much academic writing about EU law in English, to which many American academics, or academics based in the US, were contributing (Arnull, 2008: 417–21). A famous 1981 piece by Eric Stein of the University of Michigan Law School (Stein, 1981) was an early sign of the break with doctrinal tradition. Also influential was Joseph Weiler's well-known article in the first volume of the *Yearbook of European Law* (Weiler, 1981).

The movement gathered pace in 1986 with the publication, under the general editorship of Mauro Cappelletti, Monica Seccombe and Weiler himself, of the multivolume series, *Integration Through Law*. That series was the fruit of a project, based at the European University Institute, which set out 'to examine the role of law in the process of European integration as seen against the American federal experience' (Cappelletti *et al.*, 1986: 3). In the same year, Hjalte Rasmussen published his polemical book on the ECJ (1986). Based on ideas that took root during a year he had spent at the University of Michigan Law School, Rasmussen focused on the political role of the Court, and its effect on policy-making, to argue that excessive activism was undermining its authority and legitimacy.

A further milestone was the appearance in 1990 of *New Directions in European Community Law* by Francis Snyder, then the holder of a chair in European Economic Law at the European University Institute (1990). *New Directions* represented a sort of manifesto based on ideas first put forward by the author elsewhere (see, in particular, Snyder, 1987). The first page boldly declared:

> So far European Community law has been conceived mainly as 'black-letter law' ... Now, however, it is time to draw upon perspectives from other social sciences and to move in new directions. We must place European Community law in its social, economic and political context. Only in this way can we achieve the deeper and broader understanding – both practical and theoretical – of European Community law that is required to meet the exciting challenges of our time. (Snyder, 1990: 1)

Snyder and Weiler were among the editors of the *European Law Journal*, launched in 1995. Subtitled 'Review of European Law in

Context' and based at the European University Institute, whose Law Department had always sought to foster a contextual approach, the first issue contained an editorial by Snyder. In it, he announced: 'the journal seeks to trace a new path. The *European Law Journal* aims to represent a new approach to European law. Its main purposes are to express and to develop the study and understanding of European law in its social, cultural, political and economic contexts' (Snyder, 1995: 1).

The same year saw the publication of Jo Shaw and Gillian More's *New Legal Dynamics of European Union*, a collection of essays written mainly by younger UK scholars. Shaw's introduction declared that the collection formed 'part of a trend towards broadening the focus of legal scholarship' on European integration. 'A more sophisticated understanding', she went on,

> of the interaction between law/legal norms and processes of integration/disintegration (in the various guises in which these terms can be understood) within all areas of European studies can enrich work on integration by highlighting the particular empirical and normative visions of lawyers. (Shaw and More, 1995: 1)

The year 1995 also witnessed the arrival of the first edition of Paul Craig and Grainne de Búrca's ground-breaking *EC Law: Text, Cases and Materials* (1995), which went on to become a best-selling student text. In a remark quoted on the back cover of the third edition published in 2003, Weiler revealingly described it as 'both a law book and a book about the law'. That distinction neatly encapsulated the difference between the old and the new styles of scholarship. It had been coined by Richard Abel in a review article published in 1973. Abel described a law book as 'a work of legal doctrine. It is a study of the rules which legal institutions apply, or which regulate the behaviour of those institutions'. By contrast, a book about law was:

> a mode of *reflection* upon the legal system. Neither legal training nor professional competence is adequate qualification to write about the legal system … For this reason, efforts to understand legal action have borrowed the perspectives of other intellectual disciplines; the social sciences and the humanities have all been used to illuminate legal phenomena. (Abel, 1973: 176)

In 1993, the German Federal Constitutional Court delivered its famous Maastricht decision, in which it declared that acts adopted by the EU which exceeded the powers conferred on it by the Member States would have no effect in Germany. That decision was impossible to reconcile with the case law of the ECJ. It provoked a torrent of academic writing about the relationship between national sovereignty and a

European legal order which proclaimed itself autonomous and supreme and the issue of so-called *Kompetenz-Kompetenz*: who has ultimate authority to determine the limits of the Union's powers? Is it the ECJ or the supreme courts of the Member States? These were existential questions which could not be fully resolved through conventional legal means. A leading protagonist in the debate was Neil MacCormick, the distinguished Scots legal theorist, whose influential book, *Questioning Sovereignty*, put forward the notion of 'constitutional pluralism' as a way of accommodating constitutional conflict (MacCormick, 1999: ch. 7, 104–5, 113–21).

An editorial published in the *European Law Review* in 2003 attempted to sum up the change in climate:

> Approaches to the study of EC/EU law are much more varied now than they were when the first issue [of the *Review*] was published in November 1975. The vastly enlarged scope of the Union's activities has required specialists in a range of other areas to familiarize themselves with the essential features of its legal order ... At the same time, as some of the momentous challenges facing Europe have seemed to call for more than just technical legal exposition, so the boundaries between the law and other disciplines, notably political science and economics, have become increasingly blurred. (Arnull, 2003: 1–2)

The influence of political scientists

The growth in contextual scholarship on EU law was fuelled by the discovery of the ECJ by the political science community following the success of the internal market programme (Armstrong, 1998; Wincott, 2003). Political scientists were intrigued by the 'spectre of a supranational court eliciting the obedience of states' (Conant, 2007: 47). The political science literature on the Court, and particularly the Court's relationship with the national courts of the Member States (e.g. Burley and Mattli, 1993; Conant, 2002; Stone Sweet, 2004), offered fresh and revealing insights into its role in making the Community work.

An example is the 'inter-court competition' thesis put forward by Karen Alter, a political scientist. The central claim of that thesis, a refinement of the notion of 'judicial empowerment' developed by Weiler (1999a: 197), was that 'different courts have different interests *vis-à-vis* EC law, and that national courts use EC law in bureaucratic struggles between levels of the judiciary and between the judiciary and political bodies, thereby inadvertently facilitating the process of legal integration' (Alter, 1997: 241). According to Alter, it was the difference between the interests of lower and higher courts that was crucial. She argued that the preliminary rulings procedure enabled the former to circumvent the case law of the latter by enlisting the help of the Court of Justice. It might as a corollary threaten the authority and independence of the higher national courts (Alter, 2001: 47–52).

It was also a political scientist who offered the most convincing explanation for the variation in the number of references from each Member State. A study of 11 of the then 12 Member States (all except Luxembourg) carried out by Jonathan Golub and published in late 1996 came to the startling conclusion that national reference rates could be explained almost entirely by quantifiable economic factors:

> transnational economic interaction, as well as transnational move-ment of people constitute the underlying determinants of national reference rates. Quantifiable variables such as intra-EC trade, intra-EC agricultural trade and EU foreign residents explain cross-national variation in patterns of judicial interaction between the ECJ and the Member States. (Golub, 1996a: 23)

Other considerations, such as population levels, national litigiousness, the number of courts and judges in a national system, knowledge of Community law among lawyers and judges and national legal cultures, did not explain the cross-national variation in the frequency of refer-ences. One Member State which did not follow this pattern was the United Kingdom, where the relationship between the number of refer-ences and economic factors was much weaker. Golub sought to explain the historically low reference rate of United Kingdom courts in a separate publication (Golub, 1996b).

Political science literature such as this gave added impetus to the growing interest among lawyers in contextual questions by suggesting new lines of enquiry which involved more than the traditional task of analysing legal sources.

Scholarship in civil law countries

A monoglot EU law scholar in a Member State belonging to the civil law tradition might not recognize this account. It is true that a distant precursor of the American realist movement could be detected in France around the end of the nineteenth century with the emergence of the *école de la libre recherche scientifique*. This was a reaction to the *école de l'exégèse*, whose adherents advocated strict compliance by judges with the text of the Code Civil enacted in 1804. When the limi-tations of that approach became apparent, the new school developed under the influence of legal writers, notably Gény and Saleilles (Bell *et al.*, 2008: 33–4). This 'allowed the judge a greater freedom with the text of the Code and encouraged him to construe the Code not simply logically and systematically, but in the light of the requirements of society as it developed, the actual usages and practices in the relevant areas of commerce, and also the results of the researches of sociologists and comparative lawyers' (Zweigert and Kötz, 1998: 96).

These ideas did not, however, produce as profound an impact as in the United States. In civil law countries, the role of academic lawyers is quite different to their role in countries belonging to the common law tradition (Vogenauer, 2006; Braun, 2006). 'Common Law comes from the court, Continental law from the study; the great jurists of England were judges, on the Continent professors' (Zweigert and Kötz, 1998: 69). Thus, in England there used to be a convention (now abandoned) that the authors of books and articles about the law could not be cited in court while they were still alive (Sugarman, 1986: 53–4). By contrast, in the civil law systems, legal writing (*la doctrine*) has long been accorded considerable significance by the courts, whose law-making function is not openly acknowledged. Important judgments are the subject of academic commentary which will be taken into account by the courts in the future. In the absence of a doctrine of binding precedent, a critical academic consensus against a judgment may result it its being revisited by the courts.

Legal writing also helps to systematize fields of law, particularly those which have never, or only recently, been codified. When a new code is introduced commentaries will soon appear (Twining *et al.*, 2003: 937; see also Vogenauer, 2006: 630). These shape analysis of the code before the courts have had a chance to pronounce on specific provisions. Even in areas which have been codified for some time, practitioners routinely turn to textbooks and commentaries for a concise account of the applicable rules and their place within the legal system as a whole.

In civil law countries, prevailing academic opinion may therefore be regarded 'as a "*de facto*" or "indirect" source of law with strong persuasive authority' (Twining *et al.*, 2003: 937; see also Vogenauer, 2006: 651–3; Braun, 2006: 677–8). Moreover, collective judgments and the absence of dissenting opinions mean that individual judges rarely enjoy the same prominence within the national legal community as their common law counterparts, who normally deliver individual judgments under their own names. 'Contrast this to the prestigious position of law professors whose names are associated with legal innovations, whose views are widely debated, and who, especially in Italy and France, have close connections to the political sphere and often get elected to the highest offices' (Twining *et al.*, 2003: 939; see also Vogenauer, 2006: 656).

That is not to say that there has been no movement in the direction travelled by academics in the US and the UK (see Twining *et al.*, 2003: 940; Bix, 2003: 981; Vogenauer, 2006: 661). Most EU law scholars are not monoglot and English has become their *lingua franca*. This has brought writers from different legal backgrounds into dialogue with each other and made them compete for contracts with the top publishers and space in the leading journals. The European University Institute is producing scholars from all over Europe and beyond who are imbued with its contextual and interdisciplinary ethos (Hunt and Shaw, 2008). But it remains the case that much civil law scholarship is largely doctrinal in character (Vogenauer, 2006: 657, 660).

Changing content

Substantive scope

Alongside the birth of these new methodologies, there has been a profound change in the substantive scope of the law of the EU since the SEA of 1986. Before then, EC law was regarded as having three basic components: the nature of the Community legal order (with a focus on the relationship between Community law and the national laws of the Member States); institutions and decision-making; and the common market (essentially the free movement of goods, persons and services, competition, and perhaps social policy). In the curriculum of a typical British university law school, Community law would be treated as a specialized subject much like company law or family law or employment law. It was not initially a 'core' subject that law students had to take in order to gain exemption from legal professional examinations.

The landscape has since been transformed. In terms of its extent (if not its nature), EU law now resembles not a specialist area of national law but a national system in its own right with its own specialist areas: the area of freedom, security and justice; the protection of fundamental rights; external relations; EC company law; EC intellectual property law; EC consumer law; EC environmental law; EC energy law; the law of economic and monetary union – one could go on. This has had at least two consequences. First, it has meant that EU law is no longer regarded as an arcane subject of interest only to a few enthusiasts. It is now taken seriously by national lawyers who have found their own areas of specialization increasingly affected by it. Conversely, EU law specialists have found it more and more difficult to keep abreast of developments across the entire field and necessary to specialize within it. Just as no one could seriously claim expert knowledge of English or French or American law, only the foolhardy would now claim expertise in EU law as a whole.

Effect

There are two reasons why in the present context the growth in the substantive scope of the law of the EU matters. One is that it has affected the intellectual climate. The enthusiasm for the integration process that characterized much of the early literature on EC law was less evident in the new contextual and interdisciplinary literature that began to appear in the 1980s. The climate became even more critical when contributions to the literature began to be made by specialists in areas of national law which were being increasingly affected by EC initiatives. These specialists were likely to be unforgiving when such initiatives seemed to disrupt national legal frameworks which had been carefully crafted over long periods of time. The result is that scholarship on EU law is no longer the preserve of disciples of Jean Monnet. This to some extent mirrors contemporary attitudes to the EU among the general public and should be welcomed: academics ought to subject the EU to critical scrutiny.

The second reason is at once more technical and less benign. It is that the inability of specialists to keep track of the field as a whole may lead to its fragmentation. Why is this important? The uniform application of Community law has traditionally been treated as essential because the internal market could not function if the relevant rules did not have the same effect in all the Member States. The famous preliminary rulings procedure, which enables national judges to ask the ECJ for guidance on questions of Community law that need to be decided before they give judgment, reflects this concern. It is also reflected in the Treaty provisions governing recourse to the Court of Justice from the European Court of First Instance, which in some cases is only permitted where there is a threat to 'the unity or consistency of Community law' (see Article 225(2) and (3) of the EC Treaty). Within the Court of Justice, a case may be assigned to the Grand Chamber (composed of 13 of the 27 judges) or even the full Court (composed of all the judges) if it wishes to correct an inconsistency that may have emerged in the case law of smaller formations. A properly functioning internal market remains a cornerstone of the Union and the consistency of its various policies is essential to its capacity to achieve its objectives. That capacity risks being undermined if legal scholars and practitioners do not, as part of their training, receive a reliable account of general principles or are unable subsequently to keep that account up to date.

Future challenges

The challenges confronting legal scholars working on the EU in the early twenty-first century are therefore both methodological and substantive.

Methodology

Methodologically speaking, the European legal academy needs to find a way of encouraging contextual and interdisciplinary writing, while at the same time continuing to nurture doctrinal work. This proposition is not controversial. Duxbury, contrasting legal scholarship in the United States and England, observes: 'to put the point crudely, the English have preferred the microscope to the telescope, the Americans vice versa; both preferences can be commended, and both can be criticized' (Duxbury, 2003: 972). Bix argues that 'there is now some risk that scholars will underestimate the autonomy of law – not give enough attention to what is specific to law and to legal reasoning. It remains valuable to focus on what is distinctive to law' (Bix, 2003: 976). There is, he says, 'a measure of autonomy not only in legal reasoning generally, but also some autonomy in the reasoning of each individual legal system' (ibid.: 984). The multiple legal autonomies represented in the EU are perhaps one of the features that make its law such a rich subject for both doctrinal and contextual study. The importance of balance was also recognized in the documentation relating to the 2008 UK Research Assessment Exercise. The Law Unit of Assessment was described as including 'all doctrinal, theoretical, empirical, comparative or other studies of law and legal phenomena' (RAE, 2006: 23). The Law subpanel announced that it would assess the significance of the research outputs submitted to it 'in a way that takes into account the diversity of academic research in law' (ibid.: 24).

Some of the leading American protagonists in the debate would approve. Edwards, perhaps the harshest critic of the theoretical turn in US legal scholarship, was at pains to emphasize that he did 'not doubt for a moment the importance of theory in legal scholarship' and that 'it is undoubtedly valuable for law students to learn economics or moral theory' (Edwards, 1992: 35, 39). His main point, he said, was that 'pure theory should not wholly displace the production of treatises or articles that, *inter alia*, focus on legal doctrine' (ibid.: 57). Essentially the same view was held by Posner, an economic analyst of law (Posner, 1981: 1115), described by Edwards as 'a pioneer of "law and" scholarship' (Edwards, 1992: 36). Posner maintained that 'disinterested legal-doctrinal analysis of the traditional kind remains the indispensable core of legal thought' (Posner, 1987: 777). Indeed, in the early 1980s he advocated action by law schools 'to attract and retain lawyers who will do doctrinal research, a form of legal scholarship whose importance has not been diminished by the growth of other forms' (Posner, 1981: 1129).

The need for catholicity in approaches to EU law is also recognized by prominent theoretical scholars of the subject. Snyder, for example, acknowledges that teaching and research in EC law should continue 'certain established lines of enquiry. This includes the tradition of highly sophisticated scholarship concerning legal doctrine' (Snyder, 1990: 14). Contextual and interdisciplinary study, he thought, would partly build on this work. Kenneth Armstrong cautions against political science accounts of the Court of Justice 'without law' (Armstrong, 1998: 158). Shaw concedes that some of the European studies literature on EU law 'could itself be strengthened by a greater sensitivity to the specificities of the law and of legal norms' (Shaw and More, 1995: 10; cf. Walker, 2005: 588–9).

If a climate of diversity is to be fostered, tolerance needs to be extended across disciplinary boundaries and latent hostility between different camps dispelled. As Hunt and Shaw explain, 'there is inevitably something of a disciplinary scepticism held by one academic community towards another' (Hunt and Shaw, 2008). Lawyers may regard political science literature as written by people who have not actually read the legislation or the cases and have made sometimes elementary mistakes about the true legal position. They may find some of its conclusions banal. Thus, Conant refers to a consensus among political scientists on two findings: 'the ECJ does not appear to favour large over small states and is most likely to agree with the legal analysis of the Commission' (Conant, 2007: 53). For their part, political scientists may find legal scholarship – perhaps even this chapter – dry and technical and devoid of theoretical basis. Conant observes that legal scholarship:

> tends to be factually descriptive and/or normatively prescriptive ... political scientists may consider the evidence presented in legal scholarship to be anecdotal and find arguments about the evolution of law to be conflated with normative philosophy about the way an author wishes case law to develop rather than an empirically grounded account of the current state of law. (Conant, 2007: 46–7)

Within the discipline of law, the law school 'must make itself ... a place where scholars of different approaches and ideologies accord each other the mutual respect they deserve' (Edwards, 1992: 51). Unfortunately, the modern American tendency to marginalize doctrinal scholarship has sometimes infected EU law scholarship. A well-known early example is the response of Martin Shapiro, a political scientist and professor of law at the University of California, Berkeley, to a paper by Ami Barav, then one of Europe's leading scholars of EC law. Barav's paper, he said,

> is a careful and systematic exposition of the judicial review provisions of the 'constitution' of the European Economic Community, an exposition that is helpful for a newcomer to these materials. But it represents a stage of constitutional scholarship out of which American constitutional law must have passed about seventy years ago (although remnants of it are still to be found). It is constitutional law without politics. Professor Barav presents the Community as a juristic idea; the written constitution as a sacred text; the

professional commentary as a legal truth; the case law as the inevitable working out of the correct implications of the constitutional text; and the constitutional court as the disembodied voice of right reason and constitutional teleology. (Shapiro, 1980: 538)

Shapiro's remarks are dripping with disdain. Barav's paper is of no value to anyone other than 'a newcomer' to the subject. It represents a type of scholarship which has become almost completely outmoded in more advanced (that is, American) academic circles. The premises on which it is based are absurd. Yet there is evidence that doctrinal scholars can be equally dismissive of other approaches to legal scholarship. In her book, *Legal Academics: Culture and Identities*, Cownie observed that the existence of 'fundamentally different approaches to law clearly brings with it the possibility of conflict between legal academics'. While acknowledging that 'conflict of the extreme kind experienced in some US law schools appeared to be unknown among the English legal academics I interviewed', Cownie drew attention to 'the attempted marginalisation of socio-legal scholars' and student resistance to approaches other than the traditional doctrinal one (Cownie, 2004: 59).

Substance

On the substantive side, few would now deny that all European law students should have some knowledge of EU law. Indeed, EU law became a 'core' subject for law degrees conferring exemption from legal professional examinations in England and Wales in 1995. There may, however, be less agreement than there once was about what the core should comprise. When dealing with decision-making, can one make sense of the current procedures without considering earlier iterations? To what extent is it necessary to deal with comitology and the open method of coordination? To what extent should one deal with national case law on the effect of EU law in the legal orders of the Member States? To what extent should one cover the second and third pillars (a dilemma that would not be wholly dispelled by the Treaty of Lisbon)? After the Charter, how much attention should be given to the protection of fundamental rights and the prospect of EU accession to the European Convention on Human Rights? Is it necessary to deal with the free movement of capital (the Treaty provisions on which were fundamentally recast at Maastricht) alongside the free movement of goods, persons and services? If so, does one also cover the law of economic and monetary union? How in a general course can one say anything meaningful about EC competition law, a huge subject which has long been the subject of comparative and interdisciplinary analysis? How does one tell the story of the Constitutional Treaty and the Treaty of Lisbon? In research-led law schools, the way such questions are answered is likely to both reflect and shape the scholarly interests of those involved in teaching the subject.

The difficulty of keeping up with developments across the whole range of the Union's competences is not confined to scholars: it is far from clear that the Court of Justice has the range of expertise necessary to deal effectively with the growing diversity of its case load. Under the present system, members of the Court are appointed by the Member States acting collectively on the basis of national nominations (see Article 223 of the EC Treaty). Although the Treaty deals with the personal qualifications required of members (essentially competence and independence), it does not say anything about the needs of the institution as a whole. Moreover, where there is more than one vacancy, there is no formal mechanism for coordinating national nominations. This makes it difficult to ensure the appointment of members with expertise in areas of emerging importance. The Treaty of Lisbon would require Member States to consult a panel of senior lawyers before making an appointment (see Article 255 of the Treaty on the Functioning of the EU). That panel would be able to comment on the appropriateness of a nominee's expertise, but the final decision would remain with the Member States. They are traditionally reluctant to override national nominations and it seems unlikely that a Member State would withdraw a nomination at that late stage of the procedure except in wholly exceptional cases. The Court's origins lie in the civil rather than the common law tradition and it has become common for its Advocates General to refer to legal scholarship in their opinions. Against that background, expert scholarly analysis can provide a measure of assistance to the Court in dealing with cases in new areas in which its members lack expertise.

The 2004 and 2007 enlargements have brought a range of further challenges. Some replicate those of earlier enlargements: the need to educate national lawyers in the new Member States (though that task becomes ever more difficult as the substantive scope of Union law grows); the need to persuade national courts to accept and apply unfamiliar concepts. But the history since the end of the Second World War of the 12 new entrants differs fundamentally from that of the other 15 Member States. The new entrants face particular difficulties in adapting to the legal demands of membership and may find it especially hard to accept doctrines like the primacy of Union law and State liability in damages for breaching that law. All this offers a rich vein of material for academic scrutiny and analysis. At the same time, scholarly examination of the 'judicial architecture' of the Union is likely to continue as the Court of Justice and the Court of First Instance grapple with the implications of enlargement for their working methods and caseload (Wallace, 2007: 16–19).

Conclusion

EU law as a subject of academic study has changed radically since the accession of the United Kingdom to the then EC in 1973. Then the subject was the preserve of specialists, many of whom were self-taught. Now the subject has entered the mainstream of the discipline of law, one which must be approached as *both* a distinct system of its own *and* an integral part of the legal systems of the Member States. Its substantive content has grown exponentially with successive revisions of the Treaties. This process has confronted specialists with the challenge of familiarizing themselves with new areas and reappraising the fundamental principles of the legal order whilst offering them the opportunity to specialize in new fields.

On top of this, there has been a huge growth in contextual and interdisciplinary literature about legal issues, some of it written by lawyers, some of it written by academics working in other disciplines. Doctrinal work may as a result sometimes seem unfashionable, but there is perhaps something inherent in the European project that makes it unlikely ever to be eclipsed. So much of EU law involves the application of common rules within a variety of national legal frameworks, the replacement of divergent national rules in particular areas with common European standards, and the adoption at the level of the Union of principles and values derived from the national systems. These exercises raise issues of enormous doctrinal complexity which call out for scholarly analysis. Reinhard Zimmermann looks forward to the emergence of an 'organically progressive' legal science transcending national boundaries and supplying 'a common legal "grammar" for discussing general legal questions and evaluating possible solutions' (Zimmermann, 1996: 605). This is surely more a task for doctrinalists than for contextualists and interdisciplinarians.

Moreover, as suggested above, doctrinal writers provide the foundations on which contextual and theoretical accounts of EU law are built. This may be illustrated by Weiler's book, *The Constitution of Europe*, where he says, in the context of the protection of human rights in the Community legal order, that the story of the leading cases:

> has been told so many times as to obviate the necessity of recapitulation. Likewise, of equal tedium is the investigation into the legal basis and formal constitutional legitimacy of this act of so-called judicial activism by the European Court whereby the Court put in place, or discovered, an unwritten Bill of Rights against which to check the legality of Community measures. (Weiler, 1999a: 108)

The reader is then referred to another author's work for an account of the doctrinal background (though Weiler's use of the word 'tedium' is telling). Similarly, in a paper on the free movement of goods, Weiler announces: 'I will present snapshots of some of the most significant cases in the area of free movement of goods, cases so well known as to obviate the necessity of any detailed description' (Weiler, 1999b: 350).

This approach is only possible because other writers have conducted the necessary doctrinal analysis (Cownie, 2004: 55). Indeed, in the first footnote to his paper on the free movement of goods, Weiler acknowledges his intellectual debt to what he calls a 'Pentateuch' of 'masters', at least two of which are classical works of doctrinal analysis (Weiler, 1999b: 349). The danger is that theoretical and contextual writers may feel absolved of the need to set out the premises on which their claims are based. Readers who are unfamiliar with the doctrinal literature, or who lack the training necessary to engage with the primary sources, may consequently form an inaccurate view of the law and the way in which legal uncertainty has been confronted. This reinforces the need for clear and accessible doctrinal analysis of both legislative texts and the decisions of the courts.

As in other fields of legal scholarship, however, the influence of contextual and interdisciplinary literature has been such that few academic writers on EU law are now doctrinal in the old sense of confining themselves to describing the rules without regard to their context. Indeed, there are now books which show how doctrinal and contextual approaches to law might be integrated (e.g. Craig and de Búrca, 1995; Dehousse, 1998; Chalmers *et al.*, 2006). We are nearly all contextual now, though some are undoubtedly more so than others.

References

Abel, R. (1973) 'Law Books and Books about Law', *Stanford Law Review* 26: 175–228.

Alter, K. (1997) 'Explaining National Court Acceptance of European Court Jurisprudence: A Critical Evaluation of Theories of Legal Integration', in A.-M. Slaughter, A. Stone Sweet and J. Weiler (eds) *The European Court and National Courts – Doctrine and Jurisprudence* (Oxford: Hart Publishing) 227–52.

Alter, K. (2001) *Establishing the Supremacy of European Law: The Making of an International Rule of Law in Europe* (Oxford: Oxford University Press).

Armstrong, K. (1998) 'Legal Integration: Theorizing the Legal Dimension of European Integration', *Journal of Common Market Studies* 36: 155–74.

Arnull, A. (2003) 'The Future of the European Law Review', *European Law Review* 28: 1–2.

Arnull, A. (2008) 'The Americanization of EU Law Scholarship' in A. Arnull, P. Eeckhout and T. Tridimas (eds) *Continuity and Change in EU Law: Essays in Honour of Sir Francis Jacobs* (Oxford: Oxford University Press) 415–31.

Bates, S.J., Finnie, W., Usher, J. and Wildberg, H. (eds) (1983) *In Memoriam J.D.B. Mitchell* (London: Sweet & Maxwell).

Bell, J., Boyron, S. and Whittaker, S. (2008) *Principles of French Law*, 2nd edn (Oxford: Oxford University Press).

Bix, B. (2003) 'Law as an Autonomous Discipline' in Cane, P. and Tushnet, M. (eds) *The Oxford Handbook of Legal Studies* (Oxford: Oxford University Press) 975–87.

Braun, A. (2006) 'Professors and Judges in Italy: It Takes Two to Tango', *Oxford Journal of Legal Studies* 26: 665–81.

Brown, L.N. and Jacobs, F. (1977) *The Court of Justice of the European Communities*, 1st edn (London: Sweet & Maxwell).

Burley, A.-M. and Mattli, W. (1993) 'Europe Before the Court: A Political Theory of Legal Integration', *International Organization* 47(1): 41–76.

Cappelletti, M., Seccombe, M. and Weiler, J. (eds) (1986) *Integration Through Law: Europe and the American Federal Experience, Volume 1, Book 1*, (Berlin: Walter de Gruyter).

Chalmers, D., Hadjiemmanuil, C., Monti, G. and Tomkins, A. (2006) *European Union Law* (Cambridge: Cambridge University Press).

Conant, L. (2002) *Justice Contained: Law and Politics in the European Union* (Ithaca and London: Cornell University Press).

Conant, L. (2007) 'Review Article: The Politics of Legal Integration', *Journal of Common Market Studies Annual Review of the European Union in 2006* 45(1): 45–66.

Cownie, F. (2004) *Legal Academics: Culture and Identities* (Oxford: Hart Publishing).

Craig, P. and de Búrca, G. (1995) *EC Law: Text, Cases and Materials* (Oxford: Oxford University Press).

Dehousse, R. (1998) *The European Court of Justice: The Politics of Judicial Integration* (London: Macmillan).

Duxbury, N. (2003) 'A Century of Legal Studies' in P. Cane and M. Tushnet (eds) *The Oxford Handbook of Legal Studies* (Oxford: Oxford University Press) 950–74.

Edwards, H. (1992) 'The Growing Disjunction Between Legal Education and the Legal Profession', *Michigan Law Review* 91: 34–78.

Golub, J. (1996a) 'Modelling Judicial Dialogue in the European Community: The Quantitative Basis of Preliminary References to the ECJ', European University Institute Working Paper RSC No 96/58.

Golub, J. (1996b) 'The Politics of Judicial Discretion: Rethinking the Interaction Between National Courts and the European Court of Justice', *West European Politics* 19(2): 360–85.

Hartley, T. (1981) *The Foundations of European Community Law* (Oxford: Clarendon Press).

Hunt, J. and Shaw, J. (2008) 'Fairy Tale of Luxembourg? Reflections on Law and Legal Scholarship in European Integration' in Phinnemore, D. and Warleigh Lack, A. (eds) *Reflections on European Integration: 50 Years of the Treaty of Rome* (Basingstoke: Palgrave Macmillan): forthcoming.

Lasok, D. and Bridge, J. (1973) *An Introduction to the Law and Institutions of the European Communities* (London: Butterworth).

MacCormick, N. (1999) *Questioning Sovereignty: Law, State, and Nation in the European Commonwealth* (Oxford: Oxford University Press).

Mégret, J. (1970–) (ed.) *Le droit de la Communauté économique européenne: commentaire du traité et des textes pris pour son application* (Brussels: Editions de l'Université de Bruxelles).

Posner, R. (1981) 'The Present Situation in Legal Scholarship', *Yale Law Journal* 90: 1113–30.

Posner, R. (1987) 'The Decline of Law as an Autonomous Discipline: 1962–1987', *Harvard Law Review* 100: 761–80.

RAE (Research Assessment Exercise) (2006) 'Panel Criteria and Working Methods, Panel J,' RAE 01/2006 (J) (Higher Education Funding Council for England).

Rasmussen, H. (1986) *On Law and Policy in the European Court of Justice: A Comparative Study in Judicial Policymaking* (Dordrecht: Martinus Nijhoff).

Schepel, H. and Wesseling, R. (1997) 'The Legal Community: Judges, Lawyers, Officials and Clerks in the Writing of Europe', *European Law Journal* 3: 165–88.

Schermers, H. (1976) *Judicial Protection in the European Communities* (Deventer: Kluwer).

Shapiro, M. (1980) 'Comparative Law and Comparative Politics', *Southern California Law Review* 53: 537–42.

Shaw, J. (2003) 'The European Union: Discipline Building Meets Polity Building' in P. Cane and M. Tushnet (eds) *The Oxford Handbook of Legal Studies* (Oxford: Oxford University Press).

Shaw, J. and More, G. (eds) (1995) *New Legal Dynamics of European Union* (Oxford: Clarendon Press).

Slaughter Burley, A.-M. (1993) 'International Law and International Relations Theory: A Dual Agenda', *American Journal of International Law* 87: 205–39.

Snyder, F. (1987) 'New Directions in European Community Law', *Journal of Law and Society* 14: 167–82.

Snyder, F. (1990) *New Directions in European Community Law* (London: Weidenfeld and Nicolson).

Snyder, F. (1995) 'Editorial', *European Law Journal* 1: 1–4.

Stein, E. (1981) 'Lawyers, Judges, and the Making of a Transnational Constitution', *American Journal of International Law* 75: 1–27.

Stone Sweet, A. (2004) *The Judicial Construction of Europe* (Oxford: Oxford University Press).

Sugarman, D. (1986) 'Legal Theory, the Common Law Mind and the Making of the Textbook Tradition' in W. Twining (ed.) *Legal Theory and Common Law*, (Oxford: Basil Blackwell).

Twining, W., Farnsworth, W., Vogenauer, S. and Tesán, F. (2003) 'The Role of Academics in the Legal System' in P. Cane and M. Tushnet (eds) *The Oxford Handbook of Legal Studies* (Oxford: Oxford University Press) 920–49.

Vandersanden, G. and Barav, A. (1977) *Contentieux Communautaire* (Brussels: Bruylant).

Vogenauer, S. (2006) 'An Empire of Light? II: Learning and Lawmaking in Germany Today', *Oxford Journal of Legal Studies* 26: 627–63.

Walker, N. (2005) 'Legal Theory and the European Union: A 25th Anniversary Essay', *Oxford Journal of Legal Studies* 25: 581–601.

Wallace, H. (2007) 'Adapting to Enlargement of the European Union: Institutional Practice since May 2004' (Brussels: Trans European Policy Studies Association).

Weiler, J. (1981) 'The Community System: The Dual Character of Supranationalism', *Yearbook of European Law* 1: 267–306.

Weiler, J. (1999a) *The Constitution of Europe: 'Do the New Clothes have an Emperor?' and other Essays on European Integration* (Cambridge: Cambridge University Press).

Weiler, J. (1999b) 'The Constitution of the Common Market Place: Text and Context in the Evolution of the Free Movement of Goods' in P. Craig and G. de Búrca (eds) *The Evolution of EU Law* (Oxford: Oxford University Press).

Wincott, D. (2003) 'Containing (Social) Justice? Rights, EU Law and the Recasting of Europe's "Social Bargains"', *European Law Review* 28: 735–49.

Wyatt, D. and Dashwood, A. (1980) *The Substantive Law of the EEC* (London: Sweet & Maxwell).

Zimmermann, R. (1996) 'Savigny's Legacy: Legal History, Comparative Law, and the Emergence of a European Legal Science', *Law Quarterly Review* 112: 576–605.

Zweigert, K. and Kötz, H. (1998) *Introduction to Comparative Law*, tr. T. Weir (3rd edn) (Oxford: Clarendon Press).

Chapter 9

New Directions in Europeanization Research

Claudio M. Radaelli and Theofanis Exadaktylos[1]

Fifty years since the inception of European integration, political scientists are increasingly attracted by the theoretical and empirical puzzles of how to establish if and how the EU has changed representation, governance and public policy in the member states and beyond. Broadly speaking, this is the domain of Europeanization research. In this chapter, we first make the argument that the concern with Europeanization is somewhat in the genes of the academic study of European integration. In a sense, this field of research has always existed. But in another sense, Europeanization as a distinct research field is increasingly prominent, as shown by several literature reviews and internet sites[2] dedicated to this topic (Olsen, 2002; Börzel and Risse, 2003; Graziano and Vink, 2007; Lenschow, 2005; Axt *et al.*, 2007; Schimmelfennig, 2007).

Accordingly, we will first present classic ways to make observable propositions about Europeanization, rooted in neofunctionalist and liberal intergovernmentalist integration theories, multilevel governance, and comparative public policy. Then we will move on to the more recent field that is commonly associated with the label 'Europeanization'. One point throughout the chapter is that Europeanization is not a new theory, but provides interesting ways to engage with existing theories of international politics, theories of the policy process and theories of governance. Hence, before we set out to search for the Holy Grail of the new Europeanization theory (something that does not exist and in our view should not even exist), we need to reflect on if and how Europeanization *concepts*, *mechanisms*, and *explanations* add to our theoretical *acquis*. If they add something useful, they can corroborate existing theories, rather than requiring the development of a new theory.

After discussing definitional and conceptual issues, we will introduce the substantive scope and the territorial extension of Europeanization. The next step will be entirely dedicated to explanation: what do the existing models explain and how? This will bring us right into the territory of causal explanation. We will look at a sample of highly cited articles to review the causal structure of scholarship on Europeanization. We will then compare our sample with more recent articles to see whether the field is going in some new directions or, alternatively, whether the highly cited articles have somewhat already formatted the field. In concluding we will take stock of our analysis and present some questions for future research.

Classic (but implicit) expectations about Europeanization

As mentioned, Europeanization has always been around scholarly work on European integration politics. In this section we consider classic integration theories, the relatively more recent approaches of multilevel governance and historical institutionalism, and the comparative public policy research on compliance, transposition of EU legislation and implementation.

Classic theories of European integration do not use the language of Europeanization, yet they come very close to formulating clear observable predictions on how integration processes transform state structures (a point made by Bulmer, 2006). For neofunctionalists, integration shifts loyalty and political dynamics from the national to the EU level. In this logic, policies like the single market and the EMU, established with the Treaty on European Union (TEU) (1992), make the economic fate of the eurozone countries one and indivisible. The ECJ has redefined the scope and role of national legislation versus EU law – a massive displacement of power from national legislatures to the Community of Courts operating in the EU (Stone Sweet and Brunell, 1998). Pressure groups and transnational society reorient their activity towards the EU level, following the power shift towards Brussels. The institutionalization of Europe (Stone Sweet and Sandholtz, 1997) provides an expectation about Europeanization: the nation state will gradually dissolve some of its essential properties into the institutions of the EU. In this context, recent work has shown that the institutionalization of the single market has not created deregulated economies. Political power has not been significantly reduced to the advantage of the market. Rather, it has been shifted towards the EU institutions (Jabko, 2006).

The expectations of liberal-intergovernmentalist theories of European integration could not be more different. Historians like Alan Milward and political scientists like Andrew Moravcsik have argued that integration makes the nation state stronger, not weaker (Milward, 1992; Moravcsik, 1998). This is because national leaders enter EU negotiations with preferences that are often well defined. If they know what they want, member states negotiate EU institutional bargains only when there is an economic or political benefit from cooperation. They then 'lock in' the outcome of their bargain in an institutional choice, typically by signing a treaty (Moravcsik, 1999). Integration Europeanizes national politics in the sense of creating more executive capacity to deal with international political and economic externalities, and also by increasing the power of the executive in relation to elected assemblies and pressure groups. The previous example of EMU can therefore be seen in a totally different way. EMU – the argument goes – has made the core executives stronger. In some cases it has been a lever for domestic, government-led reforms that would have otherwise been blocked by Parliament and the unions (on Italy see Della Sala, 1997; Dyson and Featherstone, 1996).

A second way in which existing theoretical work has shed light on the dynamics of Europeanization arises out of the conceptual approaches labelled 'multilevel governance' (MLG) (Hooghe and Marks, 2001) and historical institutionalism (HI) (Pierson, 2004; Bulmer, 2009). MLG designates a profound transformation of politics that integrates both vertical and horizontal levels in dense networks. In turn, these networks involve both public and private actors. For multilevel governance theorists, therefore, Europeanization is a process in which power is redefined (within networks) as much as it is redistributed (between centre and periphery, between state actors and private actors). In HI, Europeanization is a process of slow but big movements – in contrast with the intergovernmental emphasis on treaties, HI scholars are more interested in what goes on between one treaty revision and another (Pierson, 2006). In HI theorizing, Europeanization would look like the evolutionary process through which unforeseen contingencies (such as ECJ decisions) lock in the member states in temporal causal sequences that are difficult to revert.[3]

A third, and classic, way to study Europeanization, yet again without explicitly having used this term until recently, is through comparative public policy analysis, and more particularly through examining the transposition of EU law into national legislation, compliance with EU rules and more generally implementation (Dimitrakopoulos and Richardson, 2001; Falkner *et al.*, 2005). Since no perfect implementation is possible, this strand of research does not argue that Europeanization will make the national and EU level systems more similar (with power all redirected towards the EU institutions, or recalibrated around national executives, or meshed in policy networks). The expectation is one of variable country and policy outcomes. A key reason for this is that responses to European integration depend on implementation capacity and bureaucratic cultures, both of which vary. National bureaucracies may have become the agents of implementation of EU policies at the domestic level, but whilst the EU proposes a model of delivery based on new public management values of control – via evaluation, autonomy and bureaucratic legitimacy by efficient results and intense consultation with stakeholders – bureaucracies in countries as diverse as France, Germany and Italy are anchored in cultures of parliamentary control and the separation of politics and administration (Damonte, 2007).

Definitional issues

Expectations about Europeanization can be drawn from propositions put forward by integration theorists and comparative analysts. But the field that we nowadays associate with Europeanization is distinctively different, for three important reasons. First, it takes the issue of defining the nature, substantive scope and territorial extension of Europeanization explicitly. A difference with integration theories is that these theories are concerned with the explanation of the ontology of European integration (that is, why do the member states create institutions at the EU level?), whilst Europeanization scholars take the presence of EU institutions for granted and explore 'post-ontologically' how the political system of the EU is or is not transforming the state, party politics and public policies. Second, it goes beyond the narrow focus of classic integration theories with state structures and the emphasis of implementation studies on public policies. Without denying these important dimensions, Europeanization as a research programme covers politics, policy and polity, as shown by Vivien Schmidt (2002, 2006). Third, Europeanization is more theoretically and methodologically aware of the problems of explaining processes, whilst the classic reasoning is arguably more concerned with outcomes. In fact, most scholars see it as a process, not an outcome. The interest in outcomes has not withered away, but at the margin more efforts are put into describing how Europeanization as process affects policy, politics and polity, and with what consequences it affects the nature of governance, identities and representation at the national and subnational level.

Turning to definitions, it is fair to say that this is a still contested domain. However, there is some common ground in the definitions that have been proposed over the last ten years or so. One point that most definitions have in common is the identification of Europeanization with the domestic impact of European integration. This is what Lenschow, in her recent textbook review, calls the *top-down* view of the concept (Lenschow, 2005). All scholars accept that this is a dimension of Europeanization, but some think there are also *bottom-up* dimensions, and, perhaps *roundabout* effects too (ibid.) – in essence, a circular process with multiple feedback loops. Let us briefly look at some examples of definitions.

Risse *et al.* (2001: 3) include within Europeanization 'the emergence and development at the European level of distinct structures of governance'. Héritier (2001: 3) and her associates contribute to the top-down approaches by specifying that Europeanization is 'a process of influence deriving from European decisions and impacting on member states' policies and political administrative structures'. Olsen's (2002) four-way definition is the most inclusive, covering diverse issues such as adjustment to Europe and the process of political integration. Giuliani

(2004) instead goes for a strict definition, calling Europeanization the process of institutionalization of Europe. Dyson and Goetz (2003: 20) seem to be informed by circular notions of the concept when they speak of a 'complex interactive top-down and bottom-up process in which domestic polities, politics and public policies are shaped by European integration and in which domestic actors use European integration to shape the domestic arena'. Bomberg and Peterson (2000) collapse Europeanization to the horizontal transfer of policies – and by doing so, they shed light on diffusion across the member states. Indeed, by using Europeanization in this way they suggest that mutual influence, transfer, benchmarking and lesson-drawing do not necessarily presuppose that the EU is there all the time to provide Europeanizing templates. A country can also imitate or import or learn from another bilaterally, although the EU often provides the architectures and the procedures for horizontal transfer, like in the case of the open method of coordination (de la Porte and Pochet, 2002; Zeitlin *et al.*, 2005; Nedergaard, 2007).

But though broad definitions are useful, they obviously suffer from lack of precision. For example, what does 'to shape the domestic arena' mean in terms of clearly measurable processes and outcomes? And if Europeanization is also the path to political integration, how do we disentangle positive from normative issues? Further, if Europeanization covers the emergence of EU structures as well as the impact of these structures on domestic systems, we may not see the difference between ontological and post-ontological analysis mentioned above.

Ladrech has made an important step with his notion of 'an incremental process reorienting the direction and shape of politics to the degree that EU and political dynamics become part of the organizational logic of national politics and policy-making' (Ladrech, 1994: 69). Drawing on Ladrech, Radaelli has argued that Europeanization consists of processes, rather than outcomes. Specifically, processes of (a) construction; (b) diffusion; and (c) institutionalization of formal and informal rules, procedures, policy paradigms, styles and 'ways of doing things'. It also consists of shared beliefs and norms that are first defined and consolidated in the EU policy process and then incorporated in the logic of domestic (national and subnational) discourse, identities, political structures, and public policies (Radaelli, 2003: 30). Thus, Europeanization is an interactive process, rather than a simple process of unidirectional reaction to 'Europe'. It covers both the notion of Europeanization as 'domestic impact of Europe' (or pressure) and Europeanization as creative usages of Europe (Jacquot and Woll, 2004).

In this approach, the presence of a clearly defined European policy is neither a sufficient nor a necessary condition for Europeanization to take place. If a clearly defined EU policy exists, the system of interaction at the domestic level may or may not be influenced. It depends, as

Ladrech would put it, on whether the EU policy template is incorporated in the organizational logic of the domestic constellations of actors or not. Without policy instructions from Brussels, and even without decisions to create EU public policy *tout court*, domestic constellations of actors can still be influenced by the ideas, discussions, suggested policy templates, etc. discussed in the EU arena. What is necessary for Europeanization to occur (albeit not sufficient) is the presence at the EU level of a forum of discussion, an arena for negotiation, or a political architecture for interaction and discourse.

Here we come to an important point – well synthesized by Lenschow (2005) in the two notions of Europe as pressure and Europe as usage. On the one hand, European integration can put pressure on the member states, so that change will be brought about as a response to pressure. On the other hand, for domestic actors the EU is, apart from pressure, also an institutional repository of discourse, opportunities and levers that can suit the purposes of those who are engaged with reforms at home. These actors can use the perceived threat of action from the ECJ (for example, by arguing that reform is needed at home 'otherwise we will end up as country X who saw its laws in Sector Y struck down by the Court'), new policy instruments discussed in Brussels, or white papers and communications from the Commission to gain leverage on domestic reforms. The two levels (EU and domestic) are therefore connected both by pressure and usage.

Some authors have, it should be said, even questioned the notion of two distinct arenas by observing that 'the [domestic and EU] levels are nothing but playing fields, where actors move between one and the other, and play with them' (Ravinet, 2007: 24, our translation). Yet ultimately there are two playing fields, not just one. Ravinet's observation is nevertheless important because it draws attention to complex interaction effects, to actor-centred analysis and to the strategic linkages between EU and domestic policy arenas (Jacquot and Woll, 2004; Salgado and Woll, 2007). Carter and Smith (2008) argue that the whole notion of different levels is misleading, since it does not capture the essence of how institutional orders are created around public policy-making. To understand these orders – they conclude – one has to make use of sharp public policy analysis tools and abandon multi-level governance theorizing.

The domains

In this section we discuss the substantive and territorial scope of Europeanization. Granted that Europeanization is a process, who or what is affected by this process? To begin with, the EU can influence domestic political systems in three different ways – as *opportunity structure*, as *discourse* and as *forum*.

Beginning with the political opportunity structure (that is, a framework of rules that enables or constrains the political behaviour of actors), this is constantly affected by changes in EU rules (treaties, directives and regulations) and by the evolving jurisprudence of the ECJ. No matter whether the EU is engaged with building new markets or in correcting market failures, its impact on national-level constellations of actors is not neutral. Authors like Thatcher (2004) have rightly spoken of winners and losers in Europeanization processes to draw attention to this phenomenon.

Second, the EU has discursive impacts. In a rather obvious way, this notion covers the impact of ideas generated in Brussels. Jabko (2006) has illustrated how the idea of the single market has been propagated by the Commission in different ways depending on the target sector and the target country – this is why his book is called *Playing the Market*. But of course this also means that EU discourses are refracted, edited and interpreted at home by actors in what can be quite different ways. An example is the Saint-Malo declaration of a common defence and security policy. According to Howorth (2004), the declaration was discursively constructed by the British negotiators as a way to embed the EU in NATO, and by the French as the crucial step in making the EU autonomous from the US and NATO. Thus, ideas and strategy are intimately linked – as shown by the increasing presence of strategic constructivism in recent work (Jabko, 2006; Radaelli and Kraemer, 2008; Eberlein and Radaelli, 2010). Yet again we see 'Europe as (ideational) pressure' in some cases, and Europe as political use by domestic actors in others.

Third, the notion of 'forum' refers to the domains where the EU does not legislate, but provides architectures for the discussion of policy goals, the definition of common targets, the diffusion of innovations and the stimulation of learning processes. As mentioned, the open method of coordination has become a label to describe these types of processes. Clearly, the presence of the EU as facilitator but not as legislator (the open method is based on agreements on policy, but the reforms are carried out at the national level, not via EU law) puts the whole question of 'Europe as pressure' and 'Europe as usage' in a different light. Some authors have noted that Europeanization as forum has created the preconditions for more institutional coordination at home, and in some cases facilitated the recalibration of domestic welfare states (Zeitlin *et al.*, 2005) and foreign, defence and security policy (Smith, 2003; Major, 2005; Rieker, 2006). Others are sceptical of the possibility of bringing about policy learning and genuine experimentation 'from below' (Radaelli, 2008; but see Sabel and Zeitlin, 2007).

As mentioned, the substantive domains include policy, politics and polity. The latter covers administrative structures, executive–parliamentary relations, the role of courts and intergovernmental relations. The 'politics' dimension of Europeanization is about effects on public opinion and electoral behaviour, party competition, pressure groups and social movements. Poguntke *et al.* (2007) show that Europeanization is changing the balance of power within parties, giving more resources to the segment of party elites and officers dealing with EU affairs, and empowering the party-in-office versus the parliamentary party. The Europeanization of public opinion is critical when it comes to the future of European integration and EU-wide policies with direct impact on the domestic sphere, for example support for the common currency (Banducci *et al.*, 2003, 2009).

Crucial in this field of research is the emergence of new cleavages in domestic politics as a result of European integration. In most member states, the classic right–left cleavage has lost importance. But major political parties are now divided internally by an emerging new cleavage, more or less concerning European integration (Marks *et al.*, 2002; Edwards, 2007, 2009).

The policy domain includes the effects on constellations of actors, their material and ideational resources, the emergence of new policy instruments, and implementation structures. Two authors have linked policy, politics and polity in far-reaching claims about Europeanization. Mair (2001) has argued that integration had produced an imbalance: parties contest elections in national political systems by supplying different options for policy to the electorate. Yet policies are decided in Brussels, where there is no proper system of democratic representation and party politics. Hence political competition at the domestic level becomes irrelevant in terms of choosing between one policy option and another, but citizens cannot make up for this by engaging in a fully democratic EU-level arena. Schmidt (2006) takes an institutional discursive approach to European integration, but comes to a similar conclusion: the EU is *policy without politics*, whilst the national systems are *politics without policy*. The democratic deficit – this is the innovative implication of her reasoning – is not a matter of EU constitutional politics. It is indeed profoundly rooted in national political systems. These two examples show how Europeanization can be used to bridge the gap between positive and normative analysis, tackling issues of democracy and accountability.

One final word on the territorial scope. Although most authors are concerned with the impact of the EU, there is no logical reason why Europeanization should be confined to EU-ization (Wallace, 2000). There are other institutions in Europe that trigger Europeanization, such as bilateral agreements and the Council of Europe. But because of its unique political role and its profound impact on public policies, public opinion, party politics and polity, the EU is and will be the main focus of Europeanization scholars. Looking at the targets of Europeanization, yet again there is no reason to consider only the member states. The EU has an external dimension that affects countries that trade with the member states or obtain aid. The most studied of the external dimensions of Europeanization is the impact of integration on candidate countries in the context of accession processes (Agh, 1999; Grabbe, 2001; Schimmelfennig and Sedelmeier, 2004; Schimmelfennig, 2007). Others have investigated how countries that have no intention of joining the EU are being Europeanized via agreements with the EU, trade and the incorporation in their legislation of single market regulations. Switzerland is perhaps the most paradigmatic case (Fischer *et al.*, 2002). Take taxation, one of the most sacred Swiss cows in the policy debate, to illustrate this point: recent EU agreements on direct taxation have forced Switzerland to negotiate and partially adapt its tax rules to 'match' the EU 2003 directive on the taxation of savings (Afonso and Maggetti, 2006).

Explanation

How does one establish that European integration has a causal effect on domestic political systems? This is a difficult question given the complexity of Europeanization processes. Researchers can wrongly attribute causality to EU-level variables, whilst the changes observed may be the result of global forces or domestic-level variables. There is the risk of assuming that if some domestic changes look similar to 'what Brussels wants', this must be an instance of Europeanization. It is even more difficult to establish, given a certain change at the domestic level, how globalization, European integration and domestic forces have contributed to the change. One option is to be explicit and rigorous in formulating rival alternative hypotheses. Hence, a research design on Europeanization should always control for the null hypothesis that European integration 'does not matter'. It should also specify rival hypotheses that tell us what factors, other than Europeanization, may have generated the outcome.

Another valuable approach to this type of complexity is to formulate clear theoretical expectations about the mechanisms of Europeanization. Here we have a baseline model and a bottom-up research design. The two are conceptually different, yet in a single project one can draw on both of them to reduce bias from different sources (Quaglia and Radaelli, 2007). The baseline model was put forward by Caporaso, drawing on his previous work with Risse and Green Cowles (Caporaso, 2007). Caporaso's research design is based on a process that starts with the presence of EU-level decisions or EU-level phenomena, for example a new public policy. To create change, the EU must create some adaptational pressure at the domestic level. Pressure is mediated by intervening variables at the domestic level. If pressure is very low, there will be no change. If pressure requires fundamental change there also will be no change, perhaps because a country has not achieved the necessary administrative capacity to comply with EU rules or implement policies agreed in Brussels. In intermediate situations, however, pressure will create change. Domestic change has a feedback effect on the EU, thus closing the loop. Pressure – drawing on the template provided by Börzel and Risse (2003) – is clarified in terms of 'goodness of fit', which is not just the fit or lack thereof between EU and domestic policies, but covers structural-institutional fits as well (Caporaso, 2007). Intervening variables are grounded in either social constructivism or rational choice institutionalist frameworks (Börzel and Risse, 2003). The two broad interpretations – rational choice and social constructivism – are treated as complementary rather than mutually exclusive.

Since empirically there is no neat separation between the logic of appropriateness and the logic of choice, the question remains what should a researcher test exactly, and on the basis of what type of research design? Radaelli (2003) suggests process-tracing based on temporal causal sequences. Empirically, process-tracing starts from the set of actors, ideas, problems, rules, styles and outcomes at the domestic level at time zero – in short, the domestic system at a given time. Then the analyst process-traces the system over the years and identifies the critical junctures or turning points – for example, when major ideational change takes place, or the constellation of dominant actors is altered, or when the major problem is redefined (Radaelli and Pasquier, 2007). For each juncture, the question becomes: was the cause of this major change domestic, or did the change come from exogenous variables like the EU-level variables or global-level variables? In order to assess the contribution of the variables from outside the domestic system, the researcher goes 'up' – from the domestic level to the EU – and controls for the causal patterns. Causality is examined *in vivo* by looking at temporal causal sequences.

Within this discussion on causality and how to draw inferences from empirical evidence, some authors have also made progress in identifying typologies of mechanisms (Knill and Lehmkuhl, 2002) and outcome (Héritier *et al.*, 2001). Schmidt (2002) has made a distinction between the mechanisms involving structural variables and the special ways in which discourse has a causal impact and may transform structural variables. She shows how discourse can change preferences, remodel policy problems and enable or constrain actors, without exercising a direct causal effect on them.

Another strand of the literature on Europeanization focuses on the complexity of causal chains in the context of temporal sequences connecting major EU policies, from EMU to domestic changes (Dyson, 2000: 646–7; 2002). Most of Dyson's research is concerned with avoiding the pitfall of prejudging the role of European policies. In his carefully designed collection of case studies on EMU and domestic changes, Dyson and his associates show how previous work on EMU exaggerated the influence of the EU in domestic political change (Dyson, 2002). Recent work by Stolfi (2008) shows how the notion of the EU as external constraint bringing about domestic change has obfuscated the more important role of domestic policy communities. Interestingly, Stolfi uses the bottom-up research design to substantiate his theoretical claims, thus connecting the methodological discussion with empirical analysis.

Finally, other authors have entered the debate on research design by using the notion of control group. The question is simple: even if n EU member states are experiencing change, it may well be that k countries outside the EU are also going through the same process of change – for example because they are all part of a global process of diffusion. Saurugger (2005), in her study of interest groups in the EU, introduces a test variable studying the activities of actors outside the Union. Levi-Faur (2004) in his study of the liberalization of the telecom and electricity industries in the EU measures the net impact of Europeanization as compared to other factors like globalization trends by considering a Latin American and a rich and developed countries control group.

A look at bibliometric data

In this section, we carry on with the discussion of the field by considering simple bibliometric information. We deal with methodological aspects first, and then compare established and emerging literature. Due to the complex role of causality in this field, awareness of research design issues in Europeanization is on the rise. Most of the debate is about important trade-offs, such as conceptual analysis versus measurement, parsimony versus richer explanations, Pierson-type analysis of temporal causal sequences or more classic treatment of time, and baseline research design versus bottom-up designs. This reflects a much wider discussion on research design that has occupied mainstream political scientists for quite a while, especially since the publication of the landmark book *Designing Social Inquiry* by King, Keohane and Verba (1994).

In applying the gist of this discussion to Europeanization, the following categories of trade-offs in causal analysis have been identified:

1. Cause of effects versus effects of causes;
2. Concept formation versus measurement;
3. Complex notions of causation (including multiple-conjunctural causation) versus singular linear causation;
4. Omitted variables bias versus multicollinearity: operationalized as a rich set of independent variables versus parsimony;

5. Time as a qualitative factor in politics versus time as quantity of years;
6. Mechanism-oriented research versus variable-oriented;
7. Top-down versus bottom-up designs.

Some of the trade-offs have been already explained and others, such as explanation rooted in *mechanisms* versus *variables-oriented explanation*, are well known to students of political science. In the debate on Europeanization, the mechanisms have been classified in 'positive integration', 'negative integration' and 'framing' (Knill and Lehmkuhl, 1999). Bulmer and Radaelli distinguish between 'horizontal' and 'vertical' mechanisms (Bulmer and Radaelli, 2005). They also argue that Börzel and Risse's (2003) mechanism of 'goodness of fit' is only one possible explanation of Europeanization, particularly useful for positive integration. The other two explanations are 'regulatory competition' (in which the issue is not to adapt to EU templates, but to respond to market incentives created by negative integration) and 'learning' via facilitated coordination (in policies such as asylum, foreign and security, social inclusion, enterprise and pensions). Oliver Trieb has added to the debate the observation that politics can alter the direction of change predicted by the 'goodness of fit' explanation. In fact, party identification and the shifts in governmental majorities may lead even a poorly fitting country to adapt to EU policy and comply better than countries with high fit (Treib, 2003; Falkner *et al.*, 2005).

'Cause of effects' versus 'effects of causes' deserves a few words of explanation. One of the most important overarching goals of a research design is to produce valid descriptive and causal inferences about significant incidents in the world of political science (Brady and Collier, 2004: 221). 'Cause of effects' refers to studies that start with a dependent variable in terms of outcomes – for example, constrained policy autonomy – and investigates the possible cause, be it global economic interdependence or European integration. 'Effects of causes' is typical of studies that are interested in tracking down how a specific cause, for example European integration, has different effects, for example on domestic politics and policy.

We also need to introduce 'complex causation' versus 'singular linear causation'. Complex causation includes non-linear econometric models (such as structural model equations), multiple conjunctural causation, qualitative comparative analysis, equifinality, increasing returns, punctuated equilibria and models where the causal logic changes before and after a threshold level of a variable (Ragin, 1987, 2000; Hall, 2003; Pierson, 2004). The concept is typically applied to research designs with a small N sample as it refers to the explanation of a particular outcome rather than the generalization of average causal effects.

'Omitted variables bias' versus 'multicollinearity' is a trade-off between trying to reduce bias generated by neglecting some important variables and reducing bias arising out of the correlation between independent variables. The more one includes independent variables in the explanation, the higher the likelihood of multicollinearity problems – e.g. two or more explanatory variables are correlated to such a degree that it is impossible to separate their causal effects (King *et al.*, 1994: 119). This issue can be addressed by collecting additional observations to provide more leverage in the differentiation of the causal effects (ibid.: 123). However, according to Brady and Collier (2004: 48), increasing the number of observations 'make[s] it harder to achieve other important goals, such as maintaining independence of observations, measurement validity, and causal homogeneity'. We operationalize this trade-off as one between parsimony (the obvious way to avoid multicollinearity) and explanations based on a rich set of variables (the intuitive way to avoid omitted variables bias).

We compiled a first sample on the literature on Europeanization based on the Social Science Citation Index (search on 'Europeanization' and 'Politics'; period 1997–2007), from which we extracted the most frequently cited articles of the discipline. We then excluded review articles, normative articles without any empirical analysis, industrial relations articles and statistical artefacts (there are a few articles with Europeanization somewhere in the abstract but no real engagement with this topic). This left us with 32 Europeanization articles, cited at least five times. We created a control group of 32 highly cited articles on European integration politics (a much broader field) with similar criteria.

On average, Europeanization articles are still several citations away from the pack of highly cited articles on the politics of European integration. Further, Europeanization scholars are disproportionately more interested in policy analysis (including of course regulation, transposition of directives, comitology and implementation analysis), country-based case studies and historical narratives. Highly cited control group articles are much more diverse, with several articles on the substance of law-making and voting in the EU institutions, public opinion and identity, as well as public policy and modes of governance.

We created a scorecard which included the six trade-offs – plus the trade-off specific to Europeanization studies only for sample A. Each trade-off was split into three categories. If an observation was in accordance with one of the two options of the trade-off it was marked with the value '1', otherwise it was marked with '0'. Observations that fell under the 'not applicable' option were marked with a '−1' value, although in the data analysis the category was not considered as a 'missing case'. In terms of scoring the actual sample, upon construction of the survey protocol we employed ourselves as the two coders and utilized intercoder reliability. Intercoder reliability may not increase the validity of the actual scoring in a sample size similar to ones of this exercise, but it increases transparency and congruence (Krippendorf, 2004).

When we started coding, it turned out that most of the articles do not show awareness of the methodological trade-offs mentioned above. The authors do not have explicit sections on research design; neither do they discuss whether they are more likely to have a problem of multicollinearity or a problem of omitted variables bias. In consequence, we had to extrapolate the choice made by the author in terms of research design by carefully considering the substance of the article. In some cases, however, the trade-offs are genuinely not applicable to the study in question, hence a value of –1 was assigned.

Turning to our findings, Table 9.1 compares the results for sample A (that is, Europeanization) and sample B (our control group). Table 9.2, in particular, shows that most Europeanization articles are based on the top-down research design (21, against only 5 bottom-up articles). Both samples (Table 9.1) show a balanced distribution between cause of effects and effects of causes – albeit in the control group with a slight orientation towards the former. Turning to the trade-off between concept and measurement, we expected to find Europeanization articles more interested in developing the concept rather than measurement, and the opposite for the control group. This is because the field of Europeanization is relatively new. Hence – we reasoned – researchers will spend more time in discussing their concepts. In addition, the review articles on Europeanization (Olsen, 2002; Radaelli, 2003; Lenschow, 2005) suggest that definitional issues and concept formation have somewhat been prominent. The highly cited articles, by contrast, seem to suggest that there is a preference for measurement. This characteristic features in the control group too.

On the type of causation (Table 9.1, column 3), yet again the two samples do not show much difference, although Europeanization articles have a slight preference for complex notions of causation. This is arguably the result of a field that was created around a causation puzzle: how can one grasp the essence of the Europeanization process if there are multiple feedback loops between domestic and EU variables in this process (Radaelli, 2003)? Unsurprisingly, researchers are working with complex notions of causation in this area. Singular causation is preferred by those who think of Europeanization as an implementation of EU decisions – for these authors causation is more straightforward.

Both Europeanization articles and the control group seem to prefer a rich set of explanatory variables to parsimony (Table 9.1, column 4). Regarding time (Table 9.1, column 5) the Europeanization sample deals with the qualitative aspects of this variable more than the control group. The difference is small, however. It can be explained by noting

Table 9.1 Comparison of the Europeanization sample and the control group of highly cited articles on the politics of European integration

		Trade-offs in causal analysis																	
		1			2			3			4			5			6		
ID	Sample	Cause of effects	Effects of causes	n/a	Concept	Measurement	n/a	Complex	Singular causation	n/a	Parsimony	Rich set of independent variables	n/a	Time quantity	Time quality	n/a	Mechanism oriented	Variable oriented	n/a
1	Europeanization	16	16	0	9	23	0	16	12	4	9	19	4	12	15	5	18	14	0
2	Politics of European integration	17	14	1	8	24	0	14	14	4	12	20	0	16	13	3	12	17	3

Note: For each sample N = 32.

Table 9.2 Scorecard of the Europeanization sample

Trade-offs in causal analysis

ID	Author (Year)	Cause of effects	Effects of causes	n/a	Concept	Measurement	n/a	Top-down	Bottom-up	n/a	Compl-conjunctural	Sing. Conjunction	n/a	Parsimony	Rich set of indep var.	n/a	Time quantity	Time quality	n/a	Mech-orient	Var-orient	n/a
		\(1\)			\(2\)			\(3\)			\(4\)			\(5\)			\(6\)			\(7\)		
1	Ágh 2002	0	1	0	0	1	0	1	0	0	0	1	0	0	1	0	1	0	0	0	1	0
2	Andersen 2002	0	1	0	0	1	0	1	0	0	0	1	0	0	1	0	1	0	0	0	1	0
3	Anderson JJ 2002	0	1	0	0	1	0	1	0	0	0	1	0	0	1	0	0	1	0	0	1	0
4	Benz and Eberlein 1999	1	0	0	0	0	0	0	0	0	1	0	0	0	1	0	1	0	0	0	1	0
5	Beyers and Trondal 2004	1	0	0	0	1	0	0	1	0	0	1	0	1	0	0	0	0	−1	1	0	0
6	Börzel 1999	0	1	0	1	0	0	1	0	0	1	0	0	0	1	0	1	0	0	1	0	0
7	Börzel 2002	1	0	0	1	0	0	1	0	0	0	0	−1	0	0	−1	1	0	0	1	0	0
8	Bursens 2002	1	0	0	0	1	0	1	0	0	1	0	0	0	1	0	1	0	0	1	0	0
9	Cole 2001	1	0	0	0	1	0	1	1	0	0	1	0	1	0	0	0	1	0	1	1	0
10	Cole and Drake 2000	0	1	0	1	0	0	0	0	0	1	0	0	0	1	0	0	1	0	0	0	0
11	Dimitrova 2002	0	1	0	0	1	0	1	0	0	0	1	0	0	1	0	0	0	−1	0	1	0
12	Dyson 2000	0	0	0	0	0	0	1	0	0	0	0	−1	0	0	−1	0	1	0	1	0	0
13	Eyre and Lodge 2000	0	1	0	0	1	0	1	0	0	1	0	0	1	1	0	0	0	−1	1	0	0
14	Fulkner 2000	0	1	0	0	1	0	1	0	0	1	0	0	0	1	0	0	1	0	1	0	0

15	Fischer, Nicolet, Sciarini 2002	0	1	0	0	0	1	0	1	0	0	0	1	0	1	0	0	0	1	0
16	Gilardi 2005	1	0	0	0	0	1	0	0	−1	0	0	0	0	1	0	1	0	0	0
17	Grabbe 2001	0	1	0	1	1	0	0	0	0	0	0	1	−1	0	0	0	0	1	0
18	Harmsen 1999	1	0	0	1	0	0	1	1	0	1	0	0	0	0	1	0	0	1	0
19	Knill and Lehmkuhl 2002	1	1	0	0	1	0	1	1	0	0	−1	0	0	0	0	1	−1	0	0
20	Ladrech 2002	1	0	0	0	0	1	0	0	0	1	0	0	−1	0	0	1	0	1	0
21	Lavenex 2001	0	1	0	1	0	0	1	0	1	0	1	0	−1	0	1	0	0	1	0
22	Levi-Faur 2004	1	0	0	0	0	0	0	0	0	0	0	1	0	1	0	0	1	1	0
23	Lippert, Umbach, Wessels 2001	1	0	0	0	0	1	1	0	0	1	1	0	0	0	1	0	0	1	0
24	Lodge 2000	0	1	0	1	0	0	0	0	1	1	0	0	0	−1	1	1	0	0	0
25	Marcussen, Risse et al. 1999	1	0	0	0	1	0	0	1	0	0	1	1	0	0	0	0	1	1	0
26	Radaelli 1997	1	0	0	0	1	1	0	0	1	1	0	0	0	0	1	1	0	1	0
27	Scharpf 1997	0	1	0	0	0	0	1	1	0	1	0	0	−1	1	0	0	1	0	0
28	Schimmelfennig and Sedelmeier 2004	1	0	0	0	1	1	0	0	1	1	0	0	0	0	1	1	0	1	0
29	Schmidt 2002	1	0	0	1	0	0	1	0	0	1	0	0	0	0	1	1	0	0	0
30	Semetko, De Vreese, Peter J 2000	0	1	0	0	1	1	0	0	1	1	0	0	0	0	1	1	0	1	0
31	Smith J 2001	0	1	0	0	1	1	0	0	0	1	0	0	0	0	0	0	0	0	1
32	Warleigh A 2001	1	0	0	0	1	0	0	0	−1	1	1	1	0	0	1	0	−1	1	1
	Total observations (N = 32)	16	16	0	9	23	21	5	6	16	12	4	19	9	4	12	15	5	18	14

Table 9.3　*Comparative analysis of most-cited and most-recent articles on Europeanization*

	Enlargement	Implementation	Comparative	Citizens, identity, public opinion
Most-cited articles on Europeanization	5	13	25	16
Most-recent articles on Europeanization	0	11	18	21

that several articles on Europeanization are based on policy analysis, longitudinal case studies and/or process tracing. Since the debate on Europeanization has involved much time discussing how exactly this process works, there is a major emphasis on mechanisms that we do not find in the control group (Table 9.1, column 6).

We now contrast our 32 Europeanization articles with a sample of recently published Europeanization articles (2007 and 2008) obtained with the same keywords and the same criteria (Table 9.3). By doing so, we go beyond research design and consider the substantive issues dealt with by the Europeanization scholars in their highly cited articles. We also answer the question as to whether there is a stable trend or whether new articles are addressing different, perhaps emerging issues, with the caveat that an article can produce multiple entries, since it may deal with two categories, like 'enlargement' and 'identity'. Hence our scores do not total 32 this time.

When 'large N' is used we denote the presence of a comparative study of either all of the member states (be it the EU-15 or EU-25), or, for example, OECD countries – in other words, when it involves a broader group of countries. By CEEC, we denote the eight Central and Eastern European Countries that gained accession status in the 2004 enlargement: Poland, the Czech Republic, Slovakia, Slovenia, Hungary, Latvia, Lithuania and Estonia. 'Eurozone' implies the first 12 member states that had adopted the euro: France, Germany, Italy, Spain, Portugal, Ireland, the Netherlands, Belgium, Luxembourg, Austria, Finland and Greece. Comparing the most-cited and the most-recent articles, some interesting features emerge (Table 9.3). Enlargement seems much less popular than in the past, due to the completion of a big round of accessions to the EU. Implementation analysis is and seems to remain a stable feature. The interest in comparison is somewhat dwindling. Due to the vicissitudes of the constitutional project, more attention is paid to emerging issues of identity, public opinion, representation

Table 9.4   *Policy areas*

	Most-cited	Most-recent
Environmental policy	5	1
Competition/internal market policy (broadly)[*]	5	3
Economic policy (broadly)[**]	3	6
Refugee/immigration policy	2	0
Social policy[***]	1	4
Urban/regional policy	1	2
Minority rights/equality policy	0	3
Foreign policy	0	2
Cohesion policy	0	1
Agricultural policy	0	1

[*] Competition and internal market include areas of free movement of labour, electricity, telecommunications, transportation, taxation, etc.

[**] Economic policy is an umbrella category that includes EMU, fiscal policy, research and innovation as defined in the Lisbon Strategy, budget issues and public sector restructuring.

[***] Social policy includes areas of social welfare, income protection and health care.

Table 9.5   *Country selection as case studies*

	Most-cited	Most-recent
Large N	8	8
CEEC	4	3
Eurozone	1	0
Non-geographic	1	1
France	7	5
Germany	7	2
UK	5	1
Belgium	2	1
Hungary	2	3
Austria	1	1
Czech Republic	1	2
Denmark	1	4
Estonia	1	1
Italy	1	4
Netherlands	1	1
Poland	1	4
Slovenia	1	2
Spain	1	1
Sweden	1	1
Switzerland	1	1
Bulgaria	0	1
Greece	0	2
Romania	0	1
Russia	0	1
Turkey	0	1

and scope of governance, bringing Europeanization research closer to some issues in the normative turn in European studies. Economic and social policies are more prominent in the recent articles, whilst the number of articles on environmental policy decreases when we move from the highly cited to the most-recent articles (Table 9.4). As for the member states, work on the big three (France, Germany and the UK) tops the list of highly cited papers, but new articles are more evenly distributed – with Poland and Denmark well represented, as well as Italy (Table 9.5). Finally, the number of large N studies is exactly the same in the two groups.

Conclusions

Europeanization is still a much debated and, to some extent, controversial concept. But different definitions share some common ground. Turning to explanation, Europeanization has assisted political scientists in organizing different types of mechanisms for change, such as EU pressure, regulatory competition and learning via facilitated coordination (Bulmer and Radaelli, 2005). The 'goodness of fit' hypothesis of the baseline model has opened up an empirically rich debate on how exactly countries respond to adaptational pressure, and qualifications about the role of party politics and party identification have been added (Treib, 2003). Others have explored more general models that include the 'goodness of fit' but track down causality from the bottom-up perspective (Radaelli, 2003). Research on implementation has been reinvigorated by the academic turn towards Europeanization. The comparison of most-recent and most-cited articles shows that the field is not stable, and the choice of specific topics is changing. This can be an indicator of an expanding field, but can also show that researchers have not settled around core topics.

On balance, although this strand of European studies is still controversial and the discussion is lively, and there is evidence of symbolic, even faddish engagement with the term 'Europeanization', we do not share the pessimism of Lenschow (2005) about the state of the art. To blame Europeanization for not having reached the status of a theory is unfair. Europeanization is not trying to become a new theory with its own ad hoc vocabulary. Instead, it helps us to organize concepts and orchestrate mainstream theories of political science, political economy and international relations (Hassenteufel and Surel, 2000; Featherstone and Radaelli, 2003). The aim is to make the whole field of European studies more integrated with major theories.

Looking to the future, research should usefully explore more ambitious questions, such as: what does Europeanization tell us about the politics of integration, power and legitimacy? Does it give new insights for classic middle-range concepts and theories of comparative policy analysis, such as policy learning and implementation analysis? And does it provide methodological innovation?

Europeanization is a process of power generation. After having discussed 'Europe as usage' and 'Europe as pressure', scholars should try to formulate general statements about 'Europeanization as socialization' – considering the power shifts implied by changes in European identities and most importantly policy paradigms (Quaglia *et al.*, 2008; Radaelli and Banducci, 2008). Here, 'Europeanization as socialization' could usefully cross roads with the literature on the clash of capitalisms (Schmidt, 2002; Menz, 2005; Callaghan, 2008).

Another central theme is discourse (Schmidt, 2002). Actors use the EU instrumentally, to provide, via discourse creation, legitimacy for choices already taken at home (Kallestrup, 2002). Domestic actors can also refer to norms and ideas originally displayed for different purposes in a post-decisional mode to entrap their opponents (Schimmelfennig, 2001). However, we should consider testing the post-decisional legitimizing use of EU policies and commitments. In the current climate, it is not at all certain that the EU can be used to produce more legitimacy at home – public opinion sentiments seem to go in the other direction. Hence policy-makers may find it impossible to draw on the EU to generate legitimacy if the EU itself generates hostility and opposition. On a different but somewhat related issue, research on EU discourses has shown the ambiguous political roles of myths created with the intention to justify EU policies, such as 'learning', 'participation' and 'voluntarism' (Alam, 2007; Ravinet, 2007; Smismans, 2008).

For comparative policy analysts, a disappointing feature of early studies was the implicit adoption of simplistic theories of implementation. Scholars seemed surprised to observe that EU policies were filtered by domestic actors and institutions, and that the end result was not convergence. However, this is absolutely conventional and even obvious in the light of any contemporary model of implementation. Eventually, some attempts to fertilize Europeanization research with the insights of sophisticated theories of implementation are emerging (Zahariadis, 2008).

The final issue is methods and research design. We have dedicated a whole section of this chapter to show what Europeanization scholars are doing about trade-offs in causal analysis. The main question is still how to measure the causal role of the European factors in domestic changes. European Studies has always been beleaguered by the small *n* problem when dealing with quantitative methods. Qualitative research has faced the problem of going beyond the uniqueness of the EU and ad hoc conceptualization. The following are some examples of how the emerging literature is dealing with methodological complexities. Precision on measures of Europeanization of national legislation (the issues raised by public policy, of which legislation is only a component, are still daunting) can be increased by using indicators sensitive to breadth, countries and policy domains (Töller, 2007). Longitudinal analysis can be used to combine the historical perspective with systematic controls on 'test cases' outside the EU (Levi-Faur, 2004; Saurugger, 2005). Process-tracing and the bottom-up research design have successfully controlled for the two directions of causality – from the EU to the member states, and vice versa – in areas as diverse as foreign policy, gender equality and telecoms (Thatcher, 2004; Martisen, 2007; Exadaktylos, 2008). In turn, bottom-up and top-down designs provide two different ways to run the same story, so that the bias created by one design is reduced by the other (Quaglia and Radaelli, 2007). These are only partial solutions to some methodological problems – and the list of problems is very long indeed. Since there are classic problems faced by researchers working on international politics and domestic change, future research should integrate Europeanization with major disciplines rather than trying to solve the problems with ad hoc theorizing.

Notes

1. We wish gratefully to acknowledge the support of the Jean Monnet Chair in EU Policy Analysis at the University of Exeter. Neill Nugent kindly sent us suggestions and comments and provided major help in focusing this chapter. We wish to thank him for his friendly and firm stewardship.
2. Queen's University at Belfast has a site dedicated to Europeanization papers, see http://www.qub.ac.uk/schools/SchoolofPoliticsInternationalStudies andPhilosophy/Research/PaperSeries/EuropeanisationPapers/
3. We found two examples of linkages between Europeanization and HI: a theoretical paper by Daniel Wincott (2004) and an empirical study by Lene Pedersen (2006).

References

Afonso, A. and Maggetti, M. (2006) 'Bilaterals II: Reaching the Limits of the Swiss Third Way', in C.H. Church (ed.) *Switzerland and the European Union. A Close, Contradictory and Misunderstood Relationship* (London: Routledge) 215–33.

Agh, A. (1999) 'Europeanization of Policy-making in East Central Europe: The Hungarian Approach to EU Accession', *Journal of European Public Policy* 6(5): 839–54.

Alam, T. (2007) 'Quand la vache folle retrouve son champ. Une comparaison trasnationale de la remise en ordre d'un secteur d'action publique'. Lille, CERAPS. PhD.

Axt, H.-J., A. Milososki, and O. Schwarz (2007) 'Europäisierung – ein weites Feld: Literaturbericht und Forschungsfragen', *Politische Vierteljahresschrift* 48(1): 136–49.

Banducci, S.A, Karp, J. and Loedel, P.H. (2003) 'The euro, economic interests and multi-level governance: Examining support for the common currency', *European Journal of Political Research* 42(5): 685–703.

Banducci, S., Karp, J. and P. Loedel (2009) 'Economic interests and public support for the Euro', *Journal of European Public Policy* 16(4): 564–81.

Bomberg, E., and Peterson, J. (2000). Policy Transfer and Europeanization: Passing the Heineken Test?, *Queen's Papers on Europeanisation*, 2–2000, http://www.qub.ac.uk/schools/SchoolofPoliticsInternationalStudiesandPhilos ophy/FileStore/EuropeanisationFiles/Filetoupload,38445,en.pdf.

Börzel, T. and T. Risse (2003). 'Conceptualising the Domestic Impact of Europe: The Politics of Europeanization', in K. Featherstone and C. M. Radaelli (eds) *The Politics of Europeanization* (Oxford: Oxford University Press) 57–80.

Brady, H. and Collier, D. (2004) *Rethinking Social Inquiry: Diverse Tools, Shared Standards* (Oxford: Rowman & Littlefield).

Bulmer, S. (2006) 'Theorizing Europeanization', in P. Graziano and M. P. Vink (eds) *Europeanization: New Research Agendas* (Basingstoke: Palgrave Macmillan) 46–58.

Bulmer, S. (2009) 'Politics in Time meets the politics of time: historical institutionalism and the EU timescape', *Journal of European Public Policy* 16(2): 307–324.

Bulmer, S. and Radaelli, C. (2005) 'The Europeanization of National Policy', in S. Bulmer and C. Lequesne (eds) *The Member States of the European Union* (Oxford: Oxford University Press) 338–59.

Callaghan, H. (2008) *How Multi-level Governance Affects the Clash of Capitalisms*, paper presented at the APSA annual meeting, Boston, MA.

Caporaso, J. A. (2007) 'The Three Worlds of Regional Integration Theory', in P. Graziano and M. P. Vink (eds) *Europeanization: New Research Agendas* (Basingstoke: Palgrave Macmillan) 22–34.

Carter, C. and A. Smith (2008) 'Revitalizing public policy approaches to the EU "territorial institutionalism", fisheries and wine', *Journal of European Public Policy* 15(2): 263–81.

Damonte, A. (2007) 'Changing tools to catch the beast', *EUSA Biennial Conference*. Montreal, Canada.

Porte, C. de la and P. Pochet (2002) *Building Social Europe through the Open Method of Coordination.* (Brussels: Peter Lang).

Della Sala, V. (1997) 'Hollowing Out and Hardening the State. European Integration and the Italian Economy', *West European Politics, 20*(1): 14–33.

Dimitrakopoulos, D., and Richardson, J. (2001) 'Implementing EU public policy', in J. Richardson (ed.) *European Union: Power and Policy-Making* (London: Routledge) 335–56.

Dyson, K. (2000) 'EMU as Europeanization: Convergence, diversity and contingency', *Journal of Common Market Studies* 38(4): 645–66.

Dyson, K. (ed.). (2002) *European States and the Euro.* (Oxford: Oxford University Press).

Dyson, K., and Featherstone, K. (1996) 'Italy and EMU as "Vincolo Esterno": Empowering the Technocrats, Transforming the State', *South European Society and Politics* 1(2): 272–99.

Pierson, P. (2004). *Politics in Time: history, institutions and social analysis.* (Princeton: Princeton University Press).

Poguntke, T., Aylott, N., Ladrech, R. and Luther, K. R. (2007) 'The Europeanisation of national party organisations: A conceptual analysis', *European Journal of Political Research* 46(6): 747–71.

Quaglia, L., De Francesco, F. and Radaelli, C. M. (2008) 'Committee governance and socialization in the European Union', *Journal of European Public Policy* 15(1): 155–66.

Quaglia, L. and Radaelli, C. M. (2007) 'Italian politics and the European Union: A tale of two research designs', *West European Politics* 30(4): 924–43.

Radaelli, C. M. (2003) 'The Europeanization of public policy', in K. Featherstone and C. Radaelli (eds)', in *The Politics of Europeanization* (Oxford: Oxford University Press) 27–56.

Radaelli, C. M. (2008) 'Europeanization, policy learning and new modes of governance', *Journal of Comparative Policy Analysis* 10(3): 239–54.

Radaelli, C.M. and Banducci, S.A. (2008) 'Bureaucratic elites in the European Union: Socialization, institutional effects and policy domains', paper delivered to the annual meeting of the American Political Science Conference, Boston, 27–31 August.

Radaelli, C.M. and Kraemer, U.S. (2008) 'Governance Areas in EU Direct Tax Policy', *Journal of Common Market Studies* 46(2): 315–36.

Radaelli, C., and Pasquier, R. (2007) 'Conceptual Issues', in M. P. Vink and P. Graziano (eds) *Europeanization: New research agendas* (Basingstoke: Palgrave Macmillan) 35–45.

Ragin, C. (1987) *The Comparative Method: moving beyond qualitative and quantitative strategies* (Berkeley: University of California Press).

Ragin, C. C. (2000) *Fuzzy-set Social Science* (Chicago: University of Chicago Press).

Ravinet, P. (2007) *La genèse et l'institutionalisation du processus de Bologne: Entre chemin de traverse et sentier de dépendance.* Ecole doctorale de Sciences-Po, Cevifop, Paris.

Rieker, P. (2006) 'From Common Defence to Comprehensive Security: Towards the Europeanization of French Foreign and Security Policy', *Security Dialogue* 37(4): 509–28.

Risse, T., Caporaso, J. A. and Cowles, M. G. (2001) 'Europeanization and domestic change: "Introduction"', in M. G. Cowles, J. A. Caporaso and T. Risse (eds) *Transforming Europe: Europeanization and Domestic Change* (Ithaca: Cornell University Press) 1–20.

Sabel, C.F. and Zeitlin, J. (2007) 'Learning from Difference: The New Architecture of Experimentalist Governance in the European Union', *European Governance Papers*, No. C-07–02, http://www.connex-network .org/eurogov/pdf/egp-connex-C-07–02.pdf.

Salgado, R. and C. Woll (2007) 'L'européanisation et les acteurs non-éta- tiques. L'Europe en action' in B. Palier and Y. Surel (eds) *L'européanisation dans une perspective comparée* (Paris: L'Harmattan) 145–91.

Saurugger, S. (2005) 'Europeanization as a methodological challenge: The case of interest groups', *Journal of Comparative Policy Analysis* 7(4): 291–312.

Schimmelfennig, F. (2001) 'The community trap: Liberal norms, rhetorical action, and the Eastern enlargement of the European Union', *International Organization* 55(1): 47–80.

Schimmelfennig, F. (2007) 'Europeanization beyond Europe. Living Reviews in European Governance', *http://europeangovernance.livingreviews.org/ Articles/lreg-2007–1/, 2007–1*.

Schimmelfennig, F., and Sedelmeier, U. (2004) 'Governance by conditionality: EU rule transfer to the candidate countries of Central and Eastern Europe', *Journal of European Public Policy* 11(4): 661–79.

Schmidt, V. A. (2002) 'Europeanization and the mechanics of economic policy adjustment', *Journal of European Public Policy* 9(6): 894–912.

Schmidt, V. A. (2006) *Democracy in Europe: The EU and National Polities.* (Oxford: Oxford University Press).

Sindbjerg Martinsen, D. (2007) 'The Europeanisation of Equality between Genders. Who Controls the Scope of Non-discrimination?', *Journal of European Public Policy* 14(4): 544–62.

Smismans, S. (2008) 'New Modes of Governance and the Participatory Myth', *West European Politics* 32(5): 874–95.

Smith, M. (2003) 'The framing of European foreign and security policy: towards a post-modern policy framework?', *Journal of European Public Policy* 10(4): 556–75.

Stolfi, F. (2008) 'The Europeanization of Italy's Budget Institutions in the 1990s', *Journal of European Public Policy* 15(4): 550–66.

Stone Sweet, A. and Brunell, T. L. (1998) 'Constructing a supranational constitution: Dispute resolution and governance in the European Community', *American Political Science Review* 92(1): 63–81.

Stone Sweet, A. and Sandholtz, W. (1997) 'European integration and supranational governance', *Journal of European Public Policy* 4(3): 297–317.

Thatcher, M. (2004) 'Winners and losers in Europeanization: reforming the national regulation of telecommunications', *West European Politics* 27: 284–309.

Töller, A.E. (2007) 'Measuring the Europeanization of Public Policies – But how? A research note', *FoJus Diskussionspapiere*, No. 1/2007, http://users .ox.ac.uk/~polf0035/Diskussionspapier%201_2007%20Toeller.pdf.

Treib, O. (2003) 'EU governance, misfit and the partisan logic of domestic adaptation: An actor-centered perspective on the transposition of EU directives', EUSA biennial conference, Nashville, USA, 27–29 March.

Wallace, H. (2000) 'Europeanisation and Globalisation: Complementary or Contradictory Trends?', *New Political Economy* 5(3): 369–82.

Wincott, D. (2004) 'Policy change and discourse in Europe: Can the EU make a "square meal out of a stew of paradox?"', *West European Politics* 27(2): 354–63.

Zahariadis, N. (2008) 'Europeanization as program implementation: Effective and Democratic?', *Journal of Comparative Policy Analysis* 10(3): 221–38.

Zeitlin, J., Pochet, P. and Magnusson, L. (2005) *The Open Method of Coordination in Action: The European Employment and Social Inclusion Strategies* (Brussels: Peter Lang).

Chapter 10

Political Economy

Michelle Egan[1]

Introduction

The literature on the political economy of European integration is vast and crosses different disciplines. Scholars have sought, both theoretically and empirically, to capture the type, sequence and pace of economic integration.[2] Each debate surrounding the political economy of European integration is anchored in a particular intellectual paradigm.[3] While we have conceptual and theoretical explanations about the processes and outcomes of integration drawn from international relations and comparative politics,[4] the political economy literature has contributed the economics of information, transaction cost theory, principal–agent approaches, historical economy and bounded rationality to our understanding of how economic institutions change and evolve in seeking to coordinate national economies at the regional level. Recent emphasis has been placed upon the political and economic consequences of the choice of institutions, and upon the politics of institutional design (Scharpf, 1988; Weingast, 1995; Tsebelis, 2004). Some scholars argue that the consolidation of the market is characterized by incremental change and evolution, while others argue that the process is one of punctuated equilibrium (North, 1990). Much work has also focused on the role of interests, drawing on the differential ability of actors to solve their collective action problems at the European level, not least by building coalitions in which concentrated interests rather than diffuse interests have shaped European policy outcomes (Frieden, 1991; Weber and Hallerberg, 2001; Woll, 2008). Emphasis is also given to the role of norms and ideas in fostering economic change, generating a wealth of new research agendas in comparative politics, international relations and political economy (McNamara, 1998; Schmidt, 2006; Jabko, 2007).

Much of the political economy of European integration has sought to understand the role played by a relatively wide range of institutions and actors in shaping market outcomes. In looking at the relationship between political authority and economic structures in the European context, attention has shifted towards the different components of economic governance in the EU (Egan, 2001; Sapir *et al.*, 2004; Begg,

2008). Initially, scholars had focused on trade liberalization (see, for example, Pinder, 1968), with the predominant focus of research in the first decades of European economic integration being on either the terms of trade effects (Viner, 1950) or firm behaviour and market structure (Jacquemin and De Jong, 1977; Pelkmans, 1984). Consequently, there was little research on how international institutions structure bargaining and influence outcomes, or on how such joint management and coordination of mixed economies has transformed domestic political economies. As political economy as a field has developed, research on the EU has drawn upon theories of international trade, collective action and political institutions to understand and measure the effects of trade protection, non-tariff barriers, exchange rate regimes, regulatory competition and market liberalization. It has also raised fundamental issues of governance. The European integration project has transformed the role of the state and government practices to stabilize and regulate markets, while at the same time implementing and searching for new innovative mechanisms to manage and steer the economy. These debates about the relationship between political authority and markets have left ample room for normative concerns about the appropriate nature of economic governance.

This chapter focuses on key issues and developments at the core of European economic integration due to transformations of the global economy. Questions concerning the political foundations of markets became central to European studies as scholars addressed the consequences of growing economic interdependence, including rising imports, demands for protection, monetary instability and distributive conflict (Goldthorpe, 1984; Lake, 2006). As international economic relations were politicized in Europe, political scientists began to focus on interstate economic cooperation, drawing on the role of institutions in aggregating interests, the preferences of different societal actors and the distributional effects of domestic economic policies. The transfer of these issues to the European level has intensified debates about the conditions for economic growth, the impact of liberalization and the effort to address market failures. What are the conditions for the political sustainability of market integration? What are the functions of public and private authorities in both market formation and stabilization? What are the trade-offs between the benefits of international economic cooperation and the ability to pursue domestic welfare policies? What are the effects of greater competition and liberalization on income distribution within countries, and what political responses do they provoke? How has European integration fostered the restructuring of property rights? To answer these and other questions scholars have examined the institutional foundations of economic performance by focusing on macroeconomic stabilization, privatization and property rights, and the politics of regulation and redistribution in the EU.

The chapter begins with a brief survey of developments in fostering the single market, which is at the centre of any debate about European political economy. The second section shifts the level of analysis by focusing on subsequent scholarship and debates about the impact of market integration at the domestic level. The third section focuses on the relationship between the regional and global level by examining the dynamics and consequences of globalization for European integration. The fourth section addresses the normative implications of European economic governance. Finally, out of these various currents, I suggest that more research is needed in some areas, and I also propose several new directions for further research. Some of these directions derive from scholarship beyond traditional international relations theories to include the more general study of economic sociology, economic geography and economic history as they explore long run economic trends, relational and spatial networks, and economic outcomes embedded in wider social and political relations. Comparisons can also be drawn to other political contexts in ways that move EU studies beyond a narrow focus on a unique regional experiment.

Early developments and debates in European economic integration

The fundamental idea of a common or internal market is that 'economic frontiers' between national markets are diminished to allow for the mobility of goods, services and production factors. In the early post-war years, there was considerable support for such market integration in Western Europe, partly on economic but partly also on political grounds (Maier, 1977; Milward, 1992). Economically, Europe was seen in many quarters to need an international framework which would increase the rate of economic growth, secure employment, modernize European economies and pursue social citizenship. This would overcome the disruptive consequences generated by economic disintegration in the 1930s and 1940s, creating a more significant form of integration that would fit more easily into the process of industrial collaboration and integration that began in the eighteenth and nineteenth centuries (Pollard, 1981).

Initial political economy assessments of European integration concentrated on the substantive benefits of specific economic policy coordination (Camps, 1965; Curzon, 1974). This work focused on the coordination of liberalization initiatives and the need to ensure credible commitments through incentives and investments to promote trade, currency convertibility and managed production (Diebold, 1959; Asbeek Brusse, 1997a; Eichengreen, 2006). Much attention was paid to the various options of collective economic regulation, including the

International Trade Organization, the Council of Europe and the General Agreement on Tariffs and Trade (Asbeek Brusse, 1997b). Trade liberalization, the reduction of trade barriers and monetary stability were all viewed as key pillars in the plan to bring a stable and peaceful Europe back onto the world stage. The economic policies developed in a situation of 'embedded liberalism' (Ruggie, 1982) – where countries benefited from the protective barriers of capital exchange controls, fixed but adjustable exchange rates, and optional barriers to trade – which helped to consolidate very different systems of economic management and development. Drawing on theories of international political economy, European integration involved two basic policy objectives: the liberalization of exchange of goods and services, and the provision of socio-economic collective goods (Moravscik, 1993). One manifestation of this resurgence of post-war European integration was the rise of so-called intra-industry trade (Grubel and Lloyd, 1975). Unlike international trade in the nineteenth century, an increasing share of global trade was taking place between countries with similar resource endowments which traded similar types of goods – mainly manufactured products traded among industrial countries (Bernanke, 2006). The process was successful in the early period of European integration due to rapid economic growth, which masked the contradiction inherent between trade liberalization and the mixed economy and welfare state (Pelkmans, 1984).[5]

Scholarly interest in market integration waned in the 1970s as, especially in the aftermath of the two oil price crises of that decade, slower growth, recession and unemployment created problems for further cooperation (Tsoukalis, 1997; Griffiths, 2006). The two crises brought new political demands and pressure for national industrial policy, and protectionism returned to the top of the political agenda. The issue of European-wide industrial policy did receive some attention from scholars, although the bulk of research focused on how such factors as wage bargaining, industrial relations, welfare states and corporate governance at the national level impacted upon economic competitiveness, trade openness and democratic stability (Goldthorpe, 1984; Katzenstein, 1985; Jones, 2008). Much was written about how national governments proved unable to deal with a myriad of problems and became mired in stagflation. Gradually, recessionary impulses pushed states into monetarism as Keynesian demand management was abandoned and, together with fiscal policies designed to stabilize or lower deficits, governments shifted towards market incentives. Such functional convergence – which has been termed the 'competition state model' (Cerny, 1997) – emphasized 'sound' monetary policy, deflationary policy, wage restraint, minimal government budget deficits, privatization and liberalization of state-owned enterprises, and the promotion of an attractive climate for foreign direct investment, while still allowing states to retain highly diverse configurations of political–economic arrangements.

The single market programme

The high level of economic interdependence between West European countries made continuing protectionism in the 1970s and 1980s costly and visible (Pelkmans, 1984; Cecchini *et al.*, 1988). The EC's response to this problem was the launch in the mid-1980s of the single market programme to integrate national markets. This sparked a wave of mergers and acquisitions and corporate restructuring, as firms sought to take advantage of economies of scale, focusing on the benefits of market unification (Padoa-Schioppa *et al.*, 1988; Emerson, 1988; Pelkmans and Winters, 1988).

As progress with the internal market and then the single currency rekindled interest in the integration project, political economists came to offer a variety of explanations to account for the resurgence of activity in market integration. These explanations have identified a number of causal factors: information technology and financial market developments (see, for example, Moran, 1991; Sandholtz, 1992); societal interest group mobilization (Sandholtz and Zysman, 1989; Frieden, 1991; Cowles, 1995; Friedan and Rogowski, 1996; Van Apeldoorn, 2000); policy diffusion (Moran, 1991; Majone, 1997); and domestic political and economic factors and various interactions among them (Moravscik, 1991, 1993; Milner, 1999). New ideas about markets and competition also emerged in response to changing conditions in the European economy (Radaelli, 1999; Jabko, 2007). These approaches offered differing views about the transmission mechanisms that spur an integrated economy, with emphasis placed on the macroeconomic and external conditions, and the preferences of interest groups.

The repercussions from revitalizing the single market have not been confined to the member states, with the consequence that the external impact of European market regulation on surrounding states as well as competitors has also generated significant scholarly interest (Eeckhout, 1994; Young, 2002, 2004; Meunier, 2005). Initial assessments of the impact of the '1992 programme' led Messerlin (2001) to argue that a combination of contingent protection and non-tariff measures continued external protection, whereas Hanson (1998) suggested that in fact external liberalization accompanied internal liberalization. Yet the degree of regulatory alignment with single market rules varies across preferential trade agreements. Of particular interest have been the ways in which the impact and effect of the single market has been extended to neighbouring states through bilateral and multilateral agreements, stabilization and association agreements, and EU accession negotiations (Vachudova, 2005; Gstöhl, 2008).

The single market in practice: unfinished business

The single market has fundamentally changed the economic mode of governance in Europe. Many subsequent policy initiatives owe their genesis to the single market, with economic and monetary union, for instance, being launched to promote economic efficiency, and the coordination of environmental, social and merger policies being aimed at preventing conflict between different regulatory regimes. In recent years, increased attention has turned to the performance or functioning of the single market through an expansion of impact assessment and monitoring mechanisms (Radaelli, 2005). This has included the modernization and reform of public authorities through regulatory simplification and administrative reform (Egan, 2007). Now attention has turned towards making the European market project deliver, with sustained efforts by the European institutions to promote the better functioning of the internal market (Ilkovitz *et al.*, 2007). Such an emphasis fits closely with current research on compliance and implementation that draws attention to problems in specific sectors, as well as administrative capabilities and institutional constraints in coordinating across markets and sectors (Falkner *et al.*, 2005).

The actual operation of the single market has led to research on problems encountered with the mutual recognition principle in practice (Pelkmans, 2007; Nicoläidis and Schmidt, 2007), as well as the blockages in such areas as public monopolies, takeovers and patents (Smith, 2005). Despite the appearance of a single market, at least in comparison to other regional trade blocs, there is increased focus on the still significant 'home bias' in consumption and investment patterns (Delgado, 2006). Overall, the rising tide of cross-border transactions has meant that the internal market has extended to cover most of the goods sector and select service sectors, and made significant progress in capital market liberalization and intellectual property rights. Yet there is often a segmentation of analysis on the single market, both across disciplines and sectors.

Market liberalization in goods has garnered much attention, with much emphasis on, for example, pivotal case law rulings, the role of private regulatory authority and standard setting, and the innovation of mutual recognition (Egan, 2001; Schmidt, 2007). After decades of lagging behind the other freedoms, services have generated significant case law aimed at allowing more room for home-country rules and regulatory arbitrage (Hatzopolous, 2008). Legal analysts have documented the expansion of treaty rules concerning services, including reference to mutual recognition and home-country control despite stalled legislative developments and political resistance.[6] Political science has focused on services of a 'general interest', but research on market freedoms in health care policies, professional services and business services has lagged in comparison to research on other regulatory or compensatory policies, such as competition and regional policies. Substantial economic analysis has indicated that the single market still has untapped potential, especially in the area of services and network industries (Pelkmans, 2007; Lejour, 2008). Economists have drawn attention to the relationship between services liberalization, innovation and competitiveness, drawing on theoretical insights from trade and innovation theory to illustrate the potential dynamic effects for productivity growth in the single market (Lejour, 2008).

For labour, the growing restrictions on labour mobility and the inefficiencies this creates has drawn increased attention (ECB, 2006). While political analysis has focused on the strength of domestic preferences and bargaining to explain the restrictions on labour movements, legal analysis has focused on treaty amendments, legislative changes and fundamental rights provisions, resulting in a shift from the rights of workers to the rights, more generally, of citizens and non-nationals (Grabbe, 2006). This legal analysis reflects the fact that the objectives of the provisions in the treaty regarding market freedoms have always been much debated, often reflecting tensions between the purely welfare and efficiency goals and social values.

While the internal market has (supposedly) eliminated the possibility of using public sector industries as an employment buffer, has reduced industrial development strategies, and has restricted use of selective state aids and public procurement through promoting a European-wide competition policy, current protectionist pressures have not abated. There are increased concerns about the impact of the financial crisis on the single market as a further deepening of the single market can effectively be ruled out given the current backlash against liberalization.

New modes of governance

Economic policy coordination has increasingly been promoted through 'softer' modes of governance, as efforts to promote market coordination have fostered new mechanisms and instruments that have developed as alternatives to legally enforceable legislation. In attempting to modernize the European economy, the EU has pushed forward a wide-ranging reform programme – the Lisbon Agenda – aimed at promoting knowledge and innovation, as well as structural reform to enhance competitiveness by completing the single market. Although cutting across many policy areas, the strategy has led to increased focus on the so-called OMC which emphasizes the deliberation, persuasion and learning efforts that the EU can apply in policy fields that have hitherto been under exclusive national competence. Such a policy represents a shift from the traditional model of growth promotion within the EU, based on lowered barriers to trade and intensified competition, to more direct measures tackling productivity and growth – including investment in research, promotion of technology and innovation based on prescriptive policies. The new modes of governance based on a premise of institutionalized policy learning, has expanded beyond the core of economic policy coordination to areas such as innovation, taxation and environmental policy. Assessments of the effectiveness of OMC vary (Zeitlan *et al.*, 2005; Toemmel and Verdun, 2008).

Much scholarly attention has been given to the emergence of different forms of governance in promoting coordination in the Lisbon strategy (Héritier, 2002; Eberlein, 2003). Scholars have studied changes in production and exchange relationships based on shifts that have been taking place from formal rules (harmonization, mutual recognition and market based instruments) to more flexible means of compliance (soft law, coercion, guidance and benchmarking) (Héritier, 2002; Toemmel and Verdun, 2008). Some have focused on the capacities of different governance mechanisms for handling different kinds of market transactions, by comparing how successfully both hard and soft law mechanisms can integrate and coordinate markets, and how coordination among public and private actors can foster or hinder collective action (Dehousse and Joerges, 2002; Egan, 2008b; Schmidt, 2008). Others have focused on the rationale for non-hierarchical modes of coordination in social, competition, employment and environmental policies, with varying emphases placed on ideational, institutional and interest explanations. As such, research on new modes of governance – like that of the single market – offers differing views about the transmission mechanisms that foster market coordination, drawing on different theoretical perspectives and causal factors as various as interest mobilization, judicial reasoning, market externalities, institutional constraints and domestic preferences.

Lisbon and the single market

Despite the emphasis on new modes of governance in understanding the evolving relationship between state and market, public and private goods, and formal and informal laws, such changes have generated substantial criticism about whether the Lisbon Agenda – and its soft forms of coordination – have in fact influenced national reform programmes.

In assessing the main structural impediments to growth, Pelkmans has argued that there needs to be a better focus on the realities of member-state responsibility for economic growth, as most of the levers of macroeconomic performance are national, and the political capacity to deliver reforms has become increasingly difficult as resistance has sharpened over further efforts to promote the openness of the EU economy (Pelkmans, 2008). Despite EU efforts to promote European industry and competitiveness, through structural adjustment of certain industries, product standardization and promotion of risk capital, the European economy is underperforming (Alesina and Giavazzi, 2006). However, the success of Lisbon is important for the single market as a means to create synergies and complementarities that encourage innovation and growth, promote structural reforms through deregulation of labour and product markets, increase research and development spending and further market liberalization (Sapir *et al.*, 2004; Alesina and Giavazzi, 2006). Although the single market is built on a different logic and far stronger legal and political commitments than Lisbon, there needs to be more work done on the recent changes in internal market strategies that include new decentralized and network-based approaches, social impact assessments, and flexible governance.[7] And there needs to be greater understanding of how EU-led strategies to promote competitiveness are hampered by institutional and budgetary constraints, and how supposedly new market integration efforts often reflect the repackaging and reframing of prior instruments and policies (Pelkmans, 2006).

In widening the scope of the internal market beyond market liberalization, some scholars have expressed concern that the growth of voluntary, cooperative and soft law options that is inherent in some policy programmes, including the Lisbon Agenda, undermines the functioning of the internal market (see, for example, Hanf, 2008). Others, however, argue that although deliberative modes of governance are often viewed as more legitimate and democratic, the focus given to informal and indirect regulatory instruments in shaping markets has drawn attention away from the growing legalization and new patterns of juridification that have emerged in the single market. There needs, it is argued, to be a corresponding emphasis on judicial remedies such as private litigation, infringement proceedings, decentralized and delegated enforcement, and state liability. Modes of governance are not static and changes in governance in the EU are often a function of internal market developments.

Impact of integration on national economies

A central aspect of current research in EU studies is the impact of market integration on domestic polities, economies and societies. The dramatic increases in cross-border trade in goods and services, the effects of trade liberalization and capital mobility, and increased regulatory coordination raise new questions about the autonomy of nation states and the impact of greater competition and economic reform on different groups in society. A growing number of EU scholars have shifted their attention from the process of European integration to that of Europeanization, focusing on the factors that affect policy outcomes (Knill and Lenschow, 1998; Knill and Lehmkuhl, 1999; Börzel and

Risse, 2000; Schmidt, 2007). Such discussions of governance transformations at the European level bear directly on debates about the long term institutional development of different models of capitalism (Menz, 2005). Early in the development of this debate the focus was on why growth rates and economic development differed in post-war capitalist economies (Shonfield, 1965; Katzenstein, 1985; Schmidt, 2002). Government policies differed widely, leading observers to focus on the relative competitiveness of different economic policy regimes. Following this tradition of political economy in sociology and political science, prominent approaches to understanding markets in Europe have focused on the different models of market organization and sectoral governance (Schonfield, 1965; Katzenstein, 1985; Schmidt, 2002; Thatcher, 2004). Yet interestingly, one feature of governance across Europe in the 1970s and 1980s – neocorporatist arrangements that were seen as delivering superior economic performance by organizing business, labour and the state – have not been transferred to the European level (Cameron, 1984; Streeck and Schmitter, 1991; Streeck, 1996).

Subsequent research on factors determining economic growth has sought to distinguish between liberal market economies (LME) and coordinated market economies (CME), with these two models reflecting fundamentally different approaches to the organization of European economies. Known as the 'varieties of capitalism' debate (see, for example, Berger and Dore, 2006; Crouch and Streeck, 1997; Hollingsworth and Boyer 1997; Hall and Soskice, 2001; cf. Kitschelt *et al.*, 1999), this research outlines the institutional and social structure of the economy in industrial countries, focusing on explaining the resilience of distinctive national models based on economic performance, state capacity and institutional embeddedness (Zysman, 1994). This approach has considerable virtues and has led to a second generation of research in which the impact of European integration – Europeanization – on national modes of governance has generated a substantial scholarly literature (Schmidt, 2001; Menz, 2005).

The structure and strategy of the firm have also been much studied, with research showing that these tend to be derived from the national institutional framework without much consideration of the impact of regionalization on entrepreneurship and management strategies. Such adjustment strategies that firms have undertaken in response to changing economic and regulatory conditions in the single market have been under-researched, even though the impact of geographical distribution of production, industrial concentration, diversification and business practices may be affected by market integration. The current work on Europeanization also fails to incorporate a subnational variation in how different sectors are regulated (Kitschelt, 1991; Crouch and Farrell, 2004). A greater emphasis on the role of regional and local economies, modes of production and industrial districts can provide additional insights into the institutional foundations of economic performance (Sabel and Piore, 1984; Locke, 1995; Crouch, 2001).

In recent years, attention has also turned towards the transformation of economic relations in post-communist Eastern Europe, as enlargement has fostered major changes in market transactions, particularly with regard to production, trade and investment and corporate restructuring (McDermott, 2002; Grabbe, 2006). With post-communist countries making a transition to market capitalism, it was politically expedient for Central and Eastern Europe (CEE) policy-makers to claim to be emulating Western models given the influence of international financial institutions and foreign governments that were keen to promote neoliberal economic orthodoxy (Grabbe, 2000; Orenstein, 2001). However, past legacies and industrial networks have a great impact on economic modernization efforts in East European markets, and it is debatable whether emerging models of capitalism are even comparable with advanced economies at all, given the diversity of institutional solutions adopted during post-communist transition (Stark and Bruszt, 1998; Bohle and Greskovits, 2007). A large body of scholarly work indicates that the CEE countries differ in the functioning of labour markets, the extent of state regulation of the economy, industrial relations systems and various microlevel institutions in work practices, motivation and norms of economic behaviour (Bohle and Greskovits, 2003; Crowley, 2005; Greskovits and Bohle, 2007).[8] Despite efforts to map the varieties of capitalism framework in and distinguish the diversity of LME and CME in Central and Eastern Europe (Buchen, 2006), both international forces and state capacity play key roles in determining institutional choices. The transition to democratic capitalism was influenced by the EU, as part of the regions' internal integration into global markets. However, the transition strategies varied based on domestic social and political forces, as well as the extent to which post-communist states relied on functioning states and institutions from the socialist system, or were able to introduce rapidly market reforms and changes (Bohle and Greskovits, 2004, 2007). Market reforms have been examined extensively by scholars of enlargement, who have focused on issues of conditionality, norms and policy transfer, but have paid less attention to how corruption and rent seeking can distort and delay the intended forms of democratization and economic development (Woodruff, 1999; Vachudova, 2005; Grabbe, 2006).

Impact of integration on welfare states

Initially, the study of the welfare state and economic integration remained largely separate concerns. Though they seemed contradictory, the continuous strengthening and expansion of the public economy was essential for market integration. Rodrik (1997) and Garrett (1998) have pointed to the importance of compensatory mechanisms in which social welfare policies ensure economic openness (see also Cameron, 1978). Yet the EC/EU treaties made virtually no provision for redistributive instruments of policy. Instead, welfare state regimes have evolved in different national contexts (Esping Anderson, 1990) so that institutional variations between European welfare states persist in terms of social inclusion, benefit structures, financing regulations and organizational arrangements. The institutional diversity makes it difficult to coordinate welfare systems at the European level, not least because the EU lacks the resources required to engage in large scale redistributive policies (Rhodes, 1993). However, Leibfried and Pierson (1995) note that although national welfare states maintain the prime institutions for social policy in Europe, they do so only within a constrained 'multi-tiered system'. Ever growing market integration undermines both the autonomy and the sovereignty of national welfare states (Leibfried and Pierson, 1995). While some scholars have focused on the growth of European social policy (Falkner, 2003; Caporaso and Tarrow, 2009), as well as specific policy domains such as gender (see Chapter 13), labour (Menz, 2005) or immigration (Menz, 2009), many express concern for the absence of centralized social protection (Streeck, 1996; Scharpf, 2002) and the transformation of social solidarity as Europe adjusts to intensified market pressures, leading to economic insecurity and social exclusion for growing segments of the population (Ferrara, 2005).

While a social dimension is clearly evident in some policies, EU social policy largely takes the form of social regulation which needs to be compatible with the neoliberal economic order (Majone, 1993). Majone's argument, which stresses the efficiency-improving aspects of such regulation, fits with the broader shift in political discourse, away from social solidarity and redistribution towards production and market citizenship in the context of social policy initiatives. The subsequent expansion of social policy in terms of employability, investment and lifelong learning in the Lisbon Agenda – reminiscent of third-way efforts – is about successful market participation not social redistributive policies that underpin national welfare regimes.

The emphasis on market competition has also increased interest in the nature of European governance in the social policy domain. Streeck has argued that many EU social polices are based on neovoluntarism in which non-binding recommendations have replaced or altered traditional modes hierarchical of governance. Others argue that the importance of non-state mechanisms in compensating for market failures has increased as public–private networks at all levels, from local partnerships to supranational neocorporatist arrangements, may provide solutions to the pressures upon welfare states (Falkner, 2003); cf. Streeck and Schmitter, 1991). While earlier theorists claimed a fiscal crisis (O'Connor, 1973), a crisis of government over-load (Rose and Peters, 1978) and a crisis of legitimacy (Habermas, 1976), in relation to social democracy and social policy, Scharpf has tied such concerns about legitimacy and effectiveness to the European level. He has suggested (1996) that to avoid competition between different national social rules, member states should commit themselves to EU-level regulations that establish multilevel social standards to avoid social dumping. Exploring relations between the welfare regimes and market-making is of increasing concern, especially in determining the effects on growth and productivity and income distribution (Iverson, 2005).

Another debate has focused on whether increased market liberalization and trade openness in the European context will undermine the welfare state as fiscal policy is constrained by capital mobility and as large budget deficits are constrained by exchange rate coordination and monetary union. Much of the literature has argued that different types of welfare states have proven relatively resilient. Empirical work has shown that the capacity for adaptation (or recalibration) maintains essential redistributive elements and that, as a result, welfare cutbacks and reforms have been strictly limited in scope (Pierson, 1994, 1996; Levy, 1999) Scholars have also identified the dilemmas facing governments given their respective institutional environments as they face different problems with regard to the 'service economy trilemma' (Iverson and Wren, 1998). What is less certain is the extent to which European integration has constrained the tools and strategies available to national governments to mitigate the effects of the market. On the one hand, social pacts appear to be driving welfare state modernization and modifying wage bargaining at the national level (Rhodes, 2001). On the other hand, the EU may foster 'supranational embedded liberalism', activating new social and political bargains by legally and politically constraining market exchanges in the single market (Caporaso and Tarrow, 2009). Efforts at reforming and modernizing labour markets, industrial relations and social welfare at the EU and national levels will continue to attract substantial research attention (Scharpf, 1999; Zeitlan and Trubek, 2003)

Reconfiguration of property rights: privatization and regulatory design

The comprehensive programmes of economic liberalization and privatization in both Western and Eastern Europe since the 1980s were supposed to dismantle the rents of import substitution and *dirigisme* as macroeconomic stabilization, microeconomic restructuring and institutional redesign – and therefore political restructuring – would pave the way for economic growth. Reversing nationalization, a formerly very important form of governance in Western Europe, and state owned enterprises, as had operated in Central and Eastern Europe, these newer ways of operating have entailed the redefinition of the public and private sphere. Property is transferred from public to private ownership and economic functions and provisions are privatized. Europe has consequently instituted new forms of control and oversight, as privatization has been accompanied by the emergence of regulatory agencies as a new form of public intervention. There may be said to be the formation of a regulatory system across Europe, which has transformed the organization of the economy and (re)embedded the European market through regulation (Majone, 1993, 1996).

Applying theories of delegation, much research has focused on the emergence in Europe of non-majoritarian institutions – such as central banks, regulatory agencies, anti-trust authorities and courts – which have become especially prominent in the area of economic management (Majone, 1996; Sbragia, 2003). Majone argues that this is the optimal strategy to enhance efficiency, promote general welfare and the public interest by insulating decisions from political control. Thus, the trade-offs between accountability and performance have increasingly been addressed by expanding the scope of bureaucratic delegation. From monetary policy to defence, and administration of justice to utility regulation, these policies rely extensively on technical expertise and grant extensive decision-making power to autonomous, supranational agencies shielded from the electorate (Epstein and O'Halloran, 1999; Pollack, 2003). However, European scholarship increasingly questions the democratic legitimacy of counter-majoritarian processes and the way in which the design of regulation and the creation of regulatory agencies generate problems in establishing accountability in democratic polities. At the EU level, scholars have focused on the different institutional forms, the dynamics of regulatory cooperation and competition, the formal controls across different issue areas, and the range of agencies to illustrate the advance of regulation as a new mode of governance (Vos, 2005).

However, few EU scholars have critically examined the changing structure of economic governance in Central and Eastern Europe, even though privatization there has led to the concentration of assets and ownership, resulting in unhealthy lending practices with significant moral hazard, as exemplified in financial crises in Latvia, Poland, Hungary and Romania (McDermott, 2002). The high social costs, both in terms of economic performance and the capacity of the state to provide public goods for the development of the market economy in CEEs, deserve further study.

Also meriting further study is the issue of corruption which, though by no means being confined to CEEs, affects the proper functioning of the market economy. Whereas competition enhances economic vitality and political accountability, corruption weakens political and economic institutions and diminishes the benefits of economic liberalization. Since the mid-1990s a series of problematic transfers of property in CEEs has undermined the creation of stable market-sustaining institutions, perhaps creating a 'rentier state' (Woodruff, 1999; Appel, 2001). It has also given society as a whole a cushion from transitional recession through informal activities and non-monetary market outlets. Scholars interested in European enlargement have, however, paid comparatively little attention to how corruption and rent-seeking can distort and delay the intended forms of democratization and economic development (Woodruff, 2004). As Bruszt (2002) has emphasized, market preservation requires that there is an appropriate mix of institutional norms and practices to promote economic freedoms, and as such the quality of market institutions in newly acceded countries deserves more attention than it has been typically given in the enlargement literature.

Globalization and regionalism

European integration has not occurred in isolation; the international dimension matters. Scholars have debated extensively the relationship between Europeanization and globalization (Verdier and Breen, 2001). Some argue that the two are synonymous, comprising a set of ideas centred around liberalization, deregulation and privatization, which have altered social relations and generated increased market integration (Scharpf, 2002; Katzenstein and Shiraishi, 2005). Others argue that their effects mitigate each other, as regionalism has sought to adapt to and shape the acceleration and transformation of the global economy and as the erosion of national autonomy has been compensated by closer regional cooperation (Wallace, 2000; Verdier and Breen, 2001).

Although the changes within the European political economy, as part of a larger process of structural transformation in the global economy, have generated substantial research in both comparative politics and international relations, the economic context has changed fundamentally. European integration now takes place in a situation of global sourcing of goods and services, increased tradability of goods and services, and changing patterns of trade and investment (Ilkovitz and Dierx, 2007).

As the globalization of the economy continues to advance, issues of 'deeper' integration have become increasingly important. Global economic forces have served as a major impetus for European integration and for the transformation of European national economies. But as Schmidt (2002) argues, the EU has served as a conduit for global forces by opening member states up to international markets and trade, and it has also served as a shield against them by reducing member-state vulnerability to global economic forces through monetary integration and the single market.

Researchers disagree on the basic characteristics of the globalization process, the political consequences of globalization and the relationship between the international economy and regionalization (Hay, 2000). Most observers argue that market liberalization and trade increases aggregate economic growth but also intensifies economic uncertainty and income inequality, thus generating economic winners and losers (Rodrik, 1997; Garrett, 1998). As a result, national policy choices and the ability of governments to influence growth and employment are constrained (Scharpf, 2002). This has led to specific attempts to adjust to or resist globalization, and has generated research on understanding European contestation across issues and territories (Marks and Steenbergen, 2002). An important effect of such dislocation is that – as the principle of comparative advantage suggests – the expansion of trade opportunities tends to change the mix of goods that each country produces and the relative returns to capital and labour, making the distributional impact of changes in production increasingly contested. Other scholars, however, see the changes in the global economy as extensions of the deepening of prior historical waves of internationalization and interdependence (Wallerstein, 1974; Pollard, 1981; Crafts and Venables, 2003). The surge in international trade, capital and labour flows has been accompanied by quantitative research on the history of international economic integration and, importantly, disintegration (O'Rourke and Williamson, 1999). Looking at the process of economic integration over the long term, the dysfunctional effects of prior patterns of interlocking trade and commodity markets suggests that European integration is built on a pattern of integration that differs from that of the nineteenth century, which collapsed amid failure to provide an acceptable distribution of benefits among classes and states.[9]

From market embeddedness to constitutional asymmetry

The processes of democratic transition and market capitalism, the advent and extension of the single market, and the internationalization of market forces have drawn attention to trade-offs between promoting growth and efficiency and dealing with equity and distributional impacts. These and related issues have been extensively explored in the literature both empirically and normatively.

On the one hand, empirically, there are some common trajectories, variable patterns and divergent outcomes with regard to European markets (Schmidt, 2002; Hay, 2004). This invokes the current debate in political economy between those who see a process of convergence between national policies and institutions and those who see a process of sustained diversity (Berger and Dore, 1996). On the other hand, the discourse about markets reflect concerns about a whole new set of issues and priorities which are the product of global competition and which challenge patterns of domestic political-economic organization. These include the extent to which market competition and international economic pressure diminishes the capacity of states to achieve democratically legitimate political goals to mitigate the effects of the market (Scharpf, 1999: ch. 1). Such concerns reflect a growing body of work in law and political science that link normative questions about social reform that cannot be addressed in the EU's current constitutional design, with the emphasis on guaranteed economic freedoms based on an economic constitution (Dehousse and Joerges, 2002; Sabel and Gerstenberg, 2002).[10]

This social democratic critique, drawing on a tradition that dates back to Joseph Schumpeter and Karl Polanyi, argues that the economy has to be re-embedded and political control over the economy re-established. This would shift attention from the processes leading to economic liberalization towards the political and distributional effects of market reform, addressing not only issues of economic efficiency but also of social order and equity (Majone, 2000). Many observers have been increasingly sceptical of the virtues of further economic integration itself and also of the broader political viability and sustainability of European integration, asserting that the liberalization process has reached its limits as the costs associated with implementing market reforms are generating 'reform fatigue' (Tsoukalis, 2006).

On the political left, there are increased concerns that the legal emphasis on the economic provisions of the EU treaties comes at the expense of the protection of social rights.[11] The erosion of even a minimal social role for the state has become an issue of concern for scholars and practitioners. In an integrated European market, and less than integrated European polity, the constitutional asymmetry between policies promoting market efficiencies and policies promoting social protection and equality will continue to feature in debates about the future of the European economic space (Ferrara, 2005; Caporaso and Tarrow, 2009).

Future directions for research

Any suggestions for further research in the political economy field should first note how closely markets have become associated with governance. Both involve challenges to the capacity of state autonomy and authority as globalization appears to circumscribe political and economic choices by reducing the impact of territoriality. As noted above, comprehensive reform has led to state withdrawal from specific segments of market activity, as well as shifting some economic activities from public to private and from state to non-state actors, while also restructuring and reshaping state power (Nee, 2000; Bruszt, 2002; Sbragia, 2000; Schamis, 2001; Fabbrini, 2003; cf. Schmidt, 2009). In such an environment, it is sometimes forgotten that strong institutions ensuring the rule of law, contract enforcement and the protection of property rights are central to a well-functioning economy (North, 1990; Schamis, 2001; Bruszt, 2002).

These insights come from both the literature on property rights and the literature on state formation (Skowronek, 1982; Levi, 1988; North, 1990; Schamis, 2001). As a result, future scholarship could more fruitfully explore the relationship between market integration and state-building.[12] The transformation generated by European integration has ensured that the overall capacity of states to constitute and preserve market order, enforce competition and regulate economic transactions has evolved in both Western and Eastern Europe (Bruszt, 2002). Yet when we consider the efforts at market creation in Europe, the process has much in common with earlier efforts at consolidating divergent economies, since it involves reconceptualizing the role of the state in the economy, dealing with the developmental consequences of the economy, and establishing the necessary legal and regulatory frameworks to preserve markets (Polanyi, 1944).

State building

European integration has led to unprecedented alterations in domestic institutional configurations as market reforms have fostered new norms, rules and organizational changes irrespective of the nature of the economic and political regime. This in turn highlights the main impact of the political economy of European integration in which the deeper institutional effects of market expansion are similar to historical state-building efforts (Fligstein, 1996; McNamara, 2002; Fabbrini, 2003; Egan, forthcoming).[13] As studies of state-making in Europe have always been attentive to the constitutive impact of the global economy and geopolitics in shaping domestic institutions and policies, there is a good starting point for understanding broadly similar processes elsewhere and across time (Tilly, 1990; Ertman, 1997). Understanding other past cases is crucial to putting today's discussions of European political economy into their proper intellectual and historical context.

As European integration progresses, the demand for a coherent account of European economic history, rather than a series of national histories, or specific policy histories, has led some scholars to argue that the contemporary debate on consolidating markets has many historical parallels (McNamara, 2002; Egan, 2008a). The United States offers a particularly valuable model for cross-level historical analysis since early advocates often referred to the economic success of the country as evidence of the advantages of a large integrated economy (Scitovsky, 1958). The Spaak Report, which provided a conceptual and political basis for the founding of the European Communities, made clear that the formation of a Continent-wide common market along the lines of the United States was a feasible option (Spaak, 1956). The work of economic historians also shows that important lessons can be learned from the American experience (North, 1966; Egan, forthcoming). And yet when we think about US and EU experiences, the former is tied to state-building, which implies the internal consolidation of power, whereas the latter is tied to post-national democracy, with a different pattern and organization of power and institutions.[14] As political systems characterized by compromises and bargains based on deeply rooted territorial cleavages, both have balanced the goals of building and maintaining a centralized economic order while preserving regional and local diversity.

The US experience is thus instructive, and although it cannot be unambiguously applied to Europe (Nicolaidis and Howse, 2001) it does provide a number of useful parallels. Four of these parallels will now be identified. The first is the volatility of the transitions to modern economic growth experienced by both the US and Europe. Market integration is not linear, but it is periodically interrupted by shocks such as wars and world depressions, or by endogenous political responses to the distributional effects of globalization itself (Findlay and O' Rourke, 2007).

A second parallel is the importance of institutional frameworks for economic growth and development. These create incentives for productive activity as opposed to rent-seeking activity, and an environment in which property rights are defined and enforced, with limits set on the right of government to interfere with those rights. Sbragia argues that the rule of law and well-defined legal and judicial mechanisms for resolving conflicts among parties are critical for a market economy (Sbragia, 2000: 245; see also Egan, 2001). Just as the American government used the interstate commerce clause to expand its regulatory powers and address internal barriers to trade, so the European courts have exploited single market rules to extend their responsibility into regulating areas such as social policy, health and safety and the environment that can impact cross-border trade. A significant related parallel is the way that law has opened-up opportunities by reducing much of the cost of innovation and entrepreneurship.

A third parallel is that the reductions of political barriers to trade in Europe are having an effect analogous to the reduction of technological barriers to trade in the United States in the nineteenth century (Findlay and O'Rourke, 2003). Business historians have focused on the ways in which expanding markets and technological change altered the economic environment with the systematic reorganization of production in the United States. European integration has also drawn attention to changes in modes of production from mass production to flexible specialization and post-Fordism, as well as technology transfer and communications technology in changing market practices. European accounts of the relationship between the role of law and institutions in shaping the market, the entrepreneurial energy and effort to enhance the productive power of the economy, and the mobilization of interests in shaping economic development and integration, are reminiscent of the American experience.

And a fourth parallel is the way in which the economic transformation of the US led to profound social and cultural changes (Hays, 1984). The spread of the market was shaped by political debate on the future of the polity. It created economic and social instabilities and unrest, with efforts to mobilize and organize aimed at stopping the competitive economic and social order. Americans remained divided not over the market per se, but also over the kind of market society they wanted and how to compensate for socially problematic effects of the market system (Licht, 1995). Market integration in the United States was also characterized by wide variation in technology and corporate governance arrangements, differential growth and uneven development that suggests that different paths or models of capitalism were part of the process of industrialization and integration in the US (Bensel, 1990). Market consolidation pointed to the need for regulative intervention of the market to deal with consequences for society at large, including the effects on social order, justice and equality. A residual welfare state was created in terms of labour protection, though unionization was often viewed as inimical to the American common market (Skocpol, 1992). The recurrent theme here is the presence of distributive conflict in the integration process, with competition over the allocation of resources and contestation over different economic and social values (Jones, 2006; Hooghe and Marks, 2009). Thus, the contemporary debate in the EU on how to resolve the governance dilemma has a decided historical parallel in the US (Egan, forthcoming).

Geography and markets

A second avenue of future research concerns geography and markets. The international integration of markets and the decentralization of authority within nation states are two defining trends in Europe. Regional specialization is another likely consequence of economic integration (Krugman, 1991). The relationship between regional economic specialization and European integration deserves more attention. Economic geographers examine the spatial aspects of enterprise embeddedness. There is a considerable literature on regional economic development in Europe, and the clustering of linked industrial activities in specific locations (Krugman, 1991; Crouch, 2001). Yet despite the implications of regional economic specialization, regional business cycles, locational economies of scale and regional disparities in development within Europe, the focus in integration studies has been on redistributive mechanisms, such as structural and cohesion funds, as economic integration has created pressures to modify market outcomes to correct market failures (Hooghe, 1998). Current analyses of European regulatory policy do not focus on the territorial implications of such policies (Sbragia, 2004: 210).

Regional and local governments face some of the same contradictions of the state in terms of coordination, management and control over policies. Europeanization processes can however have very different impacts on regions and territories. While regional governments have a profound effect on public finances, sharing tax revenue and tax power, such reconfiguring of state redistribution mechanisms as well as their role in economic growth and development is often separated from broader regulatory developments at the EU level (Sbragia, 2004). Though localization of specialization has gone further in America than in Europe, scholars of European integration have paid less attention to changes in the market, and particularly changes in innovation and investment policies, which can affect certain territorially concentrated industries. The changing costs of distance, both within Europe and globally, has meant that production processes are becoming geographically fragmented to an unprecedented degree.

Informal markets

A third avenue of future research is the role of formal and informal markets. Much of the work on market integration in Europe has begun to address the relative differentiation between markets, which is critical as the specific characteristics of each factor market – goods, capital and labour – are different. The production of EU market institutions has tended to focus on formal rules and processes, and market specific definitions of competition and control (Fligstein, 1990). But Europe has also developed more informal institutional practices, based on trust and reciprocity that govern economic interaction (Farell, 2009). The informal sector has grown particularly rapidly in transition economies, as social protection systems have receded, unemployment has risen and labour force participation has declined. The informal sector is a critical component of many economies of Eastern Europe and the former Soviet Union, yet little attention has been given to the market challenges that this poses to newly admitted EU member states.

A key question here is whether future EU membership can credibly provide the social and political basis of market economies which continue to be undermined by the rise of the informal economy, state capture and social marginalization (Brusis, 2005). The focus on informal governance in EU studies should be applied to the effects of informal markets on European governance, including issues of corruption in the context of economic transformation processes and their institutional particularities. As was noted above, corruption undermines orderly competition and weakens political and economic institutions, and so it is welcome that some recent research has begun to focus on enhancing the capacity of states to constitute and preserve market order (Bruszt, 2000; Hellman *et al.*, 2000; Schamis, 2008). The need for an effective 'state capacity' exists not only during the process of market reform but also after the market system has been instituted.

Firms and organizations

Research has focused around three issues in relation to the dynamics of the firm. First, attention has been given to the role of business lobbying and alliances, as the centrality of the firm has been recognized in many studies of European integration, (Cowles, 1995; Coen, 2008; Woll, 2008). A second strand of literature in political economy has focused on firm strategies in terms of rent-seeking and protectionism. Firms will try to affect the constitution of markets and seek to maintain sector specific protection through collective action (Olsen, 1965). And a third strand of firm research has explored the conditions under which private actors set the conditions for market entry and promote economic coordination. Such demands for European-wide market rules has led to private governance arrangements that seek to set coordinated rules or avoid arbitration through self-regulation or voluntary coordination that do not have the force of law (Ronit and Schneider, 1999; Egan, 2001; Mattli, 2003).

Yet the study of European political economy has drawn little upon the economics of organization to understand the impact of European integration on internal issues of coordination, organizational design and managerial strategies, and also on external questions of contracting, networking and corporate control and governance (Chandler, 1977; Langlois, 2003). That said, useful advances in understanding have been made in some areas. For example, industrial organization economists have thrown light on the role of sunk costs in deterring competitive entry and generally slowing the competitive environment as expanding markets and technological change have altered the economic environment so that attractive rent-seeking possibilities can be seized only by breaking down or 'unbundling' the vertical structure of the managerial corporation (Baumol, 1982). This breakdown in the vertically integrated mode of production in Europe has triggered processes of institutional change and generated substantial research on the new governance structures that have emerged in traditional public services (Thatcher, 2004; Humphreys and Padgett, 2006). While different regulatory or political strategies can affect the acquisition of new firm capabilities, and in doing so can induce both stability and change in network structures and relationships among firms, the changes in industrial organization induced by changes in markets do not converge to a single form (Gourevitch, 1996).

Focusing on individual service and industrial sectors and how they determine whether classical comparative advantage, competitive advantage or firm alliances best explains observed trade patterns and market share is critical given the European focus on 'competitiveness'. Yet, much of the current discussion at the European level does not include the dilemmas that firms face in a changing regulatory environment: as one problem is solved and markets are stabilized, another set of issues emerges in relation to issues of competition, property rights and rules of exchange (Fligstein, 1990). The creation of regional economic markets cannot be understood simply as the reduction of transaction costs as market specific arrangements have both intended and unintended outcomes. The single market should have created a more integrated market, yet consumption and investment in the EU still remains heavily domestic in goods and assets (Delgado, 2006).[15] Although there is broad agreement that industrial organization has been transformed over the past decades in Europe, with a rise of employment in services relative to manufacturing and changes in the modes of production, the causes and effect of European integration on different forms of industrial transformation has not been adequately assessed.[16] Systematic studies of corporate restructuring in both Western and Eastern Europe, building on earlier work in industrial economics by Buiges *et al.* (1995) and more recent work by Bohle and Greskovits (2007), is warranted. Political economy needs to focus on the responsiveness of firms to the growth of European regulation and the effect on industry dynamics of the increasing use of market competition by considering how firm strategies have evolved over time in tandem with political developments.

Comparative regionalism

Research on regionalism has become overwhelmingly focused on the EU itself, with a concomitant decline of comparative regional integration studies. Yet more work is warranted for comparing or contrasting the European experience with other regional development processes (Webber and Fort, 2005; Sbragia, 2008; Farrell, 2009). Of course, the developmental trajectories and evolution of the European integration model are often used as the benchmark to measure economic integration more generally. The liberalization undertaken by the EU is often advocated by international economists, as EU trade policy has shifted from tariffs and quotas towards non-tariff barriers and subsequent expansion of the EU trade regime to include labour protection, environmental sustainability and good governance (Jones, 2006).

However, research on other nascent regional developments can provide alternative hypotheses about, for example, the role of collective institutions (Duina, 2005; Archarya, 2007). Many regional organizations have developed in the world that are accompanied by deep intraregional trade and investment ties but have more modest institutional arrangements. Efforts in Africa, Asia and Latin America have evolved over time, based on a loose and pragmatic regionalism that avoids legal binding decisions (Pempel, 2005; Balme and Bridges, 2008). They are often intended only to dismantle barriers to trade and investment, exclude mechanisms to deal with market failures, and generally provide no development strategies (Pastor, 2001). Just as research on European economic integration draws on both trade theory and industrial behaviour and market structure, research in other regional contexts might also consider the effects of reciprocal trade agreements on business and corporate strategy, state development practices, and investment and trade policy agendas. The research challenge is to examine the complementarities and synergies that occur in different regional settings that promote greater liberalization, as well as the persistent legal and cultural differences and geopolitical constraints that impede economic coordination. Differing relations between state and society, the role of colonialism and the hegemonic influence of the United States suggest that the nature of regional integration varies substantially by region (Sbragia, 2008).

Conclusions

Scholars have used institutional, international, ideational and coalitional factors to explain the process and dynamics of political economy and market reform in Europe. This chapter has emphasized, in particular, the importance of institutions in creating credible commitments, ensuring enforcement and fostering administrative capacity to ensure the sustainability of market integration. Much of the research in the political economy of European integration seeks to understand the structuring of rules, including issues of property rights, governance structures and rules of exchange. European political economy also acknowledges that the emerging system for governing includes both state and non-state actors, and that market integration depends not only on many legal and formal institutionalized sets of rules but also on many informal modes of governance.

Yet in emphasizing the importance of such matters as economic interdependence, the advent of the single market and monetary union, and the transition that many EU states have made to becoming market economies, the challenges such changes have and do involve are also recognized by political economists. The challenges are manifest perhaps most notably in the debates about whether states can still temper market competition when their policies and policy instruments have been undermined by intense economic integration (Polanyi, 1944; Scharpf, 1999; Caporaso and Tarrow, 2009). Consequently, attention is gradually shifting to sustaining market reforms in adverse circumstances without jeopardizing democratic governance (Schamis, 1999).

European integration has focused on the need to improve the *effectiveness* of public sector institutions and the *performance* of public policies through enhancing the performance of democratic institutions. This had led scholars to focus on the trade-offs between policy credibility and political legitimacy which have emerged in research and academic exchanges about delegation to non-majoritarian institutions (O'Donnell, 1994; Majone, 1996; Scharpf, 1999). As the evolving governance of the single market has changed the functional and territorial boundaries of regulatory policy, debates in political economy have ranged from the effects of the global trading system, the pressure for trade reform in Europe, and the growth of regional trade agreements to the regulatory design of institutions and their effects on accountability, legitimacy and social solidarity.

The suggestions for further research that have been made in this chapter draw upon a range of interdisciplinary scholarship that can contribute further to contemporary policy debates about knowledge and innovation, competitiveness, inequality and development in the EU. Scholars working in such fields as economic sociology, economic geography and economic history can add substantially to the work on political economy, emphasizing the institutional power relations and institutional logics operating in the political system. So, economic sociologists can show the structural and institutional sources of economic success and failure by highlighting the organizational characteristics of firms (Fligstein, 2001). Economic geography can provide an important focus on the behaviour of firms and the spatial organization and formal and informal functions of economic activity. And comparative economic history can remind us of the importance of systematically comparing experiences across time, regions and states in ways reminiscent of early studies of comparative regionalism.

In short, although there is already a widespread interest in several academic disciplines in understanding how market processes and institutional structures work and interact, there is 'substantial methodological pluralism in the field of political economy to warrant a number of avenues for future research' (Pahre, 2004: 171).

Notes

1. This chapter is a much revised version of a paper presented at the launch of the PSEUP series, 9 March 2007. Many thanks to Neill Nugent, Simon Hix, Claudio Radaelli, Wade Jacoby and Bill Burros for comments and suggestions.
2. Among the excellent survey works are Pelkmans (1984); Tsoukalis (1997); Gillingham (2003); Schmidt (2005); Jones and Verdun (2004); Eichengreen (2007); and Neal (2007).
3. For an overview, see Jones and Verdun (2004).
4. See for example, the research on neofunctionalism, LI, rational choice, historical institutionalism, federalism and constructivism.
5. Interestingly Meunier and Nicolaidis (2005) make a similar argument about EU trade policy, drawing attention to the EU as a conflicted trade power in much the same way that Pelkmans (1984) drew attention to the contradictions inherent between state and market.
6. The so-called services directive 2006/123.
7. Communication from the Commission to the EP, the Council, the European Economic and Social Committee and the Committee of the Regions – A Single Market for 21st Century Europe (COM(2007) 725 final) {SEC(2007) 1517} (SEC(2007) 1518) (SEC(2007) 1519) (SEC(2007) 1520) (SEC(2007) 1521).
8. The Baltic states have much more meagre welfare states and weak industrial relations compared to the Visegrad states. They have chosen minimal industrial policies and have introduced restrictive monetary policies (Bohl and Greskovits, 2007). By contrast, the Visegrad states have sought to protect against pressures of liberalization and market competition through social welfare policies, buttressed by protective regulation and tariffs, export zones, foreign trade and investment agencies, investment support funds, and tax exemption regimes, emphasizing policies of industrial modernization.
9. See Leon Lindberg's (2001) address to the EU Studies Association for a similar point.
10. For instance, scholars who challenged the 'constitutional asymmetry' view have promoted deliberative, rather than participatory, democratic processes through new forms of 'multilevel governance' in the EU. See Joerges and Dehousse (2002) and Zeitlan and Pochet (2005).
11. This has led to a substantial debate in Europe about the utilitarian functions of the single market.
12. Fabbrini (2003) has adopted a similar focus in linking the role of public authorities and market building in Europe and the US.
13. Schmidt has coined the expression 'regional state' to refer to the phenomenon of EU integration.
14. The EU has been variously described as a regional state (Schmidt, 2004), consociational state (Bogaards and Crepaz, 2002), regulatory state (Majone,

1996) post-modern state (Caporaso, 1996) and federal state (Sbragia, 1992).
15. There has been significant attention in the political economy literature to the importance of the institutional environment of organizations, and the influential varieties of capitalism literature have tended to emphasize the importance of national-level differences in the ways in which institutions structure economic activities.
16. Economic geography which is concerned with the location and distribution of economic activity, the spatial organization and function of business activity would provide additional insights into many of these issues concerning the role of territoriality and markets.

References

Alesina, A. and Giavazzi, F. (2006) *The Future of Europe: Reform or Decline* (Cambridge, MA: MIT Press).

Appel, H. (2001) 'Corruption and the Collapse of the Czech Transition Miracle', *East European Politics and Societies* 15(3): 523–53.

Archarya, A. (2007) 'The Emerging Regional Architecture of World Politics' *World Politics* 59(4): 629–52.

Armen, A. (1950) 'Uncertainty, Evolution, and Economic Theory,' *Journal of Political Economy* 58(3): 211–21.

Asbeek Brusse, W. (1997a) *Tariffs, Trade and European Integration, 1947–1957* (London: Macmillan).

Asbeek Brusse, W. (1997b) 'Regional Plans for European Trade, 1945–1957', in R. Griffiths (ed.) *The Economic Development of the EEC* (Cheltenham: Edward Elgar): 45–63.

Baldwin, R. and Thornton, P. (2008) *Multilateralising Regionalism* (London: CEPR).

Balme, R. and Bridges, B. (2008) *Europe–Asia Relations: Building Multilateralisms* (Basingstoke: Palgrave Macmillan).

Baumol, W. J. (1982) 'Contestable Markets: An Uprising in the Theory of Industry Structure', *American Economic Review, American Economic Association* 72(1): 1–15, March.

Begg, I. (2008) 'Economic Governance in an Enlarged Euro Area' *European Economy Economic Papers* 311, March. (Brussels: European Commission).

Bensel, R. (1990) *Yankee Leviathan: The Origins of Central State Authority in US 1859–1877* (Cambridge: Cambridge University Press).

Bensel, R. (2000) *The Political Economy of American Industrialisation, 1877–1900* (Cambridge: Cambridge University Press).

Berger, S. and Dore, R. (2006) *National Diversity and Global Capitalism* (Ithaca: Cornell University Press).

Bernanke, B. S. (2006) At the Federal Reserve Bank of Kansas City's Thirtieth Annual Economic Symposium, Jackson Hole, Wyoming, August 25, 2006 Global Economic Integration: What's New and What's Not? http://www.federalreserve.gov/newsevents/speech/bernanke20060825a.htm

Bogaards, M. and M. M. L. Crepaz (2002) 'Consociational interpretations of the European Union', *European Union Politics* 3(3): 357–81.

Bohle, D. and Greskovits, B. (2004) 'Capital, Labor and the Prospects of the Central and Eastern Europe', Harvard Working Paper 58, European Social Model in the East (Cambridge, MA: Harvard University Center for European Studies).

Bohle, D. and Greskovits, B. (2007) 'Neoliberalism, Embedded Neoliberalism, and Neocorporatism: Paths Towards Transnational Capitalism in Central-Eastern Europe', *West European Politics*, 30(3): 443–66.

Börzel, T. and Risse, T. (2000) 'When Europe Hits Home. Europeanization and Domestic Change', European Integration online Papers (EIoP), 4(15), http://*eiop*.or.at/*eiop*/texte/2000-015a.htm

Buiges, P., Jacquemin, A. and Sapir, A. (1995) *European Policies on Competition, Trade and Industry* (Edward Elgar: Aldershot).

Brusis, M. (2005) 'The Instrumental use of the European Union Conditionality: Regionalization in Czech Republic and Slovakia', *East European Politics and* Society 19(2): 291–316.

Bruszt, L. (2000) 'A Market Economy Needs an Effective State in The Transition', *Newsletter: The World Bank Group*, 11(3–4) (Washington, DC: World Bank).

Bruszt, L. (2002) 'Market Making as State Making – Constitutions and Economic Development in Postcommunist Eastern Europe', *Constitutional Political Economy* 15(1): 53–72.

Buchen, C. (2006) 'Estonia and Slovenia as Antipodes', in D. Lane and M. Myant (eds) *Varieties of Capitalism in Post-Communist Countries* (Basingstoke: Palgrave Macmillan) 65–89.

Cameron, D. (1978) 'The Expansion of the Public Economy: A Comparative Analysis', *American Political Science Review* 72(4): 1243–61.

Cameron, D. (1984) 'Social Democracy, Corporatism, Labor Quiescence and the Representation of Economic Interests in Advanced Capitalist Society', in J. Goldthorpe (ed.) *Order and Conflict in Contemporary Capitalism* (Oxford: Clarendon Press).

Camps, M. (1965) *What Kind of Europe: the Community Since De Gaulle's Veto* (Oxford: Oxford University Press).

Caporaso, J. (1996) 'The European Union and Forms of State: Westphalian, Regulatory or Postmodern', *Journal of Common Market Studies* 34(1): 29–52.

Caporaso, J. and Tarrow, S. (2009) 'Polanyi in Brussels: European Institutions and the Embedding of Markets in Society', forthcoming *World Politics*

Cecchini, P. *et al.*, (1988) *The European Challenge 1992: The Benefits of a Single Market* (Aldershot: Gower).

Cerny, P. (1997) Paradoxes of the Competition State: The Dynamics of Political Globalization, *Government and Opposition* 32(2): 251–74.

Chandler, A. (1962) *Strategy and Structure: Chapters in the History of the Industrial Enterprise* (Cambridge: MIT Press).

Chandler, A. (1969) 'The Structure of American Industry', *Business History Review* 43: 255–298, reprinted in *The Essential Alfred Chandler*: 247–92.

Chandler, A. (1978) *The Visible Hand: Managerial Revolution in American Business* (Cambridge, MA: Harvard University Press).

Chandler, A. (1977) *The Visible Hand*, (Cambridge, MA and London, England: The Belknap Press of Harvard University Press).

Chandler A. (1990) *Scale and Scope: the Dynamics of Industrial Capitalism*, (Cambridge, MA: Harvard University Press).

Coen, D. (2008) *Lobbying the European Union: Institutions, Actors and Policy*, (Oxford: Oxford University Press).

Cowles, M. G. (1995) 'Setting the Agenda for a New Europe: The ERT and EC 1992', *Journal of Common Market Studies* 33(4): 501–26.

Crafts, N.F.R. and Venables, A. (2003) 'Globalization in History: A Geographical Perspective', in M. Bordo, A. Taylor and J. Williamson (eds) *Globalization in Historical Perspective* (Chicago: University of Chicago Press) 323–64.

Crouch, C. (2001) *Local Production Systems in Europe: Rise or Demise*, (Oxford: Oxford University Press).

Crouch, C. and Streeck, W. (eds) (1997) *Political Economy of Modern Capitalism*, (Thousand Oaks: Sage).

Crouch, C. and Farrell, H. (2004) 'Breaking the Path of Institutional Development: Alternatives to the New Determinism in Political Economy,' *Rationality and Society* 16(1): 5–43.

Crowley, S. (2005) 'Overshooting the Mark: East European Labor, Varieties of Capitalism, and the Future of the European Social Model', paper presented at the annual meeting of the American Political Science Association, Washington, DC, September.

Curzon, V. (1974) *Essentials of Economic Integration: Lessons from the EFTA Experience* (London: Macmillan).

Joerges, C. and Dehousse, R. (eds), (2002) *Good Governance I Europe's Integrated Market* (Oxford: Oxford University Press).

Delgado, J. (2006) *Single Market Trails Home Bias* (Brussels: Bruegel Policy Brief).

Dell, E. S. (1959) 'Economic Integration and the American Example', *The Economic Journal* 69(273): 39–54.

Diebold, W. (1959) *The Schuman Plan: A Study in Economic Cooperation 1950–1959* (New York: Praeger).

Duina, F. (2005) *The Social Construction of Free Trade: The European Union, NAFTA, and Mercosur* (Princeton: Princeton University Press).

Eberlein, B. (2003) 'Formal and informal cooperation in single market regulation', in T. Christiansen and S. Piattani (eds) *Informal Governance in the European Union* (Cheltenham: Edward Elgar) 150–72.

ECB (European Central Bank) (2006) 'Cross-Border Labor Mobility within an Enlarged EU', Occasional Papers 52, October.

Eeckhout, P. (1994) *The European Internal Market and International Trade* (Oxford: Clarendon Press).

Egan, M. (2001) *Constructing a European Market* (Oxford: Oxford University Press).

Egan, M. (2007) 'The Single Market' in M. Cini (ed.) *European Union Politics* (Oxford: Oxford University Press) 253–60.

Egan, M. (2008a) 'The Emergence of the US Internal Market', in J. Pelkman, M. Chang and D. Hanf (eds) *The EU Internal Market in Comparative Perspective Economic, Political and Legal Analyses* (Brussels: Peter Lang).

Egan, M. (2008b) 'Governance and the Single Market' in A. Verdun and I. Toemmel (eds) *Innovative Governance in the European Union* (Boulder: Lynne Reinner) 237–69.

Egan, M. (forthcoming) *Single Markets: Economic Integration in Europe and the United States* (Oxford: Oxford University Press).

Eichengreen, B. (2006) 'European Integration' in B. R. Weingast and D. Wittman (eds) *Handbook of Political Economy,* (Oxford: Oxford University Press).

Eichengreen, B. (2007) *The European Economy Since 1945: Coordinated Capitalism and Beyond* (Princeton: Princeton University Press).

Emerson, M. (1988) *The Economics of 1992: The EC Commission's Assessment of the Economic Effects of Completing the Internal Market* (Oxford: Oxford University Press).

Epstein, D. and O'Halloran, S. (1999) *Delegating Power: A Transaction Cost Approach to Policy-Making* (Cambridge: Cambridge University Press).

Ertman, T. (1997) *Birth of the Leviathan: Building States and Regimes in Early Modern Europe* (Cambridge: Cambridge University Press).

Esping Anderson, G. (1990) *The Three Worlds of Welfare Capitalism* (Princeton: Princeton University Press).

Fabbrini, S. (2003) 'A Single Western State Model? Differential Development and Constrained Convergence of Public Authority Organisation in Europe and America', *Comparative Political Studies* 36(6): 653–78.

Falkner, G (2003) 'Social Policy', in M. Cini (ed.) *European Union Politics* (Oxford: Oxford University Press) 271–86.

Falkner, G., Treib, O., Hartlapp, M. and Leiber, S. (2005) *Complying with Europe: EU Harmonization and Soft Law in the Member States* (Cambridge: Cambridge University Press).

Farrell, H. (2009) *The Political Economy of Trust* (Cambridge: Cambridge University Press).

Ferrara, M. (2005) *The Boundaries of Welfare* (Oxford: Oxford University Press).

Findlay, B. and O'Rourke, K. H. (2003) 'Commodity Market Integration 1500–2000' in M. Bardo, A. M. Taylor and J. Williamson (eds) *Globalization in Historical Perspective* (Chicago: University of Chicago Press.)

Findlay, B. and O'Rourke, K. H. (2007) *Power and Plenty: Trade, War, and the World Economy in the Second Millennium* (Princeton: Princeton University Press).

Fligstein, N. (1990) *The Transformation of Corporate Control* (Harvard: Harvard University Press).

Fligstein, N. (1996) 'Markets as politics: a political-cultural approach to market institutions', *American Sociological Review* 61(4): 656–73.

Fligstein, N. (2003) *The Architecture of Markets: An Economic Sociology of Twenty-First-Century Capitalist Societies* (Princeton: Princeton University Press).

Fort, B. and Webber, D. (eds), (2006) *Regional Integration in East Asia and Europe* (London: Routledge).

Frieden, J. (1991) 'Invested Interests: The Politics of National Economic Policies in a World of Global Finance,' *International Organization* 45(4): 425–51.

Friedan, J. and Rogowski, R. (1996) 'The impact of the international economy on national policies: An analytical overview', in H. Milner and R. Keohane (eds), *Internationalization and Domestic Politics* (Cambridge: Cambridge University Press).

Garrett, G. (1998) *Partisan Politics in the Global Economy* (Cambridge: Cambridge University Press).

Gillingham, J. (2003) *European Integration, 1950–2003 Superstate or New Market Economy?* (Cambridge: Cambridge University Press).

Goldthorpe, J. H. (1984) *Order and Conflict in Contemporary Capitalism* (Oxford: Clarendon Press).

Gourevitch, P. (1996) 'The Macropolitics of Microinstitutional Differences in the Analysis of Comparative Capitalism' in Berger, S. and R. P. Dore (eds) *National Diversity and Global Capitalism* (Ithaca: Cornell University Press) 239–62.

Grabbe, H. (2000) 'European Integration and Corporate Governance in Central Europe: Trajectories of Institutional Change', Unpublished Paper Birmingham.

Grabbe, H. (2006) *The EU's Transformative Power. Europeanization through Conditionality in Central and Eastern Europe* (Basingstoke: Palgrave Macmillan).

Greskovits, B. and Bohle, D. (2007) 'The State, Internationalization, and Capitalist Diversity in Eastern Europe', *Competition and Change* 11(2): 89–114.

Griffiths, R. (2006) 'A Dismal Decade? European Integration in the 1970s' in D. Dinan (ed.) *Origins and Evolution of the EU* (Oxford: Oxford University Press) 169–90.

Grubel, H. G. and Lloyd, P. J. (1975) *Intra-Industry Trade: The Theory and Measurement of International Trade in Differentiated Products* (New York: John Wiley & Sons).

Gstöhl, S. (2008) 'The Internal Market's External Dimension: Political Aspects', in J. Pelkmans, D. Hanf and M Chang (eds) The *EU Internal Market in Comparative Perspective: Economic, Political and Legal Analyses* (Brussels: Peter Lang) 221–46.

Habermas, J. (1976) *Legitimation Crisis* (London: Heinemann).

Hall, P. A. and Soskice, D. (2001) *Varieties of Capitalism. The Institutional Foundations of Comparative Advantage* (Oxford: Oxford University Press).

Hancké, R., Rhodes, M. and Thatcher, M. (2007) *Beyond Varieties of Capitalism: Conflict, Contradictions, and Complementarities in the European Economy* (Oxford: Oxford University Press).

Hanf, D. (2008) 'Legal Concept and Meaning of the Internal Market', in J. Pelkmans, M. Chang and D. Hanf (eds) *The EU Internal Market in Comparative Perspective Economic, Political and Legal Analyses* (Brussels: Peter Lang).

Hanson, B. (1998) 'What Happened to Fortress Europe? External Trade Policy Liberalization in the EU', *International Organization* 52(1): 55–85.

Hatzopoulos, V. (2008) 'Legal Aspects of the Internal Market for Services' in J. Pelkmans, D. Hanf and M. Chang (eds) *The EU Internal Market in*

Comparative Perspective Economic, Political and Legal Analyses (Brussels: Peter Lang) 139–88.

Hay, C. (2000) 'Contemporary capitalism, globalization, regionalization and the persistence of national variation', *Review of International Studies* 26(4): 509–31.

Hay, C. (2004) 'Common Trajectories, variable paces, divergent outcomes? Modes of European capitalism under conditions of complex economic interdependence', *Review of Intenational Political Economy* 11(2): 231–62.

Hays, S. (1984) *The Response to Industrialism 1885–1914* (Chicago: Chicago University Press).

Hellman, J., Jones, G. and Kaufmann, D. (2000) 'Seize the State, Seize the Day: State Capture, Corruption, and Influence in Transition,' Policy Research Working Paper 2444 (Washington, DC: World Bank).

Héritier, A. (2002) 'New Modes of Governance in Europe: Policy Making without Legislating?' Working paper, IHS Political Science Series, 81.

Hollingsworth, J. R. and Boyer, R. (eds), (1997) *Contemporary Capitalism: The Embeddedness of Institutions* (Cambridge: Cambridge University Press).

Hooghe, L. (1998) 'EU Cohesion Policy and Competing Models of Capitalism', *Journal of Common Market Studies* 36(4): 457–77.

Hooghe, L. and Marks, G. (1997) 'The Making of a Polity: The Struggle Over European Integration', European Integration online Papers (EIoP) 4, http://eiop.or.at/eiop/texte/1997–004a.htm

Hooghe, L. and Marks, G. (2009) 'A Postfunctional Theory of European Integration: From Permissive Consensus to Constraining Dissensus', *British Journal of Political Science* 39: 1–23.

Humphreys, P. and Padgett, S. (2006) 'Globalization, the European Union, and Domestic Governance in Telecoms and Electricity,' *Governance* 19(3): 383–406.

Ilzkovitz, F., Dierx, A., Kovacs, V. and Sousa, N. (2007) 'Steps towards a Deeper Economic Integration: The Internal Market in the 21st Century', paper presented at the EUSA Biennial Conference Montreal May 17–19.

Iverson, T. (2005) *Capitalism, Democracy and Welfare* (Cambridge: Cambridge University Press).

Iverson, T. and Wren, A. (1998) 'Equality, employment and budgetary restraint: The trilemma of the service economy', *World Politics* 50(4): 507–46.

Jabko, N. (2007) *Playing the Market: A Political Strategy for Uniting Europe, 1985–2005* (Ithaca: Cornell University Press).

Jacquemin, A. and De Jong, H. W. (1977) *European Industrial Organisation* (New York: Wiley).

Joerges, C. and Dehousse. R. (2002) *Good Governance in Europe's Integrated Market* (Oxford: Oxford University Press).

Jones, E. (2006) 'Europe's Market Liberalization is a Bad Model for a Global Trade Agenda', *Journal of European Public Policy* 13(6): 943–57.

Jones, E. (2008) *Economic Adjustment and Transformation in Small States* (Oxford: Oxford University Press).

Jones E. and Verdun, A. (eds) (2004) *The Political Economy of European Integration: Theories and Analysis* (London: Routledge).

Katzenstein, P. (1985) *Small States in World Markets: Industrial Policy in Europe* (Ithaca: Cornell University Press).

Katzenstein, P. and Shirashi, T. (eds), (2005) *A World of Regions: Asia and Europe in the American Imperium* (Cornell: Cornell University Press).

Katzenstein, P. and Shirashi, T. (2006) *Beyond Japan: East Asian Regionalism* (Ithaca: Cornell University Press).

Kitschelt, H. (1991) 'Industrial Governance Structures, Innovation Strategies, and the Case of Japan', *International Organization*, 45(4) (October): 453–93.

Kitschelt, H., Lange, P., Marks, G. and Stephens, J. (eds) (1999) *Continuity and Change in Contemporary Capitalism* (Cambridge: Cambridge University Press).

Knill, C. and Lehmkuhl, D. (1999) 'How Europe Matters: Different Mechanisms of Europeanization', European Integration online Papers, vol. 3: 7, http://www.eiop.or.at/eiop/texte/1999–007a.htm

Knill, C. and Lenschow, A. (1998) *Change as Appropriate Adaptation: Administrative Adjustment to European Environmental Policy in Britain and Germany* European Integration online Papers (EIoP) Vol. 2 (1998) N° 1; http://eiop.or.at/eiop/texte/1998–001.htm.

Krugman, P. (1991) *Geography and Trade* (Boston: MIT Press).

Lake, D. (2006) 'Overview: International Political Economy: A Maturing Discipline', in B. Weingast and D. Wittman (eds) *Handbook of Political Economy* (Oxford: Oxford University Press) 757–77.

Langlois, R. (2003) 'The Vanishing Hand: The Changing Dynamics of Industrial Capitalism,' *Industrial and Corporate Change* 12(2): 351–85.

Lejour, A. (2008) 'Economic Aspects of the Internal Market for Services' in J. Pelkmans, D. Hanf and M. Chang (eds) *The EU Internal Market in Comparative Perspective: Economic, Political and Legal Analyses* (Brussels: Peter Lang) 115–37.

Leibfried, S. and P. Pierson, (1995) *European Social Policy: Between Fragmentation and Integration* (Washington, DC: Brookings Press).

Licht, W. (1995) *Industrializing America* (Baltimore: Johns Hopkins University Press).

Levy, J. (1999) 'Vice into Virtue: Progressive Politics and Welfare Reform in Continental Europe', *Politics and Society* 27(2): 239–73.

Levi, M. (1988) *Of Rule and Revenue* (Berkeley: University of California Press).

Lindberg, L. (2001) Acceptance Remarks, *EUSA Review*, Summer, 12–13.

Locke, R. (1995) *Remaking the Italian Economy* (Ithaca: Cornell University Press).

Maier, C. (1977) 'The Politics of Productivity: Foundations of American International Economic Policy after World War II', *International Organization*, 31(4), Special issue published as 'Between Power and Plenty: Foreign Economic Policies of Advanced Industrial States': 607–33.

Majone, G. (1993) 'The European Community: Between social policy and social regulations', *Journal of Common Market Studies* 31(2): 153–70.

Majone, G. (1996) *Regulating Europe* (New York: Routledge).

Majone, G. (1997) 'From the Positive to the Regulatory State: Causes and Consequences of Changes in the Mode of Governance', *Journal of Public Policy* 17(2): 139–67.

Majone, G. (2000) *Dilemmas of European Integration: The Ambiguities and Pitfalls of Integration by Stealth* (Oxford: Oxford University Press).

Marks, G. and Steenbergen, M. (2002) 'Understanding Political Contestation in the European Union', *Comparative Political Studies* 35(8): 879–92.

Mattli, W. (2001) 'Global private governance for voluntary standards setting: National organizational legacies and international institutional biases', Regulatory Policy Program working paper (Harvard: Harvard Business School).

Mattli, W. and Buthe, T. (2003) 'Setting International Standards: Technological Rationality or Primacy of Power?', *World Politics* 56(1): 1–42, October.

McDermott, G. (2002) *Embedded Politics: Industrial Networks and Institution Building in Post Communism* (Ann Arbor: University of Michigan Press).

McNamara, K. (1998) *The Currency of Ideas: Monetary Politics in the European Union* (Ithaca: Cornell University Press).

McNamara, K. (2002) 'State Building, the Territorialisation of Money, and the Creation of the American Single Currency' in Henning, R., Andrews, D. and Pauly, L. (eds) *Governing the World's Money* (Ithaca: Cornell University Press).

Menz, G. (2005) *Varieties of Capitalism and Europeanization: National Response Strategies to the Single European Market* (Oxford: Oxford University Press).

Menz, G. (2009) *The Political Economy of Managed Migration The Role of Unions, Employers, and Non-Governmental Organizations in a Europeanized Policy Domain* (Oxford: Oxford University Press).

Messerlin, P. (2001) *Measuring the Costs of Protection in Europe: European Commercial Policy in the 2000s* (Washington: International Institute for Economics).

Meunier, S. (2005) *Trading Voices: The European Union in International Commercial Negotiations* (Princeton: Princeton University Press).

Meunier, S. and Nicolaidis, K. (2005) 'The European Union as a Trade Power' in C. Hill and M. Smith (eds) *The International Relations of the European Union* (Oxford: Oxford University Press).

Meunier, S. and Nicolaides, K. (2006) 'The European Union as a conflicted trade power', *Journal of European Public Policy* 13(6): 906–25.

Milner, H. (1999) 'The Political Economy of International Trade', *Annual Review of Political Science* 99(2): 91–114.

Milward, A. (1992), *The European Rescue of the Nation-State* (London: Routledge).

Moran, M. (1991) *The Politics of the Financial Services Revolution: The USA, UK and Japan* (New York: St Martin's Press).

Moravsick, A. (1991) 'Negotiating the Single European Act: National Interests and Conventional Statecraft in the European Community', *International Organisation* 45: 19–56.

Moravscik, A. (1993) 'Preferences and Power in the European Community: A Liberal Intergovernmentalist Approach', *Journal of Common Market Studies* 31: 473–524.

Neal, L. (2007) *The Economics of Europe and the European Union* (Cambridge: University of Cambridge Press).

Nee, V. (2000) 'The Role of the State in Making a Market Economy', *Journal of Institutional and Theoretical Economics* 156(1): 64–88.

Nicoläidis, K. and Schmidt, S. (2007) 'Mutual Recognition 'on trial': the long road to services liberalization', *Journal of European Public Policy* 14(5): 717–34.

Nicolaidis, K. and Howse, R. (2001) *The Federal Vision* (Oxford: Oxford University Press).

North, D. (1966) *The Economic Growth of the United States (1790–1860)* (New York: W.W. Norton).

North, D. (1990) *Institutions, Institutional Change and Economic Performance* (Cambridge: Cambridge University Press).

O' Connor, J. (1973) *The Fiscal Crisis of the State* (New York: St Martin's Press).

O'Donnell, G. (1994) 'Delegative Democracy', *Journal of Democracy* 5(1): 55–69.

Olsen, M. (1965) *The Logic of Collective Action* (Harvard: Harvard University Press).

Orenstein, M. (1996) *Out of the Red: Building Capitalism and Democracy in Post Communist Europe* (Michigan: University of Michigan Press).

O' Rourke, K. and Williamson, J. (1999) *Globalization and History: The Evolution of a Nineteenth-Century Atlantic Economy* (Boston: MIT Press).

Padoa-Schioppa, T. (1987) *Efficiency, Stability and Equity* (Oxford: Oxford University Press).

Padoa-Schioppa, T. *et al.* (1988) *Efficiency, Stability, and Equity* (Oxford: Oxford University Press).

Pahre, R. (2004) 'The Political Economy of European Integration in a Spatial Model' in E. Jones and A. Verdun (eds) *The Political Economy of European Integration*, (London: Routledge) 179–90.

Pastor, R. (2001) *Towards a North American Community* (Washington, DC: Institute for International Economics).

Pelkmans, J. (1984) *Market Integration in the European Community*, (Hague: Martinus Nijhoff).

Pelkmans, J. (2002) 'Mutual Recognition in Goods and Services: An Economics Perspective', College of Europe Working Papers (Economics) No. 2 (Bruges), December.

Pelkmans, J. (2006) 'European Industrial Policy', College of Europe Working Papers (Economics) No. 15 (Bruges), July.

Pelkmans, J. (2007) 'Mutual recognition in goods: On promises and disillusions' *Journal of European Public Policy* 14(5): 699–716.

Pelkmans, J. (2008) 'Economic Concept and Meaning of the Internal Market' in J. Pelkmans, D. Hanf, and M. Chang (eds) *The EU Internal Market in*

Comparative Perspective: Economic, Political and Legal Analyses, (Brussels: Peter Lang) 29–76.

Pelkmans, J. and Winters, A. (1988) *Europe's Domestic Market* (London: Chatham House; Royal Institute of International Affairs).

Pempel, T. J. (2005) *Remapping Asia: The Construction of a Region* (Ithaca: Cornell University Press).

Pierson, P. (1994) *Dismantling the Welfare State: Reagan, Thatcher and the Politics of Retrenchment* (Cambridge: Cambridge University Press).

Pierson, P. (1996) 'The New Politics of the Welfare State', *World Politics* 48(2): 143–79.

Pierson, P. (ed.) (2001) *The New Politics of the Welfare State* (Oxford: Oxford University Press).

Pinder, J. (1968) 'Positive Integration and Negative Integration: Some Problems of Economic Union in the EEC', *The World Today*, 14 March: 88–110.

Polanyi, K. (1957) *The Great Transformation* (New York: Basic Books).

Pollack, M. (2003) *The Engines of European Integration: Delegation, Agency and Agenda Setting in the EU* (Oxford: Oxford University Press).

Pollard, S. (1981) *The Integration of the European Economy since 1815* (Hemel Hempstead: George Allen & Unwin).

Radaelli, C. M. (1999) 'Harmful Tax Competition in the European Union: Policy Narratives and Advocacy Coalitions', *Journal of Common Market Studies* 37(4): 661–82.

Radaelli, C. (2005) 'Diffusion Without Convergence: How Political Context Shapes the Adoption of Regulatory Impact Assessment', *Journal of European Public Policy* 12(5): 924–43.

Rhodes, M. (1993) 'A Regulatory Conundrum: Building a Regime for EC Social and Labour Market Policy', paper presented at European Union Studies Association (EUSA) Biennial Conference, Charleston, South Carolina.

Rhodes, M. (2001) 'The Political Economy of Social Pacts: Competitive Corporatism and European Welfare Reform', in Paul Pierson (ed.) *The New Politics of the Welfare State* (Oxford: Oxford University Press) 165–94.

Rodrik, D. (1997) *Has Globalization Gone too Far?* (Washington, DC: Institute for International Economics).

Ronit, K. and Schneider, V. (1999) 'Global governance through private organizations', *Governance* 12(3): 243–66.

Rose, R. and Peters, B. G. (1978) *Can Government Go Bankrupt?* (New York: Basic Books).

Ruggie, J. (1982) 'International Regimes, Transactions and Change: Embedded Liberalism in the Postwar Economic Order', *International Organization* 36(2): 379–415.

Sabel, C. and Gerstenberg, O. (2002) 'Directly Deliberative Polyarchy: An Institutional Ideal for Europe', in C. Joerges and R. Dehousse (eds) *Good Governance in Europe's Integrated Market* (Oxford: Oxford University Press).

Sabel, C. and Piore, M. (1984) *The Second Industrial Divide: Possibilities for Prosperity* (New York: Basic Books).

Sandholtz, W. (1992) *High-Tech Europe: The Politics of International Cooperation* (Berkeley: University of California Press).

Sandholtz, W. and Zysman, J. (1989) '1992: Recasting the European Bargain', *World Politics* 42(1): 95–128.

Sapir, A., Aghion, P., Bertola, G., Hellwig, M., Pisani-Ferry, J., Rosati, D., Viñals, J., Wallace, H., Buti, M., Nava, M. and Smith, P. M. (2004) *An Agenda for a Growing Europe: The Sapir Report* (Oxford: Oxford University Press).

Sbragia, A. M. (1992) *Euro Politics* (Washington, DC: Brookings Institution).

Sbragia, A. M. (2000) 'Governance, the State and the Market: What is Going On?', *Governance* 13(2): 235–42.

Sbragia (2003) 'Post-national democracy: a challenge to political science?', paper delivered at the introductory presentation SISP Universita degli Studi di trento.

Sbragia, A. M. (2004) 'Territory, Representation, and Policy Outcome: The United States and the European Union Compared', in C.K. Ansell and G. Di Palma (eds) *Restructuring Territoriality: Europe and the United States Compared* (Cambridge: Cambridge University Press) 205–24.

Sbragia, A. M. (2006) 'The United States and the European Union: Overcoming the Challenge of Comparing two "Sui Generis" Systems' in A. Menon, and M. Schain (eds) *Comparative Federalism: The European Union and the United States in Comparative. Perspective* (Oxford: Oxford University Press) 15–34.

Sbragia, A. M. (2008) 'Comparative Regionalism: What Might It Be?', *Journal of Common Market Studies* 46(1): 29–49.

Schamis, H. (1999) 'Distributional Coalitions and the Politics of Economic Reform in Latin America', *World Politics* 51(2): 236–68.

Schamis, H. (2001) *Reforming the State* (Michigan: University of Michigan Press).

Schamis, H. (2008) 'Avoiding Collusion, Averting Collision: What Do We Know about the Political Economy of Privatization and Corruption?' Unpublished Paper, American University.

Scharpf, F. W. (1988) 'The Joint Decision Trap', *Public Administration* 66(3): 239–78.

Scharpf, F. W. (1996) 'Economic Integration, Democracy, and the Welfare State', MPIfG Working Paper 96/2. Cologne: Max Planck Institute for the Study of Societies.

Scharpf, F. W. (1999) *Governing in Europe* (Oxford: Oxford University Press).

Scharpf, F. W. (2002) 'The European Social Model: Coping with the Challenges of Diversity' (Cologne: Max Planck Working Paper 02/8).

Schmidt, S. K. (2008a) 'Single Market Policies: From Mutual Recognition to Institution Building', in I. Toemmel and A. Verdun (eds) *Innovative Governance in the EU* (Boulder: Lynne Rienner) 179–200.

Schmidt, S. K. (2008b) 'The Internal Market Seen From a Political Science Perspective', in J. Pelkmans, D. Hanf, and M. Chang (eds) *The EU Internal*

Market in Comparative Perspective: Economic, Political and Legal Analyses (Brussels: Peter Lang) 93–111.

Schmidt, S. K. (2007) 'Mutual recognition as a new mode of governance', in Schmidt, S. K. (ed.), Special issue: Mutual Recognition as a New Mode of Governance. *Journal of European Public Policy* 14(5), 667–81.

Schmidt, V. (2001) 'Europeanization and the mechanics of economic policy adjustment', European integration on-line papers (EIOP) 5 6 2001.

Schmidt, V. (2002) *The Futures of European Capitalism* (Oxford: Oxford University Press).

Schmidt, V. (2004) 'The European Union: Democratic Legitimacy in a Regional State?', *Journal of Common Market Studies*, 42(5): 975–97.

Schmidt, V. (2006) *Democracy in Europe: EU and National Politics* (Oxford: Oxford University Press).

Schmidt, V. (2007) 'European Political Economy: Taking Labor Out, Brining the State Back In and Putting the Firm front and Center', paper presented at the conference for the 30th Anniversary Issue of *West European Politics*, European University Institute, Florence 18–19 January.

Schmidt, V. (2009) 'Putting Politics Back Into the Political Economy by Bringing the State Back in Again', *World Politics* 61(3): 516–46, July.

Schonfield, A. (1965) *Modern Capitalism. The Changing Balance of Public and Private Power* (Oxford: Oxford University Press).

Scitovsky, T. (1958) *Economic Theory and Western European Integration* (New York: Routledge).

Skocpol, T. (1992) *Protecting Soldiers and Mothers: The Political Origins of Social Policy in the United States* (Cambridge, MA: Belknap Press of Harvard University Press).

Skowronek, S. (1982) *Building an American State: The Expansion of National Administrative Capacities, 1877–1920* (Cambridge: Cambridge University Press).

Smith, M. (2005) *States of Liberalization* (New York: SUNY Press).

Spaak, P.-H. (1956) *Rapport des chefs de délégation aux Ministres des Affaires Etrangéres*, 21 April. Brussels.

Stark, D. and Bruszt, L. (eds) (1998) *Postsocialist Pathways. Transforming Politics and Property in East Central Europe* (Cambridge: Cambridge University Press).

Stark, D. and Bruszt, L. (2001) 'One Way or Multiple Paths: For a Comparative Sociology of East European Capitalism', *American Journal of Sociology* 106(4): 1129–37.

Streeck, W. (1996) Neo-Voluntarism: A New European Social Policy Regime?, in Marks, G. *et al.*, *Governance in the European Union* (London: Sage).

Streeck, W. and Schmitter, P. (1991) 'From National Corporatism to Transnational Pluralism: Organized Interests in the Single European Market', *Politics and Society* 19(2): 133–64.

Thatcher, M. (2004) 'Varieties of capitalism in an internationalized world: domestic institutional change in European telecommunications', *Comparative Political Studies* 37(7): 1–30.

Tilly, C. (1990) *Coercion, Capital and European States* (Polity: Oxford).

Toemmel I. and Verdun, A. (2008) *Innovative Governance in the European Union: The Politics of Multilevel Policy Making* (Boulder: Lynne Rienner).

Tsebelis, G. (2004) *Veto Players: How Political Institutions Work* (Princeton: Princeton University Press).

Tsoukalis, L. (1997) *The New European Economy Revisited* (Oxford: Oxford University Press).

Tsoukalis, L. (2006) 'Managing Diversity and Change in the European Union', *Journal of Common Market Studies* 44(1): 1–15.

Vachudova, M. (2005) *Europe Undivided: Democracy, Leverage, and Integration after Communism* (Oxford: Oxford University Press).

Van Apeldoorn, B. (2000) 'Transnational Agency and European Governance: the Case of the European Roundtable of Industrialists', *New Political Economy* 5(2): 157–81

Verdier, D. and Breen, R. (2001) 'Europeanization and globalization: Politics against markets in. the European Union', *Comparative Political Studies* 34(3): 227–62

Viner, J. (1950) *The Customs Union Issue* (Washington, DC: Carnegie Endowment for International Peace).

Vos, E. (2005) 'Independence, Accountability and Transparency of European Regulatory Agencies', in D. Gredin, R. Muñoz and N. Petit (eds) *Regulation Through Agencies in The EU: A New Paradigm of European Governance* (Cheltenham: Edward Elgar) 120–39.

Wallace, H. (2000) 'Europeanisation and Globalisation: Complementary or Contradictory Trends?' *New Political Economy* 5(3): 369–81.

Wallerstein, I. (1974) *The Modern World System: Capitalist Agriculture and the Origins of the European World Economy in the Sixteenth Century* (New York: Academic Press).

Weber, K. and Hallerberg, M. (2001) 'Explaining Variation in Institutional Integration in the European Union: Why Firms May Prefer European Solutions,' *Journal of European Public Policy* 8(2): 171–91.

Weingast, B. (1995) 'The Economic Role of Political Institutions: Market-Preserving Federalism and Economic Development,' *Journal of Law, Economics, and Organization* 11: 1–31.

Woodruff, D. (1999) *Money Unmade: Barter and the Fate of Russian Capitalism* (Ithaca: Cornell University Press).

Woodruff, D. (2004) 'Property Rights in Context: Privatization's Legacy for Corporate Legality in Poland and Russia', *Studies in Comparative International Development* 38(4): 82–108.

Woll, C. (2008) *Firm Interests: How Governments Shape Business Lobbying on Global Trade* (Ithaca: Cornell University Press).

Young, A. R. (2002) *Extending European Cooperation: The European Union and the 'New' International Trade Agenda* (Manchester: Manchester University Press).

Young, A. R. (2004) 'The Incidental Fortress: The Single European Market and World Trade', *Journal of Common Market Studies* 42(2): 393–414.

Zeitllan, J. and Trubek, D. (eds) (2003) *Governing Work and Welfare in a New Economy: European and American Experiments* (Oxford: Oxford University Press).

Zeitllan, J., Pochet, P. and Magnusson, L. (2005) *The Open Method of Coordination in Action: The European Employment and Social Inclusion Strategies* (Brussels: Presses Interuniversitaires Européennes – Peter Lang).

Zysman, J. (1994) 'How institutions create historically rooted trajectories of growth', *Industrial and Corporate Change* 3(1): 243–83.

Chapter 11

Monetary Union

Waltraud Schelkle

The title of this book invites us to think big and ahead. It is here taken as a licence to present selective answers to three questions: firstly, what did we think we knew about the monetary union in Europe; secondly, what do we seem to know now; and, thirdly, and most importantly, what should we know? The term monetary union and EMU will be used interchangeably, since the focus of the chapter is very much on the monetary aspects of Economic and Monetary Union.

An exercise like this cannot avoid starting with the theory of optimal currency areas (OCAs). If there was a point on which scholars in this field could agree, then it was the verdict that 'the Euro area is not an optimal currency area'. Where they disagreed was whether that really mattered. And even if it mattered, how would the currency area evolve over time: for better or worse?

In light of this damning verdict, a second topic gained in prominence over time, namely the structural adjustments required and possibly levered by a unified currency. In the run-up to EMU, reforms were first postulated in order to make EMU more flexible and thus more like an OCA. The idea was to leave fiscal policy to automatic stabilizers in the government budget, while more supply-side flexibility and financial market integration would dampen economic cycles, making stabilization to some extent redundant. The underlying nexus was soon turned around and scholars asked how governments' ability and willingness to reform can be used by the strategic use of cyclical stabilization.

This brings us to the economic governance of EMU. Monetary integration theory and its offspring, the political economy of reform, talk only about the constituent parts but not the whole of the union. For this whole, neither fully fledged federalism nor triangular policy coordination[1] were deemed feasible; some thought that these institutions were not even desirable. The Maastricht framework was instead built on the idea of credible commitment to policy rules. But how would a singularly independent and stability-oriented monetary policy work in combination with barely coordinated fiscal policies? Would the fiscal rules, enshrined in a pact between governments, remain strong enough to discipline governments or would we need the Eurogroup in the Council of Finance and Economics Ministers to play an authoritative role? And what would be the incentives for the wage bargaining parties

256

in the new regime? Would they be forced to commit to moderate wage bargains or would they free ride and thus create an inflation bias? The ongoing process of enlargement adds to the urgency pressing scholars and policy-makers for answers.

EMU *as a suboptimal currency area*

Scholars definitely thought they knew that 'the eurozone is not an optimal currency area'. Take the six standard criteria that the original theory by Mundell (1961), McKinnon (1963) and Kenen (1969) entailed. EMU has neither (1) high mobility of labour nor (2) very flexible real wage rates to compensate for the loss of the exchange rate when a country-specific, 'asymmetric' shock occurs. Economies are (3) fairly open but not enough to be counted as (4) small in the sense of taking world market prices as given and adjusting to them whenever necessary (using protection and industrial policies instead); on the contrary, price adjustment is often sluggish and employment adjustment prevails. Furthermore, (5) the economic structure of EMU member states is not similar enough so as to be susceptible to common (symmetric) shocks only. Finally, (6) no fiscal federal transfer mechanism was envisaged that would compensate member states if hit by an asymmetric shock to employment.

The list could be extended, for instance by including the sensible Fleming (1971) criterion that prospective members of an OCA should have similar inflation preferences. Each time the verdict of OCA theory on EMU turned out negative. This raises two questions: First of all, does it matter? No currency area in the world has been formed with the OCA criteria in mind. And, second, even if we now know and could apply this knowledge, how does it matter? The criteria may lead to contradictory messages and nobody knows how to weigh one over the other.[2] The most effective rebuff is contained, if not explicitly stated, in Krugman (1993): a currency area may suboptimize over time because a spatial division of labour evolves that makes it more susceptible to idiosyncratic (asymmetric) shocks. The worrying message is that member states may have qualified for a higher optimality ranking before EMU than afterwards. This leads one to the paradoxical conclusion that OCA theory is inherently inapplicable to any existing currency union.

However, Krugman's 'lessons of Massachusetts for EMU' can be given a more general and optimistic interpretation. The lessons may imply that the degree of optimality can change and possibly improve. Rose (2000) gave exactly this optimistic answer: EMU is not an OCA (and that matters) but it may become so *ex post*. A decline in exchange rate volatility will increase trade (existing firms exporting more, and more firms entering export markets), and this increased openness to each other would qualify the trading partners for an OCA. The 'Rose effect' (Mongelli and Vega, 2006: 15–16) takes off from the earlier transaction cost argument of the *One Market, One Money* report (Emerson *et al.*, 1992), specifically for the OCA criteria of openness and similarity, suggesting a tractable and quantifiable effect of trade creation.[3]

The Rose effect belongs to a whole class of endogeneity effects of monetary integration. Each of the standard criteria for an OCA are bound to change with the process of its forming. A more general rationale for endogeneity is the adjustment in expectations that takes place when a currency union is formed, analytically captured by the Lucas critique of static policy evaluation (Schelkle, 2001a, 2001b). The Rose effect results from a change in the perception and anticipation of reduced exchange rate volatility. Analogously, the degree of labour market flexibility (the Mundell criterion) was bound to evolve, especially in European labour markets, where collective wage bargains determine wage and employment adjustment. So the optimality ranking may change if the elimination of exchange rates with trading partners or the replacement of national monetary authorities by the ECB changes the perception of wage bargainers regarding feasible wage settlements. In the OCA train of thought, where the exchange rate is an effective adjustment mechanism, rational expectations of the currency union would make for more flexible real wages because exchange rate devaluations can no longer neutralize uncompetitive wage settlements.[4]

Given the negative verdict on EMU as an OCA, it is no surprise that the official Commission report, *One Market, One Money*, was rather sceptical of the original OCA theory and stressed the Pareto superiority of EMU, rather than its optimality (Emerson *et al.*, 1992). In parts, it pre-empted the optimistic version of what was later called endogenous OCA theory. But it also relied on the more defensive argument of the 'Impossible Trinity' (Padoa-Schioppa, 1990) and thus diluted the foundation for its endorsement of currency unification. The Impossible Trinity states that economies cannot have stable exchange rates, freedom of capital movements and autonomy of monetary policy simultaneously. By giving up the latter, one could have an integrated financial market and eliminate nominal exchange rate volatility. However, forming EMU to escape exchange rate volatility in the Single Market is a somewhat radical step for a problem with which governments have lived for a long time. Moreover, the theorem of the Impossible Trinity is not generally valid: it holds only for economies which experience waves of capital flight and are under permanent devaluation pressures, as Italy was in the Exchange Rate Mechanism (ERM). The Trinity can be made possible if the currency is under revaluation pressure and the central bank receives exchange reserves and sterilizes the foreign exchange inflow by restraining domestic credit creation. Managing and maintaining this disequilibrium was the foundation of Germany's hegemony in the ERM (Mélitz, 1988; De Grauwe, 1990). Other hard currency countries, like Austria and the Netherlands, practised the eminently Possible Trinity to their advantage as well. Thus, to claim that the Impossible Trinity provides a rationale for EMU amounts to saying that it was the weak currency areas that somehow managed to trick the hard currency areas into an EMU that would solve their problems. It is neither a convincing nor enticing argument for EMU.

So what do we know about the evolution of EMU, conceptualized as an aspiring OCA? It seems safe to confirm that EMU is not an OCA, will not become one in the foreseeable future and perhaps never will be. Many scholars still think that this matters and try to evaluate the structural changes guided by OCA theory. These results are interesting in their own right and I summarize them briefly, helped by an extensive review of the empirical literature in Mongelli and Vega (2006) and various studies that went into that report.

First, in the light of the original Mundell criteria for an OCA: how did mobility and the flexibility of real wages change? Labour mobility is a slow moving variable and the Single Market Programme may make a difference over time, by facilitating migration. Yet the capacity to adjust by moving workers may have been exaggerated all along. Studies such as Asdrubali *et al.* (1996) have shown that even in the United States, if an asymmetric shock to state income occurs, the most important compensation mechanism for wage dependent households is fiscal federalism, that is changes in state taxes and federal transfers. It is neither household migration (labour markets) nor returns on out-of-state asset holdings (financial markets) that bear the brunt of adjustment.

The flexibility of real wages in OECD countries was the object of study in a special report by the Directorate General of Economic and Financial Affairs (European Economy, 2005: ch. 8). The relevant measure for OCA theory is the responsiveness of real wages to unemployment (demand shock) and to productivity (supply shock). The authors provide an instructive meta-analysis that is a systematic quantitative literature review of 27 relevant studies, published between 1983 and 2003. The striking result is that the most flexible real wages can be found in economies as different as Sweden, Norway, Turkey, Japan and Switzerland. The least flexible real wages are found in New Zealand, the United States, the United Kingdom, Denmark, Canada and Spain. All other (pre-2004) EU member states are part of an intermediate group (ibid.: 61, Table 13).

Obviously, structural breaks may have taken place in the meantime, monetary unification being one of them. So the authors also look at changes that have taken place. They find that during the 1990s, real wage flexibility first decreased and then increased in most EU countries. It increased continuously in the south European member states, including Italy. Flexibility decreased throughout the 1980s and 1990s in

Finland, the Netherlands and Sweden, but also in the US (ibid.: 72). Thus, it is not possible to relate these changes conclusively to EMU.

Finally, the authors go on to provide their own estimates of real wage flexibility between 1970 and 2003 in order to correct for the publication bias that affects any meta-analysis and for which they find evidence in their set of studies: journals and authors may publish only results which are significant and have the expected signs (ibid.: 66–7). These estimates confirm that labour market flexibility, measured as the real wage response to unemployment, is comparable to and often higher than in the US (ibid.: Annex 10.1).[5] A robust finding on Continental European labour markets seems to be that employment responds less, and less fast, to changes in real wages and productivity. This can be related to labour market institutions associated with the prototypical Continental European labour market, such as protection of long-term employment relationships of a skilled workforce. Less and slower employment adjustment holds both for expansions and recessions. But the upshot of all this is that the alleged inflexibility of European labour markets, as measured by real wage responsiveness to unemployment and productivity changes, is largely a myth.[6]

It is not possible yet to say much about increasing openness and whether this would lead to more or less similarity of economic structures. Indicators are too slow moving for deciding whether the Rose or the Krugman effect, more intra-industry trade or more specialization, prevails (Mongelli and Vega, 2006: 22). The study suggests the rise in cross-border foreign direct investment within EMU as well as increasing trade in services are likely to make a difference. But then, again, these processes can lead to endogenous optimization or suboptimization.

Business cycles of euro area countries seem to have more in common with each other than with other countries. Compared to the US cycle, the Euro area cycle appears smoother (has less amplitude), while recessions and highs are more drawn out (have longer duration between peaks and troughs). Thus there were also fewer recessions than in the US between 1971 and 2003 (Giannone and Reichlin, 2006: 15–16). But whether this is due to changes of cyclical characteristics in the euro area cannot be established at this stage (ibid.: 21). These authors also looked at the nature of shocks and find that, first, common rather than asymmetric shocks are responsible for most output fluctuations. Second, the asymmetric shocks tend to have small but persistent effects; but whether the shocks are exogenous ('bad luck') or propagated by idiosyncratic responses ('bad policy') is an issue of debate (ibid.: 12–13; Mongelli and Vega, 2006: 21; Gerlach and Hoffmann, 2008).

This brings us to the guesswork and the agenda for future research. In his excellent comment, Sørensen (2006) qualifies the rather optimistic picture of a smooth and increasingly identifiable common cycle. First of all, Giannone and Reichlin (2006) leave out particularly volatile periods, such as 1990–92, when not only German reunification but also banking crises in Sweden and Finland occurred. 'For a discussion of risk sharing, I think leaving out volatile periods is exactly what we should not do: risk sharing arrangements may not be important in "normal times" but may be of crucial importance during crisis periods' (Sørensen, 2006: 29). To underline this point, there seems to have been a decline in risk sharing in the recessions 1981, 1991 and 2001 (ibid.: 32), which is worrying given that this is when collective insurance is most needed. This point is echoed by another commentator's finding, who notes that 'although cyclical dispersion has remained quite low in the past few years in the euro area as a whole, disparities in cyclical positions between the (four or five) larger Member States have increased steadily. Output gap dispersion across Germany, France, Italy and Spain has increased markedly since 2003 and now stands at its highest level since the start of stage III of EMU in 1999' (McCarthy, 2006: 42). It is obviously a problem for the European Central Bank (ECB) if the business cycles diverge between those member states that account for almost 80 per cent of euro area GDP.

But why this might be the case and whether it has anything to do with EMU is, at this stage, anybody's guess. A number of scholars have discussed both what it would mean if the exchange rate as a source of shocks were eliminated (Buiter, 2000) and under which circumstances nominal exchange rate adjustment is really less costly (De Grauwe, 2000). The non-neutrality view of the exchange rate that both Buiter and De Grauwe express,[7] refutes the OCA view of the exchange rate as a relative commodity price that can be manipulated at will. Assessing the contribution of less exchange rate volatility to greater stability in EMU, but also the transformation of current account crises into drawn out processes of losing market share to imports, is in its infancy and can now be studied with respect to a number of EMU member states such as Italy or Portugal.

This raises the more general question whether OCA theory was actually a poor guide to monetary integration in Europe. Perhaps the adjustments required should have been informed more by the theory of policy coordination under uncertainty (Brandsma and Hughes Hallett, 1984; Ghosh and Masson, 1994; Schelkle, 2001a, 2001b). For instance, Demertzis *et al.* (2000) concluded that a nascent EMU seemed to be 'held together [largely] by policy makers'. Yet, the idea of creating institutions of policy coordination was abandoned because decisive member states and the Bundesbank flatly refused to contemplate such changes in economic governance. It was very convenient that OCA theory did not talk about these implications for policy-making. Knowledge was substituted by hope, namely that it would do if we pursued market integration and candidates spent a probation period in the Maastricht 'purgatory' (Buiter, 2004) to prove their worthiness as regards inflation preferences.

Thus, for lack of empirical data, the academic community could pursue the question of what types of policy coordination or collective insurance mechanisms would be feasible and worthwhile only in theory. This turned into simulation exercises of how much a stabilization mechanism would cost if it were to provide the same insurance as the federal budget in the US did to the states (Italianer and Pisani-Ferry, 1994; Italianer and Vanheukelen, 1993). Renewed research interest may now be inspired by the conflicting findings about business cycles in EMU and the international financial crisis unfolding since the summer of 2007. Closely related is the puzzle of the 'Great Moderation', the finding that variance of output per capita and consumption growth has decreased in all OECD countries (Giannone and Reichlin, 2006: 10). Candidates for explaining this Great Moderation include inventory management of firms, steadier monetary policy intervention and deepening credit markets. The latter, monetary policy and financial market integration, could be explained by the changes that EMU brought about (Gerlach and Hoffmann, 2008). The jury on the Great Moderation is still out[8] and it may even be about to change its mind, given the turbulence in world financial markets. This provides an opportunity for research, for instance by assessing how EMU fares in these turbulent times compared to trade blocs that are less integrated in monetary terms. If future studies find that more stability in EMU is endogenous to a unified monetary policy in integrated financial markets, it would strengthen the case for exploring policy coordination and its effects, more than the nature of the monetary union, as an emerging OCA.

Structural reform

The consensus that EMU is not an OCA brought another consensus in its wake, namely that 'Europe needs to become more flexible'. The policy implications of OCA theory were increasingly turned on its head: it was used to identify the reforms necessary to move countries up in the optimality ranking. This theme has gained in practical importance. Initially it provided the link between the Single Market Programme and EMU. Obviously, nominal wage rigidity, created by collective wage bargaining, could still make for real wage flexibility if prices were flexible. But commodity prices in the EU are not very flexible, which is interpreted as the result of a lack of competition,[9] and so the Single Market Programme was seen as an essential part of monetary integration. In particular the privatization of state-owned enterprises and deregulation of protected quasi-monopolies promised to lead to more flexible relative prices (Mongelli, 2002: 18). In the meantime, the call for flexibility serves as a reason why the Employment Strategy and fiscal surveillance have to be 'streamlined', that is subject to a policy cycle closely coordinated with the Broad Economic Policy Guidelines (CEC, 2002).

How would the political economy of reform, implied by this instrumental reading of OCA theory, work?[10] The mainstream view was that the regime shift to a stability-oriented macropolicy, embodied by the ECB and the Stability Pact, would create a situation of TINA ('There Is No Alternative') or 'back-against-the-wall'. This can be used as a reform strategy if one believes that fiscal crises or austerity make reform easier because they raise awareness of the costs of the status quo and thus weaken the opposition to reform (Rodrik, 1996: 26–9). An explicit argument along these lines for EMU can be found in Calmfors (2001: 268–70). In his model, the government weighs up inflation, unemployment and labour market reforms, all of which are disliked by the majority in the electorate, who are also the dominant group in the labour market. Reforms can reduce equilibrium unemployment, but they are undertaken only if the benefits in lower expected inflation and unemployment outweigh the costs in terms of lower real wages or less employment security enjoyed by those in employment. The loss of access to countercyclical monetary and fiscal policies increases the incentive to reform. More reform and less countercyclical demand-management are socially desirable, because reform would raise the welfare of labour market outsiders, who are the political minority.

This view was part of the change in the policy consensus during the 1980s, the monetary and macroeconomic side of which has been brilliantly analysed by McNamara (1998). Little attention was paid to an alternative view that sees tensions between an ambitious agenda of structural reform and fiscal consolidation. It is based on what might be called a 'need for bribes' hypothesis, suggesting that fiscal space is required so as to allow compensation of potential or actual losers from reforms (Fernandez and Rodrik, 1991). One important argument in favour of the 'need for bribes' is that structural reforms under conditions of 'permanent austerity' (Pierson, 2001: 410) are biased towards measures which are fiscally favourable and shift costs to firms. In particular, stricter employment protection may be conceded in exchange for lower non-employment benefits. If correct, it would mean that combining labour market reform with fiscal consolidation would run into the difficulty that austerity weakens the political support for reforms. To overcome resistance, governments may engage in forms of compensation that obstruct specific Lisbon goals, such as making firms more competitive and eliminating the segmentation between insiders and outsiders of labour markets.

We know now that the focus on labour market reform, supported by OCA theory but also the OECD Jobs Strategy from 1994, has been exaggerated. Thus, the OECD's own reassessment of the Jobs Strategy ten years on calls for more careful sequencing of reforms in line with a 'need for bribes' view (OECD, 2006: 63, 100, 183). The IMF (2004a, 2004b) has explicitly tested for these competing hypotheses in the context of the EU; the OECD has followed suit (Duval and Elmeskov, 2005). Two findings are of particular relevance. First, reforms seem to be easier and more likely in good times or in an expansionary phase of the business cycle. Second, EU membership is a positive predictor of reform activism, although more for the cutting of non-employment benefits than for deregulation of employment protection.

What we know for sure is that the once firmly held belief in TINA strategies has become much more nuanced. Still, the findings are based on a relatively short time-period and a statistically small sample which keeps the experience of reform processes high on the research agenda. Comparative quantitative studies can provide taxonomies and examples for both reform strategies – the 'back against the wall' or the 'need for bribes'. One can then try and identify patterns and conditions under which the one or the other reform strategy will be more effective. A bolder interpretation would suggest that these findings can be read as evidence for 'political exchanges in the shadow of fiscal austerity'. A classification of the thrust of labour market reforms reveals that reforming governments engage in a strategy of 'two steps forward, one backwards' with respect to non-employment benefits, and that they go 'one forward, one backwards' with respect to employment protection (Boeri, 2005: Table 1). Thus, EU countries exhibited a comparatively high degree of activism that increased in the run-up to EMU, but there was no one-dimensional thrust of reform, except for a decline in generosity as regards non-employment benefits (such as early retirement or social assistance). This is in line with what the 'new politics of the welfare state' (Pierson, 2001) leads one to expect: a reduction of the generosity of benefits if outside is compensated by more protection for insiders of the labour market (Fatás *et al.*, 2003: 38–40; Saint-Paul, 2004: 13–16; Castanheira *et al.*, 2006: 12–14). This makes for little net change in overall indices of labour market reforms, although there is considerable restructuring going on.

But even if one goes for this bold interpretation of studies with a limited reach, we need to know more about the result of this restructuring. The reform process may be counterproductive if restructuring leads to liberalization of contracts and lower benefits only for those marginally employed or out of work (Brandt *et al.*, 2005: 63–4). Governments could end up creating exactly those insider–outsider labour markets that they have been urged to reform by the OECD Jobs Study.[11] This is why the IMF sided with the 'need for bribes' hypothesis and recommended accepting a temporary worsening of public finances to make reforms happen (IMF, 2004a: 115–16, 132; IMF, 2004b: 48, 58). A rise in the budget deficit at the beginning may be necessary not only to buy off opposition but also to bear the upfront costs of reforms such as implementing more effective employment agencies in preparation for welfare-to-work measures.

Finally, the impact of macroeconomic conditions and policy on reforms has been explored extensively – with no conclusive results as of now. But the impact of structural reform on the capacity of monetary and fiscal authorities to stabilize has not been studied very much. If structural reforms involve changes to long-standing benefit commitments and tax assessment practices, then there are at least three channels through which reforms might affect macroeconomic conditions and the conduct of policy. First, structural reforms could affect households' expectations of their permanent income. Contributory insurance systems in particular make commitments which households may rely on in forming their expectations. Reforms to these systems amount to a publicly endorsed breaking of commitments. They have the potential to affect the public's confidence in collective insurance and thus their precautionary savings. Second, if employment protection is reduced and job-changing becomes more frequent, household incomes could become more volatile.[12] The potential impact on household income expectations and consumption is uncertain: if increased labour market flexibility leads to lower long-term unemployment, income fluctuations might be of shorter duration if of higher frequency. Third, reforms which lower tax rates, reduce progressivity or reduce benefits for low-income and unemployed households will reduce the size of the automatic stabilizers, implying that less smoothing of disposable income relative to market income will take place (OECD, 2006: 39, ch. 5). This could also affect consumption, particularly among those households which are so constrained by their current income. Mabbett and Schelkle (2007) have only explored the third channel; more on this and the other two (or more) channels would be a welcome addition to the literature and would be relevant beyond EMU.

Economic governance

Following Allsopp and Vines (1998),[13] the assessment of what we thought we knew about economic governance focuses on fiscal policy, coordinated wage bargains and monetary policy. This covers the obviously relevant ingredients of stabilization in EMU that determine how the monetary union as a political and economic entity will behave. OCA theory did not address this question of how the union would do as a whole, with the exception of Kenen (1969) who suggested that a unified monetary policy needed some kind of fiscal federal mechanism for stabilization. It came in handy that the theory of rule-based policy provided an alternative foundation for the particular (or peculiar) set-up of fiscal governance in EMU. 'The advantage of tying one's hands' that Giavazzi and Pagano (1988) saw, in a pegged exchange rate system for an inflation-prone political economy like Italy, was generalized to any self-imposed constraint on discretionary intervention by governments. This reasoning was then applied, notably, to the Stability Pact and to the delegation of monetary policy to the singularly independent ECB.

The view that 'there is an advantage to tying one's hands' was probably the least consensual among the three views I assess here. Macroeconomists raised concern about the constraint on fiscal policy just as interest rate policy was being taken away from them, while providing no additional source of stabilization through a Community-wide budget.[14] The proponents responded that peer group pressure in the Council and monitoring by the Commission would hopefully be sufficient reminders of the rules that governments had agreed to. Up to 3 per cent deficit should give the automatic stabilizers enough room for manoeuvre while allowing governments to keep their fiscal house in long-term order (Artis and Buti, 2000).

But the hands-tying logic was not confined to fiscal policy – and would also not be enough for price stability. So how would it apply to wage bargainers? An early OECD study questioned whether the tying of government hands through a pact and an ECB would be enough to discipline wage bargainers, because the paradigm shift in monetary policy during the 1980s had not impressed wage bargainers. Egebo and Englander (1992: 52) found no credibility gains in labour markets, neither in the form of lower sacrifice ratios (the relationship between an increase in unemployment and the reduction in inflation) nor in a downward shift of expectations-augmented Phillips curves. On the contrary, the disciplinarian reasoning entails the paradox that credibility gains, which materialize in the form of lower interest rates in financial markets, ease the pressure for adjustment in labour markets by boosting demand and making borrowing cheaper (Schelkle, 2006: 676).

The implication that wage restraint may become a problem in EMU was reinforced by work based on a different conceptual basis, namely the cartel model of wage setting by Calmfors and Driffill (1988) and the notion of a signalling game of macroeconomic stabilization between central bank and trade unions (Iversen and Soskice, 1998, 2000). Both would predict that the decentralization of the wage bargain in EMU, relative to market size or monetary policy, tended to reduce wage restraint. The Calmfors-Driffill hypothesis was that the relationship between centralization and wage restraint takes the form of a hump shape, with a medium level of centralization in wage setting corresponding to high levels of the misery index (the sum of inflation and unemployment rates). But this imminent worsening of macroeconomic performance could be counteracted by complete decentralization of wage bargains, say to the firm level.

This brings us finally to the most tangible policy and institutional change that EMU entailed, namely the conduct of monetary policy. The credibility of the ECB's stance, namely to have mandated lexicographic preferences for price stability, seemed to be not really in doubt (price stability comes first in the ECB's alphabet). This is not withstanding the immediate alarmist responses that occur whenever, say, the French government asks for a broader set of goals and more equal weighting of employment. The alarmists in and outside the ECB naturally wanted to establish a taboo zone around Frankfurt. The serious debate was about the operational targets of the ECB, given all the uncertainties and the heterogeneity of the currency area for which it was making policy. Should it have a symmetric and explicit inflation target, rather than the 'not more than 2 per cent'? And how sensible is it to have a second target for money growth? Would this create noise or provide guidance? This was the direction to which not least the ECB and its research department steered the debate. Applied economists proposed talking more about a reasonable response function, thus considering the central bank more as a market participant with sensibly opportunistic behaviour than as a rule-bound guardian of economic prudence (Allsopp and Vines, 1998). Wise opportunism was advisable in light of the prevalent expectations that cyclical divergence might increase, both because of structural differences between member states and because of heterogeneous responses to similar shocks (European Economy, 2004: 42). Many scholars were also concerned that there was a problem of how the policy mix could be monitored, given the lack of formal coordination between several fiscal authorities and a central bank which was primarily concerned about its independence. However, this was noted more as a problem to be watched than as an issue for empirical study,[15] assuming that there would be a considerable mismatch between the stance of monetary policy and the aggregate fiscal balance of the euro area.

We know now that the original pact and a singularly independent, credibly stability-oriented central bank did not deliver the self-enforcing discipline that the argument for tying one's hands promised. But the evidence is not all that clear on discipline if it is assessed on what governments can be asked to control in the short run, namely the cyclically adjusted budget balance without interest payments. The evidence suggests that member states actually tried to rein in their deficits, with the exception of Portugal (Schelkle, 2007: 724–7). Since the reform of the Stability Pact in March 2005, it is in particular the countries in an Excessive Deficit Procedure that have kept their obligations, even though the 'corrective arm' of the Pact was the one that was weakened in terms of the quasi-automaticity of sanctions (Public Finances, 2007: 33–45). The jury on the working of the new fiscal framework is still out since it is only about to be tested in adversity, that is a recession.

Wage restraint was either unchanged or became tighter in the vast majority of countries (Posen and Gould, 2006). And this seems to be the case not because wage coordination became so decentralized that more and more regimes ended up on the decentralized left of the Calmfors-Driffill hump: 'the co-ordination of bargaining, which was established or reinforced in a number of countries in the run-up to monetary union, appears to have contributed to wage restraint. It is worth noting that co-ordinated bargaining did not necessarily run counter to delivering fairly differentiated wage outcomes across sectors, regions and qualifications' (European Economy, 2004: 82). Nor is there much evidence for the Iversen-Soskice argument that a perceived lack of response by a national central bank makes for an inflation bias. The Netherlands came closest and showed a strong rise in unit labour costs after entry into EMU while wage bargains had closely shadowed those of Germany before. But this seems to have been a temporary deviation. The crucial case of the German wage bargain has not followed the script; nor has the Austrian, which is a direct comparator to the Netherlands. In fact, if there is any surprise in wage adjustment after the entry into EMU, it is how little has changed, with Italy's rapidly rising labour costs providing the infamous example for more of the same. EMU seems not to have been the structural break in national wage dynamics that everybody expected.

Lastly, what about monetary policy and in particular the resulting policy mix? The ECB downgraded, de facto abandoned, the second pillar of a monetary target in 2003. Broad money (M3) growth had misbehaved so badly, exceeding its target value considerably and permanently, that the ECB decided to respond pragmatically. The bank lowered interest rates in the wake of the dot.com bubble burst, despite M3 development (Goodhart, 2006: 759–65). Since then, Taylor rules have been estimated to show that the response function of the ECB is actually not that different from the Federal Reserve Bank in the US and also not that restrictive (ibid.: Figure 8). It has to be said, however, that these estimates take 3.5 per cent as the 'natural' long-term real interest rate, which itself needs justifying. Assuming a somewhat lower long-term rate would make quite a difference to the assessment that ECB policy is not restrictive.

Surprisingly little empirical work has been done on the policy mix in EMU, which may be taken as a sign that unified monetary policy and the aggregate stance of fiscal policies are not completely out of sync. This may be a case of 'coordination without explicit cooperation' (Hughes Hallett, 2008). But we also do not find the policy mix to be very active or responsive.[16] Neither the aggregate budget balance nor the interest rate of the ECB react as strongly as the US counterparts. It has to be kept in mind, however, that the business cycle in the US is also more volatile than business cycles in the euro area.

So what should we know? The consensus that 'the Pact is dead' may have silenced too quickly any further inquiries into the impact that membership in the euro area seems to exert on budgetary policies. This impact is most noticeable with respect to countries' own pasts, not in comparison with non-EMU countries. Is the impact the much more detailed and permanent fiscal surveillance which the European Commission now exercises, with the support of Eurostat, that has, in the words of a senior Treasury official, become 'an independent auditor'? And is this more effective because the control through 'fire alarms' has been turned into 'police patrols', to use the distinction by McCubbins and Schwartz (1984)? This latter type of control can take account of the diversity of fiscal circumstances and systems and one can hope that sheer presence, rather than actual fire fighting, will do the job. Or is the impact being channelled via an increasingly assertive Eurogroup – whose existence is now officially acknowledged in the Lisbon Treaty? The one in-depth study of its working (Puetter, 2006) could not establish beyond doubt that this Council formation has any discernible impact on the operation of EMU. The Eurogroup could not prevent the erosion of the Stability and Growth Pact. Its most important function, to maintain an 'underlying working consensus' (ibid.: 151), did not make much difference to the observable behaviour of those who claimed to share it (Germany and Portugal) and those who challenged it (France and Ireland) – they all failed to comply.

A related question is whether effective automatic stabilizers at the national level and close fiscal surveillance at the EU level really do the trick of stabilization. This is probably what an updated version of Artis and Buti (2000) would say. The anecdotal evidence of a policy mix that is at least not obviously inconsistent is in their favour. But as Sørensen (2006) has warned us, we have lived through relatively 'normal' times which were not likely to test the robustness of the defences. This changed in August 2007. There is the pressing issue of who or what would assist with the crisis management, say if banks or mortgage finance markets in several member states were to collapse (Eichengreen, 2008: 25–9). This is an all the more worrying scenario if social pacts seem to have become rather temporary, event-driven institutions that come and go in the midst of a general decline of wage bargaining coordination (Hancké and Rhodes, 2005; Driffill, 2006: 742–6). It is not clear yet what this general decline in the relevance of collective wage bargains means for stability. But it is also not clear how much value added there would be in explicit policy coordination, given the well-known lags and the evidence of how hard it is to steer budget balances.

This raises the fundamental question as regards the founding rationale for the SGP. The rationale rested on the assumption that spillovers from profligate debt policies would trigger (1) interest rate rises or (2) a more inflationary policy than the ECB (and anybody else) wanted and

(3) a weakening of the euro. As plausible as, in particular, the interest rate argument is, we have not see much of this happening. In exactly those years that countries like Germany started to have an excessive deficit as defined by the Treaty, the euro started its rise against the dollar. Financial markets and their severely discredited rating agencies hardly differentiate between the treasury bonds of different countries. Is this the reason why the revised Pact has tacitly replaced the coordination rationale for fiscal rules by the concern for long-term sustainability?[17] Will this make the framework more enforceable as it is closer to the concerns of domestic policy-makers? At the same time, this shift raises questions of political legitimacy, given that it is for national parliaments to take governments to task for budgetary policies, the consequences of which are borne by resident future taxpayers.

Conclusion

The monetary union in Europe is historically without precedent (Eichengreen, 2008: 2). But our theories and conjectures were based on analogies with existing national currency areas or gold-standard-type systems of pegged exchange rates. So we should not be surprised that there were some surprises in store. What is noteworthy, above all, is how little it mattered that EMU is not an optimum currency area. Only Germany seemed to have unforeseen adjustment problems which was, as many observers noted, rather ironic, given that the policy framework followed a partial interpretation of post-war Germany; partial in that it left out the role of coordinated wage bargains and fiscal federalism. Adjustment to asymmetric shocks was not a prominent theme of ECOFIN Council resolutions, even though rising oil and commodity prices or enlargement did mean different things to different regions. But then region-specific shocks are not country-specific shocks, so exchange rate adjustment would have been of little help. Labour markets and their alleged inflexibility in Continental Europe did not prove to be the Achilles heel of the monetary union, even though they did not become flexible in an Anglo-Saxon/Scandinavian way. Countries with such labour markets, the UK, Denmark and Sweden, preferred to stay out of EMU. If there was anything noteworthy about labour market performance in EMU, then it was that moderate wage bargains kept inflation low despite the ECB missing its monetary target repeatedly. All those well-founded predictions of an inflation bias in EMU proved wrong.

It is about time that OCA theory was abandoned since it has proved such a poor guide as to who would qualify for monetary union and as to what policy-makers need to keep in mind when forming it.[18] The research agenda to replace it is vast and exciting. It revolves around the necessities and opportunities for policy coordination. I see three big themes that are relevant to understanding the working of political economies beyond EMU. First, how much stabilization or 'Great Moderation' is already provided by unifying the currency? Currency unification eliminates internal EMU currency crises and comes with a monetary policy that may be sluggish to respond but also avoids being disruptive, so much so that the euro has become a safe haven in times of financial market turmoil. Has the synchronization of business cycles made the policy mix of monetary policy with decentralized fiscal policies roughly consistent – or is coordination provided by a signalling game between ECB and the three or four big EMU member states? Second, have collective wage bargains really become less important or are they doing quietly their thing, namely providing a floor for wages and making sure that productivity gains trickle down to real wages? If not, what will contain the deflationary bias, rising earnings inequality and increasing working poverty, the latter having been observed in the EU for two decades now (OECD, 2006: 40)? Third, how closely related are the structural reform and the fiscal consolidation agenda? Under which conditions does fiscal austerity pervert reforms, notably creating or reinforcing insider–outsider segmentation of labour markets? In turn, to what extent do structural reforms weaken the stabilizing properties of tax-transfer systems by making them more 'employment friendly', that is less redistributive?

These latter considerations link the grand European project of monetary unification economically and politically with the tedious national projects of incremental welfare state reform. The guardians of the Treaty, in the Commission and the ECOFIN Council, seem to acknowledge this at long last. They have become less disciplinarian in their approach. The revision of the Pact indicated a quiet abandoning of the rule-based framework in favour of one that sets the parameters for deliberation between governments on how much policy coordination and collective responsibility is required. Research agendas have yet to catch up with policy-making as practised.

Notes

1. The triangle refers to monetary policy by the central bank, budgetary policy by the fiscal authorities and collective wage bargains between trade unions and employer associations.
2. See also the brilliant critique of OCA theory by Johnson (1969).
3. Baldwin (2006) and Mélitz (2006) suggest increases in intra-EMU trade in the range of 5–10 per cent.
4. Rational expectations mean expectations consistent with the underlying model. An alternative conceptualization of the wage bargain, along the lines of Calmfors and Driffill (1988) and Soskice (1990), is potentially less optimistic.

5. This goes along with a striking similarity of nominal wage responsiveness to output shocks in the euro area and in the US (European Economy 2004: 76).

6. 'What is more, country rankings change a lot, if other measures are used for 'labour market flexibility': 'for example, Spain is one of the least flexible countries when looking at the reaction of wages to unemployment, but one of the most flexible when looking at the response of employment to productivity. These results can be understood as evidence that focusing on the relationship between wages and unemployment to assess labour market flexibility will be extremely simplistic' (European Economy, 2005: 115).

7. For more references, see Mongelli (2002: 16).

8. See Artis *et al.* (2004) and Stock and Watson (2005) for relevant discussions. Gerlach and Hoffmann (2008) claim that the euro has contributed to the Great Moderation of volatility, but their data analysis ends in 2006.

9. This is not the only possible interpretation, as monopolistically competitive firms (despite the name, monopolistic competition is a fairly perfect form of competition) can always choose between price and quantity changes, i.e. pricing-to-the-market is a competitive strategy available to producers of a brand.

10. The following is based on Schelkle (2006) and Mabbett and Schelkle (2007).

11. See OECD (2006: 13). Reform-minded economists seem to have become aware of that and find strong, encompassing unions helpful for constructive labour market reforms (IMF, 2004b: para. 113; Castanheira *et al.*, 2006: 48). The European Commission has also noticed this problem and makes an attempt in its newly established labour market reform (LABREF) database to take the quality of reforms such as the targeting of outsiders and the participation of social partners into account (Arpaia *et al.*, 2005: 11, 17).

12. It would be relevant for social policy to know how much of the Great Moderation in output volatility also leads to lower household income volatility, especially at the lower end of the income distribution.

13. This is an excellent survey of the macroeconomic issues involved, being at the same time the introductory article to a special issue of the *Oxford Review of Economic Policy*.

14. See, for instance, Buiter *et al.* (1993) and Goodhart and Smith (1993) for early critiques of the Maastricht framework.

15. See Collignon (2001) and Hughes Hallett (2008) for further references.

16. See Federal Reserve Bank at St Louis at: http://research.stlouisfed.org/publications/iet/20060501/cover.pdf for the operating interest rate of the ECB and the Fed; and see De Grauwe (2006: Figure 7) for the cyclically adjusted aggregate balances of the two currency areas.

17. All 'age-related' public spending, for pensions, health, education and long-term care, is now closely monitored; in turn, governments that undertake systemic pension reforms can claim exemptions from the 3 per cent deficit rule if they undertake systemic pension reforms (Public Finances, 2005: Part II).

18. But see yet another attempt at revival by Corsetti (2008), on the occasion of the Commission's review of EMU after ten years.

References

Allsopp, C. and Vines, D. (1998) 'The Assessment: Macroeconomic Policy After EMU', *Oxford Review of Economic Policy* 13(3): 1–23.

Arpaia, A., Castello, D., Mourre, G. and Pierrini, F. (2005) 'Tracking labour market reforms in the EU Member States: an overview of reforms in 2004 based on the LABREF database', Economic Papers 239, Brussels: European Commission, DG Ecfin.

Artis, M. and Buti, M. (2000) '"Close to Balance or in Surplus": a policy-maker's guide to the implementation of the Stability and Growth Pact', *Journal of Common Market Studies* 38: 563–91.

Artis, M.J., Osborn, D. and Perez, P.J. (2004) 'The international business cycle in a changing world: volatility and the propagation of shocks in the G7', EABCN/CEPR Discussion Paper 4652, London: CEPR.

Asdrubali, P., Sørensen, B.E. and Yosha, O. (1996) 'Channels of Interstate Risk Sharing: United States 1963–1990', *Quarterly Journal of Economics* 111: 1081–110.

Baldwin, R. (2006) 'The euro's trade effects', ECB Working Paper 594, Frankfurt: European Central Bank.

Boeri, T. (2005) 'Reforming Labor and Product Markets: Some Lessons from Two Decades of Experiments in Europe', IMF Working Paper 05/97, Washington, DC: IMF.

Brandsma, A. and Hughes Hallett, A. (1984) 'Economic Conflict and the Solution of Dynamic Games', *European Economic Review* 26: 13–32.

Brandt, N., Burniaux, J.-M. and Duval, R. (2005) 'Assessing the OECD Jobs Strategy: Past Developments and Reforms', Economics Department Working Paper ECO/WKP(2005)16, Paris: OECD, http:/www.oecd.org/eco.

Buiter, W. (2000) 'Optimal currency areas', *Scottish Journal of Political Economy* 47(3): 213–50.

Buiter, W. (2004) 'To Purgatory and Beyond: When and How Should the Accession Countries from Central and Eastern Europe Become Full Members of the EMU?', in F. Breuss and E. Hochreiter (eds) *Challenges for Central Banks in an Enlarged EMU* (Vienna: Springer) 145–86.

Buiter, W., Corsetti, G. and Roubini, N. (1993) 'Excessive deficits: sense and nonsense in the Treaty of Maastricht', *Economic Policy* 16: 57–90.

Calmfors, L. (2001) 'Unemployment, Labor Market Reform, and Monetary Union', *Journal of Labor Economics* 19(2): 265–89.

Calmfors, L. and Driffill, J. (1988) 'Bargaining structure, corporatism and macroeconomic performance,' *Economic Policy* 3: 13–61.

Castanheira, M., Galasso, V., Carcillo, S., Nicoletti, G., Perotti, E. and Tsyganok, L. (2006) 'How to Gain Political Support for Reforms', in Boeri, T., Castanheira, M., Faini, R. and Gallasso, V. (eds), *Structural Reforms Wothout Prejudices* (Oxford: Oxford University Press) part II: 141–253.

CEC (Commission of the European Communities) (2002) *Communication from the Commission on Streamlining the Annual Economic and Employment Policy Co-ordination Cycle*, COM(2002) 487 final, Brussels: Commission of the European Communities.

Collignon, S. (2001) 'Economic Policy Coordination in EMU: Political and Institutional Requirements', Centre for European Studies Working Paper, May 2001 (Cambridge, MA: Harvard University).

Corsetti, G. (2008) 'A modern reconsideration of the Theory of Optimal Currency Areas', European Economy Economic Papers 308, European Commission: Brussels.

De Grauwe, P. (1990) 'The Cost of Disinflation and the European Monetary System', *Open Economies Review* 1: 147–73.

De Grauwe, P. (2000) *The Economics of Monetary Integration*, 4th edn (Oxford: Oxford University Press).

De Grauwe, P. (2006) 'What have we learnt about monetary integration since the Maastricht Treaty?', *Journal of Common Market Studies* 44(4): 711–30.

Demertzis, M., A. Hughes, and O. Rummel (2000) 'Is the European Union a Natural Currency Area, or is it Held Together by Policy Makers?' *Weltwirtschaftliches Archiv* 136 (4): 657–79.

Driffill, J. (2006) 'The Centralization of Wage Bargaining Revisited: What Have We Learnt?', *Journal of Common Market Studies* 44(4): 731–56.

Duval, R. and Elmeskov, J. (2005) 'The Effects of EMU on Structural Reforms in Labour and Product Markets', Economics Department Working Paper ECO/WKP(2005)25, Paris: OECD, http:/www.oecd.org/eco.

Egebo, T. and Englander, A.S. (1992) 'Institutional commitments and policy credibility: a critical survey and empirical evidence from the ERM', *OECD Economic Studies* 18: 45–84.

Eichengreen, B. (2008) 'Sui Generis EMU', *Economic Papers* 303, Brussels: DG Economic and Financial Affairs.

Emerson, M., Gros, D., Italianer, A., Pisani-Ferry, J. and Reichenbach, H. (1992) *One Market, One Money. An Evaluation of the Potential Benefits and Costs of Forming an Economic and Monetary Union* (Oxford: Oxford UP).

European Economy (2004) *EMU after 5 years*, Special Report No.1, Brussels: Directorate General of Economic and Financial Affairs.

European Economy (2005) *The contribution of wage developments to labour market performance*, Special Report No.1, Brussels: Directorate General of Economic and Financial Affairs.

Fatás, A., Hagen, J. von, Hughes Hallett, A., Strauch, R.R. and Sibert, A. (2003) *Stability and Growth in Europe: Towards a Better Pact*. Monitoring European Integration 13, London: Centre for Economic Policy Research.

Fernandez, R. and Rodrik, D. (1991) 'Resistance to Reform: Status Quo Bias in the Presence of Individual-Specific Uncertainty'. *American Economic Review* 81(5): 1146–55.

Fleming, J.M. (1971) 'On Exchange Rate Unification', *The Economic Journal* 81: 467–88.

Gerlach, S. and Hoffmann, M. (2008) 'The impact of the euro on international stability and volatility', *Economic Papers* 309, Brussels: DG Economic and Financial Affairs.

Ghosh, A.R. and Masson, P.R. (1994) *Economic Cooperation in an Uncertain World* (Blackwell: Oxford).

Giannone, D. and Reichlin, L. (2006) 'Trends and cycles in the euro area: how much heterogeneity and should we worry about it?', ECB Working Paper 595, Frankfurt: European Central Bank.

Giavazzi, G., and Pagano, M. (1988), 'The Advantage of Tying One's Hands: EMS Discipline and Central Bank Credibility', *European Economic Review* 32: 1055–82.

Goodhart, C.A.E. (2006) 'The ECB and the Conduct of Monetary Policy: Goodhart's Law and Lessons from the Euro Area', *Journal of Common Market Studies* 44(4): 757–78.

Goodhart, C.A.E. and Smith, S. (1993) 'Stabilization', *European Economy* 5: 417–55.

Hancké, B. and Rhodes, M. (2005) 'EMU and Labour Market Institutions in Europe. The Rise and Fall of National Social Pacts', *Work and Occupations* 32(2): 196–228.

Hughes Hallett, A. (2008) 'Coordination without explicit cooperation: monetary-fiscal interactions in an era of demographic change', *Economic Papers* 305, Brussels: DG Economic and Financial Affairs.

IMF (International Monetary Fund) (2004a) 'Fostering structural reforms in industrial countries' *World Economic Outlook* (April), Washington, DC: International Monetary Fund.

IMF (International Monetary Fund) (2004b) 'Euro Area Policies: Selected Issues', *IMF Country Report* 04/234, Washington, DC: International Monetary Fund.

Italianer, A. and Pisani-Ferry, J. (1994) 'The regional-stabilisation properties of fiscal arrangements', in: Mortensen, Jørgen (ed), *Improving Economic and Social Cohesion in the European Community*, Basingstoke and London, MacMillan: 155–94.

Italianer, A. and Vanheukelen, M. (1993) 'Proposals for Community stabilization mechanisms: Some historical applications', *European Economy*, Special No.5: 493–510.

Iversen, T. and Soskice, D. (1998) 'Multiple Wage-Bargaining Systems in the Single European Currency Area,' *Oxford Review of Economic Policy*, 14(3): 110–24.

Iversen, T. and Soskice, D. (2000) 'The Nonneutrality of Monetary Policy with Large Price or Wage Setters,' *Quarterly Journal of Economics* 115(1): 265–84.

Johnson, H.G. (1969) 'The "Problems" Approach to International Monetary Reform', in Mundell, R.A., Swoboda, A.K. (eds) *Monetary Problems of the International Economy* (Chicago: University of Chicago Press) 393–99.

Kenen, P.B. (1969) 'The Theory of Optimum Currency Areas: An Eclectic View', in Mundell, R.A., Swoboda, A.K. (eds) *Monetary Problems of the International Economy* (Chicago: University of Chicago Press) 41–60.

Krugman, P.R. (1993) 'Lessons of Massachusetts for EMU', in Torres, F. and Giavazzi, F. (eds) *Adjustment and Growth in the European Monetary Union* (Cambridge: Cambridge University Press) 241–61.

Mabbett, D. and Schelkle, W. (2007) 'Bringing macroeconomics back into the political economy of reform: the Lisbon Agenda and the "fiscal philosophy" of EMU', *Journal of Common Market Studies* 45(1): 81–104.

McCarthy, M. (2006) 'Comments by Mary McCarthy', in D. Giannone and L. Reichlin, *op. cit.*, 37–44.

McCubbins, M.D. and Schwartz, T. (1984) 'Congressional Oversight Overlooked: Police Patrols versus Fire Alarms', *American Journal of Political Science* 28(1): 165–79.

McKinnon, R.I. (1963) 'Optimum Currency Areas', *American Economic Review* 53: 717–25.

McNamara, K. (1998) *The Currency of Ideas* (Ithaca: Cornell University Press).

Mélitz, J. (1988) 'Monetary discipline and cooperation in the European Monetary System: a synthesis', in Giavazzi, G., Micossi, S. and Miller, M.H. (eds) *The European Monetary System* (Cambridge: Cambridge University Press) 51–79.

Mélitz, J. (2006) 'Comments on Baldwin', ECB Working Paper 594, Frankfurt: European Central Bank.

Mongelli, F.P. (2002) '"New" Views on the Optimum Currency Area Theory: What Is EMU Telling Us?', ECB Working Paper 138, Frankfurt: European Central Bank.

Mongelli, F.P. and Vega, J.L. (2006) 'What Effects is EMU Having on the Euro Area and its Member Countries? An Overview', ECB Working Paper 599, Frankfurt: European Central Bank.

Mundell, R.A. (1961) 'A Theory of Optimum Currency Areas', *American Economic Review* 51: 657–65.

OECD (2006) *OECD Employment Outlook*, Paris: Organisation for Economic Co-operation and Development.

Padoa-Schioppa, T. (1990) 'Financial and Monetary Integration in Europe: 1990, 1992 and Beyond', Occasional Paper 28, Washington, DC: Group of Thirty.

Pierson, P. (2001) 'Coping with Permanent Austerity: Welfare State Restructuring in Affluent Democracies', in Pierson, P. (ed.), *The New Politics of the Welfare State* (Oxford: Oxford University Press) ch. 13.

Posen, A.S. and Gould, D.P. (2006) 'Has EMU had any impact on the degree of wage restraint?', Working paper 06–6, Washington, DC: Institute for International Economics.

'Public Finances in EMU', (2007) annual publication in *European Economy*, no. 3, Brussels: DG Economic and Financial Affairs.

Puetter, U. (2006) *The Eurogroup. How a secretive circle of finance ministers shape European economic governance* (Manchester and New York: Manchester University Press).

Rodrik, D. (1996) 'Understanding Economic Policy Reform', *Journal of Economic Literature* 34 (March): 9–41.

Rose, A. (2000) 'One Money, One Market? The Effect of Common Currencies on Trade', *Economic Policy*, 15(30): 7–45.

Saint-Paul, G. (2004) 'Why are European Countries Diverging in their Unemployment Experience?', CEPR Discussion Paper 4328, London: CEPR.

Schelkle, W. (2001a) *Monetäre Integration. Bestandsaufnahme und Weiterentwicklung der neueren Theorie* (Heidelberg: Physica).

Schelkle, W. (2001b) 'The Optimum Currency Area Approach to European Monetary Integration: Framework of Debate or Dead End?', South Bank European Papers 2/01, South Bank University, London.

Schelkle, W. (2006) 'The theory and practice of economic governance in EMU revisited: What have we learnt about commitment and credibility?', *Journal of Common Market Studies* 44(4): 669–85.

Schelkle, W. (2007) 'EU Fiscal Governance: Hard Law in the Shadow of Soft Law?', *The Columbia Journal of European Law* 13(3): 705–31.

Sørensen, B.E. (2006) 'Comments by Bent E. Sørensen', in D. Giannone and L. Reichlin, op cit 27–36

Soskice, D. (1990) 'Wage Determination: The Changing Role of Institutions in Advanced Industrial Countries', *Oxford Review of Economic Policy* 6(4): 36–61.

Stock, J.H. and Watson, M.W. (2005) 'Understanding changes in international business cycle dynamics', *Journal of the European Economic Association* 3(5): 969–1006.

Chapter 12

Justice and Home Affairs

Christina Boswell

The area of Justice and Home Affairs (JHA) covers a broad set of themes which are not easily combinable in a coherent research agenda. The list extends from questions relating to asylum systems, immigration policies and the rights of resident non-nationals; through internal security, border control and counter-terrorism; to law enforcement and criminal justice. Each area raises distinct research questions and draws on rather different bodies of research, notably (but not exclusively) migration studies, development studies, criminology, international relations and security studies. And, as with other areas of EU cooperation, most of these questions can be analysed using a range of theories and concepts from political science, law, sociology, anthropology and economics. Arguably, the only rationale for treating these themes together is the simple fact that they have been defined by the EU as part of a common political agenda (Walker, 2004a).

Given the rather amorphous set of issues comprising JHA, it is not surprising that relatively little research covers these themes as a single package. As I shall suggest in the chapter, this is not in itself a source of weakness in JHA scholarship. What is problematic, however, is the relative insulation of different sub-areas of research from one another. Much of the research also suffers from being overly descriptive and/or normative. After reviewing the state of research, I shall suggest some ways in which scholarship could be more rigorous and better engage with relevant bodies of literature. I shall also suggest a number of areas in which studies of JHA have the potential to make a genuine contribution to the development of theories and concepts in cognate disciplines.

State of the art

Literature on JHA as a whole

It hardly needs reiterating that JHA is one of the newest and fastest growing areas of EU cooperation (Monar, 2001). It has also developed in a highly incremental and ad hoc fashion (Lavenex and Wallace, 2005), with many of the key developments being brokered in rather

278

informal fora and proceeding through operational practices which are difficult to track. This has generated a high demand for rather descriptive introductory texts which provide overviews of the latest developments (Monar and Morgan, 1995; den Boer, 1996; Ucarer, 1999; Apap, 2004; Lavenex and Wallace, 2005). Similarly, the complex legal arrangements of JHA – rendered even more opaque by the incomplete shift of certain areas to the first pillar – have been the object of a number of legal overviews (Barrett, 1997; Guild and Harlow, 2001; Denza, 2002; Walker, 2004a; Peers, 2006). But apart from these types of essentially introductory works, generally targeted at students, there are relatively few contributions that seek to cover the full array of JHA themes. As noted already, this can be largely attributed to the fact that JHA is pre-eminently a politically defined agenda, bringing together different areas of policy as part of a programme that aspires to provide 'an area of freedom, security and justice' (AFSJ) for EU citizens (Twomey, 1999).

One notable exception is literature that critiques the JHA project. A number of scholars have queried the political and organizational motives behind attempts to combine these diverse areas (Bigo, 1994, 2005; Huysmans, 2004). These approaches share a number of assumptions with the 'critical security' literature that emerged in the 1990s, seeking to expose the agendas of the politicians and security professionals constructing the 'internal security field' (Bigo, 1994). One recurring theme is how police and security officials have sought to colonize new areas of policy such as migration and border control, applying discourses, technologies and practices traditionally reserved for more conventional military threats. In this sense, AFSJ implied the merging of what were previously rather discrete policy areas, many of which were governed by more socio-economic considerations. As we shall see, this notion of 'securitization' crops up in literature on almost all areas of JHA cooperation – immigration and asylum, border control, relations with third countries, and cooperation in the area of law enforcement. It gained impetus after 9/11, with numerous studies scrutinizing European responses to the threat of Islamist terrorism. It is likely to remain an influential strand of research in this area, though, as we shall see in the next sections, it is by no means the only theoretical approach informing the growing number of JHA studies.

A second, related theme worth flagging is predominantly legal literature on problems of accountability and the perceived democratic deficit in JHA as a whole. Various legal commentators have been critical of the informal fora and quasi-independent agencies that have comprised a substantial portion of JHA cooperation, as well as the highly intergovernmental arrangements governing Title VI, or the Third Pillar. They have expressed concerns at the inadequate legal or constitutional basis for arrangements (Walker, 2004a), the absence of judicial review or parliamentary control (Neuwahl, 1995; Barrett, 1997; Peers, 2007a) and the lack of transparency in decision-making (Monar, 1995; Denza, 2002; Peers, 2006). As we shall see, this is a line of critique that emerges in literature on many of the sub-areas of JHA.

The discussion will now turn to the three sub-areas that cover the most prominent sets of themes in the JHA literature: immigration and asylum; borders, enlargement and the external dimension of JHA; and police and judicial cooperation.

Immigration and asylum

Much of the initial literature on EU cooperation on immigration and asylum was highly descriptive (Hailbronner, 1990, 1993; Callovi, 1992; Collinson, 1993; Ucarer, 1997). This is not surprising given the speed and novelty of developments in the first half of the 1990s. As cooperation became formalized under Title VI of the Maastricht Treaty on European Union (TEU) and legislation began to emerge, many scholars became highly critical of what they perceived to be the restrictive bent of policy. These contributions involved essentially normative critiques of the impact of harmonization on asylum seekers and refugees, proffered by both lawyers and political scientists (see, for example, Joly, 1992, 1996; Vedsted-Hansen, 1999; Morrison and Crosland, 2000; Guild and Harlow, 2001). Concerns about the apparent erosion of refugee rights echoed similar critiques of restrictive approaches at the national level. EU cooperation over this period was also criticized for the weak legal basis of instruments (Guild, 1999) or their general ineffectiveness (Noll, 1997; Hurwitz, 1999). These critiques of what was branded 'fortress Europe' have in turn been faulted by some authors for underplaying more liberal elements influencing policy, especially the role of market forces which have had a more inclusionary influence on immigration and asylum policy (Favell and Hansen, 2002). They are also criticized for nurturing somewhat idealized expectations about the potentially benign and liberalizing tendencies of European integration in this area (Geddes, 2006: 265).

By the late 1990s, the 'fortress Europe' critique had largely given way to analyses of the perceived 'securitization' of EU immigration and asylum policy. Much of this literature was informed by the seminal work of the Copenhagen School, which argued that immigration was becoming a 'new focus for insecurity' in Europe (Waever *et al.*, 1993: 2; see also Buzan *et al.*, 1998). By constructing immigration and asylum as a threat to European societies, politicians were able to legitimize practices that had traditionally been reserved for responding to military threats (Huysmans, 1995, 1998; Buzan *et al.*, 1998: 23–6). Especially in the wake of 9/11 and the subsequent attacks in Madrid and London, EU officials were able to introduce supposedly 'exceptional' measures that would normally have been considered unacceptable infringements of civil liberties. Other scholars focused less on public discourse, instead charting how experts and professionals attempted to expand their power by applying securitarian practices and technologies to migration control (Bigo, 2002, 2005; Huysmans, 2006). Interestingly, this Foucauldian approach has found less support from scholars with a background in migration studies, who tend to see migration policy as driven as much by market considerations as by a restrictive securitarian logic (Favell and Hansen, 2002; Boswell, 2007a).

Another area of focus has been the institutional dynamics of decision-making in this area (Myers, 1995). Scholars have charted the development of institutional arrangements within the European Commission, with the rapid evolution of the Task Force on Justice and Home Affairs into a separate Directorate-General on Justice, Liberty and Security (Ucarer, 2001). Others have noted tensions between different Directorates-General dealing with immigration issues, especially in relation to the 'external dimension' of immigration and asylum (van Selm, 2002; Boswell, 2003, 2008). There have also been a number of contributions analysing the trend towards outsourcing aspects of migration control to private companies (Lahav, 1998, 2000; Koslowski, 2000; Guiraudon and Lahav, 2000). Institutional changes in immigration and asylum appear to have opened up new opportunities for NGOs lobbying at EU level. Thus Guiraudon (2001) argues that the EU's relative insulation from electoral politics can enhance the possibilities for NGOs to exercise influence in an area which tends to be highly populist at the national level (see also Ireland, 1991; Geddes, 2000). Favell and Geddes (1999) have pointed out how such lobbying at EU level tends to be elite-led rather than 'bottom-up' societal mobilization. Gray and Statham (2005) have questioned this claim, suggesting that even grass-roots national NGOs have been quite astute in adapting strategies to target the EU level.

The question of the impact of lobbying leads to the wider question of explaining EU cooperation on immigration and asylum. Here we can split contributions into two main groups. First are those applying the conventional gamut of integration theories to explain cooperation on immigration and asylum. Of these theories, neofunctionalism initially emerged as the favourite, with a number of authors seeing cooperation as a paradigmatic case of 'functional spillover' from the Single Market project. On this account, cooperation on migration control was largely spurred on by the abolition of internal borders, which generated the need for 'flanking' measures to tighten external borders and regulate mobility between member states (Koslowski, 1998; Ucarer, 1999; Jordan *et al.*, 2003). Scholars have also stressed the role of exogenous factors in motivating cooperation, especially the rise in asylum and irregular migration from the late 1980s onwards (Ucarer, 1999), though others have criticized the notion that cooperation is propelled by a real rise in migration (Sciortino and Pastore, 2004). There have also been attempts to explain the shift of migration from the intergovernmental third pillar to the more supranational first pillar. Stetter (2000) explains this drawing on principal–agent theory, arguing that inefficiencies in intergovernmental arrangements provided incentives for governments to delegate authority to the Commission. By contrast, Caviedes (2004) stresses the caution of national governments in delegating authority, suggesting that the open method of coordination may be a good compromise for making progress in this sensitive area. Meanwhile, Thielemann (2003) has focused on the special case of burden-sharing in the area of immigration and asylum, explaining the lack of progress by drawing on rational choice theory.

The second set of explanations draws on literature on migration policy and the politics of migration, an area that has been rapidly expanding since the early 1990s. Much of this literature has charted how European states faced a series of constraints in implementing restrictive policies in the shape of economic liberalization (Hollifield, 1992; Sassen, 1998), expanding international human rights norms (Soysal, 1994), and domestic judicial and political constraints (Joppke, 1998; Hollifield, 1999). These factors all imposed a 'liberal constraint' on governments, delimiting the scope to pursue more stringent forms of migration control (Boswell, 2007b). In this context, European cooperation could be understood as a way of trying to 'regain control' (Geddes, 2003). As Guiraudon has argued (2000, 2003), officials in home affairs and justice ministries were keen to 'go European' in order to avoid domestic constitutional constraints and scrutiny. This notion of 'venue-shopping', with its focus on the power-expanding strategies of policy-makers and officials, has much in common with Bigo's account of security officials seeking out new policy fields (see above).

As Geddes has noted (2006), comparatively less attention has been devoted to policy implementation and the impact of cooperation in this area. Notable exceptions to this include a special issue of the *Journal of Ethnic and Migration Studies* which explores how organizational culture and national identities mediate patterns of implementation in different member states (Jordan *et al.*, 2003). A more recent edited collection by Faist and Ette (2007) explores implementation through the framework of different modes of 'Europeanization' in six member states. However, much of the literature on impacts and implementation has focused on acceding states and non-EU countries affected by cooperation (which is dealt with in the next section).

Borders, enlargement and the external dimension

Cooperation on JHA has had substantial ramifications for non-EU countries, notably in the context of EU enlargement. Literature in this area has focused on evaluating the goals and impacts of these developments, usually in a highly critical way. Scholars have been particularly concerned about the EU's attempts to impose the JHA and Schengen *acquis* on acceding countries. This requirement has been seen as generating a range of legal, political, social and economic problems for the Central and Eastern European countries (CEECs) (Lavenex, 1999, 2002; Mitsilegas, 2002) and is interpreted as a clear attempt at 'burden-shifting' (Byrne *et al.*, 2002; Byrne, 2003). The EU has also been criticized for its supposed double standards in this area, imposing the *acquis* while restricting possibilities for free movement on new members (Jileva, 2002). Grabbe (2000) and others have argued that the new EU border regime risked creating new barriers to ties between new member states and their neighbours to the east, with possibly grave security implications for Europe. Not least, there have been serious problems implementing these policies because of a lack of capacity in CEECs, as well as a lack of trust between different national authorities (Monar, 2004a).

The EU has also been criticized for exporting functions of migration control to a buffer region outside of the EU (Collinson, 1996). Such attempts have taken the form of readmission agreements and provisions on 'safe countries' of origin and transit, which facilitate the return of irregular migrants and asylum seekers to countries outside of the EU. There have also been increasing attempts to cooperate with third countries to combat irregular migration. These negotiations are often secretive or involve operational activities that are difficult to track. For this reason, empirical research often requires field research in quite remote parts of the world (Düvell, 2007; Collyer, 2007). From a safer location, Monar (2004b) has analysed the legal basis for the EU developing these forms of cooperation with third countries.

Authors have noted a number of tensions emerging within the 'external dimension' of JHA, including the divergence between the more 'repressive' approaches described above – which are focused on border control and combating irregular migration – and 'preventive' approaches which target migratory pressures (Boswell, 2003). Many commentators have been more sympathetic towards preventive approaches, which place the onus on providing development assistance to alleviate the 'root causes' of migration flows (Widgren, 1989, de Jong, 1999). This literature has expanded along with the development of the 'external dimension' after the 1999 Tampere Council, as well as the Commission's new 'global approach' to migration that was agreed in autumn 2005. The latter in particular has been criticized for its various internal incoherencies (Pastore, 2007), which can at least in part be attributed to organizational conflicts between different departments of the European Commission (Boswell, 2008).

While much of this literature is largely descriptive and evaluative, Lavenex and Ucarer (2002, 2004) have helped conceptualize these developments. Drawing on literature on policy transfer, they have developed a typology of the impacts of migration control on third countries along a continuum ranging from voluntary adaptation to more coercive imposition. By comparison, Gammeltoft-Hansen (2006b) conceptualizes these attempts in terms of the application of 'hard' and 'soft power' by the EU, which, if pursued too aggressively, risk being counter-productive. Lavenex has also attempted to explain the expansion of the external dimension, building on Guiraudon's 'venue-shopping' approach. In a 2006 article, she argued that the communitarization of immigration policy since the Treaty of Amsterdam has limited possibilities for states to avoid judicial and democratic scrutiny by 'going European'. Thus their preference for the external dimension represented an attempt to 'shift out' migration control functions to third countries as a means of evading such scrutiny (Lavenex, 2006).

EU cooperation on JHA has also triggered more general discussions on the borders of the EU. A number of scholars have noted the different and often contradictory functions of Europe's external borders (Zielonka, 2001; Geddes, 2005a; Berg and Ehin, 2006). In particular, Zielonka has noted the lack of an overlap between geographic and functional borders in the case of the EU. This implies that the EU cannot be characterized as a typical Westphalian state, but may be more accurately described as a neo-Medieval empire, with more flexible boundaries and overlapping polities (see also Koslowski, 1998). Berg and Ehin (2006) develop this line of argument, concluding that the discrepancy between different functions results in fragmented, incoherent border strategy.

More recently, a number of authors have noted the shift in practices and technologies of border control. Much of this is interpreted in the context of the securitization of JHA after 9/11, which added impetus to various attempts at expanding and integrating EU databases. A number of scholars associated with the EU CHALLENGE network led by Didier Bigo have criticized EU attempts to expand the contents of, and access to, database systems such as Eurodac, the Schengen Information System and the new Visa Information System (Masse, 2005; see also www.libertysecurity.org). Equally contested is the EU's cooperation with the US in the provision of advance passenger information (Zucconi, 2004; Mitsilegas, 2007a) – though concerns about data protection in this area also have a longer vintage (Raab, 1994). These developments have also been explained in the context of a more general shift away from 'fortress Europe' towards understanding border control in terms of risk management (Gammeltoft-Hansen, 2006a). This implies a focus on smarter methods of surveillance and control, designed to sift out desirable from undesirable entrants, through biometric technologies (Hampshire, 2008).

Law enforcement and judicial cooperation

This area of JHA has been the object of a growing body of literature by lawyers (Benyon *et al.*, 1994, 1995; Barrett, 1997; Peers, 2006). Arguably, the most interesting discussions have revolved around two key issues that have wide ramifications for the EU's legal framework. The first is the problem of mutual recognition of criminal law, which thus far has mainly arisen in the context of the European Arrest Warrant, but is set to become a central organizing principle of EU cooperation under the Lisbon Treaty (Blekxtoon, 2005; Mitsilegas, 2006). The expectation that courts recognize the criminal law provisions of other states has created serious constitutional problems in Germany, Poland and Cyprus (Mitsilegas, 2006; Shaw, 2007). The second issue is that of the constitutional principles governing the third pillar. In a landmark European Court decision (the *Pupino* case), the Court decided that the characteristically first pillar principle of 'indirect effect' should also govern cooperation under Title VI. A number of EU lawyers have argued that this decision contradicted the original notion that third pillar cooperation should proceed on a more intergovernmental basis and raises serious questions about the role of the Court in structuring political cooperation (Fletcher, 2005; Mitsilegas, 2007b).

Police and judicial cooperation has received relatively less attention from social and political scientists. Part of this may be because of its less glamorous image, certainly as compared to migration studies, which witnessed a phenomenal expansion in the 1990s. But it also reflects a number of methodological problems in tracking developments. Much of the activity in this area has taken the form of operational cooperation between police officials in different member states (Anderson *et al.*, 1995; den Boer, 2002a) or cooperation within semi-autonomous agencies (Lavenex and Wallace, 2005: 470–1), with developments often being propelled by informal networks of officials and experts (den Boer, 1998; Benyon, 1996; Monar, 2001; Peers 2006). Such processes are difficult to observe, requiring good access to respondents in national police forces and justice or interior ministries. Indeed, some of the most influential contributions to this area have involved fairly large-scale cross-national collaborations, such as the project conducted by Anderson and associates which involved interviewing more than 100 law enforcement officials in different member states (Anderson *et al.*, 1995).

While these features have created impediments to classic political science research methods, the informal and operational nature of cooperation has nonetheless raised a number of interesting research questions. First, the inability to chart developments through official documents or public political debate has implied a focus on the organizational sociology of cooperation. Scholars have differentiated between three main levels of cooperation: macro, meso and micro (Benyon *et al.*, 1994, 1995; den Boer, 2002a; Anderson *et al.*, 1995). 'Macro' refers to the big political decisions on cooperation made by ministers and heads of government at EU level, while 'micro' refers to cooperation on particular cases. Arguably of most interest is the mesolevel, which focuses on more informal operational cooperation between law enforcement agencies (Johnson, 2003). In practice, there is often a serious disjuncture between the goals and logic of cooperation at the macro- and mesolevels. Anderson et al. (1995: 77) found that many senior police officials were frustrated that political-level discussions and decisions did not reflect the practical realities of law enforcement on the ground. Deflem (2006), meanwhile, has applied a Weberian theory of bureaucratization to show how professional expertise and systems of expert knowledge shape operational cooperation in ways that are relatively independent of political control.

Second, the informal nature of cooperation has also sparked a debate on accountability in this area (Walker, 2000; den Boer, 2002b; Loader, 2002; Peers, 2008). Drawing on political theory concepts of legitimacy and accountability, scholars have developed various typologies for unpacking different types of accountability. Thus Walker (2000) and others differentiate between internal accountability within organizations or professional bodies and external accountability to the public. Anderson et al. (1995: 250–68) argue that the latter is generally secured through three channels: a legislative mandate, democratic scrutiny and due process. None of these three was adequate in the case of law enforcement cooperation, with the result that the EU tended to fall back on other channels of legitimation: namely, its technocratic competence and the need to bypass due process given the urgency of the problems it was addressing. More generally, many scholars agree on the need for a more robust or 'constitutionalist' legal framework (Walker, 2004b: 14–15; see also Peers, 2006 for a critique of the legal basis) – and one which addresses particular problems of multilevel plurality of institutions (Walker, 2000: 292; Loader, 2002). Some lawyers have gone even further, suggesting that the lack of judicial review in this area implies a high degree of 'legal pathology' and the emergence of a 'police state' (de Hert, 2004).

Other authors are more sanguine about the informal nature of JHA developments, emphasizing the potentially positive role of epistemic communities and technocrats in this area (Benyon, 1996, Liberatore, 2007). Such informal links can be far more effective than more formalized arrangements. Indeed, by imposing heavy bureaucratic procedures and requirements for accountability, such formalization could inhibit much of the progress already made in operational cooperation (Anderson *et al.*, 1995: 75–8). Not surprisingly, the securitization scholars have come to a rather different conclusion, seeing the role of professionals and experts in a far more sinister light. Huysmans (2004, 2006), for example, has argued that security professionals have contributed to the securitization of this area, exporting their technologies and practices to an ever-wider array of policy areas. This builds on work by Bigo, which explains these dynamics in terms of the attempts by officials to carve out a new role for themselves in a post-Cold War context (Bigo, 1994: 163).

Moving on from operations to the level of political discourse, much of the literature on these themes is fairly cynical about the rhetorical justifications of JHA cooperation. Thus, for example, Anderson et al. (1995) talk about the 'politics of the latest outrage' (see also Anderson, 1994: 9–10). In a similar vein, den Boer (1994: 193) discerns distinct 'domains of justification', with political rhetoric often revealing 'minimal empirical or analytical scrutiny'. Walker (2004b: 13) is concerned that this type of discourse can divert attention from the need to ensure proper constitutional checks and balances in the system. Arguably, this is the area of JHA that was most affected by the terrorist attacks in the US, Madrid and London. Den Boer (2002b) argued soon after 9/11 that the attacks had provided a 'political window of opportunity' to speed up cooperation on police and judicial cooperation. In particular, it precipitated agreement on a European Arrest Warrant and common definition of terrorist crimes (den Boer and Monar, 2002; Mitsilegas, 2003).

As with theories of cooperation on immigration and asylum, scholars have opted for neofunctionalist explanations (Occhipinti, 2003) or combined neofunctionalist theories with some account of exogenous sources of change (Turnbull and Sandholtz, 2001). Neofunctionalist accounts are challenged by Anderson and his colleagues (Anderson, 1994: 4–8; Anderson et al., 1995: 6–7) for whom the notion of 'functional spillover' is too deterministic and is unable to account for the precise timing and form of institutional structure adopted. Even where such accounts do incorporate the role of institutional dynamics in propelling change (so-called 'political spillover'), they fail to specify the relationship between the two dynamics (Anderson *et al.*, 1995: 94–5). Walker (2004b: 23–4), meanwhile, notes a polarization between two views of integration typically espoused by policy-makers: structural fatalism and naive separatism. Stuctural fatalism treats police cooperation as a dependent variable, contingent on the overall architecture of, and progress in, EU integration. This implies that there is limited scope for actors in this policy area to influence cooperation. Naive separatism, by contrast, develops programmes for cooperation divorced from a real understanding of the political context, creating a risk that such programmes become marginalized. The failure to realize naive separatist projects can generate frustration, encouraging a retreat back into fatalistic mode. Interestingly, scholars have observed a similar 'pendular' tendency in the area of migration policy (Sciortino and Pastore, 2004).

Diagnosis

The above overview suggests that there has certainly been a large quantity of research, covering a wide array of themes. But how should its quality be judged? I would like to suggest that we assess the health of research based on three criteria.

First, there should be a good balance between diversity and the attempt to engage with some common themes. Thus despite a plurality of approaches, there should be some engagement between different sub-areas and approaches, generating a sense of progress in the field – ideally resulting in the accumulation of a body of theoretical insights and/or empirical knowledge. Second, one would hope for an appropriate balance between theory-building and empirical enquiry. Theories and concepts should be informed by a good understanding of empirical developments (not always easy in such a rapidly evolving area); while empirical observation should be theoretically grounded and reflect on the presuppositions shaping methods of enquiry. Third, although research in this area is necessarily applied, it should aim to keep abreast of relevant developments in cognate disciplines. Ideally, scholarship should be applying and testing insights developed in areas such as EU studies, migration studies, security studies, international relations and criminology. Judged on these criteria, scholarship on JHA gets a mixed review.

Developing an *acquis* of knowledge

In terms of the first criterion, there has certainly been an accumulation of insights in a number of sub-areas or 'pockets' of research. I shall highlight three examples. The first of these is work on the reconfiguration of political opportunity structures brought about by the integration of immigration and asylum policies. New institutional arrangements and an emerging European discourse on immigration and integration have altered the power distribution between actors involved in influencing policy. It appears to have created new opportunities for NGO lobbying, at both transnational and national level. However, it has also provided new opportunities for officials to avoid domestic scrutiny, as Guiraudon's work on 'venue-shopping' (2000) has shown. This is an excellent example of the application of political sociology to explore the implications of integration for policy-making. It has triggered interesting debates that engage both political scientists and sociologists, and has been developed and applied to explain new developments such as the externalization of JHA (Lavenex, 2006).

A second area which has seen real movement is debates on law enforcement cooperation. Two related areas stand out in this respect. One is the work on different levels of police cooperation. The micro/meso/macro typology has been taken up by a number of scholars for analysing the dynamics of, and relationship between, political and operational cooperation. This has produced some fascinating insights into informal operational ties between police in different countries and their sense of frustration at the often symbolic and ill-informed discourse at ministerial level. Deflem (2006) has similarly theorized the relationship between top-down political cooperation and more autonomous operational dynamics. The related area of institutional structures and accountability has also seen a very fruitful debate, disentangling and assessing the various dimensions of legitimacy in this area.

A third area that deserves a mention is the growing literature on the apparent securitization of JHA, and especially migration. This is a good example of the application of security studies and Foucauldian approaches for critically analysing EU discourse and practice. Again, there is evidence of real movement in this subfield as scholars apply these theories and concepts to make sense of new developments, especially the implications of 9/11. Recent contributions also suggest scholars are pursuing new conceptual avenues, for example adjusting notions of securitization to capture more subtle discourses on 'unease' or 'risk' (Huysmans, 2006). Nonetheless, this line of research does suffer a number of theoretical and methodological weaknesses, which we shall return to later.

These three cases of 'good practice', however, represent fairly discrete subfields of enquiry. What is often lacking is more rigorous engagement across such subfields. For example, although the political opportunities and the securitization literature share a number of premises about the goals and strategies of those seeking to influence policy, they tend to remain within the confines of their respective bodies of literature with limited mutual engagement. This may well be attributable to their roots in rather different fields (respectively, social movements theory and neo-institutionalism, and security studies). However, as a relatively narrow area of applied research, studies on EU immigration policy can ill afford this type of compartmentalization. Theoretical diversity is well and good, but not where scholars fail to engage with other schools seeking to account for similar phenomena. Such insulation may partly explain, for example, the failure of securitization literature to capture the dynamics of migration policy-making (Favell and Hansen, 2002; Boswell, 2007a).

Similarly, analyses of policy-making in immigration and police cooperation have remained largely discrete. Thus literature on law enforcement has been much more attentive to the gap between political rhetoric and operational practice, and has displayed more cynicism about the justificatory strategies employed in this discourse. Although migration scholars analysing national policy have been similarly sceptical, much of the EU level analysis has a tendency to take discourse at

face value. Studies in this area might benefit from engaging with literature on the politics of police cooperation. Comparisons between the
areas of immigration and police cooperation could also yield interesting
insights into variation in policy-making. While both are highly populist
areas and subject to similar discursive strategies, they show interesting
divergences in terms of the constellation of actors attempting to influence policy, the role of expertise, issues of legitimation and accountability, and the readiness of governments to cede competence.

In sum, despite a number of impressive developments, this is an area
of research that remains overly fragmented (Geddes, 2006: 449–50).
Indeed, it seems to be subject to the sort of 'disjointed incrementalism'
that characterizes the policy area (Lavenex and Wallace, 2005).

Theory and empirics

It was noted earlier that many contributions in this field are highly
descriptive. This is to some degree understandable, given the difficulty
in keeping pace with complex and swiftly moving developments in
JHA. But the focus on charting developments can also lead to a rather
uncritical acceptance of political formulations of the issues. Much of the
more descriptive literature follows the sort of narrative frequently found
in EU documents, i.e. simplified accounts of the 'common problems'
that EU cooperation seeks to address and chronological lists of key
decisions attempting to address these. As some scholars have pointed
out, this implies buying into the often symbolic and ill-informed constructions of migration, criminality or terrorism employed by policy-
makers (den Boer, 1994; Geddes, 2005b; Sciortino and Pastore 2004).
Similarly, commentators on JHA often adopt unrealistic expectations
about what cooperation can achieve. Analyses of EU immigration and
asylum policy have frequently been critical of the restrictive bent of
cooperation, implying rather unrealistic beliefs about the liberalizing or
inclusive nature of the European project (Geddes, 2005b). Literature on
both immigration and police cooperation, meanwhile, has pointed to
the bipolar tendencies of debate in this area, with commentators
adhering to opposite extremes (securitizing vs liberalizing; structural
fatalism vs naive separatism; intergovernmental vs supranational).
These tendencies all imply the need for greater critical distance from
prevalent constructions of policy problems and responses. Rather than
accepting policy-makers' categorizations, academic researchers should
reflect on the political and institutional dynamics influencing such constructions, as well as the presuppositions guiding their own research
design and methodologies (Bommes and Morawska, 2005: 4).

One way of achieving such critical distance is for empirical studies to
engage with theories of policy-making. Insights from neo-institutionalism, constructivism or critical theory can all help deconstruct the

rhetoric of EU integration. A greater degree of theoretical reflection can also encourage the use of more rigorous research methods. Rather than relying on official EU documents, as many scholars do, analyses of policy-making and implementation should draw on complementary sources (media, parliamentary debates, interviews and participant observation). Such methods are especially crucial in observing informal and operational forms of cooperation and in assessing policy outcomes rather than outputs – as exemplified in recent studies by Jordan et al. (2003) and Faist and Ette (2007). Of course, this type of research is more financially and logistically demanding, and there are often problems getting access to officials, meetings and unofficial documents.

If empirical studies could be more theoretically aware, the converse holds for many theoretical contributions. In particular, theories attempting to explain cooperation often gloss over the complexity of actors, interests and goals shaping policy-making processes. Part of this simplification is unavoidable where the goal is to develop generalizable and testable theories. But in many cases, empirical claims are based on secondary sources or rather cursory discourse analyses which offer a somewhat skewed reading of events. One example is some of the recent contributions to the securitization literature, which use examples of 'securitarian' language from official EU documents to substantiate the notion that EU migration policies have become securitized (to be contrasted with the more rigorous methods used by scholars such as Bigo or Huysmans). Again, much of the problem can be traced back to deficient research methods, especially an over-reliance on political rhetoric (Boswell, 2007b).

Core disciplines and applied research

In a recent analysis of the state of migration research, Bommes and Morawska (2005: 3) pointed out that scholarship in this area is insufficiently integrated into its core disciplines. It has become out of touch with theoretical and conceptual developments in sociology, anthropology, geography and political science, and is missing opportunities for contributing to theory-building. Can the same be said of the literature on JHA? Much depends on how one defines its 'core' disciplines, but assuming they include migration studies, criminology, security studies and related disciplines then there have been some notable contributions to theory-building. I will briefly outline three such contributions which have a wider resonance.

First, theories of policy-making have been enriched by their application to issues of JHA cooperation. A key contribution in this respect is work on political opportunities and venue-shopping. Given the proliferation of fora for developing policy on aspects of JHA, this area provides excellent scope for observing and testing theories about how and why actors make use of different sites. Related to this, it can also shed light on how these actors view the requirements of legitimation: do they choose venues and instruments that enable them to score electoral points through symbolic rhetoric and decision, or do they instead prefer to work towards specific outcomes, away from the glare of public scrutiny? (See Brunsson, 2002 on the distinction between legitimation through talk, decisions and action.) By contrast, policy-making at the national level offers far more limited options for venue-shopping and correspondingly fewer opportunities for scholars to observe the strategies (and thus infer preferences) of officials and politicians. So analysis of JHA can certainly make a contribution to literature on how policy-makers and officials respond to shifting institutional opportunities.

Second, the informal and operational nature of cooperation on JHA can yield fascinating insights into the dynamics of, and impediments to, inter-organizational and cross-national coordination. In particular, cooperation between law enforcement officials requires excellent coordination and a high degree of trust. Efforts to investigate criminal activities or control irregular border crossings involve not just symbolic exchange and good will, but quite practical and effective coordination in addressing often urgent problems. Moreover, the officials involved are not typically the best suited for these activities, in terms of language or intercultural skills. One good example of research on such cooperation is the work of Johnson (2003) in exploring barriers to cross-border operational cooperation: problems of language, incompatible technologies, varied working practices, contrasting administrations and authority structures.

Third, analyses of JHA have contributed to a number of more general debates within EU studies. For example, debates on accountability and legitimacy in the area of police cooperation have helped clarify some of the shortcomings of EU institutional arrangements. Another example is theories of integration. Explanations of EU cooperation have benefited from being tested on the rather particular case of JHA cooperation (Hix and Noury, 2007). In this context, there appears to be growing interest in exploring the implications of JHA arrangements for theories of 'enhanced cooperation' (Kietz and Maurer, 2006).

Arguably, though, these three contributions have made an impact on a relatively narrow and applied area of studies: namely, theories of political opportunity structures, organizational cooperation and EU integration. If the requirement is to make a more general contribution to the tools of understanding in sociology, political science, anthropology, geography or legal theory, then most research on JHA is clearly not up to the mark. Arguably, this represents a missed opportunity. Just as JHA has provided policy-makers and officials with 'laboratories' for testing forms of cooperation (Monar, 2001), so too can this area offer excellent subject matter for testing and developing assumptions about politics and public administration. I shall explore these possibilities further in the final section.

Future directions for research

The diagnosis of JHA literature has a number of implications for a future research agenda. It suggests the benefits of less compartmentalization and more engagement across sub-areas, both in terms of debates on concepts and theories, and comparison of developments in different policy areas. It implies the need for more systematic scrutiny of official EU narratives of cooperation and correspondingly rigorous methods of observation. On a more positive note, there is real potential for innovative contributions in this area, which can add to our understanding of a number of contemporary challenges for governance and legitimacy. I would like to suggest six possible areas for future research on JHA, which have the potential to make a contribution to some of these broader debates.

Organizations

Recently, there has been increasing interest in the anthropology and sociology of EU institutions, especially the European Commission (Cram, 1994; Cini, 1996; Shore, 2000; Hooghe, 1997). The case of immigration and asylum has much to contribute here. Competence in many areas – such as economic integration of immigrants and the 'external dimension' – are highly contested between different Directorates-General. Moreover, there are various competing logics at play in policy-making, including labour market considerations, non-discrimination and human rights, internal security and border control, as well as foreign policy and development cooperation. What are the implications for the priorities, goals and organizational cultures of different parts of the Commission? How does the particular structure and institutional set-up of the Commission impact on coordination between departments, and how does this differ from parallel arrangements between ministries at the national level? What are the implications for EU policies, for example in terms of pursuing more liberal or securitization approaches?

Cognitive and technological drivers of policy

Bigo, Huysmans and Deflem have argued that expert knowledge and technologies can play a role in shaping policies in JHA. More research is needed to help pin down and measure the explanatory power of such factors. One important question is the role of expertise in legitimizing policy decisions and in removing decision-making from more democratic forms of settlement or scrutiny. Another is how the adoption of certain procedures or technologies, such as biometrics, create forms of path dependency in JHA policies. It would also be interesting to explore how securitarian discourses and practices are constrained or enhanced by the increased role of the Commission and Parliament in scrutinizing policy.

Constitutional law and political cooperation

Legal developments on judicial cooperation have sparked a number of important debates amongst EU lawyers, but political scientists have largely failed to pick up on these. The legal literature suggests that the European courts have had a significant and controversial role in trying to 'communitarize' Title VI; while the European Arrest Warrant and the question of mutual recognition raise huge issues of legitimacy and accountability for national governments. This is another area in which JHA appears to offer an exciting laboratory for exploring the dynamics of Europeanization, and especially the potentially huge role of legal rulings and framework decisions in shaping the architecture of political cooperation.

Implementation

Many areas of cooperation on immigration and asylum are highly symbolic, involving quite high profile decisions and statements, whose impact on policy at national level is difficult to measure. It would be interesting to explore how far such symbolic commitments translate into policies and practice, or whether instead one can observe 'institutional decoupling' (Meyer and Rowan, 1977). It would also be worth exploring how far member states adapt their policies and practices through processes of norm diffusion and policy learning. JHA provides excellent scope for comparing such processes across policy areas characterized by different types of cooperation (such as common regulations, joint programmes or operational coordination); or degrees of technocracy/expertise.

Legitimation

There has been a considerable body of literature exploring problems of accountability and legitimacy in JHA cooperation. Yet there has been little systematic comparison of the rather different issues arising in the areas of immigration and asylum (which raises concerns about the rights of non-nationals), and police and judicial cooperation (raising questions of domestic civil rights and accountability). While the former raise legal and ethical issues concerning rights across borders and the claims of non-citizens, the latter are concerned with more traditional issues of state legitimacy *vis-à-vis* citizens. This offers an interesting case for comparing patterns of mobilization and claims-making in the respective areas, and state/EU responses to such claims. While one would expect states to be more sensitive to claims-making on the part of citizens, in fact cooperation on police and judicial cooperation has remained far less accountable than policy on immigration and asylum.

Theories of the state

Cooperation in JHA requires states to cede some of the core areas of sovereignty: autonomy in the admission of non-nationals and their access to rights and resources; and control over arrangements for internal security. Debates on how far this represents a 'loss of control' appear to have reached an impasse, with no obvious standpoint from which to assess competing claims. One way of getting some leverage on these debates is to situate analyses of JHA within more theoretically and historically informed analyses of non-Westphalian models of governance. Alternatively, it would be interesting to explore the impact of this apparent loss of sovereignty on patterns of legitimation and mobilization at the national level. What is the impact of these developments on strategies of political mobilization and on expectations about state capacity to control migration or internal security?

Conclusion

EU cooperation in JHA throws up a fascinating set of research questions, as a growing number of scholars are finding. Part of its appeal lies in the rapid evolution of cooperation, as well as its extensive ramifications for human rights, security and welfare in both Europe and neighbouring countries. The field also provides excellent material for testing and developing theories of EU integration, public policy, political mobilization and legitimacy. Some of these aspects have been the object of stimulating research, including on topics such as the dynamics of police cooperation; the impact of shifting political opportunity structures on lobbying and venue-shopping; the (construction of) links between migration and security; and the impact of EU court rulings in shaping EU cooperation. With a growing number of graduate programmes, PhD studentships and research projects dedicated to the area, there is reason to be optimistic about the future development of the field.

However, this chapter has also highlighted a number of pitfalls in undertaking this type of research: notably, a tendency for research to be compartmentalized into discrete subfields; for it to proffer explanations that fail to go beyond the EU's own narratives of policy; and for researchers to adopt normative accounts that are either too idealistic or too cynical in their expectations about the EU. The challenge, then, is to ensure research is theoretically informed and uses rigorous research methods that go beyond merely analysing official documents. Scholars would also benefit from engaging with literature in parallel policy areas to avoid becoming overly self-referential. Where these conditions are in place, JHA scholarship has the potential to make a rich and important contribution to both empirical and theoretical knowledge.

References

Anderson, M. (1994) 'The Agenda for Police Cooperation', in M. Anderson and M. den Boer (eds) *Policing Across National Boundaries* (London: Pinter) 3–21.

Anderson, M. and Apap, J. (eds) (2002) *Police and Justice Co-operation and the New European Borders* (The Hague: Kluwer Law International).

Anderson, M., Cullen, P., den Boer, M., Gilmore, W., Raab, C., and Walker, N. (1995) *Policing the European Union* (Oxford: Clarendon).

Apap, J. (ed.) (2004) *Justice and Home Affairs in the EU: Liberty and Security Issues After Enlargement* (Brussels: Centre for European Studies).

Barrett, G. (1997) *Justice Cooperation in the EU: The Creation of a European Legal Service* (Dublin: Institute of European Affairs).

Benyon, J. (1996) 'The Politics of Police Co-operation in the European Union', *International Journal of Law, Crime and Justice* 24(4): 353–79.

Benyon, J., Morris, S., Toye, M., Willis, A. and Beck, A. (1995) *Police Forces in the New European Union: A Conspectus.* (Leicester: Centre for the Study of Public Order, University of Leicester).

Benyon, J., Turnbull, L., Willis, A., Woodward, R. and Beck, A. (1994) *Police co-operation in Europe: An Investigation* (Leicester: CSPO).

Berg, E. and Ehin, P. (2006) What Kind of Border Regime is in the Making? *Cooperation and Conflict* 41(1): 53–71.

Bigo, D. (1994) 'The European Internal Security Field: Stakes and Rivalries in a Newly Developing Area of Police Intervention', in M. Anderson and M. den Boer (eds) *Policing Across National Boundaries* (London: Pinter) 161–73.

Bigo, D. (2002) 'Security and Immigration: Toward a Critique of the Governmentality of Unease', *Alternatives* 27: 63–92.

Bigo, D. (2005) 'Frontier Controls in the European Union: Who Is In Control?' in D. Bigo and E. Guild (eds) *Controlling Frontiers: Free Movement Into and Within Europe* (Aldershot: Ashgate) 49–99.

Blekxtoon, R. (2005) 'Introduction', in Judge R. Blekxtoon and W. van Ballegooij (eds) *Handbook on the European Arrest Warrant* (Cambridge: Cambridge University Press) 5–11.

den Boer, M. (1994) 'The Quest for European Policing: Rhetoric and Justification in a Disorderly Debate', in M. Anderson and M. den Boer (eds) *Policing Across National Boundaries* (London: Pinter) 174–96.

den Boer, M. (1996) 'Justice and Home Affairs: Cooperation Without Integration' in H. Wallace and W. Wallace (eds) *Policy-Making in the European Union* (Oxford and New York: Oxford University Press) 389–409.

den Boer, M. (1998) *Taming the Third Pillar: improving the management of justice and home affairs cooperation in the EU* (Maastricht: European Institute of Public Administration).

den Boer, M. (2002a) 'Law-Enforcement Cooperation and Transnational Organized Crime in Europe' in M. R. Berdal and M. Serrano (eds) *Transnational Organized Crime and International Security: Business as Usual?* (Boulder: Lynne Rienner) 103–116.

den Boer, M. (2002b) 'Towards an Accountability Regime for an Emerging European Policing Governance', *Policing and Society* 12(4): 275–89.

den Boer, M. and Monar, J. (2002) '11 September and the Challenge of Global Terrorism to the EU as a Security Actor', *Journal of Common Market Studies* 40: 11–28.

Bommes, M. and Morawska, E. (2005) 'Introduction', in M. Bommes and E. Morawska (eds) *International Migration Research: Constructions, Omissions and the Promises of Interdisciplinarity* (Aldershot: Ashgate) 1–9.

Boswell, C. (2003) 'The "external dimension" of EU immigration and asylum policy', *International Affairs* 79(9): 619–38.

Boswell, C. (2007a) 'Migration Control in Europe After 9/11: Explaining the Absence of Securitization', *Journal of Common Market Studies* 45(3): 589–610.

Boswell, C. (2007b) 'Theorizing Migration Policy: Is There A Third Way?' *International Migration Review* 41(1): 75–100.

Boswell, C. (2008) 'Evasion, Reinterpretation and Decoupling: European Commission Responses to the "External Dimension" of Immigration and Asylum', *West European Politics* 31(3): 491–512.

Brunsson, N. (2002) *The Organization of Hypocrisy: Talk, Decisions and Actions in Organizations* (Copenhagen: Abstrakt and Liber).

Buzan, B., Waever, O. and de Wilde, J. (1998) *Security: A New Framework for Analysis* (Boulder: Lynne Rienner).

Byrne, R. (2003) 'Harmonization and Burden Redistribution in the Two Europes', *Journal of Refugee Studies* 16(3): 336–58.

Byrne, R., Noll, G., and Vedsted-Hansen, J. (2002) *New Asylum Countries? Migration Control and Refugee Protection in an Enlarged European Union* (The Hague: Kluwer Law International).

Callovi, G. (1992) 'Regulation of Immigration in 2003: Pieces of the European Community Jig-Saw Puzzle', *International Migration Review* 26: 353–72.

Caviedes, A. (2004) 'The open method of co-ordination in immigration policy: a tool for prying open Fortress Europe?' *Journal of European Public Policy* 11(2): 289–310.

Cini, M. (1996) *The European Commission: Leadership, Organisation and Culture in the European Union Administration* (Manchester: Manchester University Press).

Collinson, S. (1993) *Europe and International Migration* (London: Pinter).

Collinson, S. (1996) 'Visa Requirements, Carrier Sanctions, "Safe Third Countries" and "Readmission": The Development of an Asylum "Buffer

Zone" in Europe', *Transactions of the Institute of British Geographers* 29(1): 76–90.

Collyer, M. (2007) 'In-Between Places: Trans-Saharan Transit Migrants in Morocco and the Fragmented Journey to Europe', *Antipode* 39(4): 668–90.

Cram, L. (1994) 'The European Commission as a Multi-Organization: Social Policy and IT Policy in the EU', *Journal of European Public Policy* 1(2): 195–217.

Deflem, M. (2006) 'Europol and the Policing of International Terrorism: Counter-Terrorism in a Global Perspective', *Justice Quarterly* 23(3): 336–59.

Denza, E. (2002) *The Intergovernmental Pillars of the European Union* (Oxford: Oxford University Press).

Düvell, F. (2007) *Ukraine – Europe's Mexico? Country Report 1* (Oxford: COMPAS).

Faist, T. and Ette A. (eds) (2007) *The Europeanization of National Policies and Politics of Immigration Between Autonomy and the European Union* (Basingstoke: Palgrave Macmillan).

Favell, A. and Geddes, A. (1999) 'European Integration, Immigration and the Nation State: Institutionalising Transnational Political Action?', EUI Working Papers, RSC, 99(32).

Favell, A. and Hansen, R. (2002) 'Markets Against Politics: Migration, EU Enlargement and the Idea of Europe', *Journal of Ethnic and Migration Studies* 28(4): 581–601.

Fletcher, M. (2005) 'Extending "Indirect Effect" to the Third Pillar: The Significance of *Pupino*', *European Law Review* 30: 826–77.

Gammeltoft-Hansen, T. (2006a) *Filtering Out the Risky Migrant: Migration Control, Risk Theory and the European Union* (Aalborg: Aalborg University).

Gammeltoft-Hansen, T. (2006b) *Outsourcing Migration management: EU Power and the External Dimension of Asylum and Immigration Policy* (Copenhagen: DIIS).

Geddes, A. (2000) 'Lobbying for migrant inclusion in the European Union: new opportunities for transnational advocacy?', *Journal of European Public Policy* 7(4): 632–49.

Geddes, A. (2003) *The Politics of Migration and Immigration in Europe* (London: Sage).

Geddes, A. (2005a) 'Europe's Border Relationships and International Migration Relations', *Journal of Common Market Studies* 43(4): 787–806.

Geddes, A. (2005b) 'Migration Research and European Integration: The Construction and Institutionalization of Problems of Europe', in M. Bommes and E. Morawska (eds) *International Migration Research: Constructions, Omissions and the Promises of Interdisciplinarity* (Aldershot: Ashgate) 265–80.

Geddes, A. (2006) 'The Politics of EU Domestic Order', in K. E. Jorgensen and M. Pollack and B. J. Rosamond (eds) *Handbook of European Union Politics*. (London: Sage).

Grabbe, H. (2000) 'The Sharp Edges of Europe: Extending Schengen Eastwards', *International Affairs* 76(3): 519–36.

Gray, E. and Statham, P. (2005) 'Becoming European? British Pro-Migrant NGOs and the European Union', *European Political Communication Working Paper Series* 9(5): 1–17.

Guild, E. (1999) 'The Impetus to Harmonise: Asylum Policy in the European Union', in F. Nicholson and P. Twomey (eds) *Refugee Rights and Reality: Evolving International Concepts and Regimes* (Cambridge: Cambridge University Press) 313–35.

Guild, E. and Harlow, C. (eds) (2001) *Implementing Amsterdam: Immigration and Asylum Rights in EC Law* (Oxford: Hart).

Guiraudon, V. (2000) 'European Integration and Migration Policy: Vertical Policy-Making as Venue Shopping', *Journal of Common Market Studies* 38(2): 251–71.

Guiraudon, V. (2001) 'De-Nationalizing Control: Analyzing state responses to constraints on migration control', in V. Guiraudon and C. Joppke (eds) *Controlling a New Migration World* (London: Routledge) 31–64.

Guiraudon, V. (2003) 'The Constitution of a European Immigration Policy Domain: A Political Sociology Approach', *Journal of European Public Policy* 10(2): 263–82.

Guiraudon, V. and Lahav, G. (2000) 'A Reappraisal of the State: Sovereignty Debate', *Political Studies* 33(2): 163–95.

Hailbronner, K. (1990) 'The Right to Asylum and the Future of Asylum Procedures in the European Community', *International Journal of Refugee Law* 2(3): 341–60.

Hailbronner, K. (1993) 'The Concept of "Safe Country" and Expeditious Asylum Procedures: A Western European Perspective', *International Journal of Refugee Law* 5(1): 31–65.

Hampshire, J. (2008) 'Risk and the Migration State: The Emergence of Risk-based Migration Management in the UK', paper presented at the Council of European Studies 16th International Conference, Chicago, 6–8 March.

de Hert, P. (2004) 'Division of Competencies between National and European Levels with Regard to Justice and Home Affairs', in J. Apap (ed.) *Justice and Home Affairs in the EU: Liberty and Security Issues After Enlargement* (Brussels: Centre for European Studies) 55–99.

Hix, S. and Noury, A. (2007) 'Politics, Not Economic Interests: Determinants of Migration Policies in the European Union', *International Migration Review* 41(1): 182–205.

Hollifield, James F. (1992) *Immigrants, Markets, and States: The Political Economy of Postwar Europe* (Cambridge, MA: Harvard University Press).

Hollifield, J. F. (1999) 'Ideas, Institutions, and Civil Society: On the Limits of Immigration Control in France', in G. Brochmann and T. Hammar (eds) *Mechanisms of Immigration Control: A Comparative Analysis of European Regulation Policies* (Oxford: Berg) 59–95.

Hooghe, L. (1997) 'Serving Europe: Political Orientations of Senior Commission Officials', *European Integration Online Papers* 1(8). http://www.eiop.or.at/eiop/texte/1997–008.htm

Hurwitz, A. (1999) 'The 1990 Dublin Convention: A Comprehensive Assessment', *International Journal of Refugee Law* 11(4): 646–77.

Huysmans, J. (1995) 'Migrants as a Security Problem: Dangers of "Securitizing" Societal Issues', in R. Miles and D. Thranhardt (eds) *Migration and European Security: The Dynamics of Inclusion and Exclusion* (London: Pinter) 53–72.

Huysmans, J. (1998) 'Security! What Do You Mean? From Concept to Thick Signifier', *European Journal of International Relations* 4(2): 226–55.

Huysmans, J. (2004) 'A Foucaultian view on spill-over: freedom and security in the EU', *Journal of International Relations and Development* 7: 294–318.

Huysmans, J. (2006) *The Politics of Insecurity: Fear, Migration and Asylum in the EU* (Cambridge: Routledge).

Ireland, P. (1991) 'Facing the True "Fortress Europe": Immigrants and Politics in the EC', *Journal of Common Market Studies* 29(5): 246–71.

Jileva, E. (2002) 'Visa and Free Movement of Labour: The Uneven Imposition of the EU Acquis on the Accession States', *Journal of Ethnic and Migration Studies* 28(4): 683–700.

Johnson, E. (2003) 'Talking Across Frontiers: Building Communication Between Emergency Services', in J. Anderson, L. O'Dowd and T. M. Wilson (eds) *New Borders for a Changing Europe: Cross-Border Cooperation and Governance* (London: Frank Cass) 88–110.

Joly, D. (1992) *Refugees: Asylum in Europe?* (London: Minority Rights).

Joly, D. (1996) *Haven or Hell? Asylum Policies and Refugees in Europe* (London: Macmillan).

de Jong, C. D. (1999) 'Is There a Need for a European Asylum Policy?', in F. Nicholson and P. Twomey (eds) *Refugee Rights and Realities* (Cambridge: Cambridge University Press) 357–78.

Joppke, C. (1998) 'Why Liberal States Accept Unwanted Immigration', *World Politics* 50(2): 266–93.

Jordan, B., Strath, B. and Triandafyllidou, A. (2003) 'Contextualising Immigration Policy Implementation in Europe', *Journal of Ethnic and Migration Studies* 29(2): 195–224.

Kietz, D. and Maurer, A. (2006) *From Schengen to Prüm: Deeper Integration through Enhanced Cooperation or Signs of Fragmentation in the EU?* (Berlin: SWP).

Koslowski, R. (1998) 'European Migration Regimes, Established and Emergent', in C. Joppke (ed.) *Challenge to the Nation-State: Immigration in Western Europe and the United States* (OUP 1998) 49–86.

Koslowski, R. (2000) 'The Mobility Money Can Buy: Human Smuggling and Border Control in the European Union', in P. Andreas and T. Snyder (eds) *The Wall Around the West: State Borders and Immigration Controls in North America and Europe* (Lanham: Rowman & Littlefield) 203–18.

Lahav, G. (1998) 'Immigration and the State: The Devolution and Privatization of Immigration Control in the EU', *Journal of Ethnic and Migration Studies* 24(1): 675–94.

Lahav, G. (2000) 'The Rise of Nonstate Actors in Migration Regulation in the United States and Europe: Changing the Gatekeepers or Bringing Back the State?', in N. Foner and R. Rumbaut and S. J. Gold (eds) *Immigration Research for a New Century: Multidisciplinary Perspectives* (New York: Russell Sage Foundation).

Lavenex, S. (1999) *Safe Third Countries: Extending the EU Immigration and Asylum Policies to Central and Eastern Europe* (Budapest: Central European University Press).

Lavenex, S. (2002) 'Migration and the EU's new eastern border: between realism and liberalism', *Journal of European Public Policy* 8(1): 24–42.

Lavenex, S. (2006) 'Shifting Up and Out: The Foreign Policy of European Immigration Control', *West European Politics* 29(2): 329–50.

Lavenex, S. and Ucarer, E. (eds) (2002) *Migration and the Externalities of European Integration* (Lanham: Lexington).

Lavenex, S. and Ucarer, E. (2004) 'The External Dimension of Europeanization: The Case of Immigration Policies', *Cooperation and Conflict* 39(4): 417–43.

Lavenex, S. and Wallace, W. (2005) 'Justice and Home Affairs', in H. Wallace and W. Wallace and M. A. Pollack (eds) *Policy-Making in the EU* (Oxford: Oxford University Press) 457–80.

Liberatore, A. (2007) 'Balancing Security and Democracy, and the Role of Expertise: Biometrics Politics in the European Union', *European Journal on Criminal Policy and Research* 13(1–2): 109–37.

Loader, I. (2002) 'Policing, Securitization and Democratization in Europe', *Criminology and Criminal Justice* 2(2): 125–53.

Masse, J.-P. (2005) 'Data Surveillance and Border Control in the EU: Balancing Efficiency and Legal Protection of Third Country Nationals.' Working Paper produced by the CHALLENGE project, accessed at http://www.libertysecurity.org/article289.html (10 July 2009).

Meyer, J. W. and Rowan, B. (1977) 'Institutionalized Organizations: Formal Structure as Myth and Ceremony', *American Journal of Sociology* 83(2): 340–63.

Mitsilegas, V. (2002) 'The Implementation of the EU Acquis on Illegal Immigration by the Candidate Countries of Central and Eastern Europe: Challenges and Contradictions', *Journal of Ethnic and Migration Studies* 28(4): 665–82.

Mitsilegas, V. (2003) 'The New EU–USA Cooperation on Extradition, Mutual Legal Assistance and the Exchange of Police Data', *European Foreign Affairs Review* 8(4): 515–36.

Mitsilegas, V. (2006) 'The Constitutional Implications of Mutual Recognition in Criminal Matters in the EU', *Common Market Law Review* 43: 1277–311.

Mitsilegas, V. (2007a) 'Border Security in the European Union: Towards Centralised Controls and Maximum Surveillance', in H. Toner, E. Guild and A. Baldaccini (eds) *EU Immigration and Asylum Law and Policy; whose freedom, security and justice?* (Oxford: Hart) 359–93.

Mitsilegas, V. (2007b) 'Constitutional Principles of the European Community and European Criminal Law', *European Journal of Law Reform* 8 2/3: 301–23.

Monar, J. (1995) 'Democratic Control of Justice and Home Affairs: The European Parliament and the National Parliaments', in R. Bieber and J. Monar (eds) *Justice and Home Affairs in the European Union: The Development of the Third Pillar* (Brussels: Interuniversity Press) 243–57.

Monar, J. (2001) The Dynamics of Justice and Home Affairs: Laboratories, Driving Factors and Costs', *Journal of Common Market Studies* 39(4): 747–64.

Monar, J. (2004a) 'The EU as an International Actor in the Domain of Justice and Home Affairs', *European Foreign Affairs Review* 9: 395–415.

Monar, J. (2004b) 'Maintaining the JHA Acquis in an Enlarged Europe', in J. Apap (ed.) *Justice and Home Affairs in the EU: Liberty and Security Issues After Enlargement* (Brussels: Centre for European Studies) 37–53.

Monar, J. and Morgan, R. (eds) (1995) *The Third Pillar of the European Union* (Brussels: European Inter-University Press).

Morrison, J. and Crosland, B. (2000) *The Trafficking and Smuggling of Refugees: The End Game in European Asylum Policy?* (Geneva: UNHCR).

Myers, P. (1995) 'The Commission's Approach to the Third Pillar: Political and Organizational Elements', in R. Bieber and J. Monar (eds) *Justice and Home Affairs in the European Union: The Development of the Third Pillar* (Brussels: European Interuniversity Press).

Neuwahl, N. (1995) 'Judicial Control in Matters of Justice and Home Affairs: What Role for the Court of Justice?', in R. Bieber and J. Monar (eds) *Justice and Home Affairs in the European Union: The Development of the Third Pillar* (Brussels: European Interuniversity Press).

Noll, G. (1997) 'Prisoners' Dilemma in Fortress Europe. On the Prospects of Burden Sharing in the European Union', *German Yearbook of International Law* 40: 405–37.

Occhipinti, J. D. (2003) *The Politics of EU Police Cooperation: Toward a European FBI?* (Boulder: Lynne Rienner).

Pastore, F. (2007) *Europe, Migration and Development: Critical remarks on an emerging policy field* (Rome: CeSPI).

Peers, S. (2006) *EU Justice and Home Affairs Law* (2nd edn) (Oxford: Oxford University Press).

Peers, S. (2007a) 'The Jurisdiction of the Court of Justice over European Community Immigration and Asylum Law: Time for a Change?', in A. Baldaccini and E. Guild and H. Toner (eds) *Whose Freedom, Security and Justice? EU Immigration and Asylum Law and Policy* (Oxford: Hart).

Peers, S. (2007b) 'Salvation Outside the Church: Judicial Protection in the Third Pillar after the *Pupino* and *Segi* Judgements', *Criminal Market Law Review* 44: 883–929.

Raab, C. D. (1994) 'Police Cooperation: The Prospects for Privacy', in M. Anderson and M. den Boer (eds) *Policing Across National Boundaries* (London: Pinter) 121–36.

Sassen, S. (1998) 'The de-facto transnationalizing of immigration policy', in C. Joppke (ed.) *Challenge to the Nation-State: Immigration in Western Europe and the United States* (OUP 1998) 49–86.

Sciortino, G. and Pastore, F. (2004) 'Immigration and European Immigration Policy: Myths and Realities', in J. Apap (ed.) *Justice and Home Affairs in the EU: Liberty and Security Issues After Enlargement* (Brussels: Centre for European Studies) 191–209.

van Selm, J. (2002) 'Immigration and Asylum or Foreign Policy: The EU's Approach to Migrants and Their Countries of Origin', in S. Lavenex and E. Ucarer (eds) *Migration and the Externalities of European Integration* (Lanham: Lexington) 143–60.

Shaw, J. (2007) 'One or Many Constitutions The Constitutional Future of the European Union in the 2000s from a Legal Perspective', in *Why Europe? Possibilities and Limits of European Integration*, proceedings from Sieps' Annual Conference, 16 November 2006, ed. A. Follesdal, A. Moravcsik, J. Shaw, F. Langdal and G. von Sydow (Swedish Institute for European Policy Studies) 46–66.

Shore, C. (2000) *Building Europe: The Cultural Politics of European Integration* (London and New York: Routledge).

Soysal, Y. (1994) *Limits of Citizenship: Migrants and Postnational Membership in Europe* (Chicago: University of Chicago Press).

Stetter, S. (2000) 'Regulating migration: authority delegation in justice and home affairs', *Journal of European Public Policy* 7(1): 80–103.

Thielemann, E. (2003) 'Between Interests and Norms: Explaining Burden-Sharing in the European Union', *Journal of Refugee Studies* 16(Special Issue): 253–73.

Turnbull, P. and Sandholtz, W. (2001) 'Policing and Immigration: The Creation of New Policy Spaces', in A. S. Sweet, W. Sandholtz and N. Fligstein (eds) *The Institutionalization of Europe* (Oxford and New York: Oxford University Press) 194ff.

Twomey, P. (1999) 'Constructing a Secure Space: The Area of Freedom, Security and Justice', in D. O'Keefe and P. Twomey (eds) *Legal Issues of the Amsterdam Treaty* (Portland: Oxford University Press) 351–74.

Ucarer, E. (1997) 'Europe's Search for Policy: The Harmonization of Asylum Policy and European Integration', in E. Ucarer and D. Puchala (eds) *Immigration into Western Societies: Problems and Policies* (London: Pinter) 281–309.

Ucarer, E. (1999) 'Cooperation on Justice and Home Affairs Matters', in L. Cram, D. Dinan and N. Nugent (eds) *Developments in the European Union* (New York: St. Martin's Press) 247–65.

Ucarer, E. (2001) 'From the Sidelines to Center Stage: Sidekick No More? The European Commission in Justice and Home Affairs', *European Integration Online Papers, 5.*

Vedsted-Hansen, J. (1999) 'Europe's Response to the Arrival of Asylum Seekers: Refugee Protection and Immigration Control', *New Issues in Refugee Research*, Working Paper No. 6.

Waever, O., Buzan, B., Kelstrup, M. and Lemaitre, P. (1993) 'Introduction', in B. Buzan, O. Waever, M. Kelstrup and P. Lemaitre (eds) *Identity, Migration and the New Security Agenda in Europe* (London: Pinter).

Walker, N. (2000) *Policing in a Changing Constitutional Order* (London: Sweet and Maxwell).

Walker, N. (2002) 'The Problems of Trust in an Enlarged Area of Freedom, Security and Justice', in M. Anderson and J. Apap (eds) *Police and Justice Cooperation and the New European Borders* (The Hague: Kluwer Law International) 19–34.

Walker, N. (ed.) (2004a) *Europe's Area of Freedom, Security and Justice* (Oxford: Oxford University Press).

Walker, N. (2004b) 'In Search of the Area of Freedom, Security and Justice: A Constitutional Odyssey', in N. Walker (ed.) *Europe's Area of Freedom, Security and Justice* (Oxford and New York: Oxford University Press) 3–37.

Widgren, J. (1989) 'Europe and International Migration in the Future: The Necessity for Merging Migration, Refugee, and Development Policies', in G. Loescher and L. Monahan (eds) *Refugees in International Relations* (Oxford: Clarendon Press) 49–62.

Zielonka, J. (2001) 'How New Enlarged Borders will Reshape the European Union', *Journal of Common Market Studies* 39(3): 507–36.

Zucconi, M. (2004) 'Migration and Security as an Issue in US–European Relations', in J. Tirman (ed.) *The Maze of Fear: Security and Migration After 9/11* (New York: New Press) 142–54.

Chapter 13

Feminist Approaches

Johanna Kantola

Feminist studies of the EU seek to make sense of a field that has become enormously complex. Gender equality has been an issue in the EU since the inclusion of Article 119 on equal pay in the Treaty of Rome 1957 but has since widened to the recognition of equality between women and men as a fundamental principle of democracy for the whole EU. Gender equality is present both in gender specific policies, such as women's participation in the labour market, reconciliation of work and family, and political representation of women in parliaments, as well as informing the basic principles and functioning of the EU institutions wherever gender mainstreaming is implemented. While a few decades ago it was meaningful to study from which member state or EU institution particular policy initiatives, such as the equal pay or equal treatment directives, came from, the range of actors involved in gender policy-making has now widened, making this task ever more difficult. The 27 member states also convey multiple meanings and understandings of women, men, gender and gender equality (Verloo, 2007). Elisabeth Prugl (2007) suggests that whereas feminist research used to inquire 'how and why does the EU adopt and implement gender equality policies?', it now analyses 'how and why is gender difference constructed and gender inequality reproduced through EU policies?'.

Feminist scholars continue to struggle with some basic dilemmas. How compatible are market values, competition, efficiency and productivity with gender equality (Young, 2000)? Can women's concerns be represented in the EU without them being co-opted to the overall agenda (Stratigaki, 2004)? How to characterize the EU gender regime (Prugl, 2007)? Feminist scholars make sense of such questions by discerning different stages in EU gender policy. For example, Theresa Rees distinguishes a move from equal opportunities to positive action and to gender mainstreaming (Rees, 1998, 2005). Alternatively, Mark Bell sees the equality policy as having evolved from anti-discrimination policy to working towards substantive equality and to managing diversity (Bell, 2000, 2002). Although these policies have emerged at different times, they continue to coexist. This chapter establishes the state of art of feminist research by mapping four broad trends: (i) legislating for equal opportunities; (ii) positive action; (iii) gender mainstreaming;

305

and (iv) diversity. The chapter addresses the policy approach, its implementation and feminist critiques in relation to all four.

The latter part of the chapter focuses on current and future challenges to feminist research on the EU. These include a focus on the changes in the policy-making processes and the gendered dimensions of the open method of coordination (OMC) in particular. The fact that the EU is tackling a wide range of gender equality issues, including violence against women, trafficking in women, sexual harassment and reproductive rights, is briefly considered. This raises fundamental questions for feminist scholars and activists about the depth of EU gender equality policies. Finally, the emergence of an institutionalized women's policy network is critically assessed.

Legislating for equal opportunities

The first policy approach, legislating for equal opportunities, comes close to the feminist strategy of inclusion: women's rights are added to existing norms, laws and practices (Squires, 1999). The aim is to ensure equal treatment of women in relation to the norm of the male worker. The initial EU gender equality policy followed this trajectory. Despite the early start on the field of legislating for equal opportunities in the Treaty of Rome, not one national government undertook domestic policy changes in the 1960s to actually implement the equal pay principle of Article 119 in the Treaty of Rome (Cichowski, 2004: 501). Neither was this a key priority for the Commission that shied away from taking action towards the member states. The 1970s, however, witnessed a new period of intensification in gender policy. Major steps were taken by the Commission and the Council with the enactment of three new directives on Equal Pay 1975, Equal Treatment 1976 and Social Security 1978, which came to form the essential backbone for gender-equality policy for decades to come.

By the 1970s, equal pay had become a familiar issue for the Commission. It had been debated in the European Court of Justice during the *Defrenne* cases (Hoskyns, 1996b: 70–80). The Commission had acquired expert knowledge on the issue *vis-à-vis* the member states, which was helpful in obtaining their approval for the new directive. The UN International Women's Year 1975 created international pressure for taking action on women's rights, and this was backed up by some progressive member states such as France (Van der Vleuten, 2007: 87). Like Article 119, the Equal Pay Directive was a piece of legislation granted to women by male allies: women were not actively involved in the process which involved only very indirect forms of consultation and representation. Nevertheless, the meanings of pay and equal work were defined more extensively, allowing for broader comparisons across jobs and the inclusion of comparable work (Ostner, 2000: 28).

The Equal Treatment Directive 1976, by contrast, was rather revolutionary. Unlike equal pay, equal treatment was a new issue, and the Commission proposal was clearly ahead of national legislation. This also was the first directive that was influenced by feminist actors within the EU institutions (Van der Vleuten, 2007: 88). The directive was a far-reaching agreement that broadened the principle of equal treatment for women and men to access to employment (including promotion), vocational training and working conditions, and ruled out all forms of direct and indirect discrimination on grounds of sex, particularly by reference to marital or family status. Section 4 of the directive even allowed for positive action measures (Pillinger, 1992: 88; Ostner, 2000: 28; Van der Vleuten, 2007: 96). The Social Security Directive 1978, in turn, provided for the equalization of social security benefits for women and men and covered sickness, disability, retirement, industrial injury and occupational disease and unemployment (Pillinger, 1992: 88–9).

These three directives were adopted under unanimity voting. In order to reach consensus, the resulting legislation sometimes failed to address and clarify some sensitive issues of discrimination and equality. However, this lack of clarity created opportunities for legal activists to invoke EU rules against their own national governments (Cichowski, 2002, 2007). For example, the Equal Treatment Directive states that 'no discrimination whatsoever on grounds of sex' will be allowed under EU law. Scholars have observed that this general 'whatsoever' expression has given opportunities to both litigants and the ECJ to expand the directive's scope. This includes the Court decision that found protection against dismissal for transsexuals within the scope of EU equality law (Cichowski 2002: 231).[1]

The 1980s were a period of incremental development in EU gender policy. The first part of the decade has been called the 'hard times' and 'cold climate' (Hoskyns, 1996a: 18). It was characterized by high unemployment, deregulation, government cuts and a rhetorical emphasis on a 'flexible' workforce (Ostner and Lewis, 1995: 164). During this period only two of several proposed directives on equality were adopted, both in 1986, and both of relatively minor importance (Cichowski, 2002: 231; Van der Vleuten, 2007: 139).[2] A number of other directives were either rejected or watered down to weaker recommendations. It was not until the late 1980s, when the Council accepted the development of a new social dimension to complement the Single Market initiative and the voting system in the Council was modified, that further equality legislation was forthcoming (McCrudden, 2003: 4).

The changes that the Treaty of Maastricht (1992) introduced were significant for gender equality policy. First, there was the strengthened role

Table 13.1   *EU directives on gender equality in employment since 1992*

Year	Directive
1992	Pregnant Workers Directive
1993	Working Time Directive
1996	Parental Leave Directive
1996	Directive on Occupational Social Security
1997	Directive on the Burden of Proof
1997	Part-time Workers' Directive
2002	Equal Treatment in Employment Directive
2004	Goods and Services Directive
2006	Equal Opportunities Directive (Recast Directive)[*]

[*]The Recast Directive brought the following directives together in one single text: Equal Pay Directive 75/117, the Equal Treatment Directive 76/207 as amended by Directive 2002/73, the Occupational Social Security Directive 86/387 as amended by Directive 96/97, the Burden of Proof Directive 97/80 as amended by Directive 98/52. The Pregnant Workers Directive 92/85 and the Parental Leave Directive 96/34 are both excluded from the Recast Directive because of their different legal base (Masselot, 2007: 162).

of the Parliament; second, there was qualified majority voting in the Council in issues dealing with living and working conditions, training and equal opportunities for underprivileged groups, and health and safety protection; third, the involving of social partners, management and labour in the legislative process enabled the reintroduction and return to the legislative path in equal opportunities policy. Subsequently, employers and trade unions reached two agreements on equal opportunities that were later approved by the Council: the agreement on parental leave and the agreement on part-time work (Van der Vleuten, 2007: 149).[3] Table 13.1 lists the directives that have been adopted in the field of equal opportunities since 1992.

Article 13 of the Treaty of Amsterdam 1997 was significant in that it for the first time gave competence to the Community to take action to combat discrimination based on gender (and racial or ethnic origin, religion or belief, disability, age or sexual orientation) *outside* the field of employment. The first anti-discrimination directive on gender outside employment was the 2004 Goods and Services Directive (Masselot, 2007: 153). It prohibits discrimination in access to public premises, housing, services of a profession or trade, including banking, insurance, other financial services and transport. However, it excludes some of the initial proposals covering the representation of the sexes in the media, taxation and education (ibid.: 153–4).

Feminist scholars have often been highly critical of the EU's abilities to improve the position of women in society (Pillinger, 1992; Ostner and Lewis, 1995; Elman, 1996; Young, 2000). Over twenty years ago, Sonia Mazey suggested: 'while the Equality Directives have been useful in combating individual cases of sex discrimination, they have to date had no significant impact on the sex segregated labour market. In short, the socio-structural causes of sex discrimination lie beyond the reach of the existing Equality Directives' (Mazey, 1988: 63). Many feminists think this critique still applies and that anti-discrimination and equal opportunities polices do not challenge the structural inequalities with their narrow scope. They merely add women to existing frameworks without understanding how these practices often rely on women's subordinate positions. Furthermore, member states have in many cases not implemented the anti-discrimination directives, which, in turn, make their effectiveness ever more questionable (van der Vleuten, 2007).

Feminist social theories highlight that different forms of women's oppression in society – at home, work, schools, in politics – are interconnected, and oppression in one sphere supports and constitutes oppression in another sphere. Thus, it is not adequate merely to focus on gender inequalities in the labour market. The EU, however, was established to promote economic integration and it is widely agreed that until the Maastricht Treaty it dealt with its people as workers rather than citizens. Thus gender equality was mainly advanced in relation to the labour market. Feminists argue that the narrow focus on the labour market can, in fact, prevent women from entering it: not extending the notion of equal treatment to address women's caring role in the home has repercussions on women's ability to take up employment (Pillinger, 1992: 22). In other words, the EU's equal opportunities policy fails to consider the existence of material conditions that prevent women from exercising their rights and from having equal access to the opportunities they are offered (Ostner and Lewis, 1995; Hobson, 2000: 98; Lombardo, 2003: 161). Feminists, in contrast, have for long been interested in a broader set of issues, including violence against women, reproductive rights and abortion, care, pornography and women's political representation, and in some cases found these as more pressing concerns than access to the labour market and equal pay (see for example Elman, 1996, 2007; Rossilli, 2000; Young, 2000).

Feminist critics have seen the EU's ideological emphasis on the liberalized internal market and the primacy of economics to be in contradiction to feminist aims (Rossilli, 2000: 1; Young, 2000: 86). This explains why social policy at the European level was kept to the minimum and was regarded not as parallel to, or as setting a framework for, economic measures, but as subordinate to them (Hoskyns, 1996b: 52). The EU is argued to represent a 'dramatic shift towards a disciplinary neoliberal discourse of capitalism' which shuts the door to more welfare state oriented strategies, such as expanding the public sector to create jobs for women (Young, 2000: 83). The primacy of economics results in an instrumental conception of women and gender equality: 'the goal of the EU equality policy is to use women as a key resource to create a flexible workforce and promote a more rational management of professional and family responsibilities' (Rossilli, 2000: 8).

Positive action

Positive action measures embody a different notion of gender equality than anti-discrimination measures as they try to correct the initial disadvantage of women. Whilst legislating for equal opportunities often relies on a notion of women's sameness to men and a strategy of inclusion, positive action emphasizes women's difference from men, for example the impact of motherhood and pregnancy on women's career development. It thus promotes a feminist strategy of reversal: rejecting the male norm and valuing the qualities and characteristics associated with being a woman (Squires, 1999).

Positive actions were introduced to avoid the strict application of the principle of equal treatment, generating further inequality for women (Lombardo, 2003: 162). Positive action thus recognizes that equal treatment can reinforce existing inequalities and seeks to create a level playing field. In other words, the emphasis shifts from equality of access to creating conditions more likely to result in equality of outcome by equalizing starting positions (Rees, 1998: 34). In practice, the application of a compensatory measure means favouring, in cases of equal merit, a woman over a man.

Over the years the EU has supplemented its anti-discrimination legislation with positive action initiatives. In 1984, a Council Recommendation 84/635 on the promotion of positive action for women was issued. However, the road for positive action has been difficult. Part of this relates to the fact that positive action measures were initially put into place by using soft law measures. As a result, there was nothing to force member states to act on them (Beveridge *et al.*, 2000: 143). Furthermore, the non-binding formulations created uncertainties and confusions around positive action measures, as illustrated by ECJ cases *Kalanke* in 1995 and *Marschall* in 1997, that represent milestones on the road towards this strategy. Both cases questioned the lack of legal clarity on issues of equal opportunities and expressed the need to introduce new political strategies to overcome women's structural discrimination (Lombardo, 2003: 162).[4]

The *Kalanke* judgment showed the importance of establishing strong binding instruments, allowing relatively limited scope for interpretations that might adversely affect equality objectives as a means of tackling deeply rooted social problems like the unequal gender division of labour (Stratigaki, 2000: 41). The new provision of the Amsterdam Treaty (Article 141(4), ex 119) provided that the principle of equal treatment did not prevent the maintenance or adoption of measures providing for specific advantages in order to make it easier for the under-represented sex to pursue a vocational activity or to prevent or compensate for disadvantages in professional careers (McCrudden, 2003: 3). It thus further opened the way for positive action measures, although the form in which the concept of positive discrimination is expressed is rather weak (Lombardo, 2003: 162). In sum, the insertion of the positive action measures in the Amsterdam Treaty suggests that member states can use positive action in certain circumstances to address discrimination.

Gender mainstreaming

Gender mainstreaming, some argue, takes the EU agenda and tools in furthering gender equality beyond anti-discrimination, equal opportunities and positive action measures. Gender mainstreaming has the potential to change the masculine structures and policies by mainstreaming gender to all policy fields and legislation (Rees, 1998: 46). It means focusing on systems and structures that give rise to group disadvantage (Woodward, 2003: 68). Whereas legislating for equal opportunities relied on a notion of women's sameness to men and positive action highlighted women's difference from men, gender mainstreaming evokes the notion of gender as a relational concept. It thus calls for a focus on both women and men, constructions of femininities and masculinities, and how they impact on women's and men's positions in society. Gender mainstreaming is argued to make the position of both women and men better in society.

Gender mainstreaming has been endorsed as the official policy approach to gender equality in the EU and its member states since the Amsterdam Treaty. New member states have also been obliged to adopt a gender mainstreaming approach as a condition of joining the EU (Rees, 2005: 570; Fodor, 2006: 1). The EU defined gender mainstreaming as 'mobilising all general policies and measures specifically for the purpose of achieving equality by actively and openly taking into account at the planning stage their possible effects on the respective situations of men and women (the gender perspective)' (Commission of the European Communities, 1996).[5] In other words, gender mainstreaming assumes that women and men are differentially affected by policies and aims to integrate such knowledge into all dimensions of decision-making. It requires that from inception all policies should be analysed for their gendered impact so that they can benefit women and men equally (Hankivsky, 2005: 977). The Commission's Roadmap for Equality between Women and Men for 2006–2010 reasserts the importance of gender mainstreaming and situates it as a key tool in EU gender policy.

The transformative nature and the paradigm shift related to gender mainstreaming depend highly on the form that it takes. Feminist research shows that gender mainstreaming can take the form of an integrationist, agenda-setting or transformative policy (Lombardo, 2005; Squires, 2005, 2007b; Verloo, 2005). In its *integrationist* form, it focuses on experts and the bureaucratic creation of evidence-based knowledge in policy-making. Here gender mainstreaming addresses gender issues within existing policy paradigms. In its second, *agenda-setting* form, it entails a focus on the participation, presence and empowerment of disadvantaged groups via consultation with civil society organizations. This, in turn, involves a reorientation of the agenda rather than merely integrating a gender perspective into an existing agenda (Squires, 2005: 371). Yet, some scholars argue that mainstreaming can only adequately address inequality when it pursues a *transformative* agenda by focusing on the structural reproduction of gender inequality and aiming to transform the policy process such that gender bias is eliminated (Beveridge and Nott, 2002: 300; Squires, 2005: 370). Gender mainstreaming is not simply a neutral tool, a strategy to promote a predetermined end state of 'equality', but a governance concept which addresses the methods and principles which oversee the social interaction of political actors (Beveridge and Nott, 2002: 302; Shaw, 2002). Thus it has important implications *beyond* the specific policy areas that might be mainstreamed (Kantola and Outshoorn, 2007).

Theresa Rees suggests that there appear to be very few examples of a gender mainstreaming approach where promoting gender equality is the main policy goal (agenda-setting) in Europe. More often, gender mainstreaming is used as a means of delivering on or is subsumed under another policy (integration) (Rees, 2005: 561). Alison Woodward (2003: 75–6) is also critical of the success of gender mainstreaming in the EU. She identifies a number of problems including the fact that gender awareness required to implement successfully gender mainstreaming is 'pocketed' in the EU to policy areas of traditional female concern (gender, development, research and science policy). As a result it has had no impact on the core areas of EU policy and spending, such as agriculture, foreign policy, competition, environment and transport. Few women have been appointed to the higher decision-making posts in the bureaucracy and gender experts are rarely used in the implementation of gender mainstreaming. A number of scholars agree and conclude that the EU mainstreaming approach lacks a feminist perspective and an understanding of the structural power relations that reproduce inequalities (Booth and Bennett, 2002: 441; Lombardo and Meier, 2006: 160). Critical accounts of the successes of gender mainstreaming in different policy fields include agriculture (Prugl, 2008), trade (Hoskyns, 2007), development (Debusscher and True, 2008) and employment (Rubery, 2005; Woehl, 2008). In sum, the EU is embracing and promoting gender mainstreaming, but its own success in implementing it remains questionable.

Implementation of gender mainstreaming in member states is patchy too and there are great national variations (Liebert, 2002). A study of eight countries (Belgium, France, Ireland, Lithuania, Poland, Spain, Sweden and the UK) found that Sweden was a clear vanguard and came closest to adopting a form of gender mainstreaming that was informed by an understanding of structural gendered power relations (Braithwaite, 2005; see also Daly, 2005). In the other member states, a number of problems prevailed. First, there was a clear gap between rhetoric and practice: gender mainstreaming appeared in official documents but was not implemented. Second, there was a tendency 'to treat gender mainstreaming in an "à la carte" manner, adopting selectively some of the components of gender mainstreaming, especially some of the tools or techniques, without an overall framework' (Braithwaite, 2005: 90). The main objective was often to introduce a gender mainstreaming approach per se which turns it into an operational objective rather than an approach to achieve gender equality. Lithuania was a clear laggard and gender mainstreaming had been adopted only because of external EU pressure. Third, gender mainstreaming efforts were fragmented and adopted in select policy areas such as education. Finally, for example, in France and Greece, politicians and government officials conveniently use the term 'gender mainstreaming' to refer to a move from a focus on women to a more neutral focus on gender (which is simply understood as referring to both women and men) as the main concern of equality policy (Braithwaite, 2005). The problems in the member state and in the EU are thus similar to one another and cast some doubt on the effectiveness of gender mainstreaming in furthering gender equality.

Diversity

The latest shift in EU anti-discrimination and equality agenda is the emphasis placed on diversity and multiple discriminations. The legal basis for this was paved in the Treaty of Amsterdam Article 13 which states that 'the Council ... may take appropriate action to combat discrimination based on sex, racial or ethnic origin, age, religion or belief, disability and sexual orientation'. This has in practice broadened the legal basis for combating discrimination to six grounds. Two pieces of secondary legislation were quickly enacted. The Racial Equality Directive (2000/43/EC) extends the principle of equal treatment and protection against racial and ethnic discrimination to fields of employment and training, education, social security, healthcare and access to goods and services. The Employment Equality Directive

(2000/78/EC) enacts the principle of equal treatment of religion or belief, sexual orientation and age in the fields of employment and training.

The concern with diversity is closely associated with developments in feminist theory. The concern with multiple equality 'strands' resonates with the theoretical work on 'intersectionality' that highlights the mutual constitution of the inequalities, such as gender, race and class (Crenshaw, 1998). Intersectionality draws attention to the ways in which women and men are simultaneously positioned, not only in terms of their gender, but also by race, ethnicity, class, sexuality, age and disability. It thus results in a richer and more complex ontology than approaches that attempt to reduce people to one category at a time (Phoenix and Pattynama, 2006: 187). Intersectionality does not conceive social divisions as an additive but rather as a constitutive process (Yuval-Davis, 2006: 195). The discrimination faced by a black woman is qualitatively different from merely adding together the discrimination on the basis of gender and race.

Institutionally, this growing concern with multiple equality strands has generated equality reviews in many member states, with many recently changing their institutional arrangements for promoting equality (Kantola and Outshoorn, 2007). Several countries have created 'single equalities bodies' that bring law enforcement and implementation under one roof. Britain, for instance, has created an Equality and Human Rights Commission, which has responsibility for enforcing equality legislation on age, disability, gender, race, religion or belief, sexual orientation or transgender status (Squires, 2007a; Lovenduski, 2007). This has been the trend in CEECs too where in Lithuania the Equal Opportunities Ombudsman, formerly responsible for gender equality only, now deals with all Article 13 grounds. Meanwhile, Slovakia has created a National Centre for Human Rights, which oversees a new anti-discrimination law that applies to all six equality strands too. Other countries have opted for separate equalities bodies. Austria has created three separate Ombuds (for women and men, for ethnic belonging, religion/belief, age and sexual orientation, and for equal opportunities with regard to ethnic belonging).

Concerns about bringing together diversity and gender equality have been voiced, although a number of scholars share the normative claim that discrimination needs to be tackled in relation to all strands. First, both bringing the strands together and dealing with them separately can increase competition between inequalities. Feminists worry that the greater emphasis on, for example, race and disabilities will be at the expense of gender issues (Mazey, 2002: 229). Furthering equality in relation to some strands, such as religion, may be detrimental to gender equality. The second concern relates to the assumed similarity of inequalities. Can the inequalities be addressed with similar policies?

Mieke Verloo (2006: 222) argues in relation to gender, race, class and sexuality that these bases for inequality are so dissimilar that the tools (for example gender mainstreaming) to tackle one form of inequality cannot simply be adapted to other forms. Feminist scholars thus inquire whether the equality tools needed by diverse disadvantaged groups are sufficiently similar so that they can share institutional spaces and policies rather than each needing their own (Walby, 2005: 462). For example, statistics are useful when highlighting the economic and political costs of gender- and race-based discrimination but do not capture multiple or intersectional discrimination, which easily becomes statistically insignificant.

In conclusion, the four approaches – legislating for equal opportunities, positive action, gender mainstreaming and diversity – have been introduced separately in the EU and in this chapter. They have also been shown to rely on different notions of gender and different political strategies for equality. In practice, however, they continue to coexist. Both EU policy and feminist scholarship recognize that all four are needed to effectively combat discrimination, change gendered power structures and advance substantive equality. They often are combined with one another: for example gender mainstreaming is combined with positive action and women specific programmes, a strategy called the 'twin-track'. Feminist scholars, in turn, have explored the case for combining gender mainstreaming and diversity into 'diversity mainstreaming' (Beveridge and Nott, 2002: 311; Squires, 2005; Verloo, 2006). Currently, the political emphasis is also on gender mainstreaming and diversity. This is unfortunate if it results in the oversight or demise of the other two strategies.

Gendered changes in the policy-making process

The progress in EU gender policy has often been tied together with the fate of EU social policy. Many member states have been reluctant to give the EU a meaningful competence in the field. It is here that some of the major challenges for feminist approaches lie. Issues such as childcare, the length and the compensation for maternity, paternity and parental leaves, are the key to women's labour market participation and fall in the field of social policy in the member states. In the EU, by contrast, the rights of pregnant workers, for example, have been framed as a health issue to give the EU competence to legislate in the field. The legislative path has been fundamentally shaped by the subsidiarity principle since 1992. Subsidiarity requires that, whenever possible, action should be taken at the lowest possible level, and many feminist scholars remain unconvinced about its benefits for advancing gender equality (Hoskyns, 2000). Emphasis has also been placed on the use of voluntary codes and self-regulation, which has resulted in a proliferation of recommendations, resolutions, conclusions, guidelines, programmes, and so on. Subsequently, a new EU soft policy tool, the OMC, has emerged.[6] A number of crucial areas, such as childcare, social inclusion and labour market participation, are now being regulated via the OMC. The deregulation that the OMC implies arguably has a number of gendered consequences that are only emerging as objects of feminist scrutiny.

The gendered dimensions of the OMC are explored here in relation to childcare. Regulating for childcare through OMC takes place within the European Employment Strategy (EES). The key target of the EES is to increase the employment rate of men to 70 per cent and that of women to 60 per cent by 2010.[7] The EES promotes public provision of childcare or other supportive measures that facilitate work and family life reconciliation. The European Council of Barcelona affirmed in 2002 that member states should remove disincentives for female labour force participation and strive, in line with national patterns of provision, to provide childcare by 2010 to at least 90 per cent of children between three years old and the mandatory school age and at least 33 per cent of children under three years of age.

Highlighting the positive aspects of this agenda, Claire Annesley (2007: 199) suggests that the EES represents a move towards a 'supported European adult worker model social system' where all adults (including women) are expected to work and are supported in doing so. The new soft law tools have thus enabled the EU to make policy recommendations in areas where there are big national differences. For example, in care policies the member state models range from collectivizing care by providing tax-funded care programmes, such as paid parental leave and subsidized public childcare, to privatizing care by encouraging family members to take on such responsibilities without compensations or supporting and regulating care given by volunteers (Haas, 2003: 95). The EES and OMC have also increased the political relevance and visibility of childcare (Plantega, 2004: 8). The OMC can also lead to policy learning between member states. At minimum, countries have to provide comparable childcare data, which can help policy-makers and activists to pinpoint progress and remaining problems (Morgan, 2008).

However, more critical feminist comments have been directed at the policy-making process. First, the non-binding nature of the policy has created some problems. The OMC and the reports and recommendations that go with it are unlikely to bring about drastic changes in childcare policies in countries that seriously lag behind in terms of provision. In some cases they can result in mere 'window-dressing' (Van der Vleuten and Verloo, 2008). Furthermore, soft law, unlike hard law, does not allow interests groups to enforce compliance by calling upon a third party, such as the ECJ, on the matter (Richardt, 2005).

Notably, some women's policy actors, such as the British Equal Opportunities Commission, were very effective in using litigation strategy through the ECJ to advance gender equality legislation in Britain. This opportunity has been closed off by the new mode of governance through the OMC. Not surprisingly, the EES has not resulted in significant increases in publicly funded childcare in the member states.

Second, the influence of civil society actors is limited in EES and interest groups can only indirectly, through the Commission or the EP, influence the direction of the strategy. National action plans and EU targets are not debated in national parliaments and there is little media attention to the issue (Morgan, 2008). Rather, a small number of bureaucratic actors dominate the process of drafting the national reports to the EU (ibid.). This turns the process into a bureaucratic rather than a political or democratic process. For example, in Britain, the public visibility of the strategy has been limited and there have been little opportunities for challenging the government's interpretations of the implementation of the strategy (Richardt, 2005). As a result, women's organizations and activists have not had an impact in the implementation of its priorities. In Germany, in contrast, interest groups have succeeded in mobilizing around the policy and have had some success in influencing its implementation (ibid.: 3).

Beyond employment: violence

Feminists have long highlighted women's bodily integrity as an indication of gender equality in a given society. Violence against women, sexual harassment, reproductive rights, prostitution and trafficking in women have also entered the EU agenda over the past decade. Like childcare, they are typically addressed by means other than hard law, and the EU has a wide range of soft policy measures to combat them. Also feminist research in these fields has proliferated (Elman, 1996, 2007; Zippell, 2004, 2006; Kantola, 2006; Askola, 2007a, 2007b; Kriszán *et al.*, 2007).

The first EP resolution on violence against women dates back to 1986. The Commission, in turn, became active on the issue towards the end of the 1990s. A brief focus on violence against women is useful to highlight a further tendency and a change in European gender equality policies: it has increasingly become centred on short-term projects. The Commission's 'Daphne' Initiatives and programmes fund violence against women projects in the EU and at member-state level.[8] The majority of Daphne's funding has gone to the voluntary sector to support community-wide information and action campaigns (Elman, 2007: 101). Again this has increased the visibility of the issue and provided important information about the extent of the problem.

However, crucial areas, such as the maintenance of shelters, refuges and 24-hour helplines, require permanent funding. Furthermore, applying for EU funds is a time-consuming process and requires a lot of advance resources and skills. Women's organizations and NGOs have to devote a lot of human resources when applying for funding, which can avert attention away from their main activities. Some women's organizations, particularly in the CEECs, do not have enough initial resources to apply for funding (Roth, 2007: 473). R. Amy Elman (2007: 110) argues that concerns over the continuity of funding may have the effect of co-opting NGOs' critiques of EU policies. EU funding and the recognition that follows it can, however, offer respectability and political leverage to women's groups *vis-à-vis* their national governments. The EU can also shape the terms of the debate on a discursive level. Some of the Daphne programmes have foregrounded an understanding of domestic violence as a public health problem, which narrows down the understanding of the issue and the ways of dealing with it (Kantola, 2006; Kriszán *et al.*, 2007).

In addition to different forms of violence, a new challenge to feminist research is the politicization of reproductive rights at the EU level. Despite the ECJ ruling in 1996 on case X from Ireland, where abortion was termed a medical service and subject to free movement of goods and services (Taylor, 1999), the conservative anti-abortion stance of Ireland, Poland and Malta is having an impact on EU development policy and impeding aid to some reproductive rights projects in developing countries. The EU has not been able to reach a common stance on the issue for different UN conferences on women either, including the annual UN Commission on the Status of Women (CSW) meetings in New York. Debates on other civil rights and women's rights issues, such as the right to divorce, are currently taking place at the EU level. The Council Resolution to harmonize EU divorce laws so that transnationally married couples can choose which member state's divorce law to follow have agonized feminists in Sweden and Finland.[9] For example, in Malta, divorce is not permitted; in Ireland it takes four years; and in some other member states divorce requires establishing guilt, which goes against the liberal ethos of the Nordic countries. It is on these issues that the EU appears as a conservative actor in gender policy. Interestingly, these raise questions for feminists about how far EU gender policy should go and whether it should deal with all areas of gender equality.

Actors for gender equality

The Communications Commissioner Margot Wallström stated in February 2008 that she was fed up with the EU being governed by the 'reign of old men'. 'An inner circle of male decision-makers agree behind closed doors on whom to nominate to EU top jobs' and 'old men choose old men, as always', she said in a widely publicized interview with the Swedish daily *Sydsvenska Dagbladet* (8 February 2008). Whilst many feminists were undoubtedly jubilant for her having spoken out, others may have been disappointed about the realities of the gendered power structures of EU decision-making. On the surface, women's political representation, both in the European Parliament (31 per cent) and in the Commission (30 per cent), stands at record levels. The number of women in national governments, by contrast, varies greatly from 5 per cent in Greece to 60 per cent in Finland in 2007, and women continue to be concentrated in some (feminized) ministerial posts. This of course has consequences for the constitution of the Council, where the representation of women is at its lowest of the EU institutions. It was to these highest echelons of power that Wallström's statement seemed to be directed.

Despite her assessment, a network for women's policy and gender equality has become highly institutionalized at the EU level and feminists have started to debate the pros and the cons of its existence. These women's policy actors are needed not just to advance but also to guard women's rights as progress in gender equality need not be linear but can face setbacks. Alison Woodward (2003) uses the phrase 'velvet triangle' to describe partially institutionalized forms of cooperation in gender policy in the EU. The velvet triangle consist of, first, femocrats in the Commission and feminist MEPs; second, gender experts in academia or consultancies; and, third, the established women's movement (ibid.: 85; for a critique of the metaphor see Holli, 2008). These three sets of actors work together to ensure policy success. Woodward stresses personal ties, common biographies and career mobility between both individuals and representatives of movements and institutions in the area of European gender policy.

The European Women's Lobby (EWL) has come to represent one angle of this triangle: the 'established women's movement'. It is thus an interesting case study of a site where efforts are made to build a transnational consensus on what constitutes women's interests. Its key areas of lobbying represent a selection of issues that the members and the delegates have been able to agree upon. The actors themselves argue that effective lobbying in the EU requires the construction of common interests and shared goals, as the Commission prioritizes input from umbrella organizations like the EWL (Helfferich and Kolb, 2001: 149). This in turn points to the need to construct a transnational women's constituency, which is a challenge in the diverse context of 27 member states. Certain issues such as abortion and prostitution have proved too contentious 'with many meetings ending with some members walking out of the room' (Cichowski, 2007: 201). These represent issues where gender equality and women's interests are framed very differently across the member states (see Outshoorn, 2004; Verloo, 2007). On other issues such as positive action, after years of debate, members have been able to reach agreement and put forth a concrete policy agenda and action plan (Cichowski, 2007: 201). Lobbying for the Amsterdam Treaty represented a clear success, and the Treaty has been mentioned often in this chapter in relation to positive action, gender main-streaming and diversity.

The interest formation is not an easy process, but once consensus is achieved it is cemented in one of the EWL's policy papers that act as blueprints for lobbying. Barbara Helfferich and Felix Kolb (2001: 149–50) identify three factors that shape 'transnational interest forma-tion' in the EWL. First, the EWL has to mediate between differing national conceptions of gender equality. Some of its members, like the National Council of German Women (*Deutscher Frauenrat*), are cen-tralized and conservative organizations; others, like the Greek women's organizations, are loose and decentralized lobbies. There might also be great variation within specific countries, as for example North vs South Italy.

Second, the relations between national governments and women's organizations play a role. For example, the National Council of German Women is funded by the German government, which has pre-vented the Council from taking positions independent of the govern-ment. Other organizations have less funding and more insecurity and problems of efficiency, but have been freer to put forward new and innovative ideas. At times, however, common interest formation at the European level changes the views of national women's organizations. For example, the National Council of German women changed its views on maternity leave and took common positions advocated by the EWL against its own Conservative government (ibid.).

Third, the structures of the national and European organizations that are members of this lobbying group are very different. Some are individual membership organizations, others umbrella organizations with associations as members. This has resulted in debates about rep-resentation and voice in EWL decision-making and 'transnational interest formation' where each organization, no matter its size, has one representative (ibid.: 149). The tendency to monopolize women's voices is often multiplied by the fact that national roof organizations represent member states' women in the EWL. These roof organiza-tions can themselves be exclusionary. For example Finnish women are represented by NYTKIS,[10] which is a roof organization for political women's organizations and has in the past refused to take ethnic minority women's organizations as its members.

Despite the successful lobbying and interest representation that the EWL ensures at the EU level there have been some downsides to its existence. A combination of the EWL attempting to represent diverse interests and the Commission preferring to listen to one centralized voice has resulted in the Commission discouraging women's groups from operating autonomously from the EWL (Cichowski, 2007: 201). This emphasis on the EWL as a formal access point raises questions about whose voice is heard and whose not, which parts of the women's movement are represented and which not, in EU-level policy-making. For example, the representation of black and ethnic minority women has traditionally been poor in the EWL (Hoskyns, 1996b: 186).

The EWL has also been criticized for its slowness in including the women's organizations from the new member states of CEECs in the 2000s. Before May 2004 when ten new member states joined the EU, only Hungary and Latvia had established EWL national coordinations. The Czech Women's Union was only an associate member. Some commentators have described EWL's attitude as 'cautious' towards these organizations because of differing views on gender equality (Forest, 2006: 179). For women in East Europe, the EWL's lack of knowledge about the situation of women in the former communist countries was 'shocking' and they were disappointed about its lack of action during the accession process (Roth, 2007: 472). EWL addressed Eastern enlargement mainly through the dangers of trafficking, migration and prostitution. The first general conference about the enlargement was held only in 2003 and in that year the EWL extended its network to NGOs in the accession countries (ibid.). The fact that the lobby promotes the participation of umbrella organizations rather than individual subscriptions may also have delayed cooperation with Eastern NGOs that remained weak and acted separately (Forest, 2006: 179).

Conclusion

This chapter has aimed to cover some feminist approaches to the study of the EU. The task has been rather challenging because of the ever expanding scope of the EU gender policy. Issues, such as the detailed accounts of the Europeanization of EU gender policy (Liebert, 2003), the impact of the latest enlargement rounds from EU-15 to EU-25 and 27 (Velluti, 2005; Einhorn, 2006), gender analyses of EU foreign and security policy (Valenius, 2007) and of development policy (Lister, 2006; Debusscher and True, 2008) have been unaccounted for (see, however, Kantola, forthcoming). The four approaches that have been discussed in this chapter – legislating for equal opportunities, positive action, gender mainstreaming and diversity – are, however, relevant strategies for gender equality that underpin the diverse fields of EU gender policy. Feminist research makes clear that the form that these policies take in the EU and in the member states is highly relevant for the advancing of gender equality. For example gender mainstreaming can both be a useful tool for feminist activists or an excuse for governments to dismantle positive action programmes for women.

The key challenges relate to the institutional formation of the EU and European women's movements and here more feminist research needs to be conducted. The impact of gender policy is shaped by the gendered dimensions of the policy-making process. Social policy is increasingly advanced via the OMC. Other policy-making mechanisms, such as subsidiarity and the role of social partners, is legislation that needs to be explored too. The combined effect of deregulation and soft law may have some gendered consequences in the future.

Notes

1. Case C–13/94, *P* v. *S and Cornwell County Council*, ECR 1996, 2143.
2. The Occupational Social Security Directive and the Self Employed Directive.
3. See Guerrina (2005) on the pregnant workers and parental leave directives, and Bleijenbergh *et al.* (2004) on the part-time work directive.
4. The *Kalanke* ruling in 1995 showed that the notion of equality embedded in a positive action strategy may directly contradict the anti-discrimination notion of equality. The case arose in the context of the Bremen public sector (parks department) where an equally qualified woman was chosen over Eckhard Kalanke for the job. The local Bremen law on equal treatment stipulated that, in cases of two equally qualified persons, priority should be given to women if they are underrepresented (Young, 2000: 89). The German local, regional and federal labour courts ruled that Bremen law did not breach German Basic Law or the Civil Code and that it did not set strict quotas for women. Since it was unclear whether Bremen law was compatible with European equal treatment, the case was referred to the ECJ. The Court made the argument that national rules that *automatically* give priority to women who are equally qualified in job sectors where they are underrepresented violate the principle of equal treatment. In other words, the ECJ held the regional German law to be incompatible with the Equal Treatment Directive 1976 (Schiek, 1998: 152). In the *Marschall* case, the ECJ made some very fine distinctions between acceptable and unacceptable positive action strategies and opened inroads for preferential treatment.
5. For definitions see Council of Europe (1998: 19), Rai (2003: 16) and Rees (2005: 560).
6. Under the OMC, guidelines or objectives are fixed at the EU level and all member states are encouraged to implement national action plans to achieve these objectives. Country reports are peer reviewed by other countries and in the end the Commission makes recommendations about improvements. In the end, policy choices remain at the national level and there are no formal sanctions against member states whose performance does not match the standards (Scharpf, 2002: 625; Trubek and Trubek, 2005: 347–8).

7. Initially, gender equality was one of the four pillars of the strategy but was dropped in a restructuring of the objectives by the Commission in 2003. Only through the lobbying by the Expert Group of Gender and Employment and the European Women's Lobby was gender mainstreaming reintroduced to the strategy as a horizontal principle (Richardt, 2005). Commentators remain cautious about the advancement of gender equality in the new EES. It clearly prioritizes access to employment over the quality of jobs and over promoting gender equality in employment. Thus female labour force participation and childcare facilities remain on the agenda, but other issues like tackling the gender pay gap or gendered patterns of labour market segregation are not on the agenda (ibid.).

8. The Daphne Initiatives 1997, 1998, 1999, Daphne I 2000–03, Daphne II 2004–08.

9. EU Green Paper on applicable law and jurisdiction in divorce matters (Rome III) 2005. European Council Regulation (Rome III) was published in July 2006.

10. NYTKIS: Naisjärjestöt yhteistyössä. Kvinno-organisationer i samarbete (The Coalition of Finnish Women's Organizations for Joint Action).

References

Annesley, C. (2007) 'Lisbon and Social Europe: Towards a European "Adult Worker Model" Welfare System', *Journal of European Social Policy* 17(3): 195–205.

Askola, H. (2007a) *Legal Responses to Trafficking in Women for Sexual Exploitation in the European Union* (Oxford: Hart Publishing).

Askola, H. (2007b) 'Violence against Women, Trafficking, and Migration in the European Union', *European Law Journal* 13(2): 204–17.

Bell, M. (2000) 'Equality and Diversity: Anti-discrimination Law after Amsterdam', in J. Shaw (ed.) *Social Law and Policy in an Evolving European Union* (Oxford: Hart Publishing) 157–70.

Bell, M. (2002) *Anti-Discrimination Law and the European Union* (Oxford: Oxford University Press).

Beveridge, F. and Nott, S. (2002) 'Mainstreaming: A Case for Optimism and Cynicism', *Feminist Legal Studies* 10: 299–311.

Beveridge, F., Nott, S. and Stephen, K. (2000) 'Mainstreaming and the Engendering of Policy-Making: a Means to an End?', *Journal of European Public Policy* 7(3): 385–405.

Bleijenbergh, I., de Bruijn, J. and Bussemaker, J. (2004) 'European Social Citizenship and Gender: The Part-time Work Directive', *European Journal of Industrial Relations* 10(3): 309–28.

Booth, C. and Bennet, C. (2002) 'Gender Mainstreaming in the European Union – Towards a new conception and practice of equal opportunities?' *European Journal of Women's Studies* 9(4): 430–46.

Braithwaite, M. (2005) *Gender-sensitive and women-friendly public policies: A comparative analysis of their progress and impact.* Final Report. Equapol. A 5th Framework Programme Research Project funded by the European Commission.

Cichowski, R. A. (2002) '"No Discrimination Whatsoever" Women's Transnational Activism and the Evolution of EU Sex Equality Policy' in N. A. Naples and M. Desai (eds) *Women's Activism and Globalization: Linking Local Struggles and Transnational Politics* (London: Routledge) 220–38.

Cichowski, R. A. (2004) 'Women's Rights, the European Court, and Supranational Constitutionalism', *Law & Society Review* 38(3): 489–512.

Cichowski, R. A. (2007) *The European Court and Civil Society: Litigation, Mobilization and Governance* (Cambridge: Cambridge University Press).

Commission of the European Communities (1996) *Communication from the Commission Incorporating Equal Opportunities for Women and Men into all Community Policies and Activities*, COM (96) 67 final. (Luxemburg: Office for Official Publications of the European Communities).

Council of Europe (1998) *Gender Mainstreaming: Conceptual Framework, Methodology and Presentation of Good Practices. Final Report of Activities of the Group of Specialists on Gender Mainstreaming.* Strasbourg.

Crenshaw, K. (1998) 'Demarginalizing the Intersections of Race and Sex: A Black Feminist Critique of Antidiscrimination Doctrine, Feminist Theory, and Antiracist Politics' in A. Phillips (ed.) *Feminism and Politics* (Oxford: Oxford University Press) 314–43.

Daly, M. (2005) 'Gender Mainstreaming in Theory and Practice' in *Social Politics. International Studies in Gender, State and Society* 12(3): 433–50.

Debusscher, P. and True, J. (2008) 'Lobbying the EU for gender-equal development' in J. Orbie and L. Tortell (eds) *The EU's Role in the World and the Social Dimension of Globalisation* (London: Routledge).

Einhorn, B. (2006) *Citizenship in an Enlarging Union* (Basingstoke: Palgrave Macmillan).

Elman, R. A. (ed.) (1996) *Sexual Politics and the European Union: The New Feminist Challenge* (Oxford: Berghahn Books) 1–12.

Elman, R. A. (2007) *Sexual Equality in an Integrated Europe: Virtual Equality* (Basingstoke: Palgrave Macmillan).

Fodor, Eva (2006) 'Gender mainstreaming and its consequences in the European Union', *The Analyst* 7(1): 1–16.

Forest, M. (2006) 'Emerging Gender interest Groups in the New Member states: The Case of the Czech Republic', *Perspective on European Politics and Society* 7(2): 170–85.

Guerrina, R. (2005) *Mothering the Union: Gender Politics in the EU* (Manchester: Manchester University Press).

Haas, L. (2003) 'Parental Leave and Gender Equality: Lessons from the European Union', *Review of Policy Research* 20(1): 89–114.

Hankivsky, O. (2005) 'Gender vs. Diversity Mainstreaming: A Preliminary Examination of the Role and Transformative Potential of Feminist Theory,' *Canadian Journal of Political Science* 38(4): 977–1001.

Helfferich, B. and Kolb, F. (2001) 'Multilevel Action Coordination in European Contentious Politics. The Case of the European Women's Lobby' in D. Imig and S. Tarrow (eds) *Contentious Europeans: Protest Politics in an Emerging Polity* (Lanham: Rowman & Littlefield) 143–62.

Hobson, B. (2000) 'Economic Citizenship: Reflections Through the European Union Policy Mirror' in B. Hobson (ed.) *Gender and Citizenship in Transition* (Basingstoke: Palgrave Macmillan).

Holli, A. M. (2008) 'Feminist triangles: Conceptual analysis', *Representation* 8(2): 169–85.

Hoskyns, C. (1996a) 'The European Union and the women within: An overview of the women's rights policy' in R. A. Elman (ed.) *Sexual Politics and the European Union: The New Feminist Challenge* (Oxford: Berghahn Books) 13–22.

Hoskyns, C. (1996b) *Integrating Gender: Women, Law and Politics in the European Union* (London and New York: Verso).

Hoskyns, C. (2000) 'A study of four action programmes on equal opportunities' in M. Rossilli (ed.) *Gender policies in the European Union* (New York: Peter Lang) 43–59.

Hoskyns, C. (2007) 'Linking Gender and International Trade Policy: Is Interaction Possible?', CSGR Working Paper 217/07.

Kantola, J. (2006) *Feminists Theorize the State* (Basingstoke: Palgrave Macmillan).

Kantola, J. (forthcoming) *Gender and the European Union* (Basingstoke: Palgrave Macmillan).

Kantola, J. and Outshoorn, J. (2007) 'Changing State Feminism' in J. Outshoorn and J. Kantola (eds) *Changing State Feminism* (Basingstoke: Palgrave Macmillan) 1–19.

Krizsán, A., Bustelo, M., Hadjiyanni, A. and Kamoutis, F. (2007) 'Domestic Violence: A Public Matter' in M. Verloo (ed.) *Multiple Meanings of Gender Equality in Europe* (Budapest: Central European University Press).

Liebert, U. (2002) 'Europeanising gender mainstreaming: constraints and opportunities in the multilevel euro-polity', *Feminist Legal Studies* 10: 241–56.

Liebert, U. (2003) (ed.) *Gendering Europeanisation* (Brussels: Presses Interuniversitaires Européennes).

Lister, M. (2006) 'Gender and European Development Policy' in M. Lister and M. Carbone (eds) *New Pathways in Development: Gender and Civil Society in EU Policy* (Aldershot: Ashgate).

Lombardo, E. (2003) 'EU Gender Policy – Trapped in the Wollstonecraft Dilemma?', *European Journal of Women's Studies* 10(2): 159–80.

Lombardo, E. (2005) 'Integrating or Setting the Agenda? Gender Mainstreaming in the European Constitution-Making Process', *Social Politics* 12(3): 412–32.

Lombardo, E. and Meier, P. (2006) 'Gender Mainstreaming in the EU: Incorporating a Feminist Reading?' *European Journal of Women's Studies* 13(2): 151–66.

Lovenduski, J. (2007) 'Unfinished Business: Equality Policy and the Changing Context of State Feminism in Britain' in J. Outshoorn and J. Kantola (eds) *Changing State Feminism* (Basingstoke: Palgrave Macmillan) 144–63.

Masselot, A. (2007) 'The State of Gender Equality Law in the European Union', *European Law Journal* 13(2): 152–68.

Mazey, S. (1988) 'European Community action on behalf of women: the limits of legislation', *Journal of Common Market Studies* 27(1): 63–84.

Mazey, S. (2002) 'Gender Mainstreaming Strategies in the E.U.: Delivering an agenda?', *Feminist Legal Studies* 10: 227–40.

McCrudden, C. (2003) 'The New Concept of Equality', paper presented at the conference 'Fight Against Discrimination: The Race and Framework Employment Directives' in Trier, 31 March–1 April.

Morgan, K. J. (2008) 'Towards the Europeanization of Work-Family Policies? The Impact of the EU on Policies for Working Parents' in S. Roth (ed.) *Gender Politics in the Expanding European Union: Mobilization, Inclusion, Exclusion* (New York and Oxford: Berghahn Books) 37–59.

Ostner, I. (2000) 'From Equal Pay to Equal Employability: Four Decades of European Gender Policies' in M. Rossilli (ed.) *Gender Policies in the European Union* (Oxford: Lang) 25–42.

Ostner, I. and Lewis, J. (1995) 'Gender and the Evolution of European Social Policies' in S. Leibfried and P. Pierson (eds) *European Social Policy: Between Fragmentation and Integration* (Washington, DC: Brookings) 159–93.

Outshoorn, J. (ed.) (2004) *The Politics of Prostitution: Women's Movements, Democratic States and the Globalisation of Sex Commerce* (Cambridge: Cambridge University Press).

Phoenix, A. and Pattynama, P. (2006) 'Editorial: Intersectionality', *European Journal of Women's Studies* 13(3): 187–92.

Pillinger, J. (1992) *Feminising the Market: Women's Pay and Employment in the European Community* (London: Macmillan).

Plantenga, J. (2004) 'Investing in childcare. The Barcelona childcare targets and the European social model', Speech prepared for the conference: Childcare in a Changing World, 21–23 October, Groningen, the Netherlands.

Prugl, E. (2007) 'Gender and EU Politics' in K. E. Jørgensen, M. A. Pollack, and B. Rosamond (eds) *The Handbook of European Union Politics* (London: Sage).

Prugl, E. (2008) 'Gender and the Making of Global Markets: An Exploration of the Agricultural Sector' in S. Rai and G. Waylen (eds) *Global Governance: Feminist Perspectives* (Basingstoke: Palgrave Macmillan) 43–63.

Rai, S. (2003) 'Introduction' in S. Rai (ed.) *Mainstreaming Gender, Democratizing the State? Institutional Mechanisms for the Advancement of Women* (Manchester: Manchester University Press) 1–12.

Rees, T. (1998) *Mainstreaming Equality in the European Union* (London: Routledge).

Rees, T. (2005) 'Reflections on the uneven development of gender mainstreaming in Europe' *International Feminist Journal of Politics* 7(4): 555–74.

Richardt, N. (2005) 'Europeanization of Childcare Policy: Divergent Paths towards a Common Goal?', Paper prepared for the American Political Science Association Conference, Washington, DC, 1–4 September 2005.

Rossilli, M. (2000) 'Introduction: The European Union's Gender Policies' in M. Rossilli (ed.) *Gender Policies in the European Union* (Oxford: Lang) 1–23.

Roth, S. (2007) 'Sisterhood and Solidarity? Women's Organizations in the Expanded European Union', *Social Politics: International Studies in Gender, State and Society* 14(4): 460–87.

Rubery, J. (2005) 'Reflections on gender mainstreaming: An example of feminist economics in action?', *Feminist Economics* 11(3): 1–25.

Schiek, D. (1998) 'Sex Equality Law after Kalanke and Marschall', *European Law Journal* 4(2): 148–66.

Scharpf, F. W. (2002) 'The European Social Model: Coping with the Challenge of Diversity', *Journal of Common Market Studies* 40(4): 645–70.

Shaw, J. (2002) 'The European Union and Gender Mainstreaming: Constitutionally Embedded or Comprehensively Marginalised?', *Feminist Legal Studies* 10: 213–26.

Squires, J. (1999) *Gender in Political Theory* (Cambridge: Polity Press).

Squires, J. (2005) 'Is Mainstreaming Transformative? Theorizing Mainstreaming in the Context of Diversity and Deliberation', *Social Politics* 12(3): 366–88.

Squires, J. (2007a) 'The Challenge of Diversity: The Evolution of Women's Policy Agencies in Britain', *Politics and Gender* 3(4): 513–30.

Squires, J. (2007b) *The New Politics of Gender Equality* (Basingstoke: Palgrave Macmillan).

Stratigaki, M. (2000) 'The European Union and the Equal Opportunities Process' in Linda Hantrais (ed.) *Gendered Policies in Europe: Reconciling employment and family life* (London: Macmillan) 27–48.

Stratigaki, M. (2004) 'The Cooptation of Gender Concepts in EU Policies: The Case of 'Reconciliation of Work and Family', *Social Politics* 11(1): 30–56.

Taylor, J. (1999) 'Case X: Irish Reproductive Policy and European Influence', *Social Politics: International Studies in Gender, State and Society*, 6(2): 203–29.

Trubek, D. M. and L. G. Trubek (2005) 'Hard and Soft Law in the Construction of Social Europe: the Role of the Open Method of Co-ordination', *European Law Journal* 11(3): 343–64.

Valenius, J. (2007) 'Gender mainstreaming in ESDP missions', Chaillot Paper 101. Institute for Security Studies, European Union.

Van der Vleuten, A. (2007) *The Price of Gender Equality: Member States and Governance in the European Union* (Aldershot: Ashgate).

Velluti, S. (2005) 'Implementing Gender Equality and Mainstreaming in an Enlarged European Union – Some Thoughts on Prospects and Challenges for Central Eastern Europe,' *Journal of Social Welfare and Family Law* 27(2): 213–25.

Verloo, M. (2005) 'Displacement and Empowerment: Reflections on the Concept and Practice of the Council of Europe Approach to Gender Mainstreaming and Gender Equality', *Social Politics* 12(3): 344–65.

Verloo, M. (2006) 'Multiple Inequalities, Intersectionality and the European Union', *European Journal of Women's Studies* 13(3): 211–28.

Verloo, M. (ed.) (2007) *Multiple Meanings of Gender Equality in Europe* (Budapest: Central European University Press).

Verloo, M. and van der Vleuten, A. (2009) 'The discursive logic of ranking and benchmarking: Understanding gender equality measures in the European Union' in E. Lombardo, P. Meier and M. Verloo (eds) *The Discursive Politics of Gender Equality. Stretching, Bending and Policy-making* (London: Routledge).

Walby, S. (2005) 'Introduction: Comparative Gender Mainstreaming in a Global Era', *International Feminist Journal of Politics* 7(4): 453–71.

Woodward, A. (2003) 'Building velvet triangles: gender and informal governance' in T. Christiansen and S. Piattoni (eds) *Informal Governance in the European Union* (Cheltenham: Edward Elgar) 76–93.

Woehl, S. (2008) 'Global Governance as Neo-liberal Governmentality: Gender Mainstreaming in the European Employment Strategy' in S. Rai and G. Waylen (eds) *Global Governance: Feminist Perspectives* (Basingstoke: Palgrave Macmillan) 64–83.

Young, B. (2000) 'Disciplinary Neoliberalism in the European Union and Gender Politics', *New Political Economy* 5(1): 77–98.

Yuval-Davis, N. (2006) 'Intersectionality and Feminist Politics', *European Journal of Women's Studies,* 13(3): 193–209.

Zippel, K. (2004) 'Transnational Advocacy Networks and Policy Cycles in the European Union: The Case of Sexual Harassment', *Social Politics* 11(1): 57–85.

Zippel, K. (2006) *The Politics of Sexual Harassment: A Comparative Study of the United States, the European Union and Germany* (Cambridge: Cambridge University Press).

Chapter 14

The European Union in the World: Future Research Agendas

Karen E. Smith[1]

Academic interest in studying various aspects of the EU in the world is growing apace. In the 1970s and 1980s, a few academics identified European Political Cooperation (EPC) and EC external relations as developments well worth investigating; with the creation of the Common Foreign and Security Policy in the early 1990s, interest grew in the 'phenomenon' of European foreign and security policy; and in the last few years we have seen even more attention paid to this field.[2] The number of books on European foreign affairs is ever expanding and there is even an academic journal specifically dedicated to the study of European foreign affairs (*European Foreign Affairs Review*). Conferences such as those of the University Association of Contemporary European Studies (UACES), of the European Union Studies Association (EUSA), of the European Consortium for Political Research (ECPR) and of the British International Studies Association (BISA) usually have several panels on EU foreign and security policy. Courses on the EU's foreign relations are now offered at numerous universities around Europe and the world. The activities of FORNET, an EU-funded network of research on European foreign policy coordinated by Professor Christopher Hill, continued largely within the framework of the EU-CONSENT network of excellence, coordinated by Professor Wolfgang Wessels and funded by the EU. And the online bi-monthly journal *CFSP Forum* attracts contributions from scholars around and beyond Europe.[3] EU-funded networks have helped to strengthen links among researchers, while the European Foreign and Security Policy Studies Programme has generously supported research into European foreign and security policy and fostered an active network of younger researchers in particular.[4]

There are, however, quite fundamental questions about the EU in the world that we still need to address. Research may be increasing, but there is too little accumulation of knowledge (not enough attention is being paid to the large questions we face and to the answers that have already been suggested in the literature), and there is still a great need for more substantial empirical analysis, which has historical depth.

This chapter first sets out the core questions which should guide research on the EU in the world; it then reviews the current 'state of the art' in this field; and finally it suggests agendas for further research to fill in the gaps currently apparent in the literature.

Core questions for research on the EU in the world

Studying the EU's relations with the rest of the world, including how it comes to agree policies towards outsiders, is inherently complex. It involves:

- Multiple levels of enquiry (international, EU, national and subnational), and multiple actors at those levels.
- A moving 'target', in that the EU foreign policy system continues to develop over time, with new institutions and new policy instruments, as well as enlargement to more member states.

Three challenges for research thus arise:

- To understand and explain the evolution of the EU foreign policy system (the institutions, the formal rules, the informal norms, and so on).
- To understand and explain the policy-making process, including the output and implementation of policy.
- To understand and explain the impact of common policies (or the failure to agree common policies) on the system itself, on EU member states, and on the world.

The 'EU foreign policy system' is understood here to comprise the institutions and norms guiding the making and implementation of common foreign policies (in the name of the EU). The EU member states are the most important actors in the system, but institutional actors such as the European Commission and the High Representative for the Common Foreign and Security Policy (CFSP) also exercise influence in policy-making. The system stretches across the EU's pillars, encompassing the CFSP (which includes the European Security and Defence Policy (ESDP)), the European Community (EC) and the Justice and Home Affairs (JHA) pillars, insofar as the EC and JHA pillars deal with the outside world.[5] The term 'system' indicates that we are not investigating a tightly integrated entity such as a state or a federation but rather a set of institutions and norms which have been specifically created, and are so used (occasionally, at least), to produce common policies towards, and conduct relations with, the rest of the world. That such a system exists at all, in a world of states usually trying to assert their sovereignty and freedom of action vis-à-vis each other, is an astonishing development – and one that more than merits serious and sustained academic attention.

The research challenges can be broken down into six core questions that we should be asking about the 'EU in the world'. The plea here, in other words, is for question-driven research and, moreover, for empirically rich, question-driven research. I do not stake out preferences for a particular methodology or theoretical approach to answering those questions. Different theories (from and within different disciplines) can give us different answers to these questions, thus sparking a healthy debate.[6] Likewise, different methodologies may give us different – and richer – answers as well. The questions are deliberately broad, and answering them will also enable European foreign policy analysts to speak to larger debates within the disciplines of International Relations, European integration studies and political science in particular. The six questions which should guide our research are the following.

Why do the EU member states agree to act collectively in international relations?

This question derives from the larger question of why states cooperate in the international system, and the competing answers in the International Relations literature that have been offered to that question could be of use here, though they would need to take into consideration the specific context of the EU foreign policy system. For example, building on constructivist arguments regarding collective identity formation, we could hypothesize that through an intense process of foreign policy cooperation and institutionalization (the process by which shared standards of behaviour are developed) EU member states are developing a common identity and are thus more inclined to act collectively (Wendt, 1994: 389–90). A liberal institutionalist approach would instead emphasize the extent to which international interdependence encourages or creates space for collective action. An intergovernmentalist would focus on the roles that the shared or overlapping interests of member states, and what Roy Ginsberg (1989) calls the 'politics of scale' (the benefits of collective over unilateral action), play. Realists would consider how external threats or configurations of power might prompt collective action, as they do in prompting alliance formation, for example.

Moving away from the broad International Relations literature, pressures for collective EU action could conceivably come from 'below' the international or state levels, from domestic public opinion, interest groups and national parliaments; and/or it could be fostered by EU-level actors, namely the EU institutions and, above all, the

European Commission. Demands from outsiders could also build pressure for collective action.

Understanding whether and to what extent such pressures explain why the member states act collectively in specific cases (as well as generally) would be a fruitful avenue of research. In particular cases (such as EU policy towards Iran, or towards the western Balkans, or the Middle East conflict), researchers could investigate the roles that internal and external actors – such as a *directoire* of powerful member states, small groups of other states, the European Commission, the European 'public', outsiders such as the US – have played in prompting or encouraging such action. Comparative studies of specific cases of EU collective foreign policy action could illuminate any persistent patterns in terms of which factors, or actors, tend to be most important in prompting collective action. Comparison of EU foreign policy cooperation with any similar efforts in other regions (such as the Association of South-East Asian Nations (ASEAN) or NATO) could also yield potential explanations for cooperation within the EU.[7]

How are policies made?

This question brings us further down into the details of policy-making: who are the major actors and how do they take decisions? Only as lowest common denominator bargaining or in a 'problem-solving' style? Who (among member states and various actors within them, and EU institutions) 'wins' in policy-making debates? And what is the substance of any policies on which the actors can agree? Investigations would undoubtedly need to focus on actors at the EU level and national level, but the role that interest groups or epistemic communities may be of interest too. How are policies then implemented, and with which policy instruments? This is classic foreign policy analysis (FPA), which may, or may not, require modification to be applied in the European context.[8]

Why have the institutions and decision-making procedures for making EU foreign policies evolved in the way that they have, and what impact do these have on the substance of any common policies agreed?

This question leads us into explaining the dynamics of institutional development in this field. Why are we seeing 'institutionalization' in foreign and security policy cooperation (M.E. Smith, 2004)? Is it the result of neofunctionalist spillover, or incremental intergovernmentalism, or intra-EU balancing, or even balancing behaviour by the EU as a whole?[9] And to what extent, and how, do the member states seek to protect their sovereignty at the same time as they agree to further institutional development? How do considerations of sovereign prerogatives in the foreign policy field affect institutionalization? After all, a strong intergovernmentalist argument would dismiss the possibility that much progress can be made in creating potentially sovereignty-threatening institutions and norms. Philip Gordon (1997–98: 81), for example, argued that EU member states 'will only take the difficult and self-denying decision to share their foreign policy sovereignty if the gains of common action are seen to be so great that sacrificing sovereignty is worth it, or if their interests converge to the point that little loss of sovereignty is entailed'. And he maintained that 'these conditions have not held in the past, do not currently hold, and are not likely to hold in the future'. Is this the case, and if not, why have such constraints been loosened?

Furthermore, we should look at which actors are driving the evolution of the institutions and decision-making procedures: the most powerful member states, the European Commission, or other actors? And analysts could also explore whether, how and why what David Allen first called 'Brusselization' may be leading to more common policies.[10]

A related issue is the perceived legitimacy of the EU foreign policy system, and therefore also of the output of that system. The 'democratic deficit' in the EU has attracted much scholarly attention, which has begun to spill over into the study of EU foreign policy as well (Viola, 2000; *International Spectator*, 2004; Barbé and Herranz, 2005; Oppermann and Höse, 2007). Questions for further research include: how legitimate is the EU foreign policy system? Have concerns about legitimacy influenced its development? What role do public opinion or the EP or national parliaments play in the system?

What are the limits to EU collective action?

Again, there are numerous ways to address this question, one of which is essentially to pose the opposite question to that asked right at the start: why might the member states *not* act collectively in international relations? To what extent, and why, is there a 'capabilities-expectations gap', a gap between expectations of collective EU action and the EU's capacity to deliver it (Hill, 1993; Zielonka, 1998)? How important is the 'logic of diversity' (as termed by Stanley Hoffmann (1966: 881–2) four decades ago)? Do the member states have diverging interests that the processes referred to above cannot reconcile, even over a long period of time?

Limits might also be posed by bureaucratic politics, or 'turf wars' between institutions in Brussels and/or in national capitals. How is this limiting EU collective action? Do the 'pillars' obstruct and complicate common policy-making, and if so how exactly?[11]

Analysis could also focus on the extent to which the absence of a unified community or common identity hinders collective action (the opposite of the constructivist hypothesis mentioned above). Several observers have argued that foreign policy is the expression of the identity and interests of a particular community, and until the Union becomes such a community, it will never be able to formulate and implement effective, legitimate foreign policy. David Allen maintains that foreign policy is intrinsically linked to the 'idea of a state with a set of interests identified by a government' (Allen, 1996: 303). Jean-Marie Guehenno argues that 'a European foreign policy requires a European polity, which will produce European interests' (Guehenno, 1998: 30).

Other possible answers might focus on the limits of the foreign policy instruments available to the EU and/or the restricted room for manoeuvre in the international system for the EU. Realists, for example, would note that the EU does not and cannot really use military force coercively (because the member states will not agree to go that far), and that this constitutes a serious limit to EU foreign policy aspirations – especially because the international system is more Hobbesian than Kantian, as both Kagan (2003) and Cooper (2003) assert.

What impact do the EU foreign policy institutions, decision-making procedures and common policies have on the member states?

Given their centrality in decision-making, the role that the member states play in the EU foreign policy system is obviously important for the study of EU foreign policy.[12] In turn, what effect does the system have on the member states? The concept of 'Europeanization' has recently been imported from general EU studies to see if it can be of use in the field of foreign policy. 'Europeanization' is quite a flexible term, with numerous interpretations debated in the literature. Rueben Wong (2005: 136–40) groups the different usages into five categories: national adaptation to EU processes and requirements (the EU acts as a constraint on member states); national projection (member states use the EU to achieve their own objectives); elite socialization (elites learn to think 'European' rather than just 'national'); modernization (countries in Europe's periphery modernize to fit in with the EU); and policy isomorphism (convergence of policies across Europe). The question for scholars is whether any (or all) of these forms of Europeanization is identifiable in the field of foreign and defence policy: do we see evidence of changes in national institutions, policy-making processes, policy substance, perhaps even foreign policy identity that can be attributed to Europeanization?

A related issue for enquiry is whether national foreign policy has been so transformed by the EU foreign policy system that it no longer makes sense to analyse the national context without taking into consideration the EU context. Even if there may be pockets of purely 'national' foreign policy, the argument has been made that the analysis of the foreign policy of member states requires modifying traditional FPA to capture the unique context in which the member states operate.[13]

What impact does the EU have on outsiders and international relations in general?

This question forces us to consider the effectiveness of any EU foreign policies that emerge from the EU foreign policy system, and also the EU's broader influence in the international system (as Christopher Hill and Michael Smith (2005: 404–6) have recently enjoined us to do). Considerations of effectiveness include whether the EU's policies have had the effect *intended*, that is, whether and to what extent they have achieved the results desired. This question also encompasses the *unintended* effects of EU policies – not just the foreign policies agreed, but also 'internal' policies, such as the Common Fisheries and/or Agricultural Policies.

Measuring 'effectiveness' is inherently a difficult task – how can we attribute 'success' to the EU, rather than, say, to domestic actors, or other international actors, or beneficial international developments, or just plain luck? But policy-makers – and perhaps more importantly, outsiders – do make judgements about the success or not of the implementation of policies. Of course, academic observers may argue they may not be the appropriate judgements, and subsequent policy-making may not take such 'lessons' into account, but such judgements are still made, so for scholars this should be an important part of the investigation of the policy-making process. Is the EU able to influence other actors (third countries, non-governmental actors, international organizations, and so on) to do what it wants them to do?

But this question also raises the more general issue of what impact the EU may or may not be having on international relations in general – and again, approaches to this question could go in many different directions. Does the EU serve as a model for other regions, such that processes of regionalization around the world may be prompted or encouraged by the EU? Is the EU strengthening multilateralism and the rule of international law, and if so how?[14] Or does the development and enlargement of the EU prompt balancing behaviour (and therefore potentially raise tensions in international politics)?[15]

State of the art

To some extent, the current literature on the EU and the world addresses these questions, though some more than others. But there is a lot of 'compartmentalization' in the literature – a focus on the details of quite contemporary developments in microstudies of limited scope, or engagement only with particular scholars working within the same theoretical tradition. There is also currently a trend (not to say obsession) with theorizing – and sometimes with not enough grounding in the empirical, historical record: in other words, grand claims are made about implications for theory, which may not necessarily be supported by adequate empirical evidence. Topics that currently seem to be popular in the literature are noted below, though for obvious reasons of space not everything that has been published in the field has been cited here![16]

Regarding the development of institutions and their impact on policy-making

Somewhat surprisingly, we have not yet seen a book-length account (much less an explanation) of the evolution of the EU foreign policy system in the post-Cold War period. Simon Nuttall's history of the origins of the CFSP (2000) remains the best account we have of the transition from EPC to the CFSP, and, while it may prove impossible to equal the very high quality of Nuttall's work, the lack of a book-length history of the diplomacy regarding the development of the EU foreign policy system since then is disappointing. Nor have we seen many attempts to formulate explanations of that development.[17] Instead, analysts have focused on tracking and explaining contemporary debates and developments, rather than taking a long-term view. Thus recently, for example, the origins and potential impact of the 'external relations' provisions in the Constitutional Treaty and now the Lisbon Treaty have been an area of considerable interest – particularly in the think-tank world, for obvious reasons. Analysts have been especially interested in considering whether institutions such as the new-fangled High Representative (the Foreign Minister by another name) and the European External Action Service could make a difference in terms of the convergence of member state positions, efficiency of EU decision-making and effectiveness of EU foreign policy output (see Everts and Keohane, 2003, and several contributions to *CFSP Forum*).

The development and implementation of the ESDP has been an area of considerable scholarly activity – reflecting its surprisingly rapid development since 1999. Some studies have focused on the role that the Franco-British-German trio have played in that development; others have analysed problems of coherence across institutions and pillars in particular instances; some work has considered whether a common strategic culture is developing within the EU, given both ESDP developments and the promulgation of the 2003 European Security Strategy – but only a few studies have appeared about particular ESDP missions (see Biscop, 2005; Cornish and Edwards, 2005; Merlingen and Ostrauskaite, 2006; Meyer, 2006; Howorth, 2007).

The impact of enlargement on the EU's foreign policy-making system has also attracted interest, though it is still early days for such studies (Regelsberger, 2004; Edwards, 2006; Müller-Brandeck-Bocquet, 2006). The 1995 enlargement and its implications for institutional development attracted (brief) attention mostly from scholars based in the three new member states. There is still 'space' in the literature for more investigations of the impact of enlargement on the EU foreign policy system.

Scholars – particularly younger scholars – have been quite interested in exploring the intersection between the CFSP and the JHA pillars (or rather, since the latter pillar is fast disappearing, the inclusion of issues that were part of the original JHA pillar – immigration, terrorism, organized crime, and so on – on the EU foreign policy agenda). This is a growing area of EU foreign relations, particularly since the 9/11 terrorist attacks on the US, so it is not surprising that research has followed empirical developments here. Yet recent research has tended to concentrate on immigration policy rather than – oddly – terrorism or other JHA issues, such as organized crime, though this is also beginning to change.[18]

Regarding policy-making

Similar to the case of explaining the evolution of the EU foreign policy system, there have been few attempts to put forward a book-length argument about why the EU member states act collectively in international relations – though there have been several edited collections of case studies which to some extent seek to generate broader conclusions; and there are numerous texts which describe the EU's relations with a wide variety of third countries.[19] Most work has focused on describing and explaining the development and implementation of EU policies regarding particular third countries, regions and international organizations. Little work as yet has been done to try to link the various conclusions reached in this body of literature into a more general explanation of why the member states produce common foreign policies.[20]

Some areas seem to be more popular than others, which is partly a reflection of actual EU policy priorities. EU policies towards Africa, Asia and Latin America,[21] for example, do not attract nearly as much scholarly attention as the following areas:

1. Policies towards neighbouring countries and especially the European Neighbourhood Policy (ENP) have attracted increasing attention from scholars, some of whom have redirected their energies from analysing the enlargement process to the ENP (Danreuther, 2004; Aliboni, 2005; Kelley, 2006; Weber *et al.* 2007). Much work centres

on the overlap between the enlargement and neighbourhood policies, and on the extent to which the EU can influence its neighbourhood without offering countries the perspective of eventual EU
membership. Relations with Russia have not received as much attention (Prozorov, 2006).

2. Policy towards the Mediterranean in general has for some time
   attracted considerable attention – understandably, given that one of
   the first attempts at policy coordination within EPC centred on policy
   towards the Middle East.[22] Scholarly attention is directed to the
   process of policy formulation within the EU (including the influence
   that the US may have on that process), and, to some extent, on the
   EU's impact on domestic and foreign policies in the Mediterranean
   region. Some parts of the Mediterranean are still not well covered,
   however – such as Libya, isolated by the EU until recently.

3. With a few exceptions (Lucarelli, 2000; Simms, 2001; Caplan,
   2005), the western Balkans has been given less scholarly attention
   than it merits, given the fundamental significance of that region in
   the EU's foreign relations since the early 1990s. Work has centred
   on the EU's current policies (stabilization and association policy,
   ESDP missions),[23] while the EU's roles in the various wars in the
   region have attracted less interest.

4. EU policy *towards* the US is less of a focus than transatlantic relations as a whole (long of interest to scholars of EU foreign policy),
   primarily because there is little formal 'EU foreign policy' regarding
   the US per se. Thus the scholarly emphasis has tended to fall on the
   evolution of the relationship (and particularly on that relationship
   in economic areas, above all trade) as well as on the impact that the
   US may have on processes of European *integration*, rather than on
   the actual impact the US may have on the process of EU foreign
   policy cooperation or on EU foreign policies towards other countries, regions or issues.[24]

5. The EU's policies and relations towards other regional groupings is a
   growing area of interest, as 'regionalism' appears to have gathered
   strength in areas around the world. Topics debated in this literature
   include: the extent to which the EU may be fostering regionalism
   (and regional cooperation in specific geographical areas); whether
   'inter-regionalism' may be altering the international system; whether
   that inter-regionalism may be contributing to greater EU actorness
   and a sense of EU distinctiveness, as compared to other international
   actors (Edwards and Reglesberger, 1990; Teló, 2001; Grugel, 2004;
   Söderbaum *et al.*, 2005).

6. The EU and 'multilateralism' has attracted more interest quite
   recently. The EU's relations with, and roles in, various international
   organizations, as well as its general attitude towards multilateralism,
   have all been the subject of recent work (see note 14).

The role of values and norms in the EU's foreign relations is also generating considerable interest (Lucarelli and Manners, 2006). Such investigations are often combined with 'area studies' – for example, the promotion of human rights in particular areas (Arts, 2000; Youngs, 2001; Güney and Çelenk, 2007; Warkotsch, 2007). A related research area is the use and effectiveness of political conditionality, both to prompt political reform and to try to resolve conflicts, usually in the EU's neighbourhood (Kelley, 2004; Vachudova, 2005; Schimmelfennig *et al.*, 2006; Tocci, 2007).

Regarding the impact of the EU foreign policy system on member states

Research here has recently centred on 'the Europeanization of national foreign policy'. The concept of Europeanization, however, can be quite problematic to use in the foreign policy realm: the procedures, rules, norms and policies at the EU level are largely decided on 'intergovernmentally'; EU institutions play a relatively minor role in the process compared to the member states themselves; and there are few real constraints on member states to conform to EU policies and rules (the public disarray over the invasion of Iraq in 2003 illustrating clearly how member states can ignore norms of cooperation when their interests diverge from each other). But the extent to which the member states' foreign policy interests, positions, institutions and even identity may be changing as a result of the development of EU-level foreign policy cooperation (norms, institutions and the *acquis politique*) is nonetheless a significant area for scholarly investigation (M.E. Smith, 2000; Tonra, 2001; Larsen, 2005; Vaquer i Fanes, 2005; Wong, 2006; Gross, 2007).

The EU's impact on international relations

Finally, the EU and the broader international system receives some scholarly attention, but a rather large body of work has focused on how to categorize the EU's 'identity' as an international actor – is it a civilian power, military power, ethical power, normative power, superpower, and so on (Stavridis, 2001; Manners, 2002; Moravcsik, 2002; Khanna, 2004; Teló, 2005; Whitman, 2005; McCormick, 2007; Sjursen, 2007; Aggestam, 2008).[25]

Agendas for future research

What could be added to this already copious literature? There are still large gaps in our knowledge, and some of the most glaring ones have already been referred to above. There is a great need for detailed, empirical and/or historical research: that is, for research that is theoretically informed but that nonetheless requires lots of digging around in archives, or interviewing, or wading through a wide variety of sources that are not necessarily available on the internet. (What is online can be very patchy: for example, following the reorganization of the Enlargement Directorate-General's website, it is now quite difficult to find information about previous enlargements.) It is suggested here that the following questions and issues merit further research.

The policy-making process: cross-pillar issues and coordination

The challenges of coordination between first and second pillar institutions are becoming well known to us (and if the Lisbon Treaty is eventually ratified, its implementation will give us more material to analyse), particularly in areas such as 'civilian crisis management'. But there are other similar issues which also need more investigation:

- Research on the JHA-CFSP intersection is in its early days, and the implications of the disappearance of the JHA pillar for that intersection will need further analysis in particular. What, for example, is happening to the role of interior/home affairs ministries and ministers in 'cross-pillar' policies such as the fight against terrorism?
- There is even an undeveloped area of research regarding first pillar–second pillar coordination, which is the links, or tensions, between foreign policy and development policy. This is a clear example of an area where European foreign policy analysts could reach out to foster more links with development policy analysts. For example, the links, or tensions, between security and development in EU policy in Africa deserve further examination (see, for example, Gibert, 2007; Youngs, 2007).

The policy-making process: how and why are policies made?

There is still much room here for detailed, empirical research – especially comparisons across policies. Why have the member states taken decisions to launch particular ESDP missions? A comparison across the 20 or so cases would be quite useful, and could even give us clues about how the ESDP might develop, at least in the short term.

Taking an historical approach could also be highly illuminating. For example, many of the theories or explanations of why the EU has enlarged itself refer solely to the 2004/07 enlargements (and sometimes beyond). Rarely – if ever – do we use such contemporary explanations 'backwards', to see if they are helpful in explaining previous rounds of enlargement (and if not, why not).[26] There is then quite considerable scope for an historical, comparative approach to explaining why the EU has enlarged.

Comparison with other regions is also needed: it is striking that in the UN context there appear to be blocs that are even more united than the EU (Africa Group, Organisation of the Islamic Conference, and, until the 1995 enlargement, the Nordic Group), and most of these blocs are often vigorous in their opposition to the EU. What is going on there (balancing behaviour against the EU?), and how does it compare to what is going on within the EU?

The impact of the institutions on the policy-making process

To what extent has institutionalization – and the related (or identical?) process of 'Brusselization'– actually prompted foreign policy cooperation and the formulation and implementation of common foreign policies? Going further, can we really claim that 'socialization' is occurring in Brussels? Of course, there are obvious difficulties facing researchers here: how can we identify and prove that socialization occurs?[27] However, if we cannot 'operationalize' this concept, then perhaps we should direct our research energies elsewhere. But if we think that the concept is promising, then uncovering socialization will require – at a minimum – a lot of interviewing and in-depth, detailed research. And its effects would also need to be explored: is it really leading to a convergence of views on interests, values and policies? What effect does it have on the substance of policies? How does enlargement affect institutionalization, socialization and cooperation? And is socialization in Brussels offset by countervailing pressures from national officials?

The impact of institutions on policy-making processes is also an area where European foreign policy analysts could reach out to legal analysts (see Eeckhout, 2005; De Baere, 2008): what impact is the 'legalization' (M.E. Smith, 2001) of the CFSP having on the substance of policies agreed, and on the attitude of policy-makers towards the CFSP (do they see themselves as making 'law')?

The impact of the EU foreign policy system on the member states

Further detailed research is also needed on the impact of the EU on national foreign policy-making. This can build on research on 'Europeanization', or foreign policy analysis, or constructivist insights about socialization. Large-scale comparative studies would be of great interest here – and should obviously include the new member states.

We need a much better idea of what is going on in national capitals, the 'depth' of involvement of national officials in EU foreign policy processes, the proportion of national officials that must deal with the EU, and their attitudes towards EU cooperation. It may in fact be that most national officials deal rarely with EU affairs: for example, national officials involved with the 'greater Middle East' may not necessarily be informed of or interested in what the EU is doing in that respect. Can national foreign policy officials build successful careers while avoiding 'all things European', as anecdotal evidence from the UK suggests? By interviewing only officials involved in EU processes, we may miss the larger picture: we may think the EU is more important in national processes than it is. Of course we may also discover that, in fact, in some (or all) states the EU actually is quite a significant factor (and the reasons for variations across countries and over time would merit exploration). But we do not yet have enough information to be able to state this either way.

Such research should then link into studies on what is happening in Brussels: we should connect what is happening in national capitals to the questions posed at the start of this chapter: why do the member states act collectively? What are the limits to collective action? How are EU foreign policies made?

We should take a longer perspective as well. It would be interesting, for example, to know whether policy-makers are aware of the history of EU cooperation, and how or whether it affects how they interact within the system. I have heard a Council secretariat official state that the CFSP began in 1999: her point was that we shouldn't judge the member states harshly if CFSP doesn't work perfectly because the system is still new and everyone is still learning to cooperate. Yet six member states have had 37 years (and another three almost as many) of cooperation within a formal framework for foreign policy cooperation. Surely this is long enough for there to have been some impact on member states, for 'socialization' to occur, for 'identity change' to be evident (as constructivists might argue). If – as many argue – the UK is 'not really European' or not 'Europeanized' after 34 years inside the EU (and constructive and active participation in EPC/CFSP/ESDP), then perhaps there are limits to socialization: but then the question arises as to why this is the case.

The UK is not the only 'difficult' case here. We should ask the same questions of other countries. And we could gain insights from comparing 'problem cases', member states with 'adjustment problems' in the European foreign policy system, such as Greece in the 1980s, perhaps Denmark in the 1990s and Cyprus now. Are there similarities in these cases? How and why do they eventually adjust? And are there any broad lessons there? How do other member states deal with them?

The EU's impact on the world

Much more research needs to be done on the EU's influence in the wider world. In particular, we need to learn much more about the EU's impact on the international system: are we, as some realists have argued, even seeing 'soft balancing' now? Is the EU a model for other regions, for international relations? Is it a 'power'? We also need to compare the EU's actual impact on foreign governments with that of other actors, including other international organizations, states and domestic groups.

Too often, we lapse into assertions that the EU has either considerable or little influence, without the backing of clear, substantial evidence for such influence. 'Proving' the EU has influence (or not, and what sort and why) requires considerable empirical research (and particularly a lot of interviewing and reading of materials not in an EU language) to be conducted outside the EU, and necessarily involving non-EU based scholars. The view from Delhi, Moscow, Beijing, Tokyo, Cape Town, Accra, Jerusalem, Tehran, Caracas or Washington, DC (and so on) is bound to be different from the view from Brussels and EU national capitals – and might lead to considerable revision of our views on EU power and influence.[28] This sort of research could go from investigating the effectiveness of EU aid policies (in particular countries, sectors and regions), to analysing the EU's influence in international diplomatic processes, to gauging the extent to which major powers consider the EU to be an actor, or even a power, worth listening to. This means separating out EU influence from that of other domestic and international actors – an inherently difficult task – but unless we try to get to the bottom of this, we are left with unsubstantiated assertions about the EU's place/role/influence in the world.[29] Doing research on these themes should entail 'us' physically leaving the EU and venturing into other countries, and should entail the involvement of researchers from outside the EU in joint research projects with those based inside the EU.

This suggestion also means that I think that we should turn our attention to analysing what kind of power the EU wields and with what effect, rather than debating what kind of power the EU *is*. Debates about whether the EU is or is not a civilian power, a normative power, a super-power, and so on, are not really leading us anywhere right now – certainly not to firm answers to the core questions listed at the start of this chapter. We should instead engage in a debate about what the EU does, why it does it, and with what effect, rather than about what it is.

Conclusion

In conclusion, the field of study on the EU's foreign and security policy system offers up numerous research challenges but also numerous interesting questions to pursue. Much research is ongoing, but there are still many gaps to fill. We need more in-depth empirical research. We could also do more to make our work relevant to other disciplines and areas of study. We should be able to speak to a wider audience of academics and analysts, and draw in a wider circle of scholars from other disciplines. We must speak to scholars outside the EU and involve them in joint research endeavours. Finally, there is still work to do to 'accumulate knowledge': to summarize important findings and to stimulate research to contribute further findings to build up our collective knowledge.

Notes

1. An initial version of this chapter was presented to a Palgrave research symposium in March 2007, and then on the occasion of the Anna Lindh Award ceremony in Brussels, in October 2007. I am very grateful to all those participants on both occasions who offered useful comments and further questions to address. Thanks also to William Wallace and Jan Zielonka for their feedback on this chapter.
2. Classic works from the 1970s and 1980s include: Allen and Wallace (1977); Sjöstedt (1977); de Schoutheete (1980); Allen *et al.*, (1982); Hill (1983); Ifestos (1987); Pijpers *et al.* (1988); Ginsberg (1989). And from the 1990s: Rummel (1990); Holland (1991); Nuttall (1992); Hill (1993, 1996); Regelsberger *et al.* (1997); Peterson and Sjursen (1998).
3. Available on the FORNET website (www.fornet.info) and the EU-CONSENT website (www.eu-consent.net).
4. The EFSPS programme is sponsored by three foundations (Riksbankens Jubileumsfond, Volkswagen Stiftung and Compagnia di Sao Paolo) and run by the Institut für Europäische Politik, Berlin (www.iep-berlin.de).
5. There are studies which concentrate just on the CFSP pillar (and its predecessor, European Political Cooperation), but such works are considered here to be a subset of the study of the broader EU foreign policy system.
6. Walter Carlsnaes, however, has cautioned that a wide variety of different conclusions and approaches is not a sign of health in the literature on European foreign policy, but rather a 'cacophony of dissonant voices' Carlsnaes (2004: 495). The contention here, however, is that as long as there is debate regarding different conclusions and approaches (which requires analysts to be aware of, and consciously engage with, the variety out there), then the scope of our understanding should increase. Right now it is more important to conduct careful empirical research than to seek one dominant approach explaining the evolution and workings of the system (if indeed such an approach could ever be found).
7. The EU is obviously a unique international actor, in that no other collectivity can match the institutionalization and output of its foreign policy system, but this should not preclude comparison with any attempts at collective foreign policy making elsewhere (including comparison of explanations for such attempts). Ben Tonra (2000) identifies a divide in the literature on

EU foreign policy between scholars who consider the EU *sui generis* and those who take a comparative perspective.

8. A very traditionalist interpretation of FPA would preclude its use with respect to EU-level foreign policy, because the EU is not a state. However, several analysts have argued that EU foreign policy can be likened to national foreign policy and hence analysed using similar tools. Hazel Smith (2002: 1) argues that 'the European Union does indeed have a foreign policy and that it can be analysed in pretty much the same way we can analyse that of any nation-state'. Taking this argument even further, Brian White (2001) explicitly aims to show how FPA can be used to analyse European foreign policy. Carlsnaes (2004: 505–7) pleads for a more synthetic FPA which could then also be used to analyse European foreign policy.

9. Barry Posen (2006) argues that balancing US power is the motivation behind the development of the ESDP. EU member states fear abandonment (because the US has the capacity to ignore them) and want to have a greater influence in international relations.

10. 'Brusselization' is usually understood as the shift in the composition of officials involved in CFSP/ESDP from those based in national capitals to those based in Brussels: a growing number of CFSP/ESDP institutions and policy-makers are now located in Brussels (Allen, 1998: 56–8). Gisela Müller-Brandeck-Bocquet (2002) argues that Brusselization is leading to a new form of governance in CFSP.

11. There has been some initial work done on this; see for example Santopinto (2007) and Schroeder (2006).

12. Though, oddly, there are only a few book-length treatments of this subject. See, for example, Hill (1983, 1996) and Manners and Whitman (2000a).

13. Ian Manners and Richard Whitman consider that national foreign policy has been so transformed through EU membership that 'transformational FPA' is a more appropriate approach. Henrik Larsen suggests that, depending on the extent to which a state conducts foreign policy in a particular issue area within the EU, traditional or transformational FPA will be more useful. See Manners and Whitman (2000b) and Larsen (2005: 209–21).

14. This is one question explored in Laatikainen and Smith (2006); see also Jörgensen (2006) and Wouters *et al.* (2006).

15. A decade ago, Richard Rosecrance (1998) argued that the EU was unique in international relations, because even as it became more powerful (larger, richer, with more capabilities), it did not repel other countries and spark balancing behaviour (as realists would predict), but instead it attracted them, as third countries sought to strengthen their relations with it. However, the EU's continued enlargement and the development of the European defence policy (aimed at providing the EU with greater capabilities for intervention) might change that dynamic; the question is at least worth taking into consideration.

16. Books have been cited more often than articles, simply because books can provide a more in-depth treatment of the subject. Alas, English-language publications also dominate the references here, a reflection primarily of my own linguistic limitations as well as of the increasing tendency for scholars to write and publish in English, regardless of whether their native language is English or not.

17. M.E. Smith (2004) deals primarily with the evolution of the system up to the creation of CFSP. Key EU foreign policy documents from the 1990s (and some commentary) are included in Hill and Smith (2000).

18. Several EU-funded research networks and projects have been examining this intersection, including Challenge (www.libertysecurity.org) and the team on the external aspects of internal security working within the EU-Consent network. See also Boswell (2003); Monar (2004); Rees (2005); Lavenex (2006); Spence (2007); and Edwards and Meyer (2008). In retrospect it is striking how little attention was paid to the overlap between the international crime-fighting agenda and foreign policy in the literature on European foreign policy before 9/11.

19. Some of the works published since 2000 include: H. Smith (2002); Tonra and Christiansen (2004); Bretherton and Vogler (2004); Carlsnaes *et al.* (2004); Holland (2004); Mahncke *et al.* (2004); Casarini and Musu (2007); Keukeleire and MacNaughtan (2008).

20. Mea culpa: as Ben Tonra noted (2000: 165), my own work on the EU's policy towards Central and Eastern Europe argues that it is a unique case and not one from which we could necessarily draw general conclusions (K.E. Smith, 2004). This may or may not prove to be the case, but only a trawl through the literature and additional case studies will reveal this.

21. Such areas are (cursorily) covered in the broad surveys of the EU's policies with the rest of the world, but there are only a few in-depth studies, such as: Holland (2002); Smith (1995); Balme and Bridges (2008). The EU's relations with 'rising powers' such as Brazil, China, India and South Africa have received scant attention.

22. Older works include Shlaim and Yannopoulos (1976) and Allen and Pijpers (1984). More recent work includes: Jünemann (2004); Youngs (2006); Bicchi (2007).

23. Most of this work is in the form of journal articles or book chapters; one exception is O'Brennan (2007).

24. But see Gegout (2002). A sample of the literature on transatlantic relations includes: Lundestad (1998); Peterson and Pollack (2003); Gordon and Shapiro (2004); McGuire and Smith (2005).

25. The debate about 'civilian power Europe' has a long and rich history; see, for example, Duchêne (1973) and Bull (1982).

26. For a wide-ranging discussion of theorizing EU enlargement, see Schimmelfennig and Sedelmeier (2005).

27. For a recent (and fairly solitary) attempt in this respect, see Juncos and Pomorska (2006). They argue that 'internalization' of behavioural rules has not occurred, but that diplomats abide by them to obtain desired outcomes (a strategic calculation). They also note that research still needs to be done on whether socialization has an impact on the policy process and outcomes.

28. There has been some work done recently on what outsiders think of the EU. See Ortega (2004); Chaban *et al.* (2006); Lucarelli (2007a, 2007b); Elgström (2007). Yet Elgström (2007: 964) has argued that much empirical work still needs to be done on 'if, or to what extent, outsiders' perceptions actually have an influence on the EU's chance to achieve its goals'.

29. One exception to this tendency is Tocci (2007) in which she analyses specifically the EU's influence in several different conflicts (frozen or otherwise)

on the EU's periphery. Another is the wide-ranging work by Ginsberg (2001), in which he argues that the EU has considerable 'political impact' on international actors and issues.

References

Aggestam, L. (ed.) (2008) 'Ethical Power Europe?', *International Affairs* 84(1).

Aliboni, R. (2005) 'The geopolitical implications of the European Neighbourhood Policy', *European Foreign Affairs Review* 10(1).

Allen, D. (1996) 'The European Rescue of National Foreign Policy?', in C. Hill (ed.) *The Actors in Europe's Foreign Policy* (London: Routledge).

Allen, D. (1998) '"Who speaks for Europe?" The search for an effective and coherent external policy' in J. Peterson and H. Sjursen (eds) *A Common Foreign Policy for Europe?* (London: Routledge).

Allen, D. and Wallace, W. (1977) 'European Political Cooperation: procedure as a substitute for policy?' in H. Wallace, W. Wallace and C. Webb (eds) *Policy-Making in the European Communities* (Chichester: John Wiley).

Allen, D., Rummel, R. and Wessels, W. (eds) (1982) *European Political Cooperation: Towards a Foreign Policy for Western Europe* (London: Butterworth Scientific).

Allen, D. and Pijpers, A. (eds) (1984) *European Foreign Policy-Making and the Arab-Israeli Conflict* (The Hague: Martinus Nijhoff).

Arts, K. (2000) *Integrating Human Rights into Development Cooperation: The Case of the Lomé Convention* (The Hague: Kluwer Law International).

Balme, R. and Bridges, B. (eds) (2008) *Europe-Asia Relations: Building Multilateralisms* (Basingstoke: Palgrave Macmillan).

Barbé, E. and Herranz, A. (eds) (2005) *The Role of Parliaments in European Foreign Policy* (Barcelona: Observatory of European Foreign Policy).

Bicchi, F. (2007) *European Foreign Policy Making toward the Mediterranean* (New York: Palgrave).

Biscop, S. (2005) *The European Security Strategy: A Global Agenda for Positive Power* (Aldershot: Ashgate).

Boswell, C. (2003) 'The External Dimension of EU Immigration and Asylum Policy', *International Affairs* 79(3).

Bretherton, C. and Vogler, J. (2004) *The European Union as a Global Actor* (2nd edn) (London: Routledge).

Bull, H. (1982) 'Civilian Power Europe: A Contradiction in Terms?', *Journal of Common Market Studies* 21(2).

Caplan, R. (2005) *Europe and the Recognition of New States in Yugoslavia* (Cambridge: Cambridge University Press).

Carlsnaes, W. (2004) 'Where Is the Analysis of European Foreign Policy Going?', *European Union Politics* 5(4).

Carlsnaes, W., Sjursen, H. and White, B. (eds) (2004) *Contemporary European Foreign Policy* (London: Sage).

Casarini, N. and Musu, C. (eds) (2007) *European Foreign Policy in an Evolving System* (Basingstoke: Palgrave Macmillan).

Chaban, N., Elgström, O. and Holland, M. (2006) 'The European Union as Others See It', *European Foreign Affairs Review* 11(2).

Cooper, R. (2003) *The Breaking of Nations: Order and Chaos in the Twenty-First Century* (London: Atlantic Books).

Cornish, P. and Edwards, G. (2005) 'The Strategic Culture of the European Union: A Progress Report', *International Affairs* 81(4).

Dannreuther, R. (ed.) (2004) *European Union Foreign and Security Policy: Towards a Neighbourhood Strategy* (London: Routledge).

De Baere, G. (2008) *Constitutional Principles of EU External Relations* (Oxford: Oxford University Press).

Duchêne, F. (1973) 'The European Community and the Uncertainties of Interdependence', in M. Kohnstamm and W. Hager (eds) *A Nation Writ Large? Foreign-Policy Problems before the European Community* (London: Macmillan).

Edwards, G. (2006) 'The New Member States and the Making of EU Foreign Policy', *European Foreign Affairs Review* 11(2).

Edwards, G. and Regelsberger, E. (eds) (1990) *Europe's Global Links: The European Community and Inter-Regional Cooperation* (London: Pinter).

Edwards, G. and Meyer, C. (eds) (2008), 'EU and Terrorism' (Special Issue), *Journal of Common Market Studies* 46(1).

Eeckhout, P. (2005) *External Relations of the European Union: Legal and Constitutional Foundations* (Oxford: Oxford University Press).

Elgström, O. (2007) '"Outsiders" Perceptions of the European Union in International Trade Negotiations', *Journal of Common Market Studies* 45(4).

Everts, S. and Keohane, D. (2003) 'The European Convention and EU Foreign Policy: Learning from Failure', *Survival* 45(3).

Gegout, C. (2002) 'The Quint: Acknowledging the Existence of a Big Four-US Directoire at the Heart of the European Union's Foreign Policy Decision-Making Process', *Journal of Common Market Studies* 40(2).

Gibert, M. (2007) 'Monitoring a Region in Crisis: The European Union in West Africa', Chaillot Paper 96 (Paris: EU Institute for Security Studies).

Ginsberg, R. (1989) *The Foreign Policy Actions of the European Community* (Boulder: Lynn Rienner).

Ginsberg, R. (2001) *The European Union in International Politics: Baptism by Fire* (Lanham: Rowman and Littlefield).

Gordon, P. (1997–98) 'Europe's Uncommon Foreign Policy', *International Security* 22(3).

Gordon, P. and Shapiro, J. (2004) *Allies at War: America, Europe and the Crisis over Iraq* (Washington, DC: Brookings Institution).

Gross, E. (2007) 'The Europeanisation of National Foreign Policy? The Role of the EU CFSP/ESDP in Crisis Decision-making in Macedonia and Afghanistan', PhD thesis, London School of Economics.

Grugel, J. B. (2004) 'New Regionalism and Modes of Governance – Comparing US and EU Strategies in Latin America', *European Journal of International Relations* 10(4).

Guehenno, J-M. (1998) 'A Foreign Policy in Search of a Polity', in J. Zielonka (ed.) *Paradoxes of European Foreign Policy* (The Hague: Kluwer Law International).

Güney, A. and Çelenk, A. (2007) 'The European Union's Democracy Promotion Policies in Algeria: Success or Failure?', *Journal of North African Studies* 12(1).

Hill, C. (ed.) (1983) *National Foreign Policies and European Political Co-operation* (London: George Allen & Unwin).

Hill, C. (1993) 'The Capability-Expectations Gap, or Conceptualizing Europe's International Role', *Journal of Common Market Studies* 31(3).

Hill, C. (ed.) (1996) *The Actors in Europe's Foreign Policy* (London: Routledge).

Hill, C. and Smith, K. E. (eds) (2000) *European Foreign Policy: Key Documents* (London: Routledge).

Hill, C. and Smith, M. (2005) 'Acting for Europe: Reassessing the European Union's Place in International Relations', in C. Hill and M. Smith (eds) *International Relations and the European Union* (Oxford: Oxford University Press).

Hoffmann, S. (1966) 'Obstinate or Obsolete? The fate of the nation state and the case of Western Europe', *Daedalus 95*.

Holland, M. (ed.) (1991) *The Future of European Political Cooperation: Essays in Theory and Practice* (London: Macmillan).

Holland, M. (2002) *The European Union and the Third World* (Basingstoke: Palgrave Macmillan).

Holland, M. (ed.) (2004) *Common Foreign and Security Policy: The First Ten Years* (London: Continuum).

Howorth, J. (2007) *Security and Defence Policy in the European Union* (Basingstoke: Palgrave Macmillan).

Ifestos, P. (1987) *European Political Cooperation: Towards a Framework of Supranational Diplomacy?* (Aldershot: Avebury).

International Spectator, The (2004) 'Democratic Accountability of the EU and the Role of the European Parliament', 39(2).

Jörgensen, K. E. (2006) 'A Multilateralist Role for the EU?' in O. Elgström and M. Smith (eds) *The European Union's Roles in International Politics: Concepts and Analysis* (London: Routledge).

Juncos, A. E. and Pomorska, K. (2006) 'Playing the Brussels Game: Strategic Socialisation in the CFSP Council Working Groups', *European Integration online papers*, 10.

Jünemann, A. (2004) *Euro-Mediterranean Relations After September 11. International, Regional and Domestic Dynamics* (London: Frank Cass).

Kagan, R. (2003) *Of Paradise and Power: America and Europe in the New World Order* (London: Atlantic Books)

Kelley, J. (2004) *Ethnic Politics in Europe: The Power of Norms and Incentives* (Princeton: Princeton University Press).

Kelley, J. (2006) 'New Wine in Old Wineskins: Promoting Political Reform through the European Neighbourhood Policy', *Journal of Common Market Studies* 44(1).

Keukeleire, S. and MacNaughtan, J. (2008) *The Foreign Policy of the European Union* (Basingstoke: Palgrave Macmillan).

Khanna, P. (2004) 'The Metrosexual Superpower', *Foreign Policy*, July/August.

Laatikainen, K. V. and Smith, K. E. (eds) (2006) *The European Union at the United Nations: Intersecting Multilateralisms* (Basingstoke: Palgrave Macmillan).

Larsen, H. (2005) *Analysing the Foreign Policy of Small States in the EU: The Case of Denmark* (Basingstoke: Palgrave Macmillan).

Lavenex, S. (2006) 'Shifting Up and Out: The Foreign Policy of European Immigration Control', *West European Politics* 29(2).

Lucarelli, S. (2000) *Europe and the Breakup of Yugoslavia* (The Hague: Kluwer Law International).

Lucarelli, S. (ed.) (2007a) 'Beyond Self-Perception: The Others' View of the European Union', *European Foreign Affairs Review* 12(3).

Lucarelli, S. (2007b) 'European Political Identity and the Others' Images of the EU: Reflections on an Under-explored Relationship', *CFSP Forum* 5(6).

Lucarelli, S. and Manners, I. (eds) (2006) *Values and Principles in European Union Foreign Policy* (London: Routledge).

Lundestad, G. (1998) *Empire by Integration: The United States and European Integration, 1945–1997* (Oxford: Oxford University Press).

Mahncke, D., Ambos, A. and Reynolds, C. (eds) (2004) *European Foreign Policy: From Rhetoric to Reality?* (Brussels: Peter Lang).

Manners, I. (2002) 'Normative Power Europe: A Contradiction in Terms?', *Journal of Common Market Studies* 40(2).

Manners, I. and Whitman, R. (eds) (2000a) *The Foreign Policies of European Union Member States* (Manchester: Manchester University Press).

Manners, I. and Whitman, R. (2000b) 'Conclusion', in I. Manners and R. Whitman (eds) *The Foreign Policies of European Union Member States* (Manchester: Manchester University Press).

McCormick, J. (2007) *The European Superpower* (Basingstoke: Palgrave Macmillan).

McGuire, S. and Smith, M. (2005) *The European Union and the United States: Competition and Convergence in the Global Arena* (Basingstoke: Palgrave Macmillan).

Merlingen, M. and Ostrauskaite, R. (2006) *European Union Peacebuilding and Policing: Governance and the European Security and Defence Policy* (London: Routledge).

Meyer, C. (2006) *The Quest for a European Strategic Culture: Changing Norms on Security and Defence in the European Union* (Basingstoke: Palgrave Macmillan).

Monar, J. (2004) 'The European Union as an International Actor in the Domain of Justice and Home Affairs', *European Foreign Affairs Review* 9(3).

Moravcsik, A. (2002) 'The Quiet Superpower', *Newsweek*, 17 June.

Müller-Brandeck-Bocquet, G. (2002) 'The New CFSP and ESDP Decision-Making System of the European Union', *European Foreign Affairs Review* 7(3).

Müller-Brandeck-Bocquet, G. (ed.) (2006) *The Future of European Foreign Security and Defence Policy After Enlargement* (Baden-Baden: Nomos).

Nuttall, S. (1992) *European Political Co-operation* (Oxford: Clarendon).

Nuttall, S. (2000) *European Foreign Policy* (Oxford: Oxford University Press).

O'Brennan, J. (2007) *The EU and the Western Balkans* (London: Routledge).

Oppermann, K. and Höse, A. (2007) 'Public Opinion and the Development of the European Security and Defence Policy', *European Foreign Affairs Review* 12(2).

Ortega, M. (ed.) (2004) 'Global Views on the European Union', Chaillot Paper 72 (Paris: European Union Institute for Security Studies).

Peterson, J. and Sjursen, H. (eds) (1998) *A Common Foreign Policy for Europe? Competing Visions of the CFSP* (London: Routledge).

Peterson, J. and Pollack, M. (eds) (2003), *Europe, America, Bush: Transatlantic Relations in the Twenty-First Century* (London: Routledge).

Pijpers, A., Regelsberger, E., Wessels, W. and Edwards, G. (eds) (1988) *European Political Cooperation in the 1980s: A Common Foreign Policy for Western Europe?* (Dordrecht: M. Nijhoff).

Posen, B. (2006) 'European Union Security and Defence Policy: Response to Unipolarity?', *Security Studies* 15(2).

Prozorov, S. (2006), *Understanding Conflict Between Russia and the EU: The Limits of Integration* (Basingstoke: Palgrave Macmillan).

Rees, W. (2005) 'The External Face of Internal Security', in Hill, C. and Smith, M. (eds) *International Relations and the European Union* (Oxford: Oxford University Press).

Regelsberger, E. (2004) 'The Impact of EU Enlargement on the CFSP: Growing Homogeneity of Views among the Twenty-Five', *CFSP Forum* 1(3).

Regelsberger, E., de Schoutheete de Tervarent, P. and Wessels, W. (eds) (1997) *Foreign Policy of the European Union: From EPC to CFSP and Beyond* (Boulder: Lynne Rienner).

Rosecrance, R. (1998) 'The European Union: A New Type of International Actor' in Zielonka, J. (ed.) *Paradoxes of European Foreign Policy* (The Hague: Kluwer Law International).

Rummel, R. (ed.) (1990) *The Evolution of an International Actor: Western Europe's New Assertiveness* (Boulder: Westview).

Santopinto, F. (2007) 'Why the EU Needs an Institutional Reform of its External Relations', GRIP Note d'Analyse, 19 June (available at www.grip.org).

Schimmelfennig, F. and Sedelmeier, U. (eds) (2005) *The Politics of European Union Enlargement: Theoretical Approaches* (London: Routledge).

Schimmelfennig, F., Engert, S. and Knobel, H. (2006) *International Socialization in Europe: European Organizations, Political Conditionality and Democratic Change* (Basingstoke: Palgrave Macmillan).

de Schoutheete, P. (1980) *La coopération politique européenne* (Brussels: Editions Labor).

Schroeder, U. C. (2006) 'Converging Problems – Compartmentalised Solutions: The Security-Development Interface in EU Crisis Management', *CFSP Forum* 4(3) (www.fornet.info).

Shlaim, A. and Yannopoulos, G. N. (eds) (1976) *The EEC and the Mediterranean Countries* (Cambridge: Cambridge University Press).

Simms, B. (2001) *Unfinest Hour: Britain and the Destruction of Yugoslavia* (London: Allen Lane).

Sjöstedt, G. (1977) *The External Role of the European Community* (Farnborough: Saxon House).

Sjursen, H. (ed.) (2007) *Civilian or Military Power? European Foreign Policy in Perspective* (London: Routledge).

Smith, H. (1995) *European Union Foreign Policy in Central America* (London: Macmillan).

Smith, H. (2002) *European Union Foreign Policy: What it Is and What it Does* (London: Pluto Press).

Smith, K. E. (2004) *The Making of EU Foreign Policy: The Case of Eastern Europe*, 2nd edn (Basingstoke: Palgrave Macmillan).

Smith, M. E. (2000) 'Conforming to Europe: The Domestic Impact of EU Foreign Policy Co-operation', *Journal of European Public Policy*, 7(4).

Smith, M. E. (2001) 'The Legalization of EU Foreign Policy', *Journal of Common Market Studies* 39(1).

Smith, M. E. (2004) *Europe's Foreign and Security Policy: The Institutionalization of Cooperation* (Cambridge: Cambridge University Press).

Söderbaum, F., Stålgren, P. and Van Langenhove, L. (eds) (2005) 'The EU as a Global Actor and the Role of Interregionalism' (Special Issue), *Journal of European Integration* 27(3).

Spence, D. (ed.) (2007) *The European Union and Terrorism* (London: John Harper).

Stavridis, S. (2001) 'Why the "Militarising" of the European Union is Strengthening the Concept of a *"Civilian Power Europe"'*, Robert Schuman Centre Working Paper 2001/17 (Florence: European University Institute).

Telò, M. (ed.) (2001) *European Union and New Regionalism: Regional Actors and Global Governance in a Post-hegemonic Era* (Aldershot: Ashgate).

Teló, M. (2005) *Europe: A Civilian Power?* (Basingstoke: Palgrave Macmillan).

Tocci, N. (2007) *The EU and Conflict Resolution: Promoting Peace in the Backyard* (London: Routledge).

Tonra, B. (2000) 'Mapping EU Foreign Policy Studies', *Journal of European Public Policy* 7(1).

Tonra, B. (2001) *The Europeanisation of National Foreign Policy: Dutch, Danish and Irish Foreign Policy in the European Union* (Aldershot: Ashgate).

Tonra, B. and Christiansen, T. (eds) (2004) *Rethinking European Union Foreign Policy* (Manchester: Manchester University Press).

Vachudova, M.A. (2005) *Europe Undivided: Democracy, Leverage and Integration after Communism* (Oxford: Oxford University Press).

Vaquer i Fanes, J. (2005) 'Spanish Policy Towards Morocco (1986–2002): The Impact of EC/EU Membership', PhD thesis, London School of Economics.

Viola, D. (2000) *European Foreign Policy and the European Parliament in the 1990s: An Investigation into the Role and Voting Behaviour of the European Parliament's Political Groups* (Aldershot: Ashgate).

Warkotsch, A. (2007) 'The Rhetoric-Reality Gap in the EU's Democracy Promotion in Central Asia', *CFSP Forum* 5(1) (www.fornet.info).

Weber, K. Smith, M.E. and Baun, M. (eds) (2007) *Governing Europe's Neighbourhood: Partners or Periphery?* (Manchester: Manchester University Press).

Wendt, A. (1994) 'Collective Identity Formation and the International State', *American Political Science Review* 88(2).

White, B. (2001) *Understanding European Foreign Policy* (Basingstoke: Palgrave Macmillan).

Whitman, R. (2005) 'Muscles from Brussels: The Demise of Civilian Power Europe?', in Elgström, O. and Smith, M. (eds) *The European Union's Roles in International Politics: Concepts and Analysis* (London: Routledge).

Wong, R. (2005) 'The Europeanization of Foreign Policy', in Hill, C. and Smith, M. (eds) *International Relations and the European Union* (Oxford: Oxford University Press).

Wong, R. (2006) *The Europeanisation of French Foreign Policy: France and the EU in East Asia* (Basingstoke: Palgrave Macmillan).

Wouters, J., Hoffmeister, F. and Ruys, T. (eds) (2006) *The United Nations and the European Union. An Ever Closer Partnership* (The Hague: T.M.C. Asser Press).

Youngs, R. (2001) *The European Union and the Promotion of Democracy: Europe's Mediterranean and Asian Policies* (Oxford: Oxford University Press).

Youngs, R. (2006) *Europe and the Middle East: In the Shadow of September 11* (Boulder: Lynne Rienner).

Youngs, R. (2007) 'Fusing Security and Development: Just another Euro-platitude?', FRIDE Working Paper 43, Madrid.

Zielonka, Z. (1998) *Explaining Euro-Paralysis* (London: Macmillan).

Chapter 15

Europe and Globalization

Wade Jacoby and Sophie Meunier

Globalization is a source of endless debate in both popular and scholarly literatures. In the case of Europe, the causes and effects of globalization are difficult to isolate from those of the effects of deeper regional integration, often referred to as 'Europeanization'. Since globalization has occurred in tandem with regional integration, it leads to questions that are specific to the European case. Has the EU subversively acted as a Trojan Horse that helped bring globalization into the heart of Europe, or instead has the EU been Europe's best defence against its negative effects? Are regional integration and globalization two facets of the same phenomenon? Do they reinforce each other or contradict each other?

Many studies in economics and international political economy have addressed the question of how globalization and regionalization are related, but globalization scholars have not looked much at the EU (Lawrence, 1996; Baldwin, 1997; Baldwin *et al.*, 1999; Hettne *et al.*, 1999; Landau, 2001). In turn, EU scholars have not looked much at globalization (Wallace, 2000). It is commonplace in literature reviews on globalization to point out the increasing use of the term 'globalization' and its variants. Yet the most comprehensive 'mapping' of EC-EU studies doesn't even use the word 'globalization' (or 'global') at all (Keeler, 2005). Moreover, the first ten years of the European Integration Online Papers produced exactly two papers with 'global' in the title, and none with the term 'globalization' (or 'globalisation'). The *Journal of Common Market Studies* shows seven articles since 2000 with 'global' in the title, though in some of these cases 'global' seemed to be deployed as a synonym for something like 'bilateral relations at a great distance' (e.g. EU–Mexican relations).

To be sure, there is a Europeanist literature on globalization, but one reason for its modest size is the veritable explosion of literature on 'Europeanization' (Olsen, 2002; Featherstone and Radaelli, 2003; and see Chapter 9). This literature deals with an important aspect of the internationalization of European political economies and, to a certain extent, has crowded out some scholarship that might otherwise have been pitched as globalization. As we will see, one important strand of scholarship has tried to sort out the effects of globalization and Europeanization – two hard-to-define processes taking place simultaneously. This chapter provides a compact exploration of the state of the field on the complex relationship between globalization and the EU and sketches a range of questions that still remain. We start by reviewing the multiple definitions of 'globalization'. The second section surveys how scholars have studied the impact of globalization on the EU, while section three looks at the European imprint on globalization. We end by highlighting a research agenda centred on the question – partly empirical, partly normative – of whether the EU can help the Europeans 'manage' globalization.

Globalization and Europe: scope and definition

Globalization is a huge topic – sometimes so huge as to spark despair among scholars. Yet even scholars who suggest that the concept of globalization might be better abandoned have also proposed ways of refining and keeping it (Rosamond, 2005).[1] Innumerable studies have looked at its manifestation in areas such as crime, terrorism, disease, culture, sports, education and religion. This essay concentrates on economic aspects of globalization, fully mindful of the truncation of the account. This choice excludes in particular the literature on globalization's impact on European democracy (Axtman, 1998; Hooghe, 2003; Kuper, 2007). Our chapter also has a decidedly contemporary bent even though there exist several fine works on the history of globalization in Europe (Murphy, 1998; Wallace, 2000; O'Rourke, 2002; Berger, 2003). These omissions are regrettable, but a single review can only encompass so many themes.

Even the large literature on economic aspects of globalization still contains multiple definitions. Scholte (2000: 15–17) summarizes five major definitions in the social sciences, and each of them is present in the Europe-based literature.[2] First, globalization as internationalization – emphasizing cross-border flows – is present in a lively debate about whether Europe is most affected by its own regional integration or by transactions with more distant actors (Weber, 2001). Second, globalization defined as liberalization – especially the removal of state regulations on economic transactions – is exemplified in debates about whether the EU (in particular, the Commission) is an instigator of liberalization or rather an insulator against liberalization (Hay, 2007). Third, globalization as universalization – the spread of human artifacts to corners of the globe far from their creation – is present in discussions about the EU's ability to externalize its own rules, especially in an effort to 'manage globalization' (Lamy, 2004). Fourth, globalization as Westernization or modernization is featured in investigations of the diffusion of contemporary EU practices to aspirant member states (Jacoby, 2004) or close geographical neighbours (Kelley, 2006).

Fifth, globalization as deterritorialization – or the reconfiguration of geography, so that social space is no longer mapped primarily in terms of (especially national) borders (Giddens, 1990; Scholte, 2000, 2002; Katzenstein, 2005).

A crucial issue for scholars of globalization in Europe is a definition of globalization that clearly differs from regional integration, a second powerfully transformative force affecting the EU. While some early literature often used interchangeably the concepts of globalization, internationalization and regionalization, the rise of the concept of Europeanization has led scholars to try to be more precise. Such precision has not led to agreement, but it has led to somewhat more self-conscious definitions. To an extent, these definitions track findings in predictable ways. Broad definitions – such as Weber and Posner's (2001) use of factor 'mobility' as the key indicator – are linked to a broad appreciation of globalization as a powerful force in Europe (though clearly one mediated by other factors) (cf. Hiscox, 2002). By contrast, definitions that demand of globalization a degree of physical distance from Europe that allows us to distinguish it from regional processes tend also to downplay the effects of globalization in favour of more focus on Europeanization (cf. Hirst and Thompson, 1996; Hay, 2006).

Several scholarly and popular sources purport to measure globalization with some precision. Most show steady increases in the degree of globalization since the early 1970s. After major contractions in trade and, even more markedly, capital flows after September 2001, it now appears that accounts of the demise of globalization were premature (for a summary of this debate, see Held and McGrew, 2007: 3–5). The Swiss Institute for Business Cycle research maintains an annual index comprised of 24 social, economic and political variables gathered for 122 countries for over 30 years. Europe shows by far the highest absolute levels of globalization in all three areas, and indeed of the world's 15 'most globalized countries' in the period 2001–07, the first 14 are European (no. 15 is Canada; the US is no. 22), and 13 are EU members (non-member Switzerland is in fourth place).[3] Since 2000, the Foreign Policy/AT Kearney Index tracks 'economic, technological, personal and political integration' through 12 indices. The 2007 data has non-European locations (Singapore and Hong Kong) in the first two locations, but still has 11 EU states (plus Switzerland and Norway) in the top 20 of their aggregate index.[4]

With these indices, scholars can disaggregate the concept of globalization in many ways and seek more precision in tests of specific manifestations of globalization – including non-economic ones, such as flows of international telephone calls and number of international treaties ratified. Yet while these indices usefully break down globalization into many different kinds of flows, they obviously continue to privilege state territoriality. For the first four definitions above, this move has few costs. To the extent that globalization is defined as the transcendence of territory, however, such indices are often 'meaning-less' (Rosamond, 2005: 33).

The impact of globalization on Europe

There is a vibrant literature on the ways in which globalization has affected Europe. As noted, however, most of that literature lacks any specific focus on the EU. Rather, either explicitly or implicitly, it focuses on efforts of European *states*, and occasionally of *regions* (cf. Ansell *et al.*, 2001; Longo, 2003), and even *cities* (cf. Brenner, 1999; Fry and Kresl, 2005) to cope with the challenges of globalization. To review this vast literature would go beyond the chapter's remit.[5] Instead, two largely empirical issues dominate much of the current lit-erature relevant to the EU. First, we see an effort to sort out the effects of globalization and Europeanization to clarify what might otherwise appear as causal overdetermination. Second, we see an effort to deter-mine whether globalization is affecting Europe in any substantial way at all or whether it is rather a rhetorical device to promote neoliberal policies.

Empirical effects: Confronting causal overdetermination

As noted, a central analytical problem is that globalization is not the only prospective cause of economic outcomes of interest – from institu-tional and policy change to growth, employment and income distribu-tion. Rather, Europeanization also looms large as a potential cause for many of these same outcomes. Since both processes happen simultane-ously in Europe, how should scholars sort out their influence?

For some authors, Europeanization dominates globalization (Fligstein and Merand, 2002; Véron, 2007). Hay (2006) argues that Europe has seen a process of 'de-globalization' since the 1960s, with the rise of European regionalism actually diminishing earlier levels of globaliza-tion. Arguing that the globalization thesis rests largely on expectations of convergence across Europe, he shows that cross-national social spending has not, in fact, converged over the past 40 years. Indeed, precisely during the purported ramp up of globalization in the 1980s, social spending increased significantly in Europe, especially in the very open Scandinavian political economies (cf. Rodrik, 1998). Hay uses gravity models to demonstrate that of the 11 European economies in his sample, only Finland shows diminished effects of distance on trade flows. All other states exhibit patterns of 'deglobalization', in which more proximate trading relations increasingly dominate cross-border exchanges (Hay, 2006: 16). Drawing similar conclusions from the FDI data, Hay argues that rather than a process of globalization, then, intra-European divergence is a result of different responses to a relatively common *ideology* of 'neo-liberalization' (ibid.: 19).[6]

By contrast, others argue that European regionalism takes a backseat to globalization as a driver of institutional and regulatory change in Europe. A pioneering work in this regard is Verdier and Breen (2001), which attempted to separate the impacts of 'market globalization' from those of the European single market and European political union. Looking at indicators in four areas (labour and capital markets, electoral competition, and centre–local government relations), they build from the idea that globalization is largely a process of 'negative integration' or deregulation (Scharpf, 1996). If Europeanization is also 'synonymous with deregulation', its effects then 'should be similar to the effects of globalization' (ibid.: 229). By contrast, moves towards political union would have preserved (or built anew) 'interventionist capability' (ibid.: 231). The fruits of such intervention would then differ from those of globalization or, indeed, of European market integration.

Verdier and Breen find that all three forces matter. In some cases, globalization – measured as trade and financial market integration – does all the causal work. In other cases, European market integration does extra work not done by globalization. Finally, in still other cases, European political integration is the result of political 'voluntarism' not explained by market processes (sometimes the outcomes of such political voluntarism can go beyond or even against what is dictated by markets). To demonstrate this logic, Verdier and Breen structure their research design around two sets of Europeanization processes – ones that interact with globalization to either accelerate or brake its effects, and ones that operate entirely independently of globalization ('*sui generis* effects').[7] In the first logic, where Europeanization and globalization are cumulative forces, we see a 'globalization plus' effect. Where European-level political forces slow globalization, we see a 'globalization minus' outcome. Similarly, where Europeanization operates in a *sui generis* fashion, it might work either through a market or voluntarist logic.

The authors find that in finance (though not trade), globalization and Europeanization together ('globalization plus') explain variation in trade-union density and variation in the choice of the level at which wage bargains are set. There is no evidence that European countries are especially able to use policy to slow these trends (indeed, rather the opposite) (244). In capital markets, while globalization has clear effects, 'market reform took place among EU countries at the same speed as among non-EU countries. We found no trace of Europeanization, let alone voluntarism, in financial markets' (ibid.: 246). Turning to politics, the authors test the proposition that as markets become more important, political parties become less important. They find that increased financial globalization is associated with higher electoral volatility outside the EU but not inside the EU. This 'insulating' capacity of the EU is a case of 'globalization minus' and evidence of a voluntarist component (ibid.: 252). On centre–regional relations, while an increase in financial globalization is associated with increasing centralization of state spending, this is not true in those European states that receive heavy allocations of structural funds (ibid.: 256). A central implication is that since Europeanization cannot really tame globalization at home, there is a compelling case for trying to do so abroad. Here, the persistence of partisan loyalties and the rise of anti-globalization politics may be a foundation for managing globalization (see also Hoffmann, 2002 on the 'clash of globalizations').

Recent extensions of this line of research include Levi-Faur (2004), who applies it to infrastructure industries (electricity and telecommunications).[8] His central question is whether Europeanization is liberalizing Europe in ways that are distinct from what globalization is doing elsewhere in the world. His basic answer is 'no'. With liberalization quite advanced there, telecom and electricity regulation are held to represent 'best cases' for the Europeanization thesis. Yet Levi-Faur finds that Europeanization does not lead to liberalization in his comparison of 14 of the old EU-15 member states with 16 Latin American countries (using a most different cases logic) and with eight wealthy non-EU democracies (a most similar logic). He also finds that liberalization also happened in areas – like privatization – that are clearly outside EU jurisdiction. Levi-Faur notes that his findings complement the Verdier and Breen findings on capital and labour, which means that four economic cases all point to no effect of Europeanization but to substantial effects of globalization. Levi-Faur notes, however, that Europeanization may matter more in the 'southern countries', following Schneider (2001), and in Central and Eastern Europe, following Jacoby (2001).[9]

Humphreys and Padgett (2006) tell a similar story about these two sectors, focusing on the cases of France and Germany but in ways that privilege the role of EU actors. Defining globalization as a combination of technological innovation and international market forces, they argue that in telecoms, where globalization mattered significantly, the sector generated pressure for regulatory change that the Commission could use to produce reforms even when member states were reluctant to go along. Where such sectoral pressure did not exist, such as in the case of electricity, the Commission had no such leverage. The authors emphasize policy transfer (for example, of the British model in telecom regulation) as a means to 'synchroniz[e] the responses of the member states to the changing international and technological environment (globalization)' (ibid.: 402). In line with the large literature on national regulatory systems and globalization noted earlier, they find that state features matter insofar as Germany's pluralist and veto-rich system makes implementation more difficult than France's centralized, executive-led system (ibid.: 401).

Friedman's revenge? globalization as rhetoric

For some scholars, the kind of research just outlined tends to fall into traps that either exaggerate globalization's causal weight (Hay, 2006) or link it too strongly to specific spatial assumptions (Rosamond, 2005: 29). Some authors (Hirst and Thompson, 1996) seem to say that the concept of globalization might better be abandoned, as their reading of the empirical evidence does not support the idea that long-distance transactions are on the rise. For others, trying to separate global processes from other spatial domains reifies the artificial divide between domestic and foreign in much international relations scholarship (Scholte, 2002: 28). Yet globalization seems here to stay in popular discussions, which are replete with economic determinism and race-to-the-bottom scenarios. Thus, despite mountains of evidence calling the simple convergence model into question (Berger and Dore, 1996; Weber, 2001; Campbell, 2004), policy-makers still seem to act as if the world were 'flat' or at least becoming more so every day (Friedman, 2007). We see this enduring enthusiasm of policy-makers for the notion of flatness to be 'Friedman's revenge' against his legion of academic critics (cf. Berger, 2005; Aronica and Ramdoo, 2006).[10]

Thus, rather than playing down globalization's effects or pointing to endemic confusion about the levels at which such effects occur, an alternative strategy is to look into the rhetorical use made of globalization by policy-makers and journalists (Mishra, 1999; Meunier, 2003). What if the public discourse about globalization in Europe is only that – discourse? Rosamond stresses that the very complexity of globalization probably contributes to the relentless simplification of the concept for use by policy elites. He argues the concept is an 'empty signifier' that is used in radically different ways by different actors at different times.

To date, we have little research that catalogues this range of differences, and this seems a fruitful avenue for research. One exception is Smith and Hay's (2008) survey of 2,000 British and Irish politicians and civil servants, which finds that almost 99 per cent of the respondents focus on globalization as an economic phenomenon. They also find that large majorities of elites believe in the basic 'hyperglobalization' thesis in which economic imperatives tie the hands of policy-makers. Of course, parliamentarians and civil servants ought to have at least as hard a time distinguishing the effects of globalization from the effects of Europeanization as do social scientists, and Smith and Hay provide ample evidence that this is so.

Cameron and Palan (2004) help explain why such a multistranded and contradictory phenomenon as globalization can be handled in such a reductionist way – with a simple story about the need for convergence along policy lines most friendly to business interests – whether the specific policy of note involves taxation levels, labour markets or welfare-state spending. Emphasizing the 'communal story telling' surrounding globalization, Cameron and Palan suggest new avenues for understanding the evolution of ideas from minor alternative to dogma.

Several related avenues for research deserve more attention in the future. First, the concept of intellectual 'anchoring' implies that respondents may cluster their answers in similar ways for different causal forces. This is exactly what we would expect if Smith and Hay are right about the level of confusion of their respondents. If that is so, however, future scholarship should deploy phone or internet surveys that, more than paper and pencil surveys, lend themselves to randomizing the order of questions.[11] Second, a basic factor analysis should show if policy-makers' responses on globalization and Europeanization 'load' on the same factors – again suggesting that they can't really tell the two phenomena apart – or whether, by contrast, different respondents who gave similar answers on one question gave very different answers to other questions.

The imprint of Europe on globalization

Europe has not only been on the receiving end of globalization. It has also been a major actor in the globalized world that it has actively contributed to creating. In the early days of European integration, the new European institutions were inward-looking, reactive to outside pressures, and their original goal was not to shape global order. Over time, however, the EU's internal actions began to impact on the rest of the world, and the EU designed policies with the specific goal of making its mark on its outside environment.

A growing scholarship is interested in analysing what exactly has been the European imprint on globalization (cf. Kierzowski, 2002; Laible and Barkey, 2006; Heisenberg, 2006; Sapir, 2007). Recent studies have been focusing on the main mechanisms through which Europe is affecting globalization: by writing the rules that are enabling globalization to take place, by transferring European regulations and standards to the global level, and by serving as a model to be emulated. In impacting on the rest of the world, the EU is also affecting its own identity and political legitimacy. Will globalization continue to be so marked by Europe in the future, as the emergent powers, especially in Asia, become stronger?

Writing the rules of globalization

Contrary to popular imagery, globalization is not an out-of-control process or 'deregulation gone wild'. It was not created by a *deus ex machina* in the 1980s. Nor is it the result of a conspiracy by profit-obsessed capitalists. Global markets – whether they relate to capital, goods, services or even labour – have strong institutional foundations. The levees through which goods, services and people flow freely today across the world have been built and adjusted by the architects of the international system, of which the EU has been a major contributor.

A burgeoning scholarly literature explores the contribution of Europe to the setting of the terms and levels of economic openness in the past three decades. The popular literature on globalization has formed the conventional wisdom that globalization is the product of the neoliberal revolution in the 1980s in the United States and the wave of deregulation that ensued. Instead, scholars are now increasingly showing that Europe did have a major role to play in enabling globalization and in (re)regulating instead of simply deregulating.

In the world of global finance, Europe played a crucial, central role in enabling financial globalization through the rules developed by the EU and by the Organisation for Economic Co-operation and Development (OECD) (Bakker, 1995; Story and Walter, 1998; Abdelal, 2007). It was indeed European policy-makers who 'conceived and promoted the liberal rules that compose the international financial architecture. The most liberal rules in international finance are those of the EU, and the United States was irrelevant to their construction' (Abdelal, 2007: 3).

The euro is another instance of a European policy scheme which has had a direct impact, voluntarily or not, on globalization. It was created for a variety of reasons, more political than economic, in large part to immunize Europe from the vagaries of international currency fluctuations and from the diktats of the 'Washington Consensus' – in other words, to protect Europe from globalization (McNamara, 1998; Jabko, 2006). In turn, by becoming a successful reserve currency, the euro has enabled Europe to set some of the rules of the game.

In the world of global trade, the EU has been, more visibly than in finance, a major player in designing the rules that enable goods and services to circulate throughout the world. Trade is, after all, the policy area where sovereignty is shared, where the EU speaks on behalf of its member states, and where national competences have been delegated to the supranational level for the longest time (Meunier and Nicolaidis, 1999; Elsig, 2002; Meunier, 2005; Young and Peterson, 2006). When and where the EU was ready for liberalization, it happened largely on its own terms.

The EU has been instrumental in shaping global economic institutions, most notably the World Trade Organization (WTO). The EU strongly supported the move from the General Agreement on Tariffs and Trade (GATT) system to the WTO in the mid-1990s. The main institutional innovation was the creation of rules for settling trade-related disputes in the WTO – including a codified set of rules for reporting violations, adjudicating disputes and implementing resolutions in order to facilitate trade liberalization in the world (Meunier, 2007; Young, 2007). These new institutions codified and locked in a set of liberal principles, which then further reinforced liberalization and the free movement of goods and services. With respect to services in particular, the EU has been extremely vocal in pressing for more market opening.

The extent of globalization also depends on the accepted boundaries of the WTO and a consensus around what policy domains are included in, and excluded from, world trade rules (Warwick Commission, 2007). The EU has been the primary driver of the expansion of such boundaries, with its insistence on the inclusion of the four 'Singapore issues' addressing and establishing rules for the conditions under which trading takes place (competition policy, transparency in government procurement, trade facilitation and investment protection) (Howse and Nicolaidis, 2003; Young, 2007). Though not successful in having these issues included as part of the formal trade agenda for now, the EU has nonetheless put them on the table, thereby potentially expanding the reach of globalization in the future.

Transferring European regulatory standards

The second mechanism through which Europe has been impacting on globalization has been through the transfer of European regulatory standards at the global level across a wide range of sectors – from financial services to food, from chemicals to telecommunications. Alone or in cooperation with the US, the EU has been instrumental in shaping international regulatory designs and playing regulatory politics (Kelemen, 2004, 2008; Drezner, 2007; Damro, 2006; Young, 2003; Mattli and Buthe, 2003; Egan, 2001; Vogel, 1997). Indeed, in some issue areas, the recent rise of European regulatory influence in global markets has occurred despite opposition from the US and despite the absence of a single European superstate (Bach and Newman, 2007). As the *Financial Times* summarized: 'there is now a growing realization in many quarters that Brussels, not Washington, is shaping the global regulatory standards companies will have to abide by' (cited in ibid.: 829).

This powerful influence on globalization stems from two main sources: the size of Europe's internal market and the strength of its own regulatory institutions. The EU has been able to exert meaningful pressure at the global level because of the sheer size of its internal market. As Drezner explains, large markets 'have a gravitational effect on producers – the larger the economy, the stronger the pull for producers to secure and exploit market access' (Drezner, 2005: 843). The EU has been able to impose many of its preferred standards on other economies, and therefore spread its imprint on globalization, thanks to the ever growing size of its internal market (Schreurs and Tiberghien, 2007; Vogler and Hannes, 2007).

The EU has also made its mark on globalization through regulatory politics because of the skills and capacities of its internal regulatory institutions. Many analysts have noted the rise of a regulatory state in Europe, whose main functions are to stimulate competition and provide social goods (Majone, 1996; Thatcher, 2002, 2007). Bach and Newman (2007) argue that the rise of the regulatory state in Europe had important implications for global public policy, first by providing an impetus for subsequent debates about global market rules, and second by providing institutional capacity and expertise. The institutional experience acquired through years of navigating the EU system has given European regulators substantial knowledge, legitimacy and the basis for policy entrepreneurship. Europe's regulatory clout has thus enabled a globalization that is not deregulated but reregulated. This influence of EU regulatory authorities on global rules has led to a world with higher standards, much in its own image (Vogel, 1997; Shaffer, 2000; Prakash and Kollman, 2003).

Serving as a model

A third mechanism by which the EU has dictated the contours of globalization is simply by being what it is – the biggest market in the world and a hybrid organization with supranational institutions, shared competences and an ability to achieve compromises between diverse interests. Both by being a region and by serving as a model, the EU has actively shaped globalization, in addition to passively receiving it.

Europe is a region, whether defined by geographical, cultural or economic criteria (Katzenstein, 2005). Even if it were not trying to impact on the rest of the world, it still would, because economic actors elsewhere would try to conform to its own internal rules and preferences – the bigger the region, the larger its impact. By making its own sovereignty compromises and setting its social and legal norms, the EU also sets, in part, the terms and levels of economic openness in the world – like the US has done, and as China will perhaps do in the future. What is true for trade and regulatory standards is also true for financial and monetary issues, where the regional monetary order achieved by the EU after several decades has enabled the emergence of the financial globalization we know today.

Europe has also shaped globalization by serving as a model for other regions of the world. Globalization looks European because many actors of globalization are, to some extent, emulating the EU (Farrell, 2007). Fioretos calls this power of attraction 'representational power': 'through its representational power, the EU exercises influence on global economic governance by exemplifying a model of how diverse market economies can coexist in a liberal economic order while respecting and promoting the principles of social progress, sustainability, transparency and subsidiarity' (Fioretos, 2009).

The EU has also become a model through persuasion and conditionality (Jacoby, 2004; Hafner-Burton, 2005; Szymanski and Smith, 2005; Vachudova, 2005; Meunier and Nicolaidis, 2006). Yes, groupings of states emulate some features of the EU, and therefore contribute to spreading these European features globally, but they do so when it is a precondition for having access to the EU internal market and other benefits. The EU offers access to its market as a bargaining chip in order to obtain changes in the domestic arena of its trading partners – from labour standards to human rights, democratic practices and the environment. It is also a way of using trade policy to pursue foreign policy, sometimes out of the limelight and on the back of the member states (Peterson, 2007).

The result is a world that looks increasingly like the 'world of regions' described by Katzenstein (2005). A world in which global rules are made not only by the EU and North America, but also by ASEAN, Mercosur and now Unasur – the Union of South American Nations created in May 2008 with the goal of boosting economic and political integration in the region. This is a world in which 'globalization' is less global and increasingly regional, thanks in large part to the successes of the EU.

Finally, one can investigate the role of the US in allowing Europe to leave its mark on globalization. Does the EU have the power to shape the rules of global markets only when its interests are aligned with those of the US? Or only when the US retreats? These are questions being pursued more systematically under the rubric of 'managed globalization' – an emerging literature studying how the EU can ease globalization for its member states (see Jacoby and Meunier, 2010). Because of its long history of trying to manage cross-border flows, Europe is particularly well suited to the effort to manage globalization and can act as a 'filter' to globalization (Wallace, 2000).

Several scholars working on a project we have organized have found that the EU's advocacy of managed globalization is not purely a rhetorical device, only used for domestic political consumption. Instead, it has been accompanied by real policy substance, with more or less success, in policy areas as diverse as the environment (Kelemen, 2010), trade (Abdelal and Meunier, 2010; Fioretos, 2010; Sbragia, 2010), and social policy (Burgoon 2010). In other policy areas, meanwhile, evidence shows the EU has been much more dependent on a regulatory agenda set by the United States, including (at least so far) the important case of financial regulation (Posner and Véron, 2010). All of the works in our project explore the major policy mechanisms through which the EU has attempted to manage globalization over the past decade – by exercising regulatory influence, empowering international institutions, enlarging the territorial sphere of EU influence, redistributing the costs of globalization and legitimizing economic patriotism. These mechanisms provide the contours of an approach to globalization that is neither ad hoc deregulation, nor old-style economic protectionism.

Conclusion: globalization and the EU's legitimacy

This chapter has reviewed the main interactions between Europeanization and globalization, asking in particular whether the EU has acted as a Trojan Horse that helped bring globalization into the heart of Europe, or whether instead the EU has been Europe's best defence against the negative effects of globalization. Europe has been both a creator and a receiver of globalization, in a kind of virtuous or vicious circle, depending on one's point of view. In the virtuous circle interpretation, the EU has created its own internal rules for market liberalization, then shaped the rules of globalization in its own image to derive maximum benefits from globalization, while shielding European citizens from its worst effects. In the vicious circle interpretation, the EU acts as a transmission belt, even an amplifier, of globalization, and it is the combined effect of globalization and Europeanization that helped to create the economic and social malaise in which European citizens find themselves today. Much more research has yet to be conducted in order to support or debunk the virtuous/vicious interpretations and provide sound ammunition for the public debate on globalization which, while long on rhetoric, is often short on facts.

Plenty of controversies remain. Some are essentially historical: was globalization built as an outgrowth of American hegemony (Ikenberry, 2007) or, as some revisionist accounts have it, must the story also include European leadership (Abdelal, 2007; Callinicos, 2007)? Other controversies turn on differences in the direction of causation: are European firms and their lobbyists essentially responding to state 'shaping' (Woll, 2008) or are at least the weakest European states still vulnerable to capture by trans-national corporations (TNCs) and interest groups (Csaba, 2007)? Still others hearken back to the conceptual disputes noted at the outset of the chapter: is territory less meaningful (Scholte, 2002) or does globalization entail a 'reterritorialization' in the form of a multidecade trend towards aggregations of supranational competencies at European, rather than national, levels (Brenner, 1999)?

Much research needs to be done on these questions, especially now that the financial crisis has revealed both the dangers and the limits of globalization for Europe. Scholars can investigate how much insulation the EU has provided, if any, against the spread of financial contagion, how united European countries have acted in response to the crisis, and whether the experience of European integration has anything to teach the rest of the world about how to soften and contain the bluntness of neoliberal globalization.

Ultimately, the relationship between European integration and globalization is tied to the issue of EU legitimacy. In the eyes of most European citizens, the EU owes its legitimacy partly to being able to protect them from the negative side-effects of globalization while shaping aggressively a globalization in Europe's image. According to many opinion polls, this is actually an area where the EU is expected to do better than nation states because it has the advantage of the power derived from size. When Europe is perceived as adequately managing globalization, it looks legitimate. Judging by the results of the various referenda on the EU lately, however, many European citizens believe that the EU performs poorly in this respect. More research should probe the extent to which the French, Dutch and Irish referenda were swung by beliefs and preferences about globalization.

But Europe's ability to shape global economic rules is limited. Most policy tools for affecting globalization and dealing with its effects are not supranational powers. Even if they were, problems would emanate from the internal diversity and the lack of preference homogeneity within the EU – certainly all member states are not equal when it comes to loathing or admiring globalization (Sapir, 2007). Problems would also come from the fact that new challenges are threatening globalization as we know it today: turbulence in financial markets, threats to the 'European social model(s)', the emergence of new economic actors, and pressures on resources such as energy, food and water. Much is written about the EU's 'normative power' to shape the beliefs and preferences of other states by the diffusion of its values (Manners, 2002; Diez, 2005; Laïdi, 2008). But can Europe still deploy this normative power to shape the rules of globalization even if its economic and geopolitical power is eroded?

After all, the ability of the EU to manage globalization is reduced daily by the rise in power of new actors in the world. Ironically, globalization was much criticized in Europe precisely during an era when globalization clearly was, in significant ways, a European construct. This era may be over soon. It is predicted that the BRIC (Brazil–Russia–India–China) economies will account for half of world income by 2050 (Brainard, 2008). Will Europeans miss the current era of globalization or even retreat from it when other actors, in Asia and Latin America, start to have a meaningful voice? Former European trade commissioner Peter Mandelson recently remarked that 'there is a sense that globalization is something that is being done to us, rather than something we can control. The consequence is rising pressure for protection; we see it in growing economic nationalism at home, a return to fashion for zero-sum thinking about resources and public goods' (Mandelson, 2008). For every purported success in managing globalization, one can adduce (so far) some clear failures, including the absence of meaningful global labour standards, standards for the hedge-fund industry and the regulation of global financial transactions. In other words, complacency would ill-suit the EU, and scholars of the EU should thus have little reason for complacency either.

Notes

1. Olsen (2002) raises similar questions about the concept of Europeanization but also concludes that it is 'premature' to abandon the term.
2. Other extensive reviews of the concept include Hirst and Thompson, 1996; Axtman, 1998; Guillén, 2001; Held and McGrew, 2007.
3. See http://globalization.kof.ethz.ch/static/pdf/press_release_2008_en.pdf.
4. The US was seventh. See http://www.foreignpolicy.com/story/cms.php?story_id=3995&page=1. Other related indices can be found at the Warwick Centre for Globalisation and Regionalisation (http://www2.warwick.ac.uk/fac/soc/csgr/index/).
5. Influential summaries scrutinizing globalization pressures on national states include Mosley 2007; Iversen 2005; Schmidt 2002; Kitschelt *et al.* 1999; Garrett 1998. On the other hand, Eichengreen's 500 page history of the European economy since 1945 does not contain globalization in its substantial index (2007).
6. Hay explicitly sees the varieties of capitalism approach as a more subtle form of the convergence expectation but with the difference that there is now two distinct models – LMEs and CMEs – upon which laggard national political economies can converge (2006: 6–7). See Hall and Soskice (2001).
7. The study also has a null effect in which Europeanization has no effect one way or the other.
8. A different framework, with application to agriculture, is used by Hennis (2001); see also Ross (1998).
9. For more on Europe as a 'conduit' for globalization, see Schmidt (2002).
10. More sympathetic is Rodrik (2007: 201–2).
11. Important applications of cognitive psychology literature to the diffusion of liberal economic policy models can be found in Weyland (2007).

References

Abdelal, R. (2007) *Capital Rules: The Construction of Global Finance* (Cambridge: Harvard University Press).
Abdelal, R. and Meunier, S. (2010) 'Europe and the Management of Globalization: Responding to Globalization Pressures', Special Issue, *Journal of European Public Policy* 17: 3. No pages (yet) available.

Ansell, C., Gonzales. V. and O'Dwyer, C. (2001) 'The Variable Geometry of European Regional Economic Development', in S. Weber (ed.) *Globalization and the European Political Economy* (New York: Columbia University Press) 65–106.

Aronica, R. and Ramdoo, M. (2006) *The World is Flat?* (Tampa: Meghan-Kiffer Press).

Axtman, R. (ed.) (1998) *Globalization and Europe: Theoretical and Empirical Investigations* (London: Pinter).

Bach, D. and Newman, A. (2007) 'The European Regulatory State and Global Public Policy: Micro-Institutions, Macro-Influence', *Journal of European Public Policy* 16(6): 827–46.

Bakker, A. (1995) *The Liberalization of Capital Movements in Europe* (Dordrecht: Kluwer Academic).

Baldwin, R. (1997) 'The Causes of Regionalism', *The World Economy* 20(7): 865–88.

Baldwin, R., Cohen, D., Sapir, A. and Venables, A. (eds) (1999) *Market Integration, Regionalism and the Global Economy* (Cambridge: Cambridge University Press).

Berger, S. (2003) *Notre première mondialisation: Leçons d'un échec oublié* (Paris: Seuil).

Berger, S. (2005) *How We Compete: What Companies Around the World Are Doing to Make it in Today's Global Economy* (New York: Doubleday Business).

Berger, S. and Dore, R. (eds) (1996) *National Diversity and Global Capitalism* (Ithaca: Cornell University Press).

Brainard, L. (2008) *America's Trade Agenda: Examining the Trade Enforcement Act of 2007* (Washington: Brookings).

Brenner, N. (1999) 'Globalization as Reterritorialization: The Re-Scaling of Urban Governance in the European Union', *Urban Studies* 36(3): 431–51.

Burgoon, B. (2010) 'Europe and the Management of Globalization: Responding to Globalization Pressures', Special Issue, *Journal of European Public Policy* 17: 3. No pages yet available.

Callinicos, A. (2007) 'Globalization, Imperialism, and the Capitalist World System' in D. Held and A. McGrew (eds) *Globalization Theory: Approaches and Controversies* (Cambridge: Polity Press) 62–78.

Cameron, A. and Palan, R. (2004) *The Imagined Economies of Globalization* (London: Sage).

Campbell, J. (2004) *Institutional Change and Globalization* (Princeton: Princeton University Press).

Csaba, L. (2007) *The New Political Economy of Emerging Europe* (Budapest: Akadémiai Kiadó).

Damro, C. (2006) 'Transatlantic Competition Policy: Domestic and International Sources of EU–US Cooperation', *European Journal of International Relations* 12(2): 171–96.

Diez, T. (2005) 'Constructing the Self and Changing Others: Reconsidering "Normative Power Europe"', *Millennium* 33(3): 613–36.

Drezner, D. (2005) 'Globalization, harmonization, and competition: the different pathways to policy convergence', *Journal of European Public Policy* 12(5): 841–59.

Drezner, D. (2007) *All Politics is Global* (Princeton: Princeton University Press).

Egan, M. (2001) *Constructing a European Market: Standards, Regulation, and Governance* (Oxford: Oxford University Press).

Eichengreen, Barry (2007) *The European economy since 1945: coordinated capitalism and beyond* (Princeton: Princeton University Press).

Elsig, M. (2002) *The EU's Common Commercial Policy: Institutions, Interests and Ideas* (Aldershot: Ashgate).

Farrell, M. (2007) 'From EU Model to External Policy? Promoting Regional Integration in the Rest of the World' in S. Meunier and R. McNamara (eds) *Making History: European Integration and Institutional Change at Fifty* (Oxford: Oxford University Press): 299–316.

Featherstone, K. and Radaelli, C. (2003) *The Politics of Europeanization* (Oxford: Oxford University Press).

Fioretos, O. (2010) 'Europe and the Management of Globalization: Responding to Globalization Pressures', Special Issue, *Journal of European Public Policy* 17: 3. No pages yet available.

Fligstein, N. and Merand, F. (2002) 'Globalization of Europeanization? Evidence on the European Economy Since 1980', *Acta Sociologica* 45: 7–22.

Friedman, T. (2007) *The World is Flat: A Brief History of the Twenty-First Century* (New York: Picador).

Fry, E. and Kresl, P. (2005) *The Urban Response to Internationalization* (Cheltenham: Edward Elgar).

Garrett, G. (1998) *Partisan Politics in the Global Economy* (New York: Cambridge University Press).

Giddens, A. (1990) *The Consequences of Modernity* (Cambridge: Polity).

Guillén, M. (2001) 'Is Globalization Civilizing, Destructive, or Feeble? A Critique of Five Key Debates in the Sociological Literature', *Annual Review of Sociology* 27: 235–60.

Hafner-Burton, E. (2005) 'Trading Human Rights: How Preferential Trade Agreements Influence Government Repression', *International Organization* 59(3): 593–629.

Hall, P. and Soskice, D. (2001) *Varieties of Capitalism* (Oxford: Oxford University Press).

Hay, C. (2006) 'What's Globalization Got to Do With It? Economic Interdependence and the Future of European Welfare States', *Government and Opposition* 41(1): 1–23.

Hay, C. (2007) 'What Doesn't Kill You Only Makes You Stronger: The Doha Development Round, the Service Directive, and the EU's Conception of Competitiveness', *Journal of Common Market Studies* 45: 25–43.

Heisenberg. D. (2006) 'Can the European Union Control the Agenda of Globalization?' in J. Laible and H. Barkey (eds) *European Responses to Globalization* (London: Elsevier) 19–40.

Held, D. and McGrew, A. (2007) *Globalization Theory: Approaches and Controversies* (Cambridge: Polity Press).

Hennis, M. (2001) 'Europeanization and Globalization: The Missing Link', *Journal of Common Market Studies* 39(5): 829–50.

Hettne, B., Inotai, A., and Sunkel, O. (1999) *Globalism and the New Regionalism* (New York: Palgrave).

Hirst, P. and Thompson, G. (1996) *Globalization in Question* (London: Polity).

Hiscox, M. (2002) *International Trade and Political Conflict: Commerce, Coalitions, and Mobility* (Princeton: Princeton University Press).

Hoffmann, S. (2002) 'The Clash of Globalizations', *Foreign Affairs* 81(4): 104–15.

Hooghe, L. (2003) 'Globalization and the European Union: Shared Governance on a Regional Scale' in H. Lazar, H. Telford and R. Watts (eds) *The Impact of Global and Regional Integration on Federal Systems: A Comparative Analysis* (Kingston: McGill-Queen's University Press) 283–327.

Howse, R. and Nicolaidis, K. (2003) 'Enhancing WTO Legitimacy: Constitutionalization or Global Subsidiarity?', *Governance* 16(1): 73–94.

Humphreys, P. and Padgett, S. (2006) 'Globalization, The European Union, and Domestic Governance in Telecoms and Electricity', *Governance: An International Journal of Policy, Administration, and Institutions* 19(3): 383–406.

Ikenberry. G.J. (2007) 'Globalization as American Hegemony' in D. Held and A. McGrew (eds) *Globalization Theory: Approaches and Controversies* (Cambridge: Polity Press) 41–61.

Iversen, T. (2005) *Capitalism, Democracy, and Welfare* (New York: Cambridge University Press).

Jabko, N. (2006) *Playing the Market: A Political Strategy for Uniting Europe, 1985–2005* (Ithaca: Cornell University Press).

Jacoby, W. (2001) 'Tutors and Pupils: International Organizations, Central European Elites, and Western Models', *Governance* 14: 169–200.

Jacoby, W. (2004) *The Enlargement of the European Union and NATO: Ordering From the Menu in Central Europe* (New York: Cambridge University Press).

Jacoby, W. and Meunier, S. (2010) 'Europe and the Management of Globalization: Responding to Globalization Pressures', Special Issue, *Journal of European Public Policy* 17: 3. No pages yet available.

Katzenstein, P. (2005) *A World of Regions: Asia and Europe in the American Imperium* (Ithaca: Cornell University Press).

Keeler, J. (2005) 'Mapping EU Studies: The Evolution From Boutique to Boom Field 1960–2001', *Journal of Common Market Studies* 43(3): 551–82.

Kelemen, R. D. (2004) *The Rules of Federalism: Institutions and Regulatory Politics in the EU and Beyond* (Cambridge, MA: Harvard University Press).

Kelemen, R. D. (2010) 'Europe and the Management of Globalization: Responding to Globalization Pressures', Special Issue, *Journal of European Public Policy* 17: 3. No pages yet available.

Kelley, J. (2006) 'New Wine in Old Wineskins: Policy Adaptation in The European Neighborhood policy', *Journal of Common Market Studies* 44(1): 29–55.

Kierzowski, H. (ed.) (2002) *Europe and Globalization* (Basingstoke: Palgrave Macmillan).

Kitschelt, H., Lange, P., Marks, G. and Stephens, J. (eds) (1999) *Continuity and Change in Contemporary Capitalism* (New York: Cambridge University Press).

Kuper, A. (2007) 'Reconstructing Global Governance: Eight Innovations' in D. Held and A. McGrew (eds) *Globalization Theory: Approaches and Controversies* (Cambridge: Polity Press) 225–39.

Laible, J. and Barkey, H. (2006) *European responses to Globalization: Resistance, Adaptation, and Alternatives* (London: Elsevier).

Laïdi, Z. (2008) *Norms Over Force: the Enigma of European Power* (New York: Palgrave).

Lamy, P. (2004) 'Europe and the Future of Economic Governance', *Journal of Common Market Studies* 42(1): 5–21.

Landau, A. (2001) *Redrawing the Global Economy: Elements of Integration and Fragmentation* (New York: Palgrave).

Lawrence, R. (1996) *Regionalism, Multilateralism, and Deeper Integration* (Washington: Brookings).

Levi-Faur, D. (2004) 'On the "Net Impact" of Europeanization: The EU's Telecoms and Electricity Regimes Between the Global and the National', *Comparative Political Studies* 37(1): 3–29.

Longo, M. (2003) 'European Integration: Between Micro-Regionalism and Globalism', *Journal of Common Market Studies* 41(3): 475–94.

Majone, G. (1996) *Regulating Europe* (London: Routledge).

Mandelson, P. (2008) 'The EU and the US in a Globalised Economy: Politics and Priorities', *The Churchill Lecture*, New York, 9 June.

Manners, I. (2002) 'Normative Power Europe: A Contradiction in Terms?', *Journal of Common Market Studies* 40(2): 235–58.

Mattli, W. and Buthe, T. (2003) 'Setting International Standards: Technological Rationality or Primacy of Power?', *World Politics* 56(1): 1–42.

McNamara, K. (1998) *The Currency of Ideas: Monetary Politics in the European Union* (Ithaca: Cornell University Press).

Meunier, S. (2003) 'France's Double-Talk on Globalization', *French Politics, Culture and Society* 21(1): 20–34.

Meunier, S. (2005) *Trading Voices: The European Union in International Commercial Negotiations* (Princeton: Princeton University Press).

Meunier, S. (2007) 'Managing Globalization?', *Journal of Common Market Studies* 45(4): 905–26.

Meunier, S., and Nicolaidis, K. (1999) 'Who Speaks for Europe? The Delegation of Trade Authority in the EU', *Journal of Common Market Studies* 37(3): 477–501.

Meunier, S. and Nicolaidis, K. (2006) 'The European Union as a Conflicted Trade Power', *Journal of European Public Policy* 13(6): 906–25.

Mishra, R. (1999) *Globalization and the Welfare State* (London: Edward Elgar).

Mosley, L. (2007) 'The Political Economy of Globalization' in D. Held and A. McGrew (eds) *Globalization Theory: Approaches and Controversies* (Cambridge: Polity Press) 106–25.

Murphy, C. (1998) 'Globalization and Governance: A Historical Perspective' in R. Axtman (ed.) *Globalization and Europe: Theoretical and Empirical Investigations* (London: Pinter) 144–63.

Olsen, J. (2002) 'The Many Faces of Europeanization', *Journal of Common Market Studies* 40(5): 921–52.

O'Rourke, K. (2002) 'Europe and the Causes of Globalization, 1790–2000' in H. Kierzkowski (ed.) *Europe and Globalization* (Basingstoke: Palgrave Macmillan) 64–86.

Peterson, J. (2007) 'EU Trade Policy as Foreign Policy', paper presented at the 10th Conference of the European Union Studies Association, Montreal, CA, 17–19 May.

Posner, E. and Véron, N. (2010) 'The EU and Financial Regulation: Power Without Purpose?' *European Journal of Public Policy* 17:3. No pages yet available.

Prakash, A. and Kollman, K. (2003) 'Biopolitics in the EU and the US: A Race to the Bottom or Convergence to the Top', *International Studies Quarterly* 47: 617–41.

Rodrik, D. (1998) 'Why do More Open Economies Have Bigger Governments?' *Journal of Political Economy* 106(5): 997–1032.

Rodrik, D. (2007) *One Economics Many Recipes: Globalization, Institutions, and Economic Growth* (Princeton: Princeton University Press).

Rosamond, B. (2005) 'Globalization, the Ambivalence of European Integration and the Possibilities for a Post-Disciplinary EU Studies', *Innovation* 18(1): 23–43.

Ross, G. (1998) 'European Integration and Globalization' in R. Axtman (ed.) *Globalization and Europe: Theoretical and Empirical Investigations* (London: Pinter) 164–83.

Sapir, A. (ed.) (2007) *The Fragmented Power: Europe and the Global Economy* (Brussels: Bruegel).

Sbragia, A. (2010) 'Europe and the Management of Globalization: Responding to Globalization Pressures', Special Issue, *Journal of European Public Policy* 17: 3. No pages yet available.

Scharpf, F. (1996) 'Negative and Positive Integration in the Political Economy of European Welfare States' in G. Marks *et al.* (eds) *Governance in the European Union* (London: Sage) 15–39.

Schmidt, V. (2002) *The Future of European Capitalism* (Oxford: Oxford University Press).

Schneider, V. (2001) 'Institutional Reform in Telecommunications: The EU in Transnational Policy Diffusion' in M. Cowles, J. Caporaso and T. Risse (eds) *Transforming Europe: Europeanization and Domestic Change* (Ithaca: Cornell University Press) 60–78.

Scholte, J. (2000) *Globalization: A Critical Introduction* (New York: Palgrave).

Scholte, J. (2002) 'What is Globalization? The Definitional Issue – Again', CGSR Working Paper Series, Working Paper 109/02. Warwick: University of Warwick.

Schreurs, M. and Tiberghien, Y. (2007) 'Multi-Level Reinforcement: Explaining European Union Leadership in Climate Change Mitigation', *Global Environmental Politics* 7(4): 19–46.

Shaffer, G. (2000) 'Globalization and Social Protection: The Impact of EU and International Rules in the Ratcheting Up of US Privacy Standards', *Yale Journal of International Law* 25 (Winter): 1–88.

Smith, N. and Hay, C. (2008) 'Mapping the Political Discourse of Globalisation and European Integration in the United Kingdom and Ireland Empirically', *European Journal of Political Research* 47: 359–82.

Szymanski, M. and Smith, M. (2005) 'Coherence and Conditionality in European Foreign Policy: Negotiating the EU–Mexico Global Agreement', *Journal of Common Market Studies* 43(1): 171–92.

Story, J. and Walter, I. (1998) *Political Economy of Financial Integration in Europe: The Battle of the Systems* (Manchester: Manchester University Press).

Thatcher, M. (2002) 'Regulation After Delegation: Independent Regulatory Agencies in Europe', *Journal of European Public Policy* 9(6): 954–72.

Thatcher, M. (2007) *Internationalisation and Economic Institutions: Comparing European Experiences* (Oxford: Oxford University Press).

Vachudova, M. (2005) *Europe Undivided: Democracy, Leverage, and Integration After Communism* (New York: Oxford University Press).

Verdier, D. and Breen, R. (2001) 'Europeanization and Globalization: Politics Against Markets in the European Union', *Comparative Political Studies* 34 (Spring): 227–62.

Véron, N. (2007) 'When National Champions Are No Longer National: Europe's "New Economic Nationalism"', paper presented at the conference 'Europe and the Management of Globalization', Princeton University, 23 February.

Vogel, D. (1997) 'Trading Up and Governing Across: Transnational Governance and Environmental Protection', *Journal of European Public Policy* 4(4): 556–71.

Vogler, J. and Hannes, S. (2007) 'The European Union in Global Environmental Governance: Leadership in the Making?', *International Environmental Agreements* 7: 389–413.

Wallace, H. (2000) 'Europeanization and Globalization: Complementary or Contradictory Trends', *New Political Economy* 5(3): 369–82.

Warwick Commission (2007) *The Multilateral Trade Regime: Which Way Forward?* (Warwick: University of Warwick).

Weber, S. (ed.) (2001) *Globalization and the European Political Economy* (New York: Columbia University Press).

Weber, S. and Posner, E. (2001) 'Creating a Pan-European Equity Market' in S. Weber (ed.) *Globalization and the European Political Economy* (New York: Columbia University Press) 140–96.

Weyland, K. (2007) *Bounded Rationality and Policy Diffusion: Social Sector Reform in Latin America* (Princeton: Princeton University Press).

Woll, C. (2008) *Firm Interests: How Governments Shape Business Lobbying on Global Trade* (Ithaca: Cornell University Press).

Young, A. (2003) 'Political Transfer and "Trading Up"? Transatlantic Trade in Genetically Modified Food and US Politics', *World Politics* 55 (July): 457–84.

Young, A. (2007) 'Trade Politics Ain't What It Used to Be: The European Union in the Doha Round', *Journal of Common Market Studies* 45(4): 789–812.

Young, A. and Peterson, J. (2006) 'The EU and the New Trade Politics', *Journal of European Public Policy* 13(6): 795–814.

Chapter 16

The Future Shape of the European Union

Heather Grabbe and Ulrich Sedelmeier

Introduction

Is the future shape of the EU a question of maps, policies or culture? In other words, is its shape defined in terms of its territorial borders, or the functional reach of its rules, or by the constitutive identity of its members? The EU's territorial and functional dimensions do not necessarily overlap, as its functional reach extends beyond its borders. But they often interact. The EU's territorial shape influences its functional shape (for example because new members bring new priorities which stimulate the development of new policies) and vice versa (as the EU's functional reach expands, demands for integration from non-members increase). This chapter considers both these dimensions of the future shape of the EU.

While the EU's territorial shape is determined by the scope of its enlargement and the expansion of its membership, its functional shape depends on the reach of its external governance – that is, the extent to which its policies and norms are institutionalized and practised beyond its borders. The distinction between the EU's territorial and functional shape draws on the literature that identifies a variety of boundaries of EU political order (Smith, 1996; Lavenex, 2004). The territorial shape of the EU is determined by its institutional or organizational border, which shifts with each inclusion of a new member state. The functional shape relates to its legal or regulatory boundary, which shifts with each horizontal extension of the regulatory scope of EU rules.

The EU's territorial shape: enlargement

The EU's territorial shape is defined by the geographical borders of its members. The large-scale political debate about the geographical boundaries of Europe has been mostly raised by those opposed to further enlargement. Contributions to this debate include German Chancellor Angela Merkel's proposal to offer Turkey a privileged partnership (rather than membership); MEP Elmar Brok's call for a study to draw the EU's ultimate borders once and for all; Austrian

Chancellor Schüssel's push for a definition of the EU's absorption capacity; and French President Nicolas Sarkozy's initial mandate for the 'Groupe des Sages' to define the borders of the Union.

The EU is often portrayed as a space on the map, but in fact the Union's territorial scope has always raised tricky questions. The EU is not congruent with 'Europe' and it may never become so; it contains lacunae (e.g. Switzerland and Norway); it has often lacked territorial contiguity (e.g. Greece had no land border with the rest of the EU until Bulgaria joined); its eastern border has always been ambiguous; and its territory includes land that is not on the continent of Europe by any geographical definition, such as the islands in the Pacific and Caribbean that are part of France's overseas territories.

The EU's functional shape: external governance

At its origin, the Union was never intended to be a geographical entity, but rather a political project that would grow outwards from some countries located in Europe. Its policy coverage also grew outwards, as predicted by the functionalists. But as the Union has grown, its geographical and functional shape have rarely been coterminous. As 'differentiated integration' has grown among the member states, the EU's functional reach has been narrower than its geographical borders, such as European defence cooperation, the Schengen Treaty and Economic and Monetary Union (EMU), to which not all member states belong. The Lisbon Treaty – if it ever comes into force – will complicate matters further, because it provides for more opt-outs and gives more opportunities for 'flexible integration' or 'variable geometry'.

Conversely, the EU's functional dimension is wider than its territory: its external governance extends the impact of its rules ('Europeanization') beyond its membership. The extension of the EU's functional reach beyond its territory is often closely connected to its enlargement, as captured in the notion of enlargement as a process of gradual formal and informal 'horizontal institutionalization' of its rules and which starts before, and continues after, accession to the EU (Schimmelfennig and Sedelmeier, 2002: 503). At the same time as its internal integration has become more variegated, the EU has been reaching well beyond the borders of its member states, but in different ways in different regions. In its policies, this can be seen in areas that have not only opt-outs for some full members, but opt-ins by non-members, such as Norway, Iceland and Switzerland in the Schengen area. Other examples are the European Economic Area (EEA) agreement that extended the single market (except for agriculture) to the members of the European Free Trade Area (EFTA) (except for Switzerland), or the range of sectoral bilateral agreements with Switzerland.

The EU has extended its functional reach beyond its borders most effectively and most extensively through the process of EU enlargement and the European Neighbourhood Policy (ENP). In the case of enlargement, this incongruence of functional reach and geographical extension is largely temporary, as the EU demands alignment with its rules prior to accession. But in the ENP, the EU promotes the external adoption of its rules without the declared end-goal of membership. External governance also includes external policies of various kinds: development policy that includes a much stronger element of conditionality; trade policy that has shifted considerably from its initial focus on tariffs towards a multidimensional regulatory policy (Young, 2007); and the extension of parts of the Area of Justice, Liberty and Security to non-EU countries (e.g. migration cooperation).

Beyond the EU's policies and rules of the *acquis communautaire*, its external governance has also included the promotion of values and norms that are codified in other European institutions. For example, in the enlargement process, the EU often takes recourse to other international institutions to determine how to deal with tricky norms and questions of values – e.g. the Council of Europe on democracy matters, and the UN on conflict resolution. The transfer of norms and the spread of values comes through many different routes, such as declaratory policies and documents (e.g. the European Convention on Human Rights); small-scale projects (e.g. technical assistance, twinning); and contacts between bureaucracies and diplomatic corps. Implementation of the Lisbon Treaty would also make the case law of the European Court of Human Rights primary law of the Union, which would at once give the EU a substantial new human rights *acquis*.

This chapter first takes stock of the state of the art of research on EU enlargement and EU external governance. In both areas, the major conceptual debates have developed in particular in the context of the EU's eastern enlargement of 2004 and 2007. The chapter then reviews the EU's current practice and state of affairs with regard to enlargement and external governance after the 2004/07 enlargement to identify the key challenges for policy and future research on the shape of the EU.

The state of the art: EU enlargement and EU external governance

The EU's territorial shape: EU enlargement

The future territorial shape of the EU depends on the extent to which it continues to accept new members. The literature on EU enlargement has generated a number of insights into the conditions under which the Union enlarges. We can draw on these insights to assess the likelihood that specific non-member states are likely to join. Although the Union had already doubled its original membership before the end of the Cold War, enlargement only started to become a major research area in EU studies in the 1990s. A first wave of research focused on the determinants of EU enlargement, both on the EU side and on the side of potential new members. The second wave focused on the impact of the EU on candidate countries, which is the subject of the next section.

No general theory of EU enlargement has emerged from the empirical and conceptual literature. However, the insights of the debate fit well within the framework of the debate between rationalist and constructivist approaches to international institutions. The key questions are: under what conditions does a non-member state seek EU membership? Under what conditions do the incumbent member states offer accession? Rationalist and constructivist approaches suggest distinctive explanatory factors for both questions.

In a nutshell, for *rationalist* approaches a non-member will seek membership, and an incumbent will endorse their membership if the resulting benefits outweigh the costs (Schimmelfennig and Sedelmeier, 2002: 510–13). The types of costs and benefits that governments consider include welfare (increased economic opportunities and competition), membership benefits (budgetary transfers, influence on decision-making) and security. Individual states can also reduce their costs if they have sufficient bargaining power to shift adjustment costs to other states (e.g. to new members in accession negotiations) or increase the benefits for other states through side-payments.

The EU has never been enthusiastic about further enlargement, but neither has its territorial shape ever stopped changing. For the existing members, there is always the risk that bringing in new members will threaten their privileges, in terms of money or influence. For such reasons, France sought to keep Britain out in the 1960s and Spain out in the 1980s, while many member states were nervous about admitting the large number of poor, post-communist countries which applied to join in the 1990s. The population of the existing members has never shown a large majority in favour of enlargement, and sometimes that number has shrunk well below a majority. Yet 21 countries joined in successive rounds of enlargement and the EU's borders continued to move outwards.

For *constructivists*, questions of identity are a key determinant of enlargement. The more a non-member states identifies with the EU and its constitutive rules, the more likely it is to seek membership; and the greater the normative match between the EU and a non-member, the more likely are the incumbents to endorse its accession (ibid.: 513–15). However, there are differences in the literature as to what elements of such identity questions matter. Some authors focus primarily on a shared adherence to constitutive political rules – democracy and human rights – while others focus on a more general pan-European ethos that entails an obligation to remain open in principle and mitigates against incumbents treating it purely as a club for members to maximize their self-interest. Still others focus on specific identity constructions of the EU in relations with specific non-members (Fierke and Wiener, 1999; Sjursen, 2002; Schimmelfennig, 2003; Sedelmeier, 2005).

The factors emphasized by rationalist and constructivist accounts respectively are not necessarily mutually exclusive (at least not from a constructivist perspective). In certain cases, they might reinforce each other; for example, the membership applications in the Mediterranean enlargements of the 1980s and the 2004/07 eastern enlargements resulted both from hopes for material benefits and also from the desire to 'return to Europe' after regime changes. Other cases can be fully explained within a rationalist framework (e.g. EFTA enlargement, where there were overall economic benefits for both applicants and incumbents). By contrast, the following instances of EU enlargement are difficult to explain without drawing on constructivist insights.

Where constructivist and rationalist approaches point in opposite directions, identity might supersede material cost–benefit calculations. For example, despite potential gains from EU membership, a country might not apply or its population might not endorse membership, if it is perceived as a threat to national identity, as Gstoehl (2002) has argued for the cases of Norway and Switzerland. On the EU side, even if incumbents fear that enlargement threatens their material benefits from membership, they might still consent to the accession of a new member, as in the case of eastern enlargement, since the EU's collective identity precluded a veto as inappropriate behaviour (e.g. Schimmelfennig, 2003; Sedelmeier, 2005).

In sum, to explain the EU's changing territorial shape through enlargement, rationalist approaches emphasize the importance of material cost–benefits and bargaining power both within the domestic politics of potential applications and within and among the incumbent member states, while constructivist approaches draw attention to identity construction within the EU and potential members.

The EU's functional shape: EU external governance

The EU's functional shape extends beyond its geographical shape. The functional reach of the EU goes beyond its borders and therefore does not correspond with the reach of successive enlargements. At the same time, it is precisely in the context of enlargement that the study of EU external governance (or 'Europeanization' beyond the member states) emerged. It originated in the study of EU accession conditionality, through which the EU induces would-be members to adopt its rules prior to accession.

The main questions in the literature on EU accession conditionality are to what extent and under what conditions the EU's attempts to influence developments in candidate countries are effective (this section draws on Sedelmeier, 2006). In much of the literature this question is framed as: how effective is the EU's conditionality and what mediating factors account for variations in its effectiveness? However, conditionality – that is, offering rewards (positive incentives) for complying with the EU's demands – is not the only mechanism of EU external governance. One strand of the literature therefore contrasts conditionality with alternative mechanisms of EU influence. For example, Kelley (2004) analyses the relative importance of 'incentives' versus 'normative pressure'; Kubicek (2003) 'conditionality' versus 'convergence' (through the 'spread of norms'); and Schimmelfennig and Sedelmeier (2005) 'external incentives' versus 'social learning'.

Despite these apparent differences in language, the analytical frameworks that such studies draw on are very similar. Like the literature on EU enlargement, the theoretically informed study of the EU's external governance is largely set within the framework of institutionalist theory, and in particular the debate between rationalist institutionalism and constructivist institutionalism (see e.g. Goetz, 2002; Kubicek, 2003; Dimitrova and Steunenberg, 2004; Jacoby, 2004; Kelley, 2004; Schimmelfennig and Sedelmeier, 2005; Grabbe, 2006; Schimmelfennig *et al.*, 2006; Epstein, 2008).

Rationalist and constructivist approaches emphasize different strategies: the use of conditionality as an incentive-based strategy versus alternative strategies, such as persuasion and socialization, which depend on legitimacy and identity. Each of these approaches also identifies distinctive mediating factors – both at the EU level with regard to the EU's exercise of influence and at the domestic level in the target countries.

At the same time, while the two approaches emphasize analytically distinctive factors, many studies consider them to be at least partly complementary, and not necessarily mutually exclusive (see also Jacoby, 2004: 20–40; Schimmelfennig and Sedelmeier, 2005: 25). Indeed, as Kelley (2004) points out, in the issue area of minority policy, the EU never relied exclusively on conditionality, which was always combined with normative pressures from international institutions. In such cases, it is extremely difficult to disentangle the relative importance of either mechanism, since we can only contrast the effectiveness of exclusively normative pressure from normative pressure that is underpinned by conditionality. Likewise, Epstein (2008) emphasizes the social context of conditionality, rather than a simple either/or debate; and Johnson (2006) suggests a 'two-track' diffusion model, in which both mechanisms work simultaneously on different domestic groups of actors within the same issue area. Jacoby (2004) suggests the concept of 'embedded rationalism' as a synthesis between the various strands of institutionalist theory.

Still, most studies find that rationalist institutionalism best explains the broad patterns of compliance with EU demands by non-member states. To be sure, there is a number of cases in which the EU's influence cannot be explained adequately without attention to persuasion or socialization. Such cases include the adoption of EU policies without, or prior to, EU adjustment pressures (see e.g. Andonova, 2005; Epstein, 2008) or the internalization of certain EU rules by actors in the candidate countries even if the policies were initially adopted instrumentally (Grabbe, 2006). In other cases, the inclusion of mediating factors emphasized in constructivist approaches – in particular the 'cultural match' or positive domestic resonance of EU rules – can provide complementary, but more convincing, explanations of the domestic processes leading to the adoption of EU rules and the particular choices of rules within the scope of the EU's conditionality (see e.g. Schwellnus, 2005).

However, there is a large consensus in the literature that generally the EU's influence on non-members depended on governments' cost–benefit calculations in response to the incentives provided by the EU. Moreover, there is also a fairly large consensus on which particular factors emphasized by rationalist institutionalism are most important for such cost–benefit calculations and hence for the effectiveness of conditionality.

The key factor is *domestic costs* for governments. The EU made political requirements – such as democracy and respect for human rights – a necessary (but not sufficient) condition for its rewards. Since for authoritarian and nationalist governments the political adjustment costs could be prohibitively high, the EU's influence has crucially depended on the regime type and party political constellations in the non-member states (see e.g. Kelley, 2004; Schimmelfennig, 2005; Schimmelfennig and Sedelmeier, 2005; Vachudova, 2005; Schimmelfennig *et al.*, 2006).

However, in countries even where the domestic costs of complying with the EU's political conditions have not been prohibitively high, the EU's influence on public policy has generally been very strong. In such cases, even high adjustment costs in specific policy areas have not inhibited EU influence. In such cases, the key factor was then the *credibility* of the membership perspective, as governments discounted the adjustment cost in particular sectors against the overall benefits of membership. How did the EU increase the credibility of its rewards? Generally, the literature agrees that key elements are a consistent and meritocratic application of conditionality (i.e. that the EU *always* rewards compliance and *only* rewards compliance), along with clear and consensual messages from EU actors about what target states need to do in order to obtain the reward (Hughes *et al.*, 2004; Schimmelfennig and Sedelmeier, 2005; Vachudova, 2005; Grabbe, 2006).

For candidate countries, the main act that made the membership perspective credible was the opening of accession negotiations, which generally prompted the most far-reaching influence of the EU on public policies in the non-members. Of course membership is not the only reward that the EU offers. The EU also devised intermediate benefits as rewards for meeting certain conditions, such as preferential trade agreements and financial assistance, or policy-specific benefits such as the lifting of visa requirements.

However, the general finding in the literature of a high explanatory power of a rationalist institutionalist focus on credible incentives and adjustment costs does not mean that conditionality is always effective. While a credible membership incentive accorded the EU a generally strong influence on public policies in candidates, in specific issue-areas its impact was more limited by uncertainty and credibility problems of conditionality (see e.g. Grabbe, 2006). For example, credibility suffers if demands from the Commission and member states are inconsistent – either because some parts of the Commission initially promoted a more maximalist agenda of regionalization that is not part of the EU's *acquis* in regional policy (see e.g. Hughes *et al.*, 2004), or because some actors in the Commission informally indicated leniency in specific areas such as those of social policy (Sissenich, 2007).

In sum, the state of the art suggest that the functional reach of the EU depends on the incentives that the EU can offer. Generally, its most sizeable reward is membership; and this generally accounts for the strong influence of the EU if this incentive is credible. However, a precondition is that the EU's political conditions do not impose prohibitively high domestic adjustment costs on incumbent governments. Of course a key question is then whether the EU is powerless in such cases. Much of the literature suggests that in such cases, the EU has to hope for domestically driven electoral turnover that brings a new government into power for which the EU's political conditions do not impose prohibitive costs (see e.g. Schimmelfennig *et al.*, 2006). By contrast, Vachudova (2005) suggests that the EU has influenced domestic politics, leading to 'watershed elections', albeit indirectly: the EU empowered liberal reformers by informing electorates about the implication of their choices for the country's accession prospects and facilitating cooperation and moderation of opposition forces that helped them win power. However, the evidence for the EU being the decisive factor in such election victories often proves unconvincing in detailed studies (e.g. Haughton, 2007).

Summary

The study of both EU enlargement and EU conditionality is generally set within the debate between rationalist institutionalism and constructivist/sociological institutionalism, which identifies partly competing, partly complementary, factors that determine the EU's geographical and functional reach. With regard to the EU's geographic shape, rationalism suggests that the EU will continue to grow as long as the accession of a given country brings net benefits to both incumbents and potential members (including side-payments to shift costs), while constructivism emphasizes the importance of mutual positive identification. With regard to the EU's functional shape, rationalism suggests that the EU will obtain compliance with its rules to the extent that the rewards it offers exceed the adjustment costs for target governments, while constructivism emphasizes a target country's positive identification with the EU and the perceived legitimacy of the rules that the EU promotes and their resonance with domestic political culture.

Future research challenges on enlargement: how far and how fast will the EU's geographical shape change?

The EU's current enlargement agenda

The future research challenges and agenda on the shape of the Union relate to both the future development of its enlargement and its external governance. With regard to its geographical shape, the challenge is to gain a better understanding of how far and how fast it will continue to enlarge.

Certainly the EU is unlikely to undertake another 'big bang enlargement' on the scale of the 2004 accession of ten countries, which was in any case unprecedented in the history of the Union. Previously, the EU had taken in countries in twos and threes, and from 2007 onwards, enlargement is likely to revert to that pace, both because of caution about overstretch within the Union, and also because of the scale of the challenge for the countries of south-eastern Europe to meet the membership conditions.

The EU's current enlargement agenda comprises the countries of the western Balkans (the former Yugoslavia – apart from Slovenia, which joined in 2004 – plus Albania) Iceland and Turkey. Croatia and Iceland may well finish accession negotiations in 2011 and gain membership a couple of years or so afterwards, but the other countries will move slowly towards membership. The Balkan countries are likely to be ready for membership on different dates, even though it would be politically expedient for the EU to accept them all together, in order to promote regional cooperation and avoid bilateral disputes between new members and their neighbours. However, only Serbia has sufficient institutional capacity to move fast through the preparations to take on the obligations for membership, and that country's progress is still affected by the political aftershocks of the secession of Kosovo in February 2008 and continued difficulties in cooperation with the International Criminal Tribunal for the Former Yugoslavia. There is therefore no country of the western Balkans which looks likely to join the Union soon after Croatia, and some may take many years – particularly Kosovo.

Meanwhile, Turkey cannot join before 2014 at the earliest owing to the conclusions of the December 2004 European Council, which stated that Turkey could only come in after the current budgetary period is completed. But in any case, the controversy about the accession of Turkey in both the EU and the country itself has already slowed the pace of accession negotiations since they opened in 2005. Turkey's much larger size and its poor regions also make it harder to speed up the process.

The EU strengthened its relationship with the European successor states of the Soviet Union through the 'Eastern Partnership' endorsed by the European Council in December 2008, but it has not offered a clear membership perspective. Following the 2004 Orange Revolution in Ukraine and the Rose Revolution in Georgia, both countries hoped for membership of NATO and a clearer EU membership perspective. Although both goals became even more salient after the conflict between Georgia and Russia in summer 2008, neither has been forthcoming (in the case of NATO, despite strong US support). Still, the EU has made it clear that the door is not shut forever.

The economic and financial crisis that developed from 2008 had a double-edged impact on the prospect of future enlargement. On the one hand, the first major impact of the financial crisis on enlargement has been to reorientate the debate about enlargement from just being about south-eastern Europe, by resulting in Iceland applying for membership. The crisis all but destroyed the Icelandic economy and forced the country to seek massive external assistance. Joining the EMU appeared to Icelanders to be the best way to stabilize the situation and start the road to recovery. As the EU rapidly made it clear that EMU membership was impossible without EU membership, the overwhelming need for economic stabilization trumped the previous disincentives that prevented Iceland from applying – most notably the Common Fisheries Policy and the Common Agricultural Policy. The Icelandic government submitted its application in July 2009 after a narrow approval in parliament, with public opinion about EU membership divided. On the other hand, negative effects of the economic recession on enlargement are likely as the world economic slowdown starts to affect the real economies of the Balkans and Turkey. Economic troubles will make the accession process relatively more important in the enlargement countries, as EU membership offers a prospect of greater security in times of trouble. On the EU side, however, a deep and long recession is likely to make enlargement more unpopular, as public opinion turns against expansionist projects that bring risks and potential costs. EU policy-makers have cautioned Montenegro and Albania against submitting formal applications, not only because they do not yet meet the conditions for membership, but also because the economic and financial crisis would make an early start of accession negotiations unlikely (*Agence Europe*, 28 October 2008). Montenegro nonetheless submitted its application in December 2008 and Albania in April 2009, but these applications were initially blocked in the Council. In contrast to the Icelandic application, the member states failed for several months to reach a unanimous agreement to ask the Commission to prepare its opinion on the applications.

While in principle there is therefore still a long queue of potential applicants that are eligible for membership on the basis of Article 49 of the TEU, the pace of enlargement has slowed. Is this the end of enlargement or just a pause for digestion of the last enlargement? What predictions can we derive from the enlargement literature about the likelihood of future enlargements? To what extent do the current potential candidates pose new challenges for enlargement research? The literature suggests that enlargement will continue under the following conditions. First, there must be low net costs to incumbents; if a particular member state incurs costs, they must be neutralized through side-payments from members that expect benefits, or they must be externalized by shifting them to the new members. Second, if there are identity-related obstacles pertaining to candidates (and incumbents), these must not be so serious that they cannot be overcome by community norms. Will future enlargements be driven by the same dynamics? Will enlargement continue to expand the geographical shape of the Union, albeit more slowly than in the past? Or will the EU at some point reach a steady state?

Some of the dynamics determining the pace of the enlargement process identified by rationalist and constructivist approaches are likely to remain the same. However, a challenge for future enlargement research is that their interplay and the outcomes they produce might be very different. In the new political situation after the 2004/07 enlargement, calculations of the benefits of membership and the impact of identity politics appear to be rather more complex.

The future demand for accession

The continued strong demand for enlargement fits well with rationalist approaches, given the strong perceived benefits of membership. Most south-eastern and eastern European countries seek to join because the EU remains an attractive club. Even if many people living outside the current Union know little of the detailed demands that it makes of would-be members, such people make a rough cost–benefit calculation that the countries which belong are rich and stable, and benefit from generous redistribution towards the poorer members. A seat at the Council table gives small and medium-sized countries more say in world affairs through the EU's collective weight. And it is also beneficial in disputes with their neighbours, while those neighbours left outside have much less influence. The perception of the benefits from membership might change if the Union were to undergo a period of stagnation or 'eurosclerosis'; also, the perceived benefits might not lead to enlargement if the EU devises alternatives that would quench the thirst for membership – but currently neither appears likely.

Generally high potential welfare and security benefits notwithstanding, the calculation of the benefits of membership has become more complicated since the 2004/07 enlargement. The economic and regulatory requirements for joining are considerably higher, owing to the growth in EU policies and hence the size of the *acquis communautaire*. More importantly, the greater intensity of the EU's political conditionality front loads significant adjustment costs for potential applicants. In eastern enlargement, the benefits of membership appeared fairly straightforward: there were clear economic benefits (some costly adjustments notwithstanding) and the adjustment costs related to the EU's political conditionality were generally not too onerous. By contrast, in many of the current or future candidates, political conditionality imposes high costs, as standards of democracy and human rights are lower in these countries and the EU's demands directly affect questions of statehood and national identity.

The salience of costs arising from the political conditions that touch on questions of national identity is a key research challenge for future enlargements that underlines the importance of constructivist insights in domestic politics in potential members. Identity politics play a leading role in the western Balkans and Turkey. A new research challenge for constructivist approaches is that the kinds of identity issues involved are likely to be different from those in previous enlargements.

The fundamental constructivist hypothesis identified in the enlargement literature still holds: the more a country identifies with the EU and its constitutive rules, the more likely it is to seek membership; and the greater the normative match between the EU and a non-member, the more likely are the incumbents to endorse its accession. However, while in the eastern enlargement process questions of identity were generally a factor supporting enlargement in applicants, their impact is now much more complicated. In Central and Eastern Europe (CEE), mutual positive identification generally prevailed. There were some difficult identity issues during the negotiations – most notably minority rights questions such as Hungary's 'status law' for ethnic Hungarians living in surrounding countries and the treatment of Russian-speakers in Estonia and Latvia. Historical legacies also caused disputes, for example about restitution and the border between Slovenia and Italy, and the post-war refugees to Germany from the Czech Republic and Poland. Yet in general the goal of a 'return to Europe' through the EU accession of post-communist countries was not contested in either applicant countries or incumbents. There was much greater controversy about economic and regulatory costs than about identity issues.

This is not the case in south-eastern Europe, where identity politics are increasingly important. At the same time, the EU's normative agenda is becoming much more demanding, partly because of deficiencies in the applicant countries' democracies and respect for human rights, but also because the Union is gradually acquiring a larger and more specific set of values. Constitutive identity issues are therefore more controversial in both the enlargement countries and the existing member states. In the case of CEE, most countries easily met the EU's political conditions before starting negotiations. But the EU is much more attentive to the problems with meeting and keeping to the political conditions in the case of most Balkan countries and Turkey.

On the one hand, the EU stands for an identity which can serve as a rallying point for people trying to overcome painful national feelings resulting from recent conflict (e.g. in the Balkans) or to fulfil the historical orientation set at the foundation of the modern republic (in the case of Turkey). However, positive identification is often trumped by other identity issues in the Balkans – particularly by the issue of Kosovo in Serbia – and it is increasingly contested in Turkey. In many (potential) applicants, including the successor states of the Soviet Union, EU membership is not perceived simply as a long overdue 'return to Europe'; rather it is tied up with major questions about national identity. Whether the EU's normative agenda threatens national identity marks in some cases a major cleavage in domestic politics.

The supply side of enlargement

With regard to the EU's willingness to offer membership, some trends similar to earlier enlargements are evident: the EU still finds it difficult to say 'no' to countries which exhibit a clear will to comply with the EU's conditions and can claim to being European on some definition. Yet the Union has not opened any new membership perspectives since 2003, when the European Council at Thessaloniki gave a 'European perspective' (political code for openness to membership) to the countries of the western Balkans (Turkey gained candidate status in 1999). That offer was controversial at the time, and it resulted from a strong persuasion campaign by the 2003 Greek Presidency of the Union, whose foreign minister George Papandreou argued credibly that the future security and stability of the region depended on this offer. Even after the negative debates about enlargement following the 2004 and 2007 enlargements, this offer to the Balkans was never seriously questioned, because the EU could find no alternative policy for a region where ethnic conflict was still a real threat that would have immediate consequences for the member states.

Even with Turkey, the would-be member that has always provoked most controversy within the Union, the EU failed to develop a serious alternative to membership. There were several attempts: the EU invited Turkey to form a Customs Union in 1995 and to join 'European Conference' meetings in 1998 (which soon petered out). Both German Chancellor Angela Merkel and French President Nicolas Sarkozy argued strongly during their election campaigns for a 'privileged partnership' instead of membership – but neither managed to sell this idea to the Turks. In 2007, President Sarkozy also proposed a 'Mediterranean Union' that might have provided an alternative relationship with the Union in its original conception, but the resulting policy was merely an enhancement of the existing 'Barcelona Process' that creates closer relations with the countries of the southern and eastern Mediterranean. For as long as Turkey continues to express a strong will to join and to fulfil the EU's conditions, it will be difficult for reluctant member states to stop the accession process.

However, there are signs that some member-state governments are attempting to break the path-dependency of the accession process that in the past has proved very difficult to reverse. One sign is the debate triggered by some member states about redefining the meaning of 'accession negotiations' in the run-up to the start of negotiations with Turkey. It challenged the current understanding that the start of negotiations meant a mutual commitment to concluding them successfully, by suggesting that they might also lead to different outcomes, and by opening the possibility of permanent derogations (e.g. on free movement of labour) after accession. Another indication are the changes to the French constitution in 2005 and 2008 that will subject future enlargements to a referendum – unless both houses of parliament, meeting in Congress, approve an accession treaty with a 3/5 majority – which could conveniently take the decision out of the government's hand. At the same time, if the desire for membership fades in Turkey itself – either because signals from EU politicians destroy the credibility of the accession process or because of domestic factors – then the EU is unlikely to push Turkey into proceeding any further towards accession.

Meanwhile, Turkey's progress towards accession is making the impact of enlargement on the EU's own culture and identity a bigger issue than in previous enlargements. The prospect of Turkish accession highlights issues of cultural conflict and identity politics within the current member states – specifically the Turks already living in Germany, Belgium and other countries, but also more generally about minorities resident in nearly all member states and further immigration.

Ankara viewed with suspicion the EU's attempts during 2008 to forge a more attractive policy for both its southern and eastern neighbours through the Mediterranean Union and the Eastern Partnership respectively. The concerns were that either or both initiatives could be used as an alternative to accession for Turkey. No doubt this idea has currency in some political circles in the EU – most notably in Paris – but in practice it would be difficult for the EU to go back on its promises to Turkey made at the start of the accession negotiations. Moreover, Turkey already has a privileged partnership, in the form of its Customs Union and other links which give it a unique relationship with the Union, which makes it difficult to envisage how a 'privileged partnership' advocated by the opponents of Turkish accession could offer an attractive alternative.

What are the implications for future research of these changes in factors influencing the demand and supply of enlargement? In the last decades, the future shape of the EU was essentially determined in negotiations among the incumbents: the demand was very strong, and enlargement depended mainly on whether the incumbents agreed to it. In future enlargements it appears necessary to focus much more on domestic politics in (potential) candidate countries, as the demand side is far less certain. In these domestic debates, cleavages over questions of identity are likely to play a much more central role.

Questions of identity are much less likely than in earlier enlargements to facilitate enlargement also on the EU side. Within the Union, the current candidates are more easily perceived as having held themselves back through their own lack of determination to meet the EU's conditions, rather than being unfairly excluded by the Iron Curtain. The debate about Turkey is partly underpinned by unresolved conflicts among the incumbents about the constitutive elements of EU identity. A resulting question for future research is whether it will have to focus more on the cultural map of Europe – in terms of religion and language – than on political borders and adherence to political constitutive rules.

Future research on the EU's functional reach: the limits of external governance through conditionality

Credibility and strength of incentives

The more pronounced ambiguities about the demand for membership also have implications for the future of EU external governance because they make it harder for the EU to extend the functional reach of its rules. As the potential benefits from membership are more complicated to evaluate and more uncertain for current would-be members than it was for the countries joining in 2004/07, it has become harder to assess the future demand for enlargement. By the same token, as the benefits of EU membership have become more contested, EU accession conditionality has become weaker as a force in domestic politics in potential candidates.

The literature generally suggests that the key conditions for effective conditionality are evident net benefits from accession and a credible membership perspective. As it is harder for domestic actors to make a cost–benefit calculation about material rewards, so the goal is more contested in domestic politics, whereas there was often a consensus among the main political parties in Central Europe about the goal of membership. Moreover, the reward of accession seems further away and less than guaranteed – so overall, the process is less motivating as a domestic reform agenda.

The ambiguity about whether the benefits of membership outweigh the adjustment costs is not just a problem of incomplete information about when and whether a country might actually achieve membership as its final destination. The benefits during the journey of the accession process are also smaller. For the CEECs, the accession process reinforced a domestic political dynamic that developed its own momentum. By the time they gained the promise of membership, most of the countries had already embarked upon a major reform drive to open their economies and change the role of the state. The accession process gave a further impetus, but the tide was already moving in that direction. Moreover, the fact that some countries were already earning significant rewards from those reforms – such as higher economic growth, growing trade and inflows of foreign direct investment (FDI) – served as an incentive for the others also to follow the EU's advice. Moreover, the EU was itself willing to give some rewards earlier in the process, such as visa-free travel, than it has done for the Balkans and Turkey.

The economic situation is an important factor in the overall appetite for reform, and hence in perceptions of the costs and benefits of moving towards the EU in domestic politics. Having spent much of the 1990s preoccupied by the break-up of Yugoslavia and its aftermath, the Balkan countries missed the great post-communist reform drive and the FDI inflows stimulated both by reforms and high levels of global liquidity. Moreover, there is a considerable degree of 'Yugo-nostalgia' in the region because the relatively better performance of the Yugoslav economy before 1989 means that people do not feel that the liberal economic policies and regulatory convergence encouraged by the EU are the only way forward, as was often the case in CEE. Hence the EU's offers of access to its markets and technical assistance to reform economies do not have the same attractive power during the accession process. Moreover, inflows of FDI eased the pain of industrial restructuring – by providing alternative sources of employment when traditional industries closed down – in CEE, but these are much smaller per capita in the Balkans. Essentially, the virtuous circle between economic reforms, FDI inflows and accession prospects that worked so well in CEE (Bevan *et al.*, 2001) is not working in the Balkans.

Domestic adjustment costs are also higher because the Balkan countries are weak states. The public administrations of most countries are not able to move faster towards meeting the accession conditions, or even to take advantage of many of the interim rewards from the process, because of their lack of institutional capacity. The EU is therefore focusing much of its assistance on basic institution-building before accession negotiations can begin with more countries. Rationalist approaches will therefore need to focus much more on the capacity of countries to respond to the incentive structure – that is, their ability as well as strength of their will to do so.

Finally, rationalist approaches face the challenge of the EU's own conditionality dilemmas (see also Epstein and Sedelmeier, 2008). The EU has fewer conditionality levers at its disposal because the countries are further from membership. For example, the EU cannot really withdraw financial assistance where and when it is needed most – which is generally where countries have failed to meet the conditions. As regards other economic incentives, the EU cannot offer what the countries want most – access to agricultural markets and labour markets.

At the same time, the EU itself has a greater incentive to achieve other political goals in the Balkans long before accession. Interdependence – in the realm of security – is less asymmetrical, in the sense that not only the Balkan countries will suffer from insecurity in the region but the EU as well, e.g. through increased migration pressures, which makes it harder for the EU to withdraw its rewards if compliance is not forthcoming. The Union has also put additional conditions into the accession process for the former Yugoslav countries, in order to deal with the legacy of ethnic conflict: cooperation with the International Criminal Tribunal for the former Yugoslavia (ICTY) in The Hague, and regional cooperation. Cooperation with the ICTY became a key conditionality issue, trumping other concerns at some points in the process – for Croatia to begin accession negotiations in 2005, and for Serbia to negotiate and then implement its Stabilization and Association Agreement.

Finally for the countries involved in the ENP which might want to join the EU in the longer term, the incentive structure is even less conducive. The ENP explicitly excludes the EU's most powerful incentive – membership – even if some of the European countries (and in the Caucasus) might still perceive it as a long-term perspective. The adjustment costs are generally high, both with regard to political conditionality and regulatory alignment.

Identification and socialization

However, not only the factors that rationalists emphasize as necessary for the effectiveness of the EU's external governance are less conducive after the 2004/07 enlargements. The factors that constructivist approaches emphasize as conditions for external governance through socialization and persuasion are also generally more problematic. Positive identification is not only difficult in the Balkans – particularly in Serbia – but also increasingly in Turkey. Until the start of negotiations in 2005, the EU generally acted as a unifying force in Turkish politics, with people across the political spectrum identifying themselves as European as well as Turkish, and regarding membership as something that the EU should offer as a right, given Turkey's long-standing demand for closer integration, starting with the Association Agreement of 1963.

However, once negotiations began, the EU's democracy and human rights agenda became increasingly contested in Turkey because it interacted with the domestic debate about the principle of secularism and the role of religion in public life, and other key aspects of the Kemalist political philosophy on which the Turkish Republic had been founded in the 1920s. Parts of the EU agenda played into this debate – particularly the issues of freedom of expression, cultural rights for the Kurds and other minorities, and women's rights.

The EU has only a partial agenda for constitutive rules, and no clear answers to many of the most hotly contested issues in Turkey, such as the ban on headscarves for female university students. On this particular issue, the EU has not pronounced an opinion because there are no European standards on it. But the patchy nature of the EU's normative agenda – which is the result of historical compromises among its member states, which have not given the EU a role in many sensitive areas – can lead to the perception in Turkey that the EU's conditionality is selective, idiosyncratic and politically determined, rather than normatively consistent. It is precisely because these issues are so contested within the incumbent member states that the EU lacks a clear democracy and human rights *acquis* and tends to draw on other sources for its assessments of countries' progress (e.g. the European Court of Human Rights' case law, the Council of Europe, NGO reports). However, the Union's annual monitoring reports on developments in Turkey remained an important external reference point, so many Turks do not understand why the EU is interested in some normative issues in their country but not in others.

In 2007–08, the debate became dominated by these issues because of attempts by the military and then the judiciary to limit the powers of a government which had a large parliamentary majority. In this polarized political environment, the EU increasingly became a football in the debate about the future of the country, rather than a referee between the competing factions in the Turkish parliament and within the state institutions. The EU has changed from being a uniting force to become a point of division between the AK Party in government and the opposition. For constructivists, these developments offer a major research agenda for considering how identity politics and questions of legitimacy affect the EU's external governance in areas where the EU has only a partial formal agenda.

Future functional reach: alternatives to enlargement through flexible integration

After the 2004 enlargement, there were many calls from EU politicians for the Union to draw its final borders once and for all. But it proved hard for the EU to say no indefinitely, largely because it could not find alternatives to membership. This was impossible in the case of the Balkans – after all, the region had become an enclave in the midst of EU member states after 2007 – and very difficult for Turkey.

The only likely way the EU would be able to develop such alternatives would be through a major expansion in its functional differences – through differentiated integration or variable geometry. Essentially, if the Union were to develop major differences in the degree to which its members adhered to common policies, by expanding the number of opt-outs and special projects to which only some members belong, that might open the way to defining a second-class membership that included access to some but not all policies. Already, some member states have stayed outside major areas of integration, such as EMU (Denmark, Sweden and the UK by choice; while among the CEECs, so far only Slovenia and Slovakia have qualified since accession) and the Schengen area of passport-free travel (Ireland and the UK voluntarily, with Romania and Bulgaria still having to wait).

This kind of flexible integration has already opened possibilities for non-members to join EU policies which would previously have been closed to them. Most notably, Iceland Norway and Switzerland joined the Schengen area, meaning that their citizens can travel to most of the EU without passport controls – a significant benefit that involved EU members and non-members pooling sovereignty in the very sensitive policy of border security. Given that the EU is reaching the limits of its member states' ambitions in a number of policy areas, it is likely to develop further projects which only some members wish to join – and some where they may actively seek to exclude other member states. In addition to changing the functional shape of the Union, such a trend would open up more possibilities for non-members to join parts of the EU that they find attractive, even if they cannot or do not want to seek full membership. For example, might Ukraine or even Russia in future want to participate more fully in EU external policies, including foreign, defence and trade policies, as suggested by Grant (2006)? Might the Maghreb countries seek integration into the Schengen area under a deal that gives them an easier visa regime with the EU in return for EU control over their southern borders?

The ENP incorporates such ideas already. For example the EU's offer of 'a stake in the internal market' echoes the concept of the EEA that extended the single market to most EFTA states – without however addressing the question whether the adjustment costs for ENP partners make it an attractive option without the full benefits of membership. The Commission's communication on the 'Eastern Partnership' of December 2008 took these concepts further, offering substantially more to the EU's eastern neighbours on mobility of persons, or on gradual integration into the EU economy (through regulatory harmonization). Effectively, the Eastern Partnership offers these countries the same benefits and links with the EU as to candidate countries, but minus the promise of eventual membership. The question remains open whether without the political incentive of accession these offers are sufficiently attractive to overcome domestic disincentives.

Conclusion

In this chapter we have argued that the future shape of the Union is about its functioning as well as its territory. To some extent, this has always been the case, because attitudes towards enlargement are closely linked to the mental maps of Europeans about their continent. The Iron Curtain only fell in many people's minds in Western Europe after the 2004 accessions, and they are still adjusting to the last enlargement rather than preparing for the next one. Turkey creates a very different mental map that many Europeans find frightening, and which is linked to mental maps of their own societies.

How far and how fast will enlargement go in future? No big bang on the scale of 2004 is in prospect, as the Balkan countries are likely to be ready at different times, making it difficult to take them in as a group. But Turkey's accession would be a big bang in its own right because of its large and growing population. The EU's future territory is therefore likely to continue to change, but the timetable on which various countries might join is more ambiguous, a factor which itself diminishes the EU's capacity to influence the countries outside its current territory.

The EU's functional scope – and how well it functions – will be affected by enlargement, but it will also in turn affect the EU's own attractiveness as a destination. What shape of Union will the new countries join? Will greater differentiation make it easier for countries to become members, so that they can join bits of the European integration project at different times? How much diversity can the political project encompass? Will the Union remain sufficiently coherent to be attractive to join? If the EU becomes less popular among its existing population, will Euroscepticism also spread to would-be members? In researching these questions, both the rationalist and the constructivist approaches used to analyse previous enlargements are likely to be needed to explain outcomes, but the interplay between them is likely to change. Some of the concepts used in rationalist approaches – such as material incentive structures and conditionality – may have less power in future. Constructivist approaches will be important in taking account of the much greater significance of identity politics involved in enlargement to south-eastern Europe, both in the EU and the countries that seek to join.

Future empirical research will focus on new issues because the landscape in south-eastern Europe looks very different from that in previous enlargements, raising many new research questions and challenging hitherto dominant assumptions. The Balkan countries have weak states, less competitive economies and less FDI than did the Central Europeans, and lack a political consensus on giving priority to EU accession. Turkey's state and economy are much stronger, so it is much more capable of responding to the incentive structures of the accession process, but the country is riven by a passionate debate about secularism and the appropriate role of religion in public life, which distracts attention from the EU agenda.

The EU was able to provide answers to many of the major political questions facing the CEECs – economic transition and corresponding legal frameworks – but it has no ready-made solutions to the most urgent and emotive questions posed by south-eastern Europe – identity, culture, religion and ethnic conflict. This is a major change. In CEE, the influence of the EU was mostly perceived as benign, uniting political forces and galvanizing reformers. The incentive structure of the accession process could be used to speed the tide, whereas in south-eastern Europe, the EU is sometimes fighting the tide. In domestic debates about identity questions – which are more urgent and passionate than they were in Central Europe – the EU often becomes a political football.

Future research will therefore face the challenge of disentangling a more complex set of factors to determine the role of the EU in shaping these countries' development – both for rationalist and constructivist approaches. However, it also opens up new research agendas, particularly in identity politics and ethnic conflict. Moreover, new researchers from the enlargement countries will join the scene. Already, a large academic community in Turkey is starting to research the EU and the enlargement process. The Turkish academic community will bring new questions and a different perspective on the Union, strongly influenced by the domestic debate about the future of their country. That will itself enlarge the scope of research about enlargement.

References

Andonova, L.B. (2005) 'The Europeanization of Environmental Policy in Central and Eastern Europe', in F. Schimmelfennig and U. Sedelmeier (eds) *The Europeanization of Central and Eastern Europe* (Ithaca, NY: Cornell University Press) 135–55.

Bevan, A., Estrin, S. and Grabbe, H. (2001) 'The impact of EU accession prospects on FDI inflows to central and eastern Europe', ESRC 'One Europe or Several?' Programme Policy Paper 06/01, Sussex European Institute.

Dimitrova, A. and B. Steunenberg (2004) 'The End of History of Enlargement or the Beginning of a New Research Agenda', in A. Dimitrova (ed.) *Driven to Change: The European Union's Enlargement Viewed from the East* (Manchester: Manchester University Press).

Epstein, R.A. (2008) *In Pursuit of Liberalism: International Institutions in Postcommunist Europe* (Baltimore: Johns Hopkins University Press).

Epstein, R.A. and Sedelmeier, U. (2008) 'Beyond Conditionality: International Institutions in Postcommunist Europe after Enlargement', *Journal of European Public Policy* 15(6): 880–98.

Fierke, K. and A. Wiener (1999) 'Constructing Institutional Interests: EU and NATO Enlargement', *Journal of European Public Policy* 6(5): 721–42.

Goetz, K.H. (2005) 'The New Member States and the EU: Responding to Europe', in S. Bulmer and C. Lequesne (eds) *The Member States of the European Union* (Oxford: Oxford University Press).

Grabbe, H. (2006) *The EU's Transformative Power: Europeanization through Conditionality in Central and Eastern Europe* (Basingstoke: Palgrave Macmillan).

Grant, C. (2006) *Europe's Blurred Boundaries: Rethinking Enlargement and Neighbourhood Policy* (London: Centre for European Reform).

Gstoehl, S. (2002) 'Scandinavia and Switzerland: Small, Successful and Stubborn Towards the EU', *Journal of European Public Policy* 9(4): 529–49.

Haughton, T. (2007) 'When Does the EU Make a Difference? Conditionality and the Accession Process in Central and Eastern Europe', *Political Studies Review* 5(2): 233–46.

Hughes, J., G. Sasse and C. Gordon (2004) *Europeanization and Regionalization in the EU's Enlargement to Central and Eastern Europe: The Myth of Conditionality* (Basingstoke: Palgrave Macmillan).

Jacoby, W. (2004) *The Enlargement of the European Union and NATO. Ordering from the Menu in Central Europe* (Cambridge: Cambridge University Press).

Johnson, J. (2006) 'Two-Track Diffusion and Central Bank Embeddedness: The Politics of Euro Adoption in Hungary and the Czech Republic', *Review of International Political Economy* 13(3): 361–86.

Kelley, J.G. (2004) *Ethnic Politics in Europe. The Power of Norms and Incentives* (Princeton: Princeton University Press).

Kubicek, P. (2003) 'International Norms, the European Union, and Democratization: Tentative Theory and Evidence' in P. Kubicek (ed.) *The European Union and Democratization* London: Routledge: 1–29.

Lavenex, S. (2004) 'EU External Governance in "Wider Europe"', *Journal of European Public Policy* 11(4): 688–708.

Schimmelfennig, F. (2003) *The EU, NATO and the Integration of Europe: Rules and Rhetoric* (Cambridge: Cambridge University Press).

Schimmelfennig, F. (2005) 'Strategic Calculation and International Socialization: Membership Incentives, Party Constellations, and Sustained Compliance in Central and Eastern Europe', *International Organization* 59(4): 827–60.

Schimmelfennig, F., Engert, S. and Knobel, H. (2006) *International Socialization in Europe: European Organizations, Political Conditionality and Democratic Change* (Basingstoke: Palgrave Macmillan).

Schimmelfennig, F. and Sedelmeier, U. (2002) 'Theorizing EU Enlargement: Research Focus, Hypotheses, and the State of Research', *Journal of European Public Policy* 9(4): 500–28.

Schimmelfennig, F. and Sedelmeier, U. (2005) 'Conclusions: The Impact of the EU on the Accession Countries', in F. Schimmelfennig and U. Sedelmeier (eds) *The Europeanization of Central and Eastern Europe* (Ithaca, NY: Cornell University Press) 210–28.

Schwellnus, G. (2005) 'The Adoption of Nondiscrimination and Minority Protection Rules in Romania, Hungary, and Poland', in F. Schimmelfennig and U. Sedelmeier (eds) *The Europeanization of Central and Eastern Europe* (Ithaca, NY: Cornell University Press) 51–70.

Sedelmeier, U. (2005) *Constructing the Path to Eastern Enlargement: The Uneven Policy Impact of EU Identity* (Manchester: Manchester University Press).

Sedelmeier, U. (2006) 'Europeanisation in New Member and Applicant States', *Living Reviews in European Governance* (http://www.livingreviews.org/lreg-2006-3).

Sissenich, B. (2007) *Building States without Society: European Union Enlargement and the Transfer of EU Social Policy to Poland and Hungary* (Lanham: Lexington Books).

Sjursen, H. (2002) 'Why Expand? The Question of Legitimacy and Justification in the EU's Enlargement Policy', *Journal of Common Market Studies* 40(3): 491–513.

Smith, M. (1996) 'The European Union and a Changing Europe: Establishing the Boundaries of Order', *Journal of Common Market Studies* 34(1): 5–28.

Vachudova, M.A. (2005) *Europe Undivided: Democracy, Leverage and Integration after Communism* (Oxford: Oxford University Press).

Young, A.R. (2007), 'Trade Politics Ain't What it Used to Be', *Journal of Common Market Studies* 45(4): 789–811.

Chapter 17

Hastening Slowly: European Union Studies – Between Reinvention and Continuing Fragmentation

William E. Paterson, Neill Nugent and Michelle Egan

Bulletins issued on the health of European integration and EU studies have often taken a pessimistic view. For example, Karl Deutsch in the 1960s argued that the integration process had reached a plateau (Deutsch *et al.*, 1967), Ernst Haas in the 1970s wrote of the 'obsolescence' of European integration (Haas, 1975) and John Mearsheimer at the beginning of the 1990s – approaching the subject from a realist perspective – saw integration as a contingent phenomenon that would fade away with the end of the Cold War (Mearsheimer, 1990). All of these intimations of mortality have proved decidedly premature. Since the mid-1980s in particular European integration has advanced rapidly, with the EU deepening and widening at pace, and with a long queue of would-be entrants at its door – despite steeply declining chances of accession.

Paralleling the growing importance of the EU there has been a huge expansion in the number of those studying it and writing about it: an expansion that was tracked in an article by John Keeler (2005). This expansion has hopefully been conveyed in the chapters of this book. There just can be no doubt about the current, almost overwhelming, popularity of EU studies. However, as in any academic field, issues remain about the quality of some of the work being undertaken, its boundaries with cognate fields and its future trajectory.

The strengths of work in EU studies are very visible. In political science, for example – the discipline approach on which this chapter is largely based – the early years of academic work centred mainly on the key institutions, but in recent decades there has been a 'theoretical turn' and more recently a 'policy turn' and a 'governance turn', resulting in a huge and varied volume of research and theorizing, much of it of very high quality.

But if volume and diversity of research are key strengths, they also bring with them the dangers of drift and of an absence of cumulative studies that will shape and reinforce a coherent body of knowledge and methodologies. Approaches can, of course, become too converging and too exclusively based on one paradigm. The example of economics in recent decades demonstrates vividly what happens when a particular and arguably too narrow approach becomes over-dominant and the discipline suffers a loss in explanatory power and a reduced capacity to connect with real world events and processes. There has been no such narrow focus within EU studies.

Disciplinary and interdisciplinary study of the EU

There has been a considerable debate within EU studies concerning where the balance should be struck between basing the analysis of European integration on discipline-based approaches and interdisciplinary-based approaches. By its nature, as an economic and political organization with appreciable legal powers, the EU has attracted economists, political scientists, legal scholars, historians and more recently sociologists. For the most part, these scholars have preferred to stick to familiar, discipline-specific modes of explanation which confer rewards and esteem in their chosen area. This is perhaps especially the case in economics, where the incentives for straying beyond the dominant paradigms remain strikingly negative. In other disciplines the picture is more mixed. Legal approaches, for example, remained largely and uncompromisingly legally based for a long period. Things began to change when, as Anthony Arnull has shown in Chapter 8, a number of American legal scholars brought a much greater openness to interdisciplinary approaches, and since then a great deal of interdisciplinary work, including on the EU, has been undertaken, though concerns are expressed that this might dilute doctrinal work.

The picture in historical studies is not dissimilar. As in the nineteenth century with national histories, some of the early histories of the European integration process had a markedly devotional character that was designed to harness a legitimating narrative in the service of the new construction. Even in some later histories there has been a tendency to measure the success or failure of policies in terms of their contribution to the integration process rather than in pure policy terms. However, as documents have become available historians have understandably concentrated increasingly on mining the archives rather than looking for more generalized explanations, with Alan Milward constituting a magnificent exception (Milward, 1992). Historians are now more ready to embrace interdisciplinarity (Kaiser, 2008), but for the most part they remain predominantly disciplinary-based. This can be a weakness that results in the missing of lots of interconnections. For example, one area among a number where the political science literature would help is in the study of the increasing institutionalization of interactions between member states, especially major states which, as N. Piers Ludlow has shown in Chapter 2, remains an underdeveloped area for historians.

Political scientists have been both the most numerous and the most visible in the EU scholarly community. In the early years political scientists were perhaps less monodisciplinary than the others. Political science at that time was a rather eclectic discipline whose practice did not demand mastery of the exclusive techniques which characterized the professional activities of economists, historians and legal scholars. As, however, political science has grown in strength and theoretical sophistication then so have pressures to 'mainstream' EU studies in political science explanations like rational choice theory grown exponentially, resulting in interest in interdisciplinarity coming under pressure. Two particular explanations account for this phenomenon. First, whereas in legal studies the US influence encouraged interdisciplinarity, in political science, as was earlier the case with economics, a partial Americanization has been overwhelmingly in the direction of 'mainstreaming'. Second, the increased importance of the EU has encouraged many mainstream political scientists to take an interest in it and, as they have done so, they have imported the toolkits with which they are familiar rather than a bespoke interdisciplinary version. Two such examples of outstanding mainline political scientists who have 'travelled' to EU studies and come to impart extensive influence on it are Fritz Scharpf and Guy Peters. This does not, of course, entirely mean that concepts and theories are not borrowed from other disciplines, but that they enter more through the medium of their adoption into mainline political science. For example, the influence of economic models on contemporary political science is very apparent, and this has been mediated into EU studies.

The overall picture on interdisciplinarity in EU studies is a complex one. It is certainly much more prevalent in legal studies than in the past, almost non-existent in economic studies, and growing from a very low base in history. Among political scientists, the attractions of mainstreaming into political science/international relations mainline explanations have proved pervasive. Political science itself continues to be interdisciplinary with a huge growth in subdisciplines such as political economy.

We are thus confronted with something of a paradox. There has, on the one hand, been a huge growth in the EU scholarly community, with many disciplines involved (though with political scientists constituting the dominant group). But, on the other hand, there are few pressures to adopt interdisciplinary modes of studying the EU. In consequence, a relatively weak convergence around dominant paradigms contrasts with a huge amount of activity.

Many academics – Alex Warleigh-Lack and David Phinnemore (2009) among them – have made the case for a more interdisciplinary approach, but, whatever the intellectual merits of this view, it is very unlikely to happen. Academics are organized in subject departments, which means that hiring, tenure and promotion will continue to be dominated by subject-specific imperatives and act as a brake on the development of an interdisciplinary EU specific approach. Within the United Kingdom, the attempt to create a rival pole through the creation of European studies departments and academic courses has had some success in terms of creating interdisciplinary curricula but not in terms of creating a distinctive interdisciplinary research agenda. And, in any event, an innovation confined to one country is no match in firepower with disciplines that are organized globally and where the United States academic community often acts as motor and exemplar. It is possible, however, that some of the EU's own research programmes that bring together transnational groups of scholars from different disciplines will produce distinctive results on issues like boundaries.

As matters stand, there is thus the ironic situation that at a point when there has been a spectacular growth in the EU studies community, the distinctive identity in theoretical terms of the subject is less pronounced than in some earlier periods. Shape has been traded off against reach.

Theoretical reflections

The neofunctional/intergovernmental inheritance

For many years – until well into the 1980s – there was a grand divide in integration theory between neofunctionalism and intergovernmentalism. The positions of the two 'sides' reflected differing views on whether integration is a self-reinforcing and transformative process that escapes to some degree the control of the member states, or, as intergovernmentalists view integration, a process that remains firmly under the control of the states (see Frank Schimmelfennig in Chapter 3). Over the years both neofunctionalism and intergovernmentalism have been developed, and in many respects have become more sophisticated. As part of this development neofunctionalism has been recalibrated into supranationalism (Sandholtz and Stone Sweet, 1998) and intergovernmentalism has been upgraded into liberal intergovernmentalism (Moravcsik, 1993, 1998). Many scholars have contributed to the debate on the respective merits of the two theories, either directly or less directly by bringing out empirical features of the development of the integration process and the operation of the EU. Johanna Kantola in Chapter 13 illustrates the latter sort of contribution, for in her chapter she shows how lack of legal clarity in the area of gender matters has resulted in extensive recourse to the supranational ECJ, which has been enormously significant in the move towards a policy of gender mainstreaming.

But, in recent years some of the heat has gone out of the supranational–intergovernmental debate, with intergovernmentalists concentrating primarily on 'grand decisions' taken by the decidedly intergovernmental European Council and supranationalists focusing more on the incremental creep of day-to-day decisions through processes in which the supranational Commission and the ECJ usually loom large. Significantly, intergovernmentalists downplay, and indeed often virtually ignore, the roles of the latter two institutions. The general relationship between the two theoretical approaches has thus increasingly become more one of division of labour than one of overlap and convergence. Derek Beach, in Chapter 5, is something of an exception to this division in that he draws out the contribution of supranational institutions to grand decisions.

The increased interest in integration theory

In contrast to the early years, which, as has just been shown, were framed by neofunctionalist and intergovernmentalist explanations, the dominant picture now is one of theoretical pluralism. Indeed, perhaps the most striking feature of EU studies in recent years has been the explosion of theoretical work, sometimes combined with empirical enquiry, but quite often framed in terms of contributions to the various debates that have swept through the field. This movement to a much stronger theoretical concentration has been fuelled both by 'real world' developments and by debates within neighbouring and relevant disciplines. As regards real world developments, these have, of course, long been key shapers of theoretical thinking. So, neofunctionalism suffered a heavy blow as a result of de Gaulle's stance in the 1965 crisis, but has, in its amended form of supranationalism, been boosted in recent years as the integration process has advanced at pace. Unsurprisingly, de Gaulle's policy led to an early version of intergovernmentalism (Hoffmann, 1966) and then, 20 and more years later, liberal intergovernmentalism was a reflection of the key roles exercised by member state governments in the making of such 'history making' decisions as the SEM programme, the SEA and EMU. More recently, the proliferation of EU policy responsibilities, the mushrooming of EU policy processes, and the scale of enlargements have been prominent amongst the real world events that have had further redefining effects on theoretical explanation, as Frank Schimmelfennig has shown in Chapter 3.

As regards the fuel stemming from debates within neighbouring and relevant disciplines, perhaps the two major intellectual influences of recent years that can be traced directly to developments in cognate fields have been the constructivist turn in international relations theory and the new institutionalism in comparative politics, both of which have transferred very easily into European integration studies and both of which have had a massive influence on European integration theoretical work. Indeed, they have played such a significant part in EU studies that they have gradually become not just importers but also exporters of theoretical thinking, as is witnessed most notably by the 'mainstreaming' of EU studies into comparative politics and international relations (Bulmer, 2009a).

A key attraction of constructivism for EU scholars has lain in its non-realist explanations and its emphasis on socialization and 'soft power'. An especially influential and much-debated application of constructivism in EU studies is the notion of the EU as a normative power that is identified particularly with Ian Manners (2002). The normative power view has spawned a veritable industry, but it is now beginning also to attract significant critiques (Hyde-Price, 2006). In this context it is difficult not to share to some degree Karen Smith's impatience, as expressed in Chapter 14: 'we should turn our attention to analysing what kind of power the EU wields and with what effect, rather than debating what kind of power the EU is. Debates about whether the EU is or is not a civilian power, a normative power, a superpower and so on are not really leading us anywhere right now ... We should instead engage in a debate about what the EU does, why it does it, and with what effect rather than about what it is.'

Concerning the attractions of new institutionalism, this has offered two clear insights: that institutions matter and how they function matters. Institutions are understood in a more encompassing manner than in the traditional sense: as rules, norms and – for some analysts – cultural constructs (Bulmer, 2009a: 118). New institutionalism is perhaps best exemplified by the work of Bulmer (1994), Pierson (1996) and Pollack (2003).

Prospects for integration theory

In the EU there have been three big 'real world' events and processes in the last two decades: the creation of EMU, the grand enlargement of 2004/07 and the moves towards a European Constitutional Treaty. The rejection of the latter by the French and Dutch people in referenda in 2005 has consigned the Constitutional Treaty to the category of unfinished business and, for the present at least, seems to have cut off any immediate theory generation. It is, of course, possible that on a slightly longer-time perspective it will generate further innovation analogous to the rise of intergovernmentalism following the empty chair crisis of 1965. In the run-up to EMU there was a great deal of work on Optimal Currency Unions, as discussed by Waltraud Schelkle in Chapter 11, but more recently attention has shifted towards economic policy coordination in response to the financial turmoil. The seeming need for such greater cooperation, coupled with the strains the eurozone

404   *Hastening Slowly*

has increasingly experienced and the possibility of further dramatic developments, are likely to give rise to a second wave of theorizing about EMU. Enlargement, by contrast, has already given rise to significant work, in both the constructivist and rationalist/institutional traditions, as detailed by Frank Schimmelfennig in Chapter 3 and Heather Grabbe and Ulrich Sedelmeier in Chapter 16. The onset of the recession and enlargement fatigue have undermined the willingness of the EU to continue to provide the very generous selective incentives which are assumed by rationalist explanations of enlargement, so explanations of future enlargements are likely, as Grabbe and Sedelmeier argue, to lean less heavily on rationalist explanations and to favour more weight being given to identity issues.

Schimmelfennig assumes in his chapter that integration theory is likely to be becalmed for some time. One reason for being tempted to agree with him is that there seem to be few new debates coming through from comparative politics or international relations that would push theoretical innovation in European integration studies for the foreseeable future. Another reason is that real world events may look, initially at least, to offer little in the way of theoretical stimuli with, for example, further enlargements likely to be small scale in nature (at least until Turkey joins) and with a relatively stable constitutional/treaty settlement having been reached.

However, there are at least three reasons for thinking that real world events may in fact lead to theoretical advances. First, there is the world recession – a very large real world event with huge implications for the EU, which hitherto has essentially been a fair weather construction. It might be expected that the recession will provide a very robust testing-bed for all the current theoretical explanations, which were framed to provide an explanation for integration in very beneficent conditions. It is perhaps time to dig out the old references to 'spillback' (Lindberg and Scheingold, 1970). Further to this, it is difficult not to envisage that the changing market–state balance which is emerging in the crisis will not fundamentally challenge conventional theories of integration, perhaps by providing more space for 'critical Marxist' theories. If this were to be the case, it would be another example of the cyclical character of much of EU theorizing, since the most extended previous essay in this tradition was written by Peter Cocks in the downturn of the early 1980s (Cocks, 1980). Second, it is difficult to believe that the collision between continuing globalization and the welling-up of new protectionist impulses will not feed back into revisions of European integration theory. Third, all European integration accounts centre around a view of the state, although they differ as to what it is and whether integration is about strengthening the state or gradually replacing it. A key question is: will there be, and indeed is there not already, a move to replace the 'hollowing out' of the state by 'infilling'?

In a very incisive summation of current deficiencies in integration theory, Frank Schimmelfennig in Chapter 3 identifies a number of current blind spots, including an overconcentration on the first pillar, on formal institutional change, and on the elite level. Many other scholars would share Schimmelfennig's views on blind spots, especially perhaps in respect of the suggestion that although policy areas outside the first pillar have been subject to a plethora of empirical studies they have been undertheorized. So, regarding JHA, which is almost the 'new frontier' of European integration, Bulmer has encouraged scholars to 'get out more' and to connect with wider theorizing about the EU rather than remaining in a JHA ghetto (Bulmer, 2009b). Christina Boswell, a JHA specialist, takes a similar position to Bulmer, pointing out in Chapter 12 that, although very significant research has been undertaken on JHA, more needs to be done to connect it to wider theorizing on the EU. Regarding the CFSP/ESDP pillar of the EU, research on it has been undertaken over a longer period than on JHA (Smith, 2008), but despite some justifiably famous theoretically based contributions – such as Christopher Hill's identification of a 'capability–expectations gap' (Hill, 1993) – it also remains an undertheorized policy area. In Chapter 14, Karen Smith provides an extensive and persuasive list of where further theoretical work is needed on the second pillar.

Frank Schimmelfennig singles out two recent contributions as opening up interesting new theoretical vistas. The first is by Stefano Bartolini (2005) who, writing in the Hirschmann/Rokkan tradition, envisages European integration as the formation of a new centre which transforms the boundaries of the nation state and opens up the possibility of new exit options with corresponding effects on actor strategies and, more widely, on the sustainability of the welfare state and European integration. The second contribution is in an ambitious 'post functionalist' piece by Lisbet Hooghe and Gary Marks (2009) that links public opinion, party competition and European integration to transcend the elite bias of integration theory. This approach stipulates the conditions under which, as Schimmelfennig puts it, 'the politics of integration follows the distributional logic assumed by intergovernmentalism and neofuntionalism and when it follows the identity logic postulated by constructivism' (p. 53, this volume). Hooghe and Marks thus illustrate, amongst other things, how the identity logic has loomed large since the late 1990s.

In recent years, the increasing unlikelihood that the EU will ever develop a state character, combined with the huge increase in the EU's policy scope – but in a manner in which participation by member states is not universal in all policies and where there is now a lack of overlap between geographical and functional boundaries – has been accompanied by attempts to capture this impressive but incomplete and somewhat fuzzy power. A notable example of this is Zielonka's notion of neo-medievalism (Zielonka, 2005). Related to this, several scholars (including Schimmelfennig, Leuffen and Rittberger in a forth-coming book) are now undertaking work that, in the cyclical tradition of EU studies, builds on the concept of 'differentiated integration', originally conceived by Eberhard Grabitz (1984) and then taken up by Alexander Stubb (1996) to provide a more systematic characterization of an integration process which no longer assumes the same intensity of participation by all members in all policy areas. The challenge is to move from mapping to providing an explanation of the EU's consider-able, and growing, variation, both within and across pillars, and also in respect of the participation of many non-member states in certain EU policies and programmes. It is a research challenge that is likely to attract increasing attention and effort, with continuing recession and future enlargements (especially if they include Turkey) likely to strengthen the differentiated character of integration. The Lisbon Treaty, which was a lowest common denominator of the reform aspirations of member states, is also likely to lead to further differentiation. So too may the election in the UK of a Eurosceptic and market-oriented future Conservative government, with some limited support from elsewhere in the EU, taking a market oriented and partly unilateralist approach route to economic policy whilst other governments take a more inter-ventionist and multilateralist approach.

For much of its history, European integration studies has been bedev-illed by the small *n* problem. The assertion of its unique *sui generis* character has seemed to foreclose any prospect of comparison and has thereby reduced its analytical interest, especially for those beyond the community of EU specialists. The move towards viewing the EU as a normal political system (Hix, 1994, 2005) greatly increases the com-parative leverage, as does the recent revival of interest in comparative regionalism (see Warleigh-Lack, 2006; Sbragia, 2008).

The example of comparative regionalism, an early interest of integra-tion theorists, should help to guard against a facile linear view where the 'delete' rather than the 'save' button is pressed on explanations that do not appear 'to fit' (Rosamond, 2006). For, as was noted above, there has been something of a cyclical character in theoretically based explanations in European integration studies. The recent archiving of all issues of the *Journal of Common Market Studies* back to its incep-tion in 1962 now provides a unique opportunity for examining this cyclical character.

Informal processes and the governance turn

In the first decades of EU studies much of the emphasis was on the explanation of formal processes and institutions, though neofunction-alism did attempt to encompass wider aspects of societal reach through the notion of *engrenage*. But even this concept remained centred at the Brussels level, with domestic institutions being conceptualized as available for capture rather than as vibrant elements in a more reciprocal governance structure. It was only in the 1990s, through the so-called 'governance turn', that a set of explanations combining both formal and informal processes emerged that did justice to the EU's character as 'a unique set of multi-level, non hierarchical and regulatory institutions, and a hybrid mix of state and non state actors' (Hix, 1998: 39). It would be hard to improve on Simon Bulmer's account of the emergence of the governance turn (Bulmer, 2009a: 116–17), the wider academic background to which was the mainstreaming of EU studies into international relations and comparative politics and the acquisition of a much wider analytical toolkit. This toolkit equipped analysts to respond to changing domestic/international boundaries occasioned by globalization, by the move at the state level away from command to a more networked form of governance, and by the hollowing out of the state – from below by the emergence of new agencies and institutions and from above by the EU and encouragement from the Commission in its White Paper on European Governance (European Commission, 2001).

The governance approach is multifaceted, but there are perhaps two especially central elements. The first is a conception of the EU as an example of MLG. In its original formulation, MLG focussed on the way in which partnership between the Commission and the regions in managing the EU's Structural Funds was eroding the control of central state authorities and was resulting in 'the emergence of multilevel governance, a system of continuous negotiation among nested governments at several territorial tiers – supranational, national, regional and local' (Marks, 1993: 392; see also Marks *et al.*, 1996). This formulation is in marked contrast to the neofunctionalist Brussels-centred view, where substate actors are viewed as useful to the degree they are available for capture, whilst in the MLG they are part of a chain of negotiation. In response to criticisms, a distinction has since been made in MLG formulations between Type 1 and Type 2 MLG, with Type 1 being reserved for more enduring layers of governance and Type 2 for more functional and ad hoc arrangements (Hooghe and Marks, 2003). The MLG approach, while not without its critics (Jordan, 2001), has, unlike some other theoretical approaches which remain more or less empty boxes, generated a huge amount of very valuable empirical work.

Another central element of the governance turn is the regulatory approach, which is identified especially with Giandamenico Majone (1996). This approach emerges from the creation of the SEM and the establishment of EU regulatory agencies carrying responsibilities for policy execution in a range of areas. The characterization of the EU as a regulatory power became and has remained very widely accepted in the EU scholarly literature, giving rise to a great deal of empirical work.

Whilst the new governance turn, drawing as it has on theoretical advances in comparative politics and international relations, has, if anything, significantly strengthened the role of political science and international relations in explanations of the EU, the phenomena it has sought to capture have posed a challenge to the traditional and very influential and positivist approach to EU law. The new governance approach picks up on the development of 'soft law', the open method of coordination, the plethora of new agencies and the range of other developments which share the common feature of the outcomes not being the hard legislative measures (black letter) that lawyers are especially equipped to deal with. One response, identified with Deidre Curtin, is that lawyers have a particular role in 'designing accountability mechanisms that are tailored to fit contemporary realities' (Curtin, 2006: 37). A non-lawyer might also think there is still a huge place for the traditional role of lawyers, however valuable the insights from other disciplines might be in a wider analysis of the EU's courts and legal system.

The new governance approach and the mechanisms it analyses have been very productive and have even been extended and adapted to the field of security in the concept of security governance (Kirchner, 2006). But, attention is now shifting. As Guy Peters and Susana Borrás have stated in Chapter 6, 'this governance style was appropriate so long as the goals and policy areas involved in European Governance were economic competition policy, and reducing internal trade barriers ... As the tasks of the EU continue to expand then also the style of governing will have to adapt'. This adaptation should, they argue, incorporate more democratic means to make and implement policy. But perhaps the challenges are even more urgent: are the present fair-weather bureaucratic governance structures fit for purpose in the foul weather of a recession, and how will they stand up to the development of a more contentious politics?

Empirical lacunae

If theoretical refinement has been a very obvious preoccupation since the early 1990s, the policy turn that has accompanied it has also been very important. It has been very welcome too because, with the notable exception of the various editions of *Policy-Making in the European Community/Union*, edited by Wallace *et al.* – which set a high standard from the first appearance of the book in 1977 – early work on policy studies was very weak empirically. It was overwhelmingly Anglo-American, scholars often lacked the requisite linguistic basis to access sources, and very often the evidence base was gleaned almost entirely from the *Financial Times*. Thankfully, this has now changed.

The subject is less Anglo-American and younger continental European scholars, who now constitute a very visible element of the EU academic community, have the requisite linguistic and analytical skills. Large research initiatives – such as those coming out of the Norwegian ARENA group, the Deutsche Forschungsgemeinschaft, the Mannheim Centre for European Social Research, and the UK Economic and Social Science Research Council's 'One Europe or Several?' Programme – have greatly strengthened the empirical base.

But, despite these advances, contributors to this volume – including Nugent and Paterson, Boswell, Kantola, Ludlow, Rittberger and Smith – have drawn attention to continuing empirical lacunae. For example, Kantola in Chapter 13 points out the deficit of work on European civic society in contrast to a huge amount of research on economic interest groups. If institutions were overemphasized in earlier years, the contents page of the *Handbook of European Union Politics* (Jørgensen *et al.*, 2006) might well suggest that we have now moved too far in the opposite direction. Nugent and Paterson suggest that there are still many unexplored issues in relation to institutions. Interestingly, the research studies on institutions post-enlargement commented on by Nugent and Paterson in Chapter 4 indicate that really valuable empirical insights can still be generated using simple analytical methods.

Despite extensive empirical research initiatives, there is still a great deal of fragmentation, with interconnections within and across particular areas being underexplored. This picture is seen, for example, in the relative lack of research that has been undertaken on the interconnections between the EU's pillars. It is seen in the lack of grounded empirical work with a historical dimension. And it is seen too, as Karen Smith shows in Chapter 14, in the relative thinness in the literature on CFSP/ESDP on the connections with work on national foreign policies. This fragmentation ultimately reflects academic priorities, where young scholars make their name much more easily with a theoretical contribution rather than with a well-grounded piece of empirical work which might well be seen as insufficiently generalizable. This applies a fortiori to an area like the EU, which is based on a range of disciplines and where it has to compete for attention with long-run and established disciplinary concentrations. In this context, solid empirical accounts are not seen as enough.

The overdue turn to domestic politics

For a very long period the interface with domestic politics was the Cinderella of EU studies. Many scholars were attracted to European integration studies by the challenge of explaining the new institutions, and some of these institutions had an interest in fostering a group of scholars who would tell their story. This need was so elemental in the early years that scholars could have an impact on how the institution conceptualized itself, with, for example, the neofunctionalist school being credited with an influence on the Commission strategy that over-played economic at the expense of political factors in the lead-up to the ill-fated clash with de Gaulle in 1965. The way in which a new group of Euro lawyers, including Anthony Arnull, who has contributed to this book in Chapter 8, familiarized the legal community with the work of the ECJ is perhaps an even more enduring example. EU scholars had a symbiotic relationship with practitioners in the EEC institutions, whom they relied on for information and other resources. There was for a long time no equivalent or visible group of officials at the national level in Europe who were available to act as interlocutors with the emerging EEC studies community, in the way that had tradi-tionally applied in the defence and foreign policy fields. And, of course, for US scholars there was no continual national interface.

In consequence, the dominant explanations of the integration process failed to address the national interface in any depth. Much theorizing was based on international relations theory, which privileges the national executive level and largely assigns internal politics to a 'black box' status. Neofunctionalism did have a 'take' on domestic politics, but it was essentially an explanation grounded in economics in which the key driving role was assigned to interest groups rather than polit-ical parties. The latter were treated as being of interest if they could be identified as playing a part in driving integration, but otherwise they were rather neglected (Haas, 1958).

Unsurprisingly, this view of domestic politics quickly proved inade-quate and shipped a huge amount of water in the 1965/66 crisis. A very significant breakthrough was made in 1983 with the publication of an article by Simon Bulmer (1983). The article sought to establish the key role of domestic structures and national attitudes towards inte-gration in the European integration policy-making process. In Bulmer's framework, four assumptions of the domestic politics approach were posited: (1) that national politics is the base unit of the EEC; (2) that different structures and patterns of politics within member states shape the interests and policy concerns of each member state; (3) that European policy needs to be understood as part of the wider policy agenda of domestic politics; (4) that national governments occupy the key position between national and European politics and that policy style is a useful tool for characterizing the way in which domestic factors shape European policies (Bulmer, 1983: 354).

Bulmer's 'bottom-up' approach reconnected with comparative poli-tics and provided a more powerful explanation of national preference formation than had hitherto been available. Until the appearance of his article there was a tendency to characterize national positions by a range of stereotypical historical and geographical factors – what may be called the Casablanca method of 'rounding up the usual suspects' (Paterson, 1995). A decade later, Andrew Moravcsik (1993), in his seminal analysis of the negotiation of the SEA, combined an explicit theory of domestic preference formation with a rationalist theory of interstate bargaining which derived ultimately from theories of international relations. Both Bulmer and Moravcsik thus offered partial accounts of the interface between the domestic and European levels, heavily oriented towards the impact on the European policy process rather than a more generalized account of the place of European integration in national political systems.

Developments in the last two decades have led to a much greater concentration on the domestic level: a concentration that looks likely to become increasingly central to EU studies. The creation of the single market and its development has been associated with a huge increase in the scope of the EU, taking it into areas that would formerly have been considered the exclusive preserve of domestic polities. These areas include not only the obvious economic areas but many others also, ranging from defence policy to gender issues. Recently, the huge expansion of JHA has also taken the EU into what were traditionally national *chasses gardées*.

Alongside the expansion in policy scope post-Maastricht, the EU has come to favour quasi-constitutional leaps forward which national elites have increasingly sought to legitimize by use of referenda. But although they have been initially attractive to national political elites, in practice referenda have proved to be risky and unpredictable and their use has led to a great deal of political mobilization and turbulence and to a corresponding increase of attention on the EU/national interface.

Another 'complication' concerning the domestic politics dimension of European integration has been that the 2004/07 enlargement has involved bringing into the Union new member states that have political institutions with quite a short history, limited expertise on the EU, and unstable party systems. These weakening factors have meant that EU politics in these member states have lacked the predictability of more established member states and have moved from the bureaucratic/technocratic level to a more controversial level.

Also, of course, the greater ubiquity of eurosceptic parties has made the national/European interface infinitely more challenged than hitherto. The deepening of market integration has promoted something of a political backlash to further efforts to promote market liberalization, as illustrated by Michelle Egan in Chapter 10. She demonstrates how single market activities challenge the welfare and economic systems of member states, posing significant problems given the increased heterogeneity of member state levels of economic development, as well as interests and preferences. Waltraud Schelkle, in her analysis of monetary policy in

Chapter 11, focuses on the need for policy coordination, and in so doing highlights that the pressures for structural reform that arise from the loss of countercyclical measures also create electoral tensions.

These various developments have gradually been reflected in the literature. The continual expansion of the EU activities and its penetration into the nooks and crannies of domestic political life have given rise to an increasingly voluminous Europeanization literature which, as Claudio Radaelli and Theofanis Exadaktylos have shown in Chapter 9, is much taken up with tracking the impact of EU policies and institutions at the national level. One very welcome development in the Europeanization literature is a trend towards cumulative studies, illustrated by the way in which an edited volume by Bache and Jordan (2006) on the Europeanization of British politics explicitly builds on the excellent earlier edited work by Dyson and Goetz on Germany (2003).

At the same time, the move towards comparative-politics explanations of aspects of European integration – with the EU being treated as a political system employing the conventional toolkit of comparative politics – has naturally impacted on the EU–domestic politics interface in many ways. For example, significant work has been undertaken on political parties, with perhaps the most ambitious being that of Poguntke *et al.* (2008), who conducted a six-country study on the degree to which national parties had adapted to European integration. A group of scholars centred on Sussex University and the Opposing Europe project have carried out much valuable research on Euroscepticism – an area that continues to be bedevilled by definitional issues (Szczerbiak and Taggart, 2008). A great deal of work has been done on European Parliament elections, but the place of European integration in national elections remains an underexplored area. It is, however, an area that is beginning to be addressed with, for example, research undertaken by Hooghe and Marks (2009) advancing compelling arguments for the view that attitudes towards European integration do affect voting in national elections.

Contentious politics

Studies of European integration long held that a 'permissive consensus' existed in the EU, which allowed national political elites a considerable policy-making latitude. Recently, however, Follesdal and Hix (2006) have questioned whether the assumed permissive consensus really is a source of strength. Low salience and apathy, seen by many as an advantage for policy-makers, are seen as weaknesses by Follesdal and Hix, who criticize the insulation of the EU from political competition and suggest a series of measures to increase such competition. They see a danger in the disconnect between the ideological contestation along the left/right dimension characteristic of the Brussels level and the attitudes of EU citizens who, as Hix argues, 'cannot understand the EU, and so will never be able to assess and regard it as an accountable system of government, nor to identify with it' (Hix, 2008: 70). The general response to the Hix and Follesdal politicization argument has, it should be said, been one of scepticism, as Berthold Rittberger demonstrates in Chapter 7. Bartolini (2006), for example, has expressed powerful reservations about Hix's suggested introduction of 'constitutive issues' touching on constitutional issues which, in his view, could lead to party splits and to a widening gap between party elites and their electorates rather than, as Hix argues, closing the gap.

But there is in fact a strong argument to be made that the EU has already entered into a period of contestation. Bartolini is surely correct when he argues that the ever expanding scope of economic and legal integration beyond the original core issues sets up a tension with domestic economic and political systems and 'places the legitimation triangle of the nation state under severer pressure, based as it is on cultural homogeneity, political participation and social sharing institutions' (Bartolini, 2005: 375). In this changed situation public perceptions weigh much more heavily. In a recent study, Vivien Schmidt (2006) has, *inter alia*, explored – through a cross-country analysis of discourse – the sustained failure of national political elites to communicate with their citizens about the EU-related changes in national democratic practices: a failure which, over time, has provided a window of opportunity for eurosceptic arguments, increased contention and weakened popular support for European integration.

Political cleavages do, of course, also reflect strong pre-existing identities. Increased contestation is thus originally an effect of the ever-deeper penetration of the EU into the interstices of domestic life, where it comes into collision with deeply rooted interests and cultural values (see Jeffery and Paterson, 2005, for the German case). One example of this is the way that religion has come to have an EU dimension, with Irish unhappiness on perceived EU threats to the Irish prohibition on abortion, the Polish desire to insert God into the European Constitutional Treaty, and, arguably too, German and Austrian reservations on the desirability of Turkey becoming an EU member.

Such long-standing contestations are now being overlaid with new and more systematic cleavage patterns, some of them made sharper as a result of the global economic crisis that set in during 2008. For most of its history, the move towards European integration has taken place in economic good times, with increasing and continuing prosperity allowing political conflicts to be bought off, as with, for example, the creation of the Structural Funds which were designed to cushion the dynamic effects of the SEM on peripheral areas and to muffle the effects on winners and losers. The recession has now produced a resource crunch, which has opened up a gaping cleavage between the new eastern members and the established members of the EU. An 'expanding periphery and a shrinking core' – the striking phrase used by Dyson and Goetz to describe the enlarged EU (Dyson and Goetz, 2003) – looks quite different in a recession. One illustration of this core–periphery tension was seen in early 2009, when the Czech Presidency displayed open anger with protectionist noises on the automobile industry emanating from French President, Nicolas Sarkozy. At the time of writing, it is unclear that 'losers' will be able to be compensated in the way that they have traditionally been in the EU, and nor is it clear what a 'foul weather EU' will ultimately look like.

Towards a balance

In many ways European Union studies is an almost unparalleled success story. Organizationally, academic associations such as the European Union Studies Association, the University Association for Contemporary European Studies, and the European Consortium for Political Research provide vibrant and transnational forums for the exchange of ideas. Many high-level publishing opportunities abound. So, for example, alongside EU-devoted journals such as the *Journal of Common Market Studies*, the *Journal of European Public Policy*, the *European Foreign Affairs Review*, the *Journal of European Integration*, *European Union Politics*, and the *European Law Journal* many other journals – such as *International Organization*, *International Affairs* and *West European Politics* – carry articles on European integration. Online EU series of articles and papers seem to appear almost by the day. EU book series also exist, including ones published by Palgrave Macmillan, Routledge and Oxford University Press. Thanks partly to the European Commission's Jean Monnet initiative – a brilliant example of the clever use of selective incentives – EU studies are very well represented in university curricula. And the EU Framework programmes provide significant selective incentives for transnational and transdisciplinary research initiatives.

There can be no doubt about the volume, diversity and increased quality and sophistication of the published output on European integration and the EU. Research achievements, theoretically underpinned in various ways, have been impressive. To use Donald Puchala's metaphor, we can now describe the principal part of the elephant and what makes it function much better than before (Puchala, 1972). But, as well as identifying knowledge that has been gained, this book has also highlighted gaps and weaknesses in our knowledge and understanding. So, for example, as Karen Smith points out in her chapter and Wade Jacoby and Sophie Meunier do in theirs, the relationships between the EU and its wider global environment remain imperfectly understood. The EU may have elephant status in respect of international trading and many regulatory matters, but in foreign and security policy terms it is, as Asle Toje (2008) puts it, a 'small power'. Do we fully understand why this is? And do we fully understand why enlargement policy – perhaps the most successful of EU foreign policies – has slowed?

More broadly in terms of the need for further research, this book has raised questions about the rigidity of boundaries between cognate academic fields, and has concluded that there is still a long way to go if a – surely desirable – genuinely interdisciplinary and transpillar approach to European studies is ever to be adopted. For as long as no such approach is adopted, a picture of the whole elephant, a grand theory, a *Gesamtkonzept*, will remain as elusive as ever.

What of the future? Almost every chapter of this book has identified a range of pressing empirical issues that will certainly keep up the current research momentum into the foreseeable future. As for theoretical endeavours, the absence of new debates in international relations and comparative politics, the slow-down in many policy areas, and enlargement fatigue, taken together, suggest that there may be a slackening pace of theory generation. But, even here much can be expected from mining the differentiated integration theme.

The great unknowable is the effect of the world recession. European integration has been a child of prosperity and any deep recession is likely both to have a considerable effect on the process and on the accompanying explanations. Even at this point we can see a changing market/ state balance, strains in the eurozone – arguably the great achievement of European integration – and a re-evaluation of globalization, though a gulf remains between the broadly pro-globalization stance of the UK government and the more guarded attitude of others. Hopes that were recently entertained for a more ambitious European 'social space' (Ferrera, 2009: 219–33) appear decidedly premature, but we do not know what the length and depth of this recession is going to be. If it is short-lived, then the effects may not be great, but if it turns out to be profound then the implications will be very far-reaching. Some EU scholars may then find themselves in the position of William Robertson, who, in an effort to overcome the popularity of David Hume as a historian, laboured long and hard on his *History of America*. Robertson's book had as its unique selling point his view of the solid foundations of the British presence in North America, but the gestation period of the book was very long and when it eventually appeared in 1777 it had been overtaken by the American Declaration of Independence in 1776 and was therefore restricted to the history of the Spanish presence in America (Robertson, 1777). Robertson was thus fated never to achieve his ambition of overtaking Hume's popularity as a historian. It is important though to bear in mind that however frustrating unforeseen events are for individual scholars, the upside of the resultant theoretical 'creative destruction' is, of course, the opportunities it presents for deeper understanding and for new reputations to be made.

References

Bache, I. and Jordan, A. (eds) (2006) *The Europeanization of British Politics* (Basingstoke: Palgrave Macmillan).

Bartolini, S. (2005) *Restructuring Europe Centre Formation, System Building and Political Structuring Between the Nation State and the European Union* (Oxford: Oxford University Press).

Bartolini, S. (2006) 'Should the Union be "Politicized"? Prospects and Risks'. Policy Paper 19 (Paris: Notre Europe) 29–50.

Bulmer, S. (1983) 'Domestic Politics and European Community Policy Making', *Journal of Common Market Studies* 21(4): 349–63.

Bulmer, S. (1994) 'The Governance of the European Union: A New Institutionalist Approach', *Journal of Public Policy* 13(4): 351–80.

Bulmer, S. (2009a) 'Institutional and Policy Analysis in the European Union: From the Treaty of Rome to the Present' in D. Phinnemore and A. Warleigh-Lack (eds) *Reflections on European Integration: Fifty Years of the Treaty of Rome* (Basingstoke: Palgrave Macmillan) 109–24.

Bulmer, S. (2009b) 'Shop Till You Drop! The German Executive as Venue Shopper in Justice and Home Affairs' in P. Bendel, A.Ette and R.Parkes (eds) *The Europeanisation of Control* (Berlin: Lit Verlag).

Cocks, P (1980 'Towards A Marxist Theory of European Integration', *International Organization* 34(1): 1–40.

Curtin, D (2006) 'European Legal Integration: Paradise Lost' in D. Curtin, A. Klip, J. A. McCahery and J. Smits (eds), *European Integration and Law* (Antwerp: Intersentia) 1–54.

Deutsch, K. W., Edinger, L., Macridis, R. and Merritt, R. (1967) *France, Germany and the Western Alliance: A Study of Elite Attitudes on European Integration and World Politics* (New York: Scribners).

Dyson, K. and Goetz, K. (eds) (2003) *Germany, Europe and the Politics of Constraint* (Oxford: Oxford University Press).

European Commission (2001) *European Governance: A White Paper*: 428, (Luxembourg: Office for Official Publications of the European Communities).

Ferrera, M. (2009) 'The JCMS Annual Lecture: National Welfare States and European Integration: In Search of "Virtuous Nesting"', *Journal of Common Market Studies* 47(2): 219–33.

Follesdal, A. and Hix, S. (2006) 'Why There is a Democratic Deficit in the EU: A Response to Majone and Moravcsik', *Journal of Common Market Studies* 44(3): 533–62.

Grabitz, E. (1984) *Abgestufte Integration. Eine Alternative zum herkoemmlichen Integrationskonzept?* (Kehl/Strassburg: Josef Molsberger).

Haas, E. B. (1958) *The Uniting of Europe: Political, Social and Economic Forces 1950–1957* (London: Stevens).

Haas, E. B. (1975) 'The Obsolescence of Regional Integration Theory', Berkeley: University of California Institute of International Studies, Research Series, 25.

Hill, C. (1993) 'The Capability-Expectations Gap, or Conceptualizing Europe's International Role', *Journal of Common Market Studies* 31(3): 305–28.

Hix, S. (1994) 'The Study of the European Community: The Challenge to Comparative Politics', *West European Politics* 17(1): 1–30.

Hix, S. (1998) 'The Study of the European Union II: The "New Governance" Agenda and its Rival', *Journal of European Public Policy* 5(1): 1–30.

Hix, S. (2005) *The Political System of the European Union* (2nd edn) (Basingstoke: Palgrave Macmillan).

Hix, S. (2008) *What's Wrong with the European Union and How to Fix it* (Cambridge: Polity).

Hoffmann, S. (1966) 'Obstinate or Obsolete? The Fate of the Nation State and the Case of Western Europe', *Daedalus* 95(3): 862–915.

Hooghe, L. and Marks, G. (2003) 'Unravelling the Central State, But How? Types of Multi-Level Governance', *American Political Science Review* 97: 233–43.

Hooghe, L. and Marks, G. (2009) 'A Postfunctionalist Theory of European Integration: From Permissive Consensus to Constraining Dissensus', *British Journal of Political Science* 39(1): 1–23.

Hyde-Price, A. (2006) '"Normative" Power Europe: A Realist Critique' *Journal of European Public* Policy 13(2): 217–34.

Jeffery, C. and Paterson, W. E. (2005) 'Germany and European Integration: A Shifting of Tectonic Plates', *West European Politics* 26(4): 59–78.

Jordan, A. (2001) 'The European Union: An Evolving System of Multilevel Governance or Government?', *Policy and Politics* 29(2): 193–208.

Jørgensen, K. A., Pollack, M. A. and Rosamond, B. (eds) (2006) *Handbook of European Union Politics* (London: Sage).

Kaiser, W. (2008) History Meets Politics: Overcoming the Interdisciplinary Volapük in Research on the EU', *Journal of European Public Policy* 15(2): 300–13.

Keeler, J. (2005) 'Mapping EU Studies', *Journal of Common Market Studies* 43(3): 551–83.

Kirchner, E. J. (2006) 'The Challenge of European Union Security Governance', *Journal of Common Market Studies* 44(5): 947–68.

Lindberg, L. and Scheingold, S. (1970) *Europe's Would-Be Polity: Patterns of Change in the European Community* (Cambridge, MA: Harvard University Press).

Majone, G. (1996) *Regulating Europe* (London: Routledge).

Manners, I. (2002) 'Normative Power Europe: A Contradiction in Terms?' *Journal of Common Market Studies* 40(2): 235–58.

Marks, G. (1993) 'Structural Policy and Multilevel Governance in the EC', in A. W. Cafruny and G. Rosenthal (eds) *The State of the European Community: The Maastricht Debates and Beyond* (Boulder: Lynne Rienner).

Marks, G. Hooghe, L. and Blank, K., (1996) 'European Integration from the 1980s: State Centric versus Multilevel Governance', *Journal of Common Market Studies* 34(3): 341–78.

Mearsheimer, J. (1990) 'Back to the Future: Instability in Europe After the Cold War', *International Security* 15: 5–57.

Milward, A. (1992) *The European Rescue of the Nation State* (London: Routledge).

Moravcsik, A. (1993) 'Preferences and Power in the European Community: A Liberal Intergovernmentalist Approach', *Journal of Common Market Studies* 31(4): 473–524.

Moravcsik, A. (1998) *The Choice For Europe: Social Purpose and State Power From Messina to Maastricht* (Ithaca: Cornell University Press).

Paterson, W. E (1995) 'Britain and the European Union Revisited: Some Unanswered Questions', *Scottish Affairs* 9: 1–12.

Pierson, P. (1996) 'The Path to European Integration: A Historical Institutional Analysis', *Comparative Political Studies* 29(2): 123–63.

Poguntke, T., Aylott, N., Carter, E., Ladrech, R. and Luther, K. R. (2008) *The Europeanization of National Political Parties: Power and Organizational Adaptation* (London: Routledge).

Pollack, M. A. (2003) *The Engines of European Integration: Delegation, Agency and Agenda Setting in the EU* (Oxford: Oxford University Press).

Puchala, D. (1972) 'Of Blind Men, Elephants and European Integration', *Journal of Common Market Studies* 10(3): 267–84.

Robertson, W (1777) *History of America*, Vols 1 and 2 (Edinburgh: Balfour).

Rosamond, B. (2006) 'The Future of European Studies: Integration Theory, EU Studies and Social Science' in M. Eilstrup-Sangiovanni (ed.) *Debates on European Integration: A Reader* (Basingstoke: Palgrave Macmillan) 448–60.

Sandholtz, W. and Stone Sweet, A. (eds) (1998) *European Integration and Supranational Governance* (Oxford: Oxford University Press).

Sbragia, A. (2008) 'Review Article – Comparative Regionalism: What Might it Be?', in U. Sedelmeier and A. Young (eds) *The JCMS Annual Review of the European Union in 2007* (Oxford: Blackwell Publishing) 29–49.

Schmidt, V. (2006) *Democracy in Europe: The EU and National Polities* (Oxford: Oxford University Press).

Smith, M. E. (2008) 'Researching European Foreign Policy: Some Fundamentals' *Politics* 13(1): 177–87.

Stubb, A. (1996) 'A Categorization of Differentiated Integration', *Journal of Common Market Studies* 34(2): 283–95.

Szczerbiak, A. and Taggart, P. (2008) *Opposing Europe? The Comparative Party Politics of Euroscepticism*, 2 Vols (Oxford: Oxford University Press).

Toje, A. (2008) 'The European Union as a Small Power or Conceptualizing Europe's Strategic Actorness', *Journal of European Integration* 30(2): 199–215.

Wallace, H., Wallace, W. and Webb, C. (1977) *Policy-Making in the European Community* (Chichester: Wiley).

Warleigh-Lack, A. (2006) '"The European Union and the Universal Process"? European Union Studies, New Regionalism and Global Governance', in K. A. Jørgensen, M. A. Pollack, and B. Rosamond (eds) *Handbook of European Union Politics* (London: Sage) 561–75.

Warleigh-Lack, A. and Phinnemore, D. (2009) 'Conclusion: Reflections on the Past and Future of European Union Studies', in D. Phinnemore and A. Warleigh-Lack (eds) *Reflections on European Integration: 50 Years of the Treaty of Rome* (Basingstoke: Palgrave Macmillan) 212–23.

Zielonka, J. (2005) *Europe as Empire: The Nature of the Enlarged European Union* (Oxford: Oxford University Press).

Index

421